4+6
8+9
0

7+6
8+9
5+7

Today's Elementary Social Studies

Dorothy Grant Hennings
George Hennings
Serafina Fiore Banich

Kean College

Rand McNally College Publishing Company/Chicago

Rand McNally Education Series
B. Othanel Smith, Advisory Editor

Sponsoring Editor   Louise Waller
Project Editor   Kevin Thornton
Designer   James A. Buddenbaum
Photo Editors   Marcia D. Golightly
                           Sharon Punches

In memory of

Caroline Zeitchel Hennings
1900–1979

80   81   82   10   9   8   7   6   5   4   3   2   1

Contents

**Part Five
The Social Studies
Curriculum**

PREFACE

From Edward Cornish, *The Study of the Future: An Introduction to the Art and Science of Understanding and Shaping Tomorrow's World.* (Washington, D.C.: World Future Society, 1977), p. 1.

Never before in the history of civilization has humankind experienced the rapid social changes that we see today. Since 1945, the world has seen "satellite television, oral contraceptives, electronic computers, photocopying machines, supersonic plane travel, and heart transplants." In the last 35 years, people have scaled the highest mountains, explored the ocean bottom, walked on the moon, and sent probes to planets beyond Earth.

The pace of change will probably accelerate, not decelerate, in the immediate future. In *The Future of the Future*, John McHale suggests that "The next 50 years may be the most crucial of all human history."

Social Studies for Today and Tomorrow

From Cornish. p. 2. See also John McHale, *The Future of the Future.* (New York: George Braziller, 1969). McHale urges us to plan for the future so that it will be a better time for humankind.

Today's Elementary Social Studies is committed to the premise that elementary social studies education should help prepare children to live in a world in which job opportunities, technologies, human relationships, and international power structures are constantly changing. Citizens must understand how this changing world works and apply their understandings to solving problems. People must be able to make judgments and decisions and act upon them, recognize and maintain their individuality, search out answers on their own, and communicate their findings to others.

Today's Elementary Social Studies presents a design for elementary social studies programs that is made up of four major strands:

A *Pedagogical Strand* showing how to organize classrooms, content, and learning sequences for teaching and learning.

An *Epistemological/Psychological Strand* based on understanding the nature of knowledge and learning;

A *Social Science Strand* that ties in an understanding of how people function, especially when faced with change;

A *Humanities Strand* that stresses understanding of the uniqueness of human beings and the distinctiveness of each individual's contribution to the society as a whole;

The result is an eclectic approach, which, for purposes of this book, is termed *dynamic*.

The Pedagogical Strand. Drawn from pedagogical theory, the first strand is based on a general agreement among educators that no one form of classroom or lesson organization meets all children's diverse needs. For children to understand and accept themselves as unique individuals—each with the potential to make a distinctive contribution to the society of which she or he is a part—they must function in a variety of learning environments. They must function in small, highly interactive groups and in large ones; they must also have the opportunity to work independently on personalized learning tasks. For this reason, the reader will find a variety of activities in *Today's Elementary Social Studies*, some of which are related to full-class instruction, some to small-group instruction, and others to personalized learning.

The Epistemological/Psychological Strand. Epistemologists, who study the nature of knowledge, make distinctions among "knowing that . . . " and "knowing how. . . ," and also the desire to use "know-how." Psychologists explain how people learn. Drawing from the work of both fields, the authors of this book propose that active involvement is requisite if one is to go beyond "knowing that," learn to "know how," and desire to use "know-how." This means involving children directly in gathering data, organizing findings into logical and creative designs, analyzing results, hypothesizing relationships, making value judgments and decisions, and taking actions based on decisions made. Because involvement is the way people come to know their world, *Today's Elementary Social Studies* provides ideas through which teachers can make active involvement a reality in social studies classrooms.

The Social Science Strand. The social sciences are sources of understanding about the way people function. Through active involvement in social studies classrooms, students should gain not only cognitive and personal skills but also understanding of basic social science concepts. Concepts from sociology, anthropology, geography, economics, psychology, political science, and history supply the young social scientist with lenses that—if compounded one upon another—make it easier to grasp relationships.

The Humanities Strand. A fourth unifying strand utilizes the humanities. The authors of the book believe that the products of human activity at its best – literature, music, dance, art, architecture, and philosophical thought–should help children to understand the human experience more fully. Through the products of human culture, students recognize the beauty and wealth of diverse cultures, as well as the fundamental needs and feelings that make all people part of the human family. Children recognize what it is within themselves that sets them apart as distinctly human; at the same time they become more aware and accepting of the qualities they alone possess that make a unique contribution possible. Accordingly, in this book, reference is made to stories, poems, first-person accounts, chants, songs, and dances that can become integral parts of the social studies experience.

The Organization of the Book

Today's Elementary Social Studies includes five major parts, each of which highlights a series of related social studies education topics:

Part One   The Social Studies; Goals, Scope, and
      Methods of Instruction
Part Two   The Basics in the Social Studies: Skills,
      Conceptual Learnings, and Values
Part Three   The Individual in the Social Studies
Part Four   Issues and Investigations Using the
      Social Sciences
Part Five   The Social Studies Curriculum

Although the book is designed so that chapters utilize those that precede them, the reader will discover many cross-references that facilitate reading chapters out of sequence.

The Margin Notes. Readers will discover three kinds of margin notes integral to the book. *Goal notes*, indicated by the letter **G**, clarify the purposes of learning activities being described in the text. *Teaching* or *instructional* notes, indicated by the letter **T**, provide related material that the reader can use in designing similar activities. Included is information about children's books, films, and games, and specific examples relating to the text. They also supply cautions, hints, and instructional cues. *Reading notes*, introduced by the letter **R**, provide references to books and articles cited within the text, as well as additional references that amplify ideas being discussed at that point. Location of each note tells where that material fits into the total social studies picture.

Idea Pages. Set off from the ongoing text, Idea Pages present specific activities that teachers can apply directly in classroom situations, adapting them to the special needs of a group. Each chapter opens with a story, example, map, graph, collage, photograph, or lesson plan that provides a classroom teaching idea. Many of these openers can be made into lessons if adjusted to the needs of a group.

Problems to Ponder/Tasks to Try. Each chapter of *Today's Elementary Social Studies* supplies one or more sections titled Problems to Ponder and Tasks to Try. Many of these can serve as content for discussion by those who are reading the book in a college-level course or workshop. To help the reader become more actively involved, Key Questions, located at the beginning of each chapter, can be used as a pre- and/or post-test.

The Index/Glossary. Some entries in the index appear in boldfaced type. These entries represent basic terms for which definitions and/or explanations can be found in the text on the pages indicated. Thus, the index serves as a modified glossary.

G goal note

T teaching or instructional note

R reading note

A Personal Statement by the Authors

To undertake to write a text on the social studies requires a considerable commitment of time and energy. The authors of this book made this commitment because they believe that people living today are responsible for their own futures and the future of the world. The world is not fixed in time and the choices people make effect the course of events. Choice is a necessity. "Refusing to choose is itself a choice."

Eric Carle tells the tale of a rooster who set out to see the world. Two cats, three frogs, four turtles, and five fish all joined the rooster; but as night fell, the rooster's new companions asked: "Where's our dinner?" "Where are we supposed to sleep?" They complained: "We're cold," "We're afraid." Now, the rooster had not made any plans for the trip around the world. He had not remembered to think about food and shelter, so he didn't know how to answer his friends. And so they all had to turn about without getting anywhere. Clearly Carle's rooster had not even thought about how to satisfy basic physiological needs.

Today we must think about basic needs and beyond if the future is to be bright. We must remember that the future is not something far off and distant without importance or relevance for us. Tomorrow quickly becomes today.

From Eric Carle, *The Rooster Who Set Out to See the World.* (New York: Franklin Watts, 1972), to help young children see the importance of planning ahead.

Acknowledgments

The authors wish to express their appreciation to all the teachers who have willingly shared ideas with them. In travels to classrooms and talks with teachers from New Jersey to Texas to Tennessee, they have found teachers who think social studies is important and who use dynamic means to involve children directly in the study of the world of people. Some of these such as Emily Davis, a fine first-grade teacher, and Linda Morrison, an equally fine second-grade teacher, are cited by name in the text. Others contributed equally; but it was impossible to mention them. To all those teachers who shared freely, the authors say, "Thank you."

Throughout the development of the manuscript librarian Dorothy Sked was most helpful in tracking down materials used in school social studies programs. In like manner, colleague Phyllis Alliston opened her collection of social studies resource materials to the authors.

The authors also thank the reviewers who posed thoughtful questions and offered excellent suggestions during various phases of manuscript development. As one author was moved to comment, "We certainly hit the jackpot!" The ideas contributed proved a lode to be mined for specific points relative to both design and content. Especially helpful were Edward Kelly, University of Northern Colorado; David Killian, Miami University; Bruce Mossman, Southwestern University; Robert Price, University of Colorado; and William Smith, Shippensburg State College.

And to the great editors at Rand McNally who have aided in the development of the book, we say—in the Ashanti, repetitive style—"Thank you, thank you, thank you." Louise Waller's thoughtful perusal of the original proposal resulted in an overall framework that led to a more tightly organized production. Kevin Thornton's careful attention to detail resulted in a book that communicates more clearly and forcefully. Charles Heinle's encouragement was also appreciated. In the process of book development, these professionals have become friends whom the authors value and respect.

Dorothy Grant Hennings
George Hennings
Serafina Fiore Banich

January 1980

Credits

Page 13 from *People on the Land*. Los Angeles: Bowmar/Noble, 1974, p. 30. Reprinted by permission of Bowmar/Noble, Publishers, Inc.

Page 33 from *Social Sciences Education Framework for California Public Schools*, published by the California State Board of Education. Reprinted with permission of the publisher.

Page 51, "A Song of Greatness" from *The Children Sing in the Far West* by Mary Austin. Copyright © 1928 by Mary Austin. Copyright renewed 1956 by Kenneth M. Chapman and Mary C. Wheelwright. Reprinted by permission of Houghton Mifflin Company.

Page 68 illustration from *Living in Families*. Teacher's Edition. Reprinted with permission of Silver Burdett, Inc.

Page 70 illustration from *Living in Families*. Teacher's Edition. Reprinted with permission of Silver Burdett, Inc.

Page 110 drawing by H. Martin; © 1975, The New Yorker Magazine, Inc.

Page 136 map from *Goode's World Atlas*. E.B. Epenshade, Jr. and J. L. Morrison, eds. 15th Edition. Illustration Copyright by the University of Chicago Department of Geography.

Page 143 maps from *Learning to Use a Globe, Set I*. Reprinted by permission of A.J. Nystrom and Company, Division of Carnation Co.

Page 165 illustration from *Exploring Our World*. Reprinted with permission of Follett, Inc., Publishers.

Page 374 illustration from *Living in Families*, p. 68. Reprinted with permission of Silver Burdett, Inc.

Page 384 from United States Department of Interior, National Park Service. Reprinted with permission.

Pages 421–22 from *Great Names in American History*. Published by Laidlaw Bros. Reprinted by permission of the publisher.

Page 435, figure 13.3 from *The Little House* by Virginia Lee Burton, Copyright © 1942 by Virginia Lee Demetrios, Copyright © renewed 1969 by George Demetrios. Reprinted by permission of Houghton Mifflin Co.

Page 462, figure 14.1 from Fenga and Freyer, Inc. Reprinted with permission.

Page 482 illustration from *Living in Families*, p. 190. Teacher's Edition. Reprinted with permission of Silver Burdett, Inc.

Page 490, figure 15.1 from *An Inseparable Linkage: Conservation of Natural Ecosystems and the Conservation of Fossil Energy* by F.H. Borman in *Bioscience*, Vol. 26, no. 12, 1976. Reprinted with permission.

Pages 531–539 from Board of Education, Baltimore County, Towson, Maryland. Reprinted with permission.

Page 552 illustration from *Working in Our World: The American Way of Life* by Lawrence Senesh © 1973, Science Research Associates, Inc. Reproduced by permission of the publisher.

Page 580 cartoon © 1965 United Feature Syndicate, Inc.

Pages 98, 480 Courtesy of James W. Ndungu, City Education Department, Nairobi, Kenya.

Photo Credits

22 Tim Carlson / Stock, Boston, Inc.; 39 Rohn Engh / Star Prairie, Wisconsin; 47 Stu Huck / Hill Photography; 72 Freer / Photo Researchers, Inc.; 87 Mary M. Thatcher / Photo Researchers, Inc.; 101 Lynn McLaren / Rapho-Photo Researchers, Inc.; 120 Michael Goss; 145 Frank Siteman / Stock, Boston, Inc.; 157 Jean-Claude Lejeune; 173 Bohdan Hrynewych / Stock, Boston, Inc.; 187 Martine Franck-VIVA / Woodfin Camp & Associates; 206 Rohn Engh; 225 Jean-Claude Lejeune; 249 Peter Southwick / Stock, Boston, Inc.; 265 Stu Huck / Hill Photography; 277 Van Bucher / Photo Researchers, Inc.; 312 Yan Lukas / Photo Researchers, Inc.; 365 Ira Kirschenbaum / Stock, Boston, Inc.; 386 Peter Menzel / Stock, Boston, Inc.; 393 The Bettmann Archive, Inc.; 431 Jean-Claude Lejeune; 453 NASA (National Aeronautics and Space Administration); 468 Jean-Claude Lejeune; 469 Rohn Engh; 494 Jim Cartier / Photo Researchers, Inc.; 542 Miriam Reinhart / Photo Researchers, Inc.; 561 Michael Goss.

Part One

The Social Studies: Goals, Scope, and Methods of Instruction

It is a time for a new
generation of leader-
ship, to cope with new
problems and new
opportunities. For there
is a new world to be
won.

John F. Kennedy,
July 4, 1960

In planning social studies programs for children,
curriculum designers must make three fundamental
decisions. They must first determine the ultimate, or
overarching, purpose to be achieved through study.
This is the "why" question. They must then determine
the basic goals to be achieved through instruction. This
is the "what" question. Then, by focusing on practical,
day-to-day teaching and learning activities, planners
must also decide how basic goals will be realized. This
is the "how" question.

Chapter 1 of **Today's Elementary Social Studies**
answers the "why" question in terms of the future.
Through the social studies, children will acquire skills,
understandings, and attitudes that will prepare them
to meet the challenges of a future far different from the
present. Chapter 1 also answers the "what" question
by identifying five basic goal areas. Ways to achieve
goals, answering the "how" question, are developed
in chapter 2, which describes a format for lesson
planning and specific strategies for involving children
actively in social studies content.

In Search of a Design
for the Social Studies

Kathalina started to school.

Kathalina goes to School.

An inquiry never starts
unless some difficulty
arises.

F. S. C. Northrop, *The*
Logic of the Sciences and
the Humanities, **p. 255**

Key Questions

What are the goals of social studies in the elementary
curriculum?

What is the role of the social sciences in elementary
social studies?

What key ideas or understandings emanate from
inquiry into society, culture, the self, political
structures, economic structures, land spaces, and the
past?

What contribution do the humanities make to the social
studies program? What contribution do the natural
sciences make?

What are the key components of a design for social
studies education geared to the needs of today and
tomorrow?

A Folktale for Today and Tomorrow: "The Devil Is Dead"

Three men of Mols once found a watch in the roadway. Picking it up and examining it, they were filled with wonder because not one of them had the slightest idea what it was.

Suddenly one of them noticed it was ticking. Thinking the devil was inside, he quickly threw it down.

Now the eldest among the three had strong views on devils, and he knew he must act fast. He found an enormous stone and dropped it on the watch. The watch smashed into a million pieces, but this courageous hero did not run away. No, not one bit! He bent down low to the shattered watch and listened in earnest to make sure that the ticking devil had stopped. There wasn't a sound! He looked around proudly for his two companions, shouting, "There you see, I made that devil shut up all right!"

A little nervously, the others gathered to see. Each listened and nodded in approval. And then on they went down the roadway, pleased that they had overcome the devil itself.

Based on Old Stories from Denmark

Introduction

Many of the folktales that people around the world have handed down from generation to generation have as their central theme the sometimes silly things people do when faced with something new. In America, there are jokes about hicks and hayseeds; in England, stories about yokels and bumpkins; and in Denmark, tales about the country folk of Mols. The Danes are particularly proud of their stories that relate what happened when the Mols folk came into contact with the inventions of modern society, and today they cherish and tell with relish tales, such as "The Devil Is Dead."

T Other Mols stories can be found in *Old Stories from Denmark* (Ebeltoft, Denmark: Elles Boghandel, undated).

The prevalence in folk literature of stories similar to "The Devil Is Dead" is indicative of humankind's general inability to function well when encountering something new or different. Clearly the three men of Mols were unprepared to handle the exigencies of a changing world. They looked at innovation from the confines of a narrow and inadequate conceptual scheme; they knew not what questions to ask to find out more information; and as they ambled on down the road, they were totally unaware of their failure to meet life's problems. In short, each lacked an inquiring mind.

One of the imperatives facing social studies educators today is to prepare students to meet tomorrow—a tomorrow filled with problems, forces, complexities, and technical devices far different from those

[handwritten in top margin: goals of social studies ① prepare students to meet tomorrow 5]

known now. Constant change is a major characteristic of life in the second half of the twentieth century; it will certainly be a confounding one in the twenty-first.

As an example of how just one small technical development has changed life significantly in the twentieth century, let us look for a moment at the recent impact of integrated circuitry. Compacted on tiny chips are the parts and circuits that can perform hundreds of processes at almost incomprehensible speeds. The result has been computers and inexpensive hand-held calculators with memory that in milliseconds can carry out computations, which previously would have occupied numbers of human minds for many days if performed by pencil and paper, or even by slide rule. Slide rules have become almost obsolete, with manufacturers turning to new products to stay in business. Jobs have been lost. New jobs requiring different skills have surfaced. The result too has been compact equipment for radio, television, and telephone transmission and reception that has revolutionized the communications industry; the impact has been felt in areas as diverse as banking, medicine, defense, education, space travel, and crime investigation. As was strikingly pointed out in *Electronics: The Continuing Revolution*, micro-circuitry increasingly governs the way people work, play, and interact.

R See *Electronics: The Continuing Revolution* (Washington, D.C.: American Association for the Advancement of Science, 1977).

Learnings for Today and Tomorrow

How do schools prepare youngsters for a future in which new technologies will be? How do we prepare them for the twenty-first century? Obviously, schools cannot foretell the innovations, job-related skills, or specific problems that will emerge. Schools, therefore, cannot provide today's students with the precise skills and answers that will be needed in the year 2000. On the other hand, schools can help children acquire five kinds of learnings with the potential to give an open perspective on problems and a willingness to accept innovation.

R Read Betty Franks and Mary Howard, "Infusing a Futures Perspective into Standard Social Studies Courses," *Social Education,* (January 1979): 24–27.

A Social Studies Goal:
Developing the Ability to Think to Solve Problems

A primary goal of the social studies in elementary school programs is the development of citizens who can perform fundamental thinking processes necessary in solving problems they meet in their own lives. These processes include ability to conceptualize, generalize, and apply knowledge to new problem situations. Regardless of the problem to be solved—whether it is to decide if an unknown object is a devil or a delight, or whether it is to decide what to do in situations having

[handwritten in right margin: ① ability to conceptualize, generalize and apply knowledge to new situations, evaluate]

far more important consequences—to solve it effectively and efficiently, one must be able to gather data about the situation, mentally process those data, and propose a solution. Having acted, one must be able to evaluate outcomes.

A Social Studies Goal: Developing the Ability to Make Value Judgments and Act on Them

A second and related goal is the development of citizens who can make sound value decisions when there is no definitive right or wrong and who are prepared to act on them. In these situations, judgments rest on both factual evidence and one's values, biases, and personal needs. To make sound decisions, a person must know how to clarify the nature of the judgment to be rendered, how to gather relevant data, and how to identify key beliefs and biases that affect the ultimate decision. Having rendered a judgment, the citizen must know the channels and procedures through which an individual in a democratic society can take action.

A Social Studies Goal: Developing an Understanding of the Way Society Works

A third goal relates to basic facts and understandings important in solving problems and making sound decisions. Social scientists have begun to identify key relationships underlying human activity. Sociologists, anthropologists, political scientists, economists, psychologists, geographers, and historians are shedding light on the nature of:

causality

change

power and status

social behavior and roles

personality and motivation

human needs

conflict and cooperation within and between societies

human dependency on others and on the environment.

These basic concepts have broad application as a citizen interprets and interacts in new situations and renders decisions before taking action. A person cannot think, decide, or act in a knowledge vacuum. Each must have a broad understanding of the way society works and has worked in the past if interpretations and decisions are to be sound.

A Social Studies Goal: Developing the Ability to Search and Communicate

To meet the future, students must also possess a wide range of basic and interrelated communication and search skills. These include interpersonal skills: the ability to use language to discuss and share ideas, as well as the ability to interpret messages that others send orally. They include parallel skills related to use and interpretation of written language—writing and reading—and of visual language—sketching, charting, graphing, and mapping. Equally valuable are the search skills: the ability to locate data in source materials, to set up experiments that produce original data, and to interpret findings. Here the study of social phenomena merges with the study of the language arts as students listen and talk together, read and write, search out ideas, and visualize these ideas as steps toward clearer interpretation and communication.

A Social Studies Goal: Developing the Ability to Maintain Personal Identity

No one lives totally alone. A person exists and functions in a variety of social, economic, religious, and political groups. To operate productively in a world filling with more people, the citizen of today and tomorrow must be able to relate to others while maintaining his or her personal identity. This goal has two related facets—the development of group social skills and a sense of personal worth. Neither facet can be ignored. Survival of humankind upon Planet Earth demands that people adjust their individual needs and wants to the needs and wants of the group. Survival also demands that people maintain their own courses of action, question group policies, suggest different actions, and contribute their unique talents to the solution of human problems. To do this, one must see value in one's self and in one's own existence.

The Learnings: A Summary to Start

These then are the overarching **goals of social studies** programs that prepare today's students for the future:

1. Students should develop the ability to perform fundamental thinking operations. Specifically, they should develop the ability to conceptualize, generalize, and apply knowledge to the interpretation of new situations and to the solution of other problems.
2. Students should develop the ability to make value decisions and take action based on them. They should develop an awareness of

Figure 1.1
The Goals of Social Studies

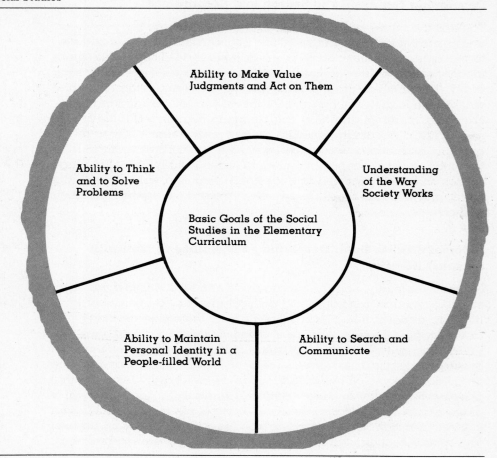

their own systems of beliefs that bear upon their moral judgments
and develop a system of beliefs in harmony with the democratic
way of life.

3. Students should develop an understanding about patterns of
   human behavior and acquire skill in raising questions based on
   their understanding of the way human societies function.

4. Students should develop related search and communication
   skills that make social investigation and interaction more
   effective.

5. Students should develop the group social skills and sense of
   personal worth necessary to maintain personal identity in a
   crowded world.

[handwritten margin note: Social science provides us with identifications/answers of questions useful in the solution of problems about human behavior, to uncover broad conceptual schemes that describe forces within human events]

Let us turn next to consider just how the social sciences and to some extent the humanities contribute to these major goals.

Widening Children's Conceptual Schemes

To identify the kinds of questions and answers useful in the solution of problems about human behavior and to uncover broad conceptual schemes that describe forces at play within human events, the educator must turn first to the **social sciences.** Social scientists analyze human events and are particularly concerned with identifying natural causes associated with them. They believe that whatever happens in human society can be comprehended most clearly through patient observation and through analysis of the relationship between a happening and other events or forces in the observable world. To this end, investigators gather data about what people do and how they do it. Based on continued observation and analysis of findings, they project generalizations about human experiences. Their ultimate objective is to synthesize observations into explanations that take into account each element of the data amassed. In this respect, social investigators are searchers after conceptual schemes, or theories, that describe and explain patterns of human behavior and can be used to predict future trends.

Inquiry into Society

Social scientists—as their very name implies—are concerned with people primarily as social beings functioning not in isolation but in groups. Observing a **society,** a group with organized patterns of interaction, they study its structure—the orderly arrangement of parts within the whole—and attempt to explain relationships.

Looking at Society. Questions of particular concern as the social scientist studies a group include the following:

How do people in the group organize their lives to take care of their basic needs?

What institutions have people developed for raising and educating the young, for educating students, for maintaining law and order, for trading goods and services, and for carrying on their beliefs and values?

What rules exist that circumscribe behavior within the group?

To what basic values do most group members subscribe?

T The way of social investigation

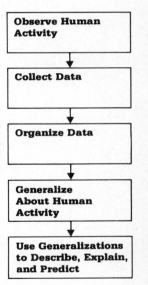

- Observe Human Activity
- Collect Data
- Organize Data
- Generalize About Human Activity
- Use Generalizations to Describe, Explain, and Predict

How have the rules and norms governing behavior changed?

What are the distinctive roles that people play within the group?

What is the status of these roles?

How have the roles people play changed? What factors have been forces for change?

What sanctions exist that tend to maintain roles, values, and rules of behavior?

Basic Understandings.   These questions are predicated on fundamental understandings about society and its functioning that sociologists and cultural anthropologists have been uncovering, especially as they have compared a society or group to other far different ones: comparisons show that

Big Ideas from **Sociology**

1. People tend to function within communities and within such institutions as the family, church, school, clan, caste, and gang.
2. The tools, buildings, handicrafts–the artifacts of a group–supply evidence as to the nature of its social structures.
3. Within social groups, there is a set of rules governing relationships among members. These rules operate as rewards and/or sanctions on the behavior of individuals.
4. Within groups, members play differing roles; roles within a group differ in the prestige or status level attributed to them.
5. Roles within groups are interdependent, making members dependent on one another.
6. Changes in rules, roles, and values come through evolutionary process and through diffusion when one group makes contact with another having a differing structure.
7. Geographic considerations determine to some extent the structure of a group, but social considerations are equally significant.
8. The roles, values, and norms of society are learned, not inborn.
9. The process of acquisition is called **socialization.**

These questions and generalizations focus directly on social structures, social organizations, and the matrix of forces at play within society. They lead to descriptions and explanations of what society is all about and thus to greater knowledge of social phenomena. In this context, the questions that typify sociological inquiry are as significant as the resulting understandings, for knowing the kinds of probes that produce useful information, students of society can raise these same questions in looking at different social structures and organizations arising in an ever-changing world.

Inquiry into Culture

The concept of **culture** as developed by the anthropologists is one that gives rise to numbers of productive questions about human experience. In *Primitive Culture*, published in 1871, E. B. Tylor defined culture to be "that complex whole which includes knowledge, belief, art, morals, law, custom, and any other capabilities and habits acquired by man as a member of society." More recently in 1965, Lucy Mair clarified this definition, writing that "A culture is the common possession of a body of people who share the same traditions; in social terms such a body is a society."

R Lucy Mair is a noted applied anthropologist. See her book, *An Introduction to Social Anthropology* (Oxford, England: Clarendon Press, 1965).

Looking at Culture. About a culture, one can ask

What complex of culture traits characterizes the acquisition and handling of food by members of the society? In this context, **culture trait** is the smallest unit of culture, consisting of either a behavior pattern or an artifact.

What complex of culture traits characterizes the religious practices of members of the society? the significant rites of passage? the courtship and marriage practices? the educational practices? the agricultural practices? the industrial practices? the discriminatory practices?

What symbols are in use within the group? What kind of language prevails? What type of literature? art? music? architecture? technological devices? Why did these kinds prevail?

What culture traits have been borrowed from other societies? forced upon the society by other societies? Why has this **acculturation** occurred?

How are young people introduced to the culture, or how does the process of **enculturation** occur?

What are the major traditions that appear to have been in existence for generations? What functions does each serve? What traditions appear to be fading in significance? Which ones appear to be gaining in significance?

What aspects of the culture are currently undergoing the most rapid change? Why are these changes occurring?

Even a cursory examination of these questions shows that each is not distinct from others; overlap obviously exists. Such overlap, however, serves the investigator, because it makes him or her look at culture traits from different perspectives.

acculturation culture traits borrowed from other societies

enculturation how young people are introduced to the culture.

Idea Page

Background information for the teacher. Throughout this book are sections set off from the ongoing text that suggest specific ways to structure learning activities being described at that point. This first *Idea Page* shows one way that the work of archeologists can be applied in the classroom.

The aim. Children will be able to describe ways we learn about past civilizations and explain relationships between artifacts and the way of life of a people.

Big Ideas from
Anthropology

The pursuit. The fact that the people who lived in Olduvai Gorge had tools tells the archeologist a number of things about those people. What kinds of tools do you think they had? If they had these tools, what kinds of activities did they carry out? Discuss these questions with your talk group.

Now list items of today that will probably be uncovered by scientists digging in your area thousands of years from now. Try to record only things that would not decay over the years. Based on your listing, write a paragraph describing human beings living in the twentieth century from the viewpoint of an investigator studying this civilization thousands of years from now. Begin with this sentence.

Twentieth Century People

From my investigation of the artifacts remaining from the twentieth century, I propose that human beings then were

_____ .

The continuation. Make a wall-sized chart based on the chart of Olduvai Gorge shown in figure 1.2. Then make a chart showing artifacts of today in layers that could possibly be found thousands of years into the future.

Figure 1.2
The Olduvai Gorge

AN ARCHAEOLOGICAL STEPLADDER

One place in the world has given us more information about early man than any other. This place is East Africa.

Olduvai Gorge is in Tanzania, which is a country in eastern Africa.

Louis and Mary Leakey have spent many years there hunting for fossils. They wanted clues about the way early man lived at Olduvai Gorge. They were very successful because Olduvai Gorge is a special place.

Olduvai Gorge is really nothing more than a very big crack in the earth. In fact, that is what a gorge is. But if you look at the walls of the gorge, you will see different layers of rock. Each layer is from a different time in the earth's history. Each layer tells a story about what the earth was like at that time.

The bottom layer of Olduvai Gorge is more than 2 million years old. Toward the top, the layers are newer.

The Leakeys found bones and tools of people in all the layers. What does that tell you about human beings?

OLDUVAI GORGE
Bones of people were found in each layer.

Mud from a lake
Old mud from a lake
Dust and pebbles (less than 500,000 years old)
Mud from swamps and lakes (between 1¼ and 1 million years old)
Yellow desert soil
Ashes from a volcano (between 2 and 1¼ million years ago)
Rock(more than 2 million years old)

The Oldest Human Skull

Dr. Richard Leakey is also an anthropologist. He is the son of Louis and Mary Leakey. In 1972, he found a human skull in Kenya, East Africa, that is 2.6 million years old.

Scientists keep finding that people are older than they thought. Now many scientists think that there may have been people on earth even earlier than 2.6 million years ago!

From *People and the Land*. Los Angeles: Bowmar/Noble, 1974, p. 30. Reprinted by permission of the publisher.

Basic Understandings. Inquiry into the nature of culture has gradually brought to light key generalizations.

1. Every society has a system of culture traits—behavior patterns and artifacts—through which members meet social and physical needs.
2. These traits include practices related to child rearing; courtship and marriage; punishment of offenders; religion; discrimination against social, sex, racial, or age groups; money and trade; agriculture and food; use of physical space and buildings; recreation and travel; and use of language.
3. All the culture traits operational within a society are interrelated. A change in one trait or the introduction of a new trait can trigger a series of changes in ripple fashion.
4. Cultures are always undergoing change as a result of the development of new knowledge within the group and contact with groups having different cultures.
5. Although all societies have culture traits that enable them to meet their basic needs, the exact traits may differ among societies.

In chapters 8 and 11, readers will find specific activities to help children discover some of these relationships for themselves. Such activities are particularly important in social studies programs that are geared to prepare young people for the future. In a world made smaller by more rapid forms of communication and transportation, groups will increasingly come into contact with other groups that possess significantly different culture traits. People must be prepared to meet other cultures by studies that make them open to different ways of doing things; people must learn to anticipate and appreciate the differences.

Inquiry into the Self

As investigators study human interaction in groups, it is sometimes of particular value to focus on the individual being—the person, the way he or she perceives the self and the world, and the way he or she functions based on these perceptions. All individuals have **basic needs** that go beyond air, food, water, rest, shelter, and clothing. These include the need for acceptance by others within the group, for achievement of personal goals, and for affection. Just how these psychological as well as physical needs are met determines in large measure the self-concept the person holds as well as the social concepts he or she develops.

Looking at the Self.   Questions that provide considerable information about individual behavior are listed below. These questions can be raised by teachers as they guide students in investigating how they themselves operate within society.

To what group does the person belong? What is the basis of his or her membership in each group?

What specific means does the person use to gain acceptance within the groups to which he or she belongs? Why does the person use these means rather than others? Does he or she employ the same means in every group to which he or she belongs? Are these means successful?

What roles does the person play in the groups?

What have been the major achievements of the individual? the major defeats? In what way has he or she been frustrated in the search for achievement?

At what levels are his or her basic physical needs (food, shelter, clothing) being satisfied? At what levels are the psychological needs being satisfied—need for recreation, mental diversion, entertainment? What are his or her hobbies?

How are the needs for affection being satisfied? In what ways has the person been frustrated in the search for affection?

How does the person view him- or herself—his or her mental capacity, physical attributes, "roots," social position, even the name he or she holds?

What beliefs, biases, values, and desires move the person to action?

The answers produced by questions like these are most critical; if large numbers of people within a society perceive their basic needs as unfulfilled, that society may well experience major dislocations.

Basic Understandings.   Youngsters in school social studies programs can begin to focus on the needs of individuals within the group by looking at themselves and asking: What are my needs? How are these needs being met? Do I like myself? Going beyond their own needs, older students can begin to develop some generalizations.

1. All human beings have basic physical needs (food, clothing, shelter) that must be met; in addition they have psychological needs (acceptance, achievement, and affection).
2. The level at which physical and psychological needs are met and the amount of frustration endured in meeting these needs determine in large measure one's concept of self and one's perception of the world.

Big Ideas from
Psychology

3. Each person perceives the world through the unique filter of one's own system of beliefs, biases, values, and attitudes. This same system is the driving motivational force behind one's actions.

Generalizations as the three outlined above are relatively simple; their simplicity, however, belies their importance. People must become more aware of and responsive to the needs of others; only with increased sensitivity will the youth of today be able to find solutions to tomorrow's increasingly complex problems.

Inquiry into Political Structures

One facet of the study of social structures is the study of political institutions operating within society and the behaviors that characterize political activity by members. Within the social sciences, political scientists focus attention on these structures, but clearly they are in the domain of other scientists as well.

Looking at Political Structures.   Questions that provide data about the nature of the political structures within a society include:

What **laws**, or codified sanctions, regulate human activity within the society?

Where does power reside in the society? How is power wielded?

In the society, how is authority of one person over another assigned?

What are the obligations of ordinary citizens to the larger society?

What rights do ordinary citizens retain?

What structures exist to carry out the legislative function? the executive function? the judicial function? the law-enforcement function?

What is the role of government in providing services to the people: fire and police protection, education, transportation facilities, health services, aid to the needy and aged, consumer protection, and protection in time of war or calamity?

How are conflicts resolved within the society? between this society and others?

Basic Understandings.   When asked about different countries studied as part of social science inquiries, the above questions lead to generalizations about the nature of political structures.

1. All societies have means—both legal and informal—of controlling the behavior of members.

Big Ideas from
Political Science

2. Societies differ in the rights retained by individuals, in the level of personal freedom afforded the individual, and in the control that the individual exerts over his or her own destiny.
3. All societies vest some authority for decision-making and social control in a person or persons who constitute authority and govern the state.
4. Societies require some means for formal lawmaking, carrying out the laws, and judging whether the law is being followed.
5. Societies differ in the basic services provided by the state; however, conduct of international relations generally is a function of the state.
6. In societies, there are numerous sources and levels of power. Members of a society differ in the degree of power each wields.
7. Governments change through evolution and revolution, but change is constant.
8. There is no single cause for conflicts within a society or among societies. Conflict can result from many diverse factors at work. The needs of society at large are often in conflict with the rights of the individual.
9. Most societies have approved means for resolving conflicts among members. Under some conditions, violence is an outgrowth of conflict.

Key words in the statements of generalizations given above—*power*, *rights*, *conflict*, *violence*—suggest how fundamental this category of social learning is. These are emotionally charged words about which people have strong opinions. In classrooms, this means that investigations must take into account underlying assumptions people have about what is right and what is wrong. Such investigations are marvelously effective contexts in which students can begin to make defendable value judgments.

Inquiry into Economic Structures

A related facet of study of social structures is inquiry into the economic institutions within a society and the behaviors that typify economic interaction and activity. In terms of the conventional divisions of social science, this study is primarily in the domain of the economist.

Looking at Economic Structures. The economist approaches human problems by asking:

What resources are available to this society for meeting the basic needs and more esoteric desires of members? What needs exist for which resources are inadequate? What means are employed to adjust demand to supply?

What structures exist for producing services and goods? for transporting services and goods? for distributing them?

What is the basis of financial exchange within the society? Who controls the exchange system—or money flow?

What jobs do people perform within society? Are jobs open equally to all those able to serve? Are there enough jobs for everyone? How do those who cannot work survive?

How is wealth distributed within the society?

How free is activity in the economic marketplace? How much control is wielded by government? by business leaders? by union leaders? by the average citizen?

How does a change in one component of the economic system affect other components?

Those who have asked these and other difficult questions are most concerned about how, on this planet of limited resources, humankind can stretch those resources to meet demands of a growing population. It is this concern that forms the focal issue of chapters 14 and 15.

Big Ideas from Economics

Basic Understandings.   If students are to be part of the solution to the problem of limited resources for the future, they must come to understand that in general:

1. Needs are limitless whereas resources are limited; the result is scarcity.
2. Scarcity implies that choices must be made among needs; all cannot be fulfilled.
3. Individuals do different jobs within a complex society; the result of this division of labor is dependency of one upon another.
4. In most societies, workers exchange their services for some kind of wage; the form that wages take differs from society to society.
5. In societies, wealth is distributed unevenly with the result being a group of haves and a group of have-nots.
6. Societies differ in the ease of entrance into jobs by members. In some, employment is dependent on membership in a particular class, caste, sex, race, religion, and/or age group.
7. The economic system is complex; a simple change can have diverse and long-range effects.
8. Basic economic decisions that all societies must make consciously or by happenstance include a.) What will be produced and in what quantity? b.) How and where shall these commodities and services be produced? c.) Who should receive the products, in

what quantities, and for what prices? d.) How much of the
society's resources both natural and human will be used for
production? e.) How much of society's resources will be
conserved?

As with the study of political structures, the study of economic structures is fraught with value related issues – issues that can be controversial. Young people in many instances will have to decide which way of
doing business is better, which form of sharing the earth's resources is
most equitable, which human need is most essential. These are questions to which there are no completely right or wrong answers.

Inquiry into Land Spaces

Society locates its towns and cities, its industrial and agricultural activity, its distribution centers, and its recreation spots in places and patterns that modern-day geographers have been attempting to analyze
in order to understand the dynamics of humankind's relationships with
the land.

Looking at Land Spaces.   Observing the way in which people
utilize land spaces, geographers ask:

Why are particular social and economic structures located as they
are? What is the relationship between the activity or activities
carried out at a site and the location of that site?

How does one population center relate to and affect other population centers?

How is the location of specific human structures–e.g., a railroad
line, an airport, an industrial complex, an electrical generating
plant–affected by geographic factors? social factors?

How does the location of limited and necessary resources affect
social structures?

What part does travel time from place to place play in the location of
sites for human activities?

How do changing means of transportation affect human activities?

How do regions of the earth differ? How do regional differences
influence the kinds of plants that can be grown, the eating habits,
building styles, recreational pursuits, and clothing of people living
there?

Idea Page

Background information for the teacher. This *Idea Page* shows how geographical understandings can be part of the elementary social studies. It can be used with a total class, small group, or individuals.

The aim. Reading information from a map. Proposing reasons for human activity. Seeing that many factors influence human behavior.

The introductory clues. The names of towns, cities, states, rivers, and lakes often tell us something about the history of a region and the people who lived there in the past. Because of this, history can at times be "read" from a map.

The pursuit. Figure 1.3 is a map of Nebraska.

List some names taken from the map of Nebraska. Then write your guess as to why that place was given its name.

From your list of guesses, can you propose reasons that explain some of the names given places on the map? List these reasons in the space below:

Places on the maps have acquired their names because of . . .

1. _____

2. _____

3. _____

Basic Understandings. Questions such as the ones outlined above are particularly useful in identifying the interactions among human activity, land spaces, and time. They have been brought to special focus on problems related to urban living. As these questions have been asked about numerous locations and spatial structures, generalizations have begun to emerge that clarify to some extent the relationships between land, time, and human activity.

Big Ideas from **Geography**

1. Regions of the world differ in their climate, ruggedness of terrain, proximity to major bodies of water, and kinds of natural resources.
2. The location and characteristics of an area, as well as the location of natural resources, have a bearing on the kinds of human activity possible at a site and the comparative wealth of nations.

Figure 1.3
Nebraska

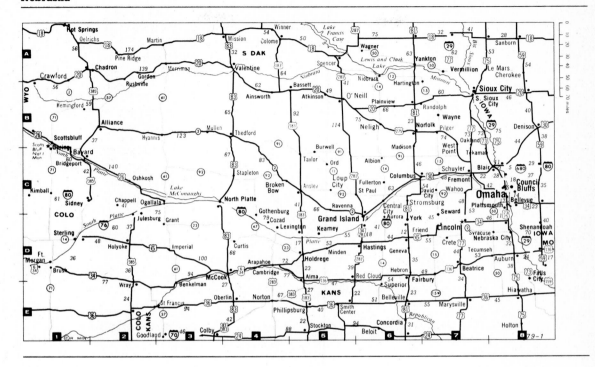

3. Geographic, as well as social, economic, and technological, factors determine the location of human activities.
4. Effective distance between points is decreased as travel time decreases. Travel time is a significant factor in the location of sites of human activity.
5. People's perceptions of places where they live and work affect their productivity, their attitudes toward their community, and the way they interact with others living there. People's perceptions of other places affect their attitudes toward people living there.

   Chapter 13 details specific investigations through which students can build these generalizations into their store of social understandings. These inquiries prove most stimulating because children are working directly with phenomena they encounter in their immediate environment.

Decision making is a natural component of historical investigations.

Decision A:
Where would you stand...
if this were July 4th, 1776, the day the
Declaration of Independence was signed?
Read the choices below, pick one and mark
your ballot at A.

1. I'd be a Patriot. I'd fight to make America free
   and independent of Britain.
2. I'd be a Loyalist (Tory). I'd be for legitimate
   British authority in America. I'd oppose
   independence.
3. I'd be neutral.
4. I'm not sure.

Inquiry into the Past

A society turns to its historians to trace what has happened in the past. The historian asks who?, when?, what?, where?, how?, and under what conditions? and then goes on to hypothesize why. In this respect, study of the past provides a record of how successfully or unsuccessfully people have met the challenges of a changing world; it provides a record of actual events in which decisions were made in terms of factors then considered important and against which present and future decisions can be weighed. Major understandings emerge as the historian unfolds the past.

Big Ideas from
History

1. Human existence is a record of constant change; change, however, does not always means progress.
2. Most major events in human history are shaped by a multitude of factors; one event in turn can trigger numerous others.

3. Every age has produced its complement of leaders who have functioned in diverse areas of human endeavor and has made its contribution to human civilization; people in some areas of the world during specific time periods have excelled in certain endeavors. These periods are known for specific contributions to the world's supply of ideas.
4. Ideas and innovations are built upon previous discoveries. Ideas are conceived within the context of the social milieu in which they emerge.
5. Human existence is a record of conflict, not a record of peace.
6. The past gives evidence of humankind's desire to find out and to explore the unknown. Humans have a curiosity that pushes them to look, search, inquire, and try the untried.
7. The past also gives evidence of humankind's tendency to gather in groups called nations to which people pledge their allegiance.

Recently, historical investigations have been gaining popularity in North America as individuals have begun to trace their family origins. A search for one's heritage builds understanding of the forces at work in society that have resulted in where one is today. For many it is a means of achieving greater self-awareness. But to be complete, this search must include an uncovering of one's ethnic and national heritages. Such a search helps one to identify where one hopes he or she and the nation will be in the future.

Putting the Social Pieces Together

Writing in *International Politics and Foreign Policy*, J. N. Rosenau charts the chief conceptual ideas of the **social sciences.** (See Figure 1.4.) Rosenau's chart makes clear that each social discipline is interested primarily in one aspect of human activity. Because discovery of knowledge in a complex world requires specialization, this is to be expected. However, the problems of the world do not come in neat

R See J. N. Rosenau, *International Politics and Foreign Policy* (New York: Macmillan, 1961).

Figure 1.4
Key Ideas and Conceptual Units
of the Social Sciences

Field	Central Organizing Idea	Chief Conceptual Unit
History	Time	Event
Geography	Place	Located area
Political science	Power	State
Economics	Scarcity	Market
Sociology	Social behavior	Social system
Anthropology	Culture	Cultural system
Psychology	Personality	Individual

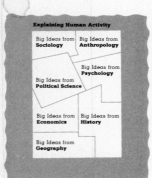

packages marked time, place, power, scarcity, and so forth. Dealing with actual problems as they occur every day, a person often considers facts related to several of the social sciences. Thus, in classrooms, it is impossible to compartmentalize study—considering history today, sociology tomorrow, and geography on another tomorrow. If knowledge is to be usable, students must put the social pieces together, develop an understanding of the multitude of forces that interact, and look at issues from a variety of perspectives.

Touching on the Uniqueness of Humankind

Social scientists deal with human activity in an attempt to generalize about it. Interestingly enough, many of the characteristics of human societies also exist within other animal societies. In some animal groups, members perform varying roles, differ in status, lay claim to territories, perform courtship rituals, and communicate clearly with one another. Conflict as well as cooperation exists, and rules govern the behavior of members.

Distinctly human qualities emerge when social scientists turn their attention to artistic, literary, philosophical, religious, and scientific endeavors. Yes, birds produce music, but they have no way to record it in a lasting form, and they cannot produce other than inborn variations on a theme. They can communicate with one another, but they have no way of recording their findings for the future so that others can gain from the experiences of the past. Each generation must begin by learning anew. Birds live their lives simply to survive from day to day with no thought as to the grand design of the world or to their own place within it. They do not systematically attempt to explain their own functioning or the social and physical environment in which they exist. Only human beings have an artistic, a musical, a literary, a philosophical, a religious, and a scientific bent.

The Humanities and the Social Sciences

To understand the nature of human activity, one must touch at some point on those characteristics that are distinctly human. In this context, the outpourings of humankind's creative and philosophical thinking are firsthand data that the social scientist analyzes to learn more about the way of life, the values, the feelings, and the beliefs of a culture.

Folktales, legends, myths, religious documents, biographies, autobiographies, and epics that have been handed down from generation to generation, first by word of mouth and then by the written word, make up one aspect of the data. By reading the literary record one can find out what people thought and valued in the past and how thoughts and values have changed over the years. By reading this record one can in some instances get a picture of how people lived in bygone days—the rituals they performed, the clothing they wore, the kinds of technological devices and tools they developed.

Music and dance also tell about the feelings, beliefs, and traditions of a people. Some forms are associated with warring, some with social activity, and some with ritualistic or religious celebrations. Both music and dance are used to tell stories, at times with the assistance of words but often without. The musical instrumentation within a society also gives a clue to the technological level achieved by a people. Some musical instruments are highly sophisticated devices, others relatively simple.

Art and architectural forms supply further evidence as to the beliefs and values of peoples past and present. These forms serve a multitude of purposes within a society. Colorful designs and sketches are used to embellish ordinary objects, to relieve the monotony of everyday living, and to make onerous tasks less difficult to bear. They are used to assign ranks to people within the group, as in the case of family crests and emblems. Art is a medium through which religious feelings are expressed; art objects are part of religious ceremonies and traditions. Cathedrals, churches, temples, and synagogues of immense size are constructed to serve as places of worship, to honor almighty beings, and to add beauty to the community. Other structures are built to represent deities, serve as time-measuring devices, tell stories, and provide shelter. Still others mark burial sites or house the bodies of the dead. Art in all its forms is used to represent the world and to express humankind's changing feelings toward the self, toward others, and toward nature. To "read" the art and architecture of a people is, therefore, to learn much about them.

Because art has communicative power, pictures were among the first forms of written language. Today social scientists study Babylonian cuneiform writing, Egyptian hieroglyphics, the Mayan glyphic script, and runic characters recorded by early Scandinavians to learn about those civilizations. In more recent days, philosophical and religious thoughts have been recorded in symbolic alphabetic writing. Through the writings of Plato, Aristotle, or St. Thomas Aquinas, a student of philosophy can come to understand the moral values and principles that have had a tremendous influence on Western thinking up to the present time.

Literature, music and dance, art, philosophy, religion, and sometimes history are the areas of learning that are generally grouped as the **humanities,** because through pursuit of them, human beings express their uniqueness. Clearly, the student of the social sciences must be a student of the humanities as well, for the products of the human mind make living not only finer and more beautiful but also more understandable.

The Natural Sciences and the Social Sciences

Where does this leave the natural sciences and technology? Does not the human mind demonstrate its uniqueness as much by its investigations of physical, biological, and social phenomena as by its artistic, musical, literary, philosophical, and religious pursuits? Surely, in using the mind to produce theoretical formulations, one is expressing one's humanness. Surely, in using the mind to create new technologies based on these formulations, one is functioning fully as a human being. For this reason, the products of scientific investigations—the theories and the technologies—cannot be considered outside the domain of social scientists.

Social scientists must be concerned with the effect of the natural sciences on society. They must at times look at the contributions of a Galileo, a Copernicus, a Pasteur, or a Curie in order to assess the impact of their discoveries on human activity. Changes in scientific thinking and in technology have resulted in significant changes in the way people operate in the world. Today science and technology are making even greater impacts. Yet critics often decry their influence, forgetting that many of the components of daily living that we take for granted are outgrowths of scientific advances. In studying human activity in the 1980s, there is simply no way that an investigator can ignore the natural sciences.

The Implications for the Social Studies Curriculum in Schools

A social studies program in the elementary school cannot divorce itself from other areas being taught and learned. This would not only be unwise from a pedagogical point of view, but it would be unsound from an epistemological view. To generalize about human functioning, one must look at both humanistic and scientific contributions to civilization and use the findings as data to be considered.

In terms of curriculum design, this means that all manner of content should become part of social studies. The teacher involves children in literary selections, art and architectural productions, musical selections, dance interpretations, philosophical ideas, religious beliefs, scientific theories, and technological devices as a way of heightening their understanding of how people function. Through this integration, the social studies is enriched as children come to understand what it is that makes them uniquely human.

The Social Studies Curriculum: A Design for Today

This chapter has proposed a design for a social studies in which key understandings from and questions raised within the social sciences unify and give direction to study. It has projected a design in which the outpourings from the humanities and to some extent the natural sciences are used as data through which students learn more about human activity and those qualities that are unique to Homo sapiens. These are two major themes found in the remaining chapters of this book. A third theme is that an integration within the social studies is essential if children are to build the conceptual framework necessary for effective problem solving and value decision making.

Skills are basic to this design. Students must learn to locate and gather data for themselves, organize these to highlight relationships, and communicate their findings, ideas, opinions, and beliefs to others. Only if young people have acquired both conceptual learnings and basic skills will they be able to function productively as citizens.

At the same time, students must also acquire the attitudes of mind and of spirit that make them open to new ideas and new ways of doing things. They must acquire an awareness of their own values, beliefs, biases, and interests so that when making decisions they operate with some understanding of why they behave as they do. They must learn to find solutions to problems by applying understandings gleaned from other situations. In short, our overarching goal as social studies educators is to help a host of dynamic young people, who have the requisite understandings, problem-solving skills, decision-making skills, search-and-communication skills, and personal-social skills, to meet the challenges of tomorrow today.

A Problem to Ponder

At the end of each chapter of this book and at points within longer chapters, the reader will encounter sections titled *A Problem to Ponder*. Here is the first problem to ponder.

Ms. Weinstein began a talking-together session by calling for volunteers to serve as chalkboard scribes. Matty, Jonathan, and Kevin volunteered their services. Anita Weinstein announced: "Let's brainstorm items of clothing you wear." As the children called out items, Kevin recorded those worn by both boys and girls; Matty, those worn only by girls; and Jonathan, those worn only by boys. The students called out items of clothing not already listed, which were generally worn by adults.

When the boards were full, the third graders analyzed their list. Their teacher queried: "What differences do we see in the kinds of clothing worn by boys and girls? by young people and adults? Under what conditions are different kinds of clothing worn?" The students organized items into categories: clothing worn on special occasions, worn for everyday activity, and worn around the house and for sleeping.

Ms. Weinstein probed further: "What makes certain clothing 'right' for boys? 'right' for girls? 'right' for adults? 'right' for young people? What makes certain clothing 'right' for some occasions? inappropriate for others?" The third graders suggested factors such as cost, warmth, comfort, and washability. They also suggested that people wear what everyone else wears. At this point, Ms. Weinstein asked the children to consider what tradition had to do with it. The children responded by offering examples of clothing traditions that are part of their culture and citing examples of changing traditions in regards to dress.

Ms. Weinstein displayed a series of pictures of people from different times and places. For each, the third graders described the dress of the people, then guessed reasons to explain why these particular clothing traditions exist. They talked of different jobs, climatic conditions, and ideas about the way people should act. Finally Ms. Weinstein displayed a photograph of Japanese people dressed in Western garb. She asked, "How can we explain the fact that these people dress as we do if their way of life is different?" The children noted that the Japanese may have borrowed their dress from the West. As the children talked, Ms. Weinstein interjected "culture trait" into the discussion. She referred to dress as a culture trait. Soon children were talking of how culture traits today are exchanged.

The third graders dispersed into groups to investigate the patterns of dress of a particular people. They were to sketch kinds of clothing, basing their sketches on pictures they would find in encyclopedias and trade books. They were to read about the way of life and discover particular patterns of dress. Later, groups shared their findings.

1. What social science understandings was Ms. Weinstein developing with her class?
2. What particular thinking skills were being developed?
3. What communication skills were being developed?
4. In what specific ways—through what activities—could Ms. Weinstein have continued to develop these learnings on successive days?

References

1. On the Goals of the Social Studies:

Flannagan, John; Shanner, William; and Mager, Robert. *Social Studies Behavioral Objectives*. Palo Alto, California: Westinghouse Learning Press, 1971.
Social Sciences Education Framework for California Public Schools. Sacramento, 1975.

2. On the Future:

Baier, Kurt; and Rescher, Nicholas, eds. *Values and the Future*. New York: Free Press, 1969.
Boulding, Kenneth. *The Meaning of the Twentieth Century*. New York: Harper & Row, 1964.
Clarke, Arthur C. *Profiles of the Future*. Rev. ed. New York: Harper & Row, 1973.
Cornish, Edward. *The Study of the Future*. Washington, D. C.: World Future Society, 1977.
Kahn, Herman; Brown, William; and Martel, Leon. *The Next 200 Years: A Scenario for America and the World*. New York: William Morrow & Co., 1976.
LaConte, Ronald; and LaConte, Ellen. *Teaching Tomorrow Today: A Guide to Futuristics*. New York: Bantam Books, 1975.
Laszlo, Ervin, et al. *Goals for Mankind: A Report to the Club of Rome on the New Horizons of Global Community*. New York: E. P. Dutton, 1977.
McHale, John. *The Future of the Future*. New York: George Braziller, 1969.
Shane, Harold. *The Educational Significance of the Future*. Bloomington, Indiana: Phi Delta Kappa Educational Foundation, 1973.
Toffler, Alvin. *Future Shock*. New York: Random House, 1970.
Toffler, Alvin, ed. *Learning for Tomorrow: The Role of the Future in Education*. New York: Random House, 1974.

2

Planning and Teaching for Active Involvement:

Creative Methods of Instruction

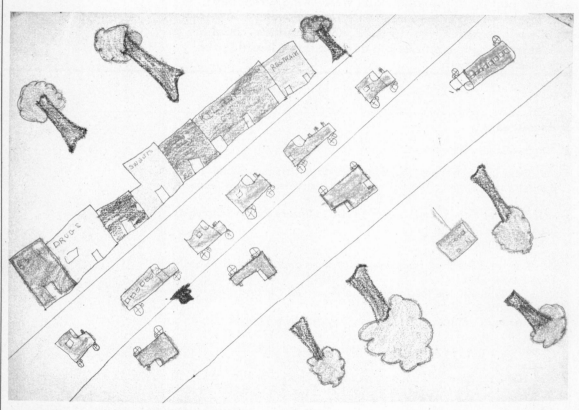

Fred is learning to express economic concepts through pictures.

It is the supreme art of the teacher to awaken joy in creative expression and knowledge.

Albert Einstein

Key Questions

What are the inherent weaknesses in a "let's-turn-to-the-next-page" approach to social studies?

What are three areas that must be considered in lesson planning? Why is each important?

Describe seven production strategies that can be part of a social studies lesson sequence. What objectives can be achieved through each?

What is the difference between role-playing and acting-out? between acting-out and chorusing-together? What objectives are achieved through these approaches?

What is the difference between gaming and simulation? Describe at least three different games and three simulations as they could be used in primary and intermediate social studies. What objectives could be achieved through each?

Figure 2.1
**Format for Lesson Planning
in the Social Studies**

Topic: _____

Major Social Studies Concept or Concepts to be Stressed (or in cases where
complex content is involved, a brief content outline):

_____

Objectives (learnings to be built or refined through the lesson):

1. _____

2. _____

Materials: _____

Procedures	**Related Key Questions and**
(sequence of learning activities):	**Structuring Remarks:**

1. Motivational Activity: _____

2. Continuing Activity: _____

3. Culminating Activity: _____

Topic of Next Lesson in Sequence: _____

Evaluation of Success of Lesson in Achieving Desired Objectives
(may be considered after the lesson has been taught):

_____

Introduction

B Teachers' negative attitudes unfortunately parallel the students'. Fred Prince in "Social Studies in Comparison with Other Subjects in the Elementary Grades, a Survey of Teacher Attitudes," in *Trends in Social Education* (Winter 1976, pp 26-30), reports that fewer than one-third of K-5 teachers who responded in a Florida study reported positive attitudes toward social studies.

Social studies can be exciting for children in the elementary grades. Students can be directly involved with fundamental concepts and generalizations as they produce a variety of materials that relate to those concepts. They can sing, dance, and recite in a manner similar to the peoples they are studying. They can act out their own feelings and reinforce factual understanding by playing games. In elementary classrooms where active involvement is the name of the social studies game, learning comes alive.

In contrast, social studies often has a negative impact on learners. Researchers who investigate children's preferences for school subjects find that students generally rate the social studies lower than most other subjects on a preference scale. The reason for this poor rating is perhaps traceable to the manner in which social studies is sometimes taught. In some classrooms, the social studies is taught by the "let's-turn-to-the-next-page" approach. The teacher with a very limited repertoire of instructional strategies starts many lessons with the statement, "Let's all turn to page 123." When the children locate the assigned place, the teacher asks, "What is the topic given in the title?" A volunteer reads the title printed on the page. The teacher then further directs, "Read the first paragraph to find out what it tells us about our topic," or—even worse—asks a student to begin the oral reading of the page paragraph by paragraph. Following the reading—through which some students stumble word by word—the children respond to a series of teacher-posed questions.

No wonder children turn thumbs down on social studies! The result of continued, repetitive use of this reading-recitation approach to instruction drains the excitement out of learning. Even more serious, the approach allows for the development of only limited skills and understandings. Vivid facts from the text may be recalled, and children may acquire some reading comprehension skills if teachers ask questions that go beyond recall. But that is it! Essentially the lesson is a poor one in reading, not an adventure into the social sciences.

Ques. One

The Way to Plan

How does a teacher avoid falling into the "let's turn to the next page" trap? The answer to this question lies in the way the teacher views lesson planning. The format for designing social studies lessons that is found in the introduction to this chapter suggests the direction that lesson planning should take. Given a particular topic to be taught, the teacher first studies the subject content to identify the key concept or concepts that will serve as integrating threads and that will pull the lesson sequence as well as the content together. These concepts are the big ideas of the social sciences—big ideas such as conflict, interdependence, change, scarcity, multiple causation. (See margin note.) Then the teacher identifies specific objectives—or student learnings—to be achieved. At this step in the lesson planning process, the teacher asks, "What specific skills, attitudes, appreciations, understandings, or facts do I want children to develop and/or refine through this experience?"

Ques. Two

T The *Social Studies Education Framework for California Public Schools* (Sacramento, 1975) identifies 18 concepts that serve as unifying threads in social studies lessons:

Citizenship
Justice
Freedom
Diversity
Culture
Resources
Multiple Causation
Needs and Wants
Property
Authority/Power
Scarcity
Social Control
Morality
Change
Conflict
Interdependence
Environment
Truth

With basic social science concepts and objectives in mind, the teacher considers the instructional strategies most likely to achieve those objectives and bring understanding of the concepts to be learned. He or she also considers the kinds of questions and leading remarks to use during chosen activity sequences. In this respect, a key element in lesson planning is the complementary pairing of instructional strategies and questioning sequences with concepts and objectives.

To succeed in this pursuit, the teacher must possess a vast repertoire of instructional strategies—in geographical terms, the teacher must have an extensive mental map comprised of hundreds of ways to structure lessons and must know the objectives that can be achieved through each strategy. And, of course, having taught the lesson—probably varying it somewhat from the original plan—he or she must be able to evaluate whether the chosen strategies did indeed achieve the planned end.

The Strategies: Ways of Teaching the Social Studies

Ques. Three

For purposes of discussion, we can categorize important social studies strategies.

1. production
2. drama
3. gaming and simulation
4. viewing
5. listening-viewing

6. search
7. sharing and discussion
8. writing
9. reading
10. brainstorming

In this chapter, we will describe those instructional approaches of a general kind (production, drama, and gaming and simulation), reserving consideration of strategies that apply to the development of basic skills and conceptual learnings to Part Two. In each case, objectives to be achieved through specific strategies are noted in the margin and/or in the introduction to the section.

All of the strategies described can be used within a variety of time frames. In some cases, a teacher may use a particular tactic as one part of a larger lesson. In other cases, a strategy can be used as the major component of a lesson or even of a series of interrelated lessons. The teacher's job—and it well may be the most creative task required of a teacher—is to weave individual strategies into a dynamic whole. Because each class is unique, because different subject content requires different approaches, no one can tell a teacher exactly how to work strategies together or how to juxtapose one with another. In this respect, the teacher is a creative designer.

Production Strategies: Doing Together

Especially with young children, understanding comes through direct, firsthand involvement with materials and events. One form active involvement can take is creating full-sized or scaled reproductions. In lower grades, this activity can comprise almost an entire lesson. In upper grades, production is more likely to be one component of a larger, ongoing learning sequence. But in either case, the key is that children are doing it together.

The Drawing Tactic

Given a written description of an object, area, or event, students can sketch their visual perceptions with crayon, marker pen or tempera and brush. For example, younger children studying contrasts between the city and the suburbs can draw their impressions, including key distinguishing features in their sketches. Studying life in the Pampas, older children can sketch the way the land appears, the kinds of homes typical of the region, and the crops that predominate.

G The student is able to translate verbal descriptions into picture form and to visualize steps in a process.

The drawing tactic is most appropriate as the class handles content containing an element of progression or change. For example, when considering how an area is changed by a new road, by war, or by the introduction of a new tool or machine, the students might sketch a series of pictures showing successive steps in the progression. Sketches can be organized as flowcharts with individual drawings tied together with arrows to indicate the direction of movement or change. Flowcharts are most useful in the study of processes: steps in steel making, in industrialization, or in urbanization of a region, or the passage of a bill through the legislature.

The drawing tactic can be used especially in primary grades to encourage students to contribute to a group endeavor. For example, each child draws one picture in a larger sequence—perhaps one event in a series, one happening in a story, one step in a process. Eventually, the drawings are pasted together so that an entire sequence is set forth in a long strip. The students can then take turns explaining their particular drawings. Or they clip the individual contributions with clothespins to a classroom sequence line, working together cooperatively to determine the most logical order. Incidentally, as the students learn to record their ideas in written form, they add words to their drawings. In kindergarten, the words can be labels supplied by the teacher and cut out and pasted on by the children. In first and second grades, youngsters can label with explanatory sentences.

T Cooperative student activity can result in the production of large murals, especially in upper-grades.

The Compiling Tactic

Children can prepare collections of materials or pictures that relate to a topic under investigation. For example, a class studying life in the North American Plains discovered that corn and wheat are important crops grown there. To find out the impact of corn and wheat on their own diets, these students searched their home cabinet shelves for products made from corn and wheat. Labels and packaging were organized onto posters. Later, studying the flood plains of China, some students discovered rice to be a major crop. Again they searched their home shelves for rice products, organized the packages into posters,

G The student is able to locate items that belong to a defined category and can display items located in a creative form.

A Problem to Ponder

Here is a picture of a city drawn by a second grader who lives in a suburb. What kinds of activities occur in cities according to this student's visualization? If you were the teacher, what things might you do to expand the child's concept of the city?

Figure 2.2

contrasted the importance of corn, wheat, and rice in their own diets, and then hypothesized whether all of these crops are important in Chinese diets.

Almost every area of social investigation lends itself to application of the compiling tactic. In some instances, students assemble collections of realia—actual objects. In others, they search magazines and old, discarded textbooks for pictures to clip. Pictures can be compiled as collages to which key words can be added for impact and interest. Actual materials can be set up as tabletop displays or in the case of very valuable materials, locked showcase displays.

The Reproduction Tactic — Objects

Upper grade youngsters studying the life of people in very early days constructed tools much in the manner that early peoples did. They used vines to bind stones to pieces of wood to form hammers; they searched for sharp rocks to serve as cutting tools; they made "spears" from long sticks and elongated rock fragments, using vines again to bind the two parts together. By making primitive tools, the sixth graders began to realize the problems inherent in toolmaking. They also began to realize the limitations imposed upon the life-style by the absence of tools that people today take for granted.

Later, the sixth graders displayed their reproductions in the school show case along with samples of modern tools. Their labels were in the form of questions: What kinds of tools did early people make? How did they make their tools? What advantage did people with tools have in comparison to those without any? What advantages do we have today as a result of the tools we have? As part of their display, the youngsters prepared charts detailing the development of tools and the significance of tools upon human activity. They mounted these charts behind their reproductions much in the manner of a museum display. Their exhibit served as a thought center for other students.

Primary grade students are especially delighted when asked to make things that relate to their social studies investigations. For example, as part of its study of Eskimo life, one second grade class made masks, embroidery, and engravings that are typically found within the Eskimo culture. Here the teacher used as reference an arts and crafts book, *Eskimo Crafts and Their Cultural Backgrounds* by Jeremy Commins (Lothrop, Lee & Shepard, 1976), that lists precise directions for making reproductions of artifacts. Another class made interesting puppet-like Vikings during a study of Scandinavia. Another created a model of the Kon-Tiki raft during a study of the South Sea Islands, and yet another made models of wagons during a transportation unit. In this respect, social studies activity can blend with art so that children not only acquire handicraft skills but an appreciation of the social studies area being studied.

G The student is able to generalize based on reproductions personally designed and created; she or he gets a "feel" for a time and place different from home base.

T Use materials creatively in model-making. Here is a bread-board converted into a colonial horn book:

T Helpful references are Helen Sattler's *Recipes for Art and Craft Materials* (New York: Lothrop, Lee & Shepard, 1973) and Richard Slade's *Modeling in Clay, Plaster, and Papier-Mâché* (New York: Lothrop, Lee & Shepard, 1968).

Idea Page

Production can involve a cooking activity as children follow recipes taken from other times and places, reproduce the culinary delight, and then sample it. Parents who have origins extending back into other lands can be helpful here, supplying recipes and assistance as the students cook.

Easy cooking activities, especially meaningful as children explore their own American backgrounds, include making:

applesauce	cranberry sauce
popcorn	peanut butter
corn bread	apple butter

Every country studied in the course of a year has an interesting dish to be sampled: tacos from Mexico, cruellers from the Netherlands, pasta from Italy, open-faced sandwiches from Denmark, to name just a few.

The Reproduction Tactic – Buildings and Communities

Young social scientists can recreate not only objects from other countries and time periods but buildings that other people have used as homes. After investigating life in different places and times, students can make reproductions of buildings from twigs, clay, and construction paper. When involved in the reproduction of tepees, igloos, stilt houses, log cabins, or cliff dwellings, youngsters experience some of the differences in everyday life resulting from the design of dwelling places. Models can be added to a mural or displayed on a desk or tabletop.

G The student demonstrates a more concrete understanding of how others live by reproducing buildings typical of a time and place.

One second-grade class made a paper reproduction of its town in colonial times. Each youngster contributed a building made from a piece of construction paper precut by the teacher. Some children designed the layout of the town, plotting the major river, ridges, and roads they found on an early map of the region. Others contributed by labeling cards for north, south, east, and west and for neighboring towns. Still others made trees, farm plots, fences, and signs for various buildings. Later, they used their reproductions as they considered changes in daily living patterns occurring from colonial days until today. In this instance, model making was a continuing activity carried out over numbers of days.

T Read Jean Kinney's *Twenty-three Varieties of Ethnic Art and How You Can Make Each One* (New York: Atheneum, 1976).

Reproduction of buildings need not be limited to the construction of colonial dwellings. Students studying life in ancient Egypt can create models of pyramids, while those studying life in the Middle Ages—the period of great cathedral building—can create reproductions of

Students who construct model towns begin to understand
the kinds of structures typically found in communities.

cathedrals complete with gargoyles and flying buttresses. The architectural features most characteristic of a particular time, place, or group are ones to consider for reproduction purposes: totem poles if Western Canada and Alaska are the focus of investigation; Easter Island statues if the South Pacific is the focus; a Stonehenge if early Britain is being considered; or, longhouses if the peoples of Borneo are being investigated. With primary children, the teacher may have to supply the materials and the design for model making, but with more mature learners, young architects can suggest ideas for both materials and design.

T See David Macaulay's *Cathedral: The Story of Its Construction* (Boston: Houghton Mifflin, 1973) and *Castles* (Boston: Houghton Mifflin, 1976), which supply drawings that youngsters can render as models.

The Reproduction Tactic – Landforms

Not only can the reproduction tactic be applied to study of buildings and communities, but it can also be applied to a study of landforms. To comprehend differences between mountains and interior plains, between plateaus and coastal plains, or between flood plains and deserts, young investigators can create reproductions of the landforms and add construction paper cutouts to represent typical foliage patterns. In like manner, they can make models to show different forms of land management—terracing, contour plowing, and so forth. In some instances, models can be made functional by constructing areas covered by different forms of vegetation—row crops, solid grass, and bare earth—and then tilting the models and pouring measured volumes of water over the surfaces. Comparisons can then be made of water-holding capacity and runoff.

In other instances, youngsters can combine reproductions of landforms with reproductions of objects to show people's use of the land. Students can make models of coal mines, offshore drilling rigs, or open-pit mines. In these cases, the models show both the engineering aspects and the layers of rock beneath the surface of the land. Such models are particularly effective in the form of dioramas—boxlike arrangements in which objects are laid out in a small box and scenery drawn on the sides of it.

> **G** The student is able to differentiate among and label a variety of landforms and can hypothesize relationships between landforms and human activity.

The Create-Your-Own-Chart Tactic

The value of charting as an instructional tactic cannot be overemphasized. Incorporated into short lessons or as part of several ongoing lessons, charts can be used in a variety of ways. Three particularly valuable kinds of charts in the social studies are group summary charts, change flowcharts, and data retrieval charts, which will be described in the following sections.

Group Summary Charts. Charting is very effective as a summarizing technique; after having investigated an area over a period of several days, students pinpoint the key ideas, laying them out clearly in chart form. Charts can be a simple listing of major points, basic terminology, or significant names. They can also consist of parallel listings of numerical data and words explaining those data, of events and possible causes of them, of names and significant happenings associated with those names, or of places and related events.

> **G** The student is able to use charts to summarize and to show relationships.

One way to compose summary charts is for students and teacher to create them together with the teacher or—in upper grades—a student serving as recorder. As the group talks about key ideas, the recorder lists them on a large chart. Especially with young learners, it is wise to stop and decide cooperatively what words should be recorded as the teacher guides the development of a chart step by step.

Charting is an equally effective small-group endeavor. Groups of students make charts that outline various aspects of a topic. If each

Figure 2.3
A Flowchart for Collecting Data
About Changes, Causes, and Events

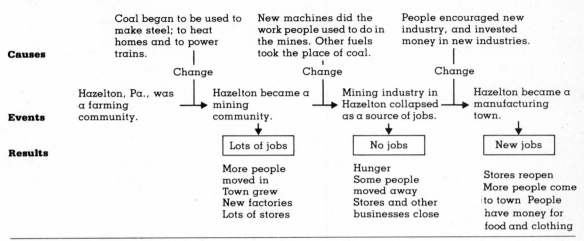

Causes — Coal began to be used to make steel; to heat homes and to power trains. | New machines did the work people used to do in the mines. Other fuels took the place of coal. | People encouraged new industry, and invested money in new industries.

Change | Change | Change

Events — Hazelton, Pa., was a farming community. → Hazelton became a mining community. → Mining industry in Hazelton collapsed as a source of jobs. → Hazelton became a manufacturing town.

Results —

Lots of jobs | No jobs | New jobs

More people moved in
Town grew
New factories
Lots of stores

Hunger
Some people moved away
Stores and other businesses close

Stores reopen
More people come to town People have money for food and clothing

Note: Use this design with any kind of content in which there is a series of changes. Start with instances where there is one change.

group assumes responsibility for a different facet, the charts can summarize major ideas of an entire unit. Posted on the bulletin board and illustrated with appropriate sketches, the series visually presents significant points. In this context, a useful technique is to make each group responsible for charting the related ideas from one social science discipline. One group, for example, outlines points about the government of an area being studied, a second outlines major ideas about geographical location, while a third considers social customs.

A Change Flowchart.   Flowcharts are a means through which a series of changing events, the causes of those events, and the results can be organized and visualized. The chart in Figure 2.3 is based on information in a third-grade textbook. (See Silver Burdett's *People and Resources*, 1979, pp. 27-41.) It suggests one possible way to record cause-and-effect relationships gleaned through informational reading. Events are laid out in blocks across the center of the chart. Causes are listed above each change. Results are listed below, as outcomes. Arrows indicate interlocking relationships.

An Information Grid.   A grid-like chart with a series of rows and columns is a useful technique when handling similar kinds of information about a number of different events, places, or people. Categories are listed at the top of columns; events, places, or people are listed in columns to the left. Facts are plotted in the resulting blocks.

Figure 2.4
Data Retrieval Chart: American Indian
Customs

Tribe	House	Forms of Food	Boats	Headdress	Money	Clothing
Hopi						
Iroquois						
Seminole						

Today information grids are often termed **data retrieval charts.** The data plotted on this type of chart can be used for developing comparisons and contrasts, generalizations, and value decisions. Figure 2.4 depicts a data retrieval chart that can be part of a comparative study of American Indian tribes. Older students complete the chart with brief summary statements, while the younger ones fill it in with representative drawings.

The Create-Your-Own-Graph Tactic

G The student translates numerical data into a graphic form and selects graphs to communicate by using them to clarify trends and make comparisons.

Students can translate into graphic form numerical data from chalkboard or wall charts, from projected transparencies, or from their texts. As they develop skill in graphing, their activity is guided step by step by the teacher; they decide what form the graph will take (line, bar, or pie), what units to set on the x and y axes, and where to plot specific points. Guided by their teacher's questions, students analyze the data on their graphs. They look for general trends, points of rapid increase, and points of rapid decrease, as well as any periods of sudden change. Analyzing together, they try to explain changes that they note. With this type of group preparation, young investigators later make graphs based on independent research.

The create-your-own-graph tactic is particularly useful, of course, with data that have a numerical dimension—population changes; changes in production of a commodity such as steel, oil, soybeans, alfalfa; relative speeds of different forms of transportation; employment figures; changes in family size; or changes in people's opinion on an issue. When data of these kinds are included in the text, graphing is a possible way of handling them—a short activity to sequence into a lesson. In other contexts, graphing can be an activity to include in a learning station, as demonstrated by the experience described on the Idea Page, page 44.

Production Strategies – A Summation

When young investigators make drawings, collections, murals, reproductions, charts, and graphs, they are actually making what Benjamin Bloom terms a **translation.** Most ideas can be expressed in a number of different forms; some are written, others pictorial, still others graphic. In making a translation, students are changing one form of communication into another. Although the process of translation requires only a relatively low level of thinking, according to Bloom, translation paves the way to higher levels of thinking. The student who has laid out data graphically or pictorially has organized them for analysis and as a result may be able to perceive relationships, trends, sequences, causes, and effects not clear before. For that reason, many experienced teachers apply production strategies early in a lesson series, sometimes relying especially on the related tactics during introductory experiences.

Most production strategies can be carried out as a total class, small group, or independent activity. An entire class can work on a production with each participant independently creating a part. In contrast, groups can produce large-scale visuals that can serve as organizing features for a report they are preparing. In these cases, several continuing work sessions may have to be dedicated to the production work. Individual students can also create pictures, models, and graphs at learning centers, which have essentially become production centers. Prepared by previous class experiences, individuals go to the center during work periods to create original visuals of material they have discussed or read.

G The student refines ability to

identify the key attributes of things,

classify based on similarities and differences observed,

generalize about relationships.

R See chapter 7 for a description of learning centers in the classroom.

Dramatizing Strategies

In selecting tactics for inclusion in lesson sequences, the teacher can also choose from a number of dramatizing strategies. In contrast to the production strategies that serve as a base for conceptualizing, dramatizing can be helpful as children build and refine human interaction skills. In dramatizing, children are working with each other and with problems of interrelationships rather than with concrete materials.

Idea Page

Background for the teacher. Children in primary grades can gather data about themselves to graph. This activity was devised by Domenica Swenson with her first grade-class.

The aim. Children become more observant about themselves and differences among them. Children compile data gathered in a graph and generalize from their graph.

Task 1. Make an eye graph and a hair graph. Count those with black, brown, hazel, and blue eyes. Color in the right number of squares on the eye color graph. Count children with black, red, brown, and blond hair. Color in the right number of squares on the hair color graph. A sample is shown in figure 2.5.

Task 2. Decide the color of most children's eyes. Decide the color of most children's hair.

The Role-Playing Tactic

ques. Four

In role-playing, students generally begin with a hypothetical problem situation presented in skeletal form. The role-playing situation can be presented in

1. A film or filmstrip sequence stopped before the resolution of the problem;
2. A brief paragraph to which students listen or that they read; the paragraph presents the basic elements of the problem on which players will elaborate;
3. A story read or heard;
4. A flat picture that depicts people interacting.

Once the scene has been set, students may volunteer for or are assigned roles to play. Without any previous discussion about how each player interprets the situation, they must extemporize dialog and actions on the spot, behaving as if they were actually in that situation.

G The student tries out ways of behaving in interpersonal situations and analyzes the impact of specific behavior options.

In turn, several groups can role-play a situation while observers watch for differences in the way a particular problem is handled. Follow-up discussion focuses on the pros and cons of various resolutions to the same problem situation. Key teacher questions to guide discussion may include: What are the different ways we can handle this kind of problem? What is likely to happen if we do this? What would happen if we don't do it? What effects does this kind of behavior have on others? What is the "right" action in this situation? What is

Figure 2.5
A Sample Hair-Eye Color Chart

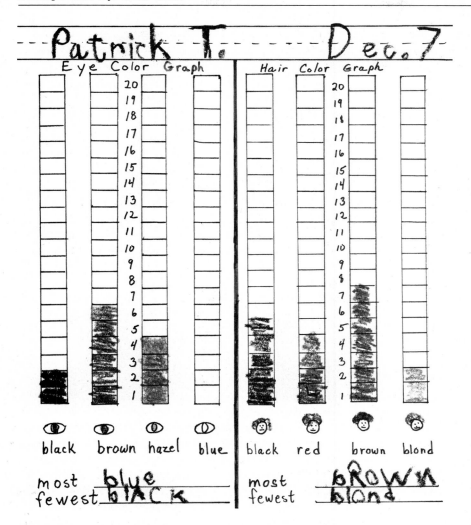

"wrong"? Are right and wrong the same in all situations? Under what conditions might it be wrong to . . . ?

Role-playing is a productive tactic to employ as children handle conflict situations in which there is an implicit moral question. Here the general design of a lesson sequence is:

1. Presentation of the problem situation in skeletal form;
2. Playing-out of the problem by several groups in turn;

3. Discussion of the different ways observed of handling this kind of situation and the conditions under which different approaches would be most appropriate.

B Read Fannie and George Shaftel's *Role-Playing for Social Values: Decision-Making in the Social Studies* (Englewood Cliffs, New Jersey: Prentice-Hall, 1967).

This design is useful even in primary grades. For example, in her kindergarten class, Roberta Stein showed a large picture of two youngsters outside a building marked library. It was raining. One boy had an armful of books. The other was sitting in a puddle next to his books. It was clear from the expressions and the stances of the boys that one had tripped the other intentionally.

Ms. Stein asked, "What building do you think this is? Where do you think the boys have been? Why does the one boy have lots of books in his arms? Why doesn't the other boy have books in his arms?" When the students had shown that they understood the dimensions of the problem, Ms. Stein said, "Let's call the boy in the puddle Kevin. The other one is Tom. If you were Kevin, what would you do next? If you were Tom, what would you do now? What would you say? Come and show me. Who would like to be Kevin? Who would like to be Tom?" In turn, several pairs of youngsters came forward to play the scene to show how they would act if they were really Kevin and Tom. In this class, the kindergartners volunteered freely, for they enjoyed the element of "let's pretend" inherent in the activity. Later, children who had not had an opportunity to play a role told how they would have acted.

The Acting-Out Tactic

In **role-playing,** students become actual participants in a problem situation—thinking, feeling, speaking, and moving much as they would if they themselves were real participants. There is no prepared script. There is no rehearsing of possible words or actions. The resolution of the problem comes about as the participants interact spontaneously with one another. In **acting-out,** on the other hand, performers do not play a role as they themselves would react if they were actually in the situation. They assume the personality, vocal and physical mannerisms, and dress of someone else. Performers act as they think the given characters would.

G The student gains skill in using vocal and body changes to communicate with others.

Acting-out is a viable tactic through which young people can gain understanding of current and historical events as well as of social customs. Understandings about what happened, why events happened as they did, why people behaved as they did, and how people lived and interacted are reflected in lines written and acted, in the props and scenery constructed, and in the costumes made and worn.

Designs for classroom acting-out sessions are varied. Some are listed on the following pages.

Dramatic activity helps children to understand the customs of other peoples and other times.

Research-Theater Companies. After some preliminary study in which the class identifies key facets of a unit topic, the students divide into research-theater companies. Each individual assumes responsibility for one facet of the topic. For example, investigative-dramatizing topics for a unit on the Revolutionary War might include:

The Winter at Valley Forge
Washington Crossing the Delaware
The Plight of Benedict Arnold
Life in Colonial Virginia
The Writing of the Declaration
  of Independence

The Stamp Act Controversy
The Boston Massacre
Life in Colonial Massachusetts
The Constitutional Convention
King George III and the British
  Parliament—Their View

Groups gather information from texts and reference books to incorporate into their scripts. They also locate ideas for costumes and scenery. Eventually, young players assume character roles, rehearse their parts, and share dramatizations that communicate major information and ideas. This design obviously requires considerable maturity on the part of students, a lengthy commitment of time, and much assistance on the part of the teacher, who must rotate among groups to guide students' research, script-writing, and rehearsal activities.

T Helpful references are Laura Ross's *Finger Puppets* (New York: Lothrop, Lee & Shepard, 1971) and *Hand Puppets* (New York: Lothrop, Lee & Shepard, 1970).

"Come by Here"), which comes from the African continent and has a long folk tradition.

A Class Production.   Students who have investigated a major topic
select one aspect for an acting-out activity in which all participate. To

Kum ba Yah

Kum ba yah, my lord. Kum ba yah!
Kum ba yah, my lord. Kum ba yah!
Kum ba yah, my lord. Kum ba yah!
    Oh lord, kum ba yah.

I am singing, lord. Kum ba yah!
I am singing, lord. Kum ba yah!
I am singing, lord. Kum ba yah!
    Oh lord, kum ba yah.

I am hoeing, lord. Kum ba yah!
I am hoeing, lord. Kum ba yah!
I am hoeing, lord. Kum ba yah!
    Oh lord, kum ba yah.

I am sowing, lord. Kum ba yah!
I am sowing, lord. Kum ba yah!
I am sowing, lord. Kum ba yah!
    Oh lord, kum ba yah.

T Use folk dances in
much the same way.

A student leader or the teacher begins the choral speaking, perhaps
clapping out the rhythm simultaneously with the hands or beating it on
a drum. On a second or third chanting, the class joins in.

Having chorused-together, young social scientists can hypothesize:
What does the chant tell us about the life-style of the people to whom it
belonged? What purpose do you think the chant served in that society?
What kind of society was it—industrial, hunting, farming? What kinds
of musical instruments would lend themselves best to the interpretation
of the piece? These questions lead directly to a consideration of religious practices, agricultural pursuits, and the relationships between
the two. They lead as well to contemplation of the function of songs and
chants in a society.

Chorusing-together is a valuable activity to include within a unit on
Native Americans. For example, the following Chippewa Indian song
is a powerful addition to the study of Indian culture.

A Song of Greatness

> When I hear the old men
> Telling of heroes,
> Telling of great deeds
> Of ancient days,
> When I hear them telling,
> Then I think within me
> I too am one of these.
> When I hear the people
> Praising great ones,
> Then I know that I too
> Shall be esteemed.
> I too when my time comes
> Shall do mightily.

from Mary Austin, *Children Sing in the Far West* (Boston: Houghton Mifflin).

One student who needs handwriting practice prints out a large chart with words from the selection and perhaps an illustrative sketch. This becomes the focal point of a bulletin board, and using it, the class cooperatively decides which lines to speak softly or quickly, and which to speak more forcefully or slowly. Together participants chorus the selection, trying out different vocal interpretations to express meanings most clearly.

Hypothesizing about the Chippewa culture is the natural next step in the lesson sequence. What was a hero to the Chippewa? What kinds of deeds were great ones? Why do you think this was the case with the Chippewa? How were stories handed down from one generation to the next? Who functioned as the historians of the group? Is our concept of a hero and great deeds the same or different today? Why do differences exist?

Songs and poems from different times and places can be used in much the same way in a variety of contexts. As young people study the westward movement across the North American prairie, such poems as Vachel Lindsay's "The Flower-fed Buffaloes" and Carl Sandburg's "Buffalo Dusk" make superb material for group chanting. Some of Langston Hughes' pieces—"The Negro," for example—correlate easily into a study of slavery. Cowhand songs, sea chanties, railroad songs, work chants—all of these can help students better understand a people or a time other than their own.

Dramatizing Strategies: A Summation

Dramatizing is fun! It also makes learning more meaningful. When role-playing, acting-out, and chorusing-together, students are *involved*; and involvement means that students are feeling, thinking, and interacting.

Gaming and Simulation Strategies

Games have become an integral part of many classrooms. Students play instructional games in which they match cards–questions with answers. They play "baseball": they move around bases driving in "runs" for their teams and amassing points by correctly answering questions "pitched" by a classmate or the teacher. Clearly such games can be developed based on social science content and vocabulary.

Game Tactics

Game tactics can be applied in almost any unit of social study. They can be used to review and reinforce terminology, facts, and ideas. In most of the games involving questions and answers, students can participate not only in the playing but in the writing of questions that are part of the action. Here are some formats that have proved workable, especially for review purposes.

G The student can ask questions that narrow the range of possible answers. The student demonstrates knowledge of basic social studies facts.

1. Twenty Questions.   In this game, the leader thinks about a particular phenomenon–an event, an object, a person, a location–associated with a unit under investigation. Players must phrase questions that gradually narrow the possibilities. Students playing twenty questions soon learn that if they are to identify the phenomenon in only twenty questions, they do not start with very specific questions. Rather they begin with broad questions such as, "Is it an historical event?" or "Is it a custom associated with the country?"

G The student is able to relate a term with its definition.

2. Crossword Puzzles.   The teacher or students can create crossword puzzles using the names and terms from a unit. Puzzles are duplicated and placed at a table where students can go in groups of two or three to complete a puzzle by writing directly on their own copy. A piece of clear acetate can be placed upon the master puzzle; students complete it by writing on the acetate with washable crayon. They can check answers by comparing with an answer key also located at the game center. The advantage of group completion of crossword puzzles is that the students can discuss possibilities before writing them down. This provides an opportunity for students to use the new terminology.

3. Crosswits. Crossword puzzles can be set up as a group activity in the manner of the TV program Crosswits. The puzzle grid should be projected with only the word numbers showing. One team then identifies the particular word number it will try. The leader reads the definition of a term, and the team tries to guess the word in question. All the words from one puzzle should focus on one element of social studies, so teams can try to guess the unifying relationship.

Students in teams can create crosswit puzzles for other teams to figure out, determining words and definitions based upon the content they are studying. Incidentally, this technique can be applied at the end of the year as a major form of review. Crossword puzzle makers must go back to units covered throughout the year. This makes identifying the topic of the puzzle more challenging and is an excellent means of reviewing the year's work.

4. Jeopardy Boards. Jeopardy boards are comprised of questions on a series of related subjects, placed on cards. The cards are arranged facedown. The questions are ranked in order of apparent difficulty. Student players select cards according to the topic categories and to the point values assigned. The question on the card selected must be answered correctly to bring the point value to the team. If it is missed, the point value is subtracted from the team's score. Again, students should participate in the production of the boards, developing questions from their viewing, listening, reading, and talking activity.

A Caution. Thoughtful analysis of the games described above makes clear that it is a rare game that carries children beyond the facts and terms of a unit to consider more complex relationships. But there are some facts and terms that need considerable review before students come to "own" them. Looked at from this point of view, games have a role to play in the social studies.

Simulation Tactics

Many authorities in the field of simulation instruction distinguish between games and simulations. In games, there is generally no attempt to replicate reality; in **simulation,** such an attempt is made. The operations, rules, and roles are similar to those in the comparable real-life situation. Some of the same bonanzas and catastrophes occur in the simulation as in real-life. By pretending to be a participant in a situation, assuming roles, adhering to rules applicable to it, and making decisions and recommendations as part of a situation, students can learn firsthand about factors—or variables—that are important. In this respect, simulations oftentimes have a greater potential than do games for getting children involved in higher-level thinking processes.

Here are some forms that simulations can assume.

1. The Assembly Line. In this simulation, students work cooperatively to complete a task. Each participant must work on all items produced by the class, performing the same component task on each one of them. For instance, students who are preparing for an open house can make invitations on an assembly line. Some become paper cutters, while others work as folders, illustrators, envelope stuffers, addressers, or envelope closers. Students who have repeated the same task over and over soon come to feel some of the same monotony that occurs on an assembly line or feel the impatience that comes about when they must wait for others. On the other hand, they may also perceive the increased efficiency that results from assembly line production.

G The student gets a firsthand feel for being a cog in the wheel.

2. The Production Team. Students who are producing a class newspaper or magazine can form production teams. There should be a team of editors, copywriters, compositors, reporters, and so forth. Each team must perform its part of the job to obtain the finished product. Students who have functioned as part of a decision-making production group and on a mechanized assembly line can compare their feelings. Why would one get considerable personal satisfaction from being a member of a production team?

G The student is able to make decisions and recommendations based on information at hand.

3. The Problems-Decision Team. Simulations can be structured around hypothetical problems to be solved. Students form teams, not to create a product but to come up with a plausible solution or a feasible recommendation for action based on data supplied. Such a problem follows.

Problem: Colonizing a New Land

You plan to start a new colony somewhere on the northern shore of Australia. Study that shore and make the following decisions. You should be able to give a reason for each decision you make.

1. What would be the best location for your settlement?
2. What kinds of tools would you take along with you?
3. What kinds of clothes would you take along?
4. What member of your group will you make colony leader?
5. How many other people would you take along? What kinds of people would you particularly like to include in your group?
6. What responsibilities would each colonist be given?
7. What social rules would you establish before you set out?
8. What tasks would you plan to do immediately upon landing? In what order would you start these plans?

Students who have already had a unit on colonization can apply their understanding of the settlers' problems to their hypothetical colonization. As a challenge, the teacher can distribute contingency cards at random to the teams after they have made colonization plans. Planners must decide what they will do based on the circumstances.

Catastrophe Cards

You encounter drought conditions.

There is a flood.

You find that the soil at the chosen site is too rocky to till.

The plow you took along with you breaks.

Your leader drowns in the river.

A dysentery epidemic strikes your settlement.

Natives try to sabotage your settlement.

There is a fight; your chief judge is killed.

Five workers stage a rebellion and try to take over settlement.

Bonanza Cards

You find a mineral lode.

The natives are friendly and offer you their extra dwellings.

There is a ready supply of a native product called Wise, which can become a basic food staple.

The soil is very fertile.

The climate is ideal—not too cold, not too hot.

A number of social studies units can be organized as simulations of the problems-decision team type. Simulations can take the form of:

a. Planning a trip through another country—that country being one currently studied.
b. Planning a trip through a particular region of their own country – students can plot out a trip from the west to east coasts of the United States, considering all the things they would need to take along if they went by car, possible stopping places and reasons for stopping there, and probable length of time for each leg of the journey.
c. Planning an airline trip around the world—participants must consider not only stops and purposes but changes in time, airline routes and schedules, differences in customs and foods, and water conditions.

d. Writing out a constitution for a new nation they are forming –
students must make decisions about who will have responsibility
for carrying out the basic tasks of government and what rights
will be guaranteed for the people.
e. Designing plans for an ideal community–simulators will make
decisions on what services will be supplied, where these services
will be located, and so forth.
f. Planning for an emergency that could strike their community –
participants decide who will do what, when.

Simulations of these kinds have been packaged commercially and
are available for the teacher who wishes to involve youngsters in the
decision making and recommendation-formulating that characterize
the best of simulation activity. One series is marketed under the name
Interact and provides the cards, forms, charts, and boards necessary
for children to make decisions on topics such as:

"Equality: A Simulation of the Struggle for Racial Equality in a
Typical American City."

"Discovery: A Simulation of Early American Colonization."

"Ecopolis: A Simulation of a Community Struggling to Solve
Ecological Problems."

"Mahopa: A Simulation of the History and Culture of the North
American Indians."

"Statehood: A Simulation of Forces Shaping a State's Past, Present
and Future."

"Dig: A Simulation in Archaeology."

The titles of these commercial packages suggest the scope of topics
open to study through simulation. A teacher who has tried the materials and approaches embodied in prepared simulations can take the
natural next step–creation of simulations based on ideas, events, concerns that children are discussing.

4. The Individual Problem to Be Solved.
Sometimes problems re-
quire that the individual devise a hypothetical plan of action. Teachers
can set the dimensions of an individual problem in the following form.

It's Up to You!
Tomorrow you learn that you have won $20,000. Decide what you
would do with this money. Set up a budget, listing on paper each thing
you would do with this money. Next to each entry, indicate why you
decided as you did.

The same approach can be used to go beyond value decision-
making to highlight principles of economics. Upper graders can become junior financiers in the following activity.

How to Invest?

You have saved $20,000. You cannot spend it. You must invest it so that you get the best growth of your money in order to go to college. Decide what you will do with your money.

This problem was given to fifth graders in a wealthy, college-oriented suburban area. Each day, the students had been bringing in the newspaper and learning how to read the stock information listed in the financial section—closing price, daily high and low, yearly high and low, dividend, even the price-earnings ratio. In addition, representatives from local banks had visited the classroom to explain the kinds of accounts they offered.

Based on these data, each student had to decide what to do with the twenty thousand dollars. Each day, they followed their investments, charting how much they had lost or gained by deciding as they did. These fifth graders quickly developed a vocabulary and an understanding of economic terms that they used like professional investment consultants. They also gained an understanding of the profit motive in the free enterprise system. A visit to a local brokerage house where they watched their stock symbols move across the board to register profits and losses proved a highlight of the economic simulation.

Similar simulations in different school settings can be structured around:

spending the weekly food budget: What should we buy to get the most out of our food dollars?

choosing a new or used car by studying folders, prices, ads, and *Consumer Reports*

selecting the best buy on almost any product

deciding on a career through a systematic analysis of self and possibilities

deciding on a college-for-the-future. Upper graders make choices after examining college catalogs, maps, and hypothetical sources of financing

Clearly, students do not actually make the purchase or follow the plotted plans; rather they propose a set of plans. They think through the pros and cons, and in so doing grow in the ability to handle the decision-making process.

Games and Simulations – A Summation and a Warning

Games and simulations have a place in elementary social studies. These strategies lead to growth in working with facts and in making decisions given certain conditions; they are good motivators, particularly of slow learners or nonreaders. Teaching social studies primarily through games and simulations, however, would be as much a mistake as teaching entirely through reading-discussion or through dramatizations. Simulations and games are often time-consuming and at times difficult to implement, as teachers who have tried the strategies are quick to remind.

Planning simulations to build into lessons and units is not a simple task, for planning means evaluating and selecting diverse tactics and weaving them systematically together so that each activity flows logically out of previous ones and leads into ones that follow. In this respect, the teacher who chooses to use simulation as part of a lesson or unit must have a clear understanding of why the activity is appropriate at that point; the direction from which the class has already come; the direction in which the class will go; and the goals sought. Used sparingly with the learnings to be achieved clearly thought out, simulations and games can be interspersed with other teaching tactics to add another dimension to the social studies.

Planning and Teaching for Active Involvement: A Summary Thought or Two

B See chapter 16 for sample units that rely on numerous and diverse strategies.

Children have relatively short attention spans. They can sit and listen attentively for only a brief time, especially if they are asked to listen to complicated content material. For this reason, teachers must include creative strategies in their lesson sequences that involve students not only intellectually but physically and emotionally as well. Comprehension comes through active involvement—by doing and making, acting-out, role-playing, singing, chorusing, and pretending. These activities must be components of the social studies, beginning in kindergarten if children are to gain a positive perception as well as an understanding of the social sciences.

Tasks to Try

1. Write a plan for a social studies lesson following the format given in the chapter introduction. Choose any topic and concepts that you wish to stress, but include at least one activity that directly involves the students. Try the lesson with a group of children if possible.
2. Locate a selection of prose or poetry that lends itself easily to interpretation through choral speaking as part of social studies

unit study. Lead a group in chorusing the piece together.
3. Devise a game that could be used for review purposes during or at the end of a unit of study. Make the necessary cards and parts. Then try it out with a group.

References

Furness, Pauline. *Role Play in the Elementary School: A Handbook for Teachers*. New York: Hart Publishing, 1976.

Glenn, Allen. "Simulations in the Instructional Sequence." *The Social Studies* 68 (1977): 23-26.

Good, Thomas; Biddle, Bruce; and Brophy, Jere. *Teachers Make a Difference*. New York: Holt, Rinehart & Winston, 1975.

Greenblat, Cathy; and Duke, Richard, eds. *Gaming-Simulation: Rationale, Design, and Applications*. New York: Halsted Press, 1975.

Heyman, Mark. *Simulation Games for the Classroom*. Bloomington, Indiana: Phi Delta Kappa, 1975.

Inbar, Michael; and Stoll, Clarice. *Simulation and Gaming in Social Science*. New York: Free Press, 1972.

Livingston, Samuel; and Stoll, Clarice. *Simulation Games: An Introduction for the Social Studies Teacher*. New York: Free Press, 1973.

McIntyre, Barbara. *Creative Drama in the Elementary School*. Itasca, Illinois: F.E. Peacock Publishers, 1974.

Nesbitt, William. *Simulation Games for the Social Studies Classroom*. 2nd ed. New York: Thomas Y. Crowell, 1971.

Norn, Robert. *The Guide to Simulations/Games for Education and Training. Academic Games*, Vol. 1. 3rd ed. Crawford, New York: Didactic Systems, 1976.

Schneider, Donald; and Roberts, Mary. "Identifying and Selecting Media for the Social Studies: A Selective Guide to Sources." *Social Education* 40 (1976): 284-288.

Shaftel, Fannie; and Shaftel, George. *Role-Playing for Social Values: Decision-Making in the Social Studies*. Englewood Cliffs, New Jersey: Prentice-Hall, 1967.

Wagner, Guy; and Gilloley, Laura. *Social Studies Games and Activities*. New York: Macmillan, 1971.

Part Two

The Basics in the Social Studies:

Skills, Conceptual Learning, and Values

> **. . . learning is a system in which content and skill are interwoven and where ideas motivate students to improve their skills.**
>
> **Lawrence Senesh.**
> ***The Social Studies.***
> **January/February, 1978**

In these days of calls for a return to "the basics," teachers must know what is basic in the social studies. For that reason, Part Two provides a framework to guide teachers in arriving at their own definitions of the phrase by describing skill areas, thinking processes, and valuing activities that many social educators have considered basic. Chapter 3 discusses ways to involve children in a variety of search and communication skills, based on the assumption that people must know how to gather information, interpret it for themselves, and share it with others if they are to function as lifelong learners. Chapter 4 focuses on reading and writing skills that can be acquired even as children learn about the way the world of people works. Chapter 5 clarifies map skills and activities appropriate at primary and intermediate levels as well as ways to expand children's concepts of time. Because conceptual learning and its application are vital within a content area in which students encounter big ideas from so many important disciplines, chapter 6 describes processes through which children develop skill in conceptualizing, generalizing, and applying their learnings to new problems. It also describes ways to help children render value-decisions that they can support with reasons.

3 Strategies for Finding Out and Sharing

Children shared their drawings during talk-time.

all questions

**Knowledge is of two
kinds. We know a
subject ourselves, or we
know where we can find
information upon it.**

Samuel Johnson, 1775

Key Questions

Why is picture reading an important skill? How can
picture reading be made an integral part of lesson
sequences in the social studies?

How can models and artifacts be used to help children
develop an understanding of human activity?

What roles do charts, diagrams, and graphs play in
the social studies?

What interpersonal listening skills should be acquired
as part of social learning? What strategies can the
elementary teacher employ to achieve these
objectives?

What is meant by basic location skills? How can
schools help children acquire location skills? How can
schools help children process the information they
have located?

What interpersonal sharing skills should be acquired
as part of social learning? What strategies can the
elementary teacher employ to reach these objectives?

Figure 3.1
A Graph to Interpret: The Energy
Outlook, 1975-1990

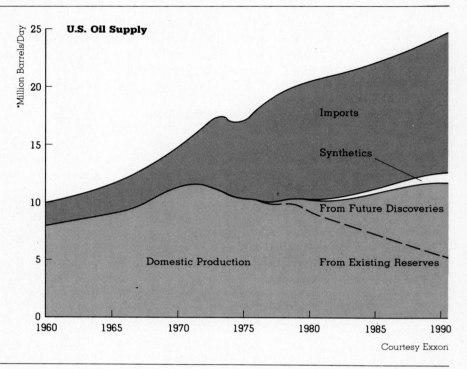

Courtesy Exxon

What does the graph in Figure 3.1 "say"? In 1975 how many barrels of oil were Americans consuming per day? What percentage of that oil was produced at home? What percentage had to be imported? Will Americans be more dependent on imported oil by 1990? By then, how many barrels of oil will Americans be consuming per day? What percentage of that oil will be imported? What percentage will come from synthetics? What percentage will come from domestic oil yet to be discovered? What factors could make the prediction for 1990 better or worse for the United States? By 1990, how many million barrels of oil will Americans be consuming per year? How does that compare to the oil consumption in 1960?

Based on the graph, can you develop a chart that presents the information in a different way? Can you convert the line graph into a bar or circle graph? Can you write a paragraph describing the U.S. oil consumption pattern in 1990? Can you explain to someone else the change in oil consumption in the United States between 1960 and 1975 and the projected consumption between 1975 and 1990? Can you locate additional references that provide information on U.S. oil consumption? Can you create written notes based on the information you locate? Can you use those notes to share your findings with others?

To answer these questions, one must possess a variety of search and communication skills. These basic skills are essential if today's students are to function as perceptive citizens. To keep abreast of changing conditions and take a defendable position on issues, citizens must be able to:

find out by listening and by interpreting pictures, objects, graphs, charts, and diagrams;

locate information in references and process it;

express ideas orally in both conversational and reportorial situations;

read and write with skill.

Viewing with Perception –
A Basic Way of Finding Out in Social Studies

One cluster of communication and search skills – the ability to look at visual materials and events and to interpret what is being "said" – brings independence as a learner. This cluster includes the ability to:

interpret relationships expressed pictorially;

perceive meanings expressed by models, objects, and artifacts;

interpret charts, diagrams, and graphs;

interpret maps and globes.

Let us look briefly at the first three skills of this cluster as each relates to social studies instruction. Because maps and globes are such key tools of the social scientist, related skills are considered in chapter 5.

Basic Picture Reading Skills

Ques Dne

Through careful analysis of pictures, students of the social sciences can gather a wealth of information, especially about the way people in different parts of the world live. Questions leading to increased understanding of a particular picture can include the following:

G The child is able to see relationships expressed pictorially.

1. Human Activity. What are the major activities of the people shown in the picture? What are the minor activities? What do the people's facial expressions, body stances, and body motions indicate about their feelings toward their activity? What does their manner of dress indicate about their way of life? their level of income?

2. Signs of Progress.   What objects in the immediate environment give a clue as to the people's way of life? What kinds of tools and technical devices are they using? In what kinds of buildings do they dwell or work? What means of transportation are evident? What means of communication are evident?

3. The Geography.   What does the visible plant and animal life tell about the climatic conditions? What kinds of geographical features (hills, mesas, rivers, etc.) are visible? In what ways do these features affect human activity?

Questions such as these can be directed at flat pictures, which are available in folders organized according to social studies themes. They can be used to interpret pictures in textbooks, encyclopedias, or magazines and to analyze 35 mm slides. When viewing films, students should not only gather information from the sound track but also from the pictures. An interesting experience is to run a film first without sound to see how many points students can garner from the visual presentation, and then rerun it with sound to encourage students to check their visual perceptions against their verbal ones. Through focused picture-reading experiences, students will learn to:

describe human activity they see in pictures;

look for clues that provide useful information about the way of life in an area—clues such as dress, tools, technical devices, building styles, and means of transportation and communication;

perceive climatic and geographical clues;

analyze relationships;

differentiate value judgments they make from factual information they gather when they look at a situation.

Interpreting Models and Artifacts

Ques. Two

Another necessary skill is the ability to view real objects and models with perception, especially artifacts—things made by humans with a view to subsequent use. "Viewing" in this context encompasses more than "looking at"; it has elements of "doing with" and "thinking about." Students handle, stroke, manipulate, sketch, label, and experiment with, going on to hypothesize functions and judge usefulness.

Observational activity is particularly relevant as children study artifacts of other cultures. Chopsticks, tatami mats, rice-paper screens, for example, are generally available in specialty shops and can be a part of study of Far Eastern cultures. Such artifacts from other cultures—as well as models of them—add to area studies. Often students will have things to loan, and parents who have traveled widely will willingly share artifacts they have collected and explain their treasures to students; local museums will loan artifacts from their collections too. When talking about them, students can consider the uses to which objects have been put and hypothesize about some of the reasons why they have survived the test of time. Observations can be jotted down, and diagrams can be drawn in individual notebooks and/or in the Class Book of Artifacts—a large-sized, loose-leaf notebook with alphabetically arranged entries, one to a page. An entry can be comprised of a labeled sketch, the name of the artifact, the area of the world where it is used, a description of its physical characteristics, and a statement about its purposes.

Observational activity can start in the early primary grades. Young children can handle objects as they sit together in talk sessions. They can propose descriptive words, which the teacher records on large charting paper. Later, students can propose descriptive sentences, selecting from the words already suggested. The result is an experience-culture chart that youngsters can read and reread; each youngster can make a copy next to a labeled diagram that he or she has drawn.

G The child is able to give a clear verbal description of an object.

From continuing activities such as these, students will learn to:

use all their senses to make thorough observations;

describe in clear verbal and visual language what they have observed;

formulate hypotheses related to the use, serviceability, and practicability of artifacts studied.

Graphic Interpretations

Three other useful tools of the social scientist are charts, labeled line drawings, and graphs, all of which depict information diagrammatically and facilitate the analysis of it.

G The child is able to interpret information presented as charts, diagrams, and graphs.

Ques. Three

Charts.   Although charts assume many forms, a tabular one is functional for consolidating information. A tabular chart presents information in a series of columns and rows—for example, a table showing the coal-producing nations in a column on the left, successive calendar years across the top, and the number of tons of coal produced each year by each country in the resulting grid. If this table is contrasted to one displaying coal-consuming nations, relationships are made strikingly clear.

T See chapter 2, pp. 40–42 for a comprehensive discussion of charts.

Materials to Study – Idea Page

What skills are being taught through activities such as those shown in Figure 3.2? What other kinds of materials could you use for the same purposes? What social science concepts are being touched upon in this type of activity?

Figure 3.2

YOUR TEST

USING YOUR PICTURES

From *Living in Families*, Teacher's Edition. (Morristown, N.J.: Silver Burdett, 1979), p. 156.

Line Drawings.   Labeled line drawings, or diagrams, can also be helpful in communicating relationships, especially structural ones. A line drawing depicts the structure of an object, generally with key components clearly labeled and with minor, distracting elements deleted. Encyclopedias are packed with labeled diagrams that clarify what an object actually is better than the accompanying text; there are diagrams of the floor plans of architectural structures like cathedrals, forts, and homes; of tools and technological devices; of topographic features; even of storm patterns. An uncluttered diagram can be reproduced, and a transparency can be made from the reproduction, which can be projected on a screen and analyzed during a discussion session. Some of the most productive classroom interpretive periods are those structured around a projected diagram or chart.

Graphs.   Many of the same instructional approaches can be applied to graphs, visuals that depict numerical relationships through a continuous or broken line (line graphs), through symbols (pictographs), through a series of columns (bar graphs), or through a series of segments cut from a whole (pie graphs). For some students, the numerical components make graphing a rather difficult skill to master. The learner must acquire the ability to:

plot and read points on a two-axis grid;

select appropriate incremental steps to be spaced out on the two axes of a graph;

interpret the data in terms of equal steps on the axes of existing graphs;

label the axes with units on the graphs under construction and interpret the labels on existing graphs;

perceive the relationships and trends in the data displayed on a graph.

Direct instruction through active involvement is imperative if students are to construct graphs based on the gathered information. Perhaps the easiest beginning is to restrict the numerical increments to one dimension of the graph with the second dimension being simply names. For example, primary students can start by graphing everyday phenomena related to themselves, labeling the increments along one axis with the cardinal numbers and the increments along the other axis with their own names. Plotted on the resulting grid is the number of days during that month that each student has been absent, the number of minutes it takes each to walk from home to the school, or the number of family members living together in their homes. From the

Figure 3.3
Some Sample Graphs

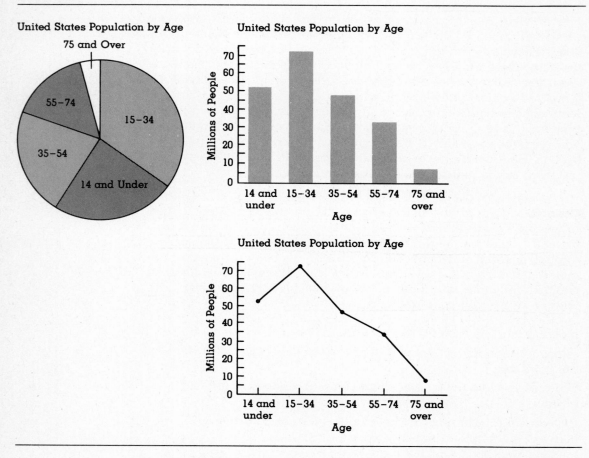

United States Population by Age

United States Population by Age

United States Population by Age

From *People and Resources*, Teacher's Edition. (Morristown, N.J.: Silver Burdett, 1979), p.232

plotted points, students can color in a bar graph or create a pictograph in which a representative number of symbols is drawn along the appropriate rows. If beginning graphs are constructed along the full length of the chalkboard, students can generalize based on the information. Simple graphing can lead to similar activities in which names of countries or states can be substituted for children's names. On the numerical axis can be information about such phenomena as the number of automobile accidents per year, metric tons of corn produced each year, or the average number of calories consumed per person.

Finding Out Through Listening and Viewing

As students investigate their world, they often must function as listeners: they listen to films or telecasts and to tapes or records while viewing filmloops or filmstrips; they participate in actual events that have both visual and oral components. As they do, children grow not only in their ability to understand human activity but to learn independently through listening and viewing.

Interpersonal Listening Skills – What They Are in the Social Studies

Listening in the social studies occurs in two rather different settings—the conversational and the presentational. In conversational situations, active speaking and listening roles are constantly shifting. Ideas put forth by one participant are picked up by another as the "conversational ball" bounces back and forth. In presentational or reportorial situations, active speaking and listening roles remain relatively constant. A major speaker (or speakers) presents ideas to which others respond nonverbally by nodding the head, by yawning, by writing or doodling, by smiling, frowning, or looking quizzically. Periodically listeners in presentational situations may respond verbally by questioning or commenting briefly.

To listen effectively to a presentation, a person must be able to:

follow the sequence of ideas presented

differentiate main from supporting ideas and facts from opinions

interpret messages sent through body language and vocal changes

supply nonverbal feedback that communicates a need for greater clarification, desire to respond verbally, agreement or disagreement, pleasure or displeasure

keep biases from affecting personal interpretations too strongly

In addition, in discussion situations, a participant must be able to formulate questions based on the ideas heard and make immediate comments as part of the give-and-take.

Interpersonal Listening Skills – Strategies for Teaching

There are numbers of strategies through which social studies teachers can work toward growth in interpersonal skills related to listening as part of content teaching. Some of these are 1) listening to think and feel, 2) noting down while listening, 3) reading along while listening, 4) audiovisuals, 5) excursions, and 6) use of experts.

Ques Four

R Read Dorothy Hennings' *Listening Aids Through the Grades*, revised edition (New York: Teachers College Press, 1979).

One way children can gather necessary information on a topic is through a tape set up in a listening center.

G The child is able to sequence events in the order given in an oral communication. The child is able to perceive relationships contained within an oral message.

Listening to Think and Feel.   Marcia Pavia, a teacher of a primary class studying colonial America, orally shared Arnold Lobel's magnificent picture storybook, *On the Day Peter Stuyvesant Sailed into Town*. As she read, she took time to display the colorful illustrations. Coming to the story end, Ms. Pavia distributed a series of short story synopsis cards, each summing up one key event in the story. Receiving cards, the students first read them aloud so that each child in the group would know what the cards said. Then the entire class cooperatively decided the order in which the cards should be placed to retell the story in the original sequence. They clipped the cards in order on the time line rope strung across one wall of the room. Because Ms. Pavia had begun by asking the students to listen so they could retell the story events, these primary youngsters had little trouble reconstructing the details they had heard.

Having helped the children recall the story order, Ms. Pavia asked them to consider the relationships and ideas. First she focused attention on details depicted in the pictures of colonial New Amsterdam:

Let's think of words to describe the buildings in the first several pictures of the book. How were the original houses of New Amsterdam different from those in New York City today? Why were they different? Let's look at the tiles around the pictures. Where do they make these tiles? Why did the illustrator of this book use tiles in this way?

The students and their teacher then considered the big ideas contained within the book: What were the problems existing in New Amsterdam? Why did the people need Peter Stuyvesant to help them clean up their town? Why do some of these problems still exist today? Why was New York called New Amsterdam in those days? To answer the last question, students found Holland and Amsterdam on a prominently displayed world map.

T A related book to use for comparison purposes is Peter Spier, *The Legend of New Amsterdam.* (New York: Doubleday, 1979).

Returning to their desks from the sharing corner where they had gathered, students made original three-part drawings based on the story. They sectioned a piece of construction paper into thirds; in the first section, they drew New Amsterdam before Stuyvesant's arrival, in the second, New Amsterdam after the eight-year clean-up, and in the third, Stuyvesant's dream of the city of the future. Later they regrouped to talk about how real Stuyvesant's dream was.

The extended sequence described above shows just how a listening/viewing activity can function in elementary social studies. The written word shared by a teacher and at times accompanied by illustrations can provide the content for talk times, for skill development sessions, and for art activity. Picture storybook material is not the only content that can be shared this way with youngsters. Most useful for listening/viewing activities are newspaper and news magazine articles clipped by the students or teachers; short and appropriate passages from such interesting volumes as *The Guinness Book of World Records* and *The World Almanac*; selections from informational books and encyclopedias. At times too, the teacher or a student can share a dictionary definition of a term met in context and with which youngsters are having trouble.

Guidelines for successful learning through listening include:

1. Share only relatively short passages. Children's attention span is short, especially in the lower grades.
2. Select passages with a vocabulary and sentence structure that children can handle; beware of passages with involved syntax.

G The child is able to listen for specific kinds of information.

3. Before sharing, prepare the students by giving them a specific task: let's listen so that you will be able to retell the story, get the main idea, decide which character did the right thing or decide how we would act if we were there.
4. Try for active responses by structuring the activity so that young people must do something physically with ideas they are hearing. A major action children can pursue is noting-down. The next section describes ways to handle note taking in social studies.

Noting-Down While Listening.   The tactics detailed under production strategies in chapter 2 are useful as part of noting down. Younger children and/or those having difficulty recording words on paper can sketch their own pictorial interpretations as the teacher reads a passage. After each main segment, the teacher pauses while students use marker pens or crayons to draw the meanings and/or feelings they have identified in an article, story, informational passage, or even a dictionary definition. The last makes for an interesting noting-down activity: the teacher reads the definition of something with which children are relatively unfamiliar—perhaps an animal or object found in a particular country being studied. The students can visualize it on paper, based upon the qualities given in the definition. Older students can respond to the material they have heard by creating maps, graphs, charts, and time lines. Obviously this activity requires practice. Numerous group sessions are necessary before students are able to note down independently.

G The child is able to formulate a set of written notes based on an informational piece received aurally. The piece will contain at least three major points.

Upper graders should also develop their verbal note taking skills. To encourage note taking, the teacher can supply a brief note taking guide that lists the following: Title of the Piece, Big Idea of Paragraph 1, Big Idea of Paragraph 2, Big Idea of Paragraph 3. The teacher announces the activity by saying, "Today I'm going to share three paragraphs. They are about the Huang Ho Plains that we plotted on our maps yesterday. First, I will read all three paragraphs. You decide what would make a good title for them." The class members listen and then spontaneously call out or brainstorm, numerous titles that a scribe records on the chalkboard. Together the class analyzes the listing and from the items shown selects one that is "best." The final selection may be by voting, since this is a judgmental thinking task. One student can record the chosen title on a duplicate of the note taking guide projected with an overhead projector; individuals record on their own.

Next the teacher announces: "Now I'm going to reread each paragraph in turn. As I read the first, see if you can compose a group of words that expresses the main idea of that paragraph. Don't think about just one fact in the paragraph. Identify the big thought that the paragraph is telling you." Following the rereading, the teacher and students identify the big idea being communicated and express it in a sentence or phrase. One student records it on the chalkboard, transparency, or charting paper by Roman numeral one while the others record it on their own guides. The same process is repeated for each paragraph in the series.

The significance of step-by-step instruction in note taking cannot be overstressed. Too often content teachers assume that upper graders can take notes independently. This is far from the truth. Structured learning sequences must be scheduled with differing kinds of content before children—even gifted ones—are able to take notes. Not only must lessons be structured to help children note main ideas but also to help them record details, steps in a set of directions, judgments, trends, and original hypotheses. The last are high-level cognitive tasks—ones that may be restricted to upper graders.

The sequence of a lesson that prepares students as independent note takers is relatively simple.

1. Introduce the way in which the session will be structured; for example—"Today let's see if we can read a news article and find answers to the five basic questions—who, what, when, where, and why." Or, "Today we will see how the editors of these two newspapers feel about this problem."

   G The child is able to function as notetaker when faced with a variety of social studies content.

2. Distribute a guide that parallels in structure the purpose identified. See Figure 3.4 for an example.
3. Read a segment of the selection, stopping at key points in order to break the material into episodes that are easy to summarize.
4. Ask questions that require participants to summarize the points made.
5. Ask one student to record the summary on a class-sized noting guide (on chalkboard, a transparency, or charting paper) while others record on individual copies.

   G The child gains the ability to use a listening guide to record significant informational content.

6. Continue reading short segments, summarizing orally, and recording.

Reading Along While Listening Along. One way to blend basic skills and social studies content is reading along while listening along. The teacher or a particularly skilled student shares a selection using the voice creatively to express meanings. Participants follow along on their own copies of the selection or on a transparency projected for them to see. After participating in a reading along while listening along activity, students can discuss ideas heard and read, note down main and subordinate ideas, create maps or charts, or convert the piece into a spontaneous dramatization. In short, almost any of the tactics detailed in this chapter can be combined with this strategy.

T Transparencies are easily created from printed matter using a thermofax machine.

Figure 3.4
Example of a Noting-down Guide

Noting Guide for Newspaper Articles

Headline of Article _____

Date of Article _____

What Happened? _____

Where? _____

To whom? _____

When? _____

Why did this happen? _____

G The child can use a combination of listening and reading skills to acquire a background of information on which he or she will later operate.

Two advantages exist with this blending of skills and content learnings. First, children with reading problems are not penalized so greatly in handling content as they would be if they had to read the information without an oral accompaniment. As a result, slow readers can still participate in meaningful follow-up activity. Second, the oral sharer serves as a model for expressive interpretation of a selection.

T See especially Caedmon's American Studies materials.

Audiovisuals.   A wealth of audiovisual materials is available today for use in social studies. The materials provide content out of which students can deepen their understanding of fundamental concepts as well as refine their note taking skills.
Rather than orally sharing a selection, do the following:

T Recent additions to the geographic list include "Egypt's Pyramids," "North American Indians Today," and "China: An Emerging Giant."

1. Share a tape or record of the selection.
2. Show a film. The National Geographic Educational Services (Washington, D.C.) is a source of striking color films.
3. Share a filmstrip—either silent or sound. Captioned strips are useful for building note taking skills. The built-in pauses between frames allow for class summarizing and noting down activity. Sound filmstrips are useful in teaching students to listen for detail. The first showing is with the sound; the second is without. Children must supply the text based on their listening. The Society for Visual Education (1345 Diversey Parkway, Chicago) has some filmstrips worthy of consideration.

T Titles from SVE to note are "South America: Land of Many Faces," "India: Tradition and Change," "African Society: Ways of Life," and "Something Difficult . . . Decisions."

4. Share a silent filmloop or series of flat pictures. Viewers figure out relationships in the pictures. Because a printed script often accompanies a loop, students can check their interpretation against it. In this context, teacher-questions are a major determinant of what viewers extract from the pictures. Social

Studies School Service (Culver Blvd., Culver City, California) supplies original newsreel footage of past events on loops. They also are a source of documentary photo aids—glossy, flat pictures that depict significant historical events.

5. Provide a current events radio or TV experience. The news, presidential news conferences, documentaries, and specials based on events in progress—all can supply content for classroom listening, viewing, thinking, and talking. Individuals can tune in to broadcasts and telecasts in the listening center, using headsets so as not to disrupt others. Later, listeners can become reporters who share what they have heard. This is an updated approach to current events, since television is fast becoming a prime source of news.

6. Assign news related radio or TV listening/viewing to students. Listeners can record on a simple noting guide the key points made in an assigned program and later share their notes with classmates. (See Figure 3.5 for an example.) Of course, teachers must be aware that this assignment cannot apply to all students; today some parents monitor children's television viewing since it interferes with reading and studying.

7. Share videocassettes on topics being studied. Some state educational TV networks loan or sell program series recorded on videocassettes. Social studies teachers should inquire whether such software is available in their state and whether hardware available in the school can be adjusted to play videotapes.

Excursions. With some topics, an excursion is the most productive way to gather data. This is true when a topic reflects some facet of the local community: community helpers and/or services, governmental processes, zoning, architecture, transportation, pollution and conservation, and commercial, agricultural, or industrial activity. The length of this list indicates that the traditional notion of a class trip to a farm, museum, or firehouse requires considerable expansion. Without a doubt, an excursion can offer a break from ordinary learning routines just as a vacation provides a change from daily living routines. But more than that, the class excursion—structured as a data-gathering investigation—releases young people to function as junior social scientists who look directly at human activity, systematically record observations, and generalize based on their data.

To serve the data-gathering purpose, an excursion must be an integral part of a class investigation. Students must prepare for a trip by identifying the phenomena they will observe and by designing an observation guide. From preparatory discussions should emerge observation guides on which students will record firsthand data. A guide may consist of:

T Two examples of videocassette programs available are 1) "Inside/Out"—a series of thirty fifteen-minute color programs that help eight-to-ten-year-olds deal with day-to-day problems through decision-making activity (National Instructional Television Center, Box A, Bloomington, Indiana 47401); 2) "Becoming Me"—twelve programs to enhance students' social and emotional growth (Great Plains National Instructional TV Library, University of Nebraska, Box 80669, Lincoln, Nebraska 68501).

G The child knows ways of noting-down data collected firsthand and can apply these techniques during on-site investigations.

**Figure 3.5
A Guide for Noting
Televised News Events**

The World Today

Name of Viewer _____   Date of Viewing _____

Program _____   Name of Newscaster or Moderator _____

What was the general topic of the program? _____

List two or three big ideas on the topic you learned from the program.

1. _____

2. _____

3. _____

Write one or two sentences telling how the program made you feel about the topic.

_____

_____

Rate the program by circling:
I felt the program was   **Good   Average   Poor.**
Tell why you rated the program as you did. _____

1. Maps or floor plans that are sketched out ahead of time and on which students plot particular features observed. (See Figure 3.6.)
2. Checklists of items; e.g., kinds of vehicles, services, and buildings. Next to entries, children record a check each time they spot a sample. This is a way to get a number count: the number of people using a particular service during a time period, the number of vehicles using a highway during a time period, or the number of industries doing business in the community. These data are the basis for projections for the future. Is there need for additional mass transit or highways to service the traffic? Are there sufficient stores to service people's needs? Should there be more stores? If so, what kinds? Although the check-off technique is perhaps the easiest form of recording in the elementary grades, these questions suggest that resulting conclusions can be amazingly complex.
3. Descriptive grid tables. Students can prepare a grid in which they name the phenomena they will see on their excursion. When they encounter a named item, they describe what they see in the appropriate block–what happens there, what is found there, where the thing is located. (See Figure 3.7 for an example.) Descriptive grids are useful if follow-up writing activity is

Figure 3.6
A Sample Map That Can Serve
as an Observation Guide for
Use on an Excursion

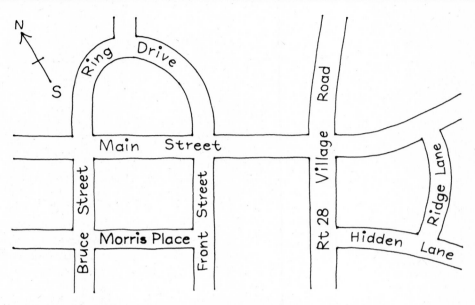

Directions. This map was drawn by some of your classmates and your teacher. It shows the major street in our "downtown area." As we walk around, draw buildings and labels to show the major places we see.

anticipated. Either individually or cooperatively with teacher guidance, students select words and phrases from their observation grids to use in paragraphs that describe their findings.

Early primary children can make similar grids by folding construction paper into four blocks. The teacher supplies labels for each phenomenon to be shared, which youngsters cut out and paste to their papers. Crayons should be taken along on the outing to be used in sketching pictures in the appropriate grid blocks.

4. Point-by-point listings. Another approach to systematic data-gathering is point-by-point listing, which can be descriptive, judgmental, or both. The data-gathering instrument is simply a numerical listing with key stops, points, concerns and/or questions noted on a sheet. Key questions are especially helpful because in preparing for the excursion young investigators must think through what it is they want to know.

T Simple portable clipboards can be constructed from pieces of plywood or hardboard and spring clips. Students record directly as they observe.

Figure 3.7
A Descriptive Grid Table

Grid Table for a Visit to Locations in Our Town

The Bank   The Service Station

The Supermarket   The Fast Food Restaurant

Some questions can be answered by looking, some by asking, others by thinking through an opinion. As information surfaces on the actual outing, observers record it next to the appropriate question, as in Figure 3.8.

Teachers must assist in the construction of point-by-point observational listings if basic understandings are to emerge. In the case of the "Observation Guide for Bakery Visitation," the class had been studying divisions of labor, profitability of businesses in order to survive, investment of money necessary to make a business work. The questions children projected were geared to get information on these components of business enterprise. In the classroom, the students were able to estimate the success of this business based on information.

Maps and floor plans, checklists, tables, and point-by-point listings can make an excursion into a productive learning experience in which basic observational, questioning, and recording skills are refined. Incidentally, these same techniques can be applied in the classroom as children gather data through audiovisual experiences and from guest speakers.

Experts.   Guides similar to the point-by-point listing described above can be developed by young social investigators as they prepare to interview an expert. In this case, the guide functions primarily as a questionnaire.

Experts can be of many kinds. They include:

1. Classroom guests who come to share ideas on a topic being investigated—local business people, community helpers, union officials, governmental officials, parents who grew up in other regions of the country or world, and senior citizens who remember what life was like in the near past.
2. Members of the school staff—a superintendent, a principal, a cafeteria worker, a custodian, or a secretary. These experts are

Figure 3.8
An Example of a Point-by-Point
Listing Guide

Observation Guide for Bakery Visitation

1. How many people do I see at work in the bakery?
2. What is each worker or group of workers doing?
3. Do the workers' jobs overlap? If so, how?
4. How many ovens are there? How expensive is each one?
5. How many customers came in while we were there?

most appropriate in the early primary grades as children learn
about their school community and in the middle grades as
students begin to encounter the principle of distribution of labor.
3. Members of specific professions and trades.
4. Neighbors, family, and community members who are
   knowledgeable on a topic being studied.

Not all interviewing need be restricted to the classroom and class
excursions; a questionnaire can be used by individuals who interview
independently outside of class. One advantage of this is that a broad
spectrum of opinions can result if each young investigator asks the
predetermined questions to one or two experts. Later each uses the
answers jotted on the guide to report findings.

Even youngsters in second grade can carry out independent interviewing if their questions are simple. For example, second graders
studying about migratory patterns of people in their community can
ask parents or guardians questions such as those in Figure 3.9.

G The child can formulate and ask questions
as a means of systemat-
ic data-gathering.

Figure 3.9
A Simple Interview Guide

How Often People Move Their Homes

Investigator: _____

Date: _____

Questions to ask:

1. How many years have you lived in this house? _____ years

2. Where did you live before you lived in this house? _____

3. Where were you born?

City: _____

State: _____

Country: _____

Finding Out Through Processing Information — Research in the Classroom

Listening-viewing is one way to find answers to a problem. A second is locating revelant reference sources and interpreting the facts, generalizations, and opinions found therein. Investigation of human activity in order to generalize, hypothesize, and predict is the essence of the social sciences. Because of this, young people should be involved in search activities. In elementary grades, these searches can take a number of related forms including searches in reference sources, direct investigation, and interviews. Through ongoing search activities children build and refine locational and information-processing skills.

Basic Locational Skills – What They Are

It has often been said that knowing where and how to find a piece of information is more vital than knowing it. The knowledge explosion makes it impossible for one to remember all the facts and ideas one will need in a lifetime; with the increase in knowledge has come a parallel increase in reference sources. As a result, locational skills are becoming more essential than they were in the past.

Specific skills related to location of information in references include the following.

Ques. Five

1. To locate words in the dictionary and to use entries to determine word meanings, usage, pronunciation, and etymology;
2. To locate information in encyclopedias;
3. To locate informational books through the use of the card catalog and the Dewey Decimal and/or the Library of Congress Classification System;
4. To locate information in specialized references such as atlases, almanacs, biographical dictionaries, special indexes, books of quotations, the thesaurus, and newspapers, magazines;
5. To know particular books and magazines that tend to offer information on special topics: e.g., *Guinness Book of World Records, The World Almanac*; pictorial volumes such as those in the Time/Life Series, the *National Geographic, Consumer Reports*;
6. To be able to develop questionnaires, opinion surveys, and interview guides through which to gather firsthand data on a subject.

Basic Locational Skills – How They Can Be Taught

Clearly teachers and librarians must design lesson sequences that focus directly on basic technical skills if young people are not to meet with frustration in locating information they need. Clearly too, the most meaningful instruction occurs at a point when skills are required to pursue a research task. For example, at the point when students are conducting biographical searches, they may find instruction on use of encyclopedia indexes particularly relevant; they may find equally relevant some guided practice in using the subject index of the card catalog and the classification numbers placed on volumes as an aid in locating them.

Here are some specific ideas for helping children develop and refine their skills.

1. Big Enough to See.   Pages of reference books, especially indexes and tables of contents, can be made big enough for all to see by being projected on a screen with an opaque projector; pages can also be converted into transparencies with the assistance of reproduction equipment. Viewing pages spread across the wall, students can interpret them guided by teacher questions: On what pages would we find information on Ethiopia? On which page would we find information on the American Stock Exchange? If you were looking up information on the American Stock Exchange, what words would you try finding in the index that might lead to relevant pages?

2. Investigating Together.   Students can become familiar with references during class or group sessions in which each participant holds a volume in hand. Students can hold volumes of encyclopedias, atlases, or almanacs; as the teacher announces questions that request specific information, they can decide whether the particular volumes they hold supply any material on the topic. Those holding relevant volumes can look up the requested information to share with the others.

3. On-the-Spot Checks.   As students participate in group discussions, they may ask for a piece of information they need but that no one knows. In such instances, the teacher should refrain from giving the answer and ask instead for on-the-spot checks into reference sources. Each week as part of the classroom helpers assignments, students can be assigned sleuthing jobs: dictionary sleuth, encyclopedia sleuth, atlas sleuth, and so on. When information about the spelling of a word is needed, the dictionary sleuth makes an on-the-spot check. When detailed factual information is needed, the encyclopedia sleuth takes off for the library.

4. This Is Guinness Week! A class can focus on a key reference each week – a reference that is spread out in a reading corner where children can go to browse. One week is "Guinness Week," another "National Geographic Week," still another "World Almanac Week," and so on. Every time a youngster goes to browse, he or she must complete an index card and record on it a "Whale of a Fact" discovered in the reference. Facts are discussed during a general talk time.

Basic Information-Processing Skills – What They Are

To locate information in reference sources is only the beginning. Students must use that information for a purpose. It is while working with investigative questions as part of unit study that information-processing skills can most purposefully be developed. Students with a problem in mind have a framework for judging what information is more significant, what is less.

Specific thinking skills involved in processing information include the ability to:

Identify main ideas; to sift main from subordinant points,
Distinguish between fact and opinion within a given source,
Summarize the ideas met in a source,
Identify significant quotations found in source materials,
Sequence ideas meaningfully.

In addition, an investigator must be able to compile a set of notes, either in written or taped form. Notes, of course, need not be kept as a formal outline; however, to be functional, notes must be clear and contain the essential information.

Basic Information Processing Skills – How They Can Be Taught

Skills as basic as these demand special attention in the upper elementary grades, and could be introduced as early as second grade. As with locational and listening/viewing skills, teachers must develop systematic learning sequences that directly focus on the skills to be learned. Too often in the past, information processing has meant copying down what the reference source included with little attempt made to sift relevant from nonrelevant, main from subordinant, fact from opinion. Here is how one sixth-grade teacher organized the search activities of his class so that skill development was an integral part.

The Reference-Search Format in the Social Studies. Mr. Avery took his twenty-six sixth graders to the library on a reference search.

Figure 3.10
An Investigative Guide

Name of Country: _____

1. Where is this country located? What are its neighbors? What is its longitude? latitude? How does this longitudinal and latitudinal position contrast to where we live?
2. What are the most important geographical features?
3. What kind of climate is found there?
4. What are the major ways people earn a living? Why have these ways become important?
5. What form of government do they have?
6. What are the ways that people enjoy themselves?
7. What has the country contributed to the world in terms of music, literature, art, and science?

Each young person went equipped with a search guide that the class had cooperatively put together based on preliminary reading and brainstorming. Before setting forth, the class had divided into search teams. The general area of study was Scandinavia and so they had decided to break up into four teams, each to focus on one of the Scandinavian countries. They had identified the questions that each team would answer and the tasks that each would complete. The questions were fundamental ones as shown in Figure 3.10; the tasks were related directly to the questions identified and resulted in materials helpful in sharing investigative data later with classmates. (See Figure 3.11 for an example.)

G The child is able to pose broad questions as a guide to his or her research activity.

Upon arrival in the library, most of the investigative teams opted for a distribution of labor. Two students worked on mapmaking, while one

Figure 3.11
A Task Sheet for Group Investigations

Group Task Sheet

1. Draw a large map of the country. Include longitude and latitude, major geographic features and bodies of water, and large cities. Do this on charting paper for later sharing.
2. Make at least four additional charts that outline important facts you uncover about the country. Label one geographic and climatic facts, a second economic facts, a third governmental facts, a fourth cultural facts.
3. If possible, locate a short literary selection—a poem or short story—by a well-known author from the country or a selection about the country. Perhaps locate a recording of a musical selection by a composer who lived there.
4. Search for pictures that show significant features of the country. Compile them in a creative manner for sharing.
5. See if you can find a filmstrip about the country. Check for this with the librarian in the school media center. Be sure to preview the strip before sharing it with the rest of us.

G The child is able to work successfully with others on a group project and locate necessary references and resources.

or two worked on each chart and another went to look for recordings, filmstrips, and pictures. In this instance, since the sixth graders had conducted several previous searches, they knew what was expected and wasted little time. Mr. Avery circulated from one team to the next, helping them locate specific references and suggesting how to lay out maps and charts.

Obviously if such search sessions are to be productive, they must be structured as tightly as the one described above. Students must know how to handle basic reference aids, and some attention must be paid to teaching the use of the card catalog, indexes, the Dewey Decimal System, and so forth. Also the assignment of specific and concrete tasks to be completed is helpful. Students are not just "looking around." They are fully involved in producing charts and maps and locating materials to share with others.

Teaching Note Taking Skills. In preparation for productive Reference-search periods, young people need preliminary work with note taking techniques. The Noting-down Task Card is helpful here with students using it in a variety of contexts. For example, before reading weekly classroom newspapers, students divide into information-processing teams, each team being responsible for one article. Team members cooperatively figure out the main idea of their article and the related sub-points. Each team should prepare a large-sized Noting-down Task Card before actually reading its article. The card should contain only two questions: 1) What is the main idea of the article? and 2) What are the important points that support the idea? After studying the article, team members can discuss possible answers to the two questions. A student records the group's answers by writing directly on the Noting-down Card. A reporter from the group can later use the card as notes when orally sharing the group's findings with the entire class. This activity can also be based on portions of the textbook or articles clipped from magazines or regular newspapers.

As students gain skill in handling references, simple Noting-down Task Cards can be replaced by more complex Search and Writing Guides, as in Mr. Avery's class. Before a period of library search, students brainstorm questions to which they could possibly find answers. In one upper-grade class in which student pairs were to find out about a patriot of their choosing, students brainstormed these questions: Where did the patriot live? When was he or she born? When did she or he die? What did he or she like to do? What made her or him a patriot? What contributions were the most important ones?

Reconsidering their questions, the fifth graders in this class selected three, decided on a logical order for composing answers in paragraphs, and set up the three questions as a Search and Write Outline.

Children who work together on research teams acquire
not only basic research skills but also the ability to work
cooperatively on a problem.

In the library, they recorded information on their guides and later used
these as outlines for writing a series of paragraphs describing their
chosen patriot. In this case, the cooperative preparation of a guide
clarified for children exactly what they were to find out.

Ques. Six

Sharing One's Findings - Reporting in the Social Studies

Perhaps the most imperative social learning a child must acquire is the ability to share his or her thoughts effectively. Oral sharing is an integral part of interpersonal situations. It is a means of making contact with others and of learning more.

Sharing Skills - What They Are in the Social Studies

The skills requisite to effective functioning as a sharer in both conversational and presentational situations are similar in some respects. A sharer must be able to:

organize thoughts so that main ideas are highlighted,

support main ideas with necessary facts, and

sequence ideas in a logical fashion.

These are thinking skills. A second grouping of skills is essentially expressive: a sharer must be able to:

relax the body to allow natural body rhythms to flow along with words,

use the body as a communication adjunct, letting the eyes, face, hands, torso, and even feet carry some of the communication burden,

use the voice as a communication adjunct, varying pitch and amplitude to maintain interest,

choose words that communicate the intended meanings and feelings.

Sharing Skills - Strategies for Teaching

Teachers who ask students to report orally on their search findings are encouraging growth in sharing skills. A major pitfall of the search-and-share approach to unit study, however, is that a sharing-time following library research can become simply a reading of paragraphs copied sometimes word for word from sources. As already discussed, a careful structuring of the search period with questions and clearly identified tasks is one way to avoid this pitfall. A second way is to pay extensive attention to expressive ways of sharing. Students need firsthand experiences in the techniques of dynamic sharing; they need to experience a variety of formats for sharing information with others and opportunity to "play with" vocal and physical aspects of sharing.

The Visual Sharing Strategy. Tasks outlined in the search section of this chapter suggest the direction that sharing sequences should take if young people are to learn to present data in a stimulating way. Rather than urging students to speak enthusiastically or to know their topic well, teachers should help them during the search phase to organize data they are gathering to insure a smooth presentation. This means *not* requiring students to take notes by writing a paper on the topic in complete sentences and paragraphs. Such a paper used as notes encourages word-by-word reading rather than an informal sharing of ideas.

Techniques more likely to result in effective sharing include these:

1. Use of Noting-down Task Cards and carefully constructed question sheets for recording information from references as detailed in pages 85–87.
2. Compilation of charts and/or transparencies for sharing findings—the presenter uses the chart as a series of notes from which to draw ideas.
3. Construction of other visuals—maps, time lines, sketches—in the form of charts, transparencies, or handouts for listeners.
4. Development of listening guides for classmates to use for noting-down during the oral report.

G The child can prepare notes and materials that facilitate sharing.

Since most of these sharing aids are visual, search-and-share tactics must merge with production tactics. If follow-up sharing is to be dynamic, the teacher must keep on the go during search periods, assisting students as they preplan and organize ideas. He or she must assist in editing material for logical sequencing of ideas by asking, "Which ideas should be presented first? Why? How are these ideas related? What would be a good summary to make at the end?"

Because so many aspects are involved in the creative presentation of informational material, use of search-and-share strategies as an entire unit is effective and efficient only with upper graders who have had previous experience handling smaller units of information. Third graders can go to the library to collect information on a limited topic and record it on a sheet in answer to two or three questions, but this activity is only one component of a larger unit.

The Creative-Sharing Strategy. Most readers know what uncreative reporting is. A person stands in one spot, drones on and on, gives one fact after another, and makes almost no eye contact with his or her listeners. In such a situation, little communication occurs between the speaker and listener. Yet unfortunately this is the way that informational sharing based on search strategies is often structured in elementary classrooms. If every unit is handled in this way, social studies can become not only unproductive but boring.

Clearly young people who report to classmates need considerable help in organizing notes for "talking from" rather than "reading from." They need help in using vocal changes and body language to express meanings dynamically. They need help too in sandwiching factual content within narrative or story sequences that they use to exemplify points they are making.

One means of achieving more creative sharing of research data is creative structuring of the sharing period. Rather than scheduling reports back to back in endless progression, the teacher can try a number of different organizational techniques.

1. An Idea Fair–Small Group Sharing.   Five students who have researched ideas on Norway become sharers. Each sits behind a table set up in a corner of the cafeteria, all-purpose room, or gymnasium. The class divides into five groups with each group going to a table to listen and talk to one of the speakers, who shares a chart of facts and ideas he or she has compiled. After about ten minutes or less, depending on the amount of material to be shared, each group rotates to another table to listen to a speaker who develops another aspect of the topic. When each group has visited each idea table, the class reconvenes, and the listeners recount as part of general class discussion what they consider to be the major points speakers have shared.

T Idea Fairs can be shared with parents. Visitors move from table to table in the gym or cafeteria, speaking informally with students on topics researched.

2. A Forum–Round Table Sharing.   Another way to structure group sharing is to gather those who have researched facets of a topic around a table set up at the front of the class. Presenters sit so that they can see each other as well as members of the larger listening group. Initially each member of the sharing team presents some basic ideas using some visual props that he or she has created. Upon completion of the presentation, the other presenters ask a question or two of the speakers.

G The child is able to share information with a class-sized group and is able to ask questions of another speaker.

Anyone who has worked with elementary-age students knows that most of them have trouble asking questions. To make this technique work, therefore, the teacher must guide the children ahead of time by supplying general kinds of questions. These include questions that ask the speaker:

a. To explain the meaning of a term used–Tell the listeners to look for new words that a speaker is using and to ask, "What did you mean when you said the word 'fjord'?"

b. To show a mentioned location by pointing to a map–Tell the listeners to look out for places mentioned by the speaker and to ask "Where is Oslo located on the map?"

c. To explain meanings and relationships—The listeners can look for specific facts and ask the speaker to try to explain why that fact is true. "You said the Norwegians do much fishing. Why is that so?" is an example of this kind of questioning pattern.

d. To give the sequence in which something happened—Listeners can be taught to ask "You mentioned that these two things happened. Which happened first?"

G The child is able to gather data by observing and questioning directly.

e. To make inferences from facts presented—Children can raise questions about possible causes: "You said that this happened. What caused it to happen?"

f. To give additional facts on a subject—"Tell me more about the way the Danes celebrate that holiday."

g. To state personal opinions and judgments—Children can raise questions that get at a speaker's feelings. "Did you like that? Would you like to live there? Why? Why not?"

As students begin to present and ask questions of one another, the teacher may wish to prepare a Forum Sheet with suggested question patterns based on the listing above. Such a questioning sheet functions also as a listening guide; students who are listening use the Forum Sheet to trigger questions to ask during follow-up talk times.

3. A Twosome. At times students may work in pairs to gather information for later sharing. To present, the twosome can sit comfortably on high stools or swivel chairs, or even cross-legged on the floor, with fellow students sitting informally nearby. The twosome presents in tandem with one making a point or two and then his or her cohort interjecting several related ideas. The give-and-take between two presenters takes the pressure off one and tends to make the presentation more stimulating.

G The child can organize ideas systematically for logical sharing.

4. Spots. Television uses short spot commercials sometimes less than a minute in length. Similar spot reports can be sequenced into classroom time. A student briefly shares a point found in reference reading, through television or radio, in discussion with parents, or in current reading of newspapers and magazines. Brief reports of this type are a good way to bring current events into the classroom, so that all youngsters are kept up-to-date with what is going on in their community and world.

G The child is able to share ideas with others as a presentational speaker.

5. The Audiovisual Break. Students who are presenting should be encouraged to break up presentations by including audiovisual materials. A recording, a tape, a short filmloop or strip, a transparency—all these can be incorporated into a reporter's presentation.

R See also chapter 3, pages 76–77.

Discussing Together

Much of everyday communication occurs in conversational discussion groups in which people interact face to face. Crucial to successful functioning here is the ability to:

Recognize feelings and interests of others and their need to participate;

Ask questions that draw silent participants into the conversation;

Make points succinctly and not monopolize the discussion;

Respond so as to carry a topic forward rather than diverting it down paths of little interest to others;

Perceive how interesting pieces of information that one possesses fit into a discussion;

Interject fun and humor by contributing an anecdote;

Feel at ease in contributing ideas to others.

These interpersonal discussion skills require considerable understanding of self, others, and the dynamics of human relationships. In this respect, they are not easy to teach. How does one begin to teach sensitivity and awareness of others? Certainly, one does not teach such an emotion-filled concept by posting "good manners signs" that exhort children to wait their turns and to make comments in terms of what has already been said.

Discussion Strategies

One way to begin is by organizing classroom activity so that small group conversations are a daily occurrence. In classrooms, conversations take the form of discussions on curricular topics, informal chats on topics of personal concern, and cooperative participation in a task. The teacher can help children grow in awareness of the needs and feelings of others by following small group talk times with a general discussion of nonverbal clues that participants received as they interacted.

Also helpful is to structure a small group discussion around topics that young people have previously researched and on which they have compiled considerable information on Noting-down Task Cards. The possession of a Noting-down Task Card gives the shy child a heightened sense of security. Successful participation that comes through sharing information from a card builds confidence in speaking to others in small groups.

The teacher should work systematically as well to encourage participation in full class discussion. As the teacher forwards discussion through questions, he or she should be aware of differences in question difficulty and in student self-confidence. When questions are simple or ask only for information contained on Noting-down Task Cards,

Figure 3.12
A Task Sheet for Upper Grades

Task Sheet: Problems in Our School

1. Brainstorm together as many problems that you can think of existing in our school. "Problems" here mean things you are dissatisfied with and would like to see changed. Write all your ideas on a piece of charting paper. You will find paper in the work center.
2. Select three problems you believe are the most important ones. By most important, we mean those that should be corrected immediately. Allow each group member to express his or her opinion before making a final selection of three by voting.
3. List the three problems on a second piece of charting paper. Place the list on the left-hand side of the chart in a column. On the right-hand side next to each problem, list the reason you selected that problem as an important one.
4. Decide on the relative importance of the three problems. Put (1) in front of the most important, (2) in front of the second, and (3) in front of the third in importance.
5. Tape up your charts so all can see them. Be ready to support your selection and rank ordering when the class meets for a general talk session.

a teacher should look for tentative nonverbal moves made by students who tend to be nonparticipants but indicate that these students know an answer. A change in eye focus, a pointing to an appropriate place in the text, or a sudden change in sitting position can be a signal to the teacher that a child wants to participate.

There are numbers of strategies upon which a teacher can draw in planning social studies discussion. A few are detailed in the sections to follow. In addition, the reader is referred to chapter 6 where questioning sequences that encourage participation in higher-level thinking are described.

Task Groups

Students can be given a specific task to be completed in small work teams. Tasks may have a production component—e.g., create a design for the class mural that will depict the major steps in the territorial growth of the United States. In contrast, tasks may be primarily cognitive—e.g., identify what you consider to be the three major problems that exist in our school community and rank order the three. In either case, to complete the task, children must communicate orally with one another, making decisions together.

G The child communicates effectively in conversational groups; as part of a group he or she works cooperatively with others.

Task Sheets

Task sheets facilitate completion of group jobs, as the exemplar shown in Figure 3.12 suggests. Task sheets like this one guide children's activity as they talk together in conversational groups. There is less tendency to "talk around" a question, a greater possibility that participants in the talk will focus on the task. Task sheets work equally well with youngsters who have just learned to read if the vocabulary and sentence patterns are kept simple and the teacher goes over the sheet with children before they begin the task.

Echo Pairs

G The child listens to what peers are saying and can repeat points made.

For this activity, the class divides into pairs. The pairs function as conversation mates. Mates begin with a given conversation task, such as talk about why (or why not):

1. You would like to live (or to visit) in the country/area we are studying;
2. A particular act or deed was wrong;
3. You like a particular character from a story or biography.

During the conversation, echo pairs not only share their own feelings or opinions, but they also listen closely so that they know how their mate feels. When the class reassembles, a mate must share with or "echo to" the total group those points his or her mate has made.

Echo pairs can be used with informational as well as evaluative content. Children in pairs can interview one another on 1) areas studied independently, 2) pictures that one interprets to the other, 3) books read and enjoyed, 4) predictions about the world of tomorrow, 5) special hobbies and interests. The interviewer reports information "echo-style" back to the class.

The Questions Panel Tactic

As students listen to a film, filmstrip, telecast, or social studies report by a peer, three can be designated as the "questions panel." These three write down questions based on the content heard. After the listening time, the panel poses its questions to the entire class. Upper graders can be guided to write questions that begin "Why . . . ?" and "How . . . ?" as well as "Who . . . ?," "What . . . ?," "When . . . ?," and "Where . . . ?"

The questions panel tactic can be varied so that it is functional with small groups and conversation pairs. One youngster becomes the question-maker for a group or pair. Others try to answer the questions based on content previously heard or read.

Talk and Report Pairs

Two youngsters can handle a problem as a pair. During their conversation time, they should prepare for a later information sharing period with the whole class. In the lower primary grades, for example, pairs of students can be given a large picture from a commercial folio set. Their task is to talk together to identify what they see in the picture. Later the two can share their description with the total group or even with another conversational pair operating in the class.

Merging Groups

The talk and report tactic detailed above suggests still another format to encourage discussion of information and ideas. Students function first within one group or pair. Later one group merges with a second so that both groups can talk together about ideas previously developed. This works especially well when the group task has been to brainstorm points. Each group lists the ideas it discussed and then makes a composite listing.

G The child can function in a variety of group settings and with others who may have different opinions, interests, and backgrounds.

Revolving Groups

At other times the teacher can apply the revolving-group tactic. Given a problem task, students first meet with two or three others to identify points and express opinions. Later group memberships shift with students going into new groups to talk about the same questions – but with a different set of participants.

This tactic is most useful when a task actually has two or three component parts. Students can complete a first part by functioning within one task group. Then as they begin to work on the second part of the task, each student moves on to become a member of a new group.

Strategies for Finding Out and Sharing: A Summary Thought or Two

If one acquires the ability to find out for oneself by viewing, listening, and processing information located through search of reference and primary sources, one is on the road toward becoming a lifelong learner. If one also acquires the ability to share one's findings orally with others, one has gained some ability to affect decisions in the future. A person with these skills can keep abreast of changing world conditions and can make an attempt to influence others and play an active role in determining the direction change will take. In this respect, the search and communication skills detailed in this chapter are among the most important learnings to be sought through education in the schools.

Tasks to Try

1. Locate a specific picture you may wish to use with a group of children. Decide on a sequence of questions that you could develop with the group to increase their ability to see relationships within visual data. Now, if you are already working with a group, share the picture and your questions. Decide: "Were the questions I asked sequenced appropriately to raise children's thinking up the cognitive ladder and to help them express their own feelings?"
2. Develop a noting card that children in primary grades could use to gather data based on a brief search of references relative to the topic: "Great Women of History." Then change the card so that it would be applicable for use by sixth graders.

References

Chapin, June; and Gross, Richard. *Teaching Social Studies Skills*. Boston: Little, Brown & Co., 1973.

Hennings, Dorothy. *Russell and Russell's Listening Aids Through the Grades*. revised ed. New York: Teachers College Press, 1979.

Jacobs, Leland. "Speaking and Listening." In *Skill Development in the Social Studies: 33rd Yearbook of the National Council for the Social Studies*, ed. by Helen Carpenter. Arlington, Virginia: NCSS, 1963, pp. 133-147.

Johnson, David; and Johnson, Roger. *Learning Together and Alone*. Englewood Cliffs, New Jersey: Prentice-Hall, 1975.

Nelson, Murry; and Singleton, H. Wells. "Small Group Decision Making for Social Action." In *Developing Decision-Making Skills: 47th Yearbook of the National Council for the Social Studies*, ed. by Dana Kurfman. Arlington, Virginia: NCSS, 1977, pp. 141-172.

Schmuck, Richard; and Schmuck, Patricia. *Group Processes in the Classroom*. Dubuque, Iowa: Wm. C. Brown, 1975.

Stanford, Gene; and Stanford, Barbara. *Learning Discussion Skills Through Games*. New York: Citation Press, 1969.

4 Strategies for Teaching Reading and Writing in the Social Studies

George used his drawings to share his ideas about the division of labor within a Kenyan family.

**Words are what hold
society together.**

**Stuart Chase,
Power of Words, 1954**

Key Questions

Why should reading and writing be part of social
studies activity?

What reading skills should be developed as part of the
social studies?

What instructional tactics help students use contextual,
structural, and dictionary clues to figure out word
meaning?

How can a teacher help children identify main and
subordinate ideas while reading?

What is an inference? How can a teacher encourage
children to make inferences as they read?

How can children learn to make supportable value
judgments as they read?

What writing skills can be taught as part of social
studies?

Describe a number of writing activities that integrate
easily with social studies.

Explain in detail how to use writing-together to teach
specific writing skills.

A place poem	Its structure
City	Place name
Active, moving, rushing, changing, Sprawling, crowded, full, mixing.	line of four adjectives line of four adjectives
Pavement, subways, cars, traffic, People, buildings, light, noise.	line of four nouns line of four nouns

An acrostic	Its structure
Past, present, future time— Everywhere, somewhere, anywhere— A man, a woman, and a child Cry out for war to End.	The first letters of the first words of lines spell the title.

Introduction

Ques. One

R For another point of view, read Robert Price's "Teaching Reading Is Not the Job of the Social Studies Teacher," *Social Education*, 42: (April 1978): 312, 314. To see the differences of opinion existing on this issue, read Bob Taylor's companion article "Teaching Reading Is Part of the Social Studies Teacher's Job," pp. 313, 315-16, 317.

Social studies programs designed to help learners handle future change effectively must include reading and writing activities. To react to change, people must be able to read to find out what is going on – to read beyond the literal comprehension level to formulate ideas and render value judgments and decisions. They must be able to communicate their ideas to others in written form. Although the spoken word forcefully delivered has the power to influence others, the written word carefully set forth is an equally powerful force that citizens can use to affect opinion. This chapter, therefore, details the objectives to be achieved through reading and writing in the social studies and offers some specific instructional strategies useful at the elementary level.

Learning-to-Read Strategies

R A helpful source of information on reading in the social studies is June Chapin and Richard Gross's "Reading," in *Teaching Social Studies Skills* (Boston: Little, Brown & Co., 1973), pp. 20-46.

In many elementary classrooms, children learn to read through the skills program incorporated in the basal reading books—a tightly sequenced series with a controlled vocabulary and carefully chosen sentence patterns. Basal reader content tends to be stories and poems. Some series include a bit of nonfiction in the form of biography and autobiography. Through this content children acquire the ability to understand print as it is used to record ideas.

Much less attention is generally paid to ways to help children gain meaning from and make value judgments based on informational

Children read to gather information; at the same time, they refine basic reading skills.

content. Informational content is readily available in elementary classrooms in the form of clipped newspaper and magazine materials (cartoons, editorials, news columns, advertisements); textbooks; reference books; and classroom newsletters and magazines. Working systematically with diverse informational content, children should learn to:

Use context to figure out meanings of technical terms

Analyze word structure to figure out meaning

Use dictionary aids to increase comprehension

Identify main ideas and significant detail

Use section headings and boldface type as a guide to interpretation of technical content;

Make inferences and judgments that go beyond facts contained in a written communication;

Identify biases and assumptions underlying ideas set forth;

Develop a logical set of notes based on readings.

Of course, most reading instruction must still occur within the structured reading program. The teacher cannot rely totally on content areas to serve as vehicles for teaching reading. If this were to take place, the big ideas, the thinking processes, the values, the attitudes, and the appreciations sought through social studies could conceivably be lost. Rather, reading skills should be taught in social studies as in all the content areas so that students learn to use reading to find out.

Contextual, Structural, and Dictionary Tactics

Ques Two

G The child learns to read content materials so that he or she is able to find out through reading. This is a basic social competency of lifelong significance.

As children read social studies content, they meet technical terms that are part of the social science disciplines. To get meaning from a page containing technical vocabulary, readers must be able to handle three kinds of clues—contextual, structural, and dictionary. Let us consider ways to help children acquire these skills as they work with the content of the social studies.

Using Definitions. Definitions of technical terms are often "tucked into" the running text of elementary social studies books. For example, in introducing the aqualung, one text begins:

In 1943, two Frenchmen invented an underwater breathing apparatus called the Aqualung.

G The child uses a variety of contextual clues to get meaning from written informational content.

The sentence is essentially a definition: Aqualung = underwater breathing apparatus. Further on, the text continues:

A third diving device—the bathyscaph—is a sphere of strong steel.

Again the definition of the term, *bathyscaph*, is tucked in at the beginning of the paragraph introducing the topic.

Students should learn to watch for such "tucked in" definitions. One way to encourage youngsters to look for meanings of new terms included in running text is the establishment of individual glossaries. During silent reading, personal glossaries—regular notebooks with pages lettered alphabetically—are placed on students' desks. Encountering a new term defined explicitly, the student flips to the appropriate alphabet page in his or her glossary and records the definition there. The definition can be noted as an equation:

Glossary, personal = regular notebooks for recording new words and definitions in alphabetical order; an aid for reading in the content areas.

Each glossary entry can later be expanded to include a sentence in which the new word is used meaningfully. This sentence can be one taken from a later portion of the text.

Time should be set aside for consideration of words recorded in glossaries. This is one way to handle the time after silent reading. Student sharers can come forward to record their "word finds" on the board. Others use glossaries or memories to suggest the meaning of the word being shared and the way that word is used in context. When differences in opinion as to pronunciation or meaning arise, the dictionary vice-president—a student whose job it is to check out problem words—refers to the dictionary entry and shares what is recorded there.

Using Descriptions. Information in texts and encyclopedias generally goes beyond definitions to supply descriptions of phenomena. For example, the paragraph that begins by defining Aqualung continues with this description:

The Aqualung is a tank that holds a breathing mixture of helium and oxygen. The tank is strapped to a diver's back. He inhales the breathing mixture through a mouthpiece. Since the diver carries his breathing mixture with him, he need not be connected to a boat, as were early divers. With the Aqualung, he can descend 200 feet beneath the surface of the water. He can stay there, moving freely for ten to fifteen minutes.

R This section follows the organization of "Reading in the Content Areas," a speech by Lillian Putnam, New Jersey Reading Association, April 1978.

Teachers who know the textual material well can identify such paragraphs as this ahead of time and use them to encourage students to build "descriptive wheels" (Figure 4.1). To make a wheel, the reader begins by labeling the technical term at the hub. Radiating from it, he or she draws spokes, recording on each a descriptive phrase.

Of course, not all descriptions contained within informational content will be as multifaceted as the one about the Aqualung. The wheel tactic, however, is still usable even when only two spokes with descriptive phrases can be drawn from the hub. Wheels can be plotted on large construction paper and suspended from lighting fixtures. In some cases, a sketch can be added to the paper. In this way words being read become a visual presence in a classroom.

T Selection on the Aqualung is from *Knowing Our Neighbors* (New York: Holt, Rinehart & Winston, 1966), pp. 95-96.

Using Synonyms. Sometimes writers build into paragraphs synonym clues to help the reader figure out the meaning of more difficult words. One might write: "The sloop danced across the water. This boat was obviously meant for sailing across the open ocean." A reader who

Figure 4.1
A Descriptive Word Wheel

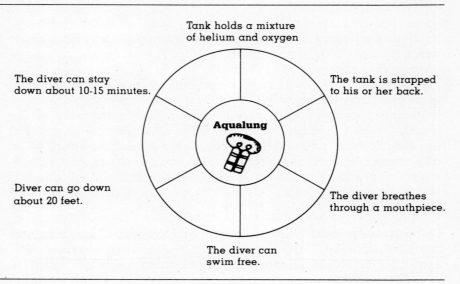

Tank holds a mixture
of helium and oxygen

The diver can stay
down about 10-15 minutes.

The tank is strapped
to his or her back.

Aqualung

Diver can go down
about 20 feet.

The diver breathes
through a mouthpiece.

The diver can
swim free.

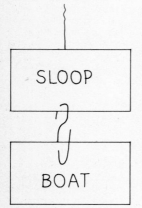

is unfamiliar with the word *sloop* may be able to figure out its meaning from its synonymous use with *boat*.

Words and their synonyms can be incorporated by readers into their personalized glossaries. Especially when terms are rather technical, sets of "synonym cards" can be strung together (Figure 4.2). To make a set, students record a known word on a card and the less familiar synonym on a second card. They connect the two with a paper clip that is opened. The set then can be hung up in the classroom.

Now as students talk together and use the more familiar term, the teacher can direct attention to the synonym cards hanging in clear view and help speakers substitute the less familiar term for the well-known one.

Figure 4.2

Using Opposites. Another kind of word clue that good writers build into informational content to help the reader handle less familiar words is an antonym—a word that means almost the opposite of the word in question. A paragraph may begin:

John Adams did not feel very contented with the convention's decision on slavery. Instead he was perturbed! "How could a country seeking freedom for all not consider the freedom of black people?" he asked himself.

A reader may not know the word *perturbed*, but juxtaposed in context with the word *contented*, the meaning becomes clear. *Perturbed = not contented*.

As students handle unit vocabulary, it sometimes is effective to build a word wall. Words printed on strips are mounted all over the wall—beneath and above the chalkboard or door, or any open space. Areas of the room can be set aside for words on different aspects of a topic. Other areas can be reserved for word pairs. There can be an antonym wall and a synonym wall. Through this tactic the vocabulary of the social science disciplines as well as more advanced general words are readily available for use in speaking and writing.

Using Structural Analysis and Word Relationships. Some children can respond correctly to test questions about prefixes, suffixes, and roots. Yet when these same students meet words comprised of these building blocks in actual context, many are unable to figure out meanings. Perhaps the reason for this lack of carry-over is failure to teach structural analysis reading skills in meaningful content areas. Social studies reading offers numerous opportunities to help children learn to apply their growing understanding of word building blocks even as they refine their understanding of basic generalizations emanating from the social science disciplines.

R See Lou Burmeister's, *Words—From Print to Meaning* (Reading, Massachusetts: Addison-Wesley, 1975), for activities to assist children with structural analysis of words.

For example, even as students meet the term "Aqualung" in their social studies reading, they can play with word relationships. What other words do children know that have *aqua* in them? What is the derivation of the word *aqua*? What is its meaning? What other roots meaning *water* do we use in building English words? Through such a question sequence, young people will begin to relate *Aqualung* to *aquatic, aquamarine, aquarium,* and *aquaplane*. Through it too, they will begin to acquire the reading habit of relating less familiar words to more familiar ones that contain some of the same word-building units.

Opportunities of this type abound in social studies reading if teachers keep alert for word relationships that are of particular importance in developing social studies understandings. For instance, as Figure 4.3 indicates, the word *communicate* comes from a Latin word meaning *to share*. How is this meaning also embodied in the English word *community? commune? communism? communion?* Similarly, if we know that the prefix *pro-* means *for*, what is a *protagonist*? And then, what is an *antagonist*? Unless students can handle word structures and relationships as they read, time spent in studying suffixes, roots, prefixes, and derivations is for naught.

G The child applies growing understanding of word-building qualities and relationships as he or she reads social studies materials.

Figure 4.3
Word Mobiles: A Tool for Visualizing
word relationships in Social Studies

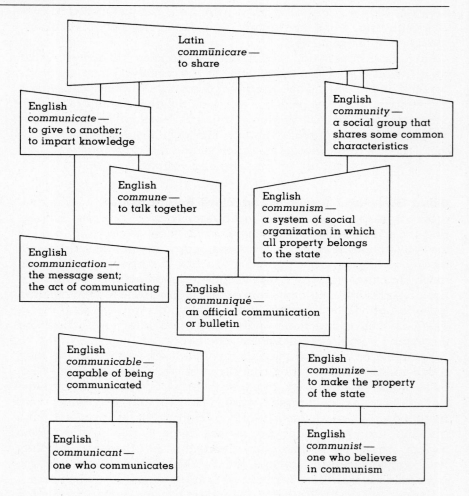

Note: The suffixes found on this chart are ones found repeatedly in social studies context: *-ism*, *-ity*, *-ist*, *-ize*, *-able*, *-tion*. Many word mobiles will contain words built from them. Through continued activity with these fundamental word components, students may gradually refine their ability to use them to unlock the meanings of familiar terms.

Using the Dictionary. Sometimes readers meet a word in context that they cannot figure out from clues contained within the passage. Even the general tone of the paragraph does not help in cracking the meaning. When this occurs and when the word is one on which the entire paragraph hangs, readers must turn to the dictionary for help.

To facilitate dictionary checking, children who are reading social studies material independently should keep dictionaries at their fingertips. If they keep their personalized glossaries available as well, they can add really difficult word demons to their lists and turn to the dictionary for the definition to record in their glossaries. These words should be starred; and during follow-up discussion, those who have checked a word in the dictionary can come forward to write it on the board and question classmates about its meaning. Other students can provide examples of how they would use it in talking about the topic under consideration. This type of follow-up work, where those who have run a dictionary check function as discussion leaders, encourages young people to spot word demons in their own reading and look up those words for later sharing.

To build skills, the teacher may select a particular entry that relates to a selection to be read and may copy it onto acetate for projection or onto a board or chart. Together students can talk of the meaning of the word, propose sentences, and interpret diacritical marks. One youngster may have to refer to that part of the dictionary that tells how the marks are used. Another may assist by checking to see if the dictionary entry provides a picture—something often as helpful as the written definition. This is generally true when words have a concrete representation in the real world. For example, in the case of the word *gorge*, Scott, Foresman's *Thorndike Barnhart Advanced Dictionary* offers this definition: "a deep, narrow valley, usually steep and rocky, especially one with a stream." Above that definition is a sharp little sketch of a gorge with stream tucked into a V-shaped valley.

In cases where meanings are clarified through pictures, students can add sketches or colored pictures clipped from magazines to their glossaries. Working with particularly important terms such as *gorge*, *fjord*, *delta*, *plateau*, *tributary*, or *distributary*, young people can make large-sized "dictionary sheets" based on material found in dictionaries, texts, and references. A sheet for *gorge* would include:

The word printed in large letters. With words of more than one
 syllable, words can be broken between syllables;
The phonetic spelling/pronunciation of the word (gorj);
The definition of the term and several model sentences;
A colored picture—either a clipping or a sketch—when the word
 applies to a phenomenon that can be visualized.

Ques. Mue

Main Idea Tactics

Upon finishing an informational passage, children should be able to identify the main idea—the key point contained within it. One way to teach reading for main ideas in social studies is through analyzing—

G The child is able to use dictionary entries to develop a better understanding of technical terms.

G The child can identify the main idea of an informational passage.

together. Children in small or class-sized groups read a paragraph silently to themselves. That paragraph is then shown on a screen with an overhead projector. As the children study the projected paragraph, the teacher queries: "What is the main idea of this paragraph? What does it tell us about?"

The students may respond with: "It tells about what happens when the river floods the plains." They then examine the paragraph to see if they can identify specific sentences that help them find the main thought.

The students and teacher then move to the next paragraph in the sequence. Usually it will be subsumed under the same boldface heading as the previous one. Thus, when the three or four paragraphs in the section have been analyzed, youngsters can study the message carried by the heading and answer the questions: "How does the boldface heading help us in working with the ideas in the three paragraphs below it? When you read the heading, *Using the land*, what kinds of ideas do you anticipate will follow? If you are making a set of written notes, how can you use this heading?"

As the last question indicates, search for main ideas can lead directly into note taking. The boldface heading becomes the major organizing point that is noted. Beneath it, students list the main point developed in each paragraph of the section. At first this is done within teacher-guided groups with one set of written notes emerging from the cooperative analysis. The notes can take form on the chalkboard or charting paper. They will be relatively simple to start. For example:

A. Using the land
   1. The importance of the river for agriculture
   2. Ways of working the land
   3. Kinds of crops grown there

Only after young investigators have had numerous group experiences noting main ideas subsumed under one heading should they attempt individual noting-down. Then such activity should flow directly into teacher-guided activity in which students share outlines they have made, perhaps by filling the chalkboard with them. The teacher and students discuss points that should be included and consider ways of tightening their notes. In this way the teacher is actually teaching basic thinking, reading, and noting skills—not simply assigning paragraphs to be read.

Detailed Reading Tactics

Children's attention should be focused on sorting significant from less significant detail. Again the teacher needs to teach this skill systematically in terms of social studies content. Guiding a group that has already read a selection silently and has gone on to note main ideas on the margin of a projected transparency, the teacher asks: "What words give detail about who? when? where? what happened first? next? why this happened?" These five W-questions serve as a useful mental checklist for the reader when identifying basic detail.

G The child can sift significant detail from informational content being read.

Again one way to structure this activity is to work from a projected transparency of the passage. Children come forward to circle "who" details, "when" details, "what" details, "where" details, and "why" details—perhaps using a different colored marker for each type. Later as they read independently, they can list the five Ws down the edge of a paper and record there the key information from a passage.

The Inferencing Tactic

Sues Four

It is possible to go beyond the details and main ideas of a passage to project conclusions and make inferences not stated directly by the writer. Look at the short paragraph below.

R See chapter 10, pages 328-342 for a summary of levels of reading and ways to assess children's growing skills.

Harriet climbed on her bicycle and started off for the store. As she rode, she checked in her pocket for the quarter her mother had given her to buy a bottle of milk at the corner grocery store. "If I ride quickly," she thought to herself as she looked up at the sky, "I will get home before dark."

Children can react to this passage by giving the main idea–that Harriet is going to the store to buy milk. They can also respond by supplying details: that she went on her bicycle and carried a quarter; that the store was on the corner. But a really perceptive reader goes beyond to infer: Did this story take place in colonial days? How do we know? Could it happen today? How do we know? What time of day was it? Did Harriet live in the country, suburbs, or city? What would be our best quess? How old was Harriet? How did Harriet feel? Everyone of these questions takes the reader beyond literal comprehension to find hidden meanings.

Social studies teachers should look for opportunities to help children probe for hidden meanings. As in the instance described above, readers can infer when an event is taking place (past, present, future; morning, noon, night) if this information is not explicitly stated in the passage; where it is taking place (in their country, somewhere else; in a rural area, in the city); the age of the participants and how they feel. In addition readers can figure out advantages and/or disadvantages accruing from a described course of action; the way one event differs from or is the same as another described in the passage; the point of view of the writer–does he or she like the person or event being described? Is he or she against this particular action?

Figure 4.4
A Cartoon for Use in Social Studies

Drawing by H. Martin; © 1975 The New Yorker Magazine, Inc.

Similar probing questions can be asked relative to cartoons that boys and girls interpret as part of investigations of current issues. With the cartoon in Figure 4.4, for example, teacher and students can ask:

What kinds of changes have occurred in this area? How do you know?

Why is the overlook now named "Split Level"? Why was it formerly called "Pleasant Valley"?

The man has a camera around his neck. Do you think he will take a picture? Why? Why not?

What message is the cartoonist trying to communicate?

These questions can lead into values clarification, which will be discussed in the next section; e.g., Do you feel that the changes implied in the cartoon are good ones? bad ones? Why?

Idea Page

Playing The Five Ws

1. Upper graders who have cooperatively and individually identified who, what, when, where, and why in paragraphs they have read sometimes enjoy an activity that converts this reading skill builder into a game. As they read an informational paragraph on their own, they write questions based on the paragraph—ones that start with the five Ws and perhaps how-questions as well. If each question is written on a separate card, cards can be taped quickly to the board—blank side facing up. Cards can be mounted according to the who, what, where, when, why, or how category to which they belong (Figure 4.5).
2. The result is a game board. Students who have read the paragraphs on which the questions are based divide into teams with each team sending a player to the board to turn over a question card to answer. Of course, no child can select one he or she has contributed.
3. A correct answer brings the team the number of points listed in the left-hand column. A wrong answer means that the number is subtracted from the score.
4. One advantage of this tactic is that students must formulate questions about material they are reading. This is a valuable skill to acquire. In upper grades students are often tested on information read. One way to prepare is to identify possible questions and to answer them as part of study.

Figure 4.5
A Question Game Board

Why (6 points)	☐	☐	☐	☐	☐
How (5 points)	☐	☐	☐	☐	☐
When (4 points)	☐	☐	☐	☐	☐
Where (3 points)	☐	☐	☐	☐	☐
What (2 points)	☐	☐	☐	☐	☐
Who (1 point)	☐	☐	☐	☐	☐
Topics of Questions:	Government	Customs	Landforms	History	Economics

Area Five **The Values Clarification Tactic**

Perhaps one of the most natural contexts in which children can clarify their developing values systems is the reading of books, stories, and poems. Here once again the questions the teacher asks about a passage determine whether children will think in judgmental terms. The teacher must go beyond factual content to question right/wrong acts, good/evil deeds, appropriate/inappropriate behavior.

Many stories written for children embody a values conflict. For the younger reader such books as the following can be used:

Betsy Byars, *The Groober* (New York: Harper & Row, 1967)	The groober attempts to keep up with his neighbors by digging a hole as magnificent as theirs. He discovers that his new magnificent hole is not half as comfortable as his little old hole.
José and Ariane Aruego, *A Crocodile's Tale* (New York: Charles Scribner's & Sons, 1972)	The crocodile plans to repay an act of kindness by eating up its benefactor. When the benefactor in turn is saved by the kindness of a monkey, he has learned to repay a kindness with another kindness.
Marcia Brown, *Once a Mouse . . .* (New York: Charles Scribner's & Sons, 1961)	A hermit changes a mouse into a tiger, but the tiger forgets who he really was and turns on the hermit. In the end the hermit changes the tiger back into a mouse.

G The child can make judgments that he or she can defend rationally.

In each case, the teacher can ask children first to retell the story to make sure they comprehend the facts of the case. But the teacher who hopes to help children make judgments as they read will ask questions that clarify the implicit moral: Can you tell about a time when you were dissatisfied with what you had and wanted what your friend had? Can you remember a time when someone you helped out didn't help you in return? Have you ever wished you were someone else? Is it good or bad to wish you had something just like somebody else has? When might it be good? When might it be bad? When someone does you a kindness, is it right or wrong to forget about the kindness? Questions such as these are not earthshaking, but they do involve children in considering right and wrong and pave the way toward deeper analysis in upper grades.

Idea Page

Background information for the teacher. Today many text series reproduce documents from the past through which young people can get a clearer perception of what life was like and how it has changed. Such documents can be used also to help children make inferences based on materials read.

The aim. The student will develop the ability to make inferences based on information contained in documents.

The task. Study the advertisement shown below (Figure 4.6). Then answer the questions.

Figure 4.6

MARSHALL & BALL
ALL THE NEW & LATEST STYLES NOW READY

All Wool Business Suits	$8, 10 12 & 15
Fine Dress Suits	$15 to 25
Men's Overcoats	$5, 6, 8, 10 to 20
Pantaloons Cut in the Correct Style	$2, 2.50, 3, 4, 5, & 6

BOYS' & CHILDREN'S CLOTHING A SPECIALTY.

Youths' School Suits	From $4 to 12
Boys' Short Suits	$2, 3, 4, 5, & 6
Children's Overcoats	From $1 to 12
Youths' Overcoats	From $4 to 16

This is the largest and most complete stock we have ever shown, and at these moderate prices we sell good substantial Clothing

MARSHALL & BALL,
CLOTHIERS,
209 & 211 MAIN STREET,

807, 809 & 811 Broad Street, Newark,
58 & 60 Newark Ave., Jersey City,

PATERSON, N. J.

1. Do you think this advertisement is a recent one? Why or why not?
2. What qualities are people looking for in their clothing? How do you know from reading this advertisement?
3. What is a *clothier*?
4. Decide: Is Marshall and Ball a large or small company? How do you know?

The Independent Reading Tactic

Not only should young investigators learn how to read social studies material but they should also use their growing skills to read these materials for pleasure. There is enjoyment to be had in reading informational content as well as in reading historical novels, stories, poems, biographies, and autobiographies. The student who has found pleasure within the covers of a book has developed an entire area within him- or herself for future growth and for future recreation. A feeling for books should be seeded early in kindergarten. Here the teacher can build anticipation by sharing fascinating books and taking children at least twice weekly to the library to select a book to carry home for reading with parents. Parents should be reminded that children will be returning home with books to read.

As children gain reading skill, the library visit becomes an exciting time to choose books for independent classroom reading. Children should be assisted in locating books that not only tell stories but supply information and ideas on topics being studied. Today there are superb picture story and informational books that are a delight to behold. Some of these integrate easily into ongoing unit study. For example, look at Barbara Kataoka's *Pictures and Pollution* (Chicago: Childrens Press, 1977). Photographs of paintings and statues assist the author in telling the pollution story.

Most teachers set up a reading table of books related to a topic to encourage children to branch out into related reading. Especially in the upper grades, students should be involved in setting up the reading display. Using their growing ability to find resources with the aid of the card catalog, a search team can head independently to the library to collect a dozen or so books to bring back. These students can use their scanning skills to look through each selection incorporated in the classroom book display. They can write up large sales captions for each selection based on their scannings. Captions are laid out with the books so that other students will have some guidance when they go to the reading table to select a book.

Problem to Ponder

Below are two reading assignments based on social studies materials. Study each to decide the kinds of skills sought through each assignment. You may want to devise a creative reading activity modeled after one of these:

Assignment 1. For several weeks we have been reading about the settlement of Nova Scotia in *People in States* (Reading,

Massachusetts: Addison-Wesley, 1973). Now go back and complete this data retrieval chart (Figure 4.7) based on pages 200-277. Do this part by yourself. You may refer back to the book as you do the chart.

Now check your chart against _____'s chart. Have him or her check yours. Together decide on three ways in which the groups living in Nova Scotia are alike and three ways in which they are different.

Assignment 2.

A. Read pages 120-127 and pages 128-134 in *Great Names in American History* to learn about the Clark brothers, George Rogers and William. Pretending you are one of these men, write your autobiography. Tell something about your childhood, your accomplishments, and those contributions for which you wish to be remembered. Do this by yourself.

B. Decide which brother made the greater contribution to America. Develop a list of reasons to support your choice. Do this with _____ and _____.

Figure 4.7
A Data Retrieval Chart

People	Where they come from	Why they came	Occupations	Sources of income
Food	Kinds	How prepared	Where obtained	How stored
Clothing	Kinds	Where obtained	How made	How worn
Shelter	Kinds	Construction materials	Where located	
Customs Traditions				

Ques Six

Writing Strategies

Not only can study in the social sciences result in material to be shared orally but it can also result in ideas recorded on paper for others to read. In this context, writing goes beyond the composition of reports, stories, and poems for correction and reading by the teacher. Ideas are recorded on paper so that fellow classmates, other members of the school community, and even adults outside the school can read and react to them. Writing is part of the total process of communication—a means of sharing with others.

Writing skills that relate directly to study in the social sciences include the ability to:

use the specialized vocabulary of the social studies in writing;

write logical reports that organize facts and ideas that were met in investigations;

write a creative composition that goes beyond actual facts but is based on facts, what today is called *faction*;

compose business and social letters that communicate ideas clearly to others;

compile short bibliographies and footnotes that include essential data about references cited;

use words and sentence patterns that communicate ideas forcefully;

use specialized writing tools—the dictionary, the thesaurus, and a dictionary of synonyms and antonyms;

make lists of related facts or outlines for use in later study and writing.

Prose Tactics

How does one begin to teach writing as part of the social studies? One point to remember is that writing activity blends naturally into other activities as students investigate social problems. Attempts to set aside distinct sessions in the social studies specifically geared to the development of writing, or even reading skills, are artificial ones. Students who have listened and talked together on a social studies topic are ready to write on that topic because they know a lot about it. Conversely, children are made ready to talk and write by reading experiences.

In social studies, writing can assume any number of creative forms. Students who have talked together about a topic, have read in reference sources, have gathered firsthand data, and/or have viewed and listened to audiovisual materials can develop their understandings on paper through the following activities.

1. Odysseys. Young writers who are studying a particular geographic region of the world can describe a hypothetical journey through that land, writing as if they were taking a cruise down a major river, hitchhiking along the highways, or visiting a friend who lives there. Most of the material is factual, but creative students can include fictional elements as well—conversations they had along the way, people they met, feelings they had. The term **faction** applies here—reports that are based on facts but incorporate fictional characters and conversations.

G The child acquires basic writing skills so that eventually he or she can use the written word to make an impact on others.

2. Diaries. Factionalized diaries can be created in which writers describe their own adventures in the past. A student can write of his or her own impressions as a member of the Lewis and Clark expedition, as a worker on the Panama Canal or Brooklyn Bridge, or as a member of Magellan's crew. Factionalized diaries should have dated, day-by-day entries just as real diaries. Entries can be short, especially with younger children who are gaining skill as writers.

G The child uses his or her growing repertoire of facts and ideas as content for writing.

3. Period newspaper and magazines. Newspapers and magazines set in a time or place being studied are an excellent means of summarizing unit activity and developing writing skills. Drawing on their background of facts and understandings, the students compile a newspaper, with each member of the class contributing. Contributions include news stories, editorials, letters to the editor, sports reports, home and family-life columns, advertising, classifieds, cartoons, comics, and so forth. Some students become headline writers; others editors and proofreaders checking for grammatical and styling improvements; others layout experts; still others printers and folders of the actual newspaper.

G The child demonstrates his or her understanding of newspaper style and structure by reproducing both. The child contributes to a group project.

Newspapers set in different time periods (Colonial Days, Middle Ages) can be compiled in different ways. A common approach is to print or type out all columns and sketch all illustrations on duplicating masters. Masters are run off on duplicating machines so that each youngster receives a final draft. The advantage of this approach is that every student has a copy to take home to share—an important achievement especially if all have a signed contribution included.

An alternative is the creation of a single edition—perhaps large sized just like a real newspaper. In this case, individual columns and illustrations are hand lettered and/or drawn by the compilers. These are stapled or glued to large pieces of white wrapping paper cut to newspaper size. The result is a mock-up of a real paper. When a single copy has been produced, it can be carried by news criers to other classes in the school to be shared orally with students there.

As a child investigates a topic, he or she can summarize
major points in paragraph or outline form.

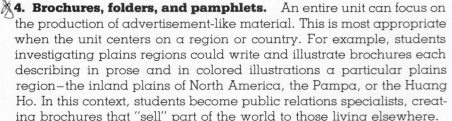

4. Brochures, folders, and pamphlets.   An entire unit can focus on
the production of advertisement-like material. This is most appropriate
when the unit centers on a region or country. For example, students
investigating plains regions could write and illustrate brochures each
describing in prose and in colored illustrations a particular plains
region—the inland plains of North America, the Pampa, or the Huang
Ho. In this context, students become public relations specialists, creating brochures that "sell" part of the world to those living elsewhere.

G The child demon-
strates understanding
and knowledge of
people, places, times,
and issues by writing
clearly about them in a
variety of forms.

5. TV and radio scripts.   Another factionalized writing task is the
compostion of TV and radio scripts. Young people who are investigating time periods from the past can recreate broadcasts and telecasts
that follow the format of "You Are There." Scripts can be simply news
reports describing in documentary fashion the step-by-step events taking place. Action-filled events are best handled in this way—"You Are
There" at the landing of the Mayflower, at the signing of the Declaration of Independence, at the Alamo, or at Fort Sumter. Or scripts can
be made for mock discussions among characters drawn from one
period of time.

6. Letters to the editor. As young people study controversial issues they may wish to state an opinion about some. What better way to express that opinion than through a letter to the editor of a local paper! Litter in the streets, rising crime rates, issues being decided by general referendum—the possibilities for this kind of writing are endless. Imagine the glow of pleasure that the young writer experiences in seeing his or her words "immortalized" in newspaper print.

G The child demonstrates understanding of point of view in a written communication by producing a piece with a definitive point of view.

7. Paragraphs of summary or description. A useful writing assignment is to ask students who have talked together or researched a topic to write a single paragraph that summarizes key points. This is a logical task that students will repeatedly be asked to complete as they move into secondary school. Descriptive paragraphs are equally important to learn to handle skillfully; for example, "Write one paragraph describing important features we associate with the Netherlands," or "Write a paragraph that describes how a set of locks operates as in the Kiel Canal."

G The child is able to summarize and outline social studies ideas in written form.

8. Outlines. Information can be organized into an outline of main and subordinate points. This is a good way to handle summary and description. For example, steps in the functioning of a set of locks or features associated with the Netherlands can be compiled in outline as well as paragraph form. Sometimes dividing the class into sections leads to interesting comparisons. One section attempts to write a paragraph of description based on a filmstrip just viewed, the other an outline of points. Results can be printed on charting paper and the young people can compare their products to determine the strengths and advantages of each approach.

9. Short, documented reports. Some young people in the upper elementary grades may be ready to compose short reports in which they quote from sources and begin to include footnotes and a bibliography. Clearly before beginning on this kind of activity, even the most able youngsters will need direct instruction in the component tasks: how to choose a passage to quote directly, how to introduce citations, how to use quotation marks, and how to lay out footnotes and bibliography. Clearly, too, reports at this level should be brief. If students are required to compile very lengthy reports on such topics as the animals of the plains, the result will be paragraphs of information copied directly from reference sources.

G The child is able to compile short, simple bibliographies and footnote entries.

General report writing is most successful if based on question-research guides developed cooperatively before students turn to references for information. Chapter 3, pages 81–87, supplies ideas on how to help children develop guides for referencing and report writing.

G The child learns to handle a variety of social studies references and books by actually producing some.

10. Original reference and trade books. There is a thrill in creating a book! For youngsters in a social studies program that book can be:

A glossary of basic terms uncovered through investigation. Each entry includes the word, its pronunciation, its meanings, a sentence to show typical use, and perhaps a sketch (Figure 4.8).

Figure 4.8
A Sample Glossary Entry

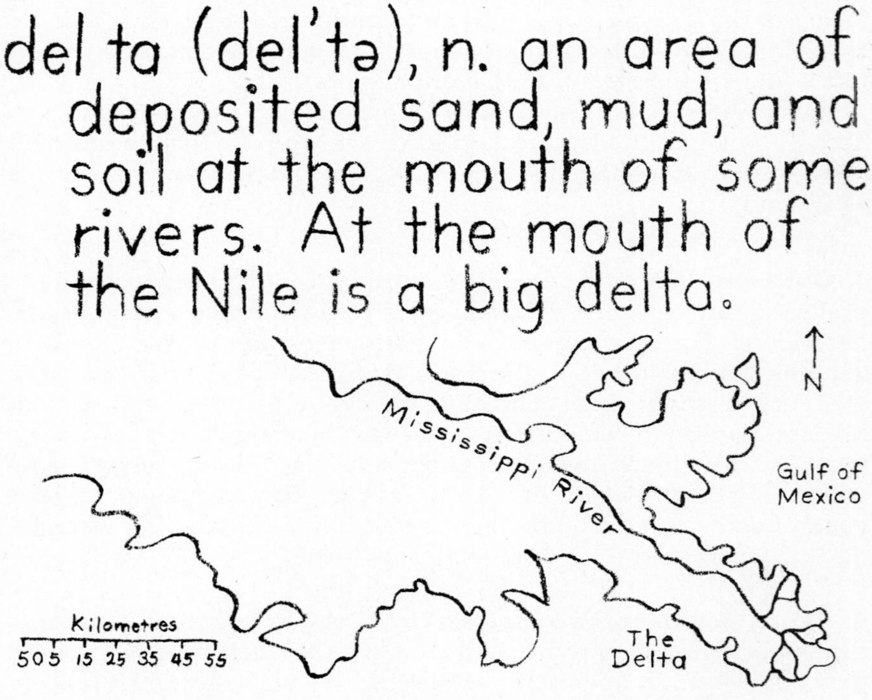
del ta (del'tə), n. an area of deposited sand, mud, and soil at the mouth of some rivers. At the mouth of the Nile is a big delta.
N
Mississippi River
Gulf of Mexico
Kilometres
505 15 25 35 45 55
The Delta

An ABC fact book. For every letter of the alphabet, writers identify a word beginning with that letter and compose a paragraph of description or explanation of the phenomenon associated with the word. A fine model for this activity is the book *Ashanti to Zulu* (New York: Dial, 1976), in which each entry tells about a group of people who live in Africa. Students can create ABC fact books on pollution, crime, population–all issues they are investigating. They can create historical or geographical fact books in which entries center on one period or place. They can create anthropological books in which each alphabetical entry tells about a particular custom or institution. The possibilities are limitless.

Encyclopedias. *Our Plains Encyclopedia! Our Encyclopedia of Transportation! Our Encyclopedia of Social Customs!* Although what children produce under such titles are not really encyclopedias, calling them by these impressive names, compiling materials written and illustrated by numbers of children within one cover, and laying these original pages in the reading center for children to use make writing productive.

The Poetry Tactic

Ques Seven In some contexts, poetry writing correlates easily with social studies. Perhaps one of the most useful forms of poetic expression of which social studies teachers should be aware is haiku. Haiku is a Japanese form consisting of three lines; the first line contains five syllables, the second seven, and the third five. When studying the people and culture of Japan, not only should youngsters create Japanese art forms and sample Japanese foods but they should try their hand at creating haiku moments. Here is a sample that has a seasonal orientation as do many of the original Japanese haikus:

> Spring flowers waken
> To a barren, greenless earth:
> Hope comes back again.

G The child comes to a better understanding of a culture by producing pieces typical of it.

Similarly, students who have heard African and American Indian chants and have learned to enjoy the regular repeating beat can create chants with similar characteristics. This kind of writing in which children play with the forms typical of a culture is ideal for pulling unit threads together. If children try art forms that also are typical of the culture and illustrate their poems with those forms, if they use their poetry-art pieces as backdrops for the classroom where they are cooking culinary treats from the culture, if they perform dances and sing songs representative of it, they will really get a feel for peoples of the world.

Writing-Together Tactics

Many teachers who have included writing activities in social studies units have been disappointed by student products. Some youngsters simply produce nothing, fiddling with pen or pencil during much of the time set aside for writing. Others pen a few lines that show little thought and general inability to express clearly what ideas they generate.

The reason for this writing failure is that writing in the content areas must be taught as carefully as we now know that reading must be taught. Young writers must be given initial guidance in how to begin a

R See *Social Education* 43 (March 1979). The focus of this issue is "Writing to Learn in the Social Studies."

Ques Eight

logical paragraph, how to organize ideas sequentially, how to move from one thought into another similar one, how to change direction, and how to conclude.

Teacher-Guided Group Writing.   Much of this initial guidance in beginning, in organizing, and in making transitions can occur as part of teacher-guided group writing. A fourth-grade teacher who has just outlined the Huang Ho plains region on a map of China (see page 128) can follow mapping with guided writing. The teacher begins with the question, "We have just outlined the Huang Ho plains. Let's see if together we can describe the location and what we know about these plains in our own words. Can someone give me one sentence that tells in what part of China the Huang Ho plains are found?"

A youngster may produce a sentence orally: "The Huang Ho plains are found in the eastern part of China." A student scribe records the sentence on board or chart.

The teacher then asks for a second sentence—perhaps one stating relationships between the river and the plains. Resulting sentences may include: "The Huang Ho flows from west to east across China." "It runs right through the plains region." "It flows into the Huang Ho Sea." "In English we call it the Yellow Sea." "The river brings water to the plains region." As students—prompted by appropriate teacher questions—suggest additional sentences, the scribe records these on the board. Initially only three or four sentences are given and recorded, especially if the topic is a rather narrow one on which children have only limited information.

Teacher-Guided Rewriting.   Having developed a rough draft of a paragraph incorporating facts that can be read from their maps, students in this fourth-grade class should go back to rework the paragraph. In reworking, students with teacher guidance voiced in the form of questions can consider:

Is there any additional information that we can read from our map that we can put into our paragraph?

Is there a better order in which our sentences should be placed?

Has the student scribe spelled all words correctly?

Is there need to change capitalization or punctuation?

Are there any words that should be added to make our paragraphs more descriptive? Are there words we should leave out?

Not all these questions should be applied to the revision of a single paragraph. The teacher must really be alert, looking quickly at what students have produced orally to see the potential for teaching a particular writing skill. If, for example, sentences are not logically arranged, the teacher can ask: "Let's look at our five sentences. Which one would make the best introductory one? What one would sensibly come next?" As children debate the most appropriate ordering of sentences, they put a number in front of each to indicate logical sequence.

Before the cooperatively composed and edited paragraph is erased, a student should copy it either into a class notebook or onto charting paper. The last makes a striking class product if ideas discussed, mapped, charted, or read are summarized daily in a paragraph devised by the group. Each day a different youngster should be the scribe. Each day another student should record the piece on charting paper, perhaps with an illustration contributed by still another student. By the time the unit is completed—which could be anywhere from two to six weeks—the class will have written an original big book that incorporates the major ideas of the unit. The big book can be shared orally with other classes studying the same unit or placed in the library for other classes to enjoy.

Writing in Teams. A technique for moving children from teacher-guided writing into individualized writing is cooperative composition in teams. After a class has composed together for several days and has had practice in working with a particular form of written expression, a team of no more than three students can create the daily journal entry, the summary paragraph, the outline of key facts, or whatever form of writing the class has been practicing. More than one team can try its hand at this group writing activity. Later writing teams share their findings with the class. The class determines by voting which entry or combination of entries should be included in the ongoing class book, script, encyclopedia, or glossary.

Students who have participated in teacher-guided group composition activity can divide into writing teams as they begin another unit or investigation. Each day the team together creates a paragraph, definition, or entry to go into their team book. Here it is sometimes helpful to encourage groups to select different kinds of writing activity. Some teams work on glossaries, others on factual ABC books, others on diaries and logs, still others on brochures. The result of unit study will be comprehensive with students compiling materials in a variety of forms.

Writing Strategies: A Summation

Many experienced teachers have commented on the industriousness of elementary students carrying out art projects in the social studies. This same industriousness can be observed in groups producing a creative written product with illustrations. To suggest that children "write" books may be an overpowering thought at first glance, but often it is the "largeness" of the idea that appeals to children. Also, as

G The child can write clearly organized informational paragraphs with punctuation and capitalization used to help communicate meanings.

G The child can work cooperatively with others to produce a clearly developed piece of written expression.

R Read Barry Beyer's article, "Pre-writing and Rewriting to Learn," *Social Education* 43 (March 1979): 187–189, 197.

this section has stressed, to make the idea work, the teacher must give attention to the details of writing, helping children acquire writing skill even as they acquire broader understanding of social science.

Strategies for Teaching Reading and Writing in the Social Studies: A Summary Thought or Two

In recent years many schools have experienced a swing back to "the basics." To many, "the basics" mean skills, specifically reading, writing, researching, systematic studying, mathematical computing, and, of course, the most basic ability–thinking. Especially in time-pressed elementary programs, this swing brings with it the distinct possibility that social investigations will be allocated a smaller proportion of school time. This is most true when skills are taught totally outside the content areas through skill-building workbooks and exercises.

The diversity of the instructional tactics detailed in the last two chapters indicates that a return to the basics should actually trigger *more*, not less, involvement in the social studies. Basic skills can be built and refined using the meaning-filled content of the social studies. Encountering the broad understandings of the social sciences and the questions investigators of them raise, students are simultaneously reading and learning to read, writing and learning to write, viewing/listening and learning to view/listen, and searching/sharing and learning to search/share.

A Problem to Ponder

Writing in the January/February 1978 issue of *The Social Studies*, Lawrence Senesh reported:

"Today, the schools and the community are rediscovering that our youth do not know how to read and write. The community is demanding more time and emphasis on the basic skills. The educators have yielded to the hue and cry. The federal government has responded to the pressures with promises of millions of dollars for reading specialists to repair the defective basic skills.

Many educators and school systems have yielded easily so that no dialogue within the school community has taken place. The educators have not explained to the community that *learning is a system in which content and skill are interwoven and where ideas motivate students to improve their skills.*"

1. What is the significance of this statement for the teaching of social studies and of skills?
2. What specific tactics detailed in this chapter can lead to the incorporation of basic reading and writing skills in the social studies?

References

Barron, Arnold; and Claybaugh, Amos. *Using Reading to Teach Subject Matter: Fundamentals for Content Teachers*. Columbus, Ohio: Charles E. Merrill, 1974.

Burns, Paul; and Roe, Betty. *Teaching Reading in Today's Elementary Schools*. Chicago: Rand McNally, 1976; especially chapter 8, "Study Skills and the Content Areas."

Carrillo, Lawrence. *Teaching Reading: A Handbook*. New York: St. Martin's Press, 1976.

Fay, Leo; and Jared, Ann. *Reading in the Content Fields*, rev. ed. Newark, Delaware: International Reading Association, 1975; an annotated bibliography of sources.

Forgan, Harry; and Mangrum, Charles. *Teaching Content Area Related to Reading Skills*. Columbus, Ohio: Charles E. Merrill, 1976.

Hennings, Dorothy. *Communication in Action*. Chicago: Rand McNally, 1978; especially chapter 8 on writing skills, and chapter 11 on reading skills.

Huss, Helen. "Reading," in *Skill Development in the Social Studies: 33rd Yearbook of the National Council for the Social Studies*. Arlington, Virginia: NCSS, 1963; see also "Writing" by Lewis Todd in the same volume.

Lunstrum, John. "Reading in the Social Studies: A Preliminary Analysis of Recent Research," *Social Education*, 40:10-18, January 1976.

Lunstrum, John. "Reading in the Social Studies," in *Developing Decision-Making Skills*, 47th Yearbook of National Council for the Social Studies. Arlington, Virginia: NSCC, 1977, pp. 109-139.

Piercey, Dorothy. *Reading Activities in Content Areas*. abridged ed. Boston: Allyn & Bacon, 1976.

Spache, Evelyn. *Reading Activities for Child Involvement*. 2nd ed. Boston: Allyn & Bacon, 1976.

Strategies for Using Maps, Globes, Clocks, Calendars, and Time Lines

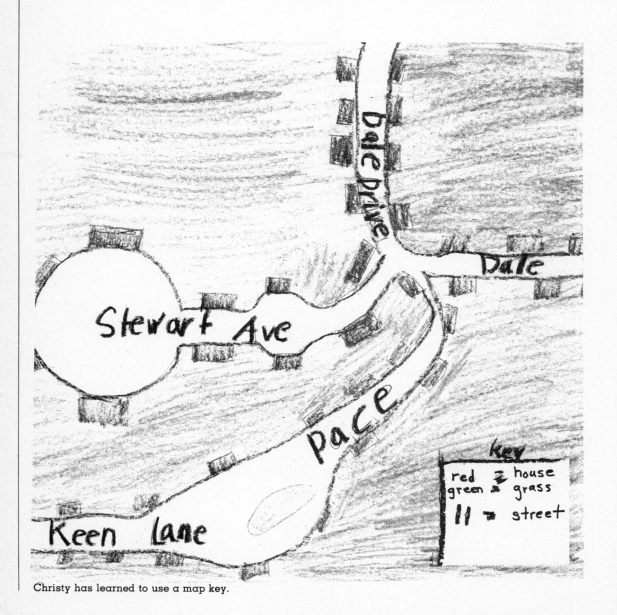

Christy has learned to use a map key.

technical
maps + globes

> **Thousands of words would be required to state the facts portrayed by a map.**
>
> **J. Paul Goode, Introduction to *Goode's School Atlas,* first edition, 1922**

Key Questions

What skills are necessary if children are to use maps and globes effectively?

What kinds of symbols are found on maps? What functions are served by a key, or legend?

Why is scaling an important characteristic of a map?

What is longitude? latitude? How does longitudinal position affect time? How does latitudinal position affect the seasonal variations?

Why is distortion an unavoidable attribute of any flat map?

Where is north? south?

What techniques can the teacher use to introduce young children to fundamental directions? cardinal directions? the earth as a sphere? the globe as a representation of the earth? simple maps? locations they should know?

What techniques can the teacher use to introduce intermediate level children to common map symbols? to the interpretation of distance and elevation on diverse maps? to latitude and longitude? to map distortion? to more complex ways of talking of direction?

How does a child's concept of time differ from an adult's?

How can we help children in the primary and intermediate grades build a concept of time sequences? day/night changes? seasonal variatons?

A Fourth-Grade Lesson to Think About

Topic: The Huang Ho Plains   **Date:** Monday, November 28

Concepts: Cause-effect; location; physical environment

Objectives:

1. Given a map of China, children will be able to outline the Huang Ho Plains and add a title, key, directional symbol, and labels.
2. On a map children can figure the direction of river flow.
3. Children will be able to describe the relationship between flood plains and the river that has formed the plains.
4. Having already studied one plains region (the western, interior plains of North America), children will be able to identify similarities and differences between the two areas.
5. Students will be able to organize a paragraph summarizing key discussion points, as part of group interaction.

Materials: globe, world map, outline maps of China, overhead projector, transparency of Huang Ho area, Laidlaw text *Regions and Social Needs*.

Procedure:

1. *Motivation and Orientation:* Children locate China on a globe and describe where China is located in relation to their own state. Others point out China and the Huang Ho on a large world map.

2. The teacher points out the Huang Ho plains on a map projected with an overhead. Children locate the area on a map in their book. They outline the boundaries of the Huang Ho Plains on a desk map. They color the area, outline the river system, put in a directional symbol, key and title.

3. Children describe the key characteristics of the Huang Ho Plains and the relationship between plains and river. Ideas as are recorded on the board.

4. Children contrast this plains area with the North American plains just studied: location, relation to river, and so forth. Similarities and differences are listed chart-style on the board.

5. Summarize the relationship between plains and river. The paragraph is recorded sentence-by-sentence on charting paper. Children work with teacher to edit the paragraph for logical development of ideas.

Related Questions:

Where on the globe is China? Find our state. Let's describe in words the location of China in relation to our state? How large is China in comparison to the United States? In what continent do we find China?

In what direction does the Huang Ho flow? How do we know? Can someone describe the plains region in this part of China—its location, shape? What is the name of the body of water to the east? What other items must we add to our maps to make them clear to a reader? What would be an appropriate title?

What is the most important feature found in the plains? Why are these plains located where they are? If you went to China, what would the area look like? How do you think the people would be using the land? What advantage would there be to live next to a big river? What disadvantage would there be?

How are these plains different from the North American plains? How are these plains similar? What kinds of geographical features would we expect to find in any plains region?

In summary, what are the major characteristics of the Huang Ho plains? What would make a good first sentence for a summary paragraph? What details should we include? How can we arrange our paragraph to make logical sense?

R Lesson plan from P. Connington, 4th grade teacher

Topic of next lesson in the sequence: Meeting basic needs—picture study. In work groups, children interpret pictures of the Huang Ho.

Introduction

Fourth graders in Pat Connington's class were making a comparative study of regions of the world. Their first focus was the plains; later they would investigate mountainous regions. In each case they were concerned with the way of life—finding out how people solve basic needs relating to food, clothing, and shelter; how geographic and climatic characteristics of a region affect existence; and how people organize their lives in social groups. Through their study, these fourth graders were gaining understanding of basic social-geographic relationships. Simultaneously they were refining their ability to use and interpret maps and globes.

T See lesson plan on page 282–85.

Map and Globe Usage Skills

The globe and the map in their many forms and varieties are two of the most useful tools of the social investigator. As in Pat Connington's classroom, the globe or map can be a source of information; rainfall, population concentrations, terrain—to name some obvious data—can be read directly from maps. A map also serves as a record of human experience; the locations and names of towns, cities, states, and provinces tell much about earlier days. Using such data, a social investigator can make inferences about human activity.

Map and Globe Skills — What Are They?

Numbers of specific skills must be acquired if one is to use maps and globes as sources of information as well as guides that help one travel from place to place. Specific competencies to develop at the primary level include the abilities to:

1. distinguish left from right
2. categorize objects according to size
3. use and react accurately to basic directional words: *up, down, in, under, through, above, below, by*
4. use the cardinal directional words: *north, south, east,* and *west*
5. navigate independently in the immediate geographic area
6. recognize the small, round globe as a representation of the earth
7. distinguish land from water areas on the globe
8. make simple maps of familiar locations, which by third grade include a title, symbols, legend, and a simple grid system
9. relate day and night changes to the rotation of earth from west to east
10. locate one's own country, state, or province on the globe

R See the 33rd Yearbook of NCSS: Skill Development in Social Studies (1963), specifically the article by Lorrin Kennamer for a listing of skills to include in a school's map and globe interpretation program.

Primary

Ques. 1

Specific competencies to develop at the intermediate level include the abilities to:

Intermediate

11. locate the continents and major oceans of the world on a globe
12. locate one's own state or province, town, or city, and familiar, well-known cities on a variety of maps (Competencies 11 and 12 often begin to be developed at the primary level.)
13. locate the poles, equator, and Tropics of Cancer and Capricorn on a globe and map
14. perceive distortions that result when a basically round earth is depicted as a flat map
15. use and interpret map symbols with ease
16. interpret and create map legends
17. read direction on a map or globe to orient it correctly in space
18. read distances off a map or globe using the scale given in the legend
19. use and interpret map grid systems, especially latitude and longitude
20. explain the cause of day and night in terms of the earth's rotation
21. relate time zones to longitude
22. read diverse kinds of information from maps and make inferences based on these data (e.g., relief maps, political maps, crop production maps, rainfall maps)
23. interpret maps that differ in projection

The Basics of Mapping

To gain control of maps and globes, one must gain control of five basic components. As the listing of specific competencies suggests, these components relate to 1) symbols, 2) direction, 3) distance, 4) grid systems, and 5) distortions that result when a sphere-shaped object is flattened out on paper. Let us look at these basic components before talking of ways to help children in the primary and intermediate grades acquire specific competencies.

Symbols.   Symbols are used on maps so that much information can be expressed with relative simplicity and in a small space. For example, on some road maps, the approximate populations of cities and towns are depicted through a series of different kinds of circles (Figure 5.1a). On the same kind of road map, other simple shapes are used to represent key information being communicated (Figure 5.1b). In each case a line or shape communicates information that in written form

Figure 5.1a
Population Symbols

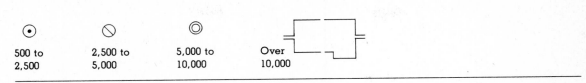

| 500 to 2,500 | 2,500 to 5,000 | 5,000 to 10,000 | Over 10,000 |

Figure 5.1b
Map Symbols

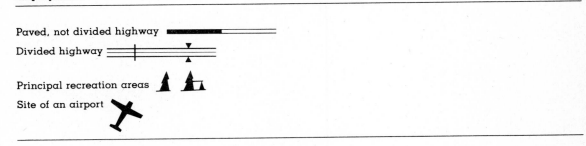

Paved, not divided highway

Divided highway

Principal recreation areas

Site of an airport

would fill considerably more space.

At times color is added to a map to communicate information. This is most common on relief maps, where shades of blue are used to indicate bodies of water, green to represent land at lower elevations, brown to show higher elevations, and white to represent glacial areas covered year round by snow. Tint is important too in relation to other symbols. A road line printed in black, for example, may be qualitatively different from one on the same map printed in red.

Ques Two

To work efficiently with map symbols, one must learn to check the key, or legend, that accompanies every map. As soon as children create their own maps, they should be taught to plot a key in a corner of the map—a listing of the symbols used with an indication of what each symbol represents.

Scale. Since areas of the world are much greater in size than those spaces occupied by them on maps and globes, **scaling** is a necessary attribute of maps. Actual space represented must be reduced, with all areas on the same map reduced proportionately. Thus, on a map, 20 kilometers may be represented by a line only 2 centimeters long. The concept of scale is made more difficult for beginning map readers by the fact that not all maps are drawn to the same scale or do not repre-

T Some scales are expressed as ratios: e.g., 1:1,000,000. This means that one map unit represents a unit one million times greater on the actual earth.

sent similar reductions of earth distances. On one, 5 centimeters may represent 100 kilometers; on another map of the same area the scale may be 2 centimeters to 100 kilometers.

Work with scale is presently made more difficult in the U.S. by the trend to "Go Metric." In Great Britain, where metric units have been in use for some time, the problem is minimized. But in Canada and the U.S., where some newer maps and globes are in metric units and others are still in miles, feet, and inches, the problem is a serious one. Students must learn to handle both sets of units: centimeters and kilometers, inches and miles. In so doing, children need not convert units from one system to another. Rather they should gradually get a feel for approximately how long kilometers and centimeters are, as well as how long miles and inches are.

The same is true as children interpret elevations on maps. Some maps show elevations in feet, others in meters. Again in working with maps, children need not convert meter elevations into feet. With the assistance of a meter stick, children gradually acquire a sense of meter length. In other words, they know about how long one meter, five meters, or fifty meters are. A multitude of measuring activities lead to this sense of distance. Students can measure everything in sight with their meter sticks and represent things measured through lines drawn to scale. Helpful here is graph paper, so that students can begin by assigning a scale value to each graph paper square: one square side = one meter, for example.

Grid Systems.   For ease in navigating their way across the earth's surface and in locating places precisely, early geographers applied the geometry of circles and spheres to the earth. Even as a circle is divided into 360 degrees, so the earth's equator line that cuts the world into northern and southern hemispheres is divided into 360 degrees by north and south running lines called longitudes, or **meridians.** By international agreement, 0 degrees longitude runs through Greenwich, England. Flying east from the Prime Meridian in Greenwich, one moves through 180 degrees of east longitude; flying west, one moves through 180 degrees of west longitude. Halfway around the world, one arrives at 180 degrees, or the approximate location of the International Date Line.

There is some relationship between longitude and time zones. Flying east, one "loses" time, for one is flying in the same direction as the earth rotates. Flying west, one "gains" time. Since the day and night period has been divided into twenty-four hour blocks, for every fifteen degrees of longitude one travels, one loses or gains an hour. Of course, a study of the time zones of Canada, the United States, and the world shows that zones do not follow exactly the lines of longitude. They twist and turn so that no large population areas located in close

T Times in key cities around the world when it is twelve midnight in London.

London
Midnight
Wednesday

New York
7 P.M.
Wednesday

Honolulu
2 P.M.
Wednesday

Tokyo
9 A.M.
Thursday

Cairo
2 A.M.
Thursday

For World Time Zones, see *Goode's World Atlas*, 15th ed., Chicago: Rand McNally, 1978, p. xii.

proximity are separated into different zones. Upper graders can hypothesize reasons for time zone divisions closest to them. They can consider the problems resulting from a time zone line cutting through a city or from no time zones at all, with each hamlet, town, and city setting its clocks directly by the sun. They can also figure the number of hours they would gain or lose if they were to travel to a distant city.

Lines of latitude girdle the earth, paralleling the Equator. For this reason they are sometimes called **parallels.** There are ninety degrees of north latitude and ninety degrees of south latitude. Key latitudes are:

0° latitude   = the equator
23½° north latitude = the Tropic of Cancer
23½° south latitude = the Tropic of Capricorn
66½° north latitude = the Arctic Circle
66½° south latitude = the Antarctic Circle

On the other hand, younger students can grow in map interpretation skills so that the introduction of longitude and latitude at a higher grade level is simplified. Youngsters in primary grades can handle simple grid systems in which a series of equidistant north-south and east-west extending lines are superimposed on maps they are making. North-south bands can be labeled A, B, C, and so forth, and east-west lines with numbers. Using this grid, students can state the approximate locations of points on their homemade maps. Similar grids can be superimposed on road maps, with cities and towns listed alphabetically by name in the side margin. Next to each name is the position according to its location within the grid. Using grid points, students in the intermediate and often in the primary grades can begin to locate on maps places within their home states.

Distortions. Obviously the most accurate representation of the sphere-shaped earth is a globe. As soon as a piece of earth is depicted on a flat surface, distortion creeps in. This can be quickly seen by comparing the shape of a familar land mass on the globe with its shapes on various projections. An example in point is Greenland, which is depicted as gigantic in size on some maps—larger even than South America, which it clearly is not. When maps are large and depict only small portions of the earth, this distortion is negligible; but whenever large areas of the earth are being represented on a flat map, distortion is a factor that must be considered.

Because distortion is present on flat maps, children in upper grades should be introduced to world maps drawn according to different projections: Mercator, polar, homolosine, interrupted. Most good school atlases include maps drawn in different ways; by studying them, young people can compare continental and land mass shapes, start-

T Some atlases to use in elementary classrooms are:

Medallion World Atlas (Maplewood, New Jersey: Hammond, 1977).

Goode's World Atlas. 15th ed. (Chicago: Rand McNally, 1978).

Concise Atlas of the Earth (Chicago: Rand McNally, 1976).

Figure 5.2
A South Polar Projection

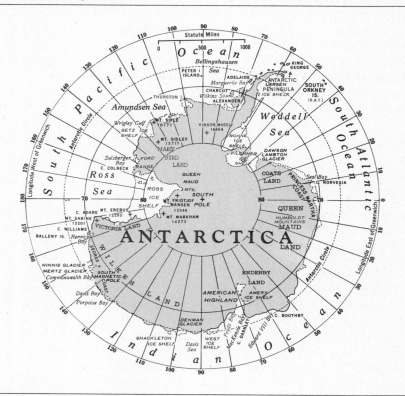

From *Worldmaster Atlas*, Chicago: Rand McNally, 1979, p. 1.

ing with a globe as a base reference. Also using polar projections, young people can refine their understanding of north, south, east, and west. On a north polar projection, north is in the center and south radiates in all directions from the pole—an interesting view of the world! See Figure 5.2 for a south polar projection.

Direction.   One of the most common misconceptions taught unintentionally to children is that north is up or toward the front. **North,** of course, is the direction in which a compass needle points, or—from a different perspective—the direction to one's right as one faces the setting sun. The latter makes sense if one remembers that the sun sets in the west and rises in the east because the earth rotates on its axis from west to east.

Actually there are two North Poles on the earth. One is the northern extremity of the earth's axis. The axis is an imaginary line extending through the center of the earth and about which it rotates completely once every twenty-four hours, resulting in day and night changes. The earth's axis is not perpendicular to the plane of its revolution around the sun. Rather the earth's axis is inclined about twenty-three and one-half degrees from the normal. This inclination, combined with the revolution of the earth in orbit around the sun, is the cause of seasonal variations, especially the changing length of daytime periods throughout the year and the number of completely sunless days that occur north of the Arctic Circle and south of the Antarctic Circle. Looking at seasons from the perspective of the northern hemisphere, the teacher should be aware of four important points in the journey of the earth about the sun.

The summer solstice is the point when, because of the inclination of the earth, the sun's direct rays reach the Tropic of Cancer. The area within the Arctic Circle is bathed in sunlight for the entire twenty-four hours. Because the northern hemisphere receives more direct heat, it is summer there and winter in the southern hemisphere.

The autumnal equinox is the point, three months later, when the sun's direct rays strike the equator. At this point every portion of the earth has twelve hours of day and twelve hours of night.

The winter solstice is the point, three months later, when the sun's direct rays strike the Tropic of Capricorn and the area within the Antarctic Circle has sunlight for twenty-four hours. Because the northern hemisphere receives less direct heat, it is winter there and summer in the southern hemisphere.

The vernal (or spring) **equinox** is the point, three months after the winter solstice, when the sun's direct rays again strike the equator. At this point every portion of the earth has twelve hours of day and twelve hours of night. It is spring in the northern hemisphere.

A second North Pole is the magnetic one, located in the upper reaches of Canada. It exists because the earth is essentially a large magnet with north and south poles just like any magnet. A compass needle actually points toward the magnetic north rather than toward the extremity of the earth's axis. Some polar projections show both the magnetic and geographic North Poles. They, as well as the globe, are useful tools with which upper graders can work as they develop a more sophisticated conception of earth directions.

A Problem to Ponder

Study the following series of diagrams (Figure 5.3) to the point where you understand the changes associated with the seasons, especially the reason why one can see the sun at midnight during the summer solstice if one is north of the Arctic Circle.

Once you have refined your own conception of these seasonal variations, try to explain it logically to a fellow classmate or teacher, or write your explanation in the space below.

**Figure 5.3
Seasonal Variations**

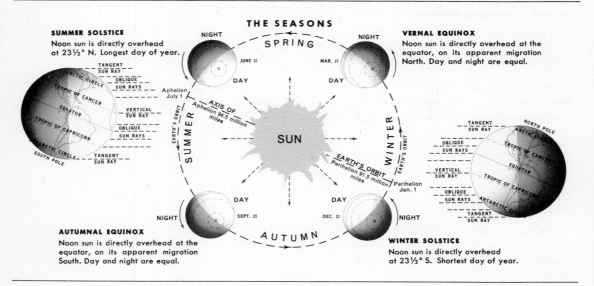

From *Goode's World Atlas*. 15th edition. Chicago: Rand McNally, 1978, p. xii.

Working with Maps and Globes in the Primary Grades

In introducing primary children to fundamental concepts related to the use of maps and globes, the teacher must keep in mind that youngsters have only begun to develop spatial concepts. For example, young children have trouble differentiating long distances. They can comprehend differences in short distances that they can perceive directly. Shown two toy cars moving different distances across a floor, children by age four can tell which one has moved farther. At this point, youngsters are still very dependent on direct perception and on their own bodies as a frame of reference.

When children begin to differentiate left from right, the body plays an equally important role. Children distinguish between the left and right sides of their bodies before applying the left/right classification to other things. Often they test for left and rightness by moving their own bodies in relation to objects "out there."

Children gradually acquire the ability to differentiate the size of objects. Early distinctions are between big and small objects. By about age five, children begin to distinguish middle-sized objects as well, especially if these are objects they can see and feel.

Because relationships between space and the child's own body are so basic in the primary grades, the child's concept of space can be extended by starting with the physical space the child is exploring and the phenomena he or she is experiencing. From this base of firsthand experiences, the child builds more involved concepts of space—concepts related to fundamental directions, scale representations, symbols, earth shape, changing day and night and seasonal patterns, and location of one's home on the earth.

R See chapter 9 for background information about the way young children think.

Learning Directions

Work with fundamental directions begins early in a child's school life. Here are some ideas to make that beginning both fun and fruitful.

Directional Words. Some of the little words of our language—*up, down, under, over, above, in, below, right, left, by, across, through, into*—embody really fundamental spatial relationships. Work with these concepts begins from the moment a child enters school. Nursery schoolers and kindergartners should have all manner of play experiences in which they move their bodies in relation to objects. Models of cars, planes, ships, horses, and carts—actually anything that moves—are fine play objects as children push them *under* tables, *across* the rug, *behind* the chair. A big tub of water adds to the learning; children push boats across the water and force them under the surface. They drop objects into the water to see which float and which sink. They fly objects, too, kites and balloons, to see them move up and down. They bounce balls up and down and throw them. Talk should accompany play, with children later telling what they did with their toys and what happened to them, using the directional words in the process.

A next stage in understanding spatial relationships is to learn to use words without handling objects directly or manipulating them in some way. Picture study is a fine activity at this point. Children study a picture to tell where the glass is, where the bear is hiding, where the car is parked, or where the dog is standing. The answer requires directional words: "The car is parked *behind* the truck."

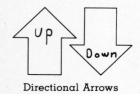

Directional Arrows

As children begin to use these words to talk about what they are seeing and doing, the teacher can help them incorporate words into their sight vocabularies. Children watch while the teacher writes the words *up* and *down* on cards shaped like arrows. Together they decide how to mount the arrow cards on the classroom walls. Students who are just learning to copy letters can make their own directional arrows and place them on the wall to clarify the meanings of *up* and *down*. In this respect spatial concepts grow as children grow in reading and writing skills.

More Complex Terminology. The teacher of kindergarten and nursery school children can make pointing-out charts (Figure 5.4) to aid in learning left and right, upper and lower, and middle.

Working with a pointing-out chart, the teacher queries, "Who can point to what is in the lower right-hand corner?" A youngster comes to point out while others say together the name of the object found there. Because this type of learning takes time, a pointing-out chart can be used more than once. Later the same kinds of questions can be used in reference to bulletin board displays located in the hall. On the way to the all-purpose room or media center, the teacher stops and asks, "What is located in the very middle of this board? in the upper left-hand corner? in the middle of the left side?"

North and South Directions. The first experiences with cardinal directions are best carried on outside, using the sun as a reference. On several mornings children go out-of-doors to find the position in the sky where the sun rises. They should carry drawing pads with them, and after several mornings' observations, draw a picture of the school with the sun in its approximate rising position. As children observe and sketch, the teacher injects the labeling term *east* into their talk: "In the morning we see the sun in the east." When children make their sketches of the morning sun, they label that direction on their pictures as east. In the late afternoon, children go out-of-doors again to look at

R East and west determined this way, will, of course, be approximations. The teacher may have to point out where the sun rises.

Figure 5.4
A Pointing-Out Chart

the sun. Where is it now? Where was it this morning in our sky? Children sketch the comparable scene, placing the sun in its westerly afternoon-evening location—a location they begin to call *west*. (Warning: do not let the children stare directly at the sun.)

Now is the time to bring out large paper directional arrows made through cooperative activity in the classroom earlier in the sequence. Children together mark the ends of one arrow *east* and *west* and lay it out on the grass pointing to the directions they have come to recognize as east and west. With the teacher's assistance, they label the second arrow ends with *north* and *south* and lay that arrow perpendicular to the first. Children look northward. What features do we see when we look from here to the north?

Using classroom windows to observe outdoor features they have already located in space, students use their drawings to figure out directions within the classroom. As we look out the windows, in what direction are we looking? A directional labeling card can be placed on the floor of the room nearest the window. The big directional arrows can be placed accurately on the floor by siting neighborhood features already located in space.

In teaching directions it is best to start with the real world rather than with maps hanging on the walls. When maps are first used, they should be placed on the floor or on desks with the north line oriented *not* to the front of the room but to the direction as it actually exists. Directional arrows spread out on the floor are most helpful at this point as children attempt to orient the map on the floor. If wall maps are used first, children may gain the misconception that north is up or north is in front—something that should be avoided from the very start.

Thinking of the Earth as a Sphere in Space

A relatively difficult idea for children to grasp is that the earth is a sphere and that it can be represented by a globe. The difficulty comes from the fact that to comprehend this idea one must be able to think at the representational level.

T Note: Young children should consider other models simultaneously: model cars, airplanes, tractors, houses. In this way they can begin to conceptualize that a model represents something in the real world. Making models is a useful activity here.

The Globe as a Model of the Earth.   Any map or globe is a representation, but because the earth approximates a sphere, the globe is the first representation of the earth a child should encounter. In primary grades a globe should be suspended with twine from the ceiling to spin in space. Children and teacher refer to it as a model of the earth, even as they make models of other things from clay. At some point they can make their own model earths, perhaps starting with a very large blue beach ball. The teacher can supply cutouts of the earth's continental masses.

The children cooperatively stick these to their beach ball as they search the globe for comparably shaped masses and decide where the shapes belong on their own model earth. Later students can add North and South Pole labels to their homemade globe. Now as children talk about places in the world—places they may even be hearing about through conversations at home—the teacher helps children locate these on their beach ball earth.

Earth-Sun Relationships.   In the later primary grades, the globe can be used to demonstrate day and night changes. A very large flashlight or filmstrip projector light beam becomes the sun. With the room otherwise darkened, the globe is gradually rotated on its axis in a counterclockwise direction. Placing a wad of clay on their own global location, children decide when that part will have day and when night. Now is the time to clarify language usage. What do we really mean when we say the sun rises in the east, sets in the west? What motion really causes the day and night changes?

Creating Maps

Simple mapping activities belong in the primary grades. Some ideas for introducing flat maps to young children are detailed in the following section.

Maps – A Plan of the Ground. Students can begin early to associate the shapes of landforms and the signs of human occupation found on globes and maps with what they see on the real earth. A simple beginning is through mapping pictures of the earth that illustrate storybooks. A case in point is *The Little Island*. It serves beautifully as content for a first mapping experience. Having listened as the teacher orally shares the book, students cooperatively sketch their own representation of the island on wrapping paper spread across the floor. They work with teacher guidance, sketching the shape of the island on paper and adding pictures of things they remember from the story and see in the illustrations. If they have had some preliminary work with directional symbols, they add a north/south/east/west arrow system to their map. Some students can contribute by coloring the land green and the ocean blue. They may even add some river lines running down the island into the sea. A child who prints clearly can add a title.

Similar activities can be developed based on stories in which the general plan of an area is described in words and pictures. As children meet each new location in a story, they plot it on a map, at first using pictures and then using representative symbols accompanied by a key. Together they decide how to plot a north/south directional arrow. After several such mapping experiences, the students can also add a grid system. The map is blocked into about six sections. The youngsters locate places by giving the reference numbers and letters of the grid. "Where is the little old woman's house found?" The answer might be, "In A-1."

Maps of an Area We Know. Another introduction to the fundamentals of mapping is the creation of a map of the street in front of the school. Again this is an outdoor, direct observation activity. The children can begin with a street plan in duplicated form supplied by the teacher that contains a sketch of the school on one side of the street. Onto the map, the children draw pictures of the houses and stores across the street. They start by drawing each building in its appropriate location. Later, teacher and children decide together on symbols to take the place of their pictures. For example, a house, store, or school can be shown symbolically as in the marginal note. Children can also talk about the advantages of using symbols rather than full-blown pictures on their maps.

Introductory maps of this simple variety can be expanded on follow-up occasions (Figure 5.6). Students add nearby streets, simple geographical features such as a stream, and additional people-made features such as bridges and railroad lines. In each case, as children decide to add a feature, they decide how to represent it on the map and add that symbol to the growing map key they have placed in a

R See Ruby Harris, *The Rand McNally Handbook of Map and Globe Usage*, 4th edition. (Chicago: Rand McNally, 1967), for creative ideas for mapmaking at the primary and beginner's level. The use of Golden Mac Donald and Leonard Weisgard, *The Little Island* (New York: Doubleday, 1946) is described there.

T Other storybooks that lend themselves easily to creative mapmaking:

Virginia Lee Burton, *The Little House* (Boston: Houghton Mifflin, 1942).

Arlene Mosel, *The Funny Little Woman*. (New York: E.P. Dutton, 1972).

Quentin Blake, *Patrick* (New York: Henry Z. Walck, Inc., 1968).

Rex Parkin, *The Red Carpet* (New York: Macmillan, 1948).

Best books for this purpose incorporate two or more locales and movement between the locales.

House

Store

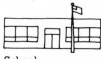

School

**Figure 5.5
A Child's Neighborhood Map**

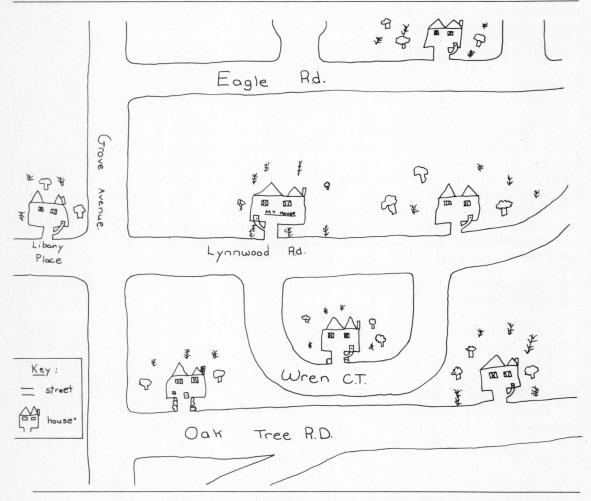

lower corner. Through actual use of symbols and keys, children gain far greater understanding than through listening to a detailed explanation given by the teacher.

Locating Places We Know

Primary-grade pupils should have some understanding of where they live on the earth. On the globe suspended by twine, a piece of clay can represent them and their home place. "Accidentally," the clay can fall off the globe on a number of occasions, especially during circle talk times—when primary youngsters assemble as a class to discuss problems and plan for activities. Children at that point can look to see if they can stick the clay back on the globe, gradually recognizing the shapes of the continents and differentiating the shape of the one on which they live.

Our Country and Our State or Province.   Eventually the children and teacher roll out a flat map of their country, laying it down on the floor with the appropriate north-south orientation. Children locate their own state or province, using the globe they have been interpreting as a guide. Once children locate home, they can take off their shoes and walk northward on the map. Those who have traveled in that direction can supply names of provinces or states located there. Children can walk south, east, and west, too. They can walk to California or British Columbia, to Maine or Quebec, explaining in words the directions in which they are walking and the distances they are covering.

The Shapes of Places We Know.   Future work with globes and maps is dependent on a sight knowledge of where big land masses are located. To find places on a globe, children must have some familiarity with the shapes of the continents. Overhead projector stencils are helpful here. Working from atlas maps, the upper primary children trace the individual continents, each onto a separate piece of tracing paper. These tracings become patterns for transferring the continental shape to a piece of thin cardboard such as that in a file folder. Having traced an outline of a continent on a file folder, children cut out the continent, leaving its outline unbroken on the folder. This outline is a stencil that can be displayed with an overhead projector. The technique can be applied to provinces, states, and countries, too. If the stencils are made to the same scale, children can superimpose them on the stage of the overhead projector to compare size; they can ask themselves, "Which is bigger, Africa or South America?"

Older students can cover a stencil opening with cellophane to which they add rivers, lakes, mountain peaks, and ridges with marker pens. The results are artistically striking; yet, at the same time, the students are building a foundation of basic geographical understandings.

Summary

The adult mind takes left and right, up and down, north and south, land and ocean for granted. The concepts embodied in these terms have become so familiar that they appear obvious. To the child's mind, however, these concepts are complex. Watch a kindergartner decide which arm to use in saluting the flag—changing from one to the other and then back again, getting the feel for the left and right by moving the body. How difficult is that seemingly simple task of remembering which arm is the right one.

T Helpful references for children include:

Sam and Beryl Epstein, *The First Book of Maps and Globes* (New York: Franklin Watts, 1959).

John Oliver, *What We Find When We Look at Maps* (New York: McGraw-Hill, 1970).

Dorothy Rhodes, *How to Read a City Map* and *How to Read a Highway Map*. (Chicago: Childrens Press, 1967, 1970).

T Can you recognize these masses?

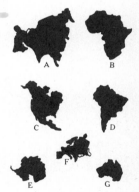

From *Learning to Use a Globe*. Chicago: A.J. Nystrom & Co., reprinted with permission.

For that reason, fundamental spatial concepts must be approached and reapproached in the primary grades, each time from a different perspective and each time building upon previous experiences. One does not teach north and south through a single lesson and assume that children will "get it." One must search for numerous creative ways to involve children directly with the concept. In general, spatial activities in the primary grades should:

Begin with what children can experience directly. Because at this stage children require a concrete base upon which to conceptualize and generalize, to begin with abstract terms is not too helpful. Young children should have opportunity to walk and look east, to hold the globe in their own hands, and to use the language of spatial directions in their singing, chorusing, and story listening.

Begin with what children know. Because children are egocentric, that which is most meaningful is what relates most directly to them. Thus children begin by mapping their school, their street, their neighborhood. Symbols plotted are for things they know firsthand. Locations are those they themselves have visited.

Working With Maps and Globes in Intermediate Grades

R A useful source for the upper-grade teacher is Haig Rushdooney, "A Child's Ability to Read Maps," *Journal of Geography,* 67 (April 1968): 213-219.

In the intermediate grades, students refine the beginning skills they have already acquired and go on to more sophisticated study. Even as young people study diverse regions of the world, periods of human history, and problems confronting people today and tomorrow, they can turn to maps and globes for information they need. In this respect, many map and globe skills can be developed as they are required.

For example, young people studying Norway as part of a larger unit on life in Scandinavia may encounter the term, Land of the Midnight Sun. This unit becomes a perfect context for consideration of why in areas north of the Arctic Circle there is sun at midnight on certain days and why during the winter there are days when the sun rarely shines. This is a perfect context for refining the understanding of how the earth's inclination and revolution result in the seasonal changes and of how latitudinal position affects life in an area. Here also young people can talk of why the population in northern Norway and Sweden is sparse and can think about the characteristics of the cultural landscape that typify the Arctic regions. And throughout, as young people talk and think, they refer to the ever-present globe and maps.

Then, too, in introducing almost any area of the world to a group of young people, a teacher can provide individual outline maps that already show certain key features—perhaps the outline of the country,

Children build map skills as they search maps for information as part of unit study.

bordering countries, and/or bordering bodies of water. The students can add to the map features significant to the inquiry in progress— perhaps railroad lines, river systems, distinct physical or political regions, and mineral deposits. Very often, by relating features they plot to those already on the map, children can generalize about causes and effects. Simultaneously they are learning to interpret and use map symbols, grid systems, and scale.

At times, of course, the intermediate-level teacher must focus on particular map and globe usage skills, so that students will have the requisite abilities to investigate independently. Let us turn next to consideration of some specific kinds of activities most useful starting about third grade.

G Children can create maps with basic components: title, grid, symbols, key, and scale; they can generalize based on data read from maps.

Idea Page

Background for the teacher. A major goal of instruction in maps and globes in intermediate grades is that students will be able to make inferences based on information contained on a map or globe. This Idea Page demonstrates a kind of activity that can be used to achieve this goal as part of history study.

The aim. Reading information from a map. Proposing explanations for information read from a map.

The introductory clues. The boundaries between states and nations have been placed where they are for a number of different reasons. You can discover some of these reasons for yourself by studying actual boundaries shown on a map.

The pursuit. Shown below are two states of the United States—New Jersey (Figure 5.6) and Missouri (Figure 5.7). Study each and explain the reason for each boundary of the state. A clue is given to get you started.

In carrying out this task, you may find some boundaries that you cannot explain. They may be ones set by treaty; their location cannot be explained simply by studying a map. You must read to find out.

The continuation.

A. From your study, propose at least three different reasons that explain the locations of boundaries on the map.
B. Now study a map of the United States. Using the reasons you have just written down, explain the location of the boundary between the United States and Canada; between the United States and Mexico; between states.

Using Map and Globe Symbols in Upper Grades

In upper elementary grades, students begin to use maps that serve a variety of purposes—those showing population, relief, rainfall, agricultural regions, industrial regions, transportation arteries, political boundaries, and climate. Study of almost any area, therefore, can be a vehicle for refining the ability to interpret symbols. Divided into map-making teams, students analyze atlas maps of the area in question and create maps, each one of which depicts a different feature. To com-

Figure 5.6
New Jersey

Explanation of boundaries

1. The eastern boundary is
   formed by the ocean. _____

2. _____

3. _____

4. _____

Figure 5.7
Missouri

Explanation of boundaries

1. _____

2. _____

3. _____

4. _____

plete the task, students must devise symbols to represent phenomena they are plotting. On a map depicting transportation arteries, for instance, they must decide how to represent railroad lines, airports, major interstate highways, toll roads, and local roads. On one depicting agricultural production, they must decide how they will represent specific crops grown and perhaps even how they will differentiate between major crop producing regions and lesser production areas.

Based on their maps, students write descriptions of the area, analyzing relationships among the features depicted. Led by teacher questions, they begin to probe why roads adhere to the patterns they do, why agricultural production is restricted to the areas it is, why population is concentrated in part of the region as it is, why some areas are sparsely populated, and why political boundaries have been set as

T Ruby Harris (1967) recommends that older students write descriptions of cities based on map information. Descriptions can include latitudinal/longitudinal location, population, proximity to other cities, bodies of water, agricultural areas, railroad lines, and relative location within a state or province, a country, or a continent.

they are. At every step of the way they are working with map symbols and accompanying legends and keys. Sometimes, too, they will have to use a grid system for enlargement purposes. To do this, they mark off a series of blocks on the small map of the area they have found. Then they draw a comparable series of grid blocks but to a larger scale on their own paper. In this way, they can make bigger maps that are a more effective means of showing key features.

Study of map symbols at some point in the upper grades should include consideration of those found on weather maps since television weather reporting utilizes them to such a great extent. Minimum competencies include the ability to recognize fronts and high and low pressure centers. Then, too, students should have some ability to interpret the radar scans that depict cloud cover and even at times the direction of airflow associated with different storm centers. Since radar scans are really crosses between pictures and maps, they supply useful concrete data for the young person who is refining his or her understanding of a map as a representation of reality.

This same integrated approach to teaching map and globe skills in a meaningful, purposeful context can be applied in a variety of social studies areas. Students can plot routes of early explorers on a map already containing river and lake systems. Later, they can hypothesize why certain areas were explored first, others second. An especially interesting context for plotting exploration routes is in reference to the exploration of the north polar region. Here students plot the Arctic Circle, the geographic and magnetic north poles, the upper reaches of Canada, the U.S.S.R., and Scandinavia. Working from the data plotted, they decide why exploration of this area occurred so much later than the exploration of Australia, New Zealand, and North America.

Mapmakers can do much the same with settlement patterns, plotting them on a map that already contains geographical features. Now they consider why settlements flourished early in certain areas, later in others. As a follow-up, they apply their growing map skills to the interpretation of map phenomena as shown on p. 146–147 Idea Page.

Interpreting Distance and Elevation

The concept of scaling has two major dimensions at the intermediate level. One relates to elevation, or altitude; the other to distance in kilometers or miles separating surface locations.

Elevation. Perhaps the most concrete way that young people can build a clear conception of elevation is through the raised relief map

T Also use commercially produced transparencies that correlate with duplicating masters. Milliken Publishing Co. (Research Blvd., St. Louis, Mo. 63132) markets transparency packets on Asia, Australia, Europe, and Latin America, as well as on the exploration and colonization of North and South America that are useful in building map skills as children encounter social studies content.

on which mountains and valleys are contoured. On a fine series of United States maps available from Hubbard Scientific (Northbrook, Illinois), elevation is shown through contour lines and through exaggerated raised relief that depicts vertical dimensions three times larger than in reality. These maps are excellent as young people learn about different kinds of landforms. On a raised relief map, mountain ridges are strikingly portrayed; even an adult will be excited when tracing the ridges with the finger and actually feeling a water gap. Young people following the routes of early settlers will have a better conception of the significance of the Cumberland Gap if they have seen and fingered it on a relief map. Those talking of the impact of great dam systems, such as that associated with the Tennessee Valley Authority, will get a clearer picture when they see the Cherokee and Douglas Dams on the same map. Those studying why centers of population clustered as they did can make realistic inferences when confronted with concrete data in visual form. A school need not buy many maps to serve this purpose. The Knoxville and Johnson City, Tennessee, maps show large population centers located in the flatter valleys, the damming of the interridge rivers to form lakes for recreational, irrigational, and power generation purposes, and the water gaps that became the major highways through the ridges for the settlers. Using these in combination with a similar map of the Hawaiian Islands, young people can contrast and compare topographic features of diverse regions and hypothesize how the differences affect human activity there.

Some maps depict elevation simply through contour lines. Young people again will get a fuller understanding by visualizing relationships. Having built a model mountain out of plaster of paris, papier mâché, or clay, young people can place it into an aquarium tank. On the side of the tank they mark off elevation in hundred meter intervals. Now they add water to the previously empty tank, bringing up the level first to the 100-meter line. At that point, with waterproof ink or pencil they draw the contour line on their mountain by tracing the line formed by the contact between water level and mountain. The process is repeated until several contour lines have been drawn, and the mountain top is under water. At that point, the mountain is lifted from the water, and the pattern of the contour lines traced on it is examined. If the mountain has been artfully constructed so that there is a steeper slope on one side and a gentler slope on the other, young investigators can discover for themselves how to interpret contour lines that are close together, and those that are further apart.

Most atlas maps show elevational changes through color changes, so that as young people are learning to handle altitude on maps, they

R See Dennis Milburn, "Children's Vocabulary," in Norman Graves, *New Movements in the Study and Teaching of Geography* (London: Temple Smith, 1972). Milburn has identified geography-related words of high frequency in everyday usage. Some relate to land forms and should be part of relief-map study. They include:

beach	marsh
canal	moor
cave	mountain
cliff	ocean
coast	river
dam	sea
hill	valley
island	volcano
lake	waterfall

are refining their ability to work with symbolic representations. A useful technique here is comparative analysis. The students can compare the color schemes and the elevation intervals set forth in map keys, asking themselves: "Why are the intervals much greater on this map than on that?" "Which color scheme communicates more clearly?"

At this point, too, young people should interpret satellite pictures of the earth's surface being sent down from space. In a sense, these pictures are almost maps—in a more modern sense of the word—for they depict topography. In this context, young people should consider how the social scientist's tools are changing and will continue to change as new technology brings innovative ways of collecting and recording data.

Distance.   In upper grades, young people refine their ability to handle map and globe scales. Road maps are helpful here, especially those that set forth the number of miles or kilometers next to stretches of highway. Regardless of the area being studied, upper graders can interpret road maps, first reading distances directly from the numbers next to major highways, then using the scale to measure distances "as the crow flies," and eventually using the scale to estimate with the eye larger distances across the map. Most useful are some of the following devices.

1. With Twine.   Students can place pins along irregular coastlines, highways, rivers and then stretch twine along the pattern of pins. The twine can later be measured to determine its length. Using the scale given in the key, students can go on to figure out the actual length of the distance involved.

2. Estimating Distance.   In estimating the distance between two points on a map, students will find it helpful to reproduce the scale of distance incorporated in the legend. Placing a card or slip of paper beneath the scale indicator, they mark off similar units. The card or slip can then be moved rapidly between the points in question to get a rough estimate of the surface distance involved. Even simpler is to mark off the scale units along the edge of the index finger, the finger becoming a "ruler" to measure the distance between points.

3. The Flexible Ruler.   A clear, plastic, flexible ruler is a great gadget for measuring distances on a globe. Using one, students can compare distance along a great circle route in contrast to the distance around the globe. Now is the time to ask why airplanes cross the pole when flying between Los Angeles and Copenhagen rather than flying via New York City.

4. Pacing Distances and Creating an Original Scale.   Students in the upper grades can learn to pace off distances as a means of constructing maps of the school and school yard to scale. All that needs to be done initially is to measure off a distance such as twenty-five meters. Students pace and repace this measured distance until they know approximately how many paces equal twenty-five meters. Now they have a simple way of estimating any distance they wish to plot on a map. Remember that each student must develop a personal scale, since pace length differs from child to child.

5. The Expanding Balloon.   A balloon blown up to medium size can become a globe on which continental masses are sketched with marker pens. As more air is forced into the balloon, students can see what relative effect this has had on items already plotted. They can ask: "What has happened to the scale? When the balloon gets bigger, are more or fewer earth kilometers represented by each centimeter of the balloon?" Again, this concrete device makes visualization of relationships easier. Children can discover that whereas initially one centimeter represented X kilometers, when the balloon expands, two centimeters may represent that same number of kilometers.

Getting Involved with Grid Systems

Fundamentally there are two kinds of **grid systems** used for plotting and locating points on maps: rectangular grids laid out on flat surfaces and grids used to segment spheres.

Rectangular Grids.   To build understanding of rectangular grids, students can draw a grid on the classroom floor with chalk and a similar grid pattern on a large piece of construction paper. Numbers can be used to mark off the rows, letters to mark off the columns. Now using this system of numbers and letters, students plot classroom tables, chairs, closets, bookcases, pianos in appropriate locations on the construction paper map. For example, the piano is located in block B-2, Jackie's desk in D-6, and so forth. Having plotted all major sites, participants can develop a key to accompany points.

T Where the classroom floor is covered with linoleum squares, these can serve as a grid. A map with a square grid is laid out on the floor. Using the floor tiles as a guide, the map can easily be transferred to the floor using a washable marker.

As Barbara Bartz (1970) has found, "Most people . . . can use the familiar 'A-10' or 'B-5' system for locating places on a road map." When children have trouble with the system, Bartz recommends comparing the idea to the game of "Bingo" that is also based on a grid system with numbers and letters. Since most young children are familiar with Bingo, work with rectangular grids is feasible even at the primary level.

R See Emrys Jones, *Towns and Cities* (London: Oxford University Press 1966). Jones describes the grid pattern in which streets such as those north of Wall Street in New York City are laid out. Students can consider such street designs and determine advantages of the scheme and possible problems that might result if the grid design were draped over hills as in San Francisco.

As young people work with rectangular grids, the teacher can give some attention to use of grids in map production. A large, gridless map of the children's home state or province should be placed on the floor for this purpose. Long, thin strips of paper can be spread out grid-style across the map and letters and numbers added to indicate the blocks. Mapmakers mark off a similar grid pattern on individual pieces of construction paper and, using the intersections of grid lines with key boundary lines depicted on the model map, they transfer the outline of the state or province to their own developing map and go on to add familiar towns and cities. Through this activity, children learn how to interpret a grid; simultaneously they are learning more about the political features of their local area.

Spherical Grids. Barbara Bartz (1970) has described the problems inherent in the interpretation of spherical grids.

When you move from a grid on a flat surface to an invisible, arbitrary grid on a ball, and try to understand the ways in which this spherical grid is rearranged as it is projected onto the flat map, there are grave perceptual and conceptual problems. Thinking and visualizing in three-dimensional space is difficult enough, but trying to derive notions in three dimensions, when you have only seen them as they are represented in distorted two-dimensional fashion, is even more difficult.

To avoid some of these problems, young people should be introduced to the concept of latitude using a large, round beach ball. On it, they draw an equator line that divides the earth into northern and southern hemispheres; they mark this line zero degrees latitude. They mark the geographic poles ninety degrees north latitude and ninety degrees south latitude. Next they stretch a piece of string from the polar site and the equator, mark off nine equal segments onto it, and use the string to mark off latitude points at ten degree intervals between pole and equator. Having done this several times for both northern and southern hemispheres, globe makers can connect points so that they have parallel lines of latitude girdling the earth. Using these lines as references and similar ones on a real globe, students add continental masses with marker pen and determine the latitudinal location of familiar areas.

Clearly, work with latitude is made more comprehensible if the students have had preliminary work with the geometry of a circle and know that by definition circles have been divided into 360 equal segments called degrees. Before encountering latitude, they should have had plenty of opportunity to play with circles, drawing them with pencil compasses and protractors and dividing the circumferences in different ways. For instance, they should have marked off the 360 degree circumference of a circle into 15-degree segments, with each 30-degree interval labeled. They should also have marked off a circle circumference into four 90-degree segments and again labeled each 30- or even 10-degree interval.

In many social studies programs, latitude is introduced first in fifth grade, longitude later in sixth. Because of the difficulty of the concept, again it appears wise to start with the globe, rather than a flat map. To their beach-ball globe, children add the arbitrary lines of longitude, starting with zero degrees longitude that passes through Greenwich, England. They study the comparable lines on a real globe and transfer similar ones onto their beach ball. Today with the advent of inexpensive Styrofoam balls, every youngster can eventually create a globe replete with lines of longitude and latitude and plot key cities based on interpretation of grid points. Later they can add hour-clock times at each fifteen degrees of longitude to show the hour it is around the world at any one point in time.

A teacher should avoid thinking that because longitude and latitude have been taught children have control of the concepts. Only through constant use will these concepts belong to children. As children talk of current events around the world, sites should be located on the globe and the latitude and longitude determined. As students talk of other countries, they should study the relationship between climate and latitude and eventually determine the time difference based on differences in longitude. Here, too, they should compare the longitudinal and latitudinal positions to their own home state or province, hypothesizing differences they have come to expect. Thus, in studying an area such as Australia, young people will be able to predict that in contrast to Canada and the United States, winter months there will be in June, July, and August. On the other hand, because Australia lies in the same latitudinal bands in the southern hemisphere as Canada and the United States occupy in the northern, there will be approximately the same range of climates in both areas. In this context, too, students in sixth grade should figure out what time it is in a country being studied when it is 8 a.m. in their own hometown.

Refining Directional Concepts

A simple hand-held magnetic compass is a functional instrument to take along on almost any field trip. If students also take along a large directional arrow system they can lay it out on the ground so that as they talk about what they are seeing, they can talk of what they see to the north, south, east, and west. If students make rough map-like sketches of an area visited—the zoo, the airport, the farm, the park—they add a directional indicator based on their compass readings.

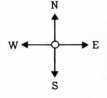

Similarly, even in upper grades flat maps should be laid out on the floor, oriented according to directions as they actually have been read from a compass. Students can take off their shoes and walk directions on the map, describing in words the directions in which they are walking. At this point, it is sometimes worthwhile to place a chair on top of the large map for children to climb on to get a satellite view of the region looking first to the east, then to the west, and so forth. Now is the time to add more sophisticated terminology: northeast, southeast, northwest, and southwest, with these terms being applied to sections of their own country and later to sections of their own province or state.

Learning to Live with Map Distortions

R Read Barbara Bartz, "Maps in the Classroom," in John Ball et al., *The Social Sciences and Geographic Education: A Reader* (New York: John Wiley, 1971).

Upper elementary students should interpret a variety of map projections and compare the treatments of land masses they know to treatments of the same masses on a globe. Barbara Bartz has provided a quick rule of thumb for handling different map projections. About a series of maps, children can ask: "Are Greenland and Mexico shown as about the same size?" In terms of actual land mass, Greenland and Mexico are equal in size—a fact that can be confirmed through globe study. Given a Mercator projection, however, students will discover that Greenland is inflated in size, for meridians are drawn parallel to one another, which they are obviously not on a spherical earth. Because Greenland is located in far northern latitudes, this means of drawing the world causes considerable size distortion.

An especially good projection for use in upper elementary classrooms is Goode's interrupted homolosine projection (Figure 5.8) readily available in *Goode's World Atlas* (15th edition, 1978, Rand McNally). An equal-area projection, it does not distort the sizes of areas. In addition, latitudes are represented by straight lines, and the shapes of continents have the least amount of distortion possible on a flat map. That there will always be distortion—whether of shape, size, scale, or direction of lines of latitude or longitude—can be demonstrated by peeling a grapefruit into segments and laying out its skin on a table surface. Participants quickly see that "something has to give."

Summary

Speaking of how to help children acquire basic map and globe usage skills, Barbara Bartz suggests that children "should only rarely have to look passively at a map hanging in front of them. More often they should have to map things themselves." These things should include the school yard, the classroom, and the route home; in addition, children should have the opportunity to convert their observations as well as numerical data into spatial form. Examples cited by Bartz include:

Figure 5.8
A Mercator, Homolographic, Sinusoidal, and Interrupted Homolosine Projections

Mercator Conformal Projection

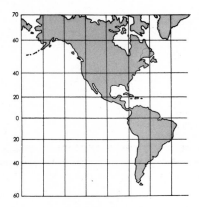

On a Mercator projection, shapes are preserved, but distances are distorted as one moves toward the poles.

Mollweide's Homolographic Projection

A Homolographic projection shows areas equal to those on a globe; however, scale is different on each parallel and meridian.

Sinusoidal Projection

A Sinusoidal projection shows areas equal to those on a globe, but only the distances along all latitudes and the central meridian are true.

Goode's Interrupted Homolosine Projection

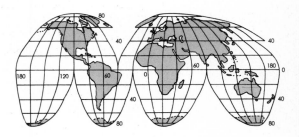

A Homolosine projection is also equiarea. It combines some qualities of both sinusoidal and homolographic projections. Because of the "breaks", each continental area is at the center of a projection, resulting in truer shapes of land masses. This is the principle of *interruption*.

From *Goode's World Atlas*, 15th Edition. (Chicago: Rand McNally, 1978), p. xi. Reprinted with permission.

R Useful booklets that teach map skills in a sequential way are *Learning to Use a Globe, Set 1* and *Learning to Use a Map* (Chicago: Nystrom & Co.). See also Kenneth Job and Lois Wolf, *Skills for Understanding Maps and Globes* (Chicago: Follett Publishing Co., 1976). It provides a series of step-by-step lesson plans.

1. making a map that shows the population of different cities based on population data
2. making a map that shows rainfall based on rainfall figures

Similar examples include:

3. making a map that shows crop production by region based on a statistical table
4. making a map that shows steel production by state based on numerical data
5. making a map that shows when states became part of the United States

As Bartz sums up, "Making one map like this is far more valuable than just looking at dozens . . . in the five or six years of social studies. The ability to make maps nearly guarantees the ability to read them, but too few children are involved in a variety of mapping experiences."

Putting Time into the Picture

Youngsters have little sense of time. What sense they do have relates to events experienced repetitively: breakfast, lunch, and supper times; the days of the week; bedtime. They comprehend the present more easily than the past and future; the immediate past more readily than the immediate future; and the immediate past more readily than the historical past. According to studies (Oakden and Sturt 1922; Bradley 1947), children have very little comprehension of the historical past until ages eleven to thirteen. That is when they begin to handle abstractions with some degree of facility as they move into the stage Piaget has termed formal operations.

Young children also have little ability to grasp the significance of the future. They may anticipate a birthday, Halloween, or a vacation. They may even plan what they will wear or do; but what children experience is the "now." For them now has the greatest meaning.

Beginning with What Children Know

R Two books to use with primary children:
Jeanne Bendick, *The First Book of Time* (New York: Franklin Watts, 1963).
Franklyn Branley, *What Makes Day and Night* (New York: Thomas Y. Crowell, 1961).

Since the events that children experience directly and repeatedly mark off time for them, these activities are the "handles" that a teacher can grasp in helping children acquire better temporal concepts. First structured experiences can include talking about things we did yesterday, we did on our vacation or will do tomorrow. As part of informal talk times, the teacher can interject key time words: *today*, *yesterday*, *tomorrow*. Later he or she can interject sequencing words as *first*, *last*, *after that*, *then*.

Children begin to work with clocks and
calendars in kindergarten and first grade.

Talking experiences can blend easily into writing-down experiences, especially in kindergarten and in first and second grades where experience charting is an ongoing activity. Coming into their room in the morning, children dictate sentences in sequence that tell what they did yesterday. They recall the events that occurred first, next, then, and finally. These sentences are recorded on charting paper by the teacher to be "read" over and over again by children. In reading, children repeat the sequence-setting words—words that help keep events in proper order.

Talking experiences blend as well into art activity. Each child draws a painting of a favorite part of today (or yesterday). Later children stand up to tell about their pictures. With the teacher's help at first, children line up to show through their picture line what happened first, second, third. To put the picture line together, the teacher must ask related questions: "Which did we do first—go to the library or the gym? Did we have lunch before going to the library? after going to the library?" In this respect, some systematic scheduling of large blocks of classroom time is helpful. Children learn the sequence of activities and this sequence becomes part of their own timekeeping.

Activities to Stretch Time Concepts at the Primary Level

Other kinds of timekeeping activities for use in K-1 include:

1. Keeping a Days of the Week Line. On Monday, children hang a card marked *Sunday* and one marked *Monday* on the line. On Tuesday, they hang up *Tuesday* next to *Monday*. Last thing on Friday, they hang up *Saturday*. Early Monday morning, a child takes down all the day-of-the-week cards and the class restrings the week day by day. To help children associate specific classroom events with days of the week, children can hang pictures beneath each day card. This can be an end-of-the-day activity, with children drawing pictures of a day's events to use as a reminder of what they did as they talk later in the week. These pictures make for easy review of the previous day's events the next morning.

2. Maintaining a Monthly Classroom Calendar. A very large calendar with space to write or draw on each day-block serves as focus for talk during last circle time—the final fifteen minutes or so of the school day when children meet as a class to talk about their day's events. Children dictate one sentence as they gather at the end of the day to decide the best happening of the day. This sentence is printed on the class's calendar block for the day so that "we will always remember it." At the end of the month, children review their immediate past to decide what the best school day of the month was.

3. Associating Months with Recurring Events. First graders can begin to associate months with events that generally occur at particular times of the year. One approach is through brainstorming and writing. The children and teacher check a calendar to find out the order of the months. The teacher lists these in time sequence on a chart. On a second chart the teacher lists activities children enjoy at different times of a year: I go swimming. I send valentines. I go skiing. I watch the snow. I rake leaves. I go trick or treating. I eat turkey. Later children write structured compositions that begin:

My best month is _____. In _____ I _____. I also _____
_____. Sometimes I _____ _____.

Children fill in the composition slots by selecting appropriate phrases from the brainstormed list.

4. Associating the Earth's Changes with Seasonal Names. Children in first grade who have lived through several changes of the seasons can cooperatively create season charts based on information they complete progressively. Coming to school at the end of August and the beginning of September, they talk about summertime activity. They listen to summer stories and poems that the teacher shares. They draw summer activity pictures. They dictate summer activity reports individually and in groups. All reports and pictures are compiled in a summertime folder.

When the seasons change, the children do the same with fall, winter, and spring until at the end of the school year, children talk about what they will do in the summer. At that point, they return to their earlier summer folder to read and look at their previous writings and drawings. At that point, too, key pages of the seasonal folders can be strung around the room in a circular pattern. Children can take turns "walking through the seasons" and describe events and activities they associate with each. Incidentally, this is a fine time for children to see the progress they have made during the year. The first folio pages will be handprinted by the teacher as a result of dictation. The last ones will be printed and created by individual children who have learned to write in sentence form.

5. Doing More with Seasons. One kindergarten teacher, Ms. Sylvia Strassberg, has devised an activity that integrates social studies, science, and language learnings as children work with seasonal changes. In the fall, she takes her youngsters outside to plant flower bulbs. In the winter, whenever the ground is free of snow, she takes her class outside to observe what is happening to the bulbs. Of course, they see nothing until early spring when the shoots poke above the ground. At this point, the children make seasonal observation booklets comprised of three pages (Figure 5.9). On the first page, each child draws what they did when they went outside to plant the bulbs. On the second, each draws winter in the garden. On the third, each draws the bulbs beginning to sprout. Ms. Strassberg gives each youngster three seasonal labels to paste to the appropriate page in their seasonal booklets. The children later dictate to the teacher sentences to go along with the pages.

6. Anticipating the Future. Children who have progressively charted days on a calendar and recorded great events on it can look ahead to months to come. As part of a first circle activity, children can

Figure 5.9
A Child's Seasonal Booklet

I planted a crocus bulb in the fall.

think about each month to come and say what they are anticipating. The linguistic format for an anticipation time is: "I can hardly wait until _____ because _____." In addition the children can write their anticipations. Assisted by the teacher, they can circle anticipated days on the calendar. As the months pass and the anticipated future becomes the present, children can say whether the event was as great as they had expected.

Then, too, youngsters can look ahead to their own futures. One first-grade group took the time to talk about what each member wanted to be when he or she grew up. At first, children reacted with limited ambitions that fit typical stereotypes. Girls wanted to be nurses, boys doctors, and so forth. But after discussion, the children expanded their perceptions. Later they wrote slotted compositions that followed this pattern:

When I grow up, I want to be a/an _____. I want to be a/an _____ because _____ _____ .

A Problem to Ponder

Here is a lesson plan designed for a first-grade group that was almost ready for second grade.

Topic: Showing time events on a line   **Concept:** Time changes

Objectives:

Materials: charting paper, marker pens, cards, tape

Procedure:	Related Questions:
1. **Motivation and Orientation:** Gather children in the afternoon to talk about things they did in the morning. Encourage wide participation.	Let's talk about some of the things we did this morning. What things did many of us do before coming to school? What things did we do on the way here? What were some of the things we did in our room this morning?
2. Review specific events of the morning. Write them in the order announced by the children, recording on charting paper.	Let's go over again what we have just been talking about. What is one thing we all did? Another? . . .
3. Have individual children read the items recorded on the chart. Give several children opportunity to read the same item.	Who can read this first sentence that Janie told us?
4. Cut up the chart between sentences. Distribute sentences to children who stand up to display their signs. Those with signs read them aloud to be sure they understand meanings.	
5. Ask children to consider the order of events. Help them through questions to get in the order in which events occurred.	Who has the part that tells what happened first? next? after that?

6. Tape the items in time order along the wall beneath the chalkboard, taping from left to right. Children will help in this.

7. Since children have been learning to tell time, ask them to think about when each event took place. Record times on cards and tape to the appropriate spot on the line.

    At what time did most of us get up?
    At what time did we come into our room?
    At what time did we go out for fair weather gym? etc.

8. Have little children come up and "walk through" their morning, moving from left to right and pausing briefly at each event card. Later children can select the event of the morning they liked best and stand by it on the line. In the order in which events happened, children tell why they liked that particular happening during the morning.

    Let's walk along our time line from early morning to noontime. Who wants to go first? As Johnny walks through the morning, let's all call out the times written on the line.

Topic of Next Lesson in the Sequence:

Questions to ponder. The objectives of this lesson have not been completed in the plan. What do you think the teacher's objectives were?

The topic of the next lesson in the sequence has also not been completed. If you were the teacher of this first grade, what kind of a lesson would you design as follow-up so that children could reinforce their understanding of how to create and "read" a time line? Remember that young children have a very limited concept of time. Time only has meaning when it relates to the self.

Activities to Refine Time Concepts in Intermediate Grades

Three basic understandings need to be refined in the upper grades—understanding of time sequences (especially in the past and the future), day and night changes and variations around the earth (especially what causes both changes and variations), and seasonal variations.

Time Sequences.   The time line is an important tool for handling time sequences, particularly sequences of historical events and steps in a set of plans to be carried out sequentially in the future. As with maps and globes, the best learning-teaching strategy is for the students to create their own. As an introduction, young people who have had some previous experience with plotting events in their own lives (see lesson sequence pages 162–163) can be given a duplicated time line on which key dates already studied in a unit have been labeled. They simply add the event that occurred at the labeled time units, taking the information from their text or from material or charts displayed around the room. For first experiences with time-line construction, some teachers have found that working together orally is most effective. The line is drawn on the chalkboard or transparency with dates already labeled. Participants come forward to contribute certain events to the line.

R Use rolls of shelf paper to create "moving time lines." Children cut stencil-like shapes into the roll of paper—each shape representing a historical event and cut in correct chronological sequence. The paper is moved across the stage of an overhead projector as students orally describe events in the sequence.

An example of the liberty bell shape that could be cut into the paper roll.

Day and Night Changes.   Study of the cause of day and night becomes more precise in the upper grades. At this point, young people redo experiments in which they shine a strong light source against a globe in a darkened room as they rotate it from west to east. They move the globe into four positions in its orbit around the sun, keeping the inclined axis of the globe parallel to itself throughout. In this way, students see that as the earth rotates, there are times when a polar region receives sun twenty-four hours, and other times when a region never sees the sun during a twenty-four hour period. At this point, too, → young people learn that it is the movement of the earth in relation to the sun that causes day and night, not the reverse; they begin to comprehend that the inclination of the earth's axis combined with its revolution around the sun causes seasonal variations in the length of day and night.

Making a diagram is a useful strategy to clarify day and night changes. As they move their model earth around the sun and rotate it on its axis, young people can convert what they are seeing into a diagram, sketching the earth in various positions and indicating whether it is day or night at their hometown when the earth is in a particular position.

Figure 5.10
A Sample Time Line

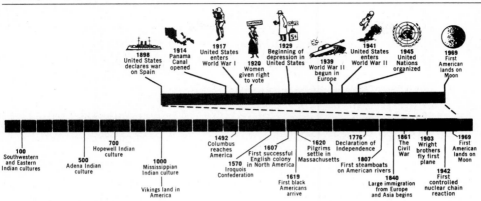

From *Exploring Our World*. Chicago: Follett, 1977. Reprinted with permission.

Seasonal Changes.   By fifth grade, students will be building their own conception of latitude, and so at that level, study of seasonal variations should relate directly to variations in latitude as well as to the revolution of the earth on its inclined axis. Again, it is best to make the situation as concrete as possible by actually demonstrating the revolution of the earth by having the students carry the globe around a central light source in an otherwise darkened room. Again diagramming is a useful means of recording observations. Diagrams should include:

the earth in the four seasonal positions, with an arrow showing revolution direction

the earth inclined at approximately twenty-three and one-half degrees in each seasonal location in its orbit

key lines of latitude: the equator, the Tropics of Cancer and Capricorn, and the Arctic and Antarctic Circles

Strategies for Using Maps, Globes, Clocks, Calendars and Time Lines: A Summary Thought or Two

Maps, globes, calendars, clocks, and time lines are fundamental tools of the social scientist and the citizen. In the future these tools will probably increase in importance as people travel more widely, often find themselves in areas they do not know, and cross time zones with greater frequency.

This chapter has introduced four major ideas about teaching map/globe usage skills and related time concepts. These ideas are:

1. Direct attention needs to be given to teaching how to use maps, globes, calendars, clocks, and time lines as sources of information. Efficient use is dependent on accurate interpretation of distance, direction, and distortion (the three d's) and of symbols, scale, and sequence (the three s's).
2. Especially in upper grades, skills needed in order to gain information from maps, globes, and time lines can be refined even as young people pursue ongoing social studies investigations.
3. Interpretational skills can best be acquired by actually making maps, globes, and time lines that serve particular purposes.
4. It is almost impossible to separate the study of the spatial relationships embodied on maps and globes from the study of time concepts. Length of day and night is dependent on latitudinal position; time zones are longitudinal bands; and in terms of human activity, time and space are interrelated entities. Study of day and night and seasonal variations have to be approached globally.

References

Anderson, Charlotte; and Winston, Barbara. "Acquiring Information by Asking Questions, Using Maps and Graphs, and Making Direct Observations." In *Developing Decision-Making Skills*, 47th Yearbook of the National Council for the Social Studies. Arlington, Virginia: NSCC, 1977, pp. 71-105.

Bartz, Barbara. "Maps in the Classroom." In Ball, John, et al. *The Social Sciences and Geographic Education: A Reader*. New York: John Wiley & Sons, 1971; originally published in *The Journal of Geography* 69, January 1970.

Bradley, N. C. "The Growth of Knowledge of Time in Children of School Age." *British Journal of Psychology* 38 (1947): 67-68.

Davis, Arnold. "Reading Maps: A Much-Needed Skill." *The Social Studies* 65, February 1974, pp. 67-71.

Downs, Roger; and Stea, David. *Maps in Minds: Reflections of Cognitive Mapping*. New York: Harper & Row, 1977.

Graves, Norman. *New Movements in the Study and Teaching of Geography*. London: Temple Smith, 1972.

Harris, Ruby. *The Rand McNally Handbook of Map and Globe Usage*. 4th ed. Chicago: Rand McNally, 1967.

Kennamer, Lorrin. "Developing a Sense of Time and Space." In *Skill Development in the Social Studies: 33rd Yearbook of the National Council for the Social Studies.* Arlington, Virginia: NSCC, 1963, pp. 148-179.

Meyers, Judith. "Map Skills Instruction and the Child's Developing Cognitive Abilities." *Journal of Geography* 72 September 1973, pp. 27-35.

Oakden, E. C.; and M. Sturt. "Development of the Knowledge of Time in Children," *British Journal of Psychology* 12 (1922): 309-336.

Karen Gunnington April 23, 1979.

Happiness Is School

Happiness is when I get good marks on my spelling and math & other subjects. The best part is not having the teacher to scold me at anytime.

Karen expresses her opinions freely.

> A person . . . can do
> and understand so much
> and so much only as he
> has observed in fact or in
> thought . . . .
>
> **Francis Bacon,**
> *Aphorisms*

Key Questions

How do people develop functional concepts? What part
does observation play in the development of concepts?

How can children perform the grouping operation in
the social studies?

What role do specific items of information play in the
generalizing process?

How can children be involved in the generalizing
process in the social studies?

How can children predict and hypothesize as part of
social studies inquiry sequences?

What kinds of value judgments do we make?

What is involved in rendering a defendable value
judgment?

What part do facts play in value decision making?

How can judgments be validated?

How can value decision making be made part of the
social studies?

Describe how you would use each of the following in
the elementary social studies: evils boards, voting,
decisions in retrospect, social action, a problems
ladder.

A Story to Think about: "The Little Red Hen"

Once there was a little red hen who on her way home discovered some grains of wheat lying in her path. To herself she said, "I will plant this grain, and when it is grown and ground, I will make it into bread."

When she arrived home, the Little Red Hen called out, "Who will help me plant the wheat?"

"Not I," replied the Dog.

"Not I," replied the Goose.

"Not I," replied the Duck.

"Very well," said the Little Red Hen, "I will do it myself." And she did.

When the wheat had grown tall, the Little Red Hen called out again, "Who will help me harvest the wheat and take it to the mill to be ground to flour?"

"Not I," replied the Dog.

"Not I," replied the Goose.

"Not I," replied the Duck.

"Very well," said the Little Red Hen, "I will do it myself." And she did.

When the Little Red Hen returned from the mill with the flour, she called out once more, "Who will help me bake the flour into bread?"

"Not I," replied the Dog.

"Not I," replied the Goose.

"Not I," replied the Duck.

"Very well," said the Little Red Hen, "I will do it myself." And she did.

And when the bread had been baked and filled the air with tantalizing aroma, the Little Red Hen called out to the Dog, the Goose, and the Duck, "Who will help me eat my bread?"

"I will," replied the Dog.

"I will," replied the Goose.

"I will," replied the Duck.

"No, you won't," said the Little Red Hen. "I planted the wheat, harvested and took it to the mill, and baked it into bread. I did all the work. Therefore, I will eat it myself!" And she did.

A traditional tale

Introduction

Most of us are familiar with the story of "The Little Red Hen." Filled with repeated phrases, the tale is a delight. Quickly the listener becomes sympathetic to the plight of the hard working hen and irritated with the dog, the goose, and the duck for refusing to help; he or she tends to cheer for the hen in the end.

But the story can go deeper than is at first apparent. Consider for one moment the complexities of the case. Why did each of the animals decline to help? Could each have had a legitimate reason for refusing? What might these reasons have been? Given valid reasons, was the hen right or wrong in not sharing her bread? What might have been the ultimate outcome of her not sharing? Are there any situations in which refusing to share scarce food is a justifiable act? Why didn't the hen explain why she wanted assistance? Was it right to tease the others by asking, "Who will help me eat my bread?" when she had no intention of sharing? And when you get down to the bottom line, did the Little Red Hen have any right to the grain she found?

To answer any one of these questions is to make a value judgment—to think through the pros and cons of the case and to decide on the rightness or wrongness of acts. The simple story of "The Little Red Hen" shows how difficult it is to render judgments that can stand the test of thorough analysis. Our immediate reaction may be to side with the conscientious hen; but as thoughtful individuals, we must go beyond superficial examination to consider extenuating circumstances and possible motivations. That there could be valid reasons behind the behavior of a nonworker is suggested by a story with a similar theme, the story of *Frederick* by Leo Lionni. Frederick sits idle while his fellow mice store food for the winter. They chide Frederick for his behavior; but when winter comes, it is Frederick who brings joy to the others by sharing poems that he has stored up during his summer of "idleness." The message here is striking: each individual may make a different contribution to the group; before criticizing we must know the facts.

T See Leo Lionni, *Frederick* (New York: Pantheon Books, 1966).

Children in schools need continued opportunity to think in a variety of patterns about a variety of questions. At times, those questions will require the formulation of judgments as in the story, "The Little Red Hen," which makes good content for a values discussion at almost any grade level. At other times, those questions will lead to the development of concepts, the projection of generalizations, and the application of knowledge to new problems. These four operations—*conceptualizing, generalizing, applying,* and *establishing values*—are the focuses of the sections that follow. These four are key tasks through which children can become actively involved with the content of the social sciences.

conceptualizing
generalizing
applying
establishing values.

Developing Strategies of Thought

R In Hilda Taba, Samuel Levine, and Freeman Elzey, "Thinking in Elementary School Children." Mimeographed. San Francisco: San Francisco State College, April 1964, p. 30.

Studies on human learning are beginning both to clarify the cognitive operations that underlie the way people think and to shed some light on the kinds of thinking in which children in school social studies should be involved. A particularly useful study is one by Hilda Taba and her associates (1964). As part of a broad investigation of thinking in elementary school children, Taba identified clusters of cognitive tasks useful in structuring inquiry sequences in classrooms. These include:

1. grouping and classification of information,
2. interpretation of data and the making of inferences, and
3. the application of known principles and facts to explain new phenomena, to predict consequences from known conditions and events, and to develop hypotheses by using known generalizations and facts.

What are these strategies of thinking all about? How do children become adept at handling them? Let us consider these two questions next.

The Strategy of Grouping and Classifying: Building Functional Concepts

Tree

As children learn about the world, they gradually attach symbolic labels to phenomena and events. The tall object with bark and leaves is a *tree*: so is the one that is shorter and has needles. As learners attach that label *tree* to myriad varieties that differ in many respects but share a number of characteristics, they are developing a **concept of "treeness."** They are learning to recognize a tree so that any new specimen is quickly assigned the verbal label *tree*.

Concepts differ in their level of abstraction. *Tree* represents a relatively concrete concept, in contrast to such abstract concepts as *honesty*, *scarcity*, *interdependence*, and *culture*. In the latter cases, there are no concrete referents to which one can point.

G Children see relationships among things as the basis of concept formation.

Perceiving the Essential Qualities of Things. According to Taba, concept formation begins with recognition of the distinctive characteristics of objects or events; the learner perceives the essential qualities of things. Two simple examples will help clarify this process of mental differentiation, which is the base of all conceptualizing. A child looking at a cat sees that it possesses four legs upon which it walks, that it purrs, that it has a specific shape, that it has a coat of fur. In this respect, the child mentally dissects the animal into its characteristic elements; he or she has begun to identify the properties of this particular object that differentiate it from others. The older learner carries on

Reading social studies material requires a student to
ponder problems of varying complexities.

this same process of differentiating when he or she looks at a familiar
worker such as a mail carrier and begins to perceive the particular
characteristics that this worker possesses: the carrier comes in a red,
white, and blue truck; brings the mail each day; wears a gray uniform.

   Careful observation is important in differentiating the attributes of
objects and events, especially in cases where concrete referents exist.
To encourage children to look carefully at things around them,
teachers can propose tasks that ask children to "look" with all their
senses: What words can we use to describe the way this object feels?
smells? looks? moves? sounds? What words can we use to describe the
uses to which it can be put? the functions it serves? the places it is
found? In relation to events, the teacher can ask children to think about
key attributes by asking: What happened first? second? next? Where
did it occur? Who was involved? When did it occur? What other events
occurred at the same time? What other events did this one lead into? By
asking these questions, the teacher is helping children develop a way
of looking at things in their environment that goes beyond the
superficial.

T The teacher as
questioner–that role is
highlighted in this chap-
ter, for it is through different kinds of questions
that children are forced
to try out different kinds
of thinking tasks.

The capacity to look at objects and events from many different perspectives is particularly important as young people handle sophisticated concepts in the social studies. Most children formulate concepts of trees, cats, and bicycles without formal instruction; they simply encounter specific examples out of which they gradually build functional concepts on their own. But as students build more sophisticated concepts of population density, political power, or tradition, the need for systematic instruction intensifies. It is at this point that the process of differentiating key attributes must consciously be pursued. Young people acquiring a concept of population density may start with a simple counting and measuring activity; going from room to room in their school, they count the number of persons at work in each area. They tabulate their findings, listing for each room the number of persons at work there. They may do the same using other phenomena that may not even involve people—counting the number of crayons left in crayon boxes that are all the same size, counting the number of cracks in each sidewalk square. Going on to work with area and volume, students may count the number of goldfish in each aquarium in the school, at the same time measuring the length, width, and height of the tank of water and calculating the volume of water in which the fish reside in each case. They may count the number of trees on different plots of land and measure the area of each plot, eventually going on to identify the number of occupants per given area.

Then, too, students can participate in simple demonstrations. Measuring an area of classroom space five meters by five meters, children themselves move into that area one by one, until all the youngsters are crowded into the twenty-five square meter space. With each additional move into the area, children calculate the population density. These specific activities, carried out by active young inquirers and later described carefully in phrases and sentences, lay the foundation for more intricate work with the concept.

Grouping. A more intricate task, according to Taba, is **grouping,** classifying together items that share one or more properties. Thus the young child seeing a Siamese cat mentally groups it with cats previously observed. The second child seeing a woman walking briskly along with a sack of mail rather than a man riding a truck enlarges the concept of mail carrier to include women as well as men. Individual students pursuing the concept of density begin to group areas and volumes into classes—those where there are many, many items found in a known volume or area, those where there is an average number of items in that volume or area, and those where there are very few items found.

In grouping, the thinker is primarily engaged in comparing and contrasting. The grouper must be able to perceive how diverse items are similar in some way and how rather similar items actually differ. To help young people develop skill in comparing and contrasting objects and events, the paramount questions are: How are these two objects or events similar? What characteristics do they share? How are they different? What characteristics do they possess that are very different? Using these questions as guides, students will develop groupings based on size, shape, color, weight, use, smell, taste, and state of motion. With little prodding, they will regroup objects already grouped according to one kind of shared attribute into new groups based on a different shared attribute. Young children in the primary grades can group all manner of things in their immediate environment—sorting blocks of differing shapes, sizes, and colors into piles; sorting school supplies found in the classroom; sorting different kinds of buildings found within their community; sorting different kinds of plants or animals they know; sorting the kinds of tools with which they are familiar; and sorting word cards that share certain verbal features into piles.

Older students can practice the grouping operation as they study countries around the world. They can sort countries according to population density, the form of government, the average annual income of families, and/or the major commodities imported or exported. More mature and gifted students will begin to see that how one groups items depends on the information for which one is looking. They will see, too, how numerical relationships can be the basis for grouping. For example, students grouping countries according to the number of barrels of oil exported yearly will be working with classes with numerical limits: countries exporting 0 to 100 million barrels yearly, countries exporting between 100 and 200 million barrels, and so on. When items are classed together in mathematical terms, the resulting data can be charted or graphed to clarify relationships.

Labeling. A third operation leading toward functional concepts is labeling—applying category labels that set forth the underlying rationale for the groupings formed. At the simplest level, the child developing a concept of *cat* begins to call all cats by that name regardless of slight differences. The second youngster attaches the label *mail carrier* to all persons who bring the mail, going on to develop more comprehensive categories such as *postal workers*—mail carriers as well as other workers—or *community helpers*—police officers, fire fighters, and mail carriers, as well as others. Likewise, the older student applies *high population density* to centers where the ratio of people to land area is great and *low population density* to centers where the ratio is small.

In this respect, labeling serves a basic human function; it makes communication among people possible as individuals attach common meanings to word symbols. It also leads the way toward a higher order

T Note again how the questions the teacher asks determine the kinds of thinking tasks children attempt.

community helpers

fire fighter

mail carrier

police officer

librarian

Figure 6.1
Up the Deductive Thinking Ladder in
Classrooms

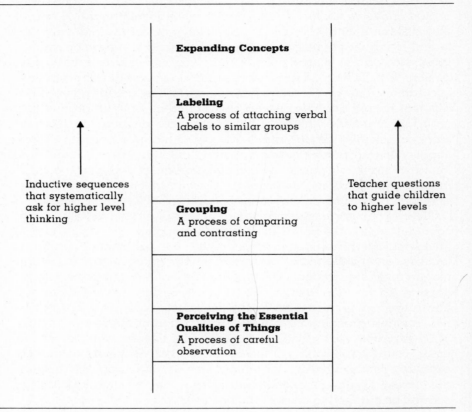

of analytical thinking, for once categories and subcategories have been delineated, investigators can study relationships among data grouped together.

In some instances, through their reading or film-viewing activities, youngsters will be able to search out and uncover labels commonly applied to phenomena under consideration. Where a category has no one label used commonly as a descriptor, students may invent their own. However, as young people deal with complex social studies concepts, at times the teacher must provide the arbitrary label in standard use within the language system. Many teachers find that the easiest way to teach the label is to interject it into ongoing discussion. Thus in the example of population density previously described, the teacher might ask the young people to think which of two fish bowls has the greater fish population density, or the larger number of fish occupying the same space. Often a term interjected directly into discussion is picked up by students who model their use after the teacher's without hearing a formal definition.

One warning before moving on! Learning formal definitions by memory is not the way functional concepts are built. Most teachers recall from personal experience how they memorized definitions of such terms as *civilization*, *values*, *nationalism*, and *ethnocentrism*. Often these memory lessons involved learning a string of words in sequence with little understanding of what the words meant.

Definitions learned in this way are quickly forgotten since the concept does not "belong" to the learner in the first place. The learner has not integrated the concept into his or her frame of understanding; it is not one that he or she would use. In contrast, meaningful concept formation is a slow process that involves many encounters with specific items or examples. These encounters provide data that learners sort into useful groups and to which they apply functional labels as they talk about experience.

The Strategy of Interpreting Data and Making Inferences: Putting Generalizations Together

A second cluster of cognitive operations relates to generalizing. In the Taba scheme these operations include:

1. gathering specific items of information,
2. processing information by explaining it, or giving reasons for specific items,
3. relating various pieces of processed information,
4. formulating generalizations—inferring generalizations based on specific relationships perceived.

Identifying Specific Information That Is Related.   The first operation in the sequence that leads to generalizing is data gathering. The thinker searches for specific instances and facts relative to a topic. Then he or she studies all the data assembled to uncover basic characteristics and to identify the most significant pieces of information. There is a vast amount of information available relative to any topic; because the thinker cannot use it all, the first step is to highlight what appears most relevant.

In the classroom, data gathering can take the form of information-backed **brainstorming.** Having read independently in a series of references, or having viewed a filmstrip or film, or having studied a map or flat picture, young social scientists go on to enumerate specific items they perceive to meet a specified criterion. For example, students looking at a map of a continent may search for cities falling within a given population range—say four to eight million. Together students

T Brainstorming is one way to amass a supply of specific items that students can later process in a variety of ways. It is one of the most valuable teaching strategies a teacher should know how to use effectively.

Figure 6.2
Climbing Higher Up the Thinking Ladder

Generalizing—A Process of Guided Discovery

D. Generalizing

1. Why do (have) all these "things" happen(ed)?

2. What basic generalizations can we propose to explain other, similar happenings?

C. Searching for Relationships

1. Are there any similarities we can see among the particular events or samples?

2. Are there any differences?

3. What are the most significant and insignificant examples or events?

4. Are there any mathematical relationships we can figure out?

5. Which is the oldest? most recent?

B. Probing for reasons—processing the data

1. Why does this event happen? What purpose does this "thing" serve?

2. Why doesn't "x" happen or be true if this particular "thing" did not happen or exist instead?

3. What might happen or be true if this particular "thing" did not happen or exist?

4. Under what conditions may "y" happen?

A. Gathering information

1. What is happening during each event in the sequence?

2. What is the chronological sequence of each event?

3. What words can we use to describe this phenomenon?

4. What are the essential characteristics of each event, sample, or phenomenon in the series?

brainstorm; searching the map, they call out and list multiple possibilities on chart or board. This same kind of information could have been gathered through reading or film viewing, or through analysis of charts and graphs. The important thing to remember is that when data to be enumerated are complex, classroom brainstorming must be information-backed. Enumerating from memory is an inadequate base for an inquiry sequence leading to productive generalizations.

Clearly, too, for brainstorming to lead to many pieces of useful data, young social scientists must understand related concepts. For example, to handle the task of identifying cities with a population falling within a given range, students must comprehend the meaning of *city* and *population*. In this respect, generalizing depends on the process of concept formation previously discussed. As numerous theorists have pointed out, concept development is the basic form of cognition, and schools must start with it to lay the foundation for generalizing.

The process of generalizing in classrooms is also dependent on the way the teacher structures a sequence. If young people are to rediscover generalizations about the nature of society, they must begin inductively as the social scientist begins—with specific data that relate to a topic. Thus as openers to inductive learning sequences, the teacher must offer statements and questions that allow students to give specific examples. In the case cited above, that opener was "Look for cities that have a population between four and eight million." Similar openers that focus on the particular rather than the general include:

1. Let's study this picture of activity within a Maori village. What specific things can we say about the way these people live?
2. Viewing this film, let's see if we can look for specific rituals that are part of the cultural heritage.
3. As you read, look for specific social problems that are found in an urban area.
4. As we study this sequence of pictures, let's list the kinds of workers who serve our community.

The result of such openers is a chalkboard or chart filled with many items that share the feature identified by teacher or students. This mass is firsthand data from which generalizations grow.

Processing Information.   A next step is to propose reasons that explain the information. To trigger thinking, the teacher must serve as guide by suggesting, "Let's focus on New York. Why do you think New York was able to grow to the size it did?" Then, "How can we explain the growth of Chicago? What was there about its location that made growth possible?" "How can we explain the growth of San Francisco?" As the students project reasons, they record these on a chart that clearly includes the city name with projected reasons arranged in columns.

Young social investigators can handle all manner of specific data in this fashion. They can enumerate specific events in history and record in parallel columns possible reasons why those events occurred when they did, where they did, or how they did. Students can list social traditions with tentative reasons that explain why these traditions have been maintained. Similarly, human institutions can be itemized with explanatory statements, and community helpers can be listed with related services performed by helpers laid out in parallel columns. In building charts of this type, young people are beginning to organize their information—process it so to speak—so that they clarify key relationships.

Relating Pieces of Processed Information.   Up to this point, young investigators have focused on specific items of information, identifying key aspects and elaborating on each. When considerable data have been accumulated and processed in this way, students turn their attention to the analysis of relationships. There are numbers of different kinds of relationships that can be perceived. One of the simplest is perceiving similarities and differences. A student, for example, might note: "Both of these cities grew as large as they did for the same reason—location on a major railroad line; City C grew for the same reason." This kind of thinking leads to comparisons and contrasts. Other thoughts lead to identification of sequential relationships, cause and effect relationships, and mathematical relationships, depending, of course, on the data at hand.

Again the teacher's opening remarks affect the direction inquiry will take. To help young investigators project relationships, the teacher may have to prime the pump with questions such as these:

Relationships based on similarities: Which items are in some way the same? How are they similar?

Relationships based on differences: Which items are very different in some respect? How are they different?

Relationships based on sequence: Of these items, which happened first? second? third? fourth? Why did they occur in this order?

Relationships based on importance: Of these items, which is most important or significant? least significant? Why?

Relationships based on ownership: Is one owned by another? possessed within another?

Relationships based on age: Which has existed longer? Which is the more recent?

Relationships based on mathematical principles: What percentage is that one compared with this? What multiple of this one is that? Is one included in or subsumed under another?

Generalizing.   As students work with relationships existing within data, at times overarching, explanatory statements of relationships emerge. At some point in an inquiry sequence, a student may announce, "Haven't water routes or railroad lines–where they are and where they go to–been important in where cities have located?" Such a statement is essentially a generalization in question form, a drawing together of points to show major relationships among them. In projecting statements such as this, the student is leaping from several examples to propose an explanation of how the world tends to operate.

The process of **generalizing** is a process of discovery. An inquirer can uncover facts–specific pieces of information. He or she can say definitively that as of this date City T has a population of X number of people. In contrast, statements of generalizations are in the realm of ideas to be discovered rather than uncovered. To generalize, a person must take an intellectual leap, going beyond facts to synthesize connections among them. In this respect, generalizing is an adventure in creative thinking, an adventure that carries the thinker from the realm of observable fact into the realm of complex thought. In describing this kind of thinking adventure, theorists use the term **inductive thinking.** Inductive thinking is that which begins with an enumeration and analysis of specific cases and proceeds to the development of general statements of conceptual relationships.

T Paul Brandwein calls the moment when children see a point for themselves, based on their own analysis of specific items of information, the EUREKA! Even as Archimedes sat in his tub contemplating how to determine the amount of space occupied by the king's crown and suddenly "got it," so children can discover some generalizations for themselves and feel the EUREKA thrill!

Idea Page

Background for the teacher. This activity demonstrates how students can compare and contrast cultural data and generalize inductively about relationships based on them. It can be used as a listening-analyzing lesson in which the stories are shared orally and the questions asked as part of a discussion. *The continuation* can serve as an independent follow-up to class discussion.

The aim. Recognizing the theme of a story; comparing and contrasting themes; perceiving relationships between recurring story themes and basic human needs.

The introductory clues. A familiar fable in western folklore is "The Milkmaid and Her Bucket of Milk."

Once there was a very poor milkmaid. She was so poor that her clothes were in rags. As she was going to market with her bucket of milk one day, she met some laughing girls. One pointed at the milkmaid and teased, "Look at poor Matilda. Her clothes are all raggedy and dirty."

The teasing made Matilda very sad. She thought to herself, "When I get to the market, I will sell my milk and buy some eggs. I will take my eggs home and let them hatch. When the chickens are grown, I will come back to the market and sell them. And with the money I will buy myself a new dress."

Because Matilda was dreaming so very hard, she failed to see the big hole in the road. She tripped and stumbled. The bucket of milk fell, and the milk spilled all over the ground.

A less familiar tale comes from India. It is called a Panchatantra story and is titled "The Poor Man and the Flask of Oil."

There once was a man who was very poor. His neighbor was a wealthy merchant who sold honey and oil. One day the merchant, who was a kindly man, sent his neighbor a flask of oil.

The poor man was very happy. He put the flask away, setting it carefully on the top shelf of his cupboard. To himself he said, "I think I will sell the oil. There is enough there for me to have money to buy at least five sheep. Then every year I would have new lambs and soon I would have a large flock. I could be rich enough to marry. We could have children. They would be tall and strong. If they do not do as I command, I would punish them with my staff."

At that he swung his staff into the air. In so doing, he knocked the flask out of the cupboard. The oil poured out, covering everything in sight with a thin film of oil.

The pursuit

What happened to the milkmaid of the first story? to the poor man in the second?

What is the message of "The Milkmaid and Her Bucket of Milk"? of "The Poor Man and the Flask of Oil"?

In what specific ways are both stories the same? different?

Why would the same kind of story appear in two cultures so far apart in the world? In thinking about this question, think about the possible purposes literature serves in a culture and the way in which stories were handed down from one generation to the next. Think about why people practice wishful thinking.

The continuation. Try to create your own version of a story that starts with high hopes and ends with the crash that kills the dream. Follow the pattern of the two stories given, using about three paragraphs and some direct conversation. Look at the way the conversation statements are punctuated in those stories and do the same in yours. In creating your story, make sure you use different characters, a different dream, and a different ending to the dream.

The Strategy of Applying Knowledge: Hypothesizing or Predicting Based on What Is Known

The ability to apply what one knows to new situations increases the worth of the facts, concepts, and generalizations one possesses and allows one to discover further relationships. Using what one knows, one can attempt to explain new phenomena, to predict consequences of acts occurring under known conditions, and to predict what will happen if conditions should change. Often it is the **deductive leap** forward into the unknown that opens up new knowledge to human understanding.

The Deductive Leap

If . . .

if . . .

if . . .

Then . . . !

Great leaps forward dot the history of investigation both in the social and natural sciences. Mendeleev's discovery of the Periodic Table of Elements is a classic case in point. Mendeleev studied the properties of the elements then known; these were the facts he had at hand. His organizing idea was to order them in repeating sequences of properties according to their atomic weights. By laying out the elements so that elements with certain properties lay in columns beneath those with similar properties, he discovered that some were missing. Based on his perception of missing elements, he made a deductive leap, predicting the existence of then unknown elements and hypothesizing the properties of these elements. His predictions led ultimately to the discovery of elements whose properties bore astonishing likenesses to those he hypothesized.

In social investigations, perfect predictions are less probable because human motivation, values, and desires play a determining role. Hypothesizing is, however, important in social science inquiry. It allows one to go beyond what is apparent to consider what may occur in the future. It allows one to consider possible outcomes after thorough analysis of conditions at hand. For that reason, opportunities should be built into social studies programs for students to think deductively–to apply their store of facts, concepts, and generalizations to inquiries into what the future holds in store.

Assembling Information and Establishing the Conditions Under Which A Generalization Can Be Applied. A search for relevant information is the first operation in the application of knowledge to new situations. The primary question here is: What are the distinguishing features of the new situation in which known generalizations will be applied? In short, what is this new situation like? This question leads an inquirer to look at all facets of the situation and develop what amounts to a complete description of it. A second operation is to analyze the generalization to determine the conditions under which it has predictive powers. Major questions here are: What are the conditions under which the generalization has held true in the past? How are these conditions similar to or different from the conditions operational in the new situation?

Intermediate youngsters can work with simple social problems that require them to use their understandings in new situations. In classrooms, hypothetical situations can involve children in the application and review of knowledge recently acquired. For example, having investigated the services supplied by local governments, young people can project a scheme for running a local government in a hypothetical community somewhat different from their own. In the data-gathering phase of their inquiry, they outline the peculiar qualities of their hypothetical community—its location, geographical scope, population, socioeconomic level, industry, and so forth. In completing this assignment in work teams, participants must draw upon factors they have learned that shape life in communities. In the second phase of data gathering, young investigators identify the kinds of tasks that must be attended to at the local level—collecting taxes, running the schools, maintaining a library, maintaining the local roads, and so forth.

To carry out this assignment, teams must reconsider what they know about community services and the relationship of services to characteristics of the community served. In reconsidering, they will talk in if-then patterns: if a community has numbers of jobless poor, then the community must assist these people; if the community sprawls over a large geographic area, then local highway maintenance can be a problem; if a community is located in the north, then snow removal must be considered. These projects are valuable in and of themselves, for young people thinking in if-then patterns are directly involved in rather complex deductive relationships. They are matching conditions with outcomes.

Predicting or Hypothesizing.   Once young people have gathered and processed data relevant to a prediction, they can hypothesize what will be true under somewhat different conditions. In the preceding example, students would propose a scheme of local government so that adequate services are provided. This can be a challenge, especially if students work in teams and each team plans for a hypothetical community of its own design. The adventure can culminate an extended study of community life with teams compiling maps, charts, and graphs to present their proposals to other class members.

Predicting need not always be such an elaborate classroom experience. Teachers can ask children to predict as part of ongoing discussion by questioning: What do you think would happen if we changed the conditions so that . . . ? What do you think would happen if we introduced the factor of . . . ? Given the way people think today, how do you predict the election would go if held right now? How do you think a particular event—an earthquake, a change of government, or an introduction of a new tool—will affect the people living there? If these questions are asked of upper elementary graders who have the necessary background, they can synthesize relationships and propose hypotheses.

Testing Hypotheses. A hypothesis is a scientific guess based on consideration of all information available. Because it represents prediction rather than certainty, a hypothesis should be put to the test of further investigation. Having predicted the effect of certain events on human activity, the social scientist goes out to see if these effects actually result. Having predicted the outcome of an election, pollsters check their projections against actual election results. In some instances, however, predictions cannot be tested completely against reality; they are too abstract or relate to events too far in the future. In such cases, hypotheses are put to the test of reason, with investigators analyzing the intricacies of the problem, laying out evidence, and developing a logical statement of support. This logical statement is their rationale.

Students who have made simple predictions should be asked the fundamental questions that force the logical testing of hypotheses: What evidence do you have to support your hypothesis? On what facts have you based your prediction? Looking back upon their own projections, young people begin to perceive the need for substantive evidence and the need to identify the limiting factors that impinge on the accuracy of their predictions. In homespun language, they begin to "hedge their bets."

Deduction in School Social Studies. Research in the development of reason in children suggests that not until later in their elementary years do youngsters have the mental capacity to carry out high level abstract thinking. Jean Piaget has identified the period from age seven to age eleven or twelve as one when through manipulation of objects, the child mentally transforms concrete data available to him or her to form generalizations and concepts based on similarities and differences among things. To Piaget this is the period of *concrete operations*. Starting about age eleven or twelve, a child begins to go beyond the concrete to use language in an abstract way. Piaget terms this period *formal operations*. Thus during most of elementary school, youngsters are growing in the ability to conceptualize and generalize—the two cognitive tasks explained earlier in this chapter. Elementary youngsters' ability to abstract, however, is more limited, and abstracting is the name of the game in the process of deduction.

Idea Page

Background information for the teacher. Use this activity as a basis for a group discussion or as an independent thinking task. It is an example of a *deductive sequence*.

The aim. Applying generalizations to the interpretation of new problem situations. Identifying specifics that support a generalization.

The introductory clues. Two big ideas we have met before are:

People all over the world are similar to us.
Other people also differ from us in certain ways.

The pursuit. The picture on p. 187 shows a person who lives in Japan.

List items you see in the picture that show you that this person is similar to you.

List items you see in the picture that show you that this person differs from you in certain ways.

The continuation. Search newspapers and magazines for pictures of people from different lands around the world. Mount your findings as a collage on colored construction paper. Beneath the collage, list items found in the pictures that show you that people all over the world are similar. Then list items that show that people differ from one another in some ways.

Predicting and hypothesizing are not total impossibilities for children in elementary grades, as teachers who have tried this mental task in classrooms have discovered. The key to success is to base predictions on a large pool of information and firsthand experience and to ask for hypotheses requiring only short leaps of the imagination. The key is also to phrase simple questions in the if-then pattern, so that students pick up this linguistic pattern to use as they voice their hypotheses about "What would happen if. . . ." Introductory activity with deduction paves the way for more elaborate activity in grades five or six and up into junior and senior high school.

Although elementary grade youngsters will be involved only in simple deductive problems, involvement is essential if they are to be prepared to meet an unknown future. Speaking of the way the human mind can use knowledge in new situations, Hilda Taba sharply summarized this importance:

The operations involved in applying principles are quite crucial to developing productive patterns of thought. . . . This is the chief process on which the transfer of knowledge depends, and therefore a crucial one for getting mileage out of what little the students are able to acquire directly during their schooling. It is the chief means for creating new knowledge by logical processes, and a way of acquiring control over wide areas of new phenomena (Taba 1964, pp. 34-35).

The process of deducing new knowledge is the top of the iceberg marked "thinking." Before one can make deductions, one must possess numbers of functional concepts and generalizations. Therefore, to point to application of knowledge as crucial in transfer is not to diminish the significance of conceptualizing and generalizing. Thinking is a complex whole in which component tasks intertwine.

Up the Thinking Ladder

Implicit in what has been said so far is the idea that thinking is not a single or simple endeavor. Rather, to know how to think is to know how to carry out numbers of interrelated cognitive processes. The word **hierarchial** is often applied to cognitive processes, because some are considered simpler, and others more complex—with the more complex tasks encompassing the simpler ones. For example, in the Taba analysis of thinking already described in this section, lower-order tasks are those that relate to concept formation, second-order tasks are those that relate to formation of generalizations, and higher-order tasks are those that relate to application of knowledge.

Another scheme for looking at the hierarchial nature of the thinking processes is Benjamin Bloom's (1956) taxonomy of educational objectives, which many teachers use as a guide in planning the kinds of questions they ask as they encourage children to think at higher and higher levels. In Bloom's taxonomy, the lowest level of cognition is knowledge. When one has knowledge, one can recall dates, definitions, names, rules, generalizations, ideas, trends, categories, and so forth. Such teacher questions as "What is the date of the Battle of Bunker Hill?" "For what does the abbreviation CIA stand?" "Who is known as the Great Compromiser?" ask for recall of knowledge. The next higher level is comprehension. In comprehending, one shows understanding of information by translating a communication into another form such as a graph, a picture, a summary, or a written explanation. When one expresses ideas, generalizations, rules, and so on in one's own words, one is involved in the comprehending task.

Although these two lower-level tasks must be performed as a base for moving up the thinking ladder, limiting a question sequence to questions that ask only for knowledge and comprehension gives children little opportunity to test their thinking on more complex tasks. In Bloom's taxonomy, higher-level tasks are application, analysis, synthesis, and—at the top—evaluation. Figure 6.3 details the meaning of these categories in the Bloom scheme and presents examples of questions subsumed under each.

R Benjamin Bloom and David R. Krathwohl, *Taxonomy of Educational Objectives: Handbook I: Cognitive Domain* (New York: Longman, 1956). See also David Krathwohl, Benjamin Bloom, and Bertram Masia, *Taxonomy of Educational Objectives, The Classification of Educational Goals, Handbook II: Affective Domain* (New York: David McKay, 1964).

Figure 6.3
Levels in Bloom's Taxonomy

6.00 Evaluation

Judgments about the goodness or weakness of materials or processes.

Questions: Is this a good book? Why do you think so? Which of these two events was the more significant one? What evidence do you have to support your judgment?

5.00 Synthesis

Arranging elements to form a whole; putting parts together in original ways.

Questions: Can you think of another way of solving the problem? Can you hypothesize how the Egyptians probably used this tool? Can you explain the meaning of this event in terms of the development of our nation?

4.00 Analysis

Figuring out how parts fit together; figuring out the relationships inherent in a communication.

Questions: What kind of advertising strategy do we find in this particular ad? How is this reference book organized? How is this newspaper organized?

3.00 Application

Using generalizations to explain particular situations.

Questions: Is there any generalization we have already discussed that applies here?

2.00 Comprehension

Translating a communication into another form; interpreting a communication by explaining or summarizing it.

Questions: How can we summarize what we have just read?
How could we express this information as a graph?

1.00 Knowledge

Recalling basic information.

Questions: Who invented the cotton gin? When did this event occur?

Thinking Activities: A Summary Listing

The single most important determinant of the kinds of thinking operations students attempt in classrooms is the question sequence that the teacher projects as he or she guides discussion, outlines personalized study tasks, and evaluates growth in learning. For that reason, emphasis in the preceding sections has been on questioning patterns. The reader may wish to go back to pages 172–189 of this chapter and underline all the suggested questions that can be asked in classroom sessions. These are the kinds of questions that lead students to conceptualize, to generalize, and eventually to apply their knowledge.

In addition, a teacher should possess a repertoire of activity frameworks that encourage students to think at higher and higher levels of cognition. Here is a summary listing of general activities that can be modified for use with diverse social studies content and that will nudge children up the thinking ladder:

1. Pictures as Puzzles. Many commercial enterprises today package folders of pictures, each structured around a single theme. Students can describe the pictures and then sort them into piles based first on one criterion, then on another. This can be done as a total class activity; later the pictures can be placed in a learning station where students individually can see if they can invent other groupings and concoct appropriate labels.

2. Factstorming and Grouping. At the culmination of a unit of study, "factstorming" can prove an exciting review technique as well as an opportunity for perceiving relationships. Students brainstorm many facts about the unit they have just completed while several serve as scribes recording the thoughts randomly on the chalkboard. When the board is filled, participants study the items and, guided by teacher questions, group those on the same facet of the topic together. A simple way to group is to circle similar items with the same color chalk.

3. Playing with Why. Whenever children study a series of events, they can chart to express relationships they are discovering. One of those relationships is the reason why the event occurred. Students list a capsule description of each event in the series down the left side of a chart; in a parallel right column, they list in brainstorming fashion many reasons why that event occurred as it did. Later they can go back and underline the most critical reasons in red; reasons of average importance in green; and the least critical reasons in blue.

4. Pin It to the Board. As students learn about a country, region, state, or province, they can develop key categories of information—specific things we know about—the climate, the topography, the plants and animals, the way people make a living, the kinds of houses in which they live, the traditions they maintain, and so forth. They pin labeling cards (climate, topography, etc.) to the bulletin board and beneath each record key facts discovered through study. When stu-

Figure 6.4
A Change Chart from Hilda Taba

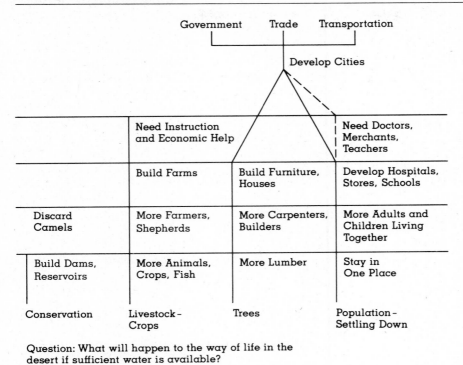

Question: What will happen to the way of life in the desert if sufficient water is available?

From Taba, Levine, Elzey, 1964.

dents have filled each column with important information, they gather for a generalizing session: they summarize the specifics into general statements that they record at the base of the bulletin board.

5. A Time Line of Facts. A time strategy can be applied to a study of a period of history. Time intervals are pinned across the top of the bulletin board: 1450-1499, 1500-1549, 1550-1559, and so forth. As students investigate the period, they list main events beneath the appropriate time category. The compiled data again make a clearly visible assembly of material about which students generalize based on a feature shared by numbers of events listed under the same time interval; for example, "this was a time of rapid exploration; this was a time when men were the adventurers and women stayed home."

6. The Practical Wish. Students who have investigated their community, school, shopping center, industrial center, government, or society can use their understanding to hypothesize the world they would like to see in the future. Projections can be in the form of individual compositions: "The School I'd Like to See," "The Society I'd Like to See," etc. When young people share their projections orally with classmates, they must be prepared to support ideas with evidence acquired through their studies.

7. One Little Change. Another relatively easy introduction to hypothesizing and predicting is thinking about the effect of one change within a total scheme of events. What would have happened if the British had won the Battle of Yorktown? What would happen if the amount of rainfall increased drastically on earth? What would happen if insects disappeared from the earth? What would happen if the glaciers suddenly began to melt as a result of a warming of the earth? How do you think the world would differ today if Hitler had not been born? Consideration of one hypothetical change can lead to consideration of other variables. Figure 6.4 shows the ramifications developed in one third-grade class when children zeroed in on the question, "What will happen to the way of life in the desert if sufficient water is available?" This visualization is a change chart. Working on their own or in task groups, students can construct similar charts based on predictive questions they are considering.

A Problem to Ponder

Children in Mr. Fritz's fourth grade searched a map for names of bodies of water. Names were listed randomly with a marker pen: Atlantic Ocean, North Sea, Indian Ocean, Lake Erie, etc. Having compiled a collage of words, students circled ocean names with red, seas with blue, and lakes with green.

Returning to the map, they projected the qualities shared by oceans, those shared by lakes, and finally those shared by seas. Size was the first quality they used to distinguish bodies of water until Mr. Fritz guided them with: "Let's compare the boundaries of lakes and seas." Students looked more carefully at the North Sea and the Adriatic. They noted that these bodies—in contrast to oceans like the Indian and the Atlantic—were marked off by land mass boundaries. Looking at lakes such as Superior, they proposed that lakes were surrounded by land.

"Let's look at the Dead Sea," Mr. Fritz suggested. "Why is that a sea?" One youngster said that it was a sea because it is salty. Others agreed that seas generally are salty; that is another characteristic. A perceptive student reminded that the Great Salt Lake is salty. At that point, students began to suggest that in general, size, kind of boundaries, and saltiness are qualities that can be used to distinguish among bodies of water, but that there are no hard and fast rules for naming.

On successive days, these fourth graders found gulfs, bays, straits, and channels on their maps. They made transparencies of examples by tracing map segments onto acetate sheets. They studied the examples projected on the screen, at times laying one on top of another to make comparisons of size and shape. They found distinguishing characteristics and recognized that exceptions exist. As they concluded their study, one gifted youngster remarked that exceptions should be expected since names are applied by people and people who do the naming may not follow the rules.

1. What fundamental understandings are being developed in this lesson sequence?
2. What thinking skills are being developed? What communication skills? What search skills?
3. What does this episode tell us about how the teacher can use gifted children in the classroom?

Learning to Make Defendable Value Decisions

One way in which people subjectively apply knowledge they have acquired is in making **value judgments** about the rightness/wrongness, advisability/inadvisability, usefulness/uselessness, beauty/ugliness, or significance/insignificance of objects, events, actions, and people. The frequent use of these value-laden terms in everyday conversation, as well as the use of related words such as good, terrible, desirable, undesirable, efficient, inefficient, valuable, valueless, indicates how the process of judging touches everyone as he or she interacts with others. Value decision making is a process of major importance in human relationships.

Kinds of Value Decisions That Must Be Made

As this listing of value-laden terms suggests, all judgments are not the same. Some are essentially moral in that they get at the rightness or

T Words that indicate that a statement may contain a value judgment are "ought to," "should," "should have," as well as more obvious evaluative terms—"good," "terrible," "dear," "nice."

wrongness of acts. When people say, *"It is wrong* to smoke in nonsmoking areas," they are stating a value judgment about the inherent goodness of an act. Another way of stating the same moral judgment is to say, "People *should not* smoke in nonsmoking areas."

In contrast, some judgments are determinations of the wiseness or foolishness, the advisability or inadvisability of a course of action. For instance, to say, "It is unwise to smoke," is not to judge the morality of the act, but rather the sensibleness of it given the knowledge of evidence at hand. Political judgments as well as economic ones are often determinations of soundness. Many personal decisions related to the use of drugs, highway speeding, diet, or other health matters fall into this category.

Still other judgments raise questions about effectiveness. Consider, for instance, this statement: "The best way to stop smoking is to go 'cold turkey'—to stop at one stroke." Obviously, the aspect of unwiseness in this statement is that smoking is a harmful thing to do; it must be given up. In addition, a judgment about effectiveness is being applied to various methods of stopping, with one being singled out as best. Effectiveness judgments are applied to all manner of plans and procedures: economic, political, and social. Almost every day every person states this kind of value judgment; he or she remarks, "The president should have done this rather than that," or "It would have been better if I had done that."

Other judgments are determinations of the importance or unimportance and the significance or insignificance of things, events, or even people. A value decision maker may state, "It is more important at this point that I take a vacation than that I finish my work." Such decisions are matters of lining up priorities. Again this type of decision abounds in everyday situations as well as in situations where national and international priorities are being established. People make importance decisions when they decide how they will spend their consumable incomes, how they will allocate their time, and in what ways they will interact with others. National leaders must make some of these same decisions as they handle the money and the interrelationships of a country.

Yet other judgments are determinations of the beauty of objects or acts. A person may remark, "I think it looks ugly to smoke." Clearly this is not a judgment of rightness or wrongness, nor of wiseness or foolishness. It is an aesthetic judgment. People tend to render decisions about the ugliness of pictures, scenery, things, acts.

Since value judgments are an omnipresent part of human interaction, it is important that young people should be systematically involved in the decision-making process as part of the social studies. This in itself is a value decision that has been made based on an analysis of human functioning. If people function often as decision makers, then

Figure 6.5
A Framework for considering
Judgmental Decision-making

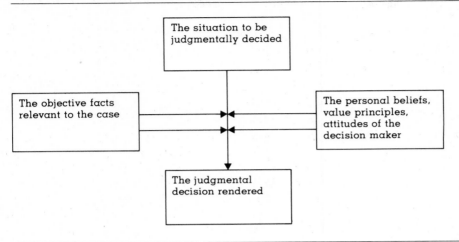

students must be prepared to make the most rational value judgments possible in given situations.

What Is Involved in Rendering a Defendable Judgment

The tasks people perform as they render a value judgment are both similar to and different from those discussed earlier as part of the application of knowledge. In the case of decisions of considerable importance, these tasks include:

1. clarifying the judgmental decision to be made and identifying possible decision options
2. gathering and organizing data related to one's own values, feelings, beliefs, and related to the facts in the case
3. making a tentative decision based on the analysis of the facts, the options, and the value principles one holds near and dear
4. testing the judgment by clarifying the assumptions underlying it
5. taking action based on a judgmental decision, if action is possible

Conceived in terms of these five tasks, to render a judgmental decision may at first appear to be a straightforward, methodical process. In practice, it is far from straightforward and not at all methodical. Rather judgmental decision making is a fluid activity. Each task is not performed in a formal sequence and is not clearly separated from other ones. Tasks actually blend together as arbitrary divisions between

R The approach to moral education given here is an analytical one. It draws heavily upon the ideas of Jerrold Coombs and Milton Meux, "Values Education," in Lawrence Metcalf, ed., *The 41st Yearbook of the National Council for the Social Studies.* (Arlington, Virginia: NCSS, 1971).

them blur. The decision maker may mull over points for hours or even days, at times going back to reconsider those pondered earlier. In so doing, he or she may chance upon new information or perceive the question in a different light. Leaning previously toward one decision, he or she may now identify and consider other options. In judgmental decisions there is no tight connecting link between facts gathered and a final decision rendered in a case. The connection is a tenuous one in which the attitudes, feelings, and value principles held by the decision maker—as well as the verifiable facts—impinge on the final judgmental decision. For that reason, a decision maker may move this way, then that way before declaring a position or taking action. Even while taking action, he or she may experience doubts as to the validity of the decision.

The sections that follow will clarify what is involved in judgmental decision making and identify ways in which children can learn to make judgments they can defend. In classrooms the tasks of decision making should be approached in a flowing, ongoing way, not separated from each other and not necessarily in the sequence given.

Clarifying the Value Decision and Identifying Options to Investigate

Before rendering a defendable judgmental decision, a person must have a clear conception of his or her problem and of possible decisions that can be rendered relative to it. The person must ask, "Am I making a moral judgment about the inherent goodness or evil of an action, or is this a determination about the wisdom of doing it?" Take, for example, the question of smoking in a nonsmoking area presented earlier. Here the decision maker could look at the problem in moral, legal, or health terms. Then, too, the decision maker must know just what it is that he or she is talking about, asking in this context, "What do we mean by a 'nonsmoking area'?"

T As with all forms of thinking in classrooms, the questions teachers ask are significant in determining the direction value decision making will take.

In classroom decision making, the teacher must raise questions that help thinkers clarify both the nature of the decision and the terms they are using. Key questions to use at this beginning point include:

What kind of a decision are we making? Are we deciding on the relative importance of these people, courses of action, events? Are we deciding on the basic goodness or evil of acts? Are we thinking in terms of the soundness of a proposed or past action? Are we making an aesthetic determination?

What do we mean by the words we are using?

Once students have isolated a problem and have clarified it, the teacher should guide them to propose possible judgments. Children propose, "We could decide X, or Y, or Z." In this case, X, Y, and Z are options to be weighed after relevant data have been collected and organized. The teacher's task here is to encourage children to consider all possible options—sensible as well as less sensible ones. Developed brainstorming style, the listing is a beginning; many other options may surface as children gather facts.

Gathering and Organizing Relevant Data Against Which to Evaluate Options

A person must have a knowledge base—a pool of facts, concepts, and generalizations—upon which to formulate a judgment; he or she must understand the intricacies of the problem situation, and all the factors having a bearing on the case. Additionally and equally important, a person must recognize those values, beliefs, feelings, and biases he or she holds that have a bearing on it. To gather relevant data is both to identify objective facts and come to a heightened understanding of the self.

Gathering Data About the Self.   What things do I like? dislike? What makes me feel good? sad? angry? tense? What things excite me? bore me? What actions of other people really stir me up? turn me off? When am I willing to act? to get involved? Answering these kinds of questions about the self not just on one or two judgmental occasions but on a continuing basis, children will come to understand more fully their own feelings, beliefs, values, and interests that often affect their judgmental decisions.

To ask students as they study a picture of two youngsters sitting outside a burned-down house clutching their charred toys, "How does this make you feel?" "Why do you feel this way?" "How do you think these children feel?" "When have you ever felt the same way?" is to begin them on the road to greater self-understanding. The questions relative to feelings are natural ones in the primary grades, especially as children

1. interact in real interpersonal situations in the classroom
2. participate in brief role-playing situations and talk about reactions
3. consider situational dilemmas as part of study of family, school, community
4. look at and talk about emotion-packed photographs
5. listen to and talk about stories in which there is an inherent values conflict

In the upper grades, young people should go beyond feeling-questions to focus on their beliefs and value principles. Students at this point should be asked to clarify the principles on which they function through such questions as: "Under what conditions is it right to do this? wrong to do it?" "Are there any circumstances when we would make a different judgment? What are they?" "What other beliefs are coloring our judgment in this case?" "If we had to choose between these two beliefs that we have identified, which would we select as more important to follow?"

These questions can be asked as an outgrowth of values problems that occur in every upper-grade classroom as individual desires come into conflict with the rights and needs of the total group and of others. When real conflicts arise, the teacher can follow up with analysis of hypothetical dilemmas. For example:

The Dilemma of the Plastic Protractor

Bruce enjoys working in the production center. His desk is next to it. One afternoon he sees Timothy take the only plastic protractor from the center. Tim slips it into his own pocket before returning to his desk.

Bruce is in the middle of doing a map project. He needs the protractor to finish it. Timothy is his good friend. They play together after school. What should Bruce do?

Handling the dilemma with a group in which pilfering of work materials is a class social problem, the teacher could:

1. begin by clarifying the problem—"Where does Bruce sit?" "Why do you think he chose to sit there?" "Why is he personally concerned about the class loss of the protractor?" "What is the relationship between Bruce and Tim?"
2. move to feelings and motives—"If you were Bruce, how would you feel?" "If you were Tim, how would you feel?" "Why would you feel this way?" "Why do you think Tim took the protractor?" "Have you ever wanted something so badly you just took it?" "How did you feel then?"
3. encourage identification of the actions Bruce could take—"What could Bruce do?" "What else could he do?" "What might be the outcome of doing this? doing that?"
4. change the conditions of the problem—"Would it make any difference in what you did if Tim were not your friend? if you did not need the protractor yourself?"

Notice that in the sequence of questions, the teacher changes the perspective of the questions. At the end, young people are talking as if they were Bruce or Tim. In so doing, the problem has become personalized. Their own feelings, values, and beliefs are at issue. And through it all they come to know themselves better—something vitally important as they go on to handle everyday judgmental decisions!

Building a Storehouse of Data Through Investigations. Not only is it important that young people "know themselves" as a basis for judgmental decision making, but it is important that they have a background of factual data relevant to a case. Often in social studies classrooms, data gathering for judgmental purposes occurs as part of unit study in which numbers of judgments are rendered based on understandings developed through the unit. This is a productive context for making decisions. Rather than talking in terms of hypothetical dilemmas as in the previous example, youngsters are handling real situations that have taken place or are taking place. For example, an historical study of the American Revolution gives rise to many value-laden questions that relate to right vs. wrong:

Was it right (morally so) for the colonials to refuse to pay the Stamp Tax? What other options did they have?

Was it right for the English to quarter their officers in the homes of the colonials without their consent?

Was it right for the new state governments to confiscate the property of the Tories?

Was it right for the colonials to develop a constitution that ignored the problems of slavery in their own country?

The same questions can be approached in terms of advisability. Were these acts wise or unwise?

Asked within a unit on the American Revolution, these questions may not require extensive data gathering. As part of their ongoing study, investigators will have seen films that build their storehouse of relevant information, read books, and participated in discussions. Specifically they may have viewed films in the National Geographic Educational Services series entitled *Decades of Decision: The American Revolution*, which present controversial issues in American history.

On the other hand, faced with a particular question within their unit, youngsters may need to identify facts that bear on the case. At the upper elementary level, these can be laid out as charts, which children devise either as part of a teacher-led group at first or as part of a small task group when they have gained experience in performing the task. A fact chart should include the question being considered, terms clearly defined, and relevant information as shown in the sample given in Figure 6.6. To gather detailed information similar to that about the Acadians compiled on the fact chart, investigators study encyclopedias, their texts, and perhaps short portions of Longfellow's "Evangeline." Having set forth the facts, students should be encouraged to express their "gut feelings" about each.

T Specific titles in the National Geographic series include "Cry Riot," "Look Back in Sorrow," "Equally Free," and "The People vs. Job Shattuck." Guidance Associates also produces filmstrips that focus on values questions within the context of interpersonal relationships.

Figure 6.6
A Decision Making Fact Chart
(Note: Ask students to express their
initial reaction to each fact they list.)

Question to be Answered: Was it morally right for the British to make the Acadians move out of Acadia when they got control of Canada in 1755 after the French and English Wars?

Fact: The Acadians had French ancestors who had lived in Canada for more than 100 years.

Fact: Acadia was a rugged land, rich in timber and game, and blessed with fine harbors.

Fact: The Acadians had worked hard to make the land serve them.

Fact: The Acadians had stayed neutral during the wars.

Fact: The British believed that the Acadians were secretly helping the French. (No one knows for sure whether they were.)

Fact: Acadia was far from England. The British could easily lose it because it was hard for them to defend.

Fact: The British had just gained control of the area. They were afraid they would lose it.

Fact: The homes and possessions of the Acadians were burned. Their lands were confiscated.

Fact: The British required that the Acadians take an oath of allegiance to England; the Acadians refused and tried to fight back.

Fact: The people were placed on ships. In the process, families were separated.

Fact: Ships unloaded the people all along the American coast. Some were taken as far as Louisiana. Some families were never reunited.

Projecting a Tentative Judgment –
Forms That Judgments Can Take

Judgments can take many different forms: forced choice among several given options, rating of options along a continuum, and creation of a statement of position. The differences can be seen in the teaching sequence given below.

To Whom Does She Belong? A Decision to Make

A third-grade class listened as their teacher orally shared the first part of the Russian folktale *The Woman of the Wood*, stopping before the end as shown in this shortened version:

Three men, overtaken by nightfall in the woods, entertained one another by telling stories. As they passed the time, the wood-carver among them whittled away at a piece of wood; by morning, he had carved a woman out of the wood. The second man, a tailor, quickly plied his craft to produce clothing that made the woman beautiful to behold. The third, a teacher, taught her to talk and to use words to think. The result was a brilliant and lovely woman whom each man claimed as his own. To resolve the problem of who should get the woman, the three went to the old wise man of the kingdom and asked: "Will you help us with our problem? To whom should this woman belong?" The old man replied. . . .

At this point in the tale, the teacher asked: "You are this old wise man; you have only three choices—the wood-carver, the tailor, the teacher; you must give the woman to one of these three. On a piece of paper make a chart like this:

My Judgment
The Wood-carver _____
The Tailor _____
The Teacher _____

Mark 1 next to your first choice, 2 next to your second choice, and 3 next to the least deserving. Be ready to explain why you chose as you did."

Later after the children had shared their ratings and orally explained the reasons behind each, the problem changed. The teacher directed: "Now write an original ending to the story in which you create your own solution—one that would be the fairest to all. Again be ready to tell why your solution is the fair one." Class time was spent listening to the endings that individuals had proposed. As children talked together, it gradually became clear that the woman should be given to none of the three. She belonged to herself and could not be given. She had a right as a human being to choose her own destiny.

In this story-based lesson sequence, two different kinds of judgments are being rendered. The first is a forced choice in which the wise person has to rank order a series of given options. Sometimes value decisions in real life require this type of judgmental ordering; the ranker, looking at a series of options, must decide which is the most deserving (or best, or most advisable, or most worthwhile), which is the next most deserving, and so on. This is what people actually do when they choose among candidates at an election.

Forced choices can take other forms as well. Some value decisions require accepting or rejecting with no in-between choices possible; the

T See Algernon Black, *The Woman of the Wood* (New York: Holt, Rinehart & Winston, 1973). It provides a finely illustrated version of the tale. Another book that can also serve as the content for value decision making is Robert L. Stevenson, *The Touchstone* (New York: Greenwillow Books, 1976). Use it with older students.

decision is either for or against, yes or no—a kind of decision people often must make in voting on issues, in determining guilt, and in deciding whether or not to carry out some questionable act. In other instances, the rating scale is more comprehensive: agrees enthusiastically, agrees to some extent, is neutral toward, disagrees to some extent, disagrees strongly.

Still other decisions require more than choosing from among given options. The person judging must analyze a situation and project an original solution—a "right" course of action, or perhaps even a series of possible options with the pros and cons outlined. Clearly under these conditions developing a value judgment is a creative as well as a moral thinking activity.

Rendering a Tentative Judgment – Ways to Project Them

The previous discussion alludes to concrete forms that tentative classroom ratings, rankings, and creative solutions to dilemmas can take. One form is voting by show of hands or by ballot. A show of hands on an issue has the advantage of asking all class members to express their opinions without speaking; it is a workable way to get young people thinking tentatively about almost any value-filled question.

Sidney Simon et al. (1972) describe a slightly more sophisticated form that classroom voting can take. Students express shades of feeling on an issue by waving their hands thumbs up to say "I agree strongly."; holding their hands thumbs up to say "I agree."; crossing their arms and holding them motionless to say "I have no opinion."; holding their hands thumbs down to say "I disagree."; and waving their hands thumbs down to say "I disagree strongly." Again this nonverbal means of offering an opinion is a simple but effective way to get children and young people to render a tentative opinion without speaking up; everyone participates, and the shy youngster who may hesitate to speak is not put on the spot.

An effective means of encouraging young people to rank order a series of events, human actions, or personalities according to their feelings toward each is the evils board—a chart listing and perhaps describing a number of different but related items to be ranked. Given a duplicated evils board, students record a 1 next to the worst evil on the board, 2 next to the evil not quite so bad, and so forth down the line. Evils boards can be devised on almost any topic students are investigating. Figure 6.7 shows one that a sixth-grade teacher, developing an ecology unit with his students, devised. On the line next to the name of the offender, students placed their individual rankings, leaving the second line for later use during group reconsideration of judgments.

R From Sidney Simon et al., *Values Clarification* (New York: Hart Publishing, 1972), pp.38-41. This book contains many specific ideas for classroom activity.

R From Dorothy Hennings, *Communication in Action*. (Chicago: Rand McNally, 1978).

Figure 6.7
An Example of an Evils Board

A Pollution Evils Board

The Litterbug _____ _____

A man is driving along an open stretch of interstate highway. He decides to have some candy, so he opens a package, pops a piece into his mouth, and tosses the wrapper out the window.

The Smokestack _____ _____

A large electrical generating plant produces power by burning a high sulfur coal. It emits thick gases into the air.

The Hog _____ _____

A child asks for an extra big piece of dessert, but finds that he or she is too full to eat the whole thing and leaves the rest to be thrown out.

The Dumper _____ _____

An oil tanker cleans its tanks by dumping what is left offshore. The oil washes ashore, gumming up miles of beach and marshland.

The Puffer _____ _____

The sign in the crowded, unventilated room reads: "No Smoking." A woman lights a cigarette and smokes until the room is filled with smoke.

Similar evils boards can be devised that list a series of

1. Wars—the Civil War, the Spanish-American War, World War I, World War II, the Vietnam War;
2. Infamous people from history, such as from the period of the American Revolution: King George III, Aaron Burr, Benedict Arnold;
3. Acts against society—treason, looting, failure to pay taxes;
4. Uninviting places to live—desert, jungle, polar ice cap;
5. Social problems—inflation, unemployment, crime.

In each case, students rank order the evils from least to most infamous.

Variations on the evils board are almost endless: most worthy person, most disliked or liked activity, most important or unimportant concern, most desirable or undesirable job, to suggest just a few. Young people can help devise value boards by brainstorming many persons, activities, concerns, or jobs they like or dislike or consider important or unimportant. Five or six of the items brainstormed can be grouped together as a values board, with items then ranked according to preferences. David Wallechinsky's *The Book of Lists* (New York: William Morrow & Co., 1977) supplies the teacher with some unique listings to

R David Wallechinsky's book, *The Book of Lists* (New York: William Morrow & Co. 1977), is a teacher, not a student reference.

be used in this way; Wallechinsky cites the five most hated and feared persons in history, the five most beloved heroes or heroines, the five worst dictators, the ten most beautiful words, and so on. Students can compile their own listings of these, rank order the items, and compare their results to those found in *The Book of Lists*.

Other concrete forms that can be used to incorporate less structured value judgments include:

1. The creative drawing—Younger children draw pictures that show the best action to take, the way they feel about something, an activity they like best, or the thing they value most. Later, during class talk time, youngsters share their pictures and tell their preferences.
2. The creative composition—Students write down what they consider the fair ending to a story, create a story of their own that shows their feelings on an issue, or devise several different endings to a story. Again oral sharing provides an opportunity for discussion of right and wrong.
3. The values card—On an index card, each student records in no more than two or three sentences his or her original solution to a value-laden dilemma. Dilemmas can be ones that occur in the present, that happened in the past, or that come up in stories.

Testing the Judgment

T Note: The word *testing* as used here is unrelated to the evaluation of performance. Rather it means, "the trial of the quality of something," as in the expression *to put to the test*. See *The American College Dictionary* (Random House).

Perhaps the single most important operation in value judging as it occurs in classrooms is testing the judgment. Judgments, after all, are not facts; rather they represent a personal interpretation of the facts. For that reason, young people should have continual opportunities to look at the judgments they have made, testing each against the facts and identifying the underlying assumptions.

Identifying Specifics. The key to getting children to review their value judgments is the verbal request that begins: "Give one specific thing. . . ." Thus children who indicate a liking for a person out of their history books, a personality of today, or a character in a novel may be asked to give one specific thing that the person did that made the children like him or her. Conversely, when children express a dislike, they can be asked to give one specific incident or act that accounts for their feelings. With more complex situations, young people can be requested to give one major advantage of the action they propose, and one major disadvantage. If several students participate in the oral search for specifics, the result will be a listing of evidence in support of a judgment or against it. Faced with such a listing, students sometimes find themselves reversing their original decision.

Trying to Reach a Consensus.   The process of arriving at a group consensus based on individual judgments is another way that young people can reconsider their thinking on issues and can begin to identify underlying assumptions—beliefs that they hold. For example, students who individually have identified the greatest hero of the Civil War as part of their investigation of forces at work during that period of American history can form small consensus teams whose task is to select one hero from among all those proposed by individual members.

Consensus comes about through discussion of the pros and cons behind the selection of each candidate—pros and cons that are listed on a judgment slate—a large sheet of charting paper that can be mounted on an easel for later sharing before the entire class. Consensus comes also through voting, with the majority view becoming the group view. It is this majority view that the group presents to the class in a "defend your choice" session. Individuals who object strenuously to the group view have the option of presenting a minority opinion.

Defending a Decision.   With young people in upper elementary grades a "defend your choice" session guided by the teacher is a productive technique to get students to consider the beliefs, biases, and values they hold that shape their ultimate choices. For example, the teacher should ask students who have selected their Civil War hero, "Why does that deed make him or her a hero or heroine? What was so great about doing that?" In response, students will begin to project such statements as "because he was thinking about other people's needs," or "because she overcame despite overwhelming odds." These statements lead to identification of fundamental assumptions upon which the students function in selecting specific heroes: "a hero is someone who thinks about other people's needs," and "a hero is someone who works for something in which he or she believes," and "a hero is someone who overcomes the impossible." Formed into a chart, these hero factors, as they can be called, function as criteria against which students can evaluate other choices.

Opportunities for defending a judgment abound in the social studies. Within almost any period of history, young people can select or rank villains and heroes, the single most magnificent act of the period and the most evil one, the worst problems, the greatest contribution to civilization, the worst disaster, the greatest discovery, and the most significant event of the period. Likewise, students investigating problems of today can select or rank the most important changes that should take place in their community, the heroes of their own community, or the most needed new recreational facility.

At times, action follows decision-making as youngsters
undertake a community clean-up project.

Taking Action Based on a Decision

R A quotation to think
about: "Every day,
every one of us meets
life situations which call
for thought, opinion
making, decision mak-
ing, and action. . . .
Everything we do, every
decision we make and
course of action we take
is based on our con-
sciously or uncon-
sciously held beliefs, attitudes, and values."
Sidney Simon (1972,
p.13).

Throughout this discussion, two terms—**decision** and **judgment**—have
been used almost interchangeably because both are generally
applied to the process through which people look at all sides of a
value-laden question and come up with a relatively subjective answer
or solution. A distinction can be made between the two words, however. In the case of a decision, once a solution has been arrived at, the
decision maker takes action based on it. Deciding that the best way to
spend one's money is to buy books, he or she goes out and does just
that. The wisdom of a decision can be tested through action. One
discovers that, regardless of the preliminary thought that went into its
formulation, the decision did not lead to the projected outcomes. In
contrast, a judgment generally is a statement of opinion replete with
the reasons that support it. Although a personal judgment may be told
to someone else and, therefore, have consequences, it is rarely put to
the test of action.

At some point, children in schools should be asked to make decisions
that result in action. Some of these can take the form of real decisions
about genuine classroom concerns. Children who have judged the
food in the school cafeteria as not good may also decide to do some-

thing about it. They may write a letter to the cafeteria head itemizing their specific concerns and making suggestions for change. That there may be unpleasant repercussions from a decision carefully thought out and implemented may become apparent to children who undertake such a project. Similarly, young people can take action by writing letters to the editor of a local paper on a community issue, by conducting a local public relations campaign in their school or community, or by speaking with concerned citizens such as the principal, or superintendent of schools, or mayor. In chapter 15, the reader will find some specific activities for this kind of social action based on decisions rendered.

In addition, students can make **decisions in retrospect**–decisions of the past in which they become involved even as they study past events. An example will clarify this instructional strategy, which is developed more fully in chapter 12. Note the structure of the sequence inherent in "Andrew Jackson's Dilemma." This sequence is 1. introduction of the facts of the case; 2. clarification of the facts and the issues; 3. tentative decision making; 4. testing the decision through group talk and through comparison to the actual decision made "back then"; 5. reconsidering the specific moral principles inherent in the situation.

An Example of Decision Making in Retrospect: Andrew Jackson's Dilemma

Step I: Introduction of Background Information Bearing on the Problem.

Children gather data through listening, reading, or viewing a filmstrip that sets forth this information:

In 1814 Andrew Jackson, allied with a number of Indian tribes, fought against and defeated the Red Sticks at the Battle of Horseshoe Bend. After that battle, a general peace reigned between the Creeks, Cherokees, Seminoles, Choctaws, and Chickasaws and the United States government, and many of the Indians who had fought beside Jackson considered him their friend. In 1828 Jackson became president of the United States. By then, Georgia had claimed rights over the lands of the Creeks and the Cherokees. Georgia said that the Cherokees had to obey Georgia law, not their own, and that the Indians could not have a separate government. Georgia asked the U.S. government to evict the Indians so that they could have complete power over Cherokee land.

The Cherokees hired a lawyer and argued the case before the U.S. Supreme Court. The Court decided in favor of the Indians. Now it was up to Jackson to decide whether to support the Court's decision and let the Indians stay on the land or whether to allow

T Information is from the filmstrip, "Jackson's Indian Policy," available through Modern Learning Aids.

the Georgians to force the Indians off. What made this a dilemma for Jackson was that he knew that the settlers would never allow the Indians to live in peace on the land. There would always be war. There would always be continued killing. Jackson had been a soldier. He knew that war and killing meant endless suffering. He hated war.

Step II: Clarifying the Facts and the Issues.

The teacher asks questions that get students to identify key facts and issues in the case: "Why was Jackson considered a friend of the Indians? Why didn't the Indians want to follow the laws of the state of Georgia? What did Georgia want the Supreme Court to rule in the case? How did the Indians hope the case would turn out? What was the Court's ruling? Why did this pose a dilemma for Jackson? Why did he want the wars to end?"

Step III: Projecting a Tentative Decision.

The teacher presents the decision that young people must make: "If you were Jackson, what would you do? Make the Indians leave? Let them stay? Do something else? On this decision sheet, write down your own decision. Later we will form groups to talk about our reasons and see if each group can agree on what was the right decision. Be sure to think out and write down the reasons why you made the decision you did." Items on the decision sheet include: "What would I do if I were Jackson; my first reason for doing this; my second reason; our group's decision; our reasons."

Step IV: Testing the Decision Through Group Thought—Arriving at a Consensus.

Have the children divide into consensus groups comprised of no more than five members. They develop a decision based on individual ones.

Step V: Defending the Decision.

Groups present their ideas to the reassembled class.

Step VI: Comparing the Decision in Retrospect to the One Jackson Made.

The teacher explains to the class that Jackson decided to expel the Indians, even though they were his friends and the Supreme Court had ruled for them. He or she then asks listener to 1. compare Jackson's decision to theirs, 2. hypothesize why he acted as he did, 3. consider the effect that emotions can play on a decision, and 4. consider why people often make decisions in retrospect that are different from those made by individuals operating within the situation.

Step VII: Rating Acts on a Continuum.

Ask the children in groups to rank order the following series of acts. At the top of the continuum they place the act they would consider most strongly when making a value decision; at the bottom they place the one to which they would give the least consideration when they are forced to make choices between things they value highly.

The Items to evaluate: telling the truth; standing by one's friends; keeping a promise; following the law; taking only that which honestly belongs to one. (Students write the given items on the lines by the numbers they choose by group consensus. Figure 6.6.)

Figure 6.8
A Continuum

Note: 1 = most valued item; 5 = least valued item.

Decisions in retrospect tend to be rather sophisticated. Because of this, use is restricted to upper elementary grades when students have a more highly developed sense of time and a more finely tuned ability to make distinctions among possible options. Young children in primary grades have still only limited powers to make decisions that involve value questions as the section to follow will point out.

Moral Reasoning in Children

Studies by Kohlberg (1971) and others suggest that there are six stages through which people pass as they develop their moral and ethical powers. These stages are listed in Figure 6.9.

According to Kohlberg's research, most adult Americans function at Stage 3 or 4. Most children tend to reason at Stage 1, although some function at higher stages. This means that most children are operating in terms of what authority figures say and reflect primarily on the punishment and reward aspects that follow a behavior act. From Kohlberg's point of view, a school should provide opportunities for children to handle dilemma-type problems that force them to operate

Figure 6.9
Kohlberg's Stages of Moral Reasoning

R Adapted from Lawrence Kohlberg and Elliot Turiel, "Moral Development and Moral Education," in *Psychology and Educational Practice*, edited by G. Lesser (Chicago: Scott, Foresman & Co., 1971), pp. 415-416. Titles given to the stages are not necessarily Kohlberg's but represent summarizations that simplify the ideas.

The Preconventional Level

Stage 1: The Punishment and Obedience Stage—At this point, people make value decisions based on earning rewards or preventing punishments. They make judgments in terms of what will please those with authority over them. Functioning at this level, the decision maker says, "I will not do that. I will get punished if I do." Or, "That is wrong because Daddy said so."

Stage 2: The I'll Scratch Your Back If You'll Scratch Mine Stage—People judge in terms of pragmatic effects. Justice is interpreted in terms of the old adage "a tooth for a tooth." What is fair or good is what best meets one's own needs.

The Conventional Level

Stage 3: The Mutual Satisfaction Stage—What is good is judged in terms of what pleases and helps others and gets their approval in return. Reasoners consider the intent as well as extenuating circumstances in rendering a judgment.

Stage 4: The Law and Order Stage—The thinker reasons in terms of fixed rules, doing one's duty, respecting authority, and maintaining the general social order for its own sake.

The Principled Level

Stages 5 and 6: People reason according to moral principles such as respect for human personality, liberty, justice, and equality. These principles have validity apart from the authority of the groups to which people belong.

R There is an element of controversy about Kohlberg's ideas. See Jack Fraenkel, "The Kohlberg Bandwagon: Some Reservations," in *Social Education*, 40 (April 1976): 216-222. It suggests that the stages of moral development explained by Kohlberg must be interpreted rather generally until they are supported by further research.

at a moral level slightly above what they typically do. Research suggests that it is possible to move children up the moral reasoning ladder to higher levels through programs that involve them in discussion of dilemmas. Kohlberg and associates advocate use of hypothetical or real-life moral dilemmas. One could hypothesize that dilemmas from history and stories would be equally effective and would bring the added advantage of letting children become familiar with important events from their own nation's past—events that could conceivably recur in the future.

Valuing Activities: A Summary Listing

Here are some brief ideas for general types of valuing activities that can be modified for use in a variety of classroom contexts:

1. Character Boxes. Young people who have completed the reading of stories and novels record the names of characters on slips of paper and drop those slips into pairs of boxes—one pair labeled good and evil; one labeled shrewd and stupid, etc. By doing this, students begin to see that evil characters can be shrewd, while good characters can at times act stupidly.

2. The Events Line. As students encounter events in a sequence, they make a label for each and clip it to a clothesline suspended across the classroom. Later they return to analyze and judge the items and hang a second label bearing a judgmental rating beneath each event—ratings such as "This was an unwise move because . . . "; "This was a fair act because . . . "; "This was a considerate act because . . . ."

3. The Personalities Line. Names of personalities encountered in a social investigation can be strung out in similar fashion along a clothesline with clothespins. Names can be printed on paper of various colors, each color representing a rank order along a five-point scale. People from the past who made the greatest contributions are ranked A and recorded on a red piece of construction paper, those with the next greatest contribution are awarded a B and recorded on orange, and so forth.

4. The Judgment Calendar. An ongoing activity in primary grades, especially in kindergarten and first grade, is the judgment calendar. At the close of the school day, children gather to talk about what they have accomplished as a class. On the calendar they record a symbolic rating next to the appropriate date (a five-star day, a four-star day, and so forth) as they give reasons to support their ratings.

5. The Problems Staircase. A visual way of setting out a series of ranked items is along a staircase (figure 6.10). In the case of problems being identified, students record the least critical problems on the bottom steps, and the most critical problems on the upper ones. The stair format can actually be used to rank personalities, acts, or things liked and disliked. If groups do this, they quickly discover that there is no correct way of ranking items. Different groups rank a series in different ways.

R For other specific ideas see:

Jack Fraenkel, *Helping Children Think and Value* (Englewood Cliffs, New Jersey: Prentice-Hall, 1973).

Leland Howe and Mary Howe, *Personalizing Education: Values Clarification and Beyond* (Philadelphia: Center for Humanistic Education, 1975).

Social Education. 39:16-39, January 1975. The issue focuses on moral education.

The School's Role as Moral Authority (Washington, D.C.: Association for Supervision and Curriculum Development, 1977).

James Jelinek, *Improving the Human Condition: A Curricular Response to Critical Realities* (Washington, D.C.: ASCD, 1978).

Figure 6.10
A Values Staircase

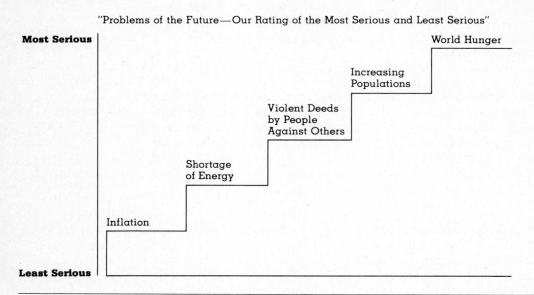

"Problems of the Future—Our Rating of the Most Serious and Least Serious"

Most Serious

World Hunger

Increasing
Populations

Violent Deeds
by People
Against Others

Shortage
of Energy

Inflation

Least Serious

Note: This values staircase represents one group's ranking. Of course, other individuals or groups
may rank items differently.

**6. Books: A Background of Data by Analyzing Reading
Materials.**   Decision making not only can take place as part of social
studies units; it can also occur as children are involved in stories as
part of the reading and literature program. Many stories—even some
encountered in basic reading books—have a value lesson that can
serve as content for a classroom judgment session. Children who have
listened to or read a story can go back to identify the facts contained in
the selection that are important in rendering a value judgment about
story characters, acts, and events.

Thinking and Valuing – A Summary Thought or Two

The teacher is the crucial variable in determining how social studies
subject matter is approached in classrooms. Chapter 1 outlined the
major understandings emanating from the social disciplines—
understandings that are fundamental if people are to interpret the
complex interaction of forces within human experience. There is not

one way that this subject content can be studied, but the way that it is handled shapes the use it will have as young people approach other problem situations in their futures. If understandings are presented as facts to be learned, little transfer will result, for students will not have acquired the requisite cognitive operations; they will have simply become proficient memorizers.

If, on the other hand, students operate intellectually on the world around them, they begin to develop the cognitive processes so essential to their future social functioning—ability to conceptualize, to generalize, to apply knowledge by predicting and hypothesizing, to make value judgments and decisions, and to look back to test their decisions, hypotheses, and predictions against the evidence that is available and actions they try out.

Teachers make this possible through the kinds of questions they ask and through the instructional activities they structure. Questions should be ones that nudge students to move up the thinking ladder. Activities should be structured so that the sequence of instruction more or less follows the sequence inherent in the thinking process: 1) data gathering, 2) data processing, 3) abstracting. Teaching and learning start inductively with the children going on later to apply their growing understanding of generalizations and principles deductively to the interpretation of new situations and the formulation of other decisions. This framework—based on steps in thinking—differs considerably from a teaching scheme in which the teacher begins by telling the students the principle, the category, the conclusion, the hypothesis, or the meaning for them to learn and repeat on another day.

A Problem to Ponder

Can you design an activity through which young people in upper elementary grades make a decision in retrospect? Check again on the structure and sequence incorporated in *Andrew Jackson's Dilemma*, pages 207–209. Following the design of that activity, create a similar sequence called *Franklin Roosevelt's Dilemma*. In 1942 America was at war with Italy, Germany, and Japan. People living on the West Coast feared invasion by Japan. At that time rumors and fears arose about the loyalty of the Japanese-Americans. Newspapers and even respected journalists wrote about suspected acts of sabotage against the war effort and many suspected the Japanese-Americans of initiating these acts. On February 13, 1942, President Roosevelt had before him Executive Order 9066, authorizing the forced evacuation of all people of Japanese ancestry, citizens and noncitizens alike, who were living on the West Coast. Roosevelt's dilemma was, "Should he sign this order that would intern these people without due process and take from them their liberty and property?"

In designing your activity sequence:

1. Use the information given above plus additional points you acquire through your reading. A good source to read is *Journey to Topaz* (New York: Charles Scribner's Sons, 1971) by Yoshiko Uchida, which tells of the incident from the point of view of a Japanese girl who experienced the event.
2. Remember not to tell the participants in the decision making how Roosevelt decided.
3. Devise a series of questions through which you could help young people probe key facts and issues.
4. Devise a sheet on which participants could record their decisions with reasons.

If you intend to work or are currently working with primary level children, create a valuing session based on a children's book of your own choosing. If you cannot find a book you consider appropriate, use Evaline Ness' *Sam, Bangs and Moonshine* (New York: Holt, Rinehart & Winston, 1966) or Byrd Baylor's *Hawk, I'm Your Brother* (New York: Charles Scribner's Sons, 1976).

References

Beyer, Barry. *Inquiry in the Social Studies Classroom: A Strategy for Teaching.* Columbus, Ohio: Charles E. Merrill, 1971.

Bloom, Benjamin; and Krathwohl, David R. *Taxonomy of Educational Objectives: Handbook I: Cognitive Domain.* New York: Longman, 1956.

Fair, Jean; and Shaftel, Fannie, eds. *Effective Thinking in the Social Studies: 37th Yearbook of National Council for the Social Studies.* Arlington, Virginia: NCSS, 1967.

Fraenkel, Jack. *Helping Children Think and Value.* Englewood Cliffs, New Jersey: Prentice-Hall, 1973.

Howe, Leland; and Howe, Mary. *Personalizing Education: Values Clarification and Beyond.* Philadelphia: Center for Humanistic Education, 1975.

Kohlberg, Lawrence; and Turiel, Elliot. "Moral Development and Moral Education," *Psychology and Educational Practice,* ed. by G. Lesser. Glenview, Ill.: Scott, Foresman and Co. 1971.

Krathwohl, David; Bloom, Benjamin; and Masia, Bertram. *Taxonomy of Educational Objectives, The Classification of Educational Goals, Handbook II: Affective Domain.* New York: David McKay, 1964.

Kurfman, Dana, ed. *Developing Decision-Making Skills: 47th Yearbook of National Council for the Social Studies.* Arlington, Virginia: NCSS, 1977.

Meehan, Eugene. *Value Judgment and Social Science.* Homewood, Illinois: Dorsey Press, 1969.

Metcalf, Lawrence, ed. *Values Education: 41st Yearbook of National Council for Social Studies.* Arlington, Virginia: NCSS, 1971.

Raths, Louis; Harmin, Merrill; and Simon, Sidney. *Values and Teaching: Working with Values in the Classroom,* 2nd ed. Columbus, Ohio: Charles E. Merrill, 1978.

Shaver, James. *Facing Value Decisions: Rationale Building for Teachers.* Belmont, California: Wadsworth, 1976.

Simon, Sidney; Howe, Leland; and Kirschenbaum, Howard. *Values Clarification: A Handbook of Practice Strategies for Teachers and Students.* New York: Hart Publishing, 1972.

Social Education, 39 (January 1975) issue focus—"Moral Education: Learning to Weigh Human Values."

Social Education, 40 (April 1976) issue focus—"Cognitive-Developmental Approach to Moral Education."

Taba, Hilda. *Teachers' Handbook for Elementary Social Studies.* Palo Alto, California: Addison-Wesley, 1967.

Taba, Hilda; Levine, Samuel; and Elzey, Freeman. "Thinking in Elementary School Children." Mimeographed. San Francisco: San Francisco State College, 1964.

Williams, David M.; and Wright, Ian. "Values and Moral Education: Analyzing Curriculum Materials." *The Social Studies,* 67 (July/August 1977): 166-172.

Williams, Norman; and Williams, Sheila. *The Moral Development of Children.* New York: Macmillan, 1970.

Part Three   The Individual in the Social Studies

It is the common wonder
of all (people), how
among so many millions
of faces there should be
none alike.

Sir Thomas Browne,
Religio Medici

A primary goal of the social studies curriculum is the development of individuals who are able to function successfully with others in groups and at the same time maintain their unique identities. Truly, among the millions of people who live on earth, no two are alike. This uniqueness is a valuable resource for the future, in which each person must contribute to the betterment of all.

Part III of this book focuses on the needs of individual learners within a group. Chapter 7 describes ways of organizing the classroom so that the uniqueness of the person is not lost, yet children learn to interact smoothly with one another. Chapter 8 highlights special needs of children: boys and girls, the gifted and talented, the slow learner, the sensory impaired, the physically handicapped, minorities, immigrants, and migrants. It describes ways of meeting diverse needs in a classroom in which all children are being mainstreamed. Chapter 9 explains the characteristics of younger children and strategies to use in teaching social studies to those in nursery and primary schools. The last chapter in the section, chapter 10, sets forth a design in which evaluation becomes an integral part of teaching and learning.

7 The Person in the Group: Organizing the Social Studies Class

Today is Thursday, January 2l, 1979. The temperature is 30°. I like Kristin because she's my friend and Alice and Annette and Kathy too.

Kathy has many friends.

not specific
no levels of moral reasoning

This self - a dot, a speck, a shadow - is from one point of view quite near to nothing. Yet it is everything . . . . It is the center of ultimate significance in the life of each person. It is the core of individual existence. It is the only existence you or I can know.

Arthur Jersild,
***When Teachers Face Themselves* (New York: Teachers College Press, 1955)**

Key Questions

What is meant by the term *self?* Why is it important for a person to develop a healthy self-concept?

How can teachers help children know themselves more fully?

What is meant by a "future-focused role image"? How can teachers help children identify futures options for themselves?

How can teachers help children accept the uniqueness they see within themselves? How can teachers help children appreciate differences in other people? How are the two learnings related?

For what purposes can total class instruction be used? How can activities be organized to achieve each of these purposes?

How can teachers use learning centers to personalize learning? How can teachers use independent study projects to meet individual needs?

On what basis should teachers divide children into work groups? Under what conditions should a teacher choose a particular means of dividing children into groups?

What guidelines can the teacher follow to maintain a classroom free of severe disciplinary problems? Why is this a particular concern of the social studies teacher?

Who are you? Why is your understanding of yourself important as you work closely with children?

Figure 7.1
A Child's Concept of Self

Introduction

Who am I? What do I like to do? What do I not like to do? What things do I do well? What things do I do poorly? What do I look like? How do I usually feel about the world, other people, myself? What is the most important thing in the world to me? What level of performance do I expect of myself? What kind of person am I?

These questions—asked by a person of him- or herself—address that part of the self of which the person is consciously aware. They address what psychologists call the **self-concept.** According to Arthur Jersild:

A person's self is the sum total of all one can call his or hers. The self includes, among other things, a system of ideas, attitudes, values, and commitments. The self is a person's total subjective environment; it is the distinctive center of experience and significance. The self constitutes a person's inner world as distinguished from the outer world consisting of all other people and things.

R From Arthur Jersild, *In Search of Self* (New York: Teachers College Press, 1952).

The self that each person finds within is a unique being, different from other selves. It is this distinctive self that the individual must come to accept fully in order to respond fully to the needs of others. Jersild stresses the relationship between acceptance of self and acceptance of others. He writes, "The self is the citadel of one's own being and worth and the stronghold from which one moves out to others."

The self does not grow within a vacuum; neither does a healthy self-concept. The self develops within a social framework. As Don E. Hamachek explains, if a person were to list the personality characteristics he or she associates with the self, each item would be influenced in some way by social interaction. Through social activity, "one hones his or her perceptions of the outside world, develops interpersonal skills, extends the intelligence, and acquires attitudes about him- or herself." Social interaction is the primary means of expanding self-awareness and understanding.

R From Arthur Jersild, *When Teachers Face Themselves* (New York: Teachers College Press, 1955), p. 135.

R See Don E. Hamachek, *Encounters with the Self* (New York: Holt, Rinehart & Winston, 1971), p. 17.

Heightening Self-Awareness and Understanding: The Search for a Healthy Self-Concept

A major goal of the social studies as set forth in the first chapter of this book is that children should develop both a sense of personal worth and the skills of social interaction as a means of maintaining their personal identities in a crowded world. Clearly at the heart of this goal is heightened self-awareness, understanding, and acceptance; in short, a healthy self-concept. Since it is through interaction with others that a person develops a mental blueprint of the self, to highlight development of a healthy self-concept as a goal of the social studies is not to diminish the importance of contact with others in groups. The person must function within groups in order to find out who he or she really is.

The School and Self-Concept

R From Don E. Hamachek, *Encounters with the Self* (New York: Holt, Rinehart & Winston, 1971). This and the next three paragraphs are based on information contained in chapter 6 of Hamachek, "Self-concept, Academic Adjustment, and Implications for Teaching Practices," pp. 174-225.

In classrooms the search for self goes on continuously. The school plays a powerful role in development of self-concept. As Hamachek writes, the school "dispenses praise and reproof, acceptance and rejection on a colossal scale. School provides not only the stage upon which much of the drama of a person's formative years is played, but it houses the most critical audience in the world—peers and teachers." In school, on a daily basis, children succeed and fail at a variety of academic and social tasks.

Self-concept has a striking impact on children's school achievement, more striking in fact than even basic intelligence. Studies of primary children's growth in reading achievement indicate that youngsters who show signs of a positive self-concept and strong ego in kindergarten are more likely to achieve high reading scores in the second grade than those with a more negative self-image. Measures of self-concept turn out to be better predictors of reading potential than do measures of intelligence. In sum, children quickly decide whether they can or cannot learn, and their perceptions of their own ability become factors in their future school achievement.

R See W. and Clifford Wattenberg, "Relation of Self-Concepts to Beginning Achievement in Reading," *Child Development*. 35:461-467, 1964.

Self-concept also affects personal adjustment in school. Studies by Williams and Cole find a strong relationship between self-concept and emotional adjustment. Children who view themselves in a positive light tend to get along better with their peers not only in school but in social activity. Those who have a negative self-concept and who are underachievers in school are less successful in relating to others. In classrooms this lack of adjustment manifests itself at times as misbehavior.

R See Robert Williams and S. Cole, "Self-Concept and School Adjustment," *Personnel and Guidance Journal*, 47:478-481, 1968.

Psychologists have raised the question of the cause-and-effect relationship between self-concept and school achievement. Does the child come to school with a negative view of the self, which in turn causes lack of achievement? Or does the child's initial failures in learning cause a negative self-concept, which then results in continued failure in school learning? One fact, however, remains clear: a relationship exists between achievement and self-image. If children are to achieve to the greatest capacity possible, schools must help children identify their own strengths so that they begin to feel positively toward themselves.

Successful participation helps children acquire a
positive self-concept.

Knowing the Self

In kindergarten and the early primary grades, children can be helped
toward a better understanding of themselves through activities that
focus directly on their bodies, their likes and dislikes, and on their
strengths, hopes, and plans. Here are some simple ideas that can be
modified for use also in middle grades.

Our Bodies — Here They Are!   Young children can begin to see and
appreciate their uniqueness by finding out more about their own
bodies. For example, try some of the following activities:

1. Measuring and weighing: At different intervals during the kindergarten year, children line up against the wall; the teacher records a mark for each child, a mark that moves up as the youngster grows. Changing weights can also be recorded.

2. Drawing: Children can draw self-portraits or prepare full-sized colored cutouts of themselves. One child lies on a piece of wrapping paper while a friend traces the body outline on the paper. Body shapes are cut out and the resulting forms are colored in. The child's name can be added somewhere on the drawing or cutout. Drawings and cutouts can become part of a large display on the bulletin board.

3. Photographing: Children can take pictures of one another using a camera that produces prints in moments. A self-photograph can be affixed to each child's desk along with a card on which his or her name is written. This makes the desk or table the child's very own.

4. Talking: Children can describe their hands, feet, noses, ears, mouths, and teeth; perhaps a magnifying glass can help them get a close-up view. A book such as Barbara Brenner's *Faces* (New York: Dutton, 1970) will help to get talk started.

My Likes and Dislikes – Here They Are!   Primary and intermediate students can gain a better understanding of their own preferences through these activities:

1. Making a likes or dislikes ladder: Children brainstorm together to list on the board things they like to do. Individually, youngsters select five items and rank them on a likes ladder. On another occasion, children work with their dislikes. They will find that some items appear on both listings, for one person's likes are another's dislikes.

2. Making a personal shield: Having done some preliminary work with identification of preferences, each child can create a personal shield, emblem, or logo that incorporates distinctive characteristics of the self. A student who is skilled with a skateboard, who enjoys swimming, and likes to be with other people a lot may create an emblem that includes a skateboard, water, and people. A second child, who really likes to sketch and paint, likes to help in the classroom, and enjoys his or her bicycle may create a shield in which paints, paint brushes, a bicycle, and people are an integral part. Some youngsters may need considerable help in identifying their interests.

3. Generalizing: Children who have made likes/dislikes ladders and personal shields can study what they have produced to see if they can find any patterns within their choices. Children can ask, "Do I tend to choose activities that relate to sports? books? people?" Teachers must encourage children to accept all pursuits and not deprecate others' preferences.

R To learn the role of the teacher in helping children develop good feelings about themselves, read Peter Brady, "Predicting Self-Concept, Anxiety, and Responsibility from Self-Evaluation and Self-Praise," *Psychology in the Schools,* 15:434-438, July, 1978.

Feelings – Let's Get Acquainted with Ourselves. Children should come to know themselves well enough so they know what excites them and what bores them. Here are some ways to put children in touch with their feelings.

1. *Poems about feelings:* Poems written for young children can help get children to talk about their own feelings. Three brief anthologies, all compiled by Lee Bennett Hopkins, belong on every primary class-room shelf: *Kim's Place* (New York: Holt, Rinehart & Winston, 1974), *Charlie's World* (Indianapolis: Bobbs-Merrill, 1972), and *Me!* (New York: Seabury Press, 1970). These little books are filled with poems that focus on children's perceptions of their own uniqueness. Starting with them, children can create their own poems about how they feel when they look in the mirror, are all alone, have an itch, bump their knees, see their shadows dance on the wall, or take a bath.

T Books like Bill Martin's *David Was Mad* (New York: Holt, Rinehart & Winston, 1967) are excellent for getting children to talk about their own feelings.

2. *Getting the "bugs" out:* Children as well as adults get "bugged" by acts that have a negative impact on them. Often consideration of specific "bugs" can lead to identification of values and principles that children hold dear. An intermediate class can begin by brainstorming acts that bug them. When the board is full, each youngster must select two from the list that he or she feels are the worst offenses people can commit against others. In choosing, each must select bugs that touch on really important, not petty, ideas and come forward to circle the two chosen. The entire class then analyzes the circled items to find out what kinds of acts bother most of us.

T Also ask children what machine they would like to be if they could be a machine for just one day and why they chose as they did.

Developing a Future-Focused Role Image

One component of a healthy and maturing self-concept is a realistic **future-focused role image** – FFRI as Harold Shane terms it. According to Shane, children need to delineate realistic, motivating concepts of the options they have in working toward a "life-role that brings satisfaction and promises self-respect and dignity." Young people today need to see themselves in "tomorrow's world of work." Shane points out that so-called prestige jobs employ only a small percentage of the work force and that "dignity, respect, and other rewards" can be achieved in "any one of many socially useful jobs." Viewed in these terms, realistic future-focused role images must be based on clear understanding of one's own talents and limitations, of pursuits that bring personal joy and contentment, and of the opportunities – the future's options – that will exist. Without this preparation, the young adults of tomorrow will "become psychologically corroded by frustration as they begin to realize that they have failed to find room at the top and as a consequence are dissatisfied as production workers, sales personnel, technicians, and so on."

R Read Harold Shane, *The Educational Significance of the Future* (Bloomington, Indiana: Phi Delta Kappa Educational Foundation, 1973), p. 46.

Idea Page

T Skeletal poem struc-
tures are from Marcy
Cromley, "Skeletal
Poems," *Journal of
Reading.* 19:292-3,
January, 1976.

Skeletal poems can be used to put children in touch with their feelings about themselves. Marcy Cromley suggests two patterns children's me-poems can take.

Me

I am _____ .

I feel _____ when

People _____ themselves.

Yesterday I was _____ .

Tomorrow I'll be _____ .

But today I am _____ .

Being me is _____

Because _____ .

I am "up" when _____ .

I am "down" when _____ .

I need _____

To keep me _____ .

Without _____ I am _____ .

But with _____ I can _____ .

I am Me! Who are You?

Who am I?

My parents think I'm _____ .

My friends think I'm _____ .

And I know that I'm _____ .

Sometimes I'm _____ .

Other times I'm _____ .

Most of the time I'm _____ .

I have a name; it's _____ .

I have a _____

That makes me different from
all the rest.

When I find out who I am

I will _____ .

Then everyone will _____

And ask, "_____?"

Sometimes I think _____ .

And life _____ .

But then _____

And _____ .

If I don't find "me"–

Perhaps _____ –

If you can help me–

_____

Children simply put their own perceptions into the given skeletal structure as Jerry did in his me-poem.

Me
I am Jerry.
I feel good when
People are nice to themselves.

Yesterday I was climbing trees.
Tomorrow I'll be riding my bike.
But today I am in school.

Being me is great
Because it is adventurous.

I am "up" when things are okay.
I am "down" when people are mad at me.
I need friends to keep me having fun.
Without friends I am bored.
But with friends I can have
lots and lots of fun.

Identifying Talents and Limitations. That each person has unique talents and limitations is a fact of life. Even the most talented individual has areas in which he or she has trouble being successful. Schools need to help youngsters identify talents upon which they can build and accept their limitations in ability, interest, and resources.

1. A talents analysis: Children can participate in a self-talent search. Youngsters begin by focusing first on a person who is highly respected—perhaps the president of their country or a well-known person of past or present who has contributed to an area in which they may wish to contribute themselves. They first list obvious talents of the person selected for analysis, then limitations. From their lists—completed through reading and researching—children begin to see that everyone has both strengths and weaknesses and that there are no perfect people in the world. This generalization develops naturally if each student works with a different noted person. It paves the way for the second half of the activity: honest and realistic identification of one's own strengths and weaknesses. Figure 7.2 is a chart on which upper graders can record these types of comparative data.

T Children can do the same with their successes and failures, starting first with successes and failures of a highly admired person and then considering their own.

2. Weaknesses That Need Not Be: At some point, children who have identified talents and weaknesses should study weaknesses listed and star those they might be able to overcome. The teacher can ask older students to select just one weakness that they can conquer with effort, outline a plan for conquering it, and then implement that plan.

Identifying Role Options, or Future Alternatives for the Self. Ask young children what they want to be "when they grow up," and typically they respond by identifying roles that are very common in the society. Schools can help young people expand their understanding of the wide range of alternative futures open to them. As part of social studies, career options should be enumerated. All youngsters can identify possible futures, the tasks workers perform in each selected job area, and the preparation required. The result of such study is the selection of several different future alternatives for the self in accordance with one's talents, strengths, and interests.

**Figure 7.2
A Self-Study Form for Assessing
Strengths and Weaknesses**

Talents and Weaknesses

Harriet Tubman   and _____

(your name here)

Harriet Tubman's Self

Her strengths or talents   Her weaknesses or handicaps

_____

_____

_____

_____

Self _____

(your name here)

My strengths or talents   My weaknesses or handicaps

_____

_____

_____

_____

This activity can begin as early as first grade. Each youngster selects three or more vocations to consider for the future. Either by writing down or by dictating to a teacher, the youngster lists what workers in each chosen job do and what things inside the self make the child want to do that work. "My Future" can be developed as individual charts on which the youngster pastes a self-portrait in the center and pictures of workers performing the chosen jobs around it.

Although clearly, as Harold Shane reminds, room in the most prestigious professions is limited, children should not be discouraged from identifying realistic options and nonstereotyped role alternatives. Girls and boys should consider options in the same manner; members of all ethnic groups have the right to work toward the same kinds of alternative futures. Children with physical handicaps should not feel that their futures must be limited. (Chapter 8 will explore these points in greater detail.)

Here particularly, children need **role models**—individuals who have successfully overcome hardships and limitations and have made real contributions. Communities are filled with individuals who find self-fulfillment and contribute to others through their jobs. To help children see all forms of honest work as a means of attaining self-respect and personal dignity, workers who visit the classroom should be representative of a variety of jobs—not just those who have made it to the top of their chosen professions. A good telephone-line worker, a happy laboratory assistant, and the manager of the corner variety store are models for children who are identifying alternative futures for themselves.

In addition, children need **value models**—people whose lives represent or represented the principles inherent in a democracy: belief in equality of opportunity for all, respect for the individual, and belief in justice and freedom. In this context, books are helpful, for in books children can read of a Martin Luther King (See Eve Merriam's *I Am a Man* [New York: Doubleday, 1971]), of an Elizabeth Blackwell (See Jean Latham's *Elizabeth Blackwell: Pioneer Woman Doctor* [New Canaan, Connecticut: Garrard, 1975]), or of a Roberto Clemente (See Jerry Brondfield's *Roberto Clemente, Pride of the Pirates* [Garrard, 1976]). Through reading, students gather data to incorporate in good times and hard times charts. Children can work again with the charts they have prepared (Fig. 7.2). The label "Good Times and Achievements" now heads the left column; "Bad Times and Failures" heads the right. Children can generalize from their charts: "What was most important to this person? In what did he or she believe? Why was he or she so willing to work and struggle so hard?" Children can apply their learnings to their own lives: "What have been my failures and successes so far? What good times have I enjoyed? What hard times have I already overcome?"

Accepting and Respecting the Uniqueness That Is the Self

Anthropologists have placed considerable emphasis in the past on the similarities that unite people. Similarities are unquestionably important, but diversity obviously exists too—a diversity that enriches the entire world. It is through the unique combination of qualities possessed that a person or culture makes a contribution. It is through uniqueness that one achieves a complete sense of personal identity. By respecting the distinctiveness that is oneself, a person is better able to respect differences in others.

Acceptance and respect for the uniqueness of each individual and culture should be developed through elementary social studies. Too often children get the feeling that to be different is for some reason to be unacceptable. The short child and the big one, the fast learner and the slower one, the quiet youngster and the loud one, the left-handed child, and the one with an uncommon name are all made to feel unacceptably different in a society that seems to put a premium on group norms. The person must maintain a unique identity if he or she is to acquire a sense of personal worth.

On Becoming a Person.   The character of Peter in Ezra Jack Keats' books is a favorite of children in kindergarten and first grade. In the first of the series, *The Snowy Day*, Peter experiences his first snow. A nursery-aged youngster, he ventures out to make footprints and angel prints in the snow and to tuck away a snowball in his pocket to keep for another day. In this book Peter is featureless, for he has not yet begun to recognize the unique person that resides inside. In later books, as Peter grows older, he learns to whistle, to stand up to neighborhood bullies, and to make friends with girls; his face takes on greater expression as his body gets bigger. Peter is becoming a unique person.

As with Peter, children in the early grades must gain a sense of "personness." Schools can help in this development through social studies unit activity in which the distinctive contribution of each person in a family or in a group is a major theme. At this stage, picture books play a significant role in the social studies, for while talking about story characters, young children begin to talk about the value of being different. The modern-day allegories written by Leo Lionni are most useful here. Books such as *Fish Is Fish*, in which a fish discovers that he cannot do what his friend the frog can do, *Pezzettino*, in which a little piece finds he is somebody in his own right and not a part of another piece, *The Greentail Mouse*, in which some mice involved in a Mardi Gras masquerade forget their true identities, and *The Biggest House in the World*, in which a little snail finds out that being bigger for him is not necessarily being better, can stimulate children to talk about their own uniqueness. When talking of stories as part of study of the child's role within the family, the teacher will find that children rather rapidly shift from using the pronouns *he* or *she* to using the pronoun *I*. They will describe times when they tried to be something or someone other than themselves and what happened as a result.

The Person I Am.   Psychologist David Johnson describes a simple but creative activity through which upper graders can broaden their growing conception of their personal uniqueness and value. He suggests that each person be given a large paper bag and several magazines that contain pictures and lettering. Colored construction paper, yarn, string, scissors, marker pens, crayons, brushes, paints, and paste should also be readily available. Each student constructs a "The Person I Am Bag" by pasting pictures and words from magazines to the outside of the bag. Yarn can be added to connect the parts. What

T Use Ezra Jack Keats, *The Snowy Day* (New York: Viking Press, 1962) with nursery and early primary youngsters. Other Keats' books include *Whistle for Willie* (Viking, 1964), *Goggles* (New York: Macmillan, 1969), and *Letter to Amy* (New York: Harper & Row, 1968).

Children must gain a sense of "personness" in early grades.

T See Leo Lionni's books: *Biggest House in the World*, 1968; *Fish Is Fish*, 1970; *Frederick*, 1966; *Greentail Mouse*, 1973; *Swimmy*, 1963; *Pezzettino*, 1975; *A Color of His Own*, 1975. All are published by Pantheon Books (New York).

R A helpful book is David Johnson's *Reaching Out: Interpersonal Effectiveness and Self-Actualization* (Englewood Cliffs, New Jersey: Prentice-Hall, 1972).

is put on the outside are those aspects of the person that he or she willingly shares with others. Inside are placed word cards, pictures, and objects that are part of the person, but which he or she is not really willing to share with others. After the construction period, Johnson advocates a sharing period in which youngsters tell about the bags. Most youngsters will readily describe the pictures and words they have affixed to the outside of their bags; after children have developed a sense of comfort with the group, they may want to share items placed inside their bags.

Johnson warns that group sharing should not focus long on any one participant. He also suggests that some children will not include any of their really positive attributes on the outsides of their bags. The teacher can encourage other students to help each child add these qualities to the outside. For example, the child who is a very fast runner but has not included this idea on the bag may do so at the urging of classmates who recognize him or her in those terms.

Drugs and the Self

The 1960s and 1970s saw enormous increase in the use of drugs for purposes other than medical treatment. These increases struck both adult and youth populations to such an extent that more drug-related programs emerged as part of health and/or social education. Most of the programs incorporated one or more of these approaches: factual, with students learning about drug types and effects in a relatively objective manner; fear-engendering, with students considering specific instances of extreme mental and physical impairments resulting from usage; legal, with students learning of the penalties associated with illicit use; and ethical, with students clarifying personal values relative to drug usage.

T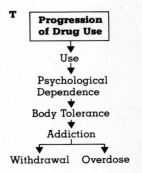

Little or no evidence exists that documents the success or failure rate of these programs, which tended to be found at the junior and senior high levels. For that reason, elementary teachers have very little to guide them if they feel a responsibility to prevent future dependency on drugs and to help youngsters who have become habitual users of one or more of the drugs listed in Figure 7.3.

What this chapter has already described regarding the need for self-respect has a bearing on the drug problem. We can hypothesize that the youngster who has a positive self-concept and a relatively clear future-focused role image is less likely to take drugs to achieve peer acceptance or to escape an existence that appears worthless. From this perspective, getting elementary youngsters to the point where they can say, "This is who I am and this is where I'm going" is a vital component of drug education.

T Read Lawrence and Mary Hepburn, "Pushing Drug Education in the Social Studies: A Rationale for Materials Selection and Reviews of Recommended Materials," *Social Education*, 38:303-308, 314, March, 1974.

Figure 7.3
Drugs Being Used for Nonmedicinal
Purposes Today

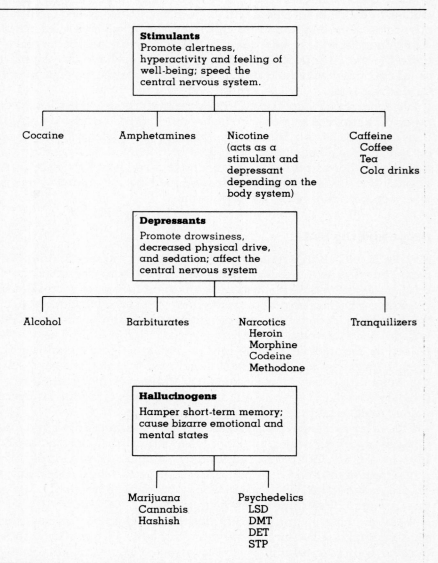

Stimulants
Promote alertness, hyperactivity and feeling of well-being; speed the central nervous system.

Cocaine   Amphetamines   Nicotine   Caffeine
                                   (acts as a   Coffee
                                   stimulant and   Tea
                                   depressant   Cola drinks
                                   depending on the
                                   body system)

Depressants
Promote drowsiness, decreased physical drive, and sedation; affect the central nervous system

Alcohol   Barbiturates   Narcotics   Tranquilizers
                                   Heroin
                                   Morphine
                                   Codeine
                                   Methodone

Hallucinogens
Hamper short-term memory; cause bizarre emotional and mental states

Marijuana   Psychedelics
Cannabis   LSD
Hashish   DMT
                 DET
                 STP

For greater detail on dependency and physiological effects, see Irwin Sherman, and Vilia Sherman. *Biology, A Human Approach.* (New York: Oxford, 1975), and Philip Applewhite, and Sam Wilson. *Understanding Biology.* (New York: Holt, Rinehart and Winston, 1978).

Of course, teachers of upper grades must at some point involve young people in values clarification relative to drug problems. Some of the newer trade books can provide a springboard for discussions. To locate specific references, teachers should check *Subject Guide to Children's Books in Print* (New York: R. R. Bowker, most recent edition) under "Narcotic Habit," "Drugs," "Drugs-Fiction," and the names of individual drugs. As Richard Gross et al. recommend in *Social Studies for Our Times*, discussions in which young people clarify their values regarding drug usage are most successful when carried out in small groups in which individuals have an opportunity to talk through beliefs, feelings, goals, and motivations.

R See Richard Gross, Rosemary Messick, June Chapin, and Jack Sutherland, *Social Studies for Our Times* (New York: John Wiley, 1978).

The Self — A Summary Statement

Development of a positive self-concept and a future-focused role image can certainly not be achieved through a daily period tagged "social studies." It is part of what some like to call **"social education,"** or even more broadly "citizenship education," which has as its goal the development of individuals who can make wise personal, social, political, and economic choices that affect themselves, their nation, and ultimately their world. In this respect, the teacher of the social studies must begin to perceive him- or herself as a social educator.

Some Tasks to Try

1. Make a "Person I Am Bag" of your own. Arthur Jersild believes that unless teachers know and accept themselves, they will have trouble accepting the uniqueness that resides in every child. When you have made your bag, talk about it with other teachers or future teachers, who in turn share their bags with you.
2. If you are unfamiliar with children's books that relate to self-identity, career concerns, or drug problems, locate several and read them to see the contribution books can make to social education, especially as a means of stimulating group talk through which students clarify their values and come to a better understanding and acceptance of self.

Organizing the Classroom to Meet the Needs of the Person in the Group

Because children should come to understand themselves fully and should develop social skills necessary for successful interaction with others, the teacher must organize social studies activities so that everyone has the opportunity to function in a variety of individual and group situations. Essentially this means scheduling classroom time and space to allow for total class involvement, individualized activity, and small group interaction.

Total Class Interaction and Involvement

Activity involving all members of a class serves a number of purposes. Specifically it provides:

1. a common base of experience on which individuals later build
2. a sense of community within the class so that all feel they belong to it
3. an arena for learning how to function as part of a relatively large listening-speaking group
4. an audience and feedback for individual and small group sharing and a time for summing up important points

A Common Base of Experience.   Social studies teachers often use total class activity as a beginning from which children branch out to pursue different but related tasks. They introduce new topics or units to the entire group, involving all children in an activity that stimulates interest in tasks to follow. To motivate, the teacher does not simply tell youngsters what they will be doing but brings them together for a time of active doing. Perhaps students cooperatively analyze information contained in a graph or time line; perhaps they plot what they already know on a projected map; perhaps they listen to a recording of a song from a culture to be studied and join in singing; or perhaps they handle objects from or look at pictures of a cultural group and hypothesize what they think they will find through study.

The total class is also the organizational unit that can be used for film and filmstrip viewing and interpretation and for listening to content material shared dramatically by the teacher. Brainstorming works well with a full class, especially when many ideas are needed for later processing. Directions that all students must follow are generally best given to the entire class to prevent unnecessary repetition by the teacher. In each of these cases, students are gathering information or know-how that they will need to pursue tasks on their own or in small groups.

A Sense of Community. Children must begin to perceive themselves as belonging to their classroom group, for to function productively together, they must have esprit de corps. A feeling of togetherness grows in a class through periods when the group completes tasks that involve everyone or talks about issues that touch on them all. Where absenteeism is a problem, a sense of community is tremendously important. Children who feel they belong to a group are less likely to be absent and are less likely to disrupt class activity.

Especially in primary grades, considerable time should be spent in talking, listening, and thinking together to build the class into a cohesive community. In some schools, times when children first come into the room in the morning and when they are preparing to leave in the afternoon are reserved for community talk. At that point children talk informally about class and school issues that concern them all as well as perform such routine housekeeping chores as taking attendance and distributing supplies. If children participate actively in chores, they are learning firsthand about their own responsibilities to groups to which they belong.

An Arena for Learning Social Group Skills. Throughout their lives people must function in groups that are relatively large. Discussing ideas in the social studies as part of a class group, children will have to:

1. listen and respond to what others are saying;
2. wait their turn, not interrupt others, and not monopolize class time;
3. use nonverbal language to send messages to others who are speaking.

set up rules

In the classroom social arena, part of the teacher's job is to help youngsters understand the need for certain amenities associated with group functioning. As David Johnson reminds, comments that focus on specific behaviors rather than imply value judgments are more helpful. Rather than saying to the youngster who has been monopolizing the discussion, "Jim, you always want to be the center of attention," the teacher may remind, "Jim, let's let José and Marcia speak now. They need a turn too." Rather than saying, "Don't you know better than to call out an answer?" the teacher encourages, "Let's all remember that if we call out an answer that means somebody else loses a turn." In this way, the teacher provides constructive, not destructive, feedback.

R See David Johnson, *Reaching Out* (Englewood Cliffs, New Jersey: Prentice-Hall, 1972).

Focus on specific behaviors rather than value judgements

A Setting for Presentations and Summing Up. When students must present individual or group findings to others, investigations gain purpose. For that reason, many teachers schedule periods when the entire class convenes to react to what others have been doing. Of course, even as they function as an audience, youngsters are learning group social skills, specifically ways of being polite to a speaker, of responding constructively, and of asking questions that require a speaker to elaborate. In the same manner, the total class can convene to sum up ideas at the end of a lesson, series of lessons, or unit.

Individualized, or Personalized, Activity

R See Harold Shane, *The Educational Significance of the Future* (Bloomington, Indiana: Phi Delta Kappa Educational Foundation, 1973), p. 63.

Personalized programs concentrate on child's own development; Don't focus on group norms

Making own decisions helps students gain a sense of responsibility toward own learning.

Harold Shane identifies as a trend in education heightened attention to **personalized programs** that concentrate on "the learner's optimum development rather than merely focusing on attempts to bring him or her up to group norms." In a personalized program, the teacher relates to each student individually, helping each formulate personal goals and standing ready to assist in the search for uniqueness.

Personalized activity in the social studies often flows out of periods of total class involvement. Children who have enjoyed a period of doing, talking, and listening together move out to explore personal interests, practice skills, and/or gather additional data. Some of these tasks are required, as would be the case when certain youngsters need more work with specific skills. Some of the tasks, however, should allow children to choose from among specified activities or in some cases to define work tasks that meet individual interests, needs, or questions. By making decisions about what tasks they will pursue, when they will pursue them, and how they will pursue them, students gain a sense of responsibility toward their own learning as they acquire efficient time allocation skills.

Personalized learning can occur at children's desks as they perform individualized work tasks with or without a co-worker. It can also occur in specialized classroom areas called **learning stations** or **learning centers.** Both kinds of individualized learning can be followed up with home study.

Personalized Activity in Specially Designated Classroom Areas

R See John I. Thomas, *Learning Centers: Opening Up the Classroom* (Boston: Holbrook Press, 1975) for a thorough discussion of learning centers.

Welcome to a combination third- and fourth-grade class in a community we will call Warrenville. As you enter the classroom, you recognize that the room has been designed to facilitate personalized instruction. About four feet from the rear wall, the teacher, Mr. Morris, has placed a row of crates that face the wall. These are filled with trade and reference books on a variety of topics and especially on those topics that are part of the third- and fourth-grade social studies curriculum. Suspended from the ceiling, just above the crates, are raised relief maps made of stiff plastic. These effectively separate the area behind the crates from the rest of the room without restricting visibility between the two areas.

On the left side of the room, the tops of the crates are covered with construction materials—glue, paper, staplers, marker pens, index cards, paints, and brushes—all readily available and waiting to be used. A table in a back corner holds hammers, nails, wood, saws, and drills. An entrance sign announces that this is *The Production Center*. Students use the center to complete a variety of work tasks; they design models and dioramas, make covers for mini-encyclopedias on social studies topics, and devise large charts, graphs, and maps. A sign-up schedule outlines times during the week when the center will open for business.

The area on the rear right-hand side of the classroom is *The Reading and Reference Center*. Atlases, almanacs, and encyclopedias line the top of the crates; several comfortable chairs fill the corners. Here students can browse through references and other books on topics that the class is studying.

In addition to the general learning center areas related to production, reading, and references, Mr. Morris typically has several other stations in his classroom. At each is a relatively structured task for individuals or small groups to complete. Suspended from the middle of the classroom ceiling, you may see the globe-study station. A cord allows the suspended globe to swing free. Beneath it are cards describing steps in the learning sequences children should follow when working at the station. Some task cards ask pupils to use the scale and the plastic ruler tied to the globe to determine the distance between cities; name the countries in which cities are located; give the direction in which one would travel when flying from one city to another; and figure out the longitude and latitude of key cities. The cards obviously differ in difficulty, for few third or fourth graders can handle longitude and latitude. To help children select tasks in accordance with their skill levels, Mr. Morris color codes the task cards following the sequence of colors in the spectrum. Students work through the tasks in the ordered sequence. An example of learning station task cards can be found in Figure 7.4.

In the Reading and Reference Center, too, Mr. Morris will at times place a task card or two that outlines a particular job that some or all of the children must complete using material found there. For example, as fourth graders study aspects of the world population problem, they simultaneously work on using almanacs and atlases as sources of information. A task card in the center might resemble the one in Figure 7.5.

The Population Data-Collecting Task Card hints at how precise directions for independent tasks must be if station activity is to succeed. Steps to be followed must be specified clearly and reviewed orally with all those who will learn at the center. If students at the center choose from among several tasks, that fact should be made clear. All the

T Some teachers also set up a *Recording and Listening Center* where students go to listen to relevant tapes and create ones to share with classmates.

T Colors to use are red, orange, yellow, green, blue, and violet. Easiest tasks are tagged in red, most difficult ones in violet.

**Figure 7.4
First Grade Learning Station Task
Cards Used as Part of a Unit on the
Understanding Self**

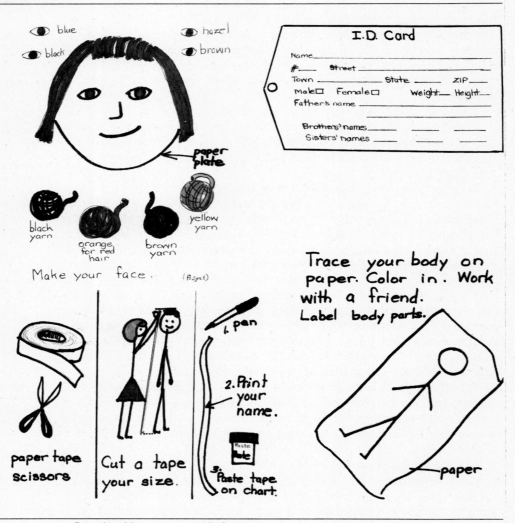

Reproduced by permission of D. Swenson

materials necessary for completion of the task should be readily available so that students will not have to move around gathering paper,
references, and pens from other locations in the room. Students must
also know what to do with their finished products—whether to take
them back to desks for future sharing, tuck them away, or affix them to
a display.

Figure 7.5
A Task Card for Use in a Learning
Station

A Population Data-Collection Task

Steps to follow:

1. Take one card from the "Cities of the World Grab Bag" hanging on the wall.
2. Using the atlas, find out where your city is located. Put an X on the map to show where your city is found.
3. Using the atlas, also find out the population of the city. Write it on your city card. Check the atlas to find out when the city had that number of people.
4. Using the most recent almanac, see what the latest population figure is for your city. Write it and the date when the population was recorded on your card. Subtract one population number from the other to find out how much larger or smaller the population has become.
5. Tack your city card to the spot you have marked with an X on the map. Be sure to put your name on your card before tacking it to the board.

Personalized Activity Through Independent Projects

Kindergarten and first-grade teachers often send youngsters to classroom work areas to complete independent projects. For example, youngsters who have viewed a filmstrip on the services provided by the school crossing guard may return to their home bases to draw a picture showing how the school crossing guard assists them. Generally in the lower primary grades, independent projects occupy a single work period with students reconvening shortly to share their projects.

With maturity, students can assume greater responsibility toward their independent projects. Making the transition to independent study activity, the teacher assigns one task that all children must complete based on an introductory activity just experienced and suggests several others from which each student selects one that is appealing. Time for independent social studies activity is scheduled on several successive days, with more rapid learners perhaps completing several optional projects outlined by the teacher or pursuing tasks that they themselves have designed relative to the topic.

Experienced teachers have discovered that to prevent confusion during initial work periods, preliminary discussion of tasks to do is essential. Together teacher and children talk about the task that everyone must do, so each child knows how and where to begin. Together they talk about each optional task and students select the one or ones they will pursue. Where some tasks involve use of limited materials, children must commit themselves to particular options before leaving the larger group to pursue chosen activities. This prevents disorder that could result from numbers of children descending on a work area that can accommodate just a few children at a time.

T A workable organizational scheme:

From talking-together times
|
To independent project times

Make tasks clear before breaking up the class!

Make "contracts" w/ directions; avoids repetition of giving directions etc. Less confusing for the child.

Contracts less for older students. Maybe make up own contracts.

Experienced teachers have also found that giving each child a contract that spells out required and optional tasks avoids repetition of directions and the confusion that comes from forgetting what one is to do next. Children use the contract sheet as a checklist; they check off items as they begin them and then recheck the items when completed. Figure 7.6 is an example of a contract for use in primary grades that spells out in detail required and optional tasks.

Older students can take greater responsibility in determining their independent study tasks. For this reason, contracts can be less specific and more tailored to individual needs. Studying a particular region, group of people, time period, or nation, children can even write their own contracts based on general guidelines and ideas provided by the teacher. Figure 7.7 is a general listing of project ideas upon which children can build as they compile folders on a topic being investigated. Figure 7.8 presents guidelines for folder construction to assure that children's independent project activity includes a variety of activities leading to different kinds of understandings and skills.

The Personalized Conference

T A workable organizational scheme:

From independent project times

To personalized conferences

To independent project times

Even in the middle grades, few elementary students can decide upon a series of independent study tasks, start to work systematically on them, and assess what they are doing without teacher guidance. Ongoing teacher-student conferences must be a part of independent study schemes if activity is to be fruitful and satisfying. In a personalized conference, the teacher helps the student:

1. identify specific tasks that meet personal needs, abilities, and interests;
2. identify sources of information and ways to collect data;
3. decide on ways to organize and present data collected;
4. plan the best sequence in which to complete tasks;
5. set up a rough schedule for beginning and finishing specific tasks;
6. assess progress periodically as the independent study activity continues.

In upper grades where project work can be extensive, each student should talk with the teacher about what he or she is doing at least every third work period. Teacher and student sit down to look at what has been done and to consider further directions for independent study. In lower grades where project work is less involved, the teacher can move from desk to desk, talking informally with youngsters.

Small Group Activity

Both full class and independent study activities can lead into small group activity. In turn small group activity can feed back into full class sharing times and prepare youngsters for further individualized study.

Figure 7.6
A Contract Sheet for Independent
Study Tasks

Contract for _____   Name _____
     (Put days of the week here)

Life on the Desert   Check when you begin and end a task.   **Begin   End**

1. *Required task:* Using the paper laid out on Shelf 2,   1. _____
   draw a picture showing how the people living in a
   desert area get their food. Then write a paragraph
   describing the kinds of foods important to people living
   on a desert and how they get their food. Use words
   from the chart we made when we talked together
   about food sources in the desert.

2. *A choice:* Read the book *The Desert Is Theirs* by Byrd   2. _____
   Baylor (New York: Charles Scribner's Sons, 1975).
   There are five copies of the book in the Reading
   Center. Write a paragraph or draw a picture showing
   how important water is to people living on a desert.

3. *A choice:* Listen to the tape in the audio-station. Go   3. _____
   there with 3 or 4 other students and take your textbook
   along. Follow the words in your text (pages 45–47) as
   you listen to the words. Know one idea from the tape
   and text to share with others at the next class session.
   Sign your name at the station after you have listened
   to the tape.

4. *A choice:* Go to the production center with 2 other   4. _____
   students. There you will find a picture of a desert
   home. Use materials in the center; make a diorama
   that shows how people live in a desert. Be ready to
   show it to the class.

5. *A choice:* Select one of the reference books from the   5. _____
   Reading Center. Read the marked section about life in
   the desert. On a piece of notebook paper, write one
   fact that you learned.

6. *A choice:* With 3 other students, go to the filmstrip   6. _____
   booth. View the strip on desert life. Go back to your
   desk and draw a picture that shows the kinds of homes
   people have in the desert. Draw a second picture that
   shows your own home. Decide how homes in the world
   differ. Why do they differ? Write your answer as a
   paragraph.

Within the social studies program, small group activities should play
a major role, for through group interaction students learn to cooperate
with others on a common undertaking, exert leadership among their
peers, communicate orally with others, and recognize the unique qualities each possesses and use them productively. Working in small

[handwritten margin note: Small group activities should be in classroom brings about interaction. Communication recognize uniqueness of students.]

Figure 7.7
Kinds of Material that Children Can
Produce and Include in an Individual
Folder

Independent Study Activities That Can Be Part of Folders

Directions: Build a folder of materials that relate to the topic we are studying. Check off items that you plan to include. Later the teacher will come to talk to you about your personal study plan.

Possible Tasks to Do: Check those you plan to do.

1. Make a map showing key physical features.   1. _____
2. Make two maps that show changes that have   2. _____
   occurred in the area during a particular time period.
3. Make a chart showing a key sequence of events or   3. _____
   steps in a process.
4. Make a model to show something important related   4. _____
   to the topic.
5. Sketch a series of drawings that show changes that   5. _____
   have occurred.
6. Do a report based on a story read. Your report can be   6. _____
   in written, outline, or pictorial form. You decide.
7. Write a paragraph describing one event, culture trait,   7. _____
   or person.
8. List key points contained under one main heading of   8. _____
   your social studies text material on the topic.
9. Write a paragraph giving your personal reaction to an   9. _____
   event, culture trait, or person. Include your reasons
   for reacting as you do.
10. Develop a glossary of key terms. Include a definition   10. _____
    of each.

Figure 7.8
Guidelines for Folder Construction

Building a Folder   Topic _____

Follow these guidelines:

1. Select a variety of tasks. Do not do only drawing activities, for example.
2. Try for full coverage of our topic. If you read and write about one part of the topic, make your map on some other part, and create a series of sketches or cartoons on still another part.
3. You may decide to work with someone else on one or two tasks. Do some tasks by yourself.
4. Set up your folder so that if a classmate were to look at it, he or she would get a good picture of the topic.
5. Select one task to do at home.
6. As you finish up your tasks, decide which one you would like to share with others in the class. There will be a sharing time later.

Figure 7.9
Ways of Organizing a Classroom
for Instruction

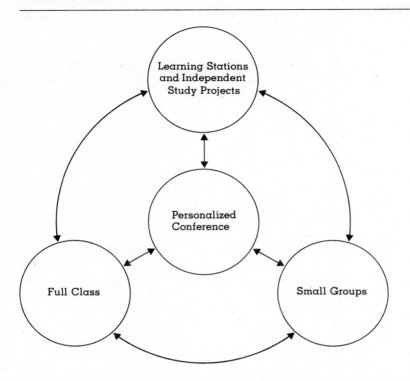

groups, children can pursue a variety of data gathering and process-ing tasks. Cooperating on these tasks with others, each student must contribute a part to a larger endeavor—one determined through group consensus. In chapter 3, page 93–95, much was said about the way groups can be used in the classroom. The reader may wish to reread the sections describing task groups, task cards, echo pairs, and revolv-ing groups.

There are several different ways to divide children into task groups. One is based on an assessment of **common needs.** If, for example, a teacher knows that four or five youngsters need additional work with a fundamental map skill, these boys and girls may be grouped together for project activity. The teacher works with them initially to develop greater understanding of concepts. At that point, the group goes to work independently on a map project that requires them to apply their new understanding. That project relates to the overall topic of unit study, which other groups are pursuing from different directions.

Grouped together to get help more of an understanding.

Grouped on common interests.

Grouped according to talented.

Children begin to see their "uniqueness" talents.

Social preferences children can pick own group.

Sociogram - info about certain patterns can be identified.

Children can at times be grouped based on **common interests.** The total class may begin a unit by deciding on subtopics that groups will investigate. One group may deal with the system of education of a country, a second with the system of government, a third with the holiday traditions, and so on. Children may decide to which group they will belong by writing their first and second choices on a slip of paper. Groups are organized based on topics of expressed interest.

Still another way of organizing task groups is based on **diverse talents.** Sometimes tasks a group will pursue will have an art component, a writing component, a musical component, and so forth. Each group will need participants who are especially talented in one of these areas. Accordingly, the teacher identifies specific roles required within each group. Children volunteer to play specified roles. One advantage of this organizational strategy is that children begin to see themselves in terms of their unique talents. The child who can locate just exactly the right reference in the library begins to see him- or herself as a rather good researcher—maybe even a technical librarian some day. The child who is called upon to sketch out the major design of a cooperative bulletin board begins to think of him- or herself as a potential commercial artist.

A fourth way of organizing work groups is based on **social preferences.** At times, experienced teachers allow students to express their choices as to co-workers. Each youngster writes down the names of two or three others with whom he or she would like to work. Using this information, the teacher organizes groups so that each child works with at least one chosen person. From this information, the teacher also can learn of the friendship patterns in a class, for although some students may name as co-workers children who will work diligently on a cooperative project, they also will name close friends.

Information about friendship patterns in a class can be compiled as a **sociogram.** Plotting the names of all children on a large sheet, the teacher draws arrows from each person to the name of those he or she chose. Analyzing the sociogram, the teacher can identify those children who are chosen very infrequently or even not at all and can then find ways to integrate these less popular children into the mainstream of classroom activity. Figure 7.10 is a sociogram constructed by asking each youngster to name the three others with whom he or she would like to work on a research project. Given the information contained in it, the reader may wish to consider how to place Karen, Robby, and Marcia in groups so that they have a positive experience that leads to growth in social skills. The reader may also wish to decide what would be the most helpful placement of the class stars—Martha, Gus, and Paul.

**Figure 7.10
A Sociogram Based on Children's
Preferences for Work Teams**

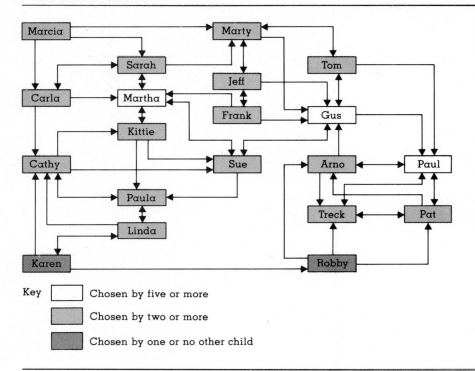

Key
◻ Chosen by five or more

▨ Chosen by two or more

▪ Chosen by one or no other child

Discipline and the Social Studies

Good discipline–a state in which each student is applying his or her energies to meaningful learning tasks and at the same time is contributing positively to the general social environment–is essential if learning is to occur in a classroom. The ability to maintain personal identity and function effectively with others is, however, a major goal of instruction in the social studies. Accordingly, the maintenance of a classroom climate that encourages compatible social living is especially important within the social studies.

Planning for All Children. The importance of adequate planning in maintaining a classroom climate conducive to learning cannot be overstressed. Children differ in their ability to perform basic tasks, in their ability to sit still for a given length of time, and in their ability to apply themselves independently to a task. They differ too in the per-

Discipline is necessary if learning is to take place!!

Reach goal!!

Togetherness is necessary.

Children differ in many ways — plans must cover differences.

sonal problems they bring with them to school and in basic social competencies—waiting their turns, helping others, or keeping their voices pitched at a low conversational level. All these factors must be considered as the teacher plans learning sequences.

Specific questions the teacher must answer in planning include:

Ways to plan. for all.

1. How shall I handle those children who finish a task ahead of the others? What other activities can they pursue until most of the class has completed the major task? Children need guidance in deciding what tasks to pursue on their own; children with nothing to do can become disruptive.
2. How shall I vary the task to meet the needs of those with a reading or learning disability? Children faced with educational tasks that are beyond them sometimes are disruptive as a means of escaping what they cannot do.
3. How shall I sequence activity so children, despite short attention spans, will be attentive throughout? What kinds of activities can I include within a sequence so that children have the opportunity to move around? Elementary school children can be involved in full-class talk activities for no more than twenty minutes. At that point, children should be placed in a small group or independent work task that requires children to draw, build, write, read, or handle.
4. How shall I explain to children what they will be doing? If children are uncertain of what is expected of them, they will often kill time—going for a drink, sharpening pencils, or dropping and picking up work tools. One way to avoid confusion resulting from lack of understanding of what to do is to have children orally review steps they are to follow during independent study times. Students also identify things they can do if they finish early—read an informational book on the subject, play a social studies game set out in a gaming center, or finish a biographical account started earlier.
5. How shall I structure the learning experience so that children must make some decisions relative to their own learning? In what ways can I provide for children's choices? The only way that children will eventually grow in ability to manage their own time productively is to be given the opportunity to do just that. For that reason, the social studies teacher should include activities in which youngsters select one or two tasks from several suggested ones and eventually propose a task or two of their own creation.

Deciding on Rules Imperative for Successful Group Living.
Rules are essential in any social group to assure the safety and rights of all members. Schools must establish rules about student and teacher

Girls and boys should participate in a wide
range of activities as a means of discovering their
unique strengths.

behavior during fire drills, during assembly programs, and during
class "migrations" through areas where other groups are involved in
study activities. They must have rules about tardiness and attendance.
In like manner, classrooms must have rules governing the level of
classroom noise acceptable when others are trying to think, governing
the thoughtful use of expensive materials, governing permission to
leave the classroom, and governing the use of learning centers.

In establishing classroom rules, teachers must take care not to make
too many rules. Too many dos and don'ts regulating relatively insignificant aspects of behavior lead to too many infractions, which the
teacher must then handle. Rules must be those essential for successful
group living, and children must understand the basis for the establishment of these fundamental rules.

Rules must be established. Be carefull not to make too many rules!

Students help sometimes establish rules

In some classrooms, students themselves develop rules. They decide how many can work at the production center at one time and how many can go to the reading center. They talk about the best way of indicating they want to leave the classroom to visit the library, bathroom, or nurse. They consider why it is important for the teacher to know where they are at all times. Students decide on ways to assure each participant a fair share of discussion time and acceptable levels of noise. Group participation in making rules, especially in the upper elementary grades, can lead to the esprit de corps that brings members into a cooperative class group.

Once rules have been established, they must be enforced with some degree of consistency. Children function better when they know where they stand; if yesterday they could walk around and talk to one another between activities and today for no understandable reason they get into trouble for doing just that, they have every right to complain about the equity of the legal system within their class. When children begin to question the fairness of teachers' actions with regard to disciplinary matters, conflict—even open rebellion—can result just as it does in society at large.

Rules enforced w/ consistency.

Children work better when they know where they stand.

Handling Potentially Explosive Situations.   In many classes there are children who have social and/or emotional problems so severe that they can lead to explosive interactions; one youngster pushes or strikes another, loses complete control and screams out loud, constantly interferes with the learnings of others, or fails to abide by the rules established for the safety and good of the group. Such situations tax the equanimity of even the calmest of teachers. To maintain a calm, steadying, composed manner, however, is perhaps the best way to prevent explosive situations from getting totally out of hand.

Being calm may be the best way to handle a situation.

Experienced teachers tend to agree that the most productive steps to take are the following:

Move before the situation explodes. If two children are feuding, physically separating them before a fight has a chance to break out may prevent a fight from taking place. If a child comes to school in a bad mood, talking with him or her and encouraging the child to sound off to someone about what is the source of frustration can prevent a later outburst.

T Read James Thompson, *Beyond Words: Nonverbal Communication in the Classroom* (New York: Citation Press, 1973) for a description of ways to use nonverbal clues as part of teaching.

Know individual children's distinctive problems. To move quickly, the teacher must be able to sense when particular children are upset; the teacher must be able to read the nonverbal signals that children send.

Reinforce positive behavior. Even the most disruptive youngsters do some things right. Advocates of behavior modification strategies suggest that behaviors that are reinforced by teacher praise will

Respond to positive behaviors ~neg. ones will gradually go away; pos ones will increase.

begin to occur more frequently. They believe that the teacher should ignore annoying but insignificant acts that children perform and concentrate on the good points. Research shows that if the teacher does this consistently, the annoying behaviors will gradually disappear, and the positive behaviors will appear more frequently.

Discuss emotionally handicapped children's behavior with school psychologists, who may be able to supply specific suggestions on how to handle a particular child.

The steps described above are easier to enumerate than to follow, and their successful implementation is dependent in many respects on teachers' understanding and acceptance of themselves and their own feelings. As Jersild reminds, teachers must see meaning in their own lives, face their own anxieties, and accept the loneliness of human existence if they are to help children in search of self.

R Read Arthur Jersild, *When Teachers Face Themselves* (New York: Teachers College Press, 1955). Although old, this book is one of the best on the topic of teacher self-understanding.

For these steps to be successful, teacher must understand self.

The Person in the Group: A Summary Thought or Two, and a Challenge

Chapter 7 has elaborated on the importance of using the social studies to help children grow in self-understanding and acceptance. Specific strategies for building positive feelings toward the self and for organizing the classroom to meet individual and social needs have been described. But these strategies alone are ineffective. According to Jersild, even teachers who make long checklists of children's interests, ask them to vote on what seem to be urgent problems, and talk to parents about individual children's needs can leave out "the one essential thing: their own direct personal involvement."

Teacher must know self!!

Teachers themselves must raise questions about the significance of everything in which they are involved. They must ask:

What does it mean? What difference does it make? What is there in the lessons we teach, the exercises we assign, the books we read, the experiences we enter into, and in all of our undertakings that can help us to find ourselves, and through us, help others in their search?

R See Arthur Jersild, *When Teachers Face Themselves*, p. 136.

In facing themselves fully, teachers must accept their own uniqueness as individuals, recognize their own needs and feelings that make them part of the human family, and perceive the meaning of their own existence. By accepting the differences they see within themselves and by perceiving the ultimate significance of themselves as persons, teachers will be better able to accept the uniqueness and the worth found within each child for whom the self is equally important.

By accepting self, teacher will be able to better accept students uniqueness.

Thoughts to Consider

1. Think about yourself by trying some of these tasks:

   a. If you could be one animal—other than a human being—for just one day, what would you choose? Why would you want to be that animal? What does your choice indicate about you as a person?

   b. If you could be someone else for just a day, who would you choose to be? Why? What does your choice indicate about you as a person?

   c. If you could have any three wishes, for what would you wish? Why? What do your wishes say about your own personal value system?

   d. What kinds of people do you generally choose to be with? Why do you choose them? What does your preference say about you as a person?

   e. What kinds of people do you generally choose not to be friendly with? Why do you feel as you do? What does your preference say about you as a person?

   f. Given the following list of adjectives, circle four that describe you best: cheerful, trusting, intelligent, thoughtful, afraid, unhappy, cautious, playful, serious, diligent, happy-go-lucky, boastful, quiet, obliging, masterful, persistent, respectful, caring, strong, uncertain, warm, willing, helpful, sensitive, shy, outgoing, content, tolerant, angry, patient, kind, alone. Now think about the words you circled: Do you like the meaning of those words? Do you like yourself?

2. Think about other "selfs" by trying some of these:

   a. Study a child you know well. Identify signals that child sends when frustrated, disturbed, or angry.

   b. Name a person that you feel understands and accepts him- or herself well. Does that person see meaning in life? How does that person handle tensions and anxiety?

   c. Name a person you feel understands and accepts him- or herself poorly. Does that person see meaning in life? Think about how you can help the person become more self-accepting. Try your plan.

R After an activity in David Johnson's *Reaching Out* (Englewood Cliffs, New Jersey: Prentice-Hall, 1972), p. 29-30.

References

Allport, Gordon. *Person in Psychology*. Boston: Beacon Press, 1968.

Campbell, David. *A Practical Guide to the Open Classroom*, 2nd ed. Dubuque, Iowa: Kendall/Hunt Publishing, 1975.

Grebstein, Lawrence, ed. *Toward Self-Understanding*. Glenview, Illinois: Scott, Foresman and Co., 1969.

Hamachek, Don. *Encounters with the Self*. New York: Holt, Rinehart & Winston, 1971.

Hamachek, Don. ed. *The Self in Growth, Teaching and Learning*. Englewood Cliffs, New Jersey: Prentice-Hall, 1965.

Jersild, Arthur. *In Search of Self*. New York: Teachers College Press, 1952.

Jersild, Arthur. *When Teachers Face Themselves*. New York: Teachers College Press, 1955.

Johnson, David. *Reaching Out: Interpersonal Effectiveness and Self-Actualization*. Englewood Cliffs, New Jersey: Prentice-Hall, 1972.

Johnson, David; and Johnson, Roger. *Learning Together and Alone: Cooperation, Competition, and Individualization*. Englewood Cliffs, New Jersey: Prentice-Hall, 1975.

Montagu, A. *On Being Human*. New York: Hawthorn Books, 1966.

Neill, A. S. *Summerhill*. New York: Hart Publishing, 1960.

Rapport, Virginia; and Parker, Mary. *Learning Centers: Children on Their Own*. Washington, D. C.: Association for Childhood Education International, 1970.

Schmuck, Richard; and Schmuck, Patricia. *Group Processes in the Classroom*. Dubuque, Iowa: William C. Brown, 1971.

Shane, Harold. *The Educational Significance of the Future*. Bloomington, Indiana: Phi Delta Kappa Educational Foundation, 1973.

Thomas, John I. *Learning Centers: Opening Up the Classroom*. Boston: Holbrook Press, 1975.

Thompson, James. *Beyond Words: Nonverbal Communication in the Classroom*. New York: Citation Press, 1973.

8

Meeting the Needs of All Children: From Side to Mainstream

My name is Frank.
I like to play football.

Frank is learning to accept his disabled arm.

not real specific

To solve the problem of education, children must be surrounded with equity and must be equitably treated, and each and every one, parent or child, must be understood to be an individual, and must have his individual rights equitably respected.

Josiah Warren,
Equitable Commerce,
1855

Key Questions

What educational commitment is embodied in Public Law 94-142?

How is *giftedness* defined? How can we enrich the school experience of the gifted?

What are the major social and curricular implications of a learning disability? What are possible causes of a learning disability? How can the social studies teacher structure learning sequences so that poor readers are actively involved in the social studies and at the same time grow in basic skills?

How can social studies teachers modify the physical arrangements of the classroom to meet the needs of the sensory impaired and the physically handicapped? What steps can teachers take to assure an emotional climate receptive to the handicapped?

What steps can social studies teachers take to assure that children overcome the limitations imposed by society's stereotyped views of what women or men can do?

What steps can social studies teachers take to assure that members of minority groups, immigrants, and migrant children overcome the limitations imposed by society's stereotyped views?

Figure 8.1
A Name Collage

Introduction

What characteristics of mind and spirit are shared by the noted men and women included in the introductory name collage? What binds them together?

Helen Adams Keller: American thinker, author, lecturer; she lost both sight and hearing at eighteen months of age.

Max Cleland: head of the Veteran's Administration during the Carter presidency; he became a paraplegic as a result of the Vietnam War.

Charles Proteus Steinmetz, born Karl August Rudolf in Germany: discoverer of the "law of hysteresis loss" and pioneer in the application of mathematics to explanations of alternating current; an immigrant; he was born with a severe back deformity.

Thomas Alva Edison: inventor of the incandescent light bulb, the phonograph, the carbon telephone transmitter, and the automatic telegraph repeater; he was almost completely deaf.

Harold Ordway Rugg: noted educator, lecturer, and professor at Columbia University; he had a noticeable stutter that he retained throughout his long career.

Booker Taliaferro Washington: founder of the Tuskegee Institute, one of the first schools for blacks in the south; he was born a slave.

Elizabeth Blackwell: American physician who opened a private dispensary in New York, which became the New York Infirmary and College for Women; she was the first known woman doctor in modern times.

Benjamin Franklin: statesperson, philosopher, and scientist; he started his career as a printer in Philadelphia with only two loaves of bread and the clothes on his back.

The late Martin Luther King, whose name also appears in the word collage, has expressed the shared relationship: "We shall overcome!" Keller, Steinmetz, Blackwell, and the others contributed in some way to the betterment of the world despite major handicaps. Some of these were physical; others were social. Yet these men and women overcame and were able to move from the side to the mainstream of human activity.

T Children can create collages bearing the names of people, places, or things that share a common feature. Classmates must see if they can discover the shared feature. The teacher can also present a name collage for children to figure out.

Exceptional Children in the Social Studies Classroom: A Legal Commitment

History relates that the public schools rendered little or no assistance in helping the individuals mentioned in the name collage perform at the highest level of which they were capable. Edison was considered unteachable by his teachers. His mother served as tutor. Steinmetz's success is often attributed to a grandmother who was kind to him and to a happy childhood in a secure home.

With passage of Public Law 94-142, however, schools have a legal responsibility to educate all children. The law states that all children are entitled to an equal education in the least restrictive environment possible. It applies particularly to those who previously were called **exceptional**: the gifted and talented, the slow or learning disabled, the physically handicapped, and the perceptually impaired. It commits schools to helping these children move into the mainstream to the greatest extent possible. In this section, let us consider the contribution of the social studies to this educational commitment.

PL. 94-142 Schools have responsibility to educate all children in a. LRE.

R Mainstreaming means that exceptional children spend part or all of the school day in a regular classroom. Read theme articles in the January 1979 issue of *Social Education*, Vol. 43, No. 1. The theme of the issue is "Mainstreaming: The Least Restrictive Environment."

The Gifted and Talented

Intelligence tests attempt to measure a child's ability to function cognitively—the ability to conceptualize, to generalize, and to apply knowledge in a deductive way. Because language is the medium through which thoughts are communicated, however, these tests also measure children's ability to handle language.

R From Lewis Terman and Maud Merrill, *Stanford-Binet Intelligence Scale, Manual for the Third Revision Form L-M* (Boston: Houghton Mifflin, 1960).

In some situations the gifted and talented are defined in terms of intelligence test scores and, therefore, in terms of language and cognitive facility. Terman and Merrill classify students with IQs between 120-140 as "superior," and between 140-170 as "very superior." Within a typical population about thirteen percent fall into these two gifted categories. On the Terman scale, an IQ over 150 represents the genius level.

To dispute the giftedness of those with stunning IQs would be senseless and indeed difficult; yet for instructional purposes any definition of giftedness that considers only performance on intelligence tests is limiting. Artistic, musical, dramatic, social, mathematical, mechanical, and leadership talents exist within the human population and can be reflections of high intelligence not necessarily correlated with the language competencies that affect performance on intelligence tests. These talents as well as those more specifically related to high language facility must be encouraged. Children who fall into all these categories have immense potential to contribute to society in the future and to the society in the classroom where they have come to learn.

Have gifted read independently—choose books of own materials.

Enrichment Through Reading. One facet of social studies for the gifted and talented is an independent reading program that encourages children to choose books to read that relate to their diverse interests. Gifted children have wide interests and intense curiosity to find out. They ask probing questions that at times can fluster a teacher who feels that he or she must "know it all." Rather than answering questions even when knowing the information, the teacher establishes books as sources to be tapped. The youngster who raises a question beyond the scope of classroom texts and references goes to the library to locate a book that will help.

R Based on "Dust Won't Gather on This Reference Shelf!" from *Instructor* 88: 148-149, October 1978.

Especially with inquisitive children, a varied and interesting supply of books must be available. A fascinating source is the *Guinness Book of World Records*, a copy of which should be on every school library shelf. Gifted children will not only use it as a reference but will read it from cover to cover. Almanacs can have the same appeal. Yearly ones for use in intermediate classrooms include *The CBS News Almanac, The Information Please Almanac, The Reader's Digest Almanac,* and *The World Almanac.* Using these, gifted children can go beyond the tasks in the regular curriculum to construct original time lines based on dates found, challenge one another with facts they have uncovered, convert statistical information into creative visual form, and write letters of inquiry to sources identified to find out even more.

At upper-elementary levels, too, able children should be encouraged to read biographies and autobiographies. From these books, they may begin to understand the contributions of exceptional people of past and present and identify areas in which they themselves may contribute in the future. Gifted children may be highly able, but they—like all children—need role models against which to pattern their own lives.

Enrichment Through Researching and Writing. Studies by the National Assessment of Educational Progress suggest that the written expression of even the brightest children in the elementary schools is not what it should be. In the social studies very able children can grow in writing and research skills so that they gain control of the basics and go beyond to skills not generally developed at the elementary level. These include the ability to:

1. scan indexes and tables of contents at a very rapid pace to locate information,
2. skim selections for information,
3. use special kinds of indexes such as *Books in Print, Readers' Guide to Periodical Literature, Webster's Biographical Dictionary,* and the *Macmillan Dictionary of Canadian Biography,*
4. prepare annotated bibliographies and compose footnotes,
5. handle quotation marks for citations,
6. use subheadings to organize written reports that focus on several aspects of a topic,
7. use a variety of sentence patterns as well as more involved punctuation patterns to express complex relationships in subject matter content,
8. use transitional words to show relationships between ideas.

When three or four youngsters in a class are ready to work on these advanced skills, the teacher can set up special skill development project groups through which advanced skills can be developed preparatory to use on a group project. Some schools are using the librarian as a resource person who takes small groups of bright students from several different classes for an hour or so each week for instruction in advanced researching and writing skills. A series such as *Doing Research and Writing Reports: Books A, B, C,* (Englewood Cliffs, N. J.: Scholastic Book Services, 1978) is helpful.

Enrichment Through Higher-Level Thinking. Very able students generally need little or no repetitive practice in order to learn. Drill time is often a waste, because gifted students have acquired a skill on the first go-round. Thinking activities in which children analyze, apply, synthesize, and evaluate should replace wasteful drill. Here are some

R See Michael Labuda's *Creative Reading for Gifted Learners* (Newark, Delaware: International Reading Association, 1974).

R See the National Assessment of Educational Progress, *Writing: National Results,* 1969-70; *Writing: Writing Mechanics,* 1972; and *Writing Mechanics,* 1969-74. (Washington, D.C.: U.S. Government Printing Office, 1970, 1972, 1975).

If necessary, teacher can set up skill development projects.

T Special atlases also intrigue the curious. See the *National Geographic Picture Atlas of Our Fifty States,* 1978. It is filled with enticing information.

Drilling "smart" students is a waste. Have them analyze, apply & evaluate & synthesize.

tasks that do not ask children to learn more facts, dates, or names but to operate intellectually on their knowledge:

1. *Ranking.* Ask students to rank order regions, countries, cities, events, causes, outcomes, or people of the past in terms of relative importance. For example, "Given four countries of Asia—the USSR, Japan, China, and India—rank order the four according to relative international importance." Students who have rank ordered should compare their orderings and explain the reasons they decided as they did. This assignment can enrich the study of almost any social studies topic.

2. *Categorizing.* Ask students to devise a scheme for categorizing people, places, or things met within a unit. Students can devise ways to categorize tools, occupations, technological devices, events, battles, and so forth.

3. *Finding a Mate or an Opposite.* Ask gifted children to identify an event, person, cause, or outcome very similar to one being studied. Later they find an example of something very different. They must explain how the two identified are similar or different.

4. *Working with Statistics.* Ask students to convert numerical data into graphs, analyze them for patterns, and generalize relationships. Understanding of percent and ratios can be applied as students handle data on the number of automobiles sold each year during a ten-year period, the amounts of corn produced each year by each of the ten major producers, the amount of oil imported this year as compared to last year by the ten largest importing nations. The possibilities for mathematical analysis are endless. A group can be named "the mathematicians"; their job is to come up quickly with mathematical relationships even as the entire class encounters data with a numerical component.

Enrichment Through Contribution. Through their school experience, gifted and talented children should recognize their obligation to use their abilities to benefit others as well as themselves. One way to help children comprehend the nature of the contribution they can make is to employ the unique talents of individual children as part of unit study.

Teachers are often amazed at the range of talents found in a heterogeneously grouped class. In some groups are capable photographers, sketchers, cartoonists, pianists, guitarists, violinists, dancers, actors, pantomimists, storytellers, writers, speakers, carpenters, whittlers, and leaders. Each has a contribution to make. As part of a study of the westward movement, for example, the fiddler in the class can share pieces that the pioneers played and sang to raise their spirits during the long journey. During study of the West, the class storyteller can share characteristic tall tales. The class artist can sketch the outline for a mural on the board, taking a leadership role in directing less capable artists to paint in portions much as the great artists of the past directed apprentices in their studios. In like manner, others can contribute by creating games for peers to play, designing learning activities related to a topic with which they are already familiar, or locating source materials for others to use.

The Learning Disabled

Children identified as slow learners are more often than not those with a reading and writing disability. These children score below grade level on reading achievement tests and have difficulty composing a simple, logical sentence. Their disability begins to be obvious in the primary grades, becomes more striking as they move up to middle and high schools, and usually results in early school leaving.

The social and curricular implications of a reading disability are numerous.

1. Since society considers literacy of prime importance, a child who fails to read by second grade may begin to view him- or herself as a general failure, a view certainly not helpful in developing a positive self-concept.
2. Since literacy is often a requirement for employment, life goals must be modified.
3. Since most school subjects rely on reading as a means of gathering information, a reading disability affects learning in the content areas. A reading problem may become a general learning problem.

Causes of reading related disabilities tend to be multiple.

Causes of Disabilities. John De Boer and Martha Dallman write that the causes of a reading-related learning disability tend to be multiple and interrelated. Reading problems can be associated with personality problems. Children who are insecure, anxious, hostile, or aggressive may approach reading with these same feelings, which then become blocks to learning. These feelings may also cause truancy, which in turn prevents children from getting the necessary remedial instruction.

Reading problems also often correlate with home conditions. A classic study by Helen Robinson in 1946 found that social, visual, and emotional difficulties were the most frequent causes of failure to learn to read. In fifty-four percent of the cases studied, family and home problems were contributing factors. When parents encourage children's early reading efforts, read aloud to them, set aside an area or

R John De Boer and Martha Dallmann, *The Teaching of Reading,* Third Edition (New York: Holt, Rinehart & Winston, 1970). Pages 446-449 provide an excellent discussion of reading disability and its causes.

R See Helen Robinson, *Why Pupils Fail in Reading* (Chicago: University of Chicago Press, 1946).

Causes: Hostile feelings, aggression, poor home conditions, social, visual, emotional difficulties.

time for reading, and provide a role model by reading newspapers, magazines, and books, children are more likely to succeed in reading. Where just the opposite is true, success is less likely.

De Boer and Dallman identify the school climate and children's early experiences with reading in school as other determinants of success. If children are asked to handle reading tasks for which they are not ready, if they develop inappropriate word-attack skills, if considerable pressure is placed on them to read, or if slow word-by-word oral reading is a typical classroom activity, students may turn off to the whole reading process.

Of course, reading disabilities may result from lack of visual or auditory acuity, overall low intelligence, poor health that keeps children out of school, or lack of experiences with words. When children come to school with a limited spoken vocabulary, they must build word meanings orally before they are able to read words with understanding.

Helping Children Overcome Reading Problems. The multiple causes of a reading-related learning disability suggest general steps the teacher can take to help slow readers, who very often are also slow writers. These steps include:

1. use of socio-drama, role-playing, and value-clarification discussions to explore concepts of self and help children identify areas of strength
2. a classroom reading environment that turns reading into an exciting, anticipated activity
3. considerable time spent in listening to both story and informational content so children grow in oral vocabulary and ability to understand sentence patterns often found in written language
4. a beginning reading program that stresses both decoding and comprehension skills

In the social studies, the teacher must find ways to prevent reading problems from affecting children's learning of social studies content and skills. Specifically the teacher must design classroom sequences so that slower children understand complex terms before reading them and have seen the visual image of words several times before trying to decode them independently.

Take, for example, a lesson in which children are learning a basic map term such as *symbol*. As children together interpret a simple outline map of their state projected with a transparency, they take turns coming to the projector to add information. "Who knows what is located in Long Beach?" the California teacher asks. A child who is intrigued by ships remembers about "The Queen" and comes forward

---

Marginal notes (handwritten):

Lots of reading materials in home is likely to make reading more successful.

Steps teacher can take to help slow learners

R Some related references to check include:

John Cawley, *The Slow Learner and the Reading Problem* (Springfield, Illinois: Charles C. Thomas, 1972).

Harry Forgan and Charles Mangrum, *Teaching Content Areas Related to Reading Skills* (Columbus, Ohio: Charles E. Merrill, 1976).

Leo Fay and Ann Jared, *Reading in the Content Fields* (an annotated bibliography), rev. ed. (Newark, Delaware: International Reading Association, 1975).

to draw a small shape of a ship at the right location on the transparency. Now students and teacher begin to refer to that little shape as a symbol for The Queen. As students offer to put in a circle for each city they know, a star for the capital city, oil rigs to show areas where oil is produced, trees to show the redwood area, and so forth, the word *symbol* is used over and over.

At a strategic point in the sequence, a child who thinks he or she knows the spelling of the term checks it in the dictionary and records it on the chalkboard. Now–as part of the social studies lesson–the teacher helps the children study the word structure: "Let's all say the word. How many syllables do we hear? How do we pronounce the first vowel sound? the second?" Slower readers are asked to respond.

Erasing the word, the teacher asks five or six children to come quickly to the board to write it again. In rapid succession, too, children offer other symbols they know–the symbol for peace, the symbol for school, or the flag symbol for their nation. As a summarizing strategy and as a way of simultaneously working on sentence skills, the teacher may then ask youngsters to write a sentence telling how a symbol is used and to list several other sentences with the word *symbol*. To help slower writers, the teacher keeps moving and may provide assistance to the child with a severe writing disability.

A reading activity can follow the writing period; children read a brief selection that includes the term or idea being stressed and that provides additional information. At this point, slower readers read about symbols in books designed for use at a lower grade level; faster readers read texts intended for use at their own level as well as other more advanced references. To ask disabled readers to gather information from texts written at a level far above their ability is to ask the impossible. It can make children feel as negatively toward social studies as they may already feel toward reading.

Designing Multifaceted Lessons for Heterogeneous Classes.
Because social studies instruction in the elementary grades generally occurs in heterogeneously grouped classes, the teacher must devise lessons that help slower students while challenging the more able. Clearly this is no easy task, but the section above hints at the way to design a lesson when pupils vary greatly in their ability to read and write. Here is a design, which, of course, the teacher must modify to meet the special needs of a class.

R Sequence is based on a creative design projected many years ago by Paul Brandwein.

1. Start with a *doing activity* that involves children with materials, pictures, objects, or maps and that provides them with a concrete base for building concepts. Slower children have trouble handling abstractions unless they have an experiential base upon which to build.

2. Schedule lots of *talking activities* so that children have the opportunity to tell what they are doing and to use new terminology in meaningful contexts. Often more able students already know the terms and slower ones can begin to model their use after that of their peers.

3. Write *new terms* on the chalkboard so that children can see them. Analyze the structure of new words as an aid to later independent decoding by children. Ask children to write the words for themselves.

4. Schedule a *writing activity* with more able students functioning independently and less able ones getting considerable teacher assistance with the basics of recording on paper. With severely disabled upper-grade students, the teacher may have to handle writing as a small-group activity and record dictated sentences on charting paper for the children. See chapter 9 for details of this strategy.

5. Include more *talking* or *sharing activities*. Students share what they have written by reading aloud their summary sentences.

6. Lead into a *reading* time with students reading about the ideas in texts and references written at grade levels they can handle. All children should not read in the same book!

R See pages 302–306.

Tapping the Talent of Slow Students.   Although academically slower students may have trouble handling reading and writing tasks, they often have talents as diverse and well developed as more gifted students. Disabled readers may be fine artists, dancers, vocalists, guitarists, or pantomimists who can contribute much to unit study. These talents should be tapped not only because units are more interesting for everyone when a wide variety of activities are included, but also because children who contribute their talents grow in self-esteem and confidence. The heightened sense of personal worth that comes through success in one endeavor may have an impact on other areas of learning. Armed with more self-confidence, pupils may attack reading with a different attitude.

Talents of slow-learners should be recognized. This in turn may have an impact on other learning tasks.

The Sensory Impaired and the Physically Disabled

Today with the implementation of Public Law 94-142, elementary classrooms are homes not only for bright, average, and slow learners, but also for the sensory impaired and the physically disabled. These children spend part or all of their school day in a regular elementary classroom, at times assisted by special teachers or translators who make possible their integration into the mainstream.

To teach children who have relatively severe visual, hearing, and/ or physical disabilities in a regular classroom requires some adjust-

Through mainstreaming, young people learn to
accept one another's handicaps.

ment in both the physical layout and the emotional climate of the class.
This can pose a problem to the social studies teacher who has organized classroom time and space based on other considerations. However, it can also prove a benefit as the following section will attempt to
clarify.

Planning the Physical Environment.   The teacher can take specific
steps to maximize the learning of sensory impaired and physically
disabled pupils in the class. In terms of the physical design of classroom space and use of materials, these steps include the following:

1. For the hearing impaired:
   Supply directions, especially for tests and tasks to be completed,
   in written as well as oral form.
   Seat the impaired near the front of the room and in the center of
   class activity.
   Arrange seats for group activity so all participants face one
   another to facilitate lipreading by the deaf.

R Good references to
consult are:

Norris Haring, ed.,
*Behavior of Exceptional
Children: An Introduc-
tion to Special Educa-
tion* (Columbus, Ohio:
Charles E. Merrill, 1974).

Samuel Kirk, *Educating
Exceptional Children.*
2nd ed. (Boston:
Houghton Mifflin, 1976).

Make sure other students do not talk when their faces are turned away from the hearing impaired.

Do not stand before a strong light source or window when speaking (this might interfere with lipreading).

2. For the visually impaired:

Seat the impaired near boards and easels to facilitate use of what vision there is.

Write in large, clear letters on boards and easels.

Supply oral directions rather than relying solely on written ones.

Use oral testing where children have trouble reading and writing.

Provide tactile experiences such as feeling relief maps, globes, and models to supplement work with pictures.

Use big maps, graphs, and charts that are relatively free of small print.

Use bright colors that the impaired with some sight can perceive.

3. For the physically disabled:

Keep a central area of classroom space clear to facilitate movement of children from desks to supply and special learning areas.

Seat children to minimize distances that must be covered to get to supplies and special learning areas.

Keep clutter off the floor.

Keep resources and supplies in easily accessible areas.

Provide seats, tables, and chairs that permit comfortable living.

In describing ways to set up classrooms to facilitate mainstreaming, specialists in the area stress the need for a design that encourages children to function independently and freely. Physically disabled children must not learn dependency although, of course, these pupils may require assistance in carrying materials, opening doors placed close together in succession, lifting materials from a floor, or getting things from high shelves.

Maintaining a Receptive Classroom Environment. The teacher can also maximize learning by establishing an emotional climate within the classroom that is accepting and respectful of the problem of the impaired and the disabled. Specific steps a teacher can take include the following:

Provide an activity for the impaired and disabled when the other students are doing an activity that is a physical impossibility for the disabled. For example, when others are involved in expressing through body motion, the immobile child can become an observer, a recorder, or even a judge. When others are involved in an intense

Disign classroom so students will function independtly

listening task, the hard-of-hearing child can be gathering information through reading if there is no interpreter present to translate speech into sign language.

Provide opportunities for the impaired to contribute to the welfare of others in the class. Handicapped children may also be gifted ones who can contribute intellectual talents to unit study by the whole class. Visually impaired children may be highly capable storytellers, speech impaired children may be highly capable writers and artists, while hearing impaired children may be fine cartographers. It is especially important for the teacher to identify the talents of special children so they too see that they have a contribution to make.

Enlist the assistance of other children to help a handicapped one. After a discussion period, for example, a rapid learner can compare written notes with those of a hard-of-hearing child to make sure that the latter has the basic points down on paper. Then, too, the physically able can render direct assistance to the physically disabled. All children should work together to keep clutter off the floor and obstacles like chairs out of main classroom thoroughfares to facilitate the movement of the visually impaired and physically disabled. Through these activities children begin to recognize their obligation to help one another.

In addition, the teacher must work on personal attitudes toward the impaired. This is most true when an impairment relates to speech, as in the case of stuttering. Many teachers do not know how to handle the stutterer in class discussions. A stutterer takes time to express a single thought. Teachers may get fidgety, ask the stutterer to speak more quickly, or even avoid calling on the stutterer all together. Speech therapists give these suggestions to the teacher:

1. Do not tell the stutterer to speak more quickly or slowly, to stop and start over, or to take a deep breath. These acts aggravate the problem.
2. Be relaxed and patient when a stutterer is speaking. Communicate these feelings and attitudes to others in the class so that the act of stuttering is accepted without a negative reaction.
3. Do not label a child in primary grades a stutterer just because he or she repeats words. All children repeat words. It is something the teacher must expect.

Learning to Respect One Another

Although everyone is unique in some way or other, students who are much brighter or slower than average and those who are sensory or physically handicapped often stand out as different from their

Children can be cruel — comes from lack of understanding & compassion.

classmates—and to be different is sometimes to feel inferior and unaccepted. Perhaps the single most difficult task that teachers must perform with regard to special children is to teach respect of individual differences to all students in the class. As all teachers know from firsthand experience, children can be cruel to those they consider different. Such cruelty arises through lack of understanding as well as lack of compassion.

Because all children at some point have functioned in a situation in which they have felt different and unaccepted, children's own experiences can supply the content for feeling-centered, value-related discussions that get at differences and lead to acceptance of them. As part of discussion periods, children can share their experiences, telling how they felt "deep down inside." In this context, the teacher can share books that describe similar situations and feelings and can explain the problems faced by the handicapped. Suitable with primary grade children are such books as:

Rebecca Caudill, *A Certain Small Shepherd* (New York: Holt, Rinehart & Winston, 1965). This is the story of a boy born mute.
Florence Heide, *Sound of Sunshine, Sound of Rain* (New York: Parents Magazine Press, 1970). This is the story of a blind boy.
Harriet Langsam Sobol, *My Brother Steven Is Retarded* (New York: Macmillan, 1977).
Sara Stein, *About Handicaps* (New York: Danbury Press, 1974).
Bernard Wolf, *Anna's Silent World* (Philadelphia: J. B. Lippincott, 1977).
Bernard Wolf, *Connie's New Eyes* (Philadelphia: J. B. Lippincott, 1977).

Suitable with upper graders are books like Judy Blume's *Blubber* (Scarsdale, New York: Bradbury, 1974); with junior high students Robert Cormier's *The Chocolate War* (New York: Dell, 1975). Both deal with harassment of individuals by a group. Although not dealing directly with the handicapped, these books clearly show what it is like to be made the scapegoat because one is different in some way. In talking about such stories, students can consider why they themselves taunt others who are different, how it feels to be the scapegoat, and why people in groups do thoughtless things they might not do by themselves.

Respect for those who are different from oneself is an essential learning in the social studies. For that reason, mainstreaming can prove advantageous to all children. When handicapped children are in the class, that class can become a social microcosm where children learn acceptance and respect through everyday interaction. Seeing a teacher operate with respect toward the gifted, slow, average, handicapped, left-handed, tall, short, fat, and thin, children may begin to

R A study unit and a listing of materials to help students learn what a handicap is can be found in "Walk a Mile in My Shoes," *Instructor.* 88:186-187, October 1978. An extended bibliography of references is given in "Books About Kids with Special Needs," by V. V. Garry, *Instructor.* 88:113-116, November, 1978.

pattern their behavior after that of a teacher who has become very important in their lives. Modeling their behavior after his or hers, children may learn to assist others who need it and look beneath appearances to judge another on the real person who lives inside.

Children will follow attitudes of teacher. (modeling) Will start to see "real" inside person.

Opening Opportunities to All: a Moral Commitment

The gifted, the slow, the sensory impaired, and the physically disabled often have not received an equal education in the least restrictive environment. The same is true of recent immigrants who cannot speak English, of those who move frequently in search of employment, and of those who have faced discrimination because of their race, ethnic background, religion, or sex. These people have found that opportunities for them are more limited than for others who belong to a more favored group. Society accepts and indeed advocates lower-level goals for some people and holds stereotyped beliefs as to what members of these groups should and should not do, trying to keep them out of the economic and social mainstreams.

Not only exceptionalities need to get an equal ed, but also immigrants.

Stereotyped Sex Roles

Women are one group for whom vocational and social opportunities have in the past been limited by traditional views. Today, however, numerous factors have led to shifting perceptions of male and female roles—a shift from agrarian to industrial society, smaller families, family planning measures, home labor-saving devices, processed foods, and growth of day-care centers. One outcome has been that more women are remaining in the work force throughout their lives; they are choosing careers that include jobs in business and computer science, medicine and dentistry, engineering and architecture, as well as in the home as full-time wives and mothers.

Options for men are increasing. Men are entering careers previously restricted to women: nursing, primary school teaching, and secretarial work; in some instances, they are choosing to assume household management responsibilities as well as those associated with child care.

On the other hand, old stereotypes persist. Men who choose to assume housekeeping and child care tasks full-time while their wives pursue careers outside the home still raise eyebrows in some circles. Women find that average salaries for them are just about half that for men, because they frequently are employed in lower paying jobs. Some careers are still essentially closed to women—for example, service in the United States Senate and Supreme Court. Since its origin in 1787, only 12 women have served in the Senate; as this book is being written only one woman serves there. No woman has ever served as a Supreme Court Justice or as President of the United States.

The Scope of the Problem.   Studies indicate that children learn at an early age the traditional roles assigned in their society to males and females. Ask a boy in kindergarten or first grade what he wants to be when he grows up, and he will talk of being a fireman, a policeman, a doctor, an engineer, or the president. It is still a rare boy who speaks of being a secretary, a nurse, or a father. In contrast, a disproportionate number of girls when asked the same question will confine choices to nurse, teacher, secretary, ballet dancer, and mother. Although sex-role stereotypes have already been internalized by age four or five, according to Jean Lipman-Bluman, these traditional views do not have a limiting influence until adolescence. It is then that children apply their beliefs to their life patterns. It is then that children's stereotyped views as well as those of society at large close off opportunities.

Numbers of factors play a part in the development of sex-role stereotypes. Of most concern to educators are those residing in the school; as Myra and David Sadker have written:

There is no subject in our elementary schools called Male Role Development or How to Be a Girl. Yet children learn their sex roles very well indeed. This learning occurs through a *hidden curriculum* that is replete with incidental learnings. As the teacher rewards or punishes certain behavior, or as children interact with school rules, rituals, and mores, they are contributing to the *hidden curriculum*. For the *hidden curriculum* consists of the learnings that children acquire not from their textbooks, but from living in and experiencing the process of schooling.

The hidden social studies curriculum takes many forms, one of which relates to language usage. Aware of this, publishers of social studies texts are changing textbook titles that use the word *man*. They are substituting terms like *fire fighter*, *police officer*, and *mail carrier* for more traditionally used terms and are avoiding the use of *he* when both men and women are being discussed. Clearly books and teachers teach roles as much by the terms they use as by the content they consider with children.

What is that content? In the social studies—which certainly should be free of stereotypes—content has been filled with male heroes. Children who study the past will learn of men who succeeded as leaders—Washington, Jefferson, Champlain, Carlton—who contributed new technologies—Howe, Edison, Fulton, Bell—who were great musicians—Beethoven, Chopin, Mozart, Berlin—who are reknowned artists—Hals, Michelangelo, Rembrandt, Monet. These lists of important people are an accurate reflection of what was. Not as many

R Read Jean Lipman-Blumen, "How Ideology Shapes Women's Lives," *Scientific American* 226:34-42 January 1972.

R From Myra and David Sadker, "Sexual Discrimination in the Elementary School," *National Elementary Principal*, 52:41, October 1972.

Development of sex-role stereotypes

women—given the social beliefs of the past—were able to make a significant contribution. And the work of many women has been ignored. On the other hand, unless social studies strives to transcend stereotyped roles for both men and women, not all people will have equal opportunity to contribute to the advance of society.

Classroom Solutions. In what ways can teachers help children overcome stereotyped views of what men and women can or cannot achieve? An easy beginning is to avoid the trap of assigning active tasks to boys and more passive ones to girls.

Do not make girls watchers and boys doers. On field trips, boys sometimes have been assigned roles as data collectors, while girls function as data recorders. Girls can collect data as effectively as boys; boys can handle secretarial tasks as effectively as girls.

Do not always make boys captains and chairpersons. The role of chairperson applies equally to all.

Do not reserve mechanical tasks for boys. Girls can hammer, saw, and drill as effectively as boys. They can operate projectors and other audiovisual equipment if given the chance.

Do not reserve sewing and cooking tasks for girls. Boys can participate in churning, sewing, and quilting activities.

Do not assign classroom housekeeping tasks based on sex. Girls and boys can move chairs, wipe counters, erase boards, etc.

Things that should be done include the following:

Widen children's views of roles by including noted women on lists of people who have and are making contributions. Here one may find female role models among modern stateswomen (including Ella Grasso, Dixie Lee Ray, Barbara Jordan, Millicent Fenwick, and the late Golda Meir), a modern artist such as Georgia O'Keefe, and an executive such as Jane Pfeiffer, NBC chairperson to whom President Carter offered a cabinet position.

Widen perceptions by bringing both men and women who have succeeded in diverse professions to the school as speakers; introduce children to female mayors, architects, doctors, postal workers, telephone workers, and engineers; introduce them to male secretaries and nurses.

Encourage girls and boys who have thought in narrow career terms to explore books that show women and men contributing in a wide range of areas.

Use language carefully. Do not talk of nurses and teachers always in terms of *she*, or carpenters and lawyers in terms of *he*. Try to avoid terms such as *chairman* and *statesman*.

T For information on women's role in the American Revolution, see Lonnelle Aikman, "Patriots in Petticoats," *National Geographic*, 148:475-493, October 1975.

[handwritten margin note: Teachers can help over come stereotyped views by not assigning active tasks to boys & passive to girls.]

Idea Page

As you study materials–text, trade, filmed, pictorial, taped–you should be alert for signs of sex, race, language, and economic stereotyping. Especially with textual materials you should also be concerned with how the needs of gifted and slow learners are being met. Here is an analysis guide for use in evaluating materials in terms of the comprehensiveness of the view they offer.

A Guide for Studying Curricular Materials

Directions: Study a set of curricular materials and the advertising brochures used in conjunction with them. Then answer the following questions:

1. Are both men and women/boys and girls given equal attention in the pictures? To answer this question, select fifteen pictures at random and count the number of each sex represented.
2. Are both males and females given equal attention in the story? To answer this question, select thirty pages of text and decide whether a male or female has the lead role.
3. Are both males and females depicted in pictures and texts performing a variety of professional and familial roles?
4. Are both males and females depicted in both active and passive pursuits?
5. Does sexism prevail in the language used?
6. Are members of various ethnic groups given attention in the pictures? Again select fifteen pictures and do a count.
7. Are members of various ethnic groups given attention in the story?
8. Are members of various ethnic groups depicted in pictures and words performing a variety of professional roles?
9. Are members of various ethnic groups depicted in leadership positions?
10. Are older citizens presented in stereotyped pursuits?
11. What is the reading level of the textual material? Generally the reading level of a social studies text series should be below the grade level at which it is to be used.
12. What kinds of enrichment activities are offered? Do these activities carry students to higher cognitive levels?
13. Are there any taped materials available for use with children who have visual problems?
14. Are handicapped people depicted in the material functioning within the mainstream?

Minorities

Racism—"the conscious and unconscious attitudes of superiority which permit and demand that a majority oppress a minority"—is a pressing concern in the U.S.—one that the Joint Commission on Mental Health of Children called "the number one public health problem facing America." Writing in the *43rd Yearbook of the National Council for the Social Studies*, Geneva Gay describes the reality of racism that "pervades the whole society and affects us all." She points out that "Some of the most devastating kinds of racism are subtle acts, committed out of habit by people who have no conscious desire or intent to relegate ethnic minorities to perpetual states of inferiority, oppression, and suppression."

The Scope of the Problem. Looking back on the period during which North America was colonized, James Banks describes the victimization of the newly arrived by those who had arrived earlier. In colonial times, the French, the Germans, the Irish, and the Scotch-Irish were discriminated against by the English because of their ethnic and religious differences. According to Banks, the goal for these and other European immigrants who were to follow—the Polish, the Italians, the Jews, the Russians, the Spanish—was to be assimilated and integrated into the mainstream. Immigrants were forced to sacrifice their ethnic ways and traditions in exchange for social acceptance, economic advancement, and personal security for them and their families. The ideal was the melting pot in which differences disappeared as newcomers assumed the dress, language, and ways of the early settlers and as intermarriage between groups blurred distinctions.

However, as Banks goes on to explain, the melting pot formula was different for nonwhite ethnics. The formula became *cultural assimilation* (assumption of dress, language, manners, and values) and *exclusion*. Members of these minority groups faced barriers that prevented them from functioning fully in the economic and social mainstreams. Certain menial jobs were considered appropriate and were, therefore, open to them; other more remunerative jobs were considered too demanding and, therefore, closed to all but a select few.

As in the case of sex-role stereotypes, ethnic-role stereotypes have a harmful effect on both members of the group to which stereotypes are applied and to the society as a whole. The striving individual is frustrated by his or her inability to get ahead despite possession of characteristics superior to some of those who make it. At the same time, society loses the contribution these individuals could make.

The schools are and have been parties to this crime; the social studies curriculum is not without blame. Here again, traditional language usage plays a part in maintaining stereotyped views. Some

R See Geneva Gay, "Racism in America: Imperatives for Teaching Ethnic Studies," in *Teaching Ethnic Studies: Concepts and Strategies*, 43rd Yearbook of the National Council for the Social Studies, James Banks, .ed. (Arlington, Virginia: National Council for the Social Studies, 1973), pp. 27-50.

R Read James Banks, "Should Integration Be a Societal Goal?" in *Controversial Issues in the Social Studies*, 45th Yearbook of the National Council for the Social Studies, Raymond Muessig, editor (Arlington, Virginia: National Council for the Social Studies, 1975), pp. 197-205.

R From Frank Hale, "Agenda for Excellence," *Phi Delta Kappan*, 60:205S, November 1978: "There are 385,000 attorneys in the U.S. . . . But there are only 4,800 black attorneys. There are 325,000 phsicians . . . but there are only 3,500 black physicians. . . ."

teachers, for instance, will talk of the Native Americans as savages, suggesting that their ways were primitive. Some books and stories offered to children sometimes reinforce such erroneous views. As a result, many children leave elementary social studies lessons believing that all Native Americans wore feathered headdresses, lived in tepees, and scalped their enemies during battle. Nothing could be farther from the truth.

Classroom Approaches.   If schools are to make good on their commitment to move all children into the economic mainstream to the greatest extent possible, clearly they must begin by making certain that erroneous and offensive stereotyped views regarding particular ethnic groups are not a hidden part of the curriculum. This is not so easy a task as it first appears. As was pointed out earlier, people are often not conscious of the racist views they hold; they behave as a matter of habit, not of thought.

Sometimes a frontal attack on a problem is the best solution. This may well be the case in dealing with misconceptions about different ethnic groups. Some educators advocate much emphasis in social studies on ethnic studies, with units developed that teach all children about blacks, Hispanics, Native Americans, white ethnics, and Hawaiians. Although knowledge about something does not necessarily bring comprehension of it, positive feelings toward or a caring about something is a first step that may lead to the other goals.

Here perhaps more than in any other context, children must work at clarifying their values and identifying principles in which they truly believe. This is the place where discussion of right and wrong is imperative, with the teacher exerting leadership in helping children commit themselves to value principles that affirm the rights of all people to equal opportunity.

New Immigrants and Migrants

The immigrants who came to the North American continent starting in the early 1600s were only the first of many. Today immigrants continue to come, bringing with them differences that set them apart. Typically they come with little material wealth, having been forced by circumstances to leave whatever valuables they possessed behind. They come with limited knowledge of English. As a result, newly arrived immigrants land on the poor end of the economic scale and generally must struggle with poverty and a society that discriminates against them because of language and cultural differences.

In a similar situation are the migrants. Often from an ethnic minority and speakers of a language other than English, migrants move in search of employment in agriculture. They are usually poor.

R See James Banks, ed., *Teaching Ethnic Studies: Concepts and Strategies, 43rd Yearbook of the National Council for the Social Studies* (Arlington, Virginia: NCSS, 1973). This book provides ideas for teaching ethnic studies as well as relevant background information.

T Use Marie Hall Ets, *Bad Boy, Good Boy* (New York: Thomas Y. Crowell, 1967) to introduce children to the problems of the immigrant in America.

Idea Page

The teacher who attempts to teach the Native American experience should know the writings of Ann Nolan Clark, who portrays Indian life with feeling and realism. Her books for the younger child include:

In My Mother's House (New York: Viking Press, 1941). This deals with life on a Pueblo Indian Reservation from the point of view of a Tewa child.

Little Navajo Bird (Viking, 1943). Ceremonial activities of the Navaho as well as the day-to-day life activities are discussed.

Secret of the Andes (Viking, 1952). This is the story of a Peruvian Indian boy.

Her books for the older child include:

Journey to the People (Viking, 1969). This is a collection of essays based on Clark's work with the Navajo, Sioux, Pueblo, and Zuni Indians.

Circle of the Seasons (Viking, 1970). Ceremonies and daily activities of the Pueblo Indians are described.

Medicine Man's Daughter (Viking, 1963). This is a story set among the Navajo Indians of today in which a girl plays a strong role.

The teacher who attempts to teach the black experience should be familiar with the writings of Ezra Jack Keats, appropriate for early primary children; the works of Lucille Clifton, for primary children; and those of Janice Udry, for primary children. Excellent and perceptive writers who have produced either prose or poetry that can be used with upper graders who are learning about the black experience include Langston Hughes, Gwendolyn Brooks, Virginia Hamilton, and June Jordon.

The Immigrant in the Schools.   Some schools that serve students whose first language is not English have extensive bilingual/bicultural programs. The goal of these programs is twofold:

1. Children should learn to communicate in and read English. Rationale: without English skills, children will be relegated to economic inferiority. In an English-speaking country, people must know the language simply to exist from day to day.
2. Children should maintain their proficiency in their first language and an appreciation and knowledge of their own ethnic traditions and heritage. Rationale: children should neither be made to feel that their own language and traditions are inferior or that they must give up that which has been so much a part of themselves.

In most instances these programs are centered in areas where students speak Spanish as their first language. They are taught by teachers who themselves are Spanish or who can speak Spanish fluently. Children maintain contact not only with the Spanish language in school but also with their own ethnic traditions and customs.

Where a child is the only non-English speaker in a class, however, the situation is far more complex. Teachers usually cannot speak the newcomer's language and they know little about the cultural traditions that are part of the newcomer's home life. Then too, because the child cannot communicate in English, he or she is placed in the "slow" group or in a class with younger children. The youngster may also dress and act somewhat differently from classmates. As a result, he or she is a ready target for other children's taunts and may begin to feel inferior as well as different and become defensive and/or withdrawn unless the teacher takes definitive steps.

Specific steps teachers can take to insure the acceptance of the immigrant child into the group include the following:

1. Teachers must not equate inability to communicate in English with general lack of intelligence. They must remember that this child does communicate well—but in another language.
2. Teachers should encourage the student who is becoming bilingual to share his or her language with the class. As the Chinese child is learning English, each day he or she can teach a word of Chinese to classmates. Many speakers of English have a strong language prejudice; many believe that their language for some reason is superior to all others. By learning about another language, children may learn to respect other languages of the world and the people who speak them.
3. Teachers should encourage a bilingual/bicultural child to share some of his or her cultural traditions with the class. A bicultural

Building a positive self-concept is especially
important in classrooms where children are
becoming bilingual.

child may be able to tell a story that is unfamiliar to the class, tell
about a holiday tradition, or show art objects that demonstrate
the forms beauty takes in his or her culture.

4. Teachers should find tasks that the child who still has trouble with
written English can perform successfully. For example, the
bilingual/bicultural child can contribute to art projects, to
mathematics projects, and to sports activities where language
difference is not a handicap. For him or her this is part of the
social studies, because through successful participation he or she
is maintaining a positive self-concept—something vitally
important if the child is to move into the economic and social
mainstreams.

R Read Arnold
Cheyney, *Teaching
Children of Different
Cultures in the Class-
room*, 2nd ed. (Colum-
bus, Ohio: Charles E.
Merrill, 1976) for specific
ideas for helping chil-
dren, especially those
who speak a different
language, achieve lan-
guage skills.

Simultaneously, the child must be given individualized instruction in
English.

Migrants. In *Go Up the Road*, Yolanda Ruiz and her family are
Mexican-Americans whose home is New Mexico but who follow the
harvests across the Southwest. Yolanda's life is one of poverty in migrant camps, of taunts—"Go home, if you don't like it here! Dirty
Mex!"—of perpetual movement from one school to another, and of
demonstrations to get something as basic as adequate medical care.

T Upper graders will be challenged by Evelyn Lampman, *Go Up the Road* (New York: Atheneum, 1972); Joe Molnar, *Graciela: A Mexican-American Child Tells Her Story* (New York: Franklin Watts, 1972); and Sandra Weiner, *Small Hands, Big Hands: Seven Profiles of Chicano Migrant Workers and Their Families* (New York: Pantheon Books, 1970).

As Yolanda's story strikingly demonstrates, the plight of migrant children is difficult, and their education is often sporadic. Poor, they become the focus of taunts from classmates. Spanish in language and Mexican in culture, they must function in an American curriculum. On the move, they hardly have time to know a teacher and a school when another dislocation strikes and they move again. Many school districts in the Southwest have adjusted their programs to meet the needs of migrant children. These programs tend to have three goals: development of a positive self-concept, heightened awareness of the migrant's own culture, and increased language skills.

1. Development of a Positive Self-Concept. Because migrant children are so likely to be the butt of classmates' taunts, development of a positive self-concept comes slowly. Some of the suggested activities for improving self-concept given in chapter 7 may be useful; however, most significant are teachers' attitudes toward the child. Teachers must be empathetic and supportive, creating an accepting environment that affects not only the migrant child but others in the class.

The very fact that the migrant youngster has traveled widely, sometimes much more widely than other students, can be put to good advantage in the social studies. Places a migrant child has visited can be plotted on a map as a means for all children to build map skills. The migrant can become an expert on these areas, sharing firsthand geographical knowledge with others. Poorer in English skills, the migrant child can share knowledge through pictures that he or she draws. Other youngsters can use these drawings for the content of picture-reading sessions out of which the class generalizes about the geography, the plant and animal life, and the customs of people living there. In this way, the migrant child begins to see that he or she belongs to this class, even if that belonging lasts but a short time. The child experiences some success, and success is essential if the child is to view him- or herself as a person of value.

2. Cultural Awareness. Where Mexican-American migrant children are in the class, the Mexican culture should be there too, for one's ethnic background is part of the self. To look positively at the self, one must view one's cultural heritage with pleasure and respect. Integration of aspects of Mexican culture into the classroom needn't be a difficult task. Mexican holidays can be celebrated in the classroom just as American ones are. Mexican heroes—Cesar Chavez, for example—should be recognized so that youngsters have role models to emulate. Without a doubt, children on the move will assimilate American manners, traditions, and values, but in the process they must not sacrifice the wealth and beauty of their own culture.

T Use Ruth Franchere, *Cesar Chavez* (New York: Thomas Y. Crowell, 1970) with children in primary grades. Use also Barbara Todd, *Juan Patricio* (New York: G. P. Putnam's Sons, 1972).

3. Language Development. Development of both English and Spanish language skills is the third goal of programs for migrant children. Mexican-Americans, like all immigrants who move into Canada and the United States, must not lose their ability to communicate in their own language and they should learn to read their first language with ease and enjoyment. Spanish is part of their selves; in teaching children English, schools should encourage children to communicate as well in Spanish so that they become truly bilingual. Of course, the ability to speak English is necessary too, if a person is to have the freedom to seek employment anywhere in the country.

Many of the strategies that involve experience charts, vocabulary lists, and slotted writing described in the next chapter can be used with children learning English as a second language as well as with primary youngsters. Working with geographical terms, for example, children can make charts that contain both the English and the Spanish equivalents. Charts dictated in Spanish to a Spanish-speaking teacher can be redictated in English, to be read and reread even as other sentences are added. The sequence of activities outlined on pages 261–262 of this chapter is equally useful here with talking, writing, and reading activities employing both Spanish and English.

From Side to Mainstream: A Summary Thought or Two

Do you remember this Old Mother Goose rhyme?

> Peter, Peter, pumpkin eater,
> Had a wife and couldn't keep her;
> He put her in a pumpkin shell
> And there he kept her very well.

Since the early beginnings of nation-states on the North American continent, we have tended to behave much in the manner of Peter Pumpkin Eater. Faced with people who were different from those in control, we have attempted to put migrants and immigrants, ethnic minorities, women, handicapped people, and slower and gifted individuals in a "pumpkin shell" to keep them out of the way. Today there are signs that the shell is breaking open. Opportunities for women, members of some minorities, and handicapped people are expanding. But there are also signs that the breaking open of the shell may be only a temporary phenomenon. Speaking of the Women's Movement but using words that can be applied to all groups that have felt the hand of discrimination, Jacquelyn Mattfield, noted educator, cautions:

R Jacquelyn Mattfield, "Perfection of the Life or of the Work," Commencement Address, delivered May 1978, Goucher College.

We cannot afford the ostrich complacency which permits selective vision. . . because we would like human nature to be different. We must not underestimate the real though inexplicable potency of age-old universal assumptions about. . . supremacy.

Mattfield's caution is one that social studies educators must take seriously. The social studies educator must not only accept fully the commitment to meet the needs of all children in the least restrictive environment but must also "person" the front lines to assure that the commitment continues.

A Quotation to Ponder

Dorothy Lee writes:

R Dorothy Lee, "Being and Value in a Primitive Culture," *The Journal of Philosophy*, 46:401-415, 1949.

Anthropologists have realized in recent years that people of other cultures not only act differently, but that they have a different basis for their behavior. They act upon different premises; they perceive reality differently, and codify it differently. In this codification, language is largely instrumental. It incorporates the premises of the culture, and codifies reality in such a way that it presents it as absolute to the members of each culture.

1. **What impact should the idea that people of different cultures perceive reality differently have on programs for children whose first language is not English and whose culture is not American?**

2. **What problems might occur as a result of differing perceptions of reality when peoples of differing language backgrounds try to interact?**

References

Banks, James A., ed. *Teaching Ethnic Studies: Concepts and Strategies, 43rd Yearbook of National Council for the Social Studies.* Arlington, Virginia: NCSS, 1973.

Burling, Robbins. *English in Black and White.* New York: Holt, Rinehart & Winston, 1973.

Cheyney, Arnold. *Teaching Children of Different Cultures in the Classroom: A Language Approach.* 2nd ed. Columbus, Ohio: Charles E. Merrill, 1976.

Cole, Robert W.; and Dunn, Rita. "A New Lease on Life for Education of the Handicapped: Ohio Copes with 94:142," in *Phi Delta Kappan,* 59:3-6, 1977.

Daniels, Arlene. "Women's Worlds," *Society,* 44-46, March/April 1978.

Haring, Norris, ed. *Behavior of Exceptional Children: An Introduction to Special Education.* Columbus, Ohio: Charles E. Merrill, 1974.

Kirk, Samuel. *Educating Exceptional Children,* 2nd ed. Boston: Houghton Mifflin, 1976.

Labuda, Michael. *Creative Reading for Gifted Learners: A Design for Excellence.* Newark, Delaware: International Reading Association, 1974.

Millman, Marcia; and Kanter, Rosabeth, eds. *Another Voice: Feminist Perspectives on Social Life and Social Science.* New York: Anchor Books, 1975.

Muessig, Raymond, ed. *Controversial Issues in the Social Studies: A Contemporary Perspective, 45th Yearbook of National Council for the Social Studies.* Arlington, Virginia: NCSS, 1975.

Smith, Robert M.; and Neisworth, John. *The Exceptional Child: A Functional Approach.* New York: McGraw-Hill, 1975.

Solomon, Edward. "New York City's Prototype School for Educating the Handicapped," *Phi Delta Kappan,* 59:7-10, 1977.

Sadker, Myra; and Sadker, David. *Now Upon a Time: A Contemporary View of Children's Literature.* New York: Harper & Row, 1977.

9

Social Studies in the Primary Years: Teaching Skills Through Content

Marty is a happy kindergartener.

Humanity shows itself in all its intellectual splendour during this tender age as the sun shows itself at dawn, and the flower in the first unfolding of the petals; and we must respect religiously, reverently, these first indications of individuality.

Maria Montessori,
The Montessori Method

Key Questions

What two dilemmas face the teacher of primary social studies?

Suggest ways that the teacher of young children can build their ability to handle representational thinking.

Describe characteristic ways that pre-operational children view the world.

Describe the thought patterns of the concrete-operationally functioning child.

Describe in detail at least ten instructional strategies for blending content and skills in primary grade classrooms.

**Figure 9.1
A Two-day Lesson Sequence
for Second Grade:**

Topic: The relationship between people and animals in Alaska
(part of a unit on Alaska)

Major Social Studies Concepts: **Grade Level:** Second
Dependency and change
                                             Date: April 28

Objectives:

1. Children are able to explain how Alaskan people used to use animals as part of
   their way of life.
2. Children are able to tell why people are less directly dependent on animals
   today.
3. Children are able to supply many adjectives that describe animals and their
   relationship to people, based on picture and poetry experiences.
4. Children are able to describe an Alaskan animal by writing a sentence that
   contains clear adjectives and verbs. The sentence should begin with a capital
   letter and end in appropriate punctuation.
5. Children are able to function cooperatively as part of a teacher-led group.

Materials: Picture folder showing people interacting with animals in Alaska;
Beyond the High Hills: Book of Eskimo Poems (World Publisher, 1971, photos by Guy
Mary-Rousselière); strips of white construction paper; pieces of construction paper
in two different colors

Procedure:	**Key Questions and Structuring Remarks:**
1. *Motivation and Orientation:* Display pictures of Alaskan animals and people.	Here are some pictures that show how the Eskimos used to use animals. Does anyone know what this animal is called? What words can we use to tell how this animal looks? moves? How big is it? What color is it? How is the person using the animal?
2. Read several poems aloud from *Beyond the High Hills*.	Why did the Eskimos hunt seals? Why were the huskies so important to the people? Today many people live in towns and cities in Alaska. Will the dogs and seals be as important to the people?
3. Cooperatively select one animal of Alaska to make into a social studies word ladder.	Which animal do you like best? Why? Let's vote to decide which one we will make into a word ladder.

4. Brainstorm descriptive phrases that fit the chosen animal. Print words given on the social studies ladder.

What words can we think of that tell about or describe our animal? Let's write them here above the animal name. What words can we think of that tell the importance of this animal to people. Let's write these words here below the animal name on our ladder.

Children orally build sentences using the words in their ladder.

Let's put sentences together by selecting some words from the top of the ladder and words from the bottom part.

Example of Social Studies Word Ladder

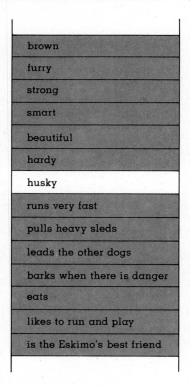

(Make the strip of adjectives one color; staple this to the major noun word.)

(Make noun word strip white.)

(Make verb phrases on a different color strip; staple it to the noun word.)

Sentences Written Based on the Ladder

The strong husky pulls the heavy sleds for the Eskimo.
The beautiful husky is a very good friend.
The smart husky barks when there is danger.
The smartest husky dog leads the other dogs.

5. Children each select another animal discussed. They create their own animal word ladders. Based on ladders, they write a series of sentences. Other animals they might use include walrus, seal, polar bear, etc.

6. Children take turns sharing their sentences and displaying their ladders. Everyone listens to each speaker to decide whether the animal in question helps people take care of a basic need—food, shelter, clothing, love, or security.

What basic need does this animal help people meet? Is this animal more threatening than it is helpful?

7. Children work together to hang up their sentences on a line strung across the classroom. (This is a cooperative physical activity that is necessary after a period of sitting and talking.)

Second Lesson in Sequence: April 29

Objectives:

1. Children are able to explain the dependency relationship that exists between people who live in cold climates and animals. They are able to use the words "dependent on" in talking about the relationship.
2. Children are able to verbalize events in the past by using the terminology used to.
3. Children can categorize various activities in terms of basic human needs: food, shelter, clothing, love, and security.
4. Children grow in the ability to write clear sentences that begin with capital letters and end with punctuation.
5. Children grow in the ability to work cooperatively on production teams.

Materials: Paper strips, paper puncher, string, pictures and sentences from previous day displayed in the room, marker pens

Procedure:

1. Motivation and Orientation: Children take turns reading a sentence written yesterday and pointing out a picture that shows the same activity. Children together decide which need (if any) is being taken care of through that activity. The child who prepared that sentence card takes it down and writes the need on the opposite side.

Key Questions and Structuring Remarks:

Let's see if we can put the sentences that we wrote yesterday with pictures that show the same meaning or idea.

Is this a way of getting food? clothing? love? shelter? security? How? Why? This is the way Eskimos used to do it. How do you think they do it today if they live in towns?

How did they used to get food? Which animals used to be used this way?

2. Vote on one animal that children believe used to be most important to the Eskimos. Cooperatively make a dependency "tie-together" as a model for later team activity.

Which animal used to be the most important one to Eskimos? Why do you say that? Let's vote to decide the most important one. What needs did that animal supply?

Example of Dependency Tie-Together

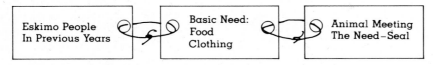

| Eskimo People In Previous Years | Basic Need: Food Clothing | Animal Meeting The Need – Seal |

Have a volunteer tie the cards together with string.

3. Hang the tie-together on the viewing line. Children work together in three-person desk teams to create other dependency tie-togethers. They choose other animals as the basis of their visuals.

In cases where an animal is a threat rather than an aid, children add the words "Basic Threat" to their tie-togethers and indicate in what respect it is a threat; e.g. polar bear – basic threat to security as well as a means of supplying clothing.

In your groups, first select an animal. One group member will make a card naming the chosen animal.

Another group member will make a card listing the basic needs supplied by that animal. The third member will make a card just like on our model tie-together. Before tying your cards together, check to be sure spelling is correct.

4. As children finish their tie-togethers they hang them on the viewing line so all can see. Later each child writes sentences that pattern in this way: People used to be dependent on the _____ because _____ . They select words from their visuals when completing their sentences.

(Based on a lesson taught by Linda Morrison, a second grade teacher.)

Introduction

Two dilemmas face the social studies teacher guiding children's learning in preschool and lower elementary programs. One is posed by the cognitive level at which primary youngsters function. Young children's ability to conceptualize is limited. They operate intellectually on their perceptions of the world in a way that is qualitatively different from that of an adult. Children handle space, time, and number concepts differently and use speech differently from adults.

The second problem is posed by the already crowded primary school program. Writing in *The Social Studies*, Joseph Harrington of Framington State College, Massachusetts, summarizes this dilemma as teachers perceive it: "I'd love to teach the children social studies, but when can I fit it in? I have reading, language arts, math, science, special subjects, and other programs. There simply isn't enough time in the day to implement a social studies curriculum."

R Read Joseph Harrington, "A Non-subject Social Studies Curriculum Guide for the Primary Grades," in *The Social Studies* 68:33-38 (January/February 1977).

Beginning Where the Child Is

Linda Morrison's lesson sequence outlined in Figure 9.1 demonstrates that these two dilemmas confronting the primary grade teacher are not irresolvable. Young children can grow in basic social studies competencies if materials and activities are presented in terms they can comprehend. Some guidelines include:

1. Use visual and concrete means as a base for talk. Words alone do not suffice at this stage.
2. Provide opportunity for young children to manipulate ideas directly through art, construction, dramatic, and physical activity—all of which go beyond the talk level and allow for active involvement rather than passive observation.
3. Place relatively complex concepts such as dependency—which is a key term in sociology and economics as well as in political science—into a context that is meaningful and interesting to young children—in this case, animals.
4. Give children specific tasks that require them to work cooperatively with others to complete a product.

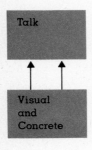

In her lesson sequence, Ms. Morrison began with pictures rather than with words so that children could verbalize descriptions based on images they had clearly in mind. She knew that children of this age are fond of animals. Therefore, she started with animals before guiding children to consider ways that humans living in Alaska were dependent on them. To help children handle dependency relationships, Linda turned to a construction activity in which children tied people and animals together with a relationship card that spelled out the dependency. The activity resulted in a product that provided a concrete representation of dependency.

In addition, Ms. Morrison asked youngsters to work in three-person teams to produce a tie-together. She did this for she knew that one of the most basic social competencies is the ability to work cooperatively and productively with others on a task. At this stage of development, however, children need considerable structure in undertaking cooperative tasks. In this case structure was achieved by beginning with a class production through which youngsters learned what was required as they attempted the task later in teams.

Saving Time by Integrating

Linda Morrison's lesson sequence also demonstrates that there is time in the school day for study of human activity 1) if social studies content is used as a vehicle for teaching reading, language arts, or mathematics; 2) if art and music activity are correlated with social studies; and 3) if social science learnings are correlated with learnings in the natural sciences.

Reading and the language arts have no specific content of their own; they are tool areas. One must read about something, talk about something, and write about something. In contrast, the social sciences and the humanities have essential content. It is this content about which children should read, write, and talk and to which they should listen in school so that they are better able to handle current and future social problems. When human activity provides the content for reading, writing, listening, speaking, drawing, and singing, children acquire fundamental understanding of social concepts and learn how to apply their understanding to the interpretation of social problems as they grow in basic skills.

The dilemmas posed by the limited cognitive development of the young child and the problem of a crowded curriculum determine the foci of this chapter. The first sections zero in on youngsters' developing ability to think and communicate and on patterns of cognitive growth. Implications for instruction are included. The second half of the chapter provides suggestions for blending social studies into the total primary school day through an integration with the skill development program.

Idea Page

A. Young children can construct tie-togethers not only to represent dependency relationships in concrete fashion but also to represent other fundamental social relationships.

B. Hints for using tie-togethers:

1. The number of cards in a tie-together can determine the number of children working on one. If there are two cards in a tie-together, put two children on a team; if there are three, include three on a team. Each child contributes a card.
2. Children also gain in handwriting and manual skills. Tie-togethers are tied together with string—a task requiring some manual dexterity on the part of youngsters. Printing the cards provides meaningful handwriting practice.
3. If they wish, young children can add pictures they draw or clip from magazines to their tie-togethers. Children who still have trouble writing can work from ideas written by the teacher on the chalkboard during a group brainstorming session. They can copy words they find there.
4. Tie-togethers with words can be used as early as mid first grade. Earlier than that, children can draw pictures that they tie together to show relationships.

**Figure 9.2
A Producer-Consumer
Tie-Together**

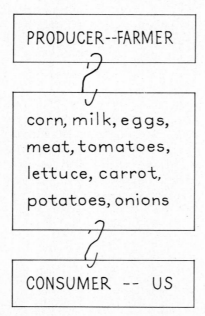

Figure 9.3
A Cause and Effect
Tie-Together

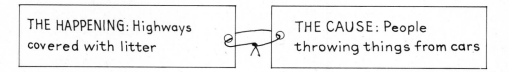

THE HAPPENING: Highways covered with litter ⟷ THE CAUSE: People throwing things from cars

Figure 9.4
A Sequence Tie-Together

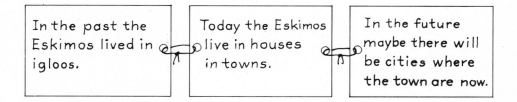

In the past the Eskimos lived in igloos. ⟷ Today the Eskimos live in houses in towns. ⟷ In the future maybe there will be cities where the town are now.

Figure 9.5
A Server-User Tie-Together

Figure 9.6
A Shared Relationship
Tie-Together

SERVER--FIRE FIGHTER

puts out fires;

rescues people;

rescues pets;

gives advice on how to prevent fire.

USER--THE COMMUNITY

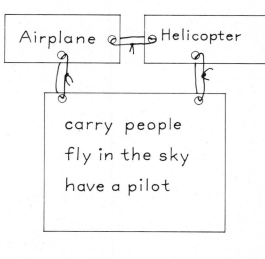

Airplane ⟷ Helicopter

carry people

fly in the sky

have a pilot

The Development of Cognitive Abilities

R See Heinz Werner, *Comparative Psychology of Mental Development* (New York: Science Editions, 1948).

In *Comparative Psychology of Mental Development*, Heinz Werner describes the cognitive functioning of the young child. According to Werner, the younger the child, the more likely he or she is to organize the world in terms of the self and of action. The child structures time in terms of personal activity; time is organized around big daily events—getting up, breakfast, snack time, going to bed. Space is mapped out in terms of the child's own body—*here* is where *I* am; *big* is bigger than *I* am; *small* is smaller than *I* am; *under* is the feel of crawling under the table; *down* is sliding down the bannister; *in* is in *my* house. In each case, what is known is known through its relation to the self and often through movement of the body.

Pre-Operational Functioning

R Check for details in Jean Piaget, *The Psychology of Intelligence* (London: Routledge and Kegan Paul, 1964). A clear explanation is also given in Celia Lavatelli, *Piaget's Theory Applied to an Early Childhood Curriculum* (Cambridge: American Science and Engineering, Inc., 1970).

Immediate and firsthand perceptions are most significant to children functioning in the **pre-operational stage** of cognitive development. Jean Piaget tells us that children from ages two to seven rely extensively on direct experience in finding out about their world. Children touch, handle, manipulate, move, and draw as they build understanding. At this stage they are dependent on appearances; to them things are what they appear to be, and young children have little ability to analyze what they see.

During the pre-operational period, children make rapid growth in language as more and more words enter their listening and speaking vocabularies. Yet children's understanding of terms they use has a long way to go; concepts are relatively simple; the understanding derived from continued experience and use in a variety of situations is still developing. Children gradually assimilate new encounters into their growing conceptual schema. They must accommodate—or change—the concepts they are refining as they meet new situations that do not fit into the concepts they hold. Through the parallel processes of assimilation and accommodation, children build their understanding of what the world—both natural and social—is all about.

Representational Thinking.   Especially important during the pre-operational stage is children's ability to use language to represent things they perceive. At first children construct in their minds mental images of what they are picking up through their senses. Many experiences and contacts with things in the environment make it possible for young children to reconstruct mental pictures even if the objects are no longer present. The children have begun to remember them.

A Problem to Ponder

A first grader approached a student teacher who was obviously pregnant and asked, "Are you married?" Receiving an affirmative reply from the teacher, the child continued, "But you don't have pierced ears. My mother says I can have my ears pierced when I get married."

In Piaget's terms, this youngster was refining her concept of "marriedness" through the twin processes of assimilation and accommodation. The child had assimilated numerous experiences with marriedness – experiences consisting of her own direct observation and explanation by adults. At this point, to her being married meant being able to have babies and being able to have your ears pierced. Faced with a situation that did not conform with her growing concept, the child had to accommodate or change that concept to take into account this new datum: a married, pregnant woman without pierced ears.

1. Identify a time or times from your own experience when you had to accommodate an idea with new data you were receiving.
2. Assume you wanted to widen children's growing understanding of dependency. Think of one concrete experience you could set up to achieve this end.

With additional experience children learn to construct mental pictures of objects when presented with only parts of them. At this point the part comes to represent the whole in children's minds. Piaget calls this the index level of representation. Later children move to the symbolic level, when a nonverbal representation has the power to evoke the mental image of the object in question. Nonverbal representation can take five forms, forms that suggest kinds of activities with which young children in nursery school and kindergarten social studies should be involved:

1. The use of the body to represent objects (imitation) – One of children's first attempts at representation often involves body movements that imitate objects and people. Children can be asked to use their bodies to imitate a fire fighter climbing a ladder, a farmer driving a tractor, an elephant pulling a log, a police officer directing traffic. These imitations help children focus their attention on human activity.

R This material is based on an excellent article by Hanne Sonquist and Constance Kamu, "Applying Some Piagetian Concepts in the Classroom for the Disadvantaged," *Young Children*, 22:231-246 (March 1967). The complete article can be found in Joe Frost, *Early Childhood Education Rediscovered: Readings* (New York: Holt, Rinehart, 1968).

2. The use of one object to represent another (make-believe)—Young children spontaneously use one object in play to represent another one. A ball of clay becomes a dragon; a box becomes the castle on the hill. In nursery school play, a wide range of materials for children to use is essential for spontaneous representation.

3. The use of utterances that characterize objects (onomatopoeia)—The sounds produced by animals and objects can come to represent real things. *Bow-wow* represents Angus, a dog, while *quack-quack* represents ducks. To help children build their skill in symbolic thinking, teachers should encourage the production of sounds. This can occur as part of informational listening in social studies. As the teacher reads to children about the work of the fire fighters, children can produce the sounds they associate with the fire department—sirens, whistles, and so forth. Or, as the teacher reads *Mike Mulligan and His Steam Engine* by Virginia Lee Burton—a story of mechanical obsolescence—children can produce engine sounds as well as telephone, horse and cart, and airplane sounds.

4. The recognition of objects in pictures—For children who have had a rich experiential background, pictures can substitute for things. Child development specialists suggest the juxtaposition of real objects with their pictorial representations to facilitate children's ability to work with symbols. It is for this reason that nursery and kindergarten rooms should be filled with many real things—from hamsters in a corner box, to brooms with which children sweep the floor after playtime, to typewriters on which children pound out letters at random. Having experienced the real thing, children talk about pictures that represent the same things.

R More detailed explanations are given on pp. 308–309.

5. The making of representations in two and three dimensions—Children can represent their mental pictures by coloring on paper, cutting out and pasting papers together, or modeling out of clay. Using a crayon, children can draw their impressions of a mother, a father, a mail carrier, a truck, a house, and so forth.

Nonverbal experiences with representation go hand in hand with verbal representation. Piaget differentiates between symbolic and sign representations. A child functioning in sign terms can mentally construct an image when hearing the word associated with the object or event in question. In contrast, symbolic representation relates to the ability to equate an object with a nonverbal equivalent—its sound, a picture of it, and so forth. Nursery and primary-grade teachers must help children use verbal signs by juxtaposing words with motor, pictorial, and real experiences. Talk must accompany action, so that children will begin to function in terms of the verbal sign.

Sign = bridge

Children's View of the World. Other characteristics of pre-operational children have been detailed by Jean Piaget, based on extensive observations of how youngsters function in diverse problem situations. Some of his findings:

1. Young children are egocentric in thinking as well as in speech. They view the world in terms of their own perspective and are unable to see a situation from another point of view.
2. They are unable to conserve—perceive that a material retains its mass despite physical transformations that are performed upon it. To the young child, mass is different if a ball of clay is rolled into a sausage shape; volume changes if an amount of liquid is poured from a tall cylinder into a flat dish. In this respect, the child is unable to go beyond appearances; what appears to be is what is.
3. Young children are at times unable to differentiate between reality and fantasy. The worlds of reality and fantasy blend so that imaginary friends seem as real as the neighbor next door.
4. Children assign life to inanimate objects. Things can feel, talk, and hurt.
5. Young children have difficulty seeing that an object possesses more than one attribute. The young child talking about a brother may talk of the brother's mother as "his mother," at that point having trouble equating "his mother" with "my mother."

T Which container holds more liquid? A or B?

The young child says B even though both vessels contain equal amounts.

Young children of about ages four to seven are able to classify objects according to their attributes if the attributes are considered one at a time. At this intuitive stage, children need many opportunities to describe objects in terms of likenesses and differences. Working from the world they know, children can think about houses, people, and workers—thinking first in terms of similarities and differences, then going on to develop categories with the assistance of the teacher, who helps them focus their attention on one set of attributes at a time. Helpful here are the words *same* and *like*. How is this one *like* that one? How are they *the same*? Helpful too in the social studies are picture folders. For example, while studying farmers, children can work with pictures showing various farm activities. The teacher asks, "What is the farmer in this picture doing? What is the farmer in this second picture doing? In what way is the farmer's work the same in both pictures?" As Smith, Goodman, and Meredith explain, "When children are confronted with things that can be categorized, practice in thinking can take place. Describing a phenomenon is a worthy exercise of the mind at this stage. Science and social studies can be the context for these thinking activities. Language development, including the skills of reading and writing, will be fostered as much by this kind of activity as by the necessary practice of those skills." (1970, p. 124)

T Comparing and contrasting should begin early in primary grades. *Scott, Foresman Social Studies* (Glenview, Illinois: Scott, Foresman and Co., 1979) begins work on this thinking skill in first grade.

R See E. Brooks Smith, Kenneth Goodman, and Robert Meredith, *Language and Thinking in the Elementary School* (New York: Holt, Rinehart & Winston, 1970).

Concrete-Operational Functioning

Jean Piaget labels the developmental period between ages seven and eleven the **concrete-operational.** At this stage, children grow in their ability to represent the world through word signs. They can handle serial order, can group objects according to space, time, and number, and can categorize in terms of two attributes at the same time. For example, younger children can gather objects into groups according to a property such as color, putting all red objects together, blue ones together, and so forth. Later, they can start again and make categories based on size. In contrast, older children can categorize based on size and color simultaneously, gathering all large red objects into a group, all large blue objects into a second group, and all small red objects into a third group. By doing this, children are demonstrating the ability to focus on two ideas at the same time—something that is very important in analyzing complex situations.

A mental operation that now emerges is reversibility. The mind can go back to a beginning point in a sequence of thought and compare what is now evident with the previous state. In this respect, the thinking of the child during the concrete-operational stage is much more flexible than it was. Children become less egocentric; they can view an event from a point of view other than their own; they can differentiate between reality and fantasy. They are able to conserve, for their minds can handle the difference between appearances and reality; given a wad of clay shaped like a sausage, they will explain that there is the same amount of "stuff" in both the sausage and the original wad. The change in shape has not affected the material present.

On the other hand, children of ages seven, eight, and nine are still highly dependent on the concrete as they mentally operate on the sense data they are receiving. Abstractions are still very difficult; children of this age have trouble theorizing unless ideas are tied directly to the concrete. For example, children now can follow the sequence of events in which a ball of clay is placed on one side of a balance scale while an equally heavy ball is placed on the opposite side. They watch as one ball is rolled out into a sausage shape and returned to the pan. They see that it is still the same weight. Now as they roll up the piece again, they are able to predict that it will still weigh the same when returned to the scale. They can hold all these events in their minds, and given the concrete nature of the problem, they can explain *why.*

By the end of first grade, most children cross the bridge between pre-operational and concrete-operational thought. They become mental "operators" upon the sense impressions they are receiving. The teacher, however, must realize that although children at this stage can predict and hypothesize, can categorize based on several properties, and can even think in terms of if–then relationships, this is only true if

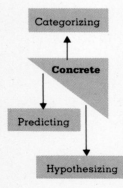

children are functioning in the realm of the concrete. At this level young people still require considerable opportunity to handle materials firsthand, look at representations of real things, and get directly involved.

Blending the Social Studies into the Primary School Day

Most of us hurry to a sale that advertises two for the price of one. The clear dollar savings are hard to resist. This is equally true for educational strategies that enable the teacher to achieve several different objectives simultaneously. Here the savings are not in dollars, but in time. Here the advantage is not added products for the money, but added learning for the time spent.

In describing her classroom, Linda Morrison commented: "A problem I am faced with as a second-grade teacher in Livingston—and I am sure that I share this problem with many other teachers in many other systems—is the ever-increasing curriculum. It seems that every year new programs are added and none are deleted. The only solution is much integration within the entire curriculum." Linda's point is well taken. The only way that we can teach both basic content and basic skills is to piggyback one upon the other.

An Example of Integration of Skills and Content

A typical unit in primary grades is "Community Helpers." Below is a sequence of three lessons through which children acquire basic understandings about the services performed by community workers while they grow in categorizing, picture-interpretation, listening, speaking, reading, and writing skills. The sequence provides a model after which primary grade teachers can pattern similar sequences.

Topic: Fire fighters   **Major Concepts:** Dependency, distribution of labor

Lesson I: Introduction to fire fighters

Grade Level: First   **Date:** March 21

Objectives:

1. Children are able to explain some of the basic services provided by fire fighters.
2. Children are able to gather information by reading pictures.

3. Children are able to categorize information under key labels: who, what, where, when, why.
4. Children are able to listen to find additional information to include in their categorized listings.
5. Children begin to know that encyclopedias are good sources of information on topics.
6. Children are able to wait their turns in a group situation.

Materials:

1. Several large pictures showing people working as fire fighters
2. Seven big pieces of charting paper, each one bearing one of the following questions at the top: Who are these community workers? Where do we find these workers? When do we find them there? What do fire fighters do at a fire? What do they wear? What equipment do they use to do their jobs? Why do people become fire fighters? (See Figure 9.7 for example.)
3. Marker pens for recording
4. *Childcraft Encyclopedia*, Volume 8: *How We Get Things*

Procedure:

1. *Motivation and Orientation:* Involve children in discussion of each of the pictures on display.
2. Focus attention on the seven charts taped to the chalkboard. Begin with "Who are these community workers?" As children brainstorm possibilities, record on the appropriate chart.

   Work with each chart in turn. Watch carefully to assure that information given for each category fits it and not another.

Related Questions and Structuring Remarks:

Can you describe what is happening in this picture? What is this fire fighter doing?

Let's see if we can think of as many answers as possible to the questions recorded on these charts. Let's first read the question on this chart together.

Is a hose something they wear? Is it a piece of equipment?
Besides wanting to help people, why else do people become fire fighters? Why do they get money for their jobs?

Figure 9.7
Sample First-Grade Charts
Dictated by Children
and Recorded by the Teacher.

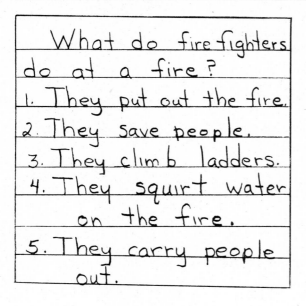

What do fire fighters
do at a fire?
1. They put out the fire.
2. They save people.
3. They climb ladders.
4. They squirt water
   on the fire.
5. They carry people
   out.

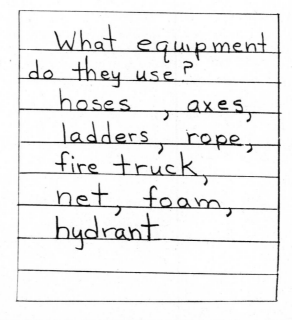

What equipment
do they use?
hoses, axes,
ladders, rope,
fire truck,
net, foam,
hydrant

3. Read the section on fire fighters in *Childcraft*. (Change fireman to fire fighter in reading.) Children listen to see if the information contained is already listed on their charts. If not, they decide to which chart the information should be added.

4. Children read charts—some individually, some chorally—to make sure they can recognize words written there.

Listen to find other facts to list on our charts. Is this information already listed? Where should we list it? Why?

Lesson II: The Service Provided by Fire Fighters

Objectives:

1. Children develop the vocabulary to use in talking about human pursuits.
2. Children are able to read words that are part of their functional listening and speaking vocabularies.
3. Children can complete sentences using words and ideas listed in front of them.
4. Children begin to handle correct sentence punctuation.
5. Children broaden their understanding of the services rendered to the community by fire fighters. They recognize their own dependency on fire fighters. They can explain the purpose served by a piece of equipment such as a fire fighter's hat.

Materials:

Charts from previous lesson, writing paper, pencils, crayons, pictures of fire fighters on display in the room, and fire fighting equipment borrowed from the local firehouse—fire fighter's hat, badge, etc.

Procedure:

1. *Motivation and Orientation:* Show the fire fighter's hat.

Related Questions and Structuring Remarks:

With whom do we associate this? Who would like to try it on? Let's look at how it fits on Jane's head. Why is it bigger in the back? Why is the brim bigger there than in the front? Is the hat a piece of clothing or a piece of equipment?

2. Refer to the charts from yesterday. Have children read hard words and phrases.

3. Display another chart that provides a beginning for writing (Figure 9.8).

**Figure 9.8
A Sample Chart**

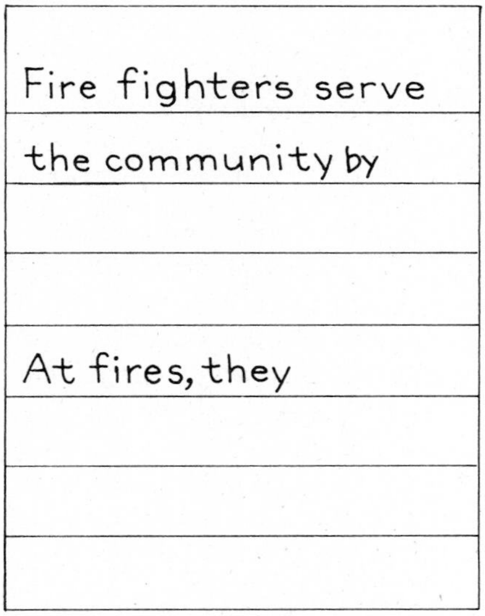

Fire fighters serve

the community by

At fires, they

Children get a duplicated copy with slots ready for writing.

4. Children who finish writing illustrate their words with a picture that they attach to the top of the paper. When all children have completed the activity, they take turns reading their productions to the class. Listeners look to see if writers have put in periods where needed.

What kinds of information did we list on this chart? Who can read one of the phrases from this chart? Who remembers what we wrote here?

Today we are each going to write a paragraph. We will take information from our charts. If you have trouble writing a word, find it on the charts. Let's all read our paragraph beginning. Can someone tell me why I wrote the first word a little to the right in the first sentence of the paragraph? To complete this paragraph, from which chart will we take words? What will this paragraph tell us? What will we put on the top line of our paper? When we come to the end of our sentence, what do we add?

Lesson III: Fire Fighting Equipment

Objectives:

1. Children refine their understanding of the services rendered by fire fighters; they are able to tell how fire fighters use different pieces of equipment.
2. Children are able to read key words related to fire fighting; they are able to write these words when provided with a visual model.
3. Children are able to wait their turns in a group situation.
4. Children are able to use pantomime to clarify concepts.

Materials: Pictures on display of fire fighters; wall-sized version of crossword puzzle on fire fighters (with words associated with the topic listed at the bottom and at least one letter for each word already incorporated in the puzzle; marker pen.

Procedure:

1. *Motivation and Orientation:* Unveil the puzzle (see Figure 9.9).
2. Children come forward taking turns in filling in a puzzle word. Each child then tells how fire fighters use that piece of equipment or how the word relates to fire fighting.
3. Children pantomime meanings where appropriate.
4. When the puzzle is completed, children take turns pointing first to a word on the puzzle, then to the correct spot on a picture that shows the meaning of the word.
5. *Follow-up:* Cover the giant puzzle and supply individual copies. Children complete puzzles at their desks and later correct them when the puzzle is unveiled again.

Related Questions and Structuring Remarks:

Today we are going to try to remember some of the things that fire fighters work with at the scene of a fire. Who can find one word at the bottom and place it where it belongs in the puzzle?

Jack, how does this word relate to fire fighting? Tod, how does the fire fighter use a net?

Marcia, can you show us how a fire fighter climbs up the ladder? slides down the pole? drives the fire truck? hangs on when the truck goes fast?

Who can find a word, point to it, and then point to a picture spot that shows the same thing as the word says?

Figure 9.9
Example of a Crossword Puzzle for Use
in First Grade

The Fire Fighter

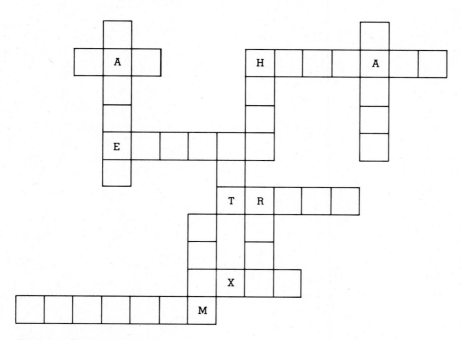

Words to place into the puzzle

axes	hat	ladder	truck
engine	hose	net	uniform
foam	hydrant	rope	water

Notes: Teachers can construct similar puzzles using words from any social studies area. Students select the words listed at the bottom to print into the appropriate location in the puzzle, explaining the meanings of the words as they go along.

Follow-up Lessons:

Children write slotted compositions on what kind of equipment fire fighters use and what kind of clothing they wear. In each case, they take information from the charts. They compile their composition pages and illustrations into a booklet on fire fighting.

Specific Strategies for Blending Content with Skills

The lesson sequence just described embodies a number of specific instructional strategies that are particularly useful with youngsters who are just learning to read and write. Even as children are learning about the work of fire fighters and about how they are dependent on these workers, they are learning to read words in meaningful contexts, write a paragraph that focuses on one topic, use words orally in talking about a topic, listen to get information, and use appropriate punctuation in writing. In this respect the strategies employed are double-barreled; they get at both content and skills.

These strategies obviously can be modified for use with different content. Much the same can be done with other community workers, with a country being studied, with neighborhood features, with the family—in fact, with all the social studies areas normally included in early primary social studies. This is possible in first grade when children have learned to decode short, commonly used words and are able to print letters in upper and lower case forms.

Because learning in the social studies in the early primary years is interrelated with learning to read and write as well as with art and music activity, let us look at some specific strategies to use.

1. Teacher-guided group compositions. The technical vocabulary youngsters learn orally in the social studies is the vocabulary they will be handling as they go on to read more about ideas under discussion and write independently. One effective way to facilitate the movement of words from children's oral vocabulary to their reading and writing vocabularies is group writing experiences, in which children together compose sentences on topics they are investigating, with the teacher serving as scribe to record sentences on the board or a chart. In chapter 4, some aspects of teacher-led group writing activity were considered as they apply within the range of elementary grades.

At primary levels, teacher-guided composition works most effectively as a summarizing device following a period of listening, viewing, and discussing. Youngsters go back to suggest sentences that summarize the major points about which they have been talking. The teacher records so that all can see, perhaps reading aloud the words while writing them down. When several sentences have been recorded, the charts can be used in several different ways, depending on the level of children's reading ability.

In kindergarten where children have only begun to recognize letters and are beginning to discriminate visually among the letters and among words, the teacher can prepare individual word cards, each one with a content word from the group composition. Youngsters can see if they can match the word card with its mate in the composition,

R *Early Years* is a magazine that provides ideas for nursery and primary teachers. *Learning, Instructor,* and *Teacher* often contain ideas for use in lower elementary classrooms.

T Ask the children, "Can you find the word on this card in our composition?"

need

We need water to live. We need food to live. We need air to live.

using that word orally as they match. As youngsters progress, they can read back the sentences they have dictated, returning on several successive days to the dictated chart to read and reread it. On other occasions the dictated composition can become a puzzle. The teacher cuts each sentence into two segments, and children attempt to put the sentences in logical order.

    For group composition to be productive requires skill on the teacher's part in drawing ideas from students and helping them phrase thoughts in sentence form. Sometimes the teacher will have to supply oral sentence beginnings that students complete. For example, if first graders are dictating about the contribution of police officers, the teacher may begin, "What are some of the things we said police officers do? Let's start our sentence with the words 'Police officers . . . . ' " With that kind of prompting one child may offer, "Police officers protect people." Others may offer sentences with similar patterns: "Police officers direct traffic." "Police officers help you if you are lost."

    After several similar sentences have been recorded, the teacher may help children by adding a final sentence, minus one key word that they have been using orally in discussion: "We _____ on police officers to do many different jobs." Participants provide the omitted word–*depend*–and it is added to the sentence, perhaps in red since it is a key concept word.

2. Words cards. Technical vocabulary encountered in group composition can be recorded in giant script on colored cards. Posted around the room on bulletin boards, walls, and windows, taped to the floor, suspended from light fixtures–these cards become a Social Studies Word Bank, a readily available source from which youngsters can draw in writing and to which they can refer during independent reading. In the case cited above where children dictated about the work of a police officer, words such as *protect*, *help*, *traffic*, and *depend* would be added to the word bank.

3. Word charting. Words and ideas relevant to a topic can be brainstormed by children and teacher working orally together. Rather than recording these on the chalkboard, the teacher records both questions and related words on charts that remain a visible part of classroom activity as a unit progresses. The charts supply words for future talking and for writing by children who have limited spelling and recording skills. Some teachers have found it helpful to number the charts so that when children later write from them, they can refer to a chart by number. The teacher can direct, "Look at chart three to get words that tell what kinds of fruits and vegetables grow in Hawaii." Incidentally, teachers of compensatory education classes in upper elementary grades have found this strategy equally useful with young people with learning deficiencies.

T Ask children: "Who can put these sentences back together?"

We need

water to live.

We need

food to live.

Then suggest, "Let's try to read our sentences."

T A Hanging Social Studies Word Bank

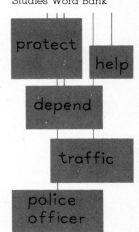

T Easy questions for beginning brainstorming start with: Who, When, Where, What, Why, and How.

See page 296 of this chapter for an example.

Idea Page

Focus: Using Textbook Materials in Primary Grades
In *You and Your Family*, the level one book in the Bowmar/Noble basal social studies called *Man and His World* (1974), two sentences on one of the pages state: "Living things have many needs. What things do you need?" This kind of questioning is characteristic of the writing style of first level books of other social studies text series as well. Questions like this—with the companion pictures also found in many first level texts—lead naturally into teacher-led group writing. A teacher records students' answers to the text question in chart form after a period of general discussion. For one possible result, see Figure 9.10.

To get children to identify food, water, air, clothes,and sleep as basic needs, the teacher asks questions such as: How do you feel when you have not eaten for many hours? What does this tell us about one kind of need we have? Who wants to tell us about a time when he or she went without food for almost all day? After children have answered these questions the teacher introduces the pattern for writing by saying, "Let's finish this sentence on our chart: "To live we need . . . ;" the teacher writes each word on the chart and asks, "Who can think of another ending to the same sentence by telling about another need we have?" In this way, words and sentence patterns are repeated making simplified material for children to reread.

Figure 9.10
A Chart Resulting from Group Writing

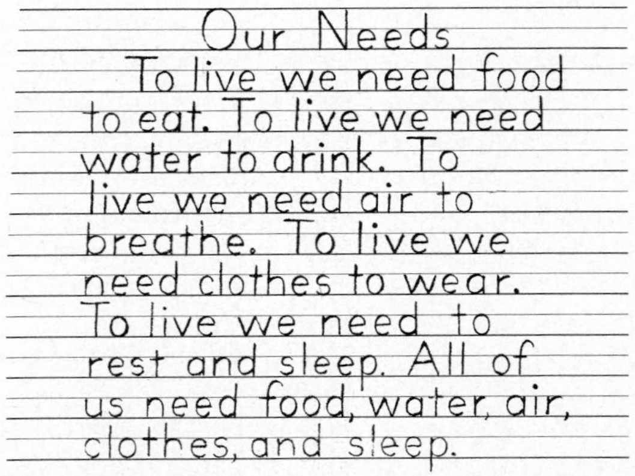

Our Needs
To live we need food to eat. To live we need water to drink. To live we need air to breathe. To live we need clothes to wear. To live we need to rest and sleep. All of us need food, water, air, clothes, and sleep.

4. Basic vocabulary charting. Also useful as a primary unit progresses are slim charts—one for each letter of the alphabet–that the teacher posts along a word wall of the classroom (See Figure 9.11). As children inquire about the spelling of common words to write into their social studies paragraphs, the teacher adds those words to the appropriate alphabet chart. As children continue to write down their social studies ideas and need the same basic vocabulary word again, the teacher responds by saying, "Look at the S chart. The word *several* is the ninth word there."

T Words are added to charts as needed so that words on each chart are not alphabetized. Emily Davis, a first-grade teacher, recommends numbering the words for ease in directing children's attention to those needed in writing.

Figure 9.11
Some Basic Vocabulary Charts

Aa	Mm	Ss
1. an	1. my	1. so
2. at	2. make	2. six
3. ask	3. mother	3. some
4. are	4. me	4. say
5.	5. man	5. should

5. Dictating and tracing. Young children should be asked to summarize ideas met in the social studies. Before youngsters are actually able to record their summaries independently, they can dictate their sentences on a one-to-one basis to the teacher, who records them lightly in printed form. Good for this purpose is paper in which a place for art work is available at the top and lines for recording sentences are found beneath. Children return to their own desks after individual dictation to darken the letters the teacher has written and to illustrate the ideas with a sketch.

6. Dictating and copying. First graders who have gained control of pencils and can form letters can take the next step–copying the words the teacher has recorded for them during individual dictation. To facilitate this copying, the teacher records every other line, leaving space for children to write their own versions. When young writers are to make copies of dictated summaries of ideas, summaries should be kept short—perhaps only two sentences at first—for writing is a time-consuming activity for those just learning to control a pencil.

R Check page 299 of this chapter for an example of this strategy in practice.

7. Slotting.   A possible next step in the sequence toward independence in recording is slotting. The teacher starts sentences for the youngsters, structuring the sentences so that children simply have to look up at the brainstormed charts of words for ones to use in completing the thought. It is at this point that numbering the brainstormed charts becomes an aid to writing. Children who need additional guidelines for beginning writing know that they must take words from a specific chart.

8. Counting and computing.   In kindergarten and first grade, children gradually acquire a broadened concept of number. Words such as *fifteen, less than, more than, greater than, take away,* and *add to* become more meaningful. This heightened meaning can come as part of counting and computing in the social studies. For example, children can:

Help to count students for work groups;

Count the number of buildings, people, animals, and vehicles in pictures;

Decide whether there are more or fewer buildings, people, animals, or vehicles in one picture as contrasted to another;

Add objects to or take objects away from categories with which they are working;

Do simple word problems in reference to a social studies topic—if five fire fighters take care of this side of town and six fire fighters take care of the other side of town, how many fire fighters are there in the whole town? This type of problem can be presented visually, as shown in Figure 9.12.

**Figure 9.12
A Sample Word Problem**

9. Involving children actively: games. Young children's short attention spans and their high activity levels require learning sequences that involve them not only in thinking but in doing. As suggested in chapter 2, using games is a strategy that allows for active involvement.

In early primary grades, matching games are appropriate. Students can match pictures of phenomena with naming cards (as in a game in which the names of fire fighters' equipment are matched with pictures). In kindergarten, before children can recognize words, youngsters can simply match two pictures of the same object.

As demonstrated in the model lesson series, crossword puzzles are feasible even in first grade if they are simplified so that the words are given in full at the bottom. At this level too, map jigsaw puzzles are appropriate content for a classroom game corner.

10. Involving children actively: let's pretend. Children in nursery school, kindergarten, and first grade love to "play at living." They play school, play doctor, play police officer, play house, and so forth. Most teachers of young children recognize the importance of play activity as a way through which youngsters come to grips with the roles and pursuits of everyday living. They encourage creative play by designing play centers into the classroom.

11. Involving children actively: pantomiming. In pantomime children express their understanding by communicating meanings physically. Pantomime can be relatively unsophisticated with children showing nonverbally how certain activities are performed. Children can pretend they are driving a fire truck, sliding down the pole in the firehouse, climbing a ladder at a fire, attaching the hose to a hydrant, climbing a tree to rescue a frightened cat; directing traffic, walking a beat, stopping a speeding car, following a suspect, helping children cross the street; driving a garbage truck, lifting up the large garbage barrels, sweeping the streets, picking up litter. With beginning pantomimists, experienced teachers start with total group involvement. All the children together–perhaps with musical accompaniment–pretend that they are directing traffic. Later pantomiming can blend with games. A single pantomimist performs an act that the teacher has suggested to him or her. Classmates must guess the activity being performed.

12. Involving children actively–role-playing. Children's enjoyment of let's pretend carries over to role-playing. In primary grades role-playing can be used to demonstrate processes and to develop skill in handling oneself in a variety of situations. In one first-grade classroom, children planned a let's pretend trip to Washington, D. C. as

R Millie Almy summarizes: "Nursery school educators, since the very beginning of the movement, have regarded play as an inherent right of the child. Moreover, they have long identified the child's play with experimentation that offers unlimited opportunities for learning." *The Bulletin of the Institute of Child Study* 28: (November 1966).

they studied their nation's capital city. As part of this lesson sequence, children took turns pretending they were at the airport buying a ticket. They had to ask for their tickets from a clerk, who would sell tickets only if purchasers gave all the necessary information. Similar role-playing activity can take place as children learn how to buy a variety of objects in a store, to check change, and to act politely in this situation.

13. Involving children actively – verbal facsimiles. Children's let's pretend activity can involve making representations that include words, once they have acquired basic handwriting skills. The first graders, who planned a trip to Washington, D. C., printed out their own airlines tickets, modeled after one supplied by the teacher. They had to record their departure point, their destination, their flight time, and their own names on the tickets.

Other representations with a verbal component that can be part of primary level social studies include making a menu, writing out a permit, writing out a bill, and making out a receipt. Such activities can be included in almost any primary unit and result in a blending of social competencies with writing skills.

14. Involving children actively — art. Chapter 2 discusses the use of art activity in the social studies. Clearly, in primary grades and at the nursery-school level, children can draw their conception of events and things in the world around them. For children who have not yet developed writing skills, the teacher can supply labels produced using spirit duplicating masters. Young artists cut out the labels and with teacher guidance paste them to the appropriate portions of their drawings, tracing over the letters with crayons. Particularly good as children create two or three related drawings are label sets like those listed below:

now/then	in the morning/at noontime/ in the evening
first/second/third	a good act/a naughty act
nighttime/daytime	a happy time/a sad time
at home/at school	a quiet place/a noisy place
summer/fall/winter/spring	near/far
teacher/student	before/after

Similarly, color/cut/paste activities can correlate with social studies. Teachers can prepare duplicated sheets comprised of a series of small pictures, all related to the social studies unit underway. Children color the pictures, cut them out, and paste them on a larger sheet organized to show relationships. For example, small pictures to color can be simple drawings of:

Key activities and places found in the state that students paste to desk-sized maps of their own state;

Important buildings in their own town (or a well-known city) that children paste on a street map;

Community helpers that students paste next to the appropriate building to show where in the community the helpers are found;

Items that children group into categories and paste on a sheet to show these groupings—for example, breakfast foods I eat, luncheon foods I eat, supper foods I eat; items related to food, to clothing, or to shelter; big things, little things;

Labels can also be added by the color, cut, and paste method.

15. Gathering background information–listening to nonfiction. Most primary teachers set aside periods for reading to children; typically the material shared is a story or poem. But young children need practice in listening to informational content as well. Listening for specific kinds of information can begin as early as nursery school.

In the lesson sequence that introduces this chapter, the teacher reads from a children's encyclopedia as students listened to find more points to add to their charts. Such an activity supplies essential background information and is effective if selections read are relatively short. In addition, library shelves are stocked with informational books that build background on a topic.

T "Clip and paste" can be used in similar ways as youngsters search magazines for pictures to clip and to paste onto maps, charts, classification grids, or data retrieval charts.

T Generally the April issue of *Social Education* contains an annotated bibliography titled "notable Children's Trade Books in the Field of Social Studies." Entries are categorized under such headings as American Heritage; Arts, Sports, and Crafts; Contemporary Concerns; Customs and Festivals; Folklore and Tall Tales; People and Nature; Native Americans; People and Places; Women; Pluralistic Cultures; Twentieth Century; Understanding Oneself and Others. Appropriate grade levels are suggested.

A Quotation to Consider

Jeanne Chall in *Learning to Read* (New York: McGraw-Hill, 1967), p. 13, has written: "The process of reading should be defined broadly to include as major goals. . . word recognition, comprehension, . . . and *the application of what is read to the study of personal and social problems.*" Study the reading material found in a typical primary reading text series and identify questions through which children could apply that content to personal and social problems. For example, a question like "Why did Marty obey his mother?" helps children think in terms of authority, power, and truth. Questions such as "Why did Marty want to go to the fair?" and "What is another reason he wanted to go?" get at multiple causation.

A young child can be helped to use reading as a
means of gathering data.

Teaching Social Studies in the Primary Years:
A Summary Thought or Two

Many of the instructional strategies described in this chapter have
been around for a long time. Originally proposed under the heading
"language experience approach," the strategies have typically
been advocated for use in building children's language skills. Little,
however, has been said about the content that should be part of the
experience.

One way to insure value of content is for the teacher to keep the
major concepts of the social sciences in mind. These become the basis
for observing, painting, cutting, pasting, discussing, listening, analyzing, categorizing, reading, writing, and vocabulary development. At
this point the reader may wish to refer back to the listing of key concepts identified as part of the *Social Sciences Education Framework for
California Public Schools* given in chapter 2. As the lessons described
in this chapter suggest, such big ideas as interdependency, diversity,
change, and needs can be put into concrete terms that the young child
can understand.

A Task to Try

Typical units included in the primary school social studies curriculum include the family, community, community helpers, and school. Select one component of such a unit such as the principal of our school, grandfathers, or the library in our town and create a series of lessons that utilize some of the strategies described in this chapter. As you develop your sequence, consider how you could help children handle the idea of change. For example, children studying about the fire fighter could brainstorm ways that fire fighting might be different in the future; they could look at old pictures to see how fire fighting was different in the past from what it is today.

References

Almy, Millie. *The Early Childhood Educator at Work*. New York: McGraw-Hill, 1974.

Bronfenbrenner, Urie. *Two Worlds of Childhood: U. S. and U.S.S.R.* New York: Simon and Schuster, 1970.

Coody, Betty. *Using Literature with Young Children*. Dubuque, Iowa: William C. Brown, 1973.

Evans, Ellis. *Contemporary Influences in Early Childhood Education*. 2nd ed. New York: Holt, Rinehart & Winston, 1975.

Flemming, Bonnie; and Hamilton, Darlene. *Resources for Creative Teaching in Early Childhood Education*. New York: Harcourt Brace Jovanovich, 1977.

Frost, Joe; and Kissinger, Joan. *The Young Child and the Educative Process*. New York: Holt, Rinehart & Winston, 1976.

Hymes, James L. *Teaching the Child Under Six*. 2nd ed. Columbus, Ohio: Charles E. Merrill, 1974.

Lavatelli, Celia. *Piaget's Theory Applied to an Early Childhood Curriculum*. Boston: Center for Media Development, 1970.

Lee, Catherine. *The Growth and Development of Children*. 2nd ed. New York: Longman, 1977.

Morrison, George. *Early Childhood Education Today*. Columbus, Ohio: Charles E. Merrill, 1976.

Wadsworth, Barry. *Piaget for the Classroom Teacher*. New York: Longman, 1978.

Steven Iannuzzi   2A
Swimmy is happy now
because___ he helped his
friends.

A listening-writing activity is a useful form of evaluation.

How dreadful it is when the right judge judges wrong!

Sophicles, *Antigone,* **Line 323**

Key Questions

Why is evaluation a key component of social studies programs?

What is meant by a teaching-learning-evaluation-reteaching cycle? How do goals fit into the cycle?

How is evaluation different from testing?

What qualities characterize an evaluation program that is internally consistent?

What is involved in assessing reading comprehension? in assessing children's ability to function at higher cognitive levels? in assessing children's growth toward social/emotional process goals?

What two means can a teacher employ in order to make his or her evaluative devices more creative?

A Pretest to Try

A third-grade teacher planned a series of lessons on Columbus to teach during October. As long-range goals, the teacher established that by the end of the series, students would:

1. Have increased their factual understanding of Columbus and his journey to America (knowledge)
2. Be able to use selected classroom and library books as sources of information (skills)
3. Have increased their appreciation of Columbus' pioneer voyage as part of their American heritage (attitudes and appreciations)

After the series was completed, the teacher gave this test to the class.
1. Columbus came to America in the year _____.
2-4. The names of his ships were the _____, _____, and _____.
5-6. Columbus' journey was paid for by the country of _____, and the queen who helped him was named _____.
7. Columbus made the journey because he was looking for _____ _____.
8-9. At that time most people thought the world was _____ in shape, but Columbus said it was _____.
10-11. Columbus called the people he found in America _____ because he thought he had reached the country of _____.
12. Columbus was brave because _____.

Directions to the reader: Answer the following questions about the Columbus sequence.

To what extent—if any—did the teacher measure each of the stated goals?

Was the evaluation procedure an effective one? If yes, give your reasons. If no, tell how you would improve it.

Do you believe the goals were worthwhile? If yes, give your reasons. If no, tell how you would change the goals so that they would be more defendable.

Assessment of student progress should be an integral part of the teaching-learning process in the social studies—not something tacked on at the end of a topic or unit. A teacher must know whether students have reached first goals before setting higher, more sophisticated ones. Without this knowledge the teacher has little basis for designing remedial sequences or planning future lesson series. He or she has little basis for judging the effectiveness of either the teaching or the learning.

R For a discussion of evaluation read *Evaluation in the Social Studies: 35th Yearbook, National Council for the Social Studies* (Arlington, Virginia: NCSS, 1965).

Designing Teaching-Learning-Evaluation-Reteaching Cycles

When evaluation is conceived as an essential part of the teaching-learning process, cycles of planning-diagnosis-teaching-learning-evaluating-reteaching-evaluating-planning-diagnosis-teaching . . . occur and recur in interlinking chains. Even as the teachers are closely involved in the teaching act, they are involved in assessing students' progress.

Starting the cycle:
1) set goals for lesson
2) must measure growth in content & process

3) Assess

Identifying Goals – Starting a Cycle

The teacher initiates a cycle of instruction by identifying important goals to be achieved through a projected sequence of lessons. To be effective, evaluation in the social studies, like that in other content areas, must measure growth along two different but related dimensions—content and process. In terms of content, the teacher must assess children's mastery of the facts, terms, and generalizations that are the substance of the investigation. The key question that the teacher asks at this point is "What are the basic terms, the big ideas, and the supporting facts that children should acquire through the projected instructional sequence?" More significantly, the teacher must identify basic process goals. These include goals that are primarily cognitive, such as the ability to analyze information, hypothesize relationships, and render judgments.

R See chapter 16 for a discussion of behavioral objectives, a way of stating desired learnings in precise terms as a base for instruction and evaluation.

Easier to determine is mastery of content.

Assessing growth in these thinking and communication skills is not an easy task. Most educators agree that it is far easier to determine mastery of content than growth in the cognitive-processing skills. After all, it is relatively simple to construct an instrument to determine whether children can recall information. Obviously, however, teachers want much more than this. As was set forth in chapter 1, teachers want to assist children in using information productively and in operating cognitively upon it.

Additionally, teachers of the social studies are concerned with processes that have a social or emotional dimension as well as a cognitive one. Important social/emotional process goals include development of a wide range of interests; development of attitudes, appreciations, and values that relate to basic issues, oneself, and others; growth in ability to work cooperatively with others; and growth in the ability to assess

R State and national assessments are becoming more widespread. For information about the purposes and the procedures relative to these assessments, read:

Jean Fair, "What Is National Assessment and What Does It Say to Us?" in *Social Education*, 38:398-403, 414 (May 1974).

Bob Taylor, "Implications of the National Assessment Model for Curriculum Development and Accountability," *Social Education*, 38:404-408 (May 1974).

Ralph Tyler and Richard Wolf, eds. *Crucial Issues in Testing* (Berkeley, California: McCutchan Publishing Corp., 1978). This reference discusses the ethical problems implicit in nationwide testing.

oneself. Again, evaluation of these goals is no easy task, but it is one that teachers must attack if they are ultimately to judge the effectiveness of their own instruction.

In summary, setting goals as part of the teaching-learning-evaluation-reteaching cycle requires consideration of both content and processes to be acquired.

Content – *Knowledge Goals:* the facts, terms, and generalizations related to the area under investigation

Process – *Cognitive Process Goals:* the skills basic to effective cognitive functioning

Social/emotional Process Goals: the social and personal skills, attitudes, appreciations, values, and interests

Although on paper, goals of instruction can be classed into three categories, in practice, of course, these learnings blend together. A person uses knowledge to feel and think. A person thinks even as he or she feels, feels even as he or she thinks.

Diagnosing What Is Already Known – Finding Out Where to Begin

The second step in planning for instruction in which evaluation is an ongoing component is to diagnose each student's strengths and weaknesses in terms of stated goals. Two questions are paramount at this stage in the cycle.

1. What information, skills, interests, appreciations, attitudes, and values do students already possess as a result of life experiences and previous instruction?
2. In what areas and at what levels do students require instruction to bring them to a higher level of proficiency?

That diagnosis is important in planning for teaching and learning becomes clear when one considers what could result if this preliminary step were skipped. A series of lessons could be taught for which children do not have necessary background. Or a series could be planned to develop skills that most children have already mastered at the desired level of proficiency. In either case, valuable learning time would be wasted, and children's attention could conceivably wander, no matter how skillful the instruction.

The reader may now wish to reconsider the sequence that opens this chapter and ask, "Would it be possible for third graders to pass the test without the lesson sequence the teacher prepared and implemented?" In this case, the teacher failed to diagnose children's background and had no way to determine whether the sequence was necessary or whether any significant growth resulted from the instruction.

Teaching, Assessing, Reteaching, Reassessing – Keeping the Cycle Going

The next four steps in the teaching-evaluation cycle are so closely bound together that it is impossible to describe them separately. They are 1) designing experiences and teaching to promote student learning; 2) assessing student progress in terms of stated goals; 3) designing additional experiences to fill educational gaps and reteaching; 4) reassessing and decision making. These four acts are what teaching in the social studies is all about!

To start to meet the goals of instruction, the teacher plans and schedules a wide variety of activities. If sessions are structured to satisfy children's interests and needs, and if children are motivated, they will join in enthusiastically. As they learn they will provide evidence of their progress or lack of it.

At this point, the teacher must be perceptive of individual student performance. He or she must informally observe behavior and periodically systematize informal observations by recording samples in the form of checklists, rating scales, and anecdotal records. Students participate in the process, assessing their own strengths and weaknesses. In addition, they produce samples of verbal and nonverbal work—sketches, maps, charts, compositions, sentences, models—that provide the teacher with other clues as to the level of learning reached. Periodically too, where appropriate, the teacher schedules formal tests to gather samples of learning.

Such continuing evaluation of student progress is especially important when one considers the purpose that evaluation is to serve. Assessment is not intended simply as a means of grading individual student performance along an A, B, C, D, F or 100-0% continuum. Rather it is primarily intended as a means of determining what additional learning experiences are necessary to bring children to the desired level of competency. Reteaching must follow assessment, with youngsters becoming involved in different kinds of activities that lead to learning they still must achieve. After reteaching, the instructor must check again to see whether additional work is still necessary. At some point, of course, the teacher must go on to other topics and units, tucking away in his or her mind students' individual learning problems, especially in the area of skills. As the class encounters different content, the teacher provides additional work with those skills.

Testing and Evaluation

The steps in an ongoing evaluation program described so far are clarified in the diagram given in Figure 10.1. This diagram highlights and summarizes the fundamental position of assessment in any instructional scheme.

T Using the community as a base for learning is described in David Armstrong and Tom Savage, "A Framework for Utilizing the Community for Social Learning in Grades 4-6," *Social Education*, 40:164-167 (March 1976). After a trip to the local business center, ask children to complete these charts:

Evidence
of
the Past

Present
Activity
in the
Center

Future
Trends

**Figure 10.1
A Flow Chart of the
Teaching – Learning –
Evaluation –
Reteaching Cycle**

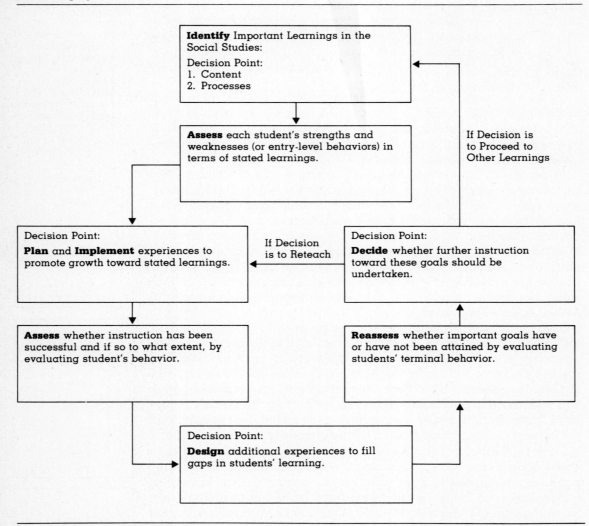

It also suggests that to equate the term *evaluation* with *testing* is to view the entire evaluative process from too narrow a perspective; **evaluation** is a much broader term with **testing** being merely one part of a larger whole. Tests are one mechanism for gathering evidence on

*Two categories of
tests ① written
② Performance*

how much students have learned. Tests typically tell how well students have mastered content and how well students can handle certain skills.

As employed by most teachers, tests fall into two categories: **written** or **performance.** Generally tests of content are written, with students either composing their knowledge in essay form or responding to short answer or objective questions. Short answer items can ask students to complete sentences by filling in blanks (This was the format the teacher in our opening selection employed.); choose from options the one that gives the best response; decide whether a statement is true or false; or match pairs of items that belong together. These same kinds of test questions can be used to assess some basic cognitive skills. In contrast, in a performance test, students are actually called upon to perform the desired task.

One can see that in some instances either a performance or a written test can be used to assess children's growth. Consider one goal from the lesson sequence presented earlier in the chapter: that students be able to use selected classroom and library books as sources of information. Relying on a written test, the teacher could ask:

To see if a book has information about Columbus, the best way to find out is by

A. looking at the pictures
B. checking the index
C. studying the table of contents
D. thumbing through the book
E. reading the title page

Relying instead on a performance test, the teacher might call upon each child individually, present him or her with a reference problem, and then observe how the child handles the book to locate the desired information.

In other instances, only direct observation of performance in real rather than test situations can give an accurate estimate of growth. This is especially true in areas related to social/emotional functioning. For example, in assessing students' ability to work and interact with others, the only acceptable means of evaluation is direct observation of students' participation in groups. When the reader remembers that goals of instruction include not only such social skills but also values, attitudes, and appreciations, it becomes clear that teachers must go beyond tests—especially written ones—if they are to analyze total performance. Figure 10.2 summarizes the distinctions between a narrow concept of testing and a much broader concept of evaluation.

R Read more about testing in terms of observable behaviors in:

Myron Marty, "Wrestling with Testing in American History," *Social Education,* 40:524-527 (November/December 1976).

Eileen Peters, "Develop Your Own Tests in Political Science," *Social Education,* 40:528-532 (November/December 1976).

R For a discussion of the shortcomings of objective test items read Robert Ebel, "The Ineffectiveness of Multiple Choice, True-False Items," *Educational and Psychological Measurement,* 38:37-44 (Spring 1978).

R See Francis Hunkins, "Rationale for Testing in the Social Studies," *Social Education* 40:504-508 (November/December 1976) for further distinctions between testing and evaluation.

Figure 10.2
Testing and Evaluation – A Contrast

Testing	Evaluation
1. Written and, sometimes, performance pre-tests are given to determine existing knowledge.	1a. Written and, sometimes, performance pre-tests are given to determine existing knowledge.
	1b. Pre-assessment can be done through teacher observation of ongoing student performance using checklists, rating scales, and anecdotal records to determine:
	how children function in groups
	how children go about searching for, organizing, and presenting data
	how children solve problems
	how children respond to issues and problems
	how children express themselves orally
	how they feel about themselves and others
	what values, attitudes, and interests are influencing their behavior.
	Observation occurs as students join in discussions, panels, debates, informal conversations, role-playing, simulations, puppet plays, and so forth.
2. Formal tests are given periodically throughout and at the end of a unit to determine progress.	2a. Formal tests are given periodically throughout and at the end of a unit to determine progress.
	2b. Periodic assessment of growth toward goals is accomplished using a variety of creative means.
	2c. Student involvement in evaluation of progress occurs on a continuing basis.

The Internal Consistency of an Evaluation Program

Internal consistency is the keystone of a sound teaching-evaluation cycle. Primary questions that relate to the internal integrity of assessment programs include:

Do the evaluative procedures and instruments actually measure the goals set forth as the teacher begins to plan for instruction?

Do procedures and measures take into account children's reading levels?

Are procedures and measures consistent with children's capacity to think, value, and perform?

These three elements are such obvious characteristics of sound evaluations that to mention them appears almost unnecessary. On the other hand, many evaluation programs suffer from the fact that there is little congruity between goals and measures of those goals.

It is in terms of internal consistency that we can begin to judge the teaching-evaluation sequence detailed at the beginning of this chapter. Does the evaluative device—in this case a simple completion test—measure growth toward the stated goals? Clearly the answer is no if we are looking at the goal related to use of reference materials. Not one question focuses on this skill. What about growth in knowledge of Columbus' voyage? Without a doubt, most of the questions are directed at assessment of students' retention of basic facts. But can the teacher be sure that children who answered all questions accurately did so as a result of the instructional sequence? As was pointed out earlier, the answer to that question is also no. Without any initial diagnosis, there is no way of knowing whether the learning was due to present or past teaching. In the case of the third goal—appreciation of the contribution Columbus made in familiarizing Europeans with what lay to the west of them—only one question—the last—touches at all on this learning. There may be some relationship between Columbus' bravery and the fear that prevented earlier Europeans from making the voyage. But can third graders perceive this relationship? Is such thinking consistent with their cognitive development? In sum, the Columbus teaching sequence suffers from internal inconsistency.

R See Gilbert Sax, *Principles of Educational Measurement and Evaluation* (Belmont, California: Wadsworth Publishing Co., 1974) for a discussion of how to judge evaluation programs.

[handwritten marginal note:] Evaluate devices; measuring goals. 1) Task Sheet 2) Written Items 3) Performance checklist

The Task Sheet – One Technique

What might have served as a suitable instrument in this particular instance? Surely the teacher's task is considerably eased if one device can be designed to measure all three goals. Here is one example of how the teacher could have structured both the introductory explanation and the assessment instrument.

The Introduction. The teacher begins, "We have been studying about Columbus for the past week. We have been learning many exciting things about him. (If the teacher feels it is necessary, he or she can schedule a short oral review at this point.) Today we will use our learning in order to solve a problem. Most Americans and many historians believe that Columbus was the greatest explorer of his time. Why is it that we think more highly of Columbus than the other explorers?

"To find the answer to this question, you will work in groups, which are listed on the board. Look for your name so that you know to which group you belong.

"Then from the books I have placed on the library table, first pick at least three and read about Columbus in them. As you read, keep a list of the things that Columbus did that made him such a great explorer. Do this part by yourself. Keep your list on this task sheet I am handing out. Everyone must complete his or her own sheet. Remember to share your books with others in the group.

"Second, when you have finished your list, take a turn with the other boys and girls in your group and read aloud what you have listed on your own task sheet. Then talk together about the questions I have written on the board: What were the new things Columbus did? Why were they so great? not so great? Was Columbus the greatest explorer? Why? Why not? What do you think America would be like if Columbus had not sailed to the west? Each person in the group will have at least one turn to talk.

"Finally, after you have talked together about these questions, write the answers to questions 4 and 5 onto your own sheet. Now before we begin, let's review the steps we will take. Who can review what we will do first?"

A sample task sheet that also serves as an evaluative device is shown in Figure 10.3. Using sheets that students complete individually, the teacher can assess growth toward the stated goals. For example, by considering the uniqueness of Columbus' feat, students are searching for information that they may or may not already have known. They are looking at that information from an analytical perspective. In this context, they are not only showing their knowledge of basic facts, but they are increasing it at the same time.

Thinking in terms of the greatness of Columbus' feat, students may give some indication of their level of appreciation of the explorer's contribution. Certainly the teacher would not try to grade children's appreciation as A, B, or C, but responses can give some evidence as to the level of thinking at which youngsters are functioning. For instance, if a child writes as his or her reason for holding Columbus in high esteem, "I like the fact that his hair was red," that youngster is operating at a lower level of cognition and valuing than one who states, "He believed in himself." If children's responses in general show lack of serious thought, the teacher is clued into the need to help them clarify their reasons and to support reasons with specific evidence.

Finally, throughout the first stages of the activity, children must use references to locate information. If they successfully complete questions 1, 2, and 3 of the task sheet, they have supplied some evidence that they have developed basic skill in working rather efficiently with references.

Figure 10.3
A Task Sheet That Also
Serves as an Evaluative Device

Columbus: An Explorer to Explore

Name: _____   Date: _____

Directions: Select three books from the table. List the title of each one on the line
provided. Write down the pages that you read in each to find out more
about Columbus. Then list three great things about Columbus you
discovered from reading each book. Then answer questions 4 and 5,
but only after you have discussed your answers to questions 1, 2, and
3 with your group members.

1. Title of book:	1. Title of book:	1. Title of book:
_____	_____	_____
2. Pages read: _____	2. Pages read: _____	2. Pages read: _____
3. Great things about Columbus:	3. Great things about Columbus:	3. Great things about Columbus:
a.	a.	a.
b.	b.	b.
c.	c.	c.

4. Columbus (was/was not) the greatest explorer because _____

_____

5. Three ways in which America might have been different if Columbus had not
made his voyage are:

a. _____

b. _____

c. _____

Written Items: A Second Technique

The teacher may wish to consider a second technique for measuring
children's growth in ability to use references—adding a test item to the
task sheet or to another evaluative device being used at that point in
the classroom. A suggested item is given below.

Directions: Draw a line from each item in Column A to the correct
answer in Column B.

A	B
If I wanted to know . . .	I would look in the . . .
1. the name of the book,	A. glossary.
2. what a word means,	B. index.
3. what a chapter tells about,	C. table of contents.
4. who wrote the book,	D. cover and title page.
5. if the book has information about Columbus,	

Of course, while this will tell the teacher if the students know how to
seek information in a reference book, it obviously does not reveal if

R Two excellent references to check on testing procedures include:

David Payne, *The Assessment of Learning: Cognitive and Affective* (Lexington, Massachusetts: D. C. Heath & Co., 1974).

W. James Popham, "Well-Crafted Criterion-Referenced Tests," *Educational Leadership*, 36:91-95 (November 1978). This article gives six steps in building tests that measure students' behavior in a clearly defined way.

they actually follow the most efficient procedures in practice. Being able to tell how to do something is a lower-level mental operation than applying the correct approach in real situations. Using this measure, the teacher must augment his or her data with firsthand observations of children as they function at the task.

Idea Page

Background for the teacher: The task sheet on Columbus described in the text and given in Figure 10.3 was designed for use with third or fourth graders. It is, therefore, relatively simple. Here are some ways it can be varied for use with students of greater capacity and/or background:

1. Students complete the task sheet independently without the stimulation of group thought and talk.
2. A modified sheet is completed first without looking through the references, relying on the memory for data. Having filled in the facts, students use references to check points they have recorded.
3. Students are not given books. They must locate their own references in the classroom or school libraries.
4. Students search for and write down actual words and phrases complete with quotation marks, selecting statements that reveal author bias and feelings. They complete the exercise by telling with which views they agree and with which they disagree.
5. Students compare Columbus with a modern explorer such as Neil Armstrong. They decide which one deserves the greater praise and support their opinions with reasons.
6. After reading three or four different accounts of Columbus' voyage, students write their own historical accounts. They exchange papers and analyze friends' accounts to identify historical bias.
7. After searching for and reading updated information that disputes Columbus as the first European to set foot in the Americas, young people tell which explorer or group deserves the honor. They cite reasons to support their choices.

Performance Checklists: A Third Technique

To guide observations of children's performance in real situations, the teacher may use a **performance checklist**. This is often a necessity because observations are usually made "on the run," memory is short-lived, and teachers generally are responsible for twenty-five or more children. Figure 10.4 supplies an example of an observation checklist that is relatively simple to use. On it a teacher records information about each youngster, checking in the appropriate column after having observed children working at the task.

R An excellent book with many practical suggestions is *Observing and Recording the Behavior of Young Children* by Dorothy Cohen and Virginia Stern (New York: Teachers College Press, 1971).

Figure 10.4
A Performance Checklist to Guide
Observations

Names of Students	The Student Correctly Uses the:												Comments
	Table of Contents			Glossary			Title Page or Cover			Index			
	Yes	No	Not Seen	Yes	No	Not Seen	Yes	No	Not Seen	Yes	No	Not Seen	

Date of Observation: _____   Situation: _____

This method of evaluation clearly reveals more about children's handling of books than the question given on page 323. However, it has weaknesses too. The teacher must be an alert and accurate observer with time to observe every child. This means that the teacher may have to restrict observation to one or two small groups during a session and may have to postpone observing others until another time. For this reason, a teacher may wish to record the date and the situation in which the observation was made at the bottom of the checklist (Figure 10.4).

Checklists for recording observations can be made more sophisticated by including gradations that indicate the frequency with which a skill is utilized. A typical gradation of frequency is:

| always | most of the time | sometimes | hardly ever | never |

In contrast, a typical gradation for rating the quality of a performance is:

| excellent | good | average | fair | poor |

Once a series of gradations has been chosen, the teacher should use it consistently. Switching from one set of evaluative words to another makes it difficult to compare one sample of recorded behavior to a second or third. Of course, if over a period of time a teacher discovers that the evaluative words chosen prove unwieldy, a change must be made.

Having selected a series of frequency and/or quality terms to use as the basis of performance observations, the teacher should think through and perhaps even write down key words and phrases that clarify the meaning of each term selected. Everyone has his or her own conception of *good*, *average*, or *poor*. In applying these evaluative terms, the teacher must attempt to be as consistent as possible.

Ways to Achieve Internal Consistency Within Teaching-Evaluative Cycles

So far in this section, emphasis has been placed on ways in which teachers can achieve internal consistency by using evaluative devices that measure specified learning goals. This recommendation, of course, assumes that teachers have thought through the important goals in the social studies they wish to teach and have clearly stated specific and observable behaviors. The reader who is uncertain how to state goals as behavioral objectives is referred to chapter 16, where the procedure is explained.

The recommendation also assumes that teachers evaluate children's progress toward all goals to be achieved through a teaching-learning sequence. It is easier to evaluate student achievement in some areas than in others; yet if teachers allow some goals to go unchecked and concentrate on those that can be more precisely measured, students quickly sense their teacher's priorities. When only lip service is given to a goal, children may also be less conscientious in pursuing it.

A second way in which internal consistency can be violated is through an evaluation device that is poorly designed. As a result, the device measures spurious factors. This can happen as an outgrowth of unclear or vague wording, which makes it difficult for children to know what is expected of them. Even with the use of simple language structures, vagueness can be a problem. Take, for example, an item such as "Columbus arrived in America in _____." Many answers are possible because of the manner in which the question is phrased: "autumn," "1492," "a boat named the Santa Maria," "an unplanned way," "the middle of October." Not knowing the category of response required, the bright child in particular agonizes over the answer and may come up with one that is unanticipated by the teacher. Instead of assessing children's knowledge of the social studies, the test becomes a game in which the student guesses what the test writer has in mind.

The reading level of the evaluative instrument can also cause problems. When the level is beyond the comprehension of many children, the instrument ceases to be a measure of growth in the social studies. It becomes a reading test, for only those who understand what is written will be able to respond appropriately. The others will struggle to read what is written. To avoid this pitfall, the language in any measuring instrument should be kept as simple as possible; words should be kept to a minimum.

In addition, spurious evaluation can result from an evaluation instrument that is too simple or advanced for those whose growth will be assessed via it. An effective assessment procedure or device is one that discriminates among students who have learned as a result of instruction and those who have not. When a test is too simple, most will do well not because they have learned through the lesson sequence but because the instrument asks for information they had at the beginning. In contrast, when a test is too difficult, many students will respond with little or no information and have no opportunity to demonstrate the knowledge they have acquired.

Evaluation and Decision Making

The explanation of measuring devices found in the preceding paragraphs points to another perspective from which the difference between testing and evaluation can be viewed. Testing, also termed **measurement**, provides raw data about progress but nothing more. Given these data, the teacher must then make judgments about students' growth. This is evaluation.

Teachers should give as much attention to analyzing the data supplied by measuring devices as they do in constructing them. In a sense, once teachers have administered a device, their job has only begun, for the results must be interpreted. Instruments can yield several kinds of data, for example:

1. How much each child has learned as a result of the teaching sequence (or in the case of pre-instructional assessment, how much each knows as a result of previous learning experiences); Data

2. Which students have or have not mastered specific cognitive or social/emotional learnings measured by the instrument;
3. Which topics or skills need further attention or reteaching.

Based on these data, the teacher must decide whether the growth is acceptable for a particular child or for the class and whether or not to proceed with further instruction on the same topic or skill.

These decisions involve some degree of teacher subjectivity, for no matter what the measuring instrument, it provides only raw data. The teacher must then place a value judgment on the sample of behavior and decide if that growth is typical, remarkable, or inadequate. On the other hand, the more accurate the data provided by an evaluative instrument, the more reliable is the teacher's basis for assigning labels. If an instrument yields information that is irrelevant, uncharacteristic, or chancy, then the teacher's judgment will be clouded by these factors. A spurious measuring device has resulted in a spurious evaluation.

Assessing Growth at Many Levels of Thinking and Feeling

Getting students prepared for The ~~teacher~~ future develop higher lebel of thinking tasks.

An integrating theme of this text is that the education of today's young people for an unknown future is best accomplished by helping them develop the ability to handle higher-level thinking tasks and modes of gathering information, solving problems, and making decisions. Testing for only information recalled is inconsistent with these goals of social studies instruction. Evaluation must be in terms of major curriculum goals, as was described in Figure 10.1.

Assessing Growth in Social Studies Content and Reading

R For further ideas on assessing reading in social studies, check:

Ronald Hash, and Mollie Bailey, "A Classroom Strategy: Improving Social Studies Comprehension," *Social Education*, 42:24-26 (January 1978).

William Rader, "Improving Critical Reading Through Consumer Education," *Social Education*, 42:18-20 (January 1978).

The previous paragraph does not imply that factual knowledge should not be measured. Indeed, just the opposite is true, since content goals (knowledge of facts, terms, and generalizations) are being sought, and this information forms the substance of an investigation. Critics of the new social studies claim that not enough attention to content has resulted in a generation of uninformed young people who know little about their own national heritage. Some teachers are further concerned about children's ability to handle reading in the social studies. To be certain that students have mastered basic reading skills and acquired knowledge of content, these teachers spend class social studies time having children read the content under their guidance—a practice that leaves no time for active involvement. The teacher is faced with a real dilemma: how to determine if students have mastered basic skills and content without utilizing the entire social studies time to do it.

In actuality, the solution is not so difficult as it first appears. Teachers check comprehension in social studies just as in their reading programs by scheduling reading for information as an independent or small group activity, while class time is used for other more dynamic involvement. In social studies there are four overlapping levels of comprehension to be evaluated.

1. Factual or literal–Questions ask for information directly stated in a passage. Giving a correct answer requires locating or remembering it with the printed lines confirming or denying the accuracy of an answer.
2. Inferential–Questions ask for information implied but not stated directly. Answering requires identification of subtle clues or reading between the lines. For inferential questions there are right and wrong answers.
3. Relational–Questions ask for relationships that go beyond what is stated explicitly or implicitly. Answers require that a reader think in terms of why and how. The accuracy of answers is determined by restudying what is printed to see that all factors have been considered. There are no right or wrong answers.
4. Critical or judgmental–Questions ask for value judgments or a critique of the author's assumptions, opinions, point of view, and/or style. Answering requires that a reader formulate a statement that can be defended by referring to specific data in the passage. There are no right or wrong answers.

To assess children's comprehension of a passage, a teacher must construct an evaluative device that questions at all four levels. The format of the device can be a straightforward task sheet as is shown in Figure 10.5, which is based on a selection from one social studies text. This question sheet would be used as follow-up to a lesson in which children study a map of Canada that shows natural features such as mountains, rapids, rivers, and rainfall, as well as land features such as railroads, mineral deposits, and so forth. As part of the preparatory work, children talk about how and where cities grow. They consider what the parallels tell about the climate of Canada and the effect climate has on city building; what role mountains have in the development of cities; where the rivers are located and the part played by rivers in the growth of cities; how railroads and mineral deposits affect city growth; and where people usually settle when they emigrate to a new area. They hypothesize the six best locations for city development in Canada. This analysis and discussion prepare young social scientists for independent text study through which the teacher can simultaneously assess children's ability to read and think at higher levels.

T An evaluative idea: Ask children in upper grades, "What changes in immigration do these graphs show? Why do you think these changes occurred?"

1820-60

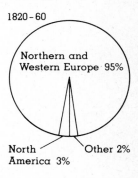

1971-74

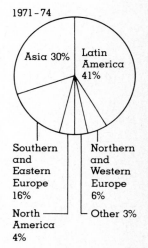

Figure 10.5
A Task Sheet That Checks Factual,
Inferential, Relational, and Critical
Comprehension

Cities in Canada

Directions: Read "Cities in Canada" found on pages 277–282 of *Man and Society.* Then answer the questions on this sheet.

1. Name the 6 largest Canadian cities and tell for what each is best known. (This is factual question–the answer is stated explicitly in the text.)

The City   **What It Is Known for**

A.

B.

C.

D.

E.

F.

2. What crops are grown in Canada? What industries does Canada have? (This is an inferential question–the answer can be inferred from goods shipped to and from cities.)

The Crops   **The Industries**

3. Why is Montreal the largest and most important commercial city in Canada? (This is a relationship question–the reader must consider geographic factors, transportation facilities, past history, and sociological factors.)

4. The book calls Hamilton the Pittsburgh of Canada and Windsor the Detroit of Canada. Match a city in the United States with each of the six Canadian cities. Give one reason for each of your choices. Then decide in which one of the six Canadian cities you would most like to live and give your reason. (This is a relationship and judgmental activity–the reader must consider numbers of interrelated factors, make a decision, and support it with reasons.)

The Canadian City	The United States City	Your Reason
A.		
B.		
C.		
D.		
E.		
F.		

The City Where You Might Want to Live: _____ Your Reasons:

The teacher can extend the task and encourage children to build on their basic comprehension in a number of ways. Possibilities include these tasks:

Read another book and compare the two authors' lists of the major Canadian cities. In what ways are they alike? different?

Write a brief report comprised of two or three paragraphs telling why one pair of Canadian/United States cities is really well matched.

Select one of the six cities, read more about it in an encyclopedia, and write a brief report on it.

Compare the sizes of the six Canadian cities given in the text with the six largest cities in the United States. Give reasons for the differences you find in city sizes. Express your data on a chart or graph.

Decide: If your family had to move to one of the Canadian cities on the list, which would you choose? Why?

Pretend you are a printer and are asked to create a brochure to attract either industry or tourists to the cities of Canada. Write the brochure and illustrate it.

Draw a seal for any of the Canadian cities. Make sure it communicates key facts about it.

Locate the six largest Canadian and United States cities on a map. Describe the patterns you see.

New York City is known as the "Big Apple," Chicago as the "Windy City." Create a nickname for one of the Canadian cities and give your reasons for choosing it.

T Children can read for more information in a reference such as *The Canada Handbook* by the Publishing Section, Information Division, Statistics Canada (Ottawa, Canada: Minister of Supply and Services), an annual publication.

Even as children work individually and in pairs at their desks or at learning stations, the teacher has opportunity to observe their performance, especially their work habits and their ability to cooperate with others. The materials that children produce are evaluated as well. Under these conditions, evaluation can hardly be separated from the teaching-learning act, for evaluation is occurring as part of ongoing activity.

Idea Page

Background for the teacher. Figure 10.6 can be used in a personalized teacher-student conference as described in chapter 7, either after a student has participated as a member of an investigative task group or after he or she has worked independently to compile a data folder. Under these conditions, teacher and student cooperatively discuss the specific behaviors listed on the checklist and decide on a rating. Both "need to improve some" and "have improved some" can be checked for a particular item. A copy of the completed checklist can be pasted inside the personal folder in which the student is compiling investigative data.

The instrument can be used also for assessing a student's cognitive growth as demonstrated during class discussions. For this purpose only items under Roman numerals II and III are checked.

Assessing Growth Toward Process Goals

T Read Francis Hunkins, "Exercises to Assess Social Studies and Citizenship: How Good Are They?" in *Social Education*, 38:415-421 (May 1974). Then following the steps in the article, construct a device to assess growth toward one of these broad citizenship goals: Students care for and share materials in the classroom. Students appreciate the ethnic and racial diversity of class members.

Traditionally, evaluation has focused on content rather than process goals. Only recently has the assessment of growth toward process goals concerned teachers and other school personnel. It was formerly assumed that if children had knowledge of content, they had mastered as well the processes for operating with this content. Today this assumption is challenged by the fact that many children know answers but are poorly equipped to gather data and utilize findings constructively. Furthermore, evaluation devices for assessing knowledge of content have a longer history and are more refined measuring tools. Because their form is more tangible, they have been used more extensively. In contrast, how a child relates to another or searches for information is but a fleeting act observed by a teacher who must record it in a subjective manner.

For these reasons teachers understandably have devoted more attention to assessing more easily verified goals. A one-dimensional evaluation, however, distorts the teacher's view of students' growth. Because children are not equally adept at all tasks, evaluation may

**Figure 10.6
Checklist of Problem-Solving
Behaviors**

Area in which I

	Need to improve a lot	Need to improve some	Have improved some	Have improved a lot
I. Gathering Data				
Uses several kinds of sources				
Uses several cases of any one kind of source				
Selects data relevant to the problem				
Keeps systematic notes				
II. Using Data				
Organizes data systematically				
Perceives relationships within data				
Separates facts from opinions				
Considers available alternatives				
III. Arriving at Conclusions				
Weighs alternatives and selects viable solution				
States solution clearly				
Supports solution with reasons				
Expresses opinion about solution				

Teacher Comments:

Student Comments:

Problem Situation:

Date:

cast them in an unduly favorable or unfavorable light unless a wide variety of techniques is employed. For example, some children are very capable of delivering an oral report, whereas others are shy and hesitant. Some can write pages about a topic, whereas others struggle to organize their thoughts into a single paragraph. Some can sail through a series of short items, whereas others ponder over every question. Some can create very original ideas, whereas others cannot extend their thinking beyond the mundane. Some can express their innermost thoughts and feelings with fervor, whereas others grapple for a mere sentence. Some lead with the exquisite poise of a patrician, whereas others hope only to get a word in edgewise. Clearly a fair picture of students' strengths and weaknesses can be determined only if many different behaviors are assessed.

Ways of Focusing on Process Skills.   Three elements are essential as the teacher constructs instruments to assess children's progress toward process goals.

R For ways to measure process and affective goals, read Bruce Tuckman, *Measuring Educational Outcomes: Fundamentals of Testing* (New York: Harcourt Brace Jovanovich, 1975).

1. Clear identification of criteria, or attributes, that describe behavior–The assessor must know what he or she is evaluating before collecting samples of behavior;
2. Relatively precise use of judgmental terms so that the degree to which criteria or attributes are manifested can be communicated–e.g., good, average, poor;
3. Involvement to some extent of children in the evaluation process.

Figure 10.7 is a sample instrument that can be used to assess individual performance as part of a class or group discussion. Figure 10.8 is a simple device for assessing an oral report by a student. The reader may wish to study those as well as Figure 10.9, which provides a sample of a device for assessing a written report, and Figure 10.10, which provides one for assessing a student product (diorama, bulletin board, booklet, model, and so forth) to see several different formats for assessing performance. In each case, the instrument can be used by teacher and/or students. In each case too, criteria are expressed as actions and begin with verbs.

Figure 10.7
Instrument for Evaluating Class or
Group Discussions

A Discussion Checklist

Directions: Put a small check in the appropriate column each time a specific behavior is observed.

Names of Children

Behaviors	Martin C.	Sara F.	José M.	Keith B.	Melissa A.
1. Asks relevant questions					
2. Presents related information					
3. Makes comparisons and contrasts					
4. Comes up with generalizations, summaries and/or conclusions					
5. Supports opinions and judgments with reasons					
6. Helps others with comments and questions					
7. Waits turn without interrupting					
8. Uses face and eyes to show interest					
(Add other items that apply to your class here)					

Date

Topic

Observer

(This form can be used by a student or teacher observer.)

General comments about the discussion as a whole:

Was the discussion worthwhile?

Were there varying opinions and many ideas?

What was accomplished?

Figure 10.8
Device for Evaluating
an Oral Presentation

An Oral Presentation Checklist

Student   Date of Presentation

Topic   Date of Conference

Subject Content	Very Good	Good	Needs Improvement
1. Covers the topic so listeners see a complete picture.			
2. Supports big ideas with interesting details.			
3. Organizes content so it is easy to follow.			
4. Presents accurate information.			
5. Draws conclusions and summarizes information at the end.			
6. Supports judgments with reasons.			

Presentation	Very Good	Good	Needs Improvement
1. Speaks in a clear and interesting voice.			
2. Uses notes without word-for-word reading.			
3. Uses visual techniques to add to the oral presentation.			
4. Uses language accurately and forcefully.			
5. Stands with ease.			
6. Looks at listeners, making eye contact.			
7. Uses body motions and facial expressions to communicate.			

Teacher Comments:

Student Comments:

**Figure 10.9
A Form for Evaluating a Written
Report (Upper Elementary)**

Written Report Checklist

	Never	Sometimes	Almost Always	Always
Content				
1. Presents accurate information.				
2. States information in own words.				
3. Organizes information in a logical sequence.				
4. Sticks to the topic.				
5. Supports main ideas with related details.				
Language Skills				
1. Writes complete sentences and punctuates them correctly.				
2. Builds each paragraph around one big idea.				
3. Uses varied vocabulary.				
4. Spells words correctly.				
5. Writes legibly.				
6. Proofreads carefully.				

	Yes	No	Not Required
Research Skills			
1. Locates information in a variety of sources			
2. Organizes notes in a logical way.			
3. Compiles sources into a bibliography.			
4. Uses quotation marks around quotations and gives sources in footnote form.			

Title of Written Report   Student Comments

Name of Student   Teacher Comments

Date of Conference

**Figure 10.10
A Form for Evaluating
a Student Project**

A Product Checklist	Satisfactory	Unsatisfactory
Content		
1. Does the project clearly demonstrate the big idea of the topic?		
2. Is factual content accurate?		
3. Is there evidence that more than one source of information was used?		
Presentation		
1. Has the work been neatly and carefully done?		
2. Are labels used where needed?		
3. Have materials been organized to show relationships?		
4. Is the design of the presentation creative?		
5. Is the overall product attractive?		

Rating

Title of Product

Name of Student

Date of Teacher/Student Conference

Student Comments

Teacher Comments

Ways of Focusing on Values, Attitudes, and Feelings. The attributes constituting the cognitive and social process skills are generally easier to define than those of values, attitudes, and feelings. Feelings and attitudes are inner dimensions of personality that can only be inferred from outward behavior. What emotion, for instance, prompts a second grader to weep when he or she is the penultimate choice for a work group? Is it rage? frustration? bitterness? hatred? sadness? tension? or happiness at not being the last one?

T Assessing feelings toward ethnic groups is discussed in James Banks, "Evaluating the Multi-ethnic Component of the Social Studies," *Social Education*, 40:538-541 (November/December 1976).

Asking the weeper may appear to be a simple solution, but often one does not know or is unable to articulate exactly what it is that brings on an emotional response. Then too, a gap exists between what a person says and how one truly feels; sometimes innermost feelings and attitudes are too frightening to voice. Furthermore, every observer brings to a situation biases and attitudes that often color his or her perceptions of what another person is saying.

For these reasons teachers must exercise extreme caution in assessing children's emotional behavior. They need to gather many observations and separate their perceptions from their interpretations. They should give children ample opportunities to express feelings, attitudes, and values in beneficial ways and then *listen* to what youngsters are saying. Some methods include:

1. Sociograms that reveal peer preferences in a wide variety of situations;
2. Interest inventories that tell about hobbies, interests, and preferences in and out of school;
3. Responses to values lessons that divulge not only attitudes but the thinking behind them;
4. Open-ended value statements structured so that no matter how a child responds (even leaving an item blank), he or she discloses attitudes and feelings;
5. Socio-dramas and role-playing structured so that children's spontaneous reactions unmask many of their feelings, attitudes, and values;
6. Suggestion boxes that permit students to offer opinions on how the class or school can be run more harmoniously or efficiently;
7. Interviews with children that focus on feelings, attitudes, and values;
8. Anecdotal records through which a teacher records incidents and samples of behavior that reveal a particular attitude, feeling, or value.

Ways of Determining Children's Feelings Toward School. Although a teacher should encourage children to express their feelings and opinions on a variety of issues, conditions, and situations, he or she has little power to affect change beyond that of any citizen. In establishing the emotional climate of the classroom, however, the classroom teacher is the principal agent and prime mover. As a base for determining possible directions for change in the classroom, students' feelings and attitudes can be appraised along several dimensions.

One dimension involves children's feelings and attitudes about the curriculum content. The teacher gathers data about these by using:

Figure 10.11
Summary Sheet for the
Primary Grades

MY DAY

Name:

Date:

Today I feel _____ because _____

What I did today	What I did not do today

My day was: great   good   fair   bad
because

1. Summary sheets on which children react to what they are doing—Figures 10.11 and 10.12 provide examples. The first is intended for use in primary grades, the second for use with intermediate students.
2. Forced-choice devices on which students rank curricular subjects and specific classroom activities according to their preferences
3. Open-ended questionnaires

These same devices can be used to find out about children's feelings about school in general.

A second dimension that the teacher should consider is children's feelings and attitudes about the classroom operation. Two samples of devices to highlight feelings are given in Figure 10.13. The first is an open-ended questionnaire on which upper graders can record responses directly. The second, the story of Helpful Hannah, can be used in oral or written form. Sharing it aloud with younger primary children, the teacher pauses at the points indicated in the story. Children orally contribute ideas, pretending they are speaking for Helpful Hannah, who has come to visit the class. When children are able to read the words for themselves, the story—with space left at key points—can be placed in a writing center where children go to write down the words that Helpful Hannah would speak.

T To understand the effect of teacher behavior on student initiative, read "Teacher Responsiveness: Pupil Initiative—Themes and Variations," by Greta Morine and Ned Flanders in *Social Education*, 38:432-439 (May 1974). Based on it, construct a learning contract that fosters student independence.

Figure 10.12
A Self-Analysis Sheet

My Production Line

Name

Week of

Stations and Independent Tasks	**Group Activities**

This week I did these stations and tasks: This week I worked on these group tasks:

Monday_____   Monday_____

Tuesday_____   Tuesday_____

Wednesday_____   Wednesday_____

Thursday_____   Thursday_____

Friday_____   Friday_____

What I liked best about the work this week was_____

because _____

What I didn't like was _____

because _____

I need to improve in _____

About me	Always	Sometimes	Never
1. My work is neat.			
2. I finish my work.			
3. I follow directions.			
4. I concentrate hard on my work.			
5. I contribute my share to group projects.			

Student's initials

Teacher's initials

T For ideas on observation instruments that measure a teacher's responses, read "Assessing and Influencing Teachers' Affective Interactions in the Classroom," by Virginia Bruininks in *Educational Technology*, 18:10-14 (July 1978).

A third dimension of classroom environment is interpersonal relationships. Teachers can encourage children to express their feelings in this area through the use of sociograms, socio-dramas, role-playing, and discussions that provide evidence about peer and child-teacher feelings and attitudes.

In response to children's stated feelings, the teacher cannot and should not affect change in all areas. On the other hand, responses can provide an incentive to change when substantial benefits to students will result. In addition, by responding to conflict, differences of opinion, and criticism, the teacher provides a model of how an open person functions.

Creative Evaluation

Evaluation devices and activities need not be routine; indeed, as the previous section has attempted to show, evaluative situations can be absorbing and challenging if the teacher has incorporated something exciting and unusual. From this point of view, creativity is as important in the design of assessment instruments as it is in the design of teaching sequences.

Creativity in Evaluation

T A current trend in the social studies is the use of documents in evaluation. Read about this in Mildred Alperin, "Develop Your Own Tests in World History," *Social Education*, 40:517-523 (November/December 1976). For example, ask children to study the painting "Washington Crossing the Delaware." Then ask, "How do you think Washington felt as he crossed the Delaware? How would you have felt if you had been with him?"

There are two ways through which the unusual can be incorporated in evaluation instruments. The first is through a format that is not ordinary. Look at Figure 10.13, and notice the differences in the formats of the two devices, each having the same purpose–the assessment of student reaction to the teacher. The response sheet is matter-of-fact; whereas the story format of Helpful Hannah is one that most children have used on only rare occasions. The tale is fun for younger children, who characteristically anthropomorphize nonhuman creatures.

The second means of interjecting the unusual into evaluation is to challenge the thinking ability of students by asking them to perform puzzle tasks. Learners are more likely to enjoy a situation that provokes them to think. Teachers cannot always construct out-of-the-ordinary evaluative instruments; but as far as possible, they should be creative in designing tasks that ask students to go beyond memory activity to apply, analyze, synthesize, evaluate, and decide.

Figure 10.13
Two Devices to Assess Children's
reaction to the Teacher

A Simple Reasons Sheet

1. I like this class because:
2. If I could change this class in some way, I would:
3. If I were the teacher, I would:
4. I get annoyed when the teacher:
5. The very best thing about the teacher is:

A Participation Story: Helpful Hannah

Once there was a bug  called Helpful Hanna. She was called this because she always tried to help others. The only problem was that she was a bug and couldn't talk, so when she had an idea , she asked the children  to speak for her.

One day Helpful Hanna  opened the door 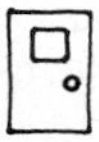 and walked right into this classroom. She saw you  and me  , the desk 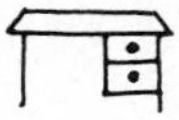 , the books  and everything else. She thought, "I like this class because. . . . ." But Helpful Hanna  could not speak, so boys and girls, let's speak for her. She said, "I like this class because. . ."

As Helpful Hanna  walked around, she saw some things she wanted to change, and she thought, "If I could change this class, I would. . ."

Then Helpful Hanna  strolled right up to the teacher's desk 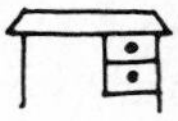 and looked at the children  and the classroom.

Then she thought, "If I were the teacher,  I would. . ."

Now Helpful Hanna  went and sat right where you  are sitting. She glanced at the teacher. "My, my," she fretted, "I get annoyed when the teacher. . .

But then Helpful Hanna  nodded her head and thought, "The very best thing about the teacher is. . ."

Very pleased that she had helped us, Helpful Hanna  crawled out of the door 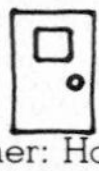 just as quietly and as quickly as she came in.

(Note to the teacher: Have children each make a set of cards, bearing a picture of Hanna, the teacher, and the children. When you get to the appropriate spots in the story, children listen and hold up the correct card.)

An Example: Entering Neverland

A teacher of an intermediate class had been working toward growth in basic map skills, specifically on children's ability to orient a map and note directions, recognize the scale of a map, compute distance, locate places on a map, express relative location, use map symbols, and compare maps and make inferences from them. Keeping these goals in mind, Ms. Fiore went on to devise the activity sheet called "Entering Neverland" to use for evaluative purposes at the end of a unit. The reader may wish to study each question first to see how well he or she can handle skills schools should be teaching children, second to identify the kind of thinking skill being employed by children as they complete each question, and third to decide whether the instrument truly measures all of the teacher's stated goals and is a creative device. In this respect, the reader can use Figure 10.14 as a way of post-testing his or her ability to handle the ideas encountered in this chapter.

**Figure 10.14
A Way to Measure Map Skills**

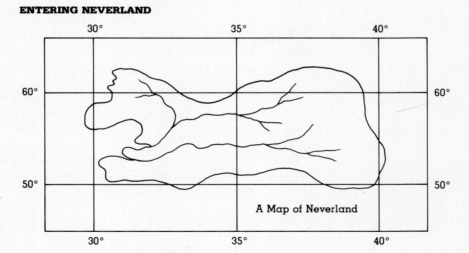

ENTERING NEVERLAND

A Map of Neverland

Directions: Study the map. Then fill in the word or phrase that best completes each item.

1-2. The two hemispheres in which Neverland is located are _____ and _____ .
3. The direction in which the rivers flow is from _____ to _____ .
4. The coast that is most suited to the location of port cities is _____ .
5. If it is 3 P.M. on the west coast of Neverland, the time on the east coast is _____ .

6. Of the meridians plotted on the map, the one which is closest to the International Date Line is _____ .

7-8. You live on Neverland. Two ways you might make a living are _____ and _____ .

9. The coast of highest elevation is _____ .

10. The coast that would probably have the densest population is _____ .

11. An adjective to describe the climate of Neverland is _____ .

12-14. Put a large dot on the most advantageous spot to locate a port. Support your site selection by giving two reasons why that spot would be advantageous.

15. The width of Neverland at its widest point from east to west coasts is _____ . Use your knowledge of the distance between lines of longitude to solve this problem.

16. Because it connects with no other land bodies, Neverland is called a/an ____ .

Evaluating Learnings in the Social Studies: A Summary Thought or Two

Evaluation in classrooms should be a continuing, integral part of the social studies program. If it is, teachers' judgments about student progress determine what teaching-learning activities will be pursued. Even as children go on to pursue these tasks, they produce additional evidence of learning or non-learning, which again the teacher considers in planning future and remedial work. Viewed from this perspective, evaluation is a key component of the teaching-learning act. It is much more comprehensive than testing, or measurement, which is merely the collection of data through written and performance devices. Data so collected must be interpreted by the teacher in terms of individual differences in attitude, ability, and previous experience.

In setting up an evaluation program, a teacher should ultimately try to assess progress in terms of all goals sought through instruction in the social studies—the lower-level content as well as cognitive and social/emotional process goals. To do otherwise is to function much as the ten blind men did when each described the elephant in terms of only the small part he had felt and each arrived at a different judgment. Unless evaluation is complete, more than likely it will be unsound.

A teacher must seek to be creative in the evaluative instruments he or she devises. Involving the children in the process of assessing their own progress, he or she must think of evaluation in very broad terms so that lines between assessing and teaching become less distinct. Evaluation need not prove a tedious and dreaded process for students. Under the right conditions, evaluation can be a challenging and exciting process for student and teacher alike.

R For discussions on standardized testing in the social studies see:

Lena Brown, "What Teachers Should Know About Standardized Tests," *Social Education*, 40:509-511, 516 (November/December 1976).

Oscar Buros, ed., *Social Studies Tests and Reviews* (Highland Park, New Jersey: Gryphon Press, 1975). This gives information on the kinds of standardized tests available in the social studies.

Robert MacKay, "How Teachers Know: A Case of Epistemological Conflict," *Sociology of Education*, 51:177-187 (July 1978).

Some Tasks to Try

Here are some tasks to try as a means of evaluating your own ability to devise creative measures of social studies learnings.

1. Create an instrument based on a passage from a social studies text that you could use to assess children's ability to comprehend content through reading. Use the sheet included in Figure 10.5 as a guide.
2. Devise an instrument for evaluating children's ability to handle bar graphs. Model your instrument after the one supplied in the text to get at children's growth in map interpretation skills.
3. Design a forced-choice instrument through which you could determine children's preferences for school subjects.
4. Design a performance checklist that you could use to assess children's ability to locate a particular book in the library. Be sure to specify precisely the component behaviors necessary to complete the task successfully. Use the checklist given in Figure 10.4 as a guide.

References

Bloom, Benjamin. *Evaluation of Student Learning.* New York: McGraw-Hill, 1971.

Brown, F. G. *Principles of Educational and Psychological Testing,* 2nd ed. New York: Holt, Rinehart & Winston, 1976.

Cohen, Dorothy; and Stern, Virginia. *Observing and Recording the Behavior of Young Children.* New York: Teachers College Press, 1971.

Gronlund, Norman. *Constructing Achievement Tests.* Englewood Cliffs, New Jersey: Prentice-Hall, 1977.

Karmel, Louis; and Karmel, Marylin. *Measurement and Evaluation in the Schools,* 2nd ed. New York: Macmillan, 1978.

Payne, David. *The Assessment of Learning: Cognitive and Affective.* Lexington, Massachusetts: D. C. Heath & Co., 1974.

Sax, Gilbert. *Principles of Educational Measurement and Evaluation.* Belmont, California: Wadsworth Publishing Co., 1974.

Thorndike, Robert; and Hagen, Elizabeth. *Measurement and Evaluation in Psychology and Education,* 4th ed., New York: John Wiley & Sons, 1977.

Tuckman, Bruce. *Measuring Educational Outcomes: Fundamentals of Testing.* New York: Harcourt Brace Jovanovich, 1975.

Part Four   Issues and Investigations Using the Social Sciences

As life is action and passion, it is required of a (person) that he should share the passion and action of the time, at peril of being judged not to have lived.

Oliver Wendell Holmes, Jr., 1884

Part Four describes issues and investigations important in preparing students to meet today's challenges. Each chapter draws upon several of the social sciences as well as upon the humanities for content and methodology. Ideas found in these chapters can be integrated into other units normally included in social studies programs.

To avoid repetition, in describing activities in each chapter, the authors have intentionally limited usage of particular social studies activities to one or two chapters in the part. For example,

Chapter 11 specifies ways of using values ladders, group writing, visuals, literature, music, and dance to teach concepts from sociology and anthropology.

Chapter 12 provides ideas for using decision-making simulations, time lines, values graphs, now-and-then charts, and documents to teach concepts from history and political science.

Chapter 13 presents ideas from economics and geography and provides suggestions for direct inquiry into the local environment and for the use of maps to show mental perceptions of geographic areas.

Chapter 14 demonstrates ways to integrate library investigation into the social studies as children apply understanding of geographic, economic, and demographic concepts to global and consumer problems.

Chapter 15 integrates the social and natural sciences by blending ideas from ecology with economic, geographic, legal, and ethical concerns. It presents ways of using legal and value decision making, role-playing, firsthand data collection, and categorization. This chapter demonstrates an updated approach to current events.

11

Joan sees herself as part of a family.

There goes many a ship to sea, with many hundred souls in one ship, whose weal and woe is common, and is a true picture of a commonwealth or a human combination or society.

Roger Williams, "Letter to the Town of Providence," 1655

Key Questions

In what respects do the concerns of physical, social, and cultural anthropologists differ? How are they the same?

What are the major foci of sociological and psychological investigations?

What methodology is characteristic of study of the social sciences?

What weaknesses do we find within some programs that attempt to develop cultural awareness?

What kinds of activities should be included in social studies programs to help children develop their understanding of cultures around the world?

Why is it especially important for children living in the United States and Canada to be involved in cultural studies?

How do sociologists use the terms *role*, *status*, *role expectations*, and *sanctions*?

Describe a series of specific activities that would help children understand their own roles in school and in family groups.

How can we help children better understand the job-oriented roles of their society without reinforcing stereotyped beliefs?

Clues to a culture – the totem pole

Figure 11.1
The Kats Totem Pole

The totem pole in Figure 11.1 records the story of Kats and his grizzly bear wife. Long ago, before you and I were alive, a man was hunting bear with his dogs. His name was Kats. In his pursuit, Kats stumbled upon a cave that was home for a pair of grizzly bears. The male grizzly, protecting his home, slapped Kats and knocked him into the cave. But the female appeared to Kats as a woman. She fell in love with him and drove the male grizzly away from the cave.

For many years, Kats and his bear wife lived happily together. They raised three cub children. Kats hunted seal and fish for his family. But Kats' bear wife–perhaps knowing that she would lose him if he were to look at or do anything with his human family–forbade him from making contact of any kind with his family.

One day, while Kats was hunting near the village, his human wife stepped in front of him. His bear wife knew immediately that Kats had committed the forbidden act, but she also knew it was not his fault. When Kats returned to the cave, she slapped him playfully. But the cub children did not realize the playfulness of the slap. They jumped upon their human father and tore him to pieces.

Up to this day, some Tlingit Indians–believing themselves to be descendents of these cub children–will not eat grizzly meat.

Introduction

ANTHROPOLOGY   SOCIOLOGY

Totem poles were carved by the people living along the coast of British Columbia and Alaska. The Tlingit were the northernmost of these people, and it is their legend of Kats and his bear wife that is depicted on the totem pole shown here.

These carved cedar monuments served different purposes. Some held the ashes of the dead. Some served as pillars supporting the rafters of community houses. Others heralded the legends that were part of the mythological history of a family or group.

Outside totem poles were essentially public documents of people with no written language but with an extensive history to be passed from one generation to the next. The figures, in sequence from top down, assisted a person already well-versed in the myths and history of the clan in relating the legend to others. Indeed, the myths were the property of the family or clan. Only those who inherited or acquired the right in some way were privileged to recite the stories. Sanctions were assessed against those breaking the rules of who could recite.

Putting People into Perspective: Anthropology and Sociology

The Tlingit totem poles reveal much about the culture of these people. The totem poles are evidence of the important objects in their lives, the customs to which they adhered, their art forms and symbols, and their social norms and rules of behavior. These aspects of culture are of special interest to anthropologists trying to understand the way of life of a people.

Anthropology is sometimes considered a study of the natural history of people, but anthropology today more nearly reflects the derivation of the term–*anthropos* = man; *logos* = discourse. It is a broad study covering the ideas, symbols and language, personality, social forms and socialization, religion, ethics, and laws of a people. It encompasses as well the study of the genetics and anatomy of humankind as a species. Let us look at some of the facets of anthropological study, going on to look briefly, too, at those aspects of sociology and psychology that are finding their way into or influencing elementary social studies programs.

Physical Anthropology

In earlier years, anthropologists took careful measurements of bones and the outside of the human body in order to classify human beings according to type and to develop correlations among various types. At that point physical anthropologists were primarily interested in finding out about the first humans and their animal ancestors and in studying the varieties of people and body types.

Today **physical anthropology** has become more process-oriented. Anthropologists work to understand how human variation and primate evolution occur. Bones are not only measured and compared, but functional complexities of muscles and bones are studied to determine how changes in physical traits arise and how these changes are significant in terms of survival of the race and adaptation to the environment. For example, Sherwood Washburn suggests that the decrease in size of the human face–particularly of jaw muscle and bone size–along with increase in brain size are related to changes in natural selection after human beings began using tools. These characteristics increased the chances of survival of beings who used tools rather than the mouth for grasping, cutting, and fighting.

Population genetics and the genetics of blood chemistry are newer aspects of anthropological study. Genetic differences and similarities in population groups–including those related to blood cells and serums–reveal relationships among people and shed light on long-term evolutionary trends.

R For information about the Northwest Coast Indians consult: Edward Keithahn, *Monuments in Cedar: The Authentic Story of the Totem Pole* (New York: Bonanza Books, Crown Publishers, 1963); Maria Ackerman, *Tlingit Stories* (Anchorage, Alaska: Amu Press, 1975). Stories such as "Kats and His Bear Wife" are part of Tlingit mythology, which incorporates the belief that animals are really people who appear as animals when away from home.

R See Sherwood Washburn, "The New Physical Anthropology," in *Readings in Anthropology*, third edition, edited by Jesse Jennings and E. Adamson Hoebel (New York: McGraw-Hill, 1972). The teacher with limited background in anthropology will find many of the articles interesting; they give an overview of the field of anthropology today.

Cultural Anthropology

Another facet of anthropology involves the study of culture. In the broad sense, people working in archeology, ethnology, and linguistics are all students of **cultural anthropology.** While a clear distinction can be made between archeology—a study of extinct cultures—and ethnology—a study of living cultures—the field of ethnology itself is fragmented into a number of overlapping subspecialties. Some ethnologists concentrate on what French anthropologist Claude Levi-Strauss calls first stages in research: they observe, describe, classify, and analyze culture traits such as tools, weapons, beliefs, and kinship structures. Other ethnologists systematically concentrate on a single culture trait such as methods of gathering food, courtship practices, or ways that group rules are enforced.

R See Claude Levi-Strauss, *Structural Anthropology* (New York: Basic Books, 1963). Levi-Strauss is one of the world's leading anthropologists.

Social Anthropology

Anthropologists interested primarily in aspects of culture call themselves cultural anthropologists, whereas those concerned with social interaction and the structure of society call themselves social anthropologists. Lucy Mair, in describing the British view of **social anthropology,** writes: "It means that we think of the *society,* not the culture, as an orderly arrangement of parts, and that our business is to detect and explain this order."

Social anthropologists tend to examine the social structure in terms of concepts such as *status, role, role expectation,* and *social control.* They think of social organization as "a network of recognized statuses and the behavior patterns followed by people who occupy those statuses." (See Gibbs, 1977.) In this context **status** means the relative rank or standing of a person within the larger social sphere in which he or she operates. A person's status is a function of the role that he or she customarily plays within the group. People within a society associate certain behavior patterns with certain roles. They come to expect those playing these roles to behave as those occupying that niche in society have behaved in the past. In this respect, people's role expectations operate as social controls, or **sanctions.**

R See Lucy Mair, *An Introduction to Social Anthropology* (Oxford, England: Oxford University Press, 1965). This book provides excellent background for the teacher who has had little formal study of social anthropology.

R See James L. Gibbs, "Social Organization," in *Horizons of Anthropology,* 2nd ed., edited by Sol Tax and Leslie Freeman (Chicago: Aldine Publishing, 1977). This book contains readings that set forth anthropological ideas as they were developing between 1964-1976.

Behavior Patterns in Societies.   While studying a group or society, social anthropologists look for behavior patterns that typify it—patterns that express individual acceptance of the rules of living as they relate to status, role, and role expectations. These rules are often unwritten. The individual learns to act and react according to the accepted patterns by growing up within the culture and by gradually assimilating the orientation to life and the world that is characteristic of the group.

Behavior patterns that characterize groups relate to kinship, to rites of passage, and to regard for the supernatural. Groups have typical ways of behaving in conversational situations, in job-related situations, and in education-related situations. The study of ways of behaving reveals stylistic forms of expression. There are the nonverbal mannerisms, postures, gestures, and facial expressions that have come to be called *body language*. There are paralinguistic intonations, speech rhythms, and pause patterns that have a basis in cultural conventions. There are also the subtle shadings of meaning associated with particular word choices and sentence order. All can be described in the study of the behavior patterns of different social groups.

To an outsider viewing a group, characteristic behavior patterns may appear strange or even irrational. This appearance comes about because the outsider does not know, accept, or feel comfortable with the rules that govern human activity in the group. The outsider judges the new group through the filter of his or her own rules —rules that may differ considerably from those of the new group.

As George Foster points out, the patterns of those living in relatively unindustrialized societies may appear irrational to those for whom technology and industrialization have been part of everyday living for many years. In a rapidly changing world, peasant societies have technology thrust upon them. Their traditional statuses, roles, role expectations, and behavior patterns are no longer totally appropriate. New ones emerge that may make little sense to an outsider but are most reasonable to those functioning within the group experiencing rapid change.

Just as people living in less technologically developed areas must alter their traditional behavior patterns in response to forces impinging upon their lives, so too must students of the social studies learn ways to adapt to the new realities resulting from increased contacts with other people. They must be open to changes in their own living patterns, for if society is to function smoothly, rules of behavior must change as conditions change. They must be open also to differences in the way others behave, learning to look at other people not in terms of their own behavior patterns but in terms of the rules underlying the society in which the others live.

Rules and the Law. Rules—implicit or stated—govern most social relations. Chess, basketball, bridge, and even hopscotch have clearly stated rules. Etiquette books set forth ways of behaving at the dinner table, at formal functions, and on being introduced to a business associate. Less explicit rules govern informal interaction among friends and strangers.

Klaus-Friedrich Koch classifies social controls existing within a group into three categories: 1) the definition of rights and duties—who should do what, when; 2) the management of disputes—how disputes among members of the group shall be handled; 3) the allocation of

R Helpful here are two popular books: Julius Fast, *Body Language* (New York: Evans, 1970) and Edward Hall, *The Silent Language* (Garden City, N.Y.: Doubleday, 1959).

R See George M. Foster, "Peasant Society and the Image of Limited Good," in Jennings and Hoebel, 1972. The article was originally printed in *American Anthropologist*, 67:293-310 (1965).

R See Klaus-Friedrich Koch, "The Anthropology of Law and Order," in Tax and Freeman, *Horizons of Anthropology*, 1977.

responsibilities for actions that injure others or take away the rights of others—how unacceptable acts shall be punished.

These ways of controlling behavior within the group can be codified in the form of legal statutes. Some societal controls are more diffuse, being handed down from one generation to the next by the process of imitation. Newcomers within a group see others behaving in certain ways and gradually assimilate these ways into their own behavior.

An interesting distinction exists between laws and the concept of law. A society may be law-abiding but have no formal written laws. Social pressures and sanctions applied by members of the group encourage people to conform to the norms of social behavior accepted by the majority of the group. In this context respect for the law refers to following social norms and values acquired as part of one's upbringing.

A Problem to Ponder

R See Lucy Mair, *An Introduction to Social Anthropology.*

In making the distinction between laws and the rule of law, Lucy Mair explains that the rule of law means "the whole process by which rules that are recognized to be binding are maintained and enforced, including the motives and values that influence judges, and all the manifold social forces that prevent the majority of people from having to come before a judge at all." There is clearly a rule of law within classrooms. List some of the ways that classroom rules are maintained and enforced, being careful not to overlook the sanctions exerted by one student upon another.

Social Forces and Religion. Anthropologists studying religious practices find that some of these activities yield unexpected results. Some religious practices help individuals feel comfortable with social norms. As people perform common rituals, friction may be lessened and cohesiveness brought to the society. In addition, rites of passage such as those related to birth, maturity, marriage, and death are incorporated into religious practices. Rituals develop to celebrate these major transition points of life within the society—rituals that structure how people behave toward one another.

R See Edward Norbeck, "The Study of Religion," in Tax and Freeman, *Horizons of Anthropology*, 1977.

When religion is viewed as part of the whole culture rather than a separate entity, its influence can be noted in almost every area of human activity—in art, music and dance, in approved play and sports, in therapy, and even in the use of drugs. According to Edward Norbeck, religion has been and continues to be an important vehicle for expressing and controlling human emotions, predispositions, and drives.

Culture and Language. Many anthropologists equate humanness with the use of symbols. Human beings are the only creatures of this earth to create and use symbols. The term **symbol** in anthropology has a very broad meaning. A red traffic light is a symbol. It stands for "stop." A flag is a symbol. It may represent a class of persons, a state, even an individual. It can signal commands and directions. These symbols are concrete; they take the form of material objects. Actions also can carry symbolic meaning. Taking one's hat off or putting it on may be signs of respect, depending on the circumstances in which the action is performed.

Children learn quickly that meaning can be assigned to objects and motions. They learn, too, that meanings assigned can be changed at will. In play a stick becomes an arrow. A moment later it is a magic wand. In Leslie White's words, "This creative faculty, that of freely, actively, and arbitrarily bestowing value upon things, is one of the most commonplace as well as the most important characteristics of man."

Systems of symbols are an inherent part of all forms of cultural expression—art and architecture, music and dance, rituals and living routines, and especially speech. Speech and writing are crucial in explaining the progress of humankind. The words, the sentence patterns, and the meanings associated with both words and sentences make communication of ideas possible. They make possible the higher-level thinking that only human beings carry on and the preservation of ideas, from generation to generation.

Horacio Fabrega, a neurolinguist, summarized the importance of language within culture: "Culture and language together influence the way a person comes to recognize and like music, the way he or she shows emotion, and, to some extent, the way he or she orients spatially." In short, the system of symbols one uses is part of one's personality and has an impact on one's social behavior. Some bilingual people who live and work in two cultural environments develop two identities—each identity functioning in the appropriate environment and performing the social behaviors accepted within that group.

Psychology and Sociology

Dividing points among psychology, sociology, and anthropology are indistinct. Terms like *identity*, *personality*, and *social behavior* are found in the lexicons of all these social sciences. In like manner there is cross-fertilization among the disciplines. For example, as Christie Kiefer points out, anthropology has taken on a more psychological orientation in recent years. Both psychologists and anthropologists of today view humankind as much more elastic and flexible in behavior patterns than was believed a few years ago. Kiefer explains that

T Symbols: what does each mean?

R See Leslie A. White, "The Symbol: The Origin and Basis of Human Behavior," in Jennings and Hoebel (1972). Originally published in *Etc.: A Review of General Semantics*, 1:229-237 (1944).

R See Horacio Fabrega, "Culture, Behavior, and the Nervous System" in *Annual Review of Anthropology*, Vol. 6 (Palo Alto, Calif.: Annual Reviews, 1977). This annual review of anthropology is published each year.

R See Christie Kiefer, "Psychological Anthropology," also in the *Annual Review of Anthropology*, Vol. 6 (1977).

people can adjust to greatly changing conditions, can redefine symbols to meet changing needs, and can continue to be resocialized throughout life. This ability to change is of great importance in a world in which changing conditions appear to be an everyday feature of living.

On the other hand, the social disciplines do differ in the foci of their study. Whereas anthropologists tend to start with the culture as the basis of their research and psychologists with the individual, sociologists focus on the social nature of human beings—the way people function in groups. They look at people's membership in groups, the causes of social conditions, and the structure and organization of groups. Sociologists look to see how each member affects the group and how the group in turn affects each member. They explore the activities of a group to learn how that group functions and is changing and what the results of these activities are.

What sociologists find out about the way groups function has a bearing on current social problems. Knowledge of social phenomena—when put to practical use—can reduce conflict. If people know who is doing what to whom and why, they have an information base upon which to make value judgments about the rightness and wrongness of acts; they have information upon which to make decisions about directions for future change.

Understandings gleaned by those who pursue the study of **psychology** have a similar potential to assist people in making decisions and value judgments. As Arthur Jersild points out, these understandings are of two related kinds. One approach to psychology centers on "norms of development, the architecture of growth, description of behavior, and measurement of traits and abilities, emphasizing what is overt and objective." A second deals with the "subjective aspect, the 'inner life' and the dimensions of the self, inquiring into the nature of . . . personal experience." In practice the two approaches tend to overlap and blend. Not only should the student of psychology look at both overt and inner aspects of the self as they interrelate, but—according to Jersild—the student gains most if, in the process of seeking to understand others, he or she seeks also to understand him- or herself. "Each person has within the self a laboratory in which he or she can, to some degree, test the meaning and implication of what has been found in the study of others."

R Arthur Jersild has written several books that focus on child and adolescent development and the implications for teachers. This quotation is from Arthur Jersild, "Foreword to the First Edition," *Psychology of Adolescence* (New York: Macmillan, 1957). See the updated edition (1974).

The People-Oriented Sciences – Their Methodology

Anthropologists, sociologists, and psychologists are involved in the business of finding out more about people. Their perspectives differ at times based on their own backgrounds and trainings and on the purpose of their investigations. Yet they share certain basic methodologi-

(handwritten margin notes: 1. objective 2. try to keep personal beliefs, biases, values from investigation 3. direct observation 4. reasons/explanations)

cal features. All social investigators strive to be objective. Humanistic concerns and the sometimes controversial aspects of study can make objectivity difficult. Nonetheless, the social scientists, like the natural scientists, must try to keep their personal beliefs, biases, and values from coloring the results of their investigations.

All social scientists use direct observation as a major means of discovery. They gather data, compile information, and describe what they see. They are searchers, observers, listeners, touchers, and recorders. But social scientists are also analysts. They look for reasons and explanations, they identify relationships, and they try to generalize based on specific data they have uncovered. The method of direct observation and objective analysis is common to all the people-oriented disciplines. It is this method that produces explanations of how human beings relate to each other and their environment.

A Problem to Ponder

Ecologists study the relationships of organisms to each other and to their environment. In what ways are anthropologists, sociologists, and psychologists actually functioning as human ecologists?

The People-Oriented Sciences in the Elementary Social Studies Curriculum

The elementary school teacher or the prospective teacher reading about the areas of investigation of interest to anthropologists, sociologists, and psychologists may already have identified ways in which these areas can be incorporated into the social studies program. Without doubt, the social scientists' emphasis on observation and analysis can be reflected in a similar emphasis in teaching. In addition, some of the major concepts stressed in social inquiry can serve as integrating threads as children look at human activity in an attempt to learn more about what makes society tick. Let us look next at specific ways this integration can be achieved, remembering as we do that in elementary schools, children do not encounter each of the social sciences as a discrete discipline, but rather they draw upon each as they attempt to find out more about the world of people.

First Thoughts: A Test

Before you read on, take this test. Next to each country or culture group, write down the two or three things, people, events, or traits you associate with it.

Holland   _____   _____   _____

Japan   _____   _____   _____

Mexico   _____   _____   _____

Egypt   _____   _____   _____

Native Americans   _____   _____   _____

Eskimos   _____   _____   _____

Investigating Cultures and Societies

Most social studies programs bring young people into contact with cultures other than their own. The general purpose of this study is to widen the outlook that youngsters have—an outlook that makes them react negatively when they encounter culture traits different from their own. In recent years, the popularity of air travel has increased the likelihood of direct encounters with diverse cultures. Numerous young Canadians and Americans are traveling all over the world and especially in Europe. Such direct contact with other cultures is a positive feature of a world made smaller. Only if people get to know—really know—people of different cultures will we be able to live harmoniously together today and tomorrow.

Schools must do their part to break down the negative perceptual barriers that separate people from one another. Children can be taught to look at other culture groups in terms of the historical, economic, and social forces that produced them. To do this, study of people of the world must not be restricted to physical geography, products, trade, and traditional folk costumes. In some classrooms in the past, too great an emphasis has been placed on narrow and stereotyped views so that children leave with a view of the Netherlands as a land of wooden shoes, tulips, dikes, and windmills; of Mexico as a land of hat dances, tacos, and serapes; of Egypt as a land of pyramids, sphinxes, and Cleopatras. Care must be taken not to equate what was with what is today. Although at one time the kimono was the typical form of dress for Japanese women, the dogsled was a major form of transportation in Alaska, and many Native Americans lived in tepees, those days are long gone. Yet in some instances, such phenomena are taught as if they continue to be the reigning way of life.

Superficialities, stereotypes, and inaccuracies need not and should not result from study of other cultures. Information about life around the world is widely available. Periodicals such as *National Geographic* and *Smithsonian* frequently include illustrated essays on people in other lands that provide background for the teacher. Some new textbooks are beautifully illustrated with up-to-date, realistic pictures, which are a pleasure for even an adult to read. Many countries have established tourist bureaus in Canada and the United States that provide complimentary brochures. Local travel agencies also supply travel brochures. Of course, the teacher must take care in using public relations materials distributed by commercial groups. Some stress the exotic in an effort to entice the tourist to visit. Although some attention to unique and interesting aspects of life in other lands adds "spice" to social studies, there needs to be much more "meat" than "spice."

Investigating What One Knows Best: One's Own Culture

One often gains a better understanding of other cultures by seeking to understand one's own. For this reason, first encounters with concepts related to culture and society are generally encounters with one's own culture. These occur as part of broad units on family, community and neighborhood, and human needs found in the primary curriculum or in specific units on culture.

Identifying Specific Examples: Artifacts of Today.   A rather simple introduction to culture and its characteristics is through artifacts. As the reader remembers, **artifacts** are material objects people use as part of their culture. The fact that an artifact is an object—concrete, observable, touchable—makes conceptualization a relatively easy task, even for primary students.

Young children begin by talking about things they use in everyday living. Items named can be recorded by the teacher on a chart labeled "Things We Use." Talk time leads into a general activity time in which youngsters search magazines for pictures of things people use. They clip the samples and paste them on a large piece of colored paper, also labeled "Things We Use." If children cannot record for themselves, the teacher can supply labels for children to color, cut out, and paste on.

Generalizing About a Culture Based on Artifacts.   Older youngsters can use artifacts to describe a culture, again focusing their attention at first on the culture they know best, their own. One form this study can take is a Calendar Quest. Working with a calendar that has

T Now evaluate your answers to the test on page 360. Did your answers involve any superficialities, stereotypes, or outdated ideas?

T The definition of *artifact* is after one given in the glossary of *People and Culture*, one book in the Bowmar/Noble Basal Social Studies Series (Los Angeles: 1974). Most good text series include glossaries at the end of each volume, especially at the intermediate level where children should acquire skill in using a glossary.

colorful pictures showing activities that are typical of the way people in America live today, students mentally toy with this problem:

You are an archeologist in the year 3000. By some miracle, the paper and colors on this calendar have survived for more than a thousand years. What can we say about the way people lived in the 1980s based on the data contained within this artifact? What things did they like to do? What things did they value?

If the calendar has been wisely chosen, participants in the simulation will probably be able to describe the custom of eating a big turkey dinner during November, of skating in February, and of decorating a tree in December. They can hypothesize the probable purposes of these human activities.

Similar studies of the things held important by Americans living in the 1980s can be carried out by looking at advertisements, catalogs, and artifacts collected by the teacher. In the last instance, the teacher collects "1980s items found during an archeological dig of hometown America in the year 3000 A.D.": a ball-point pen, a Big Mac container, a transistor radio, a fluorescent light bulb, and so forth. As a class or in small groups, students write a description of the way of life and the values of these people.

Related follow-up activities for individuals or small groups include:

1. Making a mock-up of an archeological dig conducted in the local region one thousand years from now—Students clip pictures of ten items from magazines and newspapers (or make collections of real things); they must give reasons why they feel the items selected reflect the culture of the 1980s.

2. Putting together a time capsule by choosing 20 artifacts of reasonable size to give future civilizations an accurate view of life in the 1980s—This is a good group activity in upper grades; each group must decide what to include in their capsule and must defend their choices before the entire class.

3. Writing and illustrating a glossary of artifacts of today that would help people of tomorrow understand today's way of life.

To help children consider all aspects of their culture, the teacher may have to prompt: "Is there something we should include to show people of the future how most of us spend a great deal of time? to show how we generally travel? to show the kinds of things we eat?"

Particularly important are questions that nudge young students to consider a wide cross section of culture traits and thus to communicate a complete picture of the way people live and the things they value. One text series for upper elementary grades lists six areas that an investigation of a culture should include:

1. the ways we act together, including social institutions related to family, government, education
2. the things we make and use
3. the ways we earn a living
4. the religions we believe in
5. the languages we speak
6. the ways we see beauty

These are facets around which almost any study of a people or ethnic group can be organized. Once students are aware of these basic concerns, they have guidelines for studying people in other lands.

Looking Beyond: Cultures Around the World

What do you know about the way of life today in other countries? When television commentators talk of the yen, of apartheid, or of batik, what associations come to your mind? When commentators talk of Kuwait, Bangladesh, or Tunisia, what pictures of people do you mentally see? People all over the world have similar needs, wants, and hopes, but the world is filled with differences as well—differences that children should know and consider with an open mind.

Generalizing from Artifacts of Other Cultures. Study of their artifacts is one way to learn more about the way of life of people who live in other places and times. Looking at, handling, and thinking about objects that other people use or used on a daily basis can give young social scientists a feel for that culture. Actual art objects such as a Japanese or Chinese scroll are ideal if a resourceful teacher can locate them. Characteristic tools, calendars, street maps, picture books, magazines, newspapers, musical instruments, art prints, dolls, coins, postage stamps, greeting cards, toys, ceramics, and tiles are all artifacts that tell much about the activity of the people using them.

Experiencing a Culture Through Dance, Music, and Literature. Nonmaterial components of a culture are equally valuable. The dances, music, and songs of people show the observer ways in which women and men express feelings, the kinds of things about which they feel strongly, and the forms of beauty they appreciate. Learning and participating in folk dances are integral parts of a study of cultural groups. Of course, in some cases dances represent activity of an age gone by. As was suggested in chapter 1, there is a tie-in between the social sciences and the humanities. By experiencing the art and music of people, the social scientist can learn much about what people value and appreciate. The same is true of young social scientists who seek to learn more through classroom studies.

T From *People and Culture*, Teacher's Edition (Los Angeles: Bowmar/Noble, 1974), chapter 1. This text suggests that words can be used to learn more about a culture's needs and values. For example, the Eskimos have fourteen words for snow: soft snow is *mauyak*; snow on clothes and boots is *ayak*; falling snow is *opingaut*.

T Here material similar to "Pearl Primus' Africa" (available through Miller-Brody Productions, 342 Madison Ave., New York, New York 10017) is helpful. Primus is an artist-anthropologist, and in this record set she creatively shares the legends, folktales, proverbs, songs, and music of Africa.

In the same vein, the literary heritage of a group has much to offer. Most useful are the stories, poems, and firsthand accounts written in the country itself. The study of Germany would be incomplete without some reading of the Brothers Grimm. The study of ancient Greece would be equally incomplete without some attention to Aesop's fables. The Nordic and Greek myths and the fairy tales of Hans Christian Andersen also come immediately to mind. But going beyond the obvious, the teacher will find that most library shelves hold a wealth of folklore—Russian, Chinese, Indonesian, and Indian, to name just a few.

Social studies text series are beginning to reflect the literary background of a culture. Some series use folktales, myths, and fables as primary source materials. For instance, *People in the Eastern Hemisphere*, an upper elementary book in the 1979 Silver Burdett Social Studies, introduces the chapter titled "The Jobs of Government" with a legend.

T From "Jobs of Government," *People in the Eastern Hemisphere*, Teacher's Edition (Morristown, New Jersey: Silver Burdett, 1979), p. 203.

The Chinese have a number of old stories about the earliest rulers of their country. Some of the stories tell of two *emperors*, Yao and Shun. Yao and Shun ruled long ago . . .

The stories say that Yao ruled the land fairly and well. The country was peaceful. No person attacked another or stole another's goods. When people had quarrels, they took them to Yao to settle. He was fair to all the people. A bell and a tablet hung outside Yao's door. Anyone needing the ruler's help could sound the bell at any time. Any person having a complaint could write it on the tablet. The emperor would be sure to read it. The stories say that the land enjoyed real peace in Yao's day. People did not even lock their doors at night . . .

Here an old legend is being used to help young people understand some of the jobs governments are expected to do.

Comparing Culture Traits at the Primary Level. As elementary students work with the artifacts, music, dance, and literature of people in other lands and areas of their own country, they begin to generalize about behavior patterns through which different societies meet their social and physical needs. This is a rather difficult pursuit for primary children, especially in kindergarten and first grade. To overcome the difficulty of studying people who seem very remote, many programs start by focusing on those aspects that are most meaningful to children. Rather than asking questions about the way people in a culture farm the land or worship, youngsters ask questions about how the children in the culture function as part of their families. Children in most cases have firsthand experiences with families; they are members of one and observers of others.

Through picture study, children can learn how other
groups meet basic needs (Native Americans
in Monument Valley, Utah).

Similarly, children ask questions about the play activity of children
in other lands, the holidays and the traditions that apply particularly to
children, such as Boys' Day and Girls' Day in Japan. Because most
young children have a fondness for animals, study may begin with the
kinds of animals that are pets or helpers within other cultures. In social
studies books for young children, pictures of children and animals
abound.

The activities developed in primary grades to help children learn
about diverse culture traits must also take into account the interests
of children at this point. For instance, primary children looking at
the way of life of the Japanese people find kite making and flying
much more meaningful than a discussion of the differences between
Buddhism and Shintoism.

Comparing Culture Traits in Upper Elementary Grades. As
upper graders pursue cultural studies, they go beyond observation of
artifacts and beyond simple comparisons and contrasts to identify relationships. Considering culture traits, they go beyond first impressions.

T Reproductions of artifacts from early civilizations can be obtained from Hubbard Scientific, P. O. Box 104, Northbrook, Illinois 60062. Because these are expensive, sets might be shared among schools in a district.

1. They describe specific traits, asking about each: What is it? When is it used? Where is it used? How is it used? Where does it occur? When? Under what conditions? Who is involved?
2. They determine the purpose served by a behavior pattern or artifact.
3. They track down the origin of items identified as important in a culture. Are they local? from within the country? from a nearby country? from a distant country?
4. They hypothesize possible costs.
5. They determine how long this trait has been a part of the culture; is it a recent addition or an integral part for hundreds of years?

Many culture traits are open to this kind of systematic study: common items of food, items of clothing, items related to transportation or communication, popular forms of recreation, religious practices, language, educational materials, kinds of housing, and objects or tools used for a variety of purposes.

1. A Charting Activity.   In this context, a charting-visualizing activity is useful. Young investigators in groups can focus on a particular culture and complete a culture chart. One group adds items related to the dietary staples of the people studied; another group adds items related to the sources of these staples; a third group contributes information about the costs of the foodstuffs.

From this type of chart, young investigators can project relatively sophisticated generalizations, especially if guided by teacher questions. Students might hypothesize, "Items used commonly for food in an area are those found locally or within the country, which are, therefore, relatively inexpensive." Such a generalization could emerge from the study of countries like Norway and Japan. Both have long extended coastlines. Neither has the land or feed resources for large-scale cattle or hog production. In both countries, fish is a staple within the diet. The relationships among common usage, plentiful supply, and cost are clarified as young thinkers perceive specific linkages uncovered within a society and even express these linkages in the form of visuals. (See Figure 11.2.)

T Check the titles in the National Council for Geographic Education/Great Plains National Film Library for films that might apply to culture units you are teaching. Some titles include: Scandinavia, South Africa, Amazon Basin, Australia, Poland, Indonesia, China, Mexico. Slide sets are available through Great Plains National Instructional Television Library, Box 80669, Lincoln, Nebraska 68501.

2. A Viewing Activity.   Information essential for making sound generalizations linking historical, geographic, economic, and social factors can be gathered from films and filmstrips. When filmed material is being used as an information source, several viewings are recommended. Children listen and watch to get an overview. Then they view again, with different groups looking for specific kinds of information. One group views to identify housing traditions, another to identify traditional agricultural practices and so forth. Having identified key

Figure 11.2
Conceptual Chains

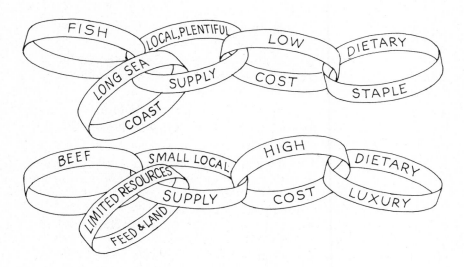

culture traits within their assigned category, viewers team up to compose description cards, purpose cards, or origins cards to add to a growing chart—a chart that can eventually include carefully drawn sketches. Pursuing this task, children should be urged to adhere to a major rule of scholarly integrity: if you can find no information, say so; don't fabricate findings!

Idea Page

Background for the teacher. This Idea Page demonstrates how to integrate some of the investigative approaches of anthropology into elementary social studies. It can be used as an independent study or as a class activity.

The aim. Generalizing based on specific cultural data (inductive thinking)

The introduction. Social scientists have found that the study of a culture's tools supplies information about the way of life of the people. It is possible to find pictures of the tools used by many different groups; for example:

Viking or Eskimo tools used for fishing, hunting, boat building, or food preparation

Tools used by Native Americans for agriculture, hunting, and clothing, jewelry, or pottery making

Tools of crafters in colonial times—blacksmiths, silversmiths, candle makers, leather workers, weavers, surveyors, and coopers (barrel makers)

The pursuit. Studying pictures and reproductions of tools, young researchers can ask some of the same questions that social anthropologists ask.

1. Of what kinds of materials were tools of that day made—stone, bone, metal, plastic, wood, or other plant matter? Why was this material used?
2. For what purposes were these tools used?
3. How convenient was it to use a particular tool? How easy or difficult was it to get a job done with it?
4. How well was this tool crafted? Was it crudely made? finely crafted? sturdy? decorated? If decorated, what do the decorations suggest?
5. What do these tools tell us about the needs and activities of those who used them? Were those needs met by the tools then available? How do we meet these needs today?

The continuation. Upper graders can consider modern tools of carpenters, kitchen workers, mechanics, and secretarial and clerical workers, asking: How have newer technologies and mass production affected the tools we use today and the work people do? They can speculate on changes they think will occur in tool production and use in the next 100 years, and they can make replicas of old tools, using them to complete tasks for which the tools were designed.

The Importance of Cultural Studies: A Brief Summary

Both the United States and Canada are multiethnic nations. If all the different groups that comprise the populations of the United States and Canada were listed, that list would fill more than a page. In the past, these two North American countries have been described as melting pots in which cultures blended and mixed to the point where differences no longer existed. In more recent years, however, people have recognized the beauty in diverse cultural traditions and realized that these traditions should not be lost. This realization has led to a renewed emphasis on the diverse components of the culture. For example, each year in New York there are street festivals honoring the contribution of various ethnic groups to our culture. Booths line Ninth Avenue, and people jam the street to sample the foods that different groups have contributed to our way of life. Music of diverse groups fills the air as songs and dances are enjoyed by people of all backgrounds. Similarly, other cities are restoring historic sections originally settled by a group that contributed significantly to the area. Los Angeles is restoring its old Spanish section, which is fast becoming a tourist center as people trace the roots of their nation. This interest in finding out more about our multiethnic cultural heritage extends as well to individuals who are searching to uncover their own origins.

T As a culmination to unit study, students can stage their own cultural street festival or create replicas of original settlements in their areas that were developed by particular ethnic groups.

Investigating Groups and Social Situations

In the study of groups four terms recur.

Roles —the parts a person plays in group or social situations

Status —the relative importance that a person, group, or role has in society

Role Expectations—people's perceptions of how those occupying specific roles should behave

Sanctions —the means that groups use to bring members' behavior in line with role expectations.

The concepts embodied in these terms are important in the study of children's activity within groups of which they are members. They are helpful too when one analyzes basic institutions—governmental, religious, agricultural, industrial—and the jobs people perform within them. Additionally *roles*, *status*, *role expectations*, and *sanctions* have application to political studies; they can be used to analyze relationships among countries. In this respect, these ideas are among the most significant of the social sciences. They are all aspects of **socialization**, which is the process whereby people are inducted into the ways of society and are prepared to function in the group. In anthropology this same process is called **enculturation**.

Investigating Children's Roles in Society

Children can begin their study of groups by identifying the groups to which they, their friends, and their parents belong; by identifying the variety of roles they play in social interaction and the expectations connected with these roles; and by making simple value judgments about roles and expectations. At upper levels, as youngsters grow in cognitive abilities, they can continue analyzing the status of different roles, observing people's behavior in group situations, and determining the sanctions that exist within groups they know.

Identifying the Groups to Which One Belongs.   Most people belong to many groups or categories. First, they belong to groups of people with whom they interact on a frequent basis. In the case of children, these groups include their family; their class in school; club groups such as Scouts, 4-H, and Brownies; and a neighborhood group of close playmates. In addition, children belong to categories—groups of people who share some common feature. A child may belong to such categories as those who are female, seven-years-old, brown-eyed, left-handed, farm dwelling, or living in Texas.

As part of a study of themselves, young children can chart the groups to which they belong. Charting can take place as part of talk time, with children suggesting first the groups to which everyone in the room belongs: the group that goes to Central School, the group that is in Ms. Morrison's first grade, or the group that lives in Warren Township. These are listed by the teacher under the title Groups We All Belong To. Later children offer to tell other groups to which they belong. These too are listed by the teacher, this time under the title Groups Some of Us Belong To. This latter listing will have general items to which many students can relate. It will also have some specific items that indicate groups to which only a very few children belong.

From this class charting experience several related activities can flow.

1. Slotted writing—The teacher supplies a duplicated sheet with introductory sentences. Children select words and phrases from their class charts to complete the sentences as in Figure 11.3.
2. Expressive drawing—Children illustrate each sentence they have completed in their slotted writing activity. Pictures and sentences can be compiled in booklet form with a title determined by the children themselves.
3. Circle grids—Youngsters divide circles into wedges. On each wedge they record the name of one group to which they belong.
4. Values-clarification—Youngsters each must think about which of all their groups is the most important one to them. Talking

T Children can make expressive drawings and write paragraphs that set forth group affiliations encountered in story and textbooks.

Figure 11.3
An Example of Slotted Writing

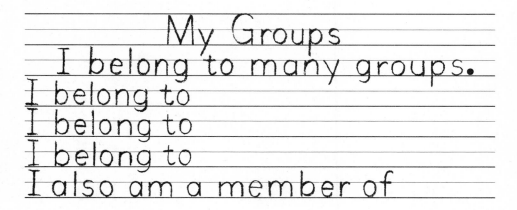

together, each tells why he or she picked a particular group.
Later youngsters can rank their groups in terms of their feelings
about each. The result can be a values staircase (Figure 11.4).

Identifying the Roles That One Plays.   As youngsters identify the
groups to which they belong they can consider the specific roles they
play within those groups: What are my roles within my family? (sister,
brother, daughter, son); What is my role within my school class? (student); What is my role within my neighborhood gang? (friend, play-
mate, leader, follower); What is my role in the Brownies? (member,
officer); What is my role on the Little League team? (shortstop, pitcher,
catcher). A similar question can be asked as children look at one institution within society—for example, the family. In this case, they ask:
What roles do people play in the family? The result can be a list of
family members. In both cases, children can express the roles listed in
the form of Relationship Chains (Figure 11.5).

Figure 11.4
A Values Staircase

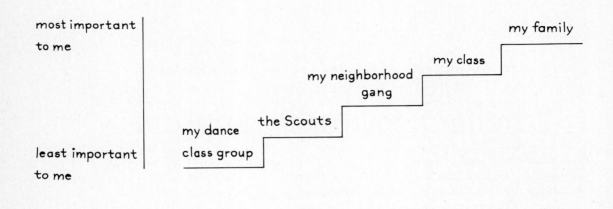

Figure 11.5
Relationship Chains

Brainstorming and Analyzing Role Expectations. Societies all over the world have tended to develop expectations about the traditional roles that people play within the group. These expectations often function as norms against which individual behavior is judged. One result of blanket application of traditional expectations is personal resentment and/or conflict. The latter is especially true when blanket expectations are applied to all those of the same sex, age, or ethnic group. As children explore their own roles in society and within the family, they need to become aware of the fallacy of applying role expectations indiscriminately to everyone occupying a particular niche.

Children at the primary level can explore role expectations in several ways.

1. Children can explore personal feelings. Did you ever not want to do something that was expected of you at home or at school? Did you ever not want to act the role of a good sister? Reacting to questions like these, children can describe times in their own lives when they felt resentful about the way they were expected to play their roles. Children can express their feelings by role-playing situations in which they are told to do something and do not follow through on the role expectations. They can express their feelings by drawing a sequence of pictures that describe a time when they did not do what was expected or they can write a brief composition.

2. Children can listen to stories about other children in family and school situations. Youngsters first listen to find out the roles that young story characters are playing. They then decide whether the characters fulfilled their roles well: Was Martin a good brother? What do we expect of people who are brothers? Did Martin do the things we expect brothers to do? In the story what made Martin want to be a good brother? When is it very right not to act the way people expect?

3. Children can identify expanded views of the roles family members play. The story and informational content children handle—even that found in social studies texts—very often present highly traditional and stereotyped role expectations. Take, for instance, the textual material shown in Figure 11.6. Here Hopi mothers and daughters are depicted carrying out cooking tasks in female groups; on other pages, Hopi fathers and sons are depicted performing hunting chores. No men are involved in the cooking and food preparation activities, for in the Hopi society these jobs were not part of their traditional role. Learning about the Hopi, primary children must learn accurately about the way these people handled certain family-work activity. We cannot

T At kindergarten and nursery levels, use such stories as Judith Viorst, *I'll Fix Anthony* (New York: Harper Row, 1969), and Patrick Mayers, *Just One More Block* (Chicago: Albert Whitman, 1970) to explore the way different people perform the role of brother.

**Figure 11.6
A Sample Page from a
First Level Text**

Hopis liked food made of corn.
Women and girls ground the corn.
They ground it into flour.
They made bread.

From *Living in Families*. Morristown, New Jersey: Silver Burdett, 1979. Drawing by Kyuzo Tsugami. Reproduced with permission of Silver Burdett Publishers.

change the past. The teacher, however, must take opportunities like this to expand children's perception of common societal roles. "Is cooking today always a female job? Tell me about some great meals your father, uncle, and grandfather have cooked for you? Why are fathers today doing more and more in terms of household tasks?"

Investigating Job-Oriented Roles in Society and the Statuses Given Them

Police officer, carpenter, mechanic, nurse, lawyer, principal, school crossing guard, and bus driver are all titles that identify work roles that adults play in society. They are positions with which children are familiar and that they study in the elementary grades. Because children have some knowledge of these roles, study of them provides the opportunity to broaden understanding of role expectations and status and to overcome sex, age, and racial stereotypes children may already have developed.

Identifying One's Own Limited Perceptions of Common Roles. As children learn more about community helpers, they should be expanding their expectations beyond traditional, stereotyped views. For example, as children describe their perceptions of the role of police officer, they may brainstorm such points as:

wears a blue uniform	is a really big man
chases robbers	is strong
gives parking tickets	has a moustache
arrests people	walks the street
has a badge	has a gun
drives a police car	is young and tall

As children brainstorm–given the state of the language in English-speaking countries–they will probably use the pronoun *he.* Here is a point when the teacher must have pictorial evidence available that contradicts the stereotyped view the children hold of police officers. Pictures should show both men and women officers, short and tall officers, younger and older officers, black, white, Asiatic, and Hispanic officers. The teacher asks, "Which of the items you listed tell about only some police officers? Which describe aspects of all those who fill the role of police officer?" Children go back to delete stereotyped items from their original list. The teacher must watch his or her own language usage; it is easy to fall into the habit of talking in terms of *he* rather than *he* and *she.* Children should come away from the study of work roles with the realization that most roles can be occupied by women or men, those who are short or tall, people who are older or younger, those of all racial or ethnic groups, those of all religious faiths, and those with some physical handicap.

Conceptualizing Based on Specific Examples: Putting Status into Clearer Perspective.

At an early age children become aware of the relative status of different roles. Status is an integral part of the folktales and legends of a society. Young children listen to stories of princes and commoners. Implied within such stories is the notion that it is somehow better to be a princess, the wife of a prince, than just one of the regular people, and children are quick to "get the point." Classroom work with status should go beyond understanding the fact that societies tend to ascribe different levels of importance to different roles. There are fundamental value questions inherent in the concept of status: Is it right for some people, groups, or jobs to be considered better than others? Is someone who occupies a job considered low in the status scheme actually inferior to someone who occupies a supposedly higher position? Why do people occupy the slots in society that they do? To what additional rights does a higher position entitle a person?

1. Listening for status-related problems. Because stories are one of the first contexts in which young children encounter problems related to status, story listening followed by discussion can be used to gain a clearer perspective. Take, for example, Gerald McDermott's retelling of the Japanese tale, *The Stonecutter* (New York: Viking Press, 1975). Children of all ages will listen intently as the teacher shares the story of the lowly stonecutter who works contentedly at his job until he sees a magnificent prince pass by. The prince is dressed in beautiful clothing and is accompanied by servants who obey his every command because he is so powerful. The stonecutter wishes he were a mighty prince. His wish is granted. He becomes the great prince only to find that there is something more powerful than him. Again he wishes. Again his wish is granted; he becomes the sun, even more powerful that the prince. The stonecutter progresses up the status ladder until he becomes what he considers to be the most powerful of all—a mountain. Then he hears the chip, chip, chip of another lowly stonecutter, cutting away at him! In the McDermott tale several words suggest status levels: *lowly*, *mighty*, *powerful*. Pictures suggest the trappings of power—differences in clothing and retinue. Words, pictures, and plot are all open to analysis by children who have listened to a dramatic reading: What is the order of power found in the story? How does the author tell us of the relative differences in status? Is it better to occupy a higher or lower position in this order? In real life what determines the position one occupies? In real life when might it be better to occupy a low position? a higher position? What should determine the position one occupies?

2. Dramatizing the nonverbal language clues that we tend to associate with low or high status.   Story listening can blend into impromptu dramatizations in which children take key character roles and act out the gestures and stances that they associate with different statuses. For example, given the story *Everyone Knows What a Dragon Looks Like* (New York: Four Winds Press, 1976), illustrated by Mercer Mayer, young people volunteer to play the emperor, the various learned men, the little boy, the old man, the old man in dragon form. The teacher prompts: "Which characters have high status or low status at the beginning? Because he is emperor, how would we expect the emperor to walk? to stand? to gesture? How do you think the boy would walk as he approached the emperor? How would he be dressed? How would the old man have walked at first? How would he have walked when he assumed the role of dragon?" In response, children practice nonverbal effects as well as lines–speaking in tones that show their relative social positions. This type of activity can be helpful for the child who has trouble reading and writing but is skilled in dramatization. Such a child may be able to use face, body, and voice to show graphically the metamorphosis from old man to powerful dragon. In the process, the child may develop a whole different concept of him or herself based on being the star rather than the nonachiever in the group.

3. Interviewing to find out about hierarchial systems that are an integral part of our culture.   Because progressive levels of responsibility and power are a component of culture today, young social scientists can collect data through interviewing those who are a part of hierarchial systems. Children can interview the following:

Local church leaders to learn of the hierarchial levels of responsibility that exist within church groups;

Parents who function or have functioned as part of a chain of command in the military;

The superintendent of schools or the president of a local university to find out the organizational structure of that particular institution;

Parents who work in relatively large industries in which there are floor supervisors, managers, executive boards, and so forth; and

Leaders in local government who can describe the levels of power in political organizations.

Through interviewing, students get down on paper a flowchart of who reports to whom, or who is in charge of whom. Students may also ask interviewees to tell the purpose served by especially tight hierarchial systems.

Idea Page

Background information for the teacher. The activities on this page help students understand that ideas from one social science discipline can be applied to problems within a related discipline.

The explanation. The terms *role, role expectations, status,* and *sanctions* are part of the vocabulary sociologists use when studying how people interact in groups. Nations interact with one another in ways that resemble somewhat the interactions among individuals. As a result, these key terms can be applied as we study the relationships that exist between and among nations.

The possibilities

1. Chart the categories to which a nation belongs (See Figure 11.7).

**Figure 11.7
Charting a Nation**

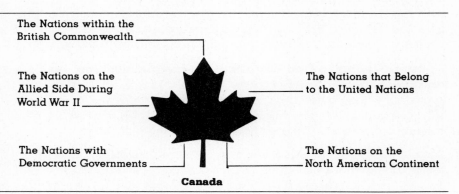

The Nations within the British Commonwealth

The Nations on the Allied Side During World War II

The Nations that Belong to the United Nations

The Nations with Democratic Governments

The Nations on the North American Continent

Canada

2. Consider the particular nation you chart. What do the group affiliations of this nation tell us about its values and way of life? Just as the company a person keeps tells us something about that person, so the company a nation keeps tells us about it.
3. Chart the roles a chosen nation plays in international affairs. Figure 11.8 shows the beginning of a chart that sets forth the roles played by the United States. Add other roles that come to mind.

Figure 11.8
The Roles of the United States

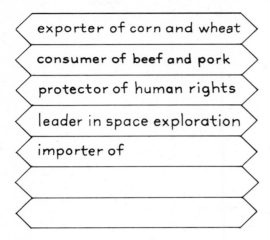

4. Put one star before those items on your chart that you consider to be favorable. Put two stars before those items that you consider to be unfavorable. Be ready to support your judgments.
5. Think about the comparative statuses of several countries in terms of some key qualities: wealth, integrity, or leadership. Place the countries chosen on a judgmental staircase (Figure 11.9) one case for each quality you choose to evaluate.

Figure 11.9
A Wealthy/Poor Staircase

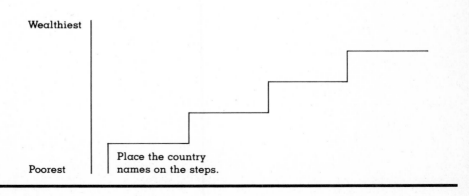

People in Society: A Summary Thought and a Look Forward

This chapter has attempted to demonstrate that important concepts from anthropology and sociology are best taught by integrating them into ongoing, larger units found within the social studies curriculum. This study includes literature, music, and dance – areas too often left only to the study of humanities. It relates to activities in which youngsters increase their ability to read, write, listen, speak, and illustrate.

In addition, major ideas from the people-oriented disciplines have application as youngsters investigate what has happened to their nation and world in the past and interpret political relationships within and among nations yesterday, today, and tomorrow.

Investigation to Enhance Understanding

R See Edward Norbeck, "The Study of Religion," in Tax and Freeman, *Horizons of Anthropology*, 1977.

Edward Norbeck describes the manner in which the anthropologist collects data. The anthropologist studies observable acts to identify the participants and the relationships among them. These acts bind the society through common use by members, smooth social interaction, and assure members of acceptance within the group.

The reader may wish to conduct an original social-anthropological investigation by focusing on the acts occurring within the social system that is the school. The reader should identify the following:

1. The roles being played by participants within the system
2. The relative status of those interacting within the system
3. The rules that govern behavior of people who learn and work in the system
4. The way these rules have come about and the way they have changed
5. The purposes served by the rules
6. The kinds of sanctions applied to enforce conformity to the rules
7. The rituals that are part of everyday living in the school

References

Barnouw, Victor. *An Introduction to Anthropology: Ethnology.* Homewood, Illinois: Dorsey Press, 1971.

Cuzzort, R. P. *Humanity and Modern Sociological Thought.* New York: Holt, Rinehart & Winston, 1969.

Jennings, Jesse; and Hoebel, E. Adamson. *Readings in Anthropology.* 3rd ed. New York: McGraw-Hill, 1972.

Keithahn, Edward. *Monuments in Cedar: The Authentic Story of the Totem Pole.* New York: Bonanza Books, Crown Publishers, 1963.

Mair, Lucy. *An Introduction to Social Anthropology.* Oxford, England: Clarendon Press, 1965.

Siegel, Bernard; Beals, Alan; and Tyler, Stephen. *Annual Review of Anthropology.* Vol. 6. Palo Alto, California: Annual Reviews, Inc., 1977.

Smyly, John and Carolyn. *The Totem Poles of Skedans.* Seattle: University of Washington Press, 1975.

Tax, Sol; and Freeman, Leslie. *Horizons of Anthropology.* 2nd ed. Chicago: Aldine Publishing, 1977.

12

People in Change: From the Past into the Future

Monique drew Abe Lincoln as part of a
biography she prepared.

Civilization is a movement and not a condition, a voyage and not a harbor.

Arnold Toynbee

Key Questions

What different approaches are used to organize the record of humankind's existence? What limitations are inherent in each of these approaches?

What basic concepts from history and political science should serve as unifying threads in the social studies taught within a democratic nation? What is the meaning of each?

How can we involve children in the study of family and community roots? What are the purposes of this study?

How can teachers use data retrieval charts as part of the study of the past? How can they use biographical writing? map activity?

In teaching national history how can teachers overcome the limitations inherent in a political approach to history? How can teachers help children hypothesize about human motivation, see people as part of a larger social arena, and develop comparisons and contrasts between past and present?

Why is it important to involve young people in decision making in retrospect?

A First-Person Account

We were absolutely, literally starved;–I do solemnly declare that I did not put a single morsel of victuals into my mouth for four days and as many nights, except a little black birch bark which I gnawed off a stick of wood, if that can be called victuals. I saw several of the men roast their old shoes and eat them, and I was afterwards informed by one of the officer's waiters, that some of the officers killed and ate a favourite little dog that belonged to one of them.–If this was not "suffering" I request to be informed what can pass under that name; if "suffering" like this did not "try men's souls," I do not know what could. (p. 124)

The army was now not only starved but naked; the greatest part were not only shirtless and barefoot, but destitute of all other clothing, especially blankets. I procured a small piece of raw cowhide and made myself a pair of moccasons, which kept my feet (while they lasted) from the frozen ground, although, as I well remember, the hard edges so galled my ancles, while on a march, that it was with much difficulty and pain that I could wear them afterwards; but the only alternative I had was to endure this inconvenience or to go barefoot, as hundreds of my companions had to, till they might be tracked by their blood upon rough frozen ground. But hunger, nakedness, and sore shins were not the only difficulties we had at that time to encounter;–we had hard duty to perform and little or no strength to perform it with. (p. 75)

> from *Narrative of the Adventures, Dangers and Sufferings of a Revolutionary Soldier* by Joseph Plumb Martin (Hallowell, Maine: Glazier, Masters and Co., 1830). Supplied through courtesy of Susan Kopczynski, Historian, Morristown National Historical Park, Morristown, New Jersey.

Introduction

The passage that opens this chapter was written down by a soldier of the American Revolution as he remembered his own adventures many years after. In June 1776 at the age of fifteen, Joseph Plumb Martin enlisted in the Continental Army for six months and subsequently was in the battles of Brooklyn, New York, Harlem, and White Plains. In December he was discharged from a regiment of Connecticut troops and spent the winter at home. In April 1777 Joseph Plumb Martin reenlisted in the Continental Army and served for the duration of the war.

That Joseph Plumb Martin endured hardships beyond our comprehension is clear from the short excerpt given here. That he did it of his own free will is equally hard for most of us to comprehend. Martin was not pressed into service as were many seamen of the Royal Navy. What motivated him to enlist when he was only fifteen? After having been in "the thick of the fighting," having been half starved, frozen, and exhausted, why did he reenlist and stick with it throughout the war? Why was young Joseph Martin willing to suffer?

We can hypothesize a number of reasons—some based on our current view of life and war. Perhaps Martin's friends enlisted, and he wanted to be with them. Perhaps he did not like his home conditions and enlisted to get away. He might have been seeking adventure and excitement. On the other hand, he might have listened to the fiery speeches of a Connecticut patriot. He might have believed that to live in a free country no longer attached to a nation across the ocean was worth all the hardships he would have to endure.

Actually all these reasons played a part, but as Martin himself wrote, he was "as warm a patriot as the best of them." Assessing the motivation of others with whom he served, he also stated: "These men . . . ventured their lives in battle and faced poverty, disease, and death for their country to gain and maintain . . . Independence and Liberty . . . ."

H **P** **S**
I **O** **C**
S **L** **I**
T **I** **E**
O **T** **N**
R **I** **C**
Y **C** **E**
A
L

T Orally share the selection by Martin with youngsters and ask this question: "Why was Martin willing to suffer?" See what kinds of hypotheses young people in grades four to six will suggest. An updated version of *Narrative* is available under the title *Private Yankee Doodle*, ed. by George Scheer (Boston: Little, Brown, 1962).

Putting the Past into Perspective: History and Political Science

Martin's *Narrative* is an authentic description and chronological record of the American Revolution from one person's perspective. It is also the moving autobiography of an ordinary soldier that takes the reader through dramatic meetings with personalities of the period, through everyday trials and tribulations, and onto the battlefront. Joseph Plumb Martin's *Narrative* is history.

Henry Steele Commager defined *history* as an "organized memory, and the organization is all important." Commager explains that the recording of history must supply order, harmony, and direction to what could be a hodgepodge of miscellaneous facts. All historical recording is incomplete, as was true in the case of Martin's *Narrative*; it is biased by the values, customs, and beliefs of the writer and the period and by the limited data upon which it is based. But in Commager's words, "How could it be otherwise?"

R See Henry Steele Commager, *The Nature and the Study of History* (Columbus, Ohio: Charles E. Merrill, 1965), pp. 2-5

The study of archaeology and history blends as
young people encounter past civilizations such
as this at Machu Picchu, Peru.

Ways of Putting the Past into Perspective

The young Revolutionary War soldier combined chronological narrative and biography in his recording of history. These are two traditional types of writing used to put the past into perspective. Other
histories focus on one period or era or on one geographic region of the
world. In some instances, study centers on events, people, or ideas of
one nation giving history a decided political orientation. Other histories are cultural. Their concern is with the way ordinary people lived
at different times and places in the past—people's art, literature, institutions, and social patterns, for example. Many great historians—from
Plutarch to Churchill—have taken yet another approach, making writing of history philosophical. Philosophers stress the underlying principles that influenced people's actions at a particular time or place.
Other writers reject history as philosophy, preferring to identify historical processes and to use history to solve the problems of past, present,
and future.

Each approach to history provides a framework for collecting, organizing, and analyzing data about the past—the purpose of history.
On the other hand, each manner of approaching history is not neces-

sarily distinct. A particular historian may actually employ several frameworks within a study. This is useful for each approach to the past has not only strengths but limitations as well.

**Figure 12.1
Steps in Historical
Research–Opening
Windows to the Past**

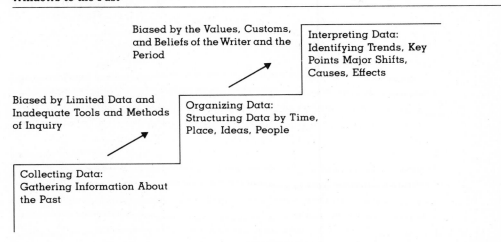

Time-Unit Approaches: Ages and Eras. The past is so long in terms of a person's short life span that it is convenient to organize the record of human activity into ages or periods. We speak of the Stone Age, the Golden Age of Greece, the Renaissance, the Elizabethan Period, Ancient History, and Modern History. This demarcation allows the historian to generalize within a shortened time frame and to compare and contrast happenings in one time unit to those in another.

On the other hand, the designation of time units and application of a label to each unit create artificial boundaries in the flow of history. When we think of the Elizabethan World (Elizabeth I: 1558-1603), we often forget that the Ming Dynasty in China (1368-1644) began about 200 years earlier, spanned Elizabeth's time, and continued another forty years. In the same way, when we talk of Modern History, we lump all those who lived before as pre-modern. Surely the ancient Greeks did not think of themselves as pre-modern.

As we apply time-unit labels, therefore, we must always be aware that in general these are based on a recent, often European-oriented perspective. The time labels with which we are most familiar–Golden Age, Enlightenment, Medieval, Renaissance–arise out of European history. Their relationship to Asian, African, and American societies is slight.

R The Ming Period is recognized for the rebuilding of Peking, the arrival of Portuguese traders in Canton, the revival of traditional culture, the export of porcelain, and the development of the novel. To find out more, check *History of China* (New York: American Heritage Publishing, 1969).

Geographic and Political Approaches. In the case of geographic approaches focusing on one area of the world, a major limitation is the narrow vision that can result. For example, speaking from the viewpoint of European-centered history, we generally say, "Columbus discovered America," or "Magellan discovered the Philippines." The implication here is that only the European world is important in history. From this narrow perspective, people such as the Native Americans or Filipinos have little importance. Many lands did not "exist" until they were discovered, claimed, and utilized by Europeans. Because much of our history has been written from the European perspective, it is difficult for us to translate "Columbus discoverd America" into "Columbus was the first Italian to set foot on American soil."

A second problem occurs when historians focus their attention on geographic regions that are essentially political units—what have come to be called **nations.** They study Spanish, Canadian, and Russian history, for example, tracing the development of these nations from some often arbitrary beginning point. Commager relates the difficulties inherent in a political orientation. First, it encourages a nationalistic, perhaps chauvinistic view of events; events are explained in terms of the effects on that particular nation-state. Second, it encourages a limited perspective that is inappropriate at a time when a world view may be necessary in the solution of economic and social problems. Then too, it exaggerates the significance of political concerns at the expense of other cultural aspects—religious, aesthetic, economic, social, and educational. One result is a stress on the great conflicts between nations and on the battles and treaties that determined the rise and fall of nations as well as the shifting of political boundaries.

R Based on H. S. Commager, *The Nature and the Study of History,* 1965, chapter 2, p. 20.

The social studies educator can also see the problems this approach may bring to the study of history at the elementary level, especially if the political or geographic unit under consideration is one's own nation. Stress may be placed on learning names of battles, treaties, wars, and capital cities. Little attention may be given to how people actually lived and felt. And perhaps most unfortunate of all, children may retain a narrow perspective; they may view events as they affect their own nation without looking beyond.

Cultural Approaches. Cultural historians focus their attention on the way of life of people. They ask: What were the major institutions—educational, political, economic, and social—through which people organized their activity? What forms did their literature, music, art, and architecture take? What ideas did they value? There are some who wonder whether this type of intellectual endeavor is really history. Is it more closely allied to cultural anthropology or sociology? Such disputes are irrelevant here, for what is important is whether the approach brings powerful relationships to light.

Speaking of cultural history, Henry Steele Commager makes an interesting point. He suggests that a cultural approach that spotlights people's everyday patterns of living has a democratizing effect. In Commager's words:

> No one can deny that history is . . . discriminatory and exclusive. It prefers to dwell with Monarchs rather than with their subjects, with Popes rather than rural vicars, with Generals rather than privates, with Statesmen rather than civil servants, with Captains of Industry and Titans of Finance rather than workingmen and clerks. It delights in the spectacular, the dramatic, and the sensational . . . .

R See Commager, 1965, p. 23.

To write and think about the lives of common people requires that one tap firsthand accounts and documents that previously went untouched. One must look at the diaries of people like Joseph Plumb Martin, at recruiting posters of the times, at tombstones, and at court documents that tell about births, deaths, marriages, litigations, punishments, taxes, and sales of slaves. Where they exist, one must peruse magazines and newspapers, calendars and catalogs, postcards and handbills. One must study the tools, the buildings, the manufacturing processes, and the transportation artifacts. And in cases where people still live who remember an event, one must gather oral history and record it on paper.

Yet even when history blends with cultural anthropology, limitations exist. Some time frames are necessary; one cannot study life patterns over too great a period. Likewise, one must usually focus study on a particular group of people. In this respect, failure to relate one group to others living at the same time becomes a possibility. The historian, after all, does not merely catalog past human activity. The historian must compare, contrast, generalize, synthesize, and even at some point judge.

R Based on Commager. "It is interpretation . . . which makes the highest demands upon the historian." See *The Nature and the Study of History*, 1965, p. 6.

A second problem arises if the student of history looks at a group as a homogenous whole, identifying only the characteristics of the people in general. The American culture has been and is still a pluralistic one. It is far from being the homogenous melting pot that some have suggested. In tracing the history of the American culture, to fail to look at component ethnic cultures–how they were distinctive, how they interacted, how they at times blended–is to get an erroneous picture of the past.

Idea Page

Background for the teacher. Reconstructions such as the one at Colonial Williamsburg provide firsthand data that students can use to hypothesize patterns of living. The following activity, for example, is based on the map of Colonial Williamsburg. The teacher supplies each youngster with a copy. Either independently or in groups, students hypothesize relationships.

The aims. Through the activity, the student will develop skill in proposing reasonable hypotheses based on pictorial evidence; the student will develop understandings about the way people lived.

The introduction to the student. A map of Colonial Williamsburg is pictured in Figure 12.2. Study it closely to see if the buildings and the design of the town tell you anything about the way of life of that time and the things the people living there considered important.

The pursuit. Answer these questions through map study.

1. In what ways did people in Colonial Williamsburg earn their living? If terms on the map are unclear to you, check them in a dictionary.
2. What was probably the main means of transportation? What evidence do you have to support your hypothesis?
3. What appears to have been one of the main ways used to light homes? What evidence do you have to support your hypothesis?
4. What do you think many of the buildings were constructed of? What evidence do you have to support your hypothesis?
5. What kind of clothing did the people wear? What is your evidence?
6. Was there a crime problem? What is your evidence?
7. Why do you think there were so many inns and taverns in a town this size?
8. The governor's palace and the capitol building are in Williamsburg. What role did this town play in the larger surrounding colony?
9. What form of recreation appears important to the people living there?
10. Were some of the people religious? What evidence do you have to support your hypothesis?

The continuation. Compose a paragraph based on your answers to the questions summarizing your hypotheses about the way people lived in Colonial Williamsburg.

Figure 12.2

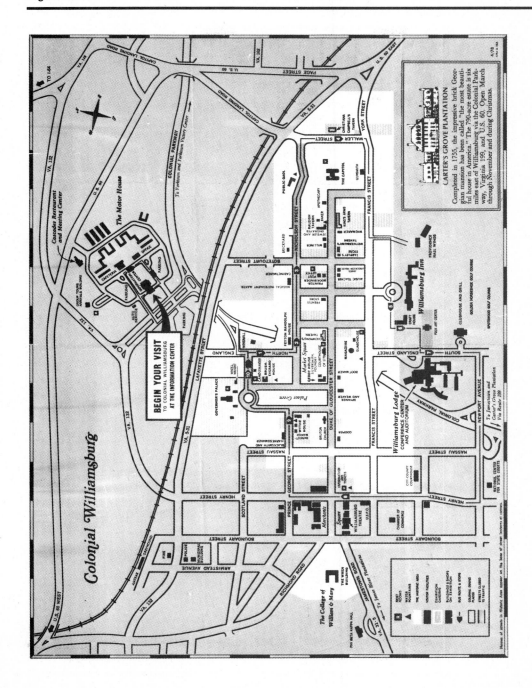

R Thomas Carlyle
wrote: "The history of
the world is but the
biography of great men
[and women]."–*Heroes
and Hero Worship*.

Personalized Approaches.   Looking at the past as do the cultural
anthropologists, we tend to think in terms of the norm – how people in
general behaved. In such an approach, the individual is easily lost.
This is not so in biography and autobiography. Here what the individual believed and thought is important. What he or she experienced
is recorded. Fortunately for those of us today who want to look at a
former time through the eyes of a person who was actually there,
many of our ancestors living between 1600 and 1900 were avid diarists.
Learned people of those times felt obliged to record on paper a day-
to-day account of their lives. Unfortunately, however, these recorders
were not generally ordinary people who worked long hours in a factory, crossed an ocean as a servant, or were enslaved. Joseph Plumb
Martin was the exception, not the rule.

Nevertheless, enough ordinary men and women did record their
impressions of their world to make possible an intimate view of the
past, not from the point of view of the Monarchs, the Popes, the Gener-
als, the Statemen, and the Captains of Industry but from the point of
view of the working people. They make it possible for us to identify as
heroes people very much like ourselves.

Nothing can substitute for a first person account. Yet historical fiction – with background information about the period accurately set
forth – can also enlighten. Stories of an early traveler's trip around
South America on the way to California during the gold rush, of the
hardships suffered by an immigrant, or of a Canadian fur trapper as
he explored the great Northwest give the reader a taste of earlier life.
Although the leading characters of historical fiction may never have
lived, others actually experienced the same hardships. Through fiction, history has become personalized.

Application to Social Studies Programs.   Faced with the limitations inherent in each approach to history, the social studies educator
clearly cannot select a single one. He or she must employ varied approaches – cultural history, political history, chronological history, or
personalized history – depending on the topic under consideration.
Through the use of varied approaches, history blends at times with
anthropology and sociology, with geography, with political science
and economics, and with psychology, literature, art, and music. In this
respect, it is a rare unit within the elementary social studies curriculum
that does not integrate history with other areas.

Major Concepts of History, Political Science, and Philosophy

To study history is to work with concepts that have a bearing on human
activity throughout all of humankind's past. Historical concepts useful
in thinking about people, ideas, events, and patterns of living in the

Original documents such as this photograph of a
picnic near Rush City, Minnesota, 1897, can
supply firsthand data that the students interpret.

past include chronological time, change, multiple causation, and multiple outcomes.

   In addition, certain concepts arise out of the political systems that
have existed in both the United States and Canada since their beginnings as nation-states. These include freedom, citizenship, and justice. Let us look briefly at the ideas embodied in these terms, since all
are important in the history of a democracy and, therefore, should be
significant threads in history-related programs in the schools.

Chronological Time.   The adult mind uses chronological time as a
way of mentally sorting out and organizing events of the past. One
tends to think: The United States purchased Louisiana *before* it purchased Alaska. Columbus probably reached the Americas *after* Lief
Erickson. At other times, one thinks more precisely: Champlain explored the St. Lawrence *in the early 1600s*, The Battle of Gettysburg
occurred in *1863*; that year marked a significant turning point in the
Civil War. In each case, having a reference point in time aids in understanding events of the past; relationships are clarified.

R See page 33 of chapter 2 for a list of major
social studies concepts
developed in *Social Sci-
ences Education
Framework for Califor-
nia Public Schools* (Sac-
ramento, California,
1975).

R See Kenneth Hilton,
"Some Practical Class-
room Remedies for
Parochialism of the Pre-
sent," *The Social
Studies*, 69:163-169
(July/August 1978) for an
excellent discussion of
ways to develop under-
standing of time rela-
tionships.

An adult uses dates and time words (before, after, early, middle, late) with an ease so deceptive that one can overlook the complexity of the relationships inherent in both. As was pointed out in chapter 5, however, children do not acquire a firm grasp of time relationships until very late in their elementary years. This poses a dilemma in the teaching of history to youngsters: How does one help students build an understanding of humankind's past when they have little ability to handle basic time relationships? Here are some possible starting points:

With very young children, encourage the use of themselves, their parents, and their grandparents as time markers and move back from there. Use terminology such as "This happened long before you were born."

Handle periods and people of the past without stress on dates. Talk in general terms: "This happened a few hundred years ago." "This is the way people used to live."

As youngsters begin to talk of specific time relationships, introduce time lines. In intermediate grades ask students to sort events in terms of before/after and early/middle/late.

Change, Multiple Causation, Multiple Outcomes: Strands That Bind the Past to the Future. A primary lesson that history teaches is the **inevitability of change.** Human history is the story of the birth, maturation, and death of individuals; the founding, movement, and demise of groups; the rise, spread, and fall of empires; the development, refinement, and obsolescence of tools; the birth, growth, and spread of ideas. Regardless of the approach employed – whether the historian focuses on a person, a cultural group, a nation, a region, or a period – one fact quickly becomes evident: It is the inevitability of change that binds the past to the present and the present to the future.

T Introduce the concept of change to young children with *Changes, Changes,* a picture book by Pat Hutchins (New York: Macmillan, 1971).

A study of the past is essentially a study of change. The historian looks at a particular time, place, or social unit and asks questions such as the following:

1. What new ideas emerged? Why did they emerge? What impact did those ideas have on people? In what ways did people react to the ideas? Did the ideas take hold? Did they die out? Why?
2. What changes occurred in the kinds of tools and devices the people used? the way people met basic needs? the way they used leisure time? the way they organized themselves in groups? the way they governed themselves and managed their economic affairs? the way they related with other groups and nations? What effect did these new ways have on everyday patterns of living? How did people handle these changes? Were they generally successful or unsuccessful in adapting to change?

3. What changes occurring in other parts of the world had an impact on this group? Were these changes more important than changes occurring at home?
4. What changes occurred in the way the people perceived themselves as individuals? as a group? as a nation? as a world member? What triggered these changes in self-perception?

As these questions suggest, consideration of **causes and effects** must accompany a study of change. Causes–often multiple in nature–trigger changes, which in turn may set in motion many interrelated events. Change, multiple causation, and multiple outcomes are among the most important concepts we have as we look at human activity. They are key concepts of history, which have application to problems in all areas of human endeavor.

Concepts Important in a Democratic State–Past and Future. School study of history should highlight major ideas implicit in a democratic system of government: freedom, justice, and citizenship. Unless students have some understanding of these political concepts, they will have little basis for interpreting the motivation and judging the actions of people living in the past.

Freedom: In a free state, the people have certain inalienable rights –the rights of free speech and a free press, free exercise of religion, peaceful assembly, petition, and freedom from unreasonable search and seizure.

Justice: Each person has the right to a trial by jury; no one can be held to answer for a crime unless on an indictment by a grand jury; laws shall apply equally to all persons; cruel and unusual punishment shall not be inflicted upon any person.

Citizenship: The right to vote shall not be withheld from any law-abiding citizen regardless of race, religion, or sex; the right to vote is a duty that each citizen should exercise; each citizen also has the responsibility to see that he or she does not trample on the rights of others, to keep knowledgeable on issues that affect the welfare of the people and the nation, and to participate actively by making opinions known.

The ideas embodied in these concepts provide a framework for studying the past history of a nation–particularly one's own: When has people's belief in freedom and justice caused them to chart a particular course of action? When has the government or individuals failed to uphold the principles of freedom, justice, and/or citizenship? Is people's belief in freedom, justice, and citizenship something they have applied to others as well as to themselves? What institutions and traditions have grown up to insure the maintenance of freedom,

R James P. Shaver has written: "Citizenship in a democratic society must involve confronting the basic ethical issues of the society and determining what action to take on those issues." See *Values of the American Heritage: Challenges, Case Studies, and Teaching Strategies,* Carl Ubbelohde and Jack Fraenkel, eds. (Arlington, Virginia: NCSS, 1976), p. vi.

R See the Bill of Rights of the United States Constitution for a complete statement of rights and responsibilities.

---

justice, and citizenship? In this context, study of the past takes on a philosophical orientation, as students talk about right and wrong, make value judgments, and discuss related issues of the present and future.

Some Definitions to Think About

R The selections by Becker and Carle are also found in Leonard M. Marsak, *The Nature of Historical Inquiry*. (New York: Holt, Rinehart & Winston, 1970).

The historical philosopher Carl Becker in "What Are Historical Facts?" *Western Political Quarterly*, 8:330-340 (September 1955) explains the purpose of study of the past:

> Its chief value, for the individual, is doubtless that it enables a person to orient him- or herself in a larger world than the merely personal . . . . This enables a person to judge the acts and thoughts of people, his own included, on the basis of an experience less immediate and restricted.

E. H. Carle in *What Is History?* (New York: Alfred A. Knopf, Inc., 1961) writes:

> The past is intelligible to us only in the light of the present; and we can fully understand the present only in the light of the past. To enable men and women to understand the society of the past and to increase their mastery over the society of the present is the dual function of history.

For what purposes do children study history in schools?

Tracing Our Own Roots in the Past

In a pluralistic culture as is found in North America, a search for personal roots in the past contributes to the society as a whole as well as to the individual. People in general are made more aware of the contributions of different groups to the exploration, settlement, and development of the continent. In addition, the individual may achieve a heightened sense of personal worth, seeing the self as part of a continuous chain of human beings – one that extends not only into the past but also into the future. Each begins to see that what he or she is and has is partly a result of what those who came before endured and conquered. And in like manner, those who come after will be dependent on what those who live today bequeath to them.

R See A. Montgomery Johnson, "Genealogy: An Approach to History," *The History Teacher* 11:193-200, (February 1978).

Investigating Family Roots

Because young children have a limited grasp of time relationships and because they find events of which they are a part most meaningful, the study of immediate family roots provides a base for looking back into the past. Since study of the family occurs in the first grade in many social studies programs, that unit can be the context for talking about children's immediate past.

A Family Tree.   As part of unit study, first graders can cooperatively diagram their family structure during talk time. Sharing descriptions of those in their families, children can generalize that different families are made up of different people. In some there may be only one child, in others, three, five, seven, or more. In some families grandmother lives with the family. In some, mother or father does not live at home. Talk can lead to a simple generalization – that all people have a mother and a father although the mother and/or a father may not be at home. Later, as an independent activity, each child draws a family tree, not necessarily his or her own, drawing a picture of father, mother, and child in the appropriate parts of the tree.

On another occasion, children can talk about grandparents; they can, through specific examples shared, conclude that both fathers and mothers have parents too. The result can be an expanded, illustrated family tree (Figures 12.3 and 12.4). For those children who do not know their parents or grandparents directly, family trees can be generalized ones. But in each case, the blank labeled ME should be a self-portrait or a photograph.

Family Roots.   As one of their first interviewing activities, youngsters can inquire at home about the countries from which their families came. Interviewing, of course, should be preceded by talk. Some children will know already that they are Irish-Americans, French-Canadians, or Native Americans, for example. Using this information, the teacher can guide children to generalize that many people living in their country and areas came from other countries around the world.

For ease in interviewing, especially since this may be the first time youngsters have gathered data in this way, together they work out a simple guide. They phrase a question cooperatively such as: From what countries did our family come? Each child prints it onto a card, which is taken home and completed with the assistance of parent or guardian. As cards are returned, the entire class takes time to add children's names to spots on the globe. In some cases, when a youngster has roots in many places, his or her family name will appear several times on the globe. This activity brings with it an added advan-

T Use "fan" or "blood-line" charts as another way of depicting family history. This is described in detail in Johnston's "Genealogy: An Approach to History."

T A study of family names fits here. Prefixes and suffixes carried by patronymic names are a clue to the national origin of a name: -ez as in *Lopez*, -vich as in *Ivanovich*, -sson as in *Ericksson*, O' as in *O'Malley*, Mc- as in *McInnes*, -s as in *Hennings*, -witz as in *Jandrowitz*, and Fitz- as in *Fitzpatrick* all mean *son of*. See Dorothy Hennings, *Words, Sounds, and Thoughts* (New York: Citation Press, 1977) for other ways to analyze family and given names.

Figure 12.3
An Extended Family Tree

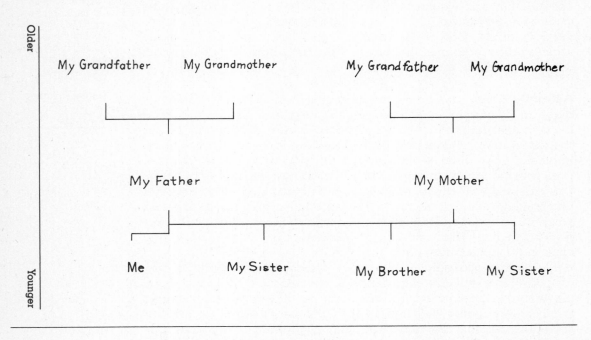

tage. Children, talking about other countries, become a bit more familiar with names of places around the world.

At upper elementary levels, young people can extend this activity, compiling all the information about family roots on a large, data retrieval chart. The chart can take the form shown in Figure 12.5, with students again getting information by interviewing family members. In intermediate grades, this activity will probably occur as part of a unit on immigration and migration. Family names, therefore, need not be restricted to class members. Young people can interview community workers, neighbors, and school personnel, gathering as many data as possible. In this context interviewing can be expanded beyond simple questions related to where, when, and how to get at both reasons and feelings. A good source here is older citizens, who may remember their own crossing of the ocean and entry into a different culture. A tape recorder can help the young investigator collect oral history without worrying about writing difficult words.

At upper levels, students should study the data to see if they can identify patterns: What groups of people settled our region? When did they generally come? What motives did they have? Did most have a difficult time when they came? Why did they endure poverty, preju-

Figure 12.4
A Family Tree Completed by a Student

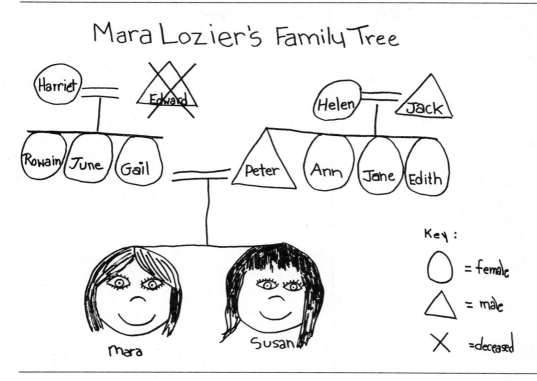

dice, and insecurity? Questions like these can lead young people to hypothesize possible relationships.

Family Biographies. In the intermediate grades biography becomes a means of extending understanding of the past. Young writers compose short family biographies that set forth their family's past. When information is limited, biographies can detail the location and date of the writer's birth and the birthplaces of parents and grandparents. In other instances, biographies may include details about how and why the parent or grandparent moved to the present location. Because ours is a highly mobile society, children themselves may have moved several times; this information can become part of the family history.

As they write biographies, young investigators should be reading biographical accounts of others. Here semi-fictional family histories such as Laurence Yep's *Dragonwings*, clarify the problems encoun-

Figure 12.5
Our Heritage: Many People Sharing One
Land – A Data Retrieval Chart

Our Heritage

Family Name	Where Our Family Came From	Why Our Ancestors Came Here	When Our Ancestors Came Here	How They Travelled Here

G Children will develop empathy with those who suffer the taunts of others and they may be less likely to assume the role of taunter. An excellent book that shows how quickly a taunter can become the recipient of taunts is Judy Blume's *Blubber* (Scarsdale, New York: Bradbury Press, 1974).

R Lawrence Yep, *Dragonwings* (New York: Harper & Row, 1975), pp. 118-119.

tered by immigrants as they arrived from across the sea. In the case of *Dragonwings*, that immigrant was Moon Shadow, a boy who came to the west coast of the United States from China to be with his father, Windrider. The book details the rich traditions of the Chinese people as they struggled to find a place in a world that was often hostile to them. It shows the discrimination that so many immigrants faced in a land founded on the principles of justice and equality. As Moon Shadow explained:

I passed by him, when he kicked me in the backs of my legs. I fell on my back, cracking my head against the ground, the breath driven out of me. Our garbage pail spilled out all over the alley. The boy leered down at me . . . . I saw a half dozen boys begin to shout.

> Ching Chong Chinaman,
> Sitting in a tree,
> Wanted to pick a berry
> But sat on a bee.

As a teacher reads a passage like this one to youngsters, the study of a family's history blends into study of a nation's history. Young people decide: Is it right or wrong to taunt others who are different? And they ask themselves: Why – if we believe in justice for all – do we do it? When have I been guilty of the same act of poor citizenship? Participants in the discussion can volunteer examples of times when they have acted just like the boys in *Dragonwings*.

Investigating Neighborhood and Community Roots

In many social studies programs, the community and neighborhood are the focus of study in the second grade. Emphasis is generally on basic physical and cultural activities in the community setting. In contrast, very little attention is given to community history; such study is feasible, however, even in the second grade, especially if there exists evidence that reminds residents what went before.

Human Roots. People living in and serving the community have diverse and often fascinating roots in the past. Children can explore these human roots as part of a study of the community. For example, children lay out a map of their town or local area, locating community buildings such as the fire and police stations, library, schools, and commercial buildings. Visiting each building as part of a Tour of Our Town, children ask a worker at each site from what country his or her family came. The worker's name and country of origin can be labeled on the appropriate site on the town map.

R A useful reference is George Mazuzan and Gerald Twomey, "Oral History in the Classroom," *The Social Studies,* 68:14-19 (January/February 1977).

Back in the classroom the map becomes a data bank. Children make a list of all the countries represented by the workers named on their map. They locate these countries on a globe or world map, indicating each location with a flag. A generalization to emerge is that people with many different family backgrounds are contributing to our community. Able students can stretch yarn from each point of origin to their town to see which worker's family has origins farthest away.

Visible Roots. Most communities have some visible evidences of past occupation. Deserted buildings are one kind of evidence – old schools, churches, barns, factories, and homes no longer in use. Buildings designed and used for one purpose but converted now to another purpose are also evidence. In addition, old country roads, abandoned railroad lines, tombstones, and buildings architecturally different from those currently being constructed, are signs of both previous occupation and change. Using firsthand data of these kinds, students in late primary (grades two and three) and intermediate levels can learn more about local history.

R See the article by Catherine Taylor, Mathew Downey, and Fay Metcalf, "Using Local Architecture as an Historical Resource: Some Teaching Strategies," *The History Teacher,* 11:175-192 (February 1978).

Here are some forms that teaching and learning can take:

1. A Memory Walk. Working from memory and their own knowledge of where things are located in their community, second graders can name buildings already plotted on a large map of their area. Orienting themselves on the map, individuals decide what map symbols represent the buildings they know and go on to describe the buildings in question: "The library is that old house made of gray stones. The town hall is that wooden, yellow building that has two stories next to the library." Thinking about the buildings they describe, children can decide which one is probably older, or which one has been there longest. They may also think of previous uses of these same buildings. For example, in many communities the library may once have been an old mansion, the town hall an old school building.

Almost every town or city has an area that stands out because the buildings there are architecturally different from others. Once children have plotted familiar landmarks on a large town map and described each, they can attempt some simple comparisons based on these architectural differences. In a city like Lubbock, Texas, comparisons are easy to make since one large area is comprised of very new buildings and the surrounding area is comprised of older homes. Children of Lubbock may know the reasons for this striking architectural contrast—a tornado in the 1970s that cut a wide path through the city. That destroyed section became the site of the modern area. In other cases, children will not know the reason for differences they have spotted. They must ask older residents to find out.

2. Do You Remember When? According to George Mazuzan and Gerald Twomey, the purpose of **oral history** is the creation of primary resources. When oral history enters the classroom, however, it brings with it another purpose; students gain a "sense of the past that often escapes them in their conventional study of . . . events." During an investigation of local history, students can find out by asking those who were there. For example, youngsters living in an apartment complex surrounded by older buildings may ask older residents of the area: "Do you remember when our apartment house wasn't here? Can you tell me what was here? What was here even before that?" Youngsters living in a suburban residential development may ask longtime residents living in older homes, "Do you remember what was here before our houses were built?"

3. Then and Now: A Map Comparison Activity. In upper grades, young people can make map comparison studies. An old road map or a town plan map is laid out next to an up-to-date version. How must our town have looked back then? Where is your house? Why isn't it on the old map? Is the up-to-date map really up-to-date? Does it show the new exit from Route 95? Why not?

Investigating Our North American Roots

At some point in most social studies programs children turn their attention to their own nation. They trace its roots from the time Europeans first explored the continent and proceed in chronological order through the present. This in-depth, year-long study typically occurs in the fifth or sixth grade when young people are better able to work with time relationships, are beginning to handle abstractions, and are beginning to look beyond their immediate sphere to find heroes with whom to identify. This study is generally more political than anthropological. Young people focus on big events in their nation's history – the founding of Plymouth and Jamestown, the writing of the Declaration of Independence and the Constitution, and the Revolutionary War in the United States; the exploration of the St. Lawrence, the founding of the Hudson's Bay Company, and the journeys of Mackenzie in Canada.

In earlier years, contact with American or Canadian history occurs on an incidental basis as children celebrate national holidays or study units on Native Americans, Eskimos, or Colonial America. Study at this level tends to be anthropological, with stress on the everyday patterns of living.

Any study of a nation's past – even by elementary children – must overcome the basic limitations inherent in political history. Study must go beyond a recounting of the facts from a narrow, nationalistic perspective. It must allow for analysis of human motivation, of related events occurring in other nations, and of the suffering one group of people has inflicted on another.

Going Beyond Facts: Hypothesizing About Human Motivation.
One way for us to study our nation's past and avoid some of the limitations of political history is to view those who lived before us as real people with feelings, concerns, doubts, and motives similar in many respects to ours today. We must develop in our minds a clear picture of individuals in the clothing of their times, walking down the streets, encountering the problems prevalent then. To get a full picture, we must know:

1. In what ways a person's life was similar to and different from ours.
2. What he or she did and said and why he or she acted that way.
3. What was going on all around that had a direct impact on him or her.
4. How he or she really felt.

Autobiographical accounts such as the one by Joseph Plumb Martin are invaluable sources for children to tap as they come into contact with their nation's past. More and more social studies texts are including this kind of material so that youngsters will have a more intimate

R Research shows that two thirds of seven-year-olds pick a personal acquaintance as their ideal, but only three percent of fifteen-year-olds mention acquaintances as ideals or heroes. See E. Macaulay, "Some Social, Age and Sex Differences Shown in Children's Choice of Ideals," *Forum of Education*, 3:105-114 (1925). This is an old but interesting study.

R An excellent reference is Edward Martin and Martin Sandler, "Rejuvenating the Teaching of United States History," *Social Education*, 35:708739 (November 1971). The article contains a thorough listing of resource materials.

view. For example, *Many Americans – One Nation*, the fifth grade book in the Bowmar/Noble social studies series, quotes this entry from the journal of the Lewis and Clark expedition:

T From *Many Americans – One Nation*, Teachers Edition (New York: Bowmar/Noble, 1974), p. 161.

November 7, 1804

Great joy in camp. We are in view of the ocean, this great Pacific Ocean which we have been so long anxious to see. And the roaring or noise made by the waves breaking on the rocky shores (as I suppose) may be heard distinctly.

Previous entries describe the suffering of the explorers as they fought cold, mountains, strong river currents, and wild animals. Faced with firsthand evidence, children can ask: "How did the explorers feel when they reached the Pacific? Why did they feel that way?"

Idea Page

Figure 12.6

MASSACRED

GEN. CUSTER AND 261 MEN THE VICTIMS.

NO OFFICER OR MAN OF 5 COMPANIES LEFT TO TELL THE TALE.

3 Days Desperate Fighting by Maj. Reno and the Remainder of the Seventh.

Full Details of the Battle.

LIST OF KILLED AND WOUNDED.

THE BISMARCK TRIBUNE'S SPECIAL CORRESPONDENT SLAIN.

Squaws Mutilate and Rob the Dead

Victims Captured Alive Tortured in a Most Fiendish Manner.

What Will Congress Do About It?

Shall This Be the Beginning of the End?

Background for the teacher. Written materials of a period often supply clues as to the feelings of the people living then. This activity shows how propaganda materials can be employed as the base for an interpretive lesson.

The aim. The student will begin to see how language has been and continues to be used to excite people's emotions.

The introduction to the student. Headlines from the Bismarck *Tribune Extra*, July 6, 1876, are shown in Figure 12.6. Underline all the words that could cause readers to build up hate against the Indians. These are called "snarl words."

The pursuit. Discuss these questions in your group:

1. Do you think the headlines exaggerated the situation? Why?

2. Why do you think the *Tribune* wrote the story in this way?

The continuation.

1. In the newspapers we have that were published yesterday, locate one story in which words were used in a way that could build up anger or hate.

2. Write a short series of headlines that you could use to build up hate against the Redcoats during the Revolutionary War that we have already studied.

Reproduced from U.S. Department of Interior, *Soldier and Brave*, Vol. XII, National Survey of Historic Sites and Buildings (Washington, D.C.: Superintendent of Documents, 1971), p. 34.

Study of the past offers opportunities to consider the feelings and motivations of people in this way. For example, similar kinds of question sequences can be developed in reference to the voyage of the Mayflower. Thinking in personal rather than event-centered terms, we can ask: "How must the Pilgrims have felt leaving their homeland behind? What was life like for them aboard the Mayflower? Why were they willing to make the hazardous trip? Why were they willing to suffer?"

Because hundreds of thousands of immigrants were to travel across oceans to make their homes in North America, and thousands more were to make the trip over land to California and Oregon, these questions can be asked over and over again. The sufferings and the motivations of migrating people—including those who landed at Plymouth—are recorded in journals and diaries that provide a realistic and often striking view of our nation's ancestors. Here, for instance, is one entry from the diary of Patrick Breen, who was a member of the Donner Party that was trapped in the high Sierras during the winter of 1847-1848:

February 26, 1848: Hungry times in camp; plenty of hides, but the folks will not eat them; we eat them with tolerably good appetite, thanks to the Almighty God. Mrs. Murphy said here yesterday that she thought she would commence on Milton and eat him. I do not think she has done so yet; it is distressing. The Donners told the California folk four days ago that they would commence on the dead people if they did not succeed that day or the next in finding their cattle . . . .

Such accounts can be compared with similar recent ones. Newspapers supply firsthand data about Laotians and Vietnamese who in recent times risked everything in their quest for a new place to live. These data and those from a past immigrating group can be compiled in a chart as shown in Figure 12.7 so that some generalizations about people's motivation can be drawn.

T The "why suffer" question can be asked in many contexts—about the voyage of the Mayflower, the settlement of Quebec, and the pioneers' journey to the Pacific.

R C. F. McGlashan, *History of the Donner Party* (San Francisco: A. L. Bancroft & Company, Printers, 1881). Reprinted in *Bridging a Continent*, 1971.

T The newspaper can be used in historical study. See Charles Berryman, "100 Ideas for Using the Newspaper in Courses in Social Science and History," *Social Education*, 37:318-320 (April 1973).

Figure 12.7
A Retrieval Chart to Use
for Comparison Purposes

	Why They Came Problems They Encountered	Why They Were Willing to Take a Chance
The Pilgrims 1620		
The Vietnamese/recent times		

Note: Any group of people can be listed at the left, with the time when they left their homeland given below.

Going Beyond Facts: Seeing People as Part of a Larger Social Arena.

A writer of fiction often embellishes his or her tale with details about the appearance, dress, manner of walk, and manner of speech of story characters. Outside ths context of the story, such details are of no significance, but the writer of fiction knows that they are important if the reader is to come to know the character as a real person and develop empathy. The same familiarity with human detail is important in understanding people of the past. It is for this reason that a multi-media approach to historical study is important at every grade level.

Pictures establish a framework for interpreting people's actions and events of the past. Through pictures, the young student of national history can see the tiny ships that carried his or her ancestors to a new homeland, the kinds of houses in which they lived, the kinds of farms and factories in which they worked, and the kinds of clothes they wore. When pictures take the form of filmed chronicles, the student can hear the words his or her ancestors spoke and in some cases have an immediate sense of being a participant.

Any study of national history is incomplete unless it includes some listening and independent reading activities that focus on real and fictionalized people of the past. At the primary level, children can read fictionalized stories such as those in the *I Can Read History* series (New York: Harper & Row, 1978). Some titles include:

Wagon Wheels by Barbara Brenner. This in the story of the Muldie family that moves to Kansas in the 1870s and endures life in a dugout house during a hard winter.

Clipper Ship by Thomas Lewis. This is the story of a clipper-ship trip to California in 1850, based on actual accounts.

It would be impossible to provide a complete description of all the fictionalized and biographical materials available for young people in intermediate grades. There are just too many good works. However, the following listing gives an idea of the general categories of reading materials available:

1. Journals or accounts based on journals. See Robert Merideth and E. B. Smith's *Pilgrim Courage* based on John Bradford's diary; their *The Quest for Columbus* based on a history written by Columbus's son; and their *Riding with Cornado* based on a first person acount. All are published by Little, Brown (Boston, 1962).
2. Eyewitness accounts. See Rhoda Hoff's *America's Immigrants: Adventures in Eyewitness History* (New York: Henry Z. Walck, 1963).
3. Songs. See Oscar Brand's *Songs of '76: A Folksinger's History* (New York: M. Evans & Co., 1973).

T Fine pictures and maps related to U.S. history can be found in the National Park Service's National Survey of Historic Sites and Buildings. There are many volumes in the series: some titles to check are *Soldier and Brave* (1971), *Prospector, Cowhand, and Sodbuster* (1967), *Colonials and Patriots* (1964), and *Explorers and Settlers* (1968) (Washington, D.C.: U.S. Government Printing Office, Superintendent of Documents.

T Other good sources of photographs, sketches, and pictures:

Roger Butterfield, ed. *The American Past* (New York: Simon & Schuster, 1966).

Alan Collins, *The Story of America in Pictures* (New York: Doubleday, 1953).

John Kouwenhoven, *The Columbia Historical Portrait of New York: An Essay in Graphic History* (New York: Doubleday, 1953).

American Heritage Pictorial Atlas of United States History (New York: American Heritage Publishing, 1966).

James Grady, *Photo-Atlas of the United States* (Pasadena, California: Ward Richie Press, 1975).

Kenneth Nebenzahl, *Atlas of the American Revolution* (Chicago: Rand McNally, 1974).

4. Reproductions of historical documents. See Wilma Hays' *Freedom* (New York: Coward, McCann & Geoghegan, 1958), that contains reproductions of documents important in American history.
5. Reproductions of primary source materials—letters, wills, etc. See *In Their Own Words: A History of the American Negro* by Milton Melzer and published by Thomas Y. Crowell (New York). There are three volumes in the series: 1964, 1965, and 1967.
6. Fictionalized accounts. See stories that have become classics in American children's literature such as Esther Forbes' *Johnny Tremain* (Boston: Houghton Mifflin, 1946) and Mark Twain's *Huckleberry Finn.* See also more recent books such as James and Christopher Collier's *My Brother Sam Is Dead* (New York: Four Winds Press, 1974); Paula Fox's *The Slave Dancer* (New York: Bradbury, 1973); Yoshiko Uchida's *Journey to Topaz* (New York: Charles Scribner's Sons, 1971).
7. Biography. See Johanna Reiss's *The Upstairs Room* (New York: Thomas Y. Crowell, 1973), for the story of Ms. Reiss's own escape as a Jewish girl from Nazi Germany.

R These categories were developed based on a discussion by Charlotte Huck of the kinds of history-related materials available for children. See Charlotte Huck, *Children's Literature in the Elementary School,* 3rd ed. updated (New York: Holt, Rinehart & Winston, 1979), pp. 544-546. The chapter "Informational Books and Biography" is most helpful.

Listening to and/or reading some of these materials gets children emotionally involved with people from the past. One may begin to see problems and situations from different perspectives and get insights into events about which one may have known nothing before.

A Problem to Ponder

Thomas Jefferson asked that these lines be inscribed on his gravestone:

Here was Buried
THOMAS JEFFERSON
Author of the
Declaration
of
American Independence
and of the
Statute of Virginia
for
Religious Freedom
and Father of the
University of Virginia

1. Why do you think Jefferson chose these three facts for his gravestone rather than the fact that he was president or that he was responsible for the Louisiana Purchase?

2. Jefferson's tombstone is an example of firsthand data on which historians rely to find out about the past. How could a fifth- or sixth-grade teacher use the inscription as part of a unit on the American Revolution?

Going Beyond the Facts: Contrasting One with Another. As was pointed out earlier, one of the greatest dangers inherent in a political study of history is the myopic view of the world that can emerge. The rest of the world is seen as important only as it affects the homeland. How does the teacher guide children as they learn about their own nation's history without encouraging a chauvinistic outlook?

Drawing upon materials that provide accounts of the past from more than one perspective is a first step. A second is to widen the sphere of study to include nations whose history paralleled but also diverged from that of the homeland. This approach allows for the natural development of contrasts.

In the case of American and Canadian history, this recommendation means that as Americans study the history of the United States and Canadians study the history of Canada, the North American continent becomes the organizing feature. Youngsters study the feelings of the people coming to the continent, the settlement patterns of North America, and the formation of nation-states. Contrasts that will develop naturally include:

The basic motivations of those coming to Canada and the United States;

The way each group viewed and treated the Indian nations;

The early exploration and settlement patterns;

The relationships existing between each of the major North American nations and England and France.

Data collected at each stage of study can be compiled in chart fashion, so that comparisons and contrasts are made clear. For example, as youngsters begin to look at exploration patterns, they ask: What areas of the continent were explored first? Why were these areas explored first? Which nations led in the explorations of the region that was to become Canada? the United States? How did these explorations affect later colonization? Answers to these questions are plotted directly on a data retrieval map, with each youngster creating a sample.

At the same time, young people can cooperatively create a set of parallel time lines that take on the appearance of a chart. (See Figure 12.8.) Significant dates are set in a column on the left side of the chart. The name of the first nation being studied heads the second column; the name of the second nation heads the third column. As significant events and people are encountered, children record them in the appropriate column adjacent to the correct time marker. The chart may have to extend onto a second bulletin board as students continue to add information to it. As in the case with the data retrieval maps described in the previous paragraph, students must stop periodically to consider: In what ways do events and people in each country mirror each other? In what ways are they different? Eventually they must ask: Why? What accounts for the similarities and differences?

Going Beyond the Facts: Contrasting Past and Present. The kinds of comparisons and contrasts just discussed are possible in the upper elementary grades, at which level most intensive study of national history tends to be included. However, simple kinds of contrasts are possible in the primary grades, especially if children are already familiar with one side of the contrast. This is true in contrasts between present and past; students compare and contrast events in which they have participated directly with similar occurrences in the past.

A relatively easy context for encouraging young children to think beyond the facts and to identify points of similarity and difference is in the study of national celebrations: Thanksgiving, 4th of July, presidential birthdays, Memorial Day, Dominion Day, and so forth. In the primary grades, much attention is given to holidays for these are significant dates in a young child's life.

Steps in the study of a national holiday that lead to consideration of similarities and differences include:

Step I Children orally share with others in the group the things they do with their family to celebrate the holiday.

Step II Students cooperatively dictate a series of sentences that tell about the holiday celebration. The teacher records the sentences on a chart. Students and teacher study the sentences to make sure they are clearly written and are in logical order.

Step III Children listen to or view material that describes the holiday as it was celebrated at an earlier time. Material can be in the form of pictures, a story read aloud by the teacher, a filmstrip or film, a televised account, or a combination of these.

Step IV Children talk about the holiday as it was celebrated in the past, getting at the reason why the holiday came to be celebrated. Children then dictate a second series of sentences for the teacher to record in chart form.

T See the *National Geographic* (September 1978) map supplement, "The Middle East and Its Early Civilizations" for an illustrated example of parallel time lines. These lines clarify time relationships among Babylonian, early Egyptian, and Phoenician civilizations.

Figure 12.8 A Comparative Time Line Data Retrieval Chart

	Organizing Data According to Time and Place	Interpreting Data
1825	War of 1812—Canada successfully defends lands against Americans.	
1800	Canada Act (1791) separated Lower and Upper Canada (Quebec and Ontario).	1782—Americans won independence including lands west to the Mississippi River. This was a time of conflict between Canada and America.
	40,000 loyalists fled from America to Canada and settled in Ontario.	
1775	Quebec Act passed guaranteeing rights (1774).	War of Independence began (1775). This was a time of nation forming on the North American continent.
	Guy Carleton, "Father of British Canada," guided the country.	
	First Continental Congress met in Philadelphia (1774).	
	French and Indian Wars ended (1763); French rule ended in North America; England got Canada and lands west to the Mississippi River.	
1750	Acadians made homes in coastal areas of U.S. and in New Orleans.	
	Acadians exiled from Nova Scotia.	
1725	French built Fort Louisbourg on Cape Breton Island to guard St. Lawrence.	
	France ceded to England all claims to Nova Scotia, Rupert's Island, and Newfoundland (1713).	This was a period of immigration.
1700	Germans, Scotch-Irish, French, Swiss, and Scotch immigrated to America (18th cent).	This was a period of conflict between competing European powers.
	French and Indian Wars (between England and France) began 1689.	
1675	William Penn became proprietor of Pennsylvania (1681) (English).	
	British seized New Netherland (1664).	
	Hudson's Bay Co. chartered by England (1670).	
	Berkeley and Carteret became proprietors of New Jersey (1664).	
	New France became a French royal colony (1663).	

Date	Canada	United States	Summary
1650		New England Confederation (1643).	Settlements grew faster in America than in Canada. Fur-trading and missionary work were found more in Canada.
	Montreal founded as Catholic mission (France, 1642).	Roger Williams founded Providence (1636); Lord Baltimore became proprietor of Maryland (1632). (English)	
1625	Jesuits arrived (1625) to preach to the Indians (French).	Dutch founded New Amsterdam about 1623.	This was a time when people came to North America to settle, to trade, and to do missionary work.
	Recollet friars arrived (1615) (French).	Plymouth Colony founded by English in 1620.	
	Hudson explored Hudson's Bay (1610) for England.	Henry Hudson explored Hudson River (1609) for Holland.	
1600	Samuel de Champlain (Father of French Canada) founded Quebec (1608).	Virginia Colony founded (1607), by English.	
1575		Spain founded St. Augustine—first city in North America—1565.	
1550		Hernando de Soto went overland from Florida to the Mississippi River (1539) for Spain.	
	Jacques Cartier (1535) sailed up the St. Lawrence to site of present day Montreal for France.		
1525	Giovanni DaVerrazano (1524) named area around Gulf of St. Lawrence "New France."	Ponce de Leon (1513) explored parts of Florida for Spain.	This was a time of exploration by England, France, and Spain.
1500	John Cabot (1497) explored eastern coast of Canada for England.	John Cabot sailed along northeast coast of U.S. for England (1498).	
		Columbus sailed across the ocean from Spain to what is today San Salvador (1492).	
1475	**Canada**	**United States**	

**Going Beyond Facts:
Categorizing Major Activity**

Youngsters build the parallel time lines on the bulletin board. They go on to identify major trends in the development of the continent. Students can contribute illustrative sketches that categorize the major activity of the period.

Step V On several following days, children return to reread their charts together. Youngsters individually draw pictures to accompany each chart.

Step VI Students who have learned to record words independently on paper create their own compositions describing the holiday. They may take words from the class charts.

Step VII Throughout the sequence, children and teacher sing songs related to the holiday. In addition, they listen to poems, stories, and informational selections.

Step VIII Toward the end of the holiday celebration in the classroom, children decide if they would rather celebrate the holiday the way we do now or the way it was celebrated long ago.

Figure 12.9 depicts two charts that children in one first grade produced as they compared Thanksgiving of today with the Pilgrims' first Thanksgiving. This first-grade class went on to another comparative study in February, making charts comparing Abraham Lincoln and George Washington based on material gleaned through listening to biographical accounts shared orally by their teacher.

Investigating Our Roots in Past Civilizations

In this section so far, emphasis has been on ways to investigate the immediate past—our family, community, and national roots that extend back only about 500 years. Clearly, civilization has roots that extend much further back than that, and at some point young people should have the opportunity to probe some of the earliest civilizations that were found in Asia, Asia Minor, Africa, and Europe.

Many of the activities already described can be adapted to study of early civilizations; many of the same questions can be raised. For this reason, few specific ideas are given here. On the other hand, in teaching about the people who lived 2000 or more years ago, one must keep in mind that much of what we know today comes to us through the efforts of archeologists who have uncovered artifacts that provide clues to how people lived then and what they valued. In this respect, school study can be modeled after the work of archeologists, with upper graders hypothesizing based on the remains of past civilizations uncovered.

Take, for example, the rise and fall of a city such as Ephesus. There, ruins excavated in relatively recent times tell about people, a city, and a civilization that existed in western Turkey 2500 years ago. Working from city plans put together by archeologists, students can hypothesize meanings, asking themselves: "What does the existence of temples to Diana and to Hadrian signify? What does the existence of large libraries, amphitheaters, and baths tell us about the way of life of these people? What does the state of architectural development indicate about the level to which civilization had progressed?" Students' hypotheses can be charted as shown in Figure 12.10.

Figure 12.9
Comparative Charts Dictated
by One First-Grade Class and
Recorded by The Teacher

The First Thanksgiving

For the first Thankgiving the Pilgrims and Indians had to shoot a turkey. The Pilgrims thanked God for what they had. The Indians and Pilgrims became friends.

At the first Thanksgiving there was no parade. Foot ball was not invented then.

Our Thanksgiving

On Thanksgiving we have turkey to eat. We are thankful for all the good food. We see all our family.

Many of us go to see foot ball games. We watch the parade on television. We like Thankgiving.

Note that the teacher helped the youngsters to organize their thoughts into paragraphs.

Figure 12.10
Making Hypotheses Based
on Uncovered Ruins

The Civilization: Ephesus

Archaeological Findings	Our Hypotheses Based on the Findings
Temple to Hadrian	Roman rulers were worshipped as gods.
Temple to Diana	People had an organized religion.
Library building	People respected learning.
Law plaques	People had a legal system.
Theaters	People had time for recreation.
Communal baths	Cleanliness was important; baths may also have been a location for socializing.

Once students have plotted the findings and hypothesized based on them, they may wish to ask the key question—What caused the fall of Ephesus? This is the time to turn to a map to look for clues to a possible answer. It is also the time to ask: "What forces could cause the fall of New York, Montreal, or San Francisco? What clues would archeologists 2000 years from now use to learn about our life and values? Will they approve or disapprove of what they find? Why?"

In this context students are using the past to interpret the present and the future. They are making value judgments about both past and present. The next step in the sequence is to formulate decisions based on available evidence. In the following section, let us turn our attention to the steps in decision making.

Becoming Part of the Past: Decision Making in Retrospect

The past is filled with decisions made. Some of these have passed the test of time; they appear to us today as wise decisions based on a clear comprehension of the relevant factors known then. In contrast, some have failed the test of time. Given what we know today, these decisions appear unwise and often unjust. Of course, decision makers of the past made their determinations within the framework of prevailing ideas and probably with much less information than is available as we decide in retrospect.

Nonetheless, decision making in retrospect offers much as a learning strategy. It offers students in upper grades the opportunity to identify relevant factors and possible alternative choices, to weigh the evidence, to present an opinion as to action that should have been taken, and to support that decision with reasons. In this section, the reader will find several examples of decision making in retrospect. They serve as models after which the reader can design similar sequences for use with young people starting about fifth grade.

To Go to War or Not Go to War

Because conflict has been a constant companion throughout human history, considerable attention should be given to the motivation that led people in the past to choose war. Some of these choices in retrospect seem senseless. Perhaps by putting ourselves in the past and considering the ramifications of a specific decision in terms of what we would do given the same situation, those of us living today may be able to learn from the past. Two designs for decision making in retrospect are 1) simplified simulations and 2) role-playing.

T Introduce the concept of conflict by sharing aloud Louise Fitzhugh and Sandra Scoppettone, *Bang Bang You're Dead* (New York: Harper & Row, 1969).

Simplified Simulations. A sequence to use in organizing classroom simulations is as follows:

1. Background information vital in a decision of the past is given to participants without the names of the conflicting parties being supplied.
2. The decision-making task is outlined with precise directions on how participants are to operate in terms of the information given. In a simplified simulation, factors are set forth on cards that young people must handle in a specified way.
3. Students make a decision individually based on the information at hand and make a group decision by voting.
4. They compare their own composite decision with the one that actually occurred in the past, which is supplied at this point by the teacher. Now they ask: "Why did those in the past decide as they did? Did the decision they made pass the test of time? What other course of action other than war could these people have chosen?"

Here is an example that can be used as part of a study of U.S. history in upper elementary grades. The activity is a sophisticated one for fifth or sixth graders.

To Go To War or Not To Go To War

Step I: Introduce the problem.

The Problem. Two groups differ on fundamental questions related to the rights of people living there. The two groups face each other across a common border. The possibility of war is very real.

Step II: Define the task to be done.

The Task. At the point of possible conflict, the two groups have different resources. The resources of each party in the conflict are described on pairs of cards. Each team will receive a set of cards (Figure 12.11).

G Through this activity, students gain in the ability to make decisions based on economic data. They learn to categorize data as assets or liabilities.

Figure 12.11
Resource Cards

Population: 9,613,000 people	Value of Manufactured Goods: $843,000,000	Miles of Canals: 1,100
Population: 13,435,000 people	Value of Manufactured Goods: $165,000,000	Miles of Canals: 3,700
Value of Agricultural Products: $566,000,000	Value of Agricultural Products: $462,000,000	Miles of Railroad: 18,000
Value of Personal Property and Land: $2,900,000,000	Value of Personal Property and Land: $4,100,000,000	Miles of Railroad: 7,000
Money in Banks: $230,000,000	Money in Banks: $102,000,000	

R Information on the cards from *Many Americans–One Nation*. (Los Angeles: Bowmar/Noble, 1974), p. 197.

The Directions

A. Sort the cards into two sets. On your desk, lay out all the cards that you believe describe situations that would be advantages to a country going to war. These are called assets. On another part of your desk, lay out all the cards that you believe would turn out to be to disadvantages in war. These are called liabilities.

B. Next, on the recording sheet, write down why each item you grouped as an asset would supply an advantage in the border war described in the introduction. (See Figure 12.12.)

Figure 12.12
A Reasons Sheet

List of Assets	Reasons You Think That a Particular Item Would Serve as an Asset
larger population	*more soldiers to fight*

Step III: Divide the class into teams. The teams—three members to each—complete the tasks.

Step IV: Reconvene the class. Teams must justify how they grouped the playing cards and share their reasoning with the total class.

Step V: Vote. You are the group that holds all the weak cards. Would you go to war? Vote yes or no.

Step VI: Redefine the situation by explaining: "The facts we have are actual ones. In the War Between the States the South held all the weak cards. The North held all the strong cards. Yet the South opted for war. Can you think of other factors that might cause a group holding such bad economic odds to go to war? Was it a wise or unwise decision? Why?"

Step VII: Hypothesize: "It took a long time for the North to win the war even though they seem to have had more assets. What other factors made this possible?"

Step VIII: Apply this to a different situation: "In the Vietnamese War, the U.S. had the economic advantage. Why couldn't the U.S. win that war?"

R For a general discussion of simulations, see pages 53-54, chapter 2. For an example of a simulation used in a different context, see chapter 15, pages 510-511.

Step IX: Generalizations that can emerge: Economic factors play a part in determining who will win a war. Psychological factors are also important and in some instances can outweigh economic liabilities. Sometimes people disregard overwhelming economic factors in their decision to fight. For them the cause for which they fight is more important than survival.

Role-Playing. Because there are always at least two sides in a conflict, role-playing in which some participants speak for one side and others speak for the opposite side provides a way of looking at fundamental considerations that lead people to choose war or not. After youngsters have studied a pre-war period in some detail, they divide into two groups, each group representing one point of view. In the case

R See Fannie and George Shaftel, *Role-Playing for Social Values: Decision-Making in the Social Studies* (Englewood Cliffs, New Jersey: Prentice-Hall, 1967).

of the American Revolution, one group might be Loyalists, who were against separation from England, and a second might be Revolutionists, who were for separation.

With sides determined by lot, the class becomes a forum. Youngsters wear signs indicating their positions, and a leader calls on participants to speak on the question, being careful to call equally on both sides. In some cases, it makes for an interesting forum to have some "undecideds"—people who have not yet made up their minds. They ask pointed questions to those who are expressing opinions. At the end of the forum, the undecideds vote on the question.

Where in the World?

The application of new technology has led to disputes in the past. One question recurs: Should a new technological device be used at all? Specifically we ask: "Should the U.S. have dropped the atomic bomb on Hiroshima? Should countries of the world continue to test nuclear weapons? Should satellites and planes such as the U-2 be used for spying on other nations?" In upper elementary grades, students can study the facts in a case. They decide in retrospect what they would have done if they had been President Truman and had to decide whether to use the A-bomb, if they had been President Eisenhower and had to decide on use of U-2 flights, or if they had been any recent president who had to decide whether to allow wiretaps in a particular instance.

A second question involves where a new technological device should be applied first. An excellent context for technological decision making is the decision as to where to lay the first intercontinental cable. Here is a design for an activity that relies on brainstorming and critical examination of options.

Where in the World?

G Through this activity, children will gain in the ability to analyze alternative ways of solving a problem. They will gain in the ability to generalize based on specific cases.

Step I: Introduce the problem.

The Background for Decision-Making: You are living in the early 1800s. At that time the only form of communication between continental masses was via ship, and ships moved very slowly. When the telegraph was invented, people began to think of laying communication wires under water. Short lengths of wire were laid beneath rivers, lakes, and bays. But the question was asked: Is it possible to connect the big continental masses via telegraph? The decision was made to try, but where was the first line to be laid?

Step II: Define the task and divide into work teams.

The Task: You are on the team that will make the final decision as to the exact location where the first intercontinental cable will be laid. Where will you lay it? In your team, start by studying the globe; then brainstorm as many possibilities as you can. Don't just name continents but identify specific points on continents that would make sensible beginning and ending points for a cable.

Step III: Critically examine the options and decide.

The Critical Analysis. As student teams complete their brainstorming, they record their options on large paper. Charts are hung around the room so they are clearly visible to all. Led by teacher questions, students consider:

Which options appear least often? most often? Why would option A be a good one? a poor one? What problems would we face if we tried option X? Would a cable between B and C be as useful as one between D and E? If a cable were to be built between T and S, who would pay for it? Would that be a problem?

As students analyze the options, they cross out from their charts those in which there appear overwhelming problems. Left with perhaps three or four viable options, they vote to decide where to build the cable.

Step IV: Compare the decision with the actual decision made in the 1850s.

The Actual Decision. "One day in 1852 several men came to visit Cyrus Field. They were planning to lay a cable from New Brunswick, on the mainland of Canada, to Newfoundland. They needed money to do this, and they had come to Cyrus Field (a very wealthy businessman) to ask for help. Field looked at a map. . . . He saw that if they could lay a cable to Newfoundland, they might be able to lay one all the way to Ireland. For the route by way of Newfoundland was the shortest route across the Atlantic. It was very close to the one Cabot followed in 1497. Field decided not to bother with the short cable between New Brunswick and Newfoundland. Linking America and Europe was a much more important task."

T From R. W. Cordier and E. B. Roberts, *History of Young America* (Chicago: Rand McNally, 1964).

Step V: Generalize. Based on the decision that students made and the actual decision as it occurred, generalize about where technological devices tend to be applied. Generalizations that may emerge include:

A. Technological developments are stimulated by the need for improved goods and services.
B. Those nations that lead in technological development are those with the money to support the costs of experimentation and the skill to implement the new ideas.
C. Because of human and financial risks, people apply new devices first where the need and chance of success are the greatest.

D. A technological development stimulates people to improve upon it.

In a similar way, young people can decide the best routes for other phenomena: a canal to carry people and materials west from New York, a transcontinental railway, a wagon trail route across the Rockies, a canal to connect the Atlantic and Pacific Oceans, or an air route between cities. In each case, students will not only have to identify alternative routes and advantages and disadvantages associated with each but will also be working with maps and globes, interpreting geographical features, and using scale to read distances. In this respect, Where in the World? simulation activities relate to a number of different learning goals.

A Matter of Life or Death

The annals of history are filled with decision points when people had to decide whether or not to take action, knowing full well that their own lives might hang in the balance. These dilemmas faced leaders and followers alike. For example:

T Use a book like Clifford L. Aderman's *The Dark Eagle: The Story of Benedict Arnold* (New York: Macmillan, 1976) to show the traitor's dilemma. The reader is left to judge Arnold's act for him- or herself. The book is for able readers; it must be shared orally with others.

The Slave's Dilemma—to escape via the Underground Railway or to remain a slave.

The Immigrant's Dilemma—to accept what one has in hand or to try for something better somewhere else.

The Senator's Dilemma—to compromise or stand firm and perhaps get nothing.

The General's Dilemma—to fight to the end or to surrender.

The Citizen's Dilemma—to pay an unfair tax in which one does not believe or to refuse to pay.

Dilemmas of these kinds are challenging to consider. The student begins by outlining the dimensions of the dilemma and determining what courses of action are open in situation X. Next he or she brainstorms possible outcomes of the proposed actions. These the student lists on a personal Dilemma Chart as shown in Figure 12.13.
With the hopes and hazards inherent in different courses of action clearly apparent, the student must decide: "Given all the conditions known, what would I have done? Why would I have done this?" The decision itself can be written independently by students who have created their own charts. Later young decision makers compare their decisions and their reasons with others in the class. Since it is a rare instance when all young people will have thought in the same way, students will quickly come to realize that different people may arrive at different decisions even though they start with the same facts.

Figure 12.13
An Example of a Personal
Dilemma Chart

The Action: *To sign the Decoration of Independence or not to sign.*

The Evaluator: *Karin Drake*

The Hopes	**The Hazards**
If we win, then we * *would be ruled by laws we make ourselves.* * *would not have English troops on our land.* * *would not have to pay taxes to England.* * *would be a separate nation.*	*If we lose, then* * *I could be shot or jailed as a traitor.* * *my family could be killed or jailed.* * *my home might be burned down.* * *my land could be taken away.* * *all my possessions could be destroyed.* * *I could be very poor.*

A Problem to Ponder

In Laidlaw's *Great Names in American History,* intended for use in fourth or fifth grades, is a description of Henry Clay's attempt to negotiate a compromise on the question of slavery and Daniel Webster's decision regarding the Great Compromise.

By 1850 the trouble between the North and the South had become so bad that there was talk of war. California wanted to enter the Union as a free state. The North wanted this, but the South was against it. This was only part of the trouble. The North wanted to make more laws against slavery. The South wanted laws that would protect slavery. The North wanted Congress to forbid slavery in new states. The South wanted the states to decide for themselves. . . .

T From *Great Names in American History* (River Forest, Illinois: Laidlaw Brothers,) pp. 167–168. This book supplies biographical accounts of many Americans associated with U.S. history up through and including J. F. Kennedy. If you use this book, supplement it with accounts of female leaders, for none are included in the volume.

A great debate . . . was to be held in the Senate. . . . John C. Calhoun was to speak for the South. Daniel Webster was to speak for the North. Henry Clay was to try to speak for the whole nation. Before the debate, Henry Clay went to the home of Daniel Webster. Clay had a plan that he thought would keep the country from splitting in two. Clay told Webster about his plan. He wanted to give the South some of the things it wanted. The North would get some of the things it wanted. But both sections would have to give up a little, too.

Webster thought a long time. . . . But finally he said, "Henry, you know I can't agree to your plan. Why, I've fought slavery all my life. Now you want me to support a plan that will strengthen slavery!"

"I know you hate slavery, Daniel," Clay argued. "But it is our only way out. The South will leave the Union if it doesn't get some of its wishes. And we are both old men, Daniel. We have both fought all our lives for our country. Do you want to see it broken up now?"

After Clay left, Webster could not sleep. He kept thinking about Clay's words. He also thought about the people he represented. The people of the North were very angry with the South. They did not want a compromise. The people in Massachusetts and all over the North would be very angry if he supported Clay's plan. . . .

On March 7, 1850, Daniel Webster rose in the Senate. . . . No one knew what Webster was going to say. Would he speak for the North? Would he, too, speak against the compromise? Daniel Webster began, "I wish to speak today . . . . "

Assume you were teaching about the Great Compromise. How could you use this selection—which actually continues on to tell what Daniel Webster said—to encourage children to become directly involved with decisions in retrospect?

Mini-Investigations: Building an Understanding of the Past as a Basis for Future Decision Making

Here are several ideas for activities to help young people better understand the complexities of situations people have faced in the past and they themselves may face in the future.

Good Buys or Rotten Deals?

Three large purchases of land mark the history of the United States: The Louisiana, Alaska, and Gadsen Purchases. Although in retrospect people generally recognize the shrewdness of these deals, at the time, they were debated. A group of young people can redebate a question as it must have been. For instance, some can be in favor of buying Alaska; others can consider it Seward's Folly. The class assembles at a hearing, with speakers having the opportunity to state their points of view. At the end of the hearing, students vote: to buy or not to buy?

Slogans

Pike's Peak or Bust! Tippicanoe and Tyler Too! Fifty-Four-Forty or Fight! Remember the Alamo! Remember the Maine! Most of us are familiar with these slogans. Some were used to garner election support. Some seem to glorify war. They all represent important themes of the past. As students encounter these and other slogans they can add them to a time line, attaching as well an index card that details the meaning of the slogan. Developed throughout an entire year's study of American or Canadian history, students can use their slogans to consider what kinds of events seemed to be important rallying points in our past? Are slogans like this helpful or harmful?

T Other slogans to include:

A Chicken in Every Pot!

A New Deal!

Children can categorize slogans according to their appeal: material goods, nationalistic pride, and so forth.

Human Lifelines-The Ups and Downs

Because life for most people is filled with ups and downs, study of historical biographies and autobiographies can be accompanied by life lines. Human life lines are plotted on a graph. On the x-axis, the student plots dates in ten-year intervals. On the y-axis the student plots a set of contrasting adjectives such as happy/sad, successful/unsuccessful, or contributing/non-contributing. It is in terms of the particular set of adjectives chosen that the student subjectively interprets particular events in the life of a person. Figure 12.14 depicts one interpretation of the life of John Paul Jones. That the activity requires subjective judgment is shown in the placement of the items "captured the Serapis" and "captured the Drake." Since many people were killed in these battles, some interpreters might not rate these events as happy ones.

T Information for the John Paul Jones life line is taken from the selection about him in *Great Names in American History*. Children can use information from this and similar books to plot lines for other historical figures.

The same judgmental approach can be employed to plot the life of a nation. Nations too have ups and downs. In this context, *up* can be interpreted as times of which citizens are particularly proud; *down* as times of which citizens are not proud. In lower grades, children can be given a set of cards to place on the graph, with each card bearing the name of a key event. The graph can be plotted on the chalkboard. The class can vote to determine how each card should be placed.

**Figure 12.14
A Subjective Lifeline for
John Paul Jones**

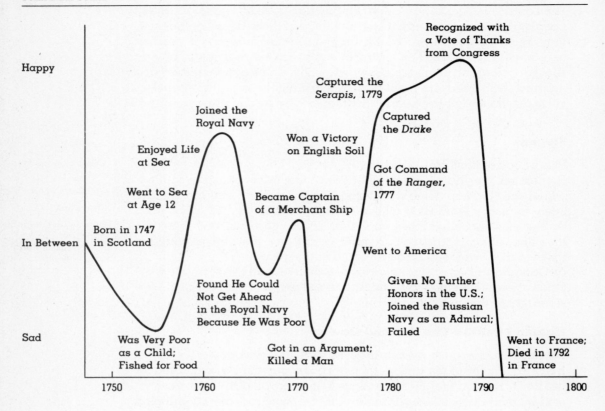

People in Change: A Summary Thought or Two

R Henry Steele Com-
mager, *The Nature and
the Study of History*
(Columbus, Ohio:
Charles E. Merrill, 1965),
p. 26.

Writing of the way people have lived in the past and live today, Henry
Steele Commager comments, "The fact is that men and women do not
live in compartments labeled 'politics' or 'law' or 'religion' or
'economics'; they live in all of these simultaneously. The same people
who write constitutions and draft laws also build houses, marry and
raise families, work at machines, write books, go to church, and fight
wars." Because this is true, school study of history must be a far-
ranging endeavor that draws understandings from all the social disciplines and the humanities and that focuses on the feelings and
beliefs of individuals. Study of the past must bring children into contact
with everyday people who made day-to-day decisions.

In contrast to other animals in the world, human beings alone have the ability to keep records of past existence and to pass this heritage on to future generations. Because of this, each generation can build on the errors and successes of previous generations. In this context, history takes on added importance. It allows for progress if men and women can learn from the past. For this reason, school study of history should encourage children to look critically at what humankind has done so that they can try to avoid the errors of those who have gone before.

A Problem to Ponder

In 1827 Massachusetts and Vermont instituted compulsory study of national history in their schools. Such requirements are common today. Do you believe that all children should study the history of their country? Support your position.

References

Commager, Henry Steele. *The Nature and the Study of History*. Columbus, Ohio: Charles E. Merrill, 1965.

Kownslar, Allan, ed. *Teaching American History: The Quest for Relevancy, 44th Yearbook of the National Council for the Social Studies*. Arlington, Virginia: NCSS, 1974.

Marsak, Leonard. *The Nature of Historical Inquiry*. New York: Holt, Rinehart & Winston, 1970.

Norling, Bernard. *Timeless Problems in History*. London: Notre Dame, 1970.

Social Education, 39 (October 1975). This issue focuses on teaching world history.

Stephens, Lester. *Probing the Past*. Boston: Allyn & Bacon, 1974.

Ubbelohde, Carl; and Fraenkel, Jack, eds. *Values of the American Heritage: Challenges, Case Studies, and Teaching Strategies, 46th Yearbook of the National Council for the Social Studies*. Arlington, Virginia: NCSS, 1976.

13

People in Their Places: Spatial Location, Time, and Human Activity

This second-grader is studying economic activity in cities.

The basic fact of today is the tremendous pace of change in human life.

Jawaharlal Nehru, *Credo,* **from the** *New York Times,* **September 7, 1958**

Key Questions

If you view the world as a chessboard, with what moves are you primarily concerned?

What is the significance of central place theory?

How can you involve young people in consideration of central place theory and help them understand the relationships between structures and processes?

How can you involve young people in the study of basic economic factors that affect them directly?

Diminishing travel time is a factor that will probably grow in significance in the future. How can you help children understand the importance of time relationships?

How can you help young people develop a world view that is less egocentric?

What do we mean by the following terms?
agglomeration - *huge group business*
services and products *- does / use*
accessibility- *availability*
constraints *-barriers*
high rent core and suburbs *middle city / outer city*
distribution of labor
mental map *- how much child really know -preference*
ignorance surface map *- can't identify everything*
                                            fill in
Into which units typically included in the social studies can you interject consideration of time, space, and human activity? *Economic / Geography*
                          Consider relationships

Figure 13.1
Illustration of Changing Land Use
Drawn by a Second Grader

Introduction

G   E
E   C
O   O
G   N
R   O
A   M
P   I
H   C
Y   S

What effect does a major highway cutting through a rural area have on the people living there? Virginia Lee Burton's Caldecott Award-winning story, *The Little House*, shows that effect. The pictures tell about the coming of the highway, traffic, buildings, subway, and eventually skyscrapers, until the little house is hidden from view by urban sprawl.

Youngsters in one second grade listened intently as their teacher shared the story with them. They then participated in a talk time during which they told about specific changes that they remembered from the story. Then each child drew a series of pictures to show the changes that come about as more and more people move into an area and connected the sketches with arrows to produce a flowchart. The sample of children's art that opens this chapter was created by one youngster in this second grade.

Clearly, through activities like this, even young children can become more aware of how human beings organize space for their own use and how this use may change as time moves on. From such simple beginnings older students can go on to analyze the factors that affect the way people organize space and time and to understand that life is affected by many factors.

T See Virginia Lee Burton. *The Little House* (Boston: Houghton Mifflin, 1942). This picture storybook can be used to develop the concept of change with children in kindergarten through grade two.

Putting Places in Perspective – Geography and Economics

Oceans, mountains, natural resources, cities, and the corn and cotton belts are all features of space and of human activity that children locate and map. However, a simple knowledge of where places are located leads to little understanding of how humans interrelate and use space. Because human activity is not static, both the geographer and the student must concentrate on interactions resulting from differences in topography, climate, and customs across the earth.

In this respect the geographer resembles the chess player who is discontent with stationary positions of pieces on a board and who is concerned with changes in movement, placement, and kinds of pieces. The chess player studies the location of each piece in relation to each other piece and the pattern of all the pieces taken together. The player makes a move after consideration of the relative positions of all the pieces or – in geographic terms – the **spatial structure** found on the board. The move of a piece from one square to another can be thought of as a **spatial process.** Each move produces a new arrangement of the chess pieces, a new location of elements with respect to one another – in short, a new spatial structure. Obviously on the chessboard spatial process and spatial structure are closely related. Indeed, one is a determinant of the other. If we filmed the moves in a chess game, leaving out the pauses for deliberation, the motion picture would show a continuously changing spatial arrangement. Process and structure have become one.

T Use a chessboard with children to explain spatial relationships. For example, some pieces can represent shops. Move one shop to a far corner. Ask: "How does this move affect the remaining shops?"

• the arrangement of things in relation to other things = *spatial structure*

• the movement of things within the structure = *spatial process*

The World as a Chessboard

Spatial structure and process are also key elements in the work of all social investigators. For example, the historian may examine the development of exploration routes from the old world to the new, noting relationships between structure and process as the routes expand, change, and increase in number. The historian is not content to identify where, but goes on to consider why. Likewise the economist charts shifting patterns of trade among cities, watching the changes in production and distribution of goods, searching for answers to the "why" questions, and even predicting future patterns based on developing trends. As communication and transportation networks—all spatial structures—change and expand, tools, modes of dress, language, and behavior patterns are carried from one culture to others. This diffusion is studied by the anthropologist, who is as concerned as other social scientists with the dynamic nature of human activity.

R See Ronald Abler, John S. Adams, and Peter Gould. *Spatial Organization: The Geographer's View of the World* (Englewood Cliffs, New Jersey: Prentice-Hall, 1971).

Because constant change is an inherent characteristic of human activity, spatial structure and process are concepts that give both professional and student investigators a framework for examining and understanding past, present, and future distributions of people and things. Out of understanding emerge plans for the future. As Ronald Abler and his associates write: "We want to know about the processes which produce spatial structures because we wish to manipulate them. . . . Man has always manipulated his social and physical environment."

T Clarify relationships of this sort with schematics:

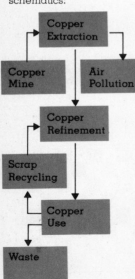

Looking at Diversities. Diversities of all kinds exist on earth. Some diversities are natural; others are human-made. We find variety in landforms and water features such as mountains, plains, and river systems; in resources such as mineral deposits and forests; in cultural features such as cities, transportation systems, and industries; and in the circulation patterns of ocean tides and currents, clear and polluted air, and migratory fish, birds, and mammals.

Differences among areas contribute to spatial interactions. Copper mined in one location is refined and converted to products in another. Wheat grown in one region is transported to and consumed in others. An industrial plant is located in one city but not in another.

Why are distributions structured as they are? What topographical characteristics, political boundaries, supply-and-demand factors, and historical sequence of events produced these particular spatial structures and triggered the interactions that we find? Why are economic spatial processes and structures—those related to production, consumption, exchange of goods and services—located as they are? As time has passed, how have processes and structures changed? How might they change in the future? These kinds of questions and problems emerge in dynamic classrooms where human activities are considered in terms of spatial processes and structures.

Children can consider the way in which modern superhighway
systems are changing their concept of distance.

Looking at Consequences.   In a world growing closer and more
crowded, other questions emerge. What are the consequences on
human behavior of a new spatial structure thrust upon established life
patterns? Suppose a new road connects a rural area of India to an
industrial or market center. What will happen? Will farmers now move
crops to the city for sale? What will happen to local markets? Will the
kinds of crops grown change? Will the habits, values, and desires of
people in the rural area begin to reflect those of the urban area? Perceiving the road as a spatial structure, the student can look at the
changes to spatial processes resulting from population shifts and from
changes in agricultural practices and societal values.

Citizens as well as social scientists are caught up in these problems.
Often the problems have immediate impact on the community in
which a citizen lives. For example, a new shopping center, utility
plant, housing complex, highway, or industrial park is to be built in or
near the community. Where exactly should it be located? An entre-
preneur may seek a location that results in the least expense and
maximum income. The local governing body may want information
about traffic patterns, service costs, and tax revenues. The environ-
mentalists may want to know about possible air and noise pollution
and about destruction of trees. Students should look at consequences
from all these perspectives; in so doing they gain some understanding
of the complexities of human problems.

T Note: This is an
example of a conflict of
interest and values.
Children can take the
parts of different parties
in such a case and hold
a mock hearing.

Idea Page

Background for the teacher. This Idea Page demonstrates one way students can consider spatial distribution on land surfaces. It can be completed as part of a thinking session. Project the map (Figure 13.2) given as a transparency. Using the questions, students analyze the map cooperatively.

The aim. Applying understanding about human activity and population locations to the interpretation of a new land area.

The introductory clues. Here is a map of two islands colonized by settlers who came by ship from a distant land.

The pursuit. Answer the following questions. Then open an atlas to find this island group and check to see if your predictions are accurate.

1. A is one of the largest cities on the two islands. Why is this situation one of the most ideal locations for city development? Why is it better than B? C? D?
2. Predict: Which island is more densely populated? Why?
3. Predict: Where do you think most of the centers of population are found? Why?
4. Predict: Where are two other major cities probably located? For each predicted city site, give reasons to support your idea.
5. Ferryboats are still important here. Where would you predict the most frequently used ferry would be located? another important ferry? Why?
6. Where would you expect to find major railroad lines? Why?
7. Today air travel is important here. Where would you expect to find major lines? Why?
8. There is considerable mountainous area on the islands. What kind of economic activity would you, therefore, expect?
9. You intend to travel here in January. What season of the year would it be? What kind of weather would you expect?
10. What will probably determine the kind of language the people speak here? the kinds of homes they live in? the kinds of clothes they wear?

Note: This activity can also be completed by students on an independent basis, or students can work in groups, regrouping as a total class to consider interpretations. As a continuation, give students other land areas to interpret.

Figure 13.2
A Map to Show Spatial Distributions
on Land Surfaces

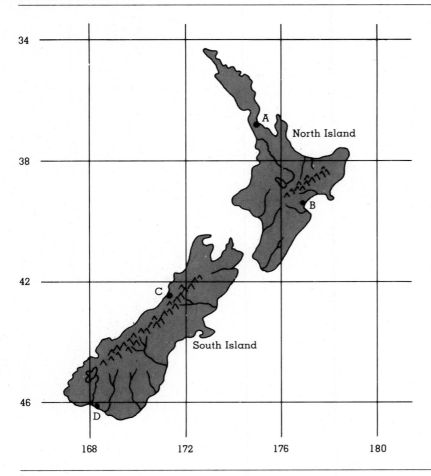

The Central Place – A Hub for Studying Structure and Process

Modern urban geographers tell us that human societies seem always to have required some kind of commercial center, or hub, where people gather to exchange goods and services. Human desire for products made by others as well as for information about people and events generates a need for a **central place.** Simple marketplaces may develop into towns that function as centers for the exchange of goods, services, and information and as centers of government. Many cities and towns today have a Market Street or City Square that had its

beginnings as a local market. Establishment of towns minimizes the distances and travel times farmers and villagers need to obtain goods and services. In turn the grouping, or the **agglomeration,** of people and services in a central and accessible place enhances interaction among people. Financial transactions are made easier and the cost of doing business is reduced. Agglomeration itself generates further growth of the central gathering place.

R Christaller's work is clearly explained in Harold Carter's *The Study of Urban Geography* (New York: John Wiley & Sons, 1976). This is a source book supplying information on central place theory and urban land-use problems.

Central Place Theory. A rationale for the location of a central place that provides goods, services, and information for itself and the surrounding region was developed in 1933 by Walter Christaller, a German geographer. According to the Christaller theory, evenly spaced settlements will develop and serve surrounding market areas. These central places are hierarchal; hamlets are the lowest order places and supply only limited goods and services; towns are of higher order, cities even higher.

Christaller pointed out that a wide area is needed between large central places so as to provide the necessary population and wealth to support them. In contrast, smaller towns and villages with more limited goods and services can survive and prosper on the less sophisticated needs of people. The smaller local population travels to a higher place to satisfy its more specialized needs. Put in modern terms, a hamlet may have an eating place and a gas station; it probably does not have a florist.

T Use flowcharts to show these relationships:

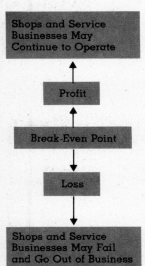

Wholesale and retail shops and service outlets are central place activities involved essentially in the profitable distribution of goods and services to people of a surrounding area. Each must do a certain amount of business to break even and meet costs. After the break-even point, or threshold, has been reached, increased business and new customers mean profit. Shops and services are dependent on easy accessibility by customers. If a store or service provides delivery to a customer's residence or place of business, reaching too far may become too costly and cut into profit. On the other hand, the size of a customer territory may be dependent on the customer's willingness to travel to see and buy the merchandise or receive the service. The customer usually weighs the buying opportunity or service to be obtained against travel cost and time.

Applying the Theory. An ideal central place theory assumes uniform resources and equal ease of movement in any direction; it also assumes a uniform distribution of population and purchasing power. Of course, these assumptions are not realistic. Central places are not evenly spaced with lower order places neatly nested and spaced between. Nonetheless evidence from many studies completed over the last two decades shows that the basic concept of central place hierar-

Figure 13.3
Urban Activity Shown in
Burton's *The Little House*

chy does reflect many aspects of the real world. Today's economists, geographers, city planners, transportation engineers, retailers, and others find the central place theory—modified by input from the many variations found in actual cases—to be a useful model for understanding societal spatial structures and processes and for solving the puzzles unique to their own professional concerns. The central place theory also is a useful framework for children to use in studying social, economic, and geographic relationships.

Investigations into Human Activity, Spatial Location, and Time

Emerging ideas about the relationships among natural features, human-made structures, and human activity, as well as about central place, provide the theoretical framework for numerous firsthand investigations that young people can pursue. Students can gain understanding of how economic activities are structured and organized by examining commercial centers and industries found in their home areas and by raising key questions about the relative location of these centers. By observing, talking about, and listing factors that influence the location and type of activity, young social scientists gain insights as to which factors are most influential. Later students can generalize, perhaps comparing the factors significant in the way that personal space is organized to the way space dedicated to commercial activity is structured.

In carrying out firsthand investigations of their immediate environment, students will be involved essentially in two interrelated and primary questions: why we choose specific locations for given activities and why we choose certain activities to carry out at specific locations. They will also be involved in thinking about why we do not always choose an ideal location for a given activity or the best activity for a given location. Many constraints operate to prevent the fusion of most appropriate activity with most suitable location.

The Shopping Center Investigation: An Opportunity for Direct Inquiry into Spatial Structures and Processes

Shopping centers—those planned agglomerations of retail businesses renting space next to one another and providing large parking areas for customers—are a characteristic of life in North America today. An excursion to a shopping center, or plaza as it is sometimes called, offers direct opportunity for firsthand collection and classification of data as young people investigate how space in the center is organized for human activity. Follow-up discussion offers the opportunity for hypothesizing and generalizing about relationships among human structures and processes.

Collecting Data.   Specific suggestions for data collection as part of this type of excursion include the following:

Divide students into three-person teams, each equipped with pencil, paper, and clipboard.

Assign activities to specific teams.

–Teams one and two: List the name of each store and the kind of merchandise sold there. One team concentrates on shops in one part of the center, the other on shops in another part.

–Teams three and four: Interview the management of selected businesses using predetermined questions. For example: How long has the business been at that location? Where was the business previously located? Why was that location selected? Is the location a profitable one?

–Teams four and five: Set up a booth to survey the characteristics of the customers. Again students work from a predetermined questionnaire: How far did you travel to come to the center? What was your means of transportation? Why did you choose this center?

–Teams six and seven: Sketch a layout map of the area.

G Through this activity students will gain in their ability to collect data through direct observation and interviews.

Survey the entire center to note the placement of buildings on the land, parking arrangements, and access patterns to highways and mass transit. The school bus can make a tour of the center, stopping periodically to allow investigators to work on a rough sketch of the entire center, including buildings, roads, bus stops, and parking lots.

A purposeful excursion obviously takes careful planning and preparation. Students who are to interview business people and customers must develop their interview guides; this may require considerable discussion about the kind of information needed and the type of questionnaire to be used. Students who are to measure and sketch a map may need to practice skills; they might first make a map of the rooms of the school to develop skill. Students must study maps of the entire area, identifying major highways near the center. If students have a clear concept of what it is they will be doing at the center and why they will be doing it, time spent on location can be used profitably.

If a group excursion is impossible, children can make individual inventories of stores found in a local shopping area based on their recollections. Each student begins with a duplicated outline plan of the shopping center stores. This plan need not be to exact scale as long as it shows the correct number and location of stores. Students can fill in appropriate names and functions.

T Plotting the locations of stores from memory is possible in grades one and two, if the commercial area is close to home and school.

Analyzing Data – A Classification Activity. With data gathered, young investigators take the next step – analyzing information. They list all the retail businesses encountered and group together those providing similar services and/or goods. Students may begin to distinguish between **goods** (saleable commodities) and **services** (acts useful to others). They may discover overlaps among categories and may find that a modified classification scheme is necessary. Possible categories include shoes, jewelry, dry cleaning, furniture, records and tapes, hardware, banks, books – categories that students can brainstorm as one or two students record on the board. The teacher helps by supplying less familiar categories: fast food, variety, appetizer, stationery, and so forth. Children may consider grouping clothing stores into men's, women's, and children's and may need help in classifying stores with multiple sales functions. Individuals carefully copy the final retail categories in a column on their own papers. Now, using their original inventory of businesses, they count how many of each kind of store was found. Perfect agreement in number is not necessary, but some form of summarizing is essential. Which kinds of businesses are found in greatest numbers? smallest numbers? Which businesses are large? small? Why?

A more sophisticated variation of this study is a comparison of a major shopping center (with at least one large department store) with a small, local shopping center (with shops clustered around a supermarket). Students living in different neighborhoods can bring in inventories of different centers to facilitate comparison and contrast. Students ask: Which kinds of shops do all shopping centers, small and large, have? Do small centers have two or more of one kind of shop? What kinds of shops do small centers have that large ones do not have? How does total store number compare in small and large centers? How many major roads and transit lines bring people to small and large centers? How much larger is the major center parking lot? Why is the lot so large? Even if young students have access only to neighborhood stores and a local supermarket center, similar comparisons can be made based on information recollected and plotted on an outline map.

Generalizing. Human geographers use the term agglomeration when they observe a number of centers of human activity coming together. Shopping centers are agglomerations – collections of retail sales outlets. Two generalizations about agglomerations that students will begin to apply as they compare concentrations of activities at large and small shopping centers are:

1. Large agglomerations are located in accessible locations. Major shopping centers need extensive parking facilities and access to highways or mass transit.

G Through this activity students gain skill in classification. Even primary youngsters can attempt simple classifications such as food businesses / non-food businesses.

G Students refine their ability to make comparisons based on data they have collected.

G Older students develop an understanding of basic economic relationships.

2. Human activities agglomerate for economic reasons. Shopping center units can share the same heating plant and common building walls. Each reaches more customers because the total traffic is heavy.

Children begin generalizing by brainstorming the factors they think about when deciding to go to a neighborhood shopping center rather than a major one and vice versa. Several children are ready at the chalkboard to list suggestions. In lower grades, the teacher can record ideas on an experience chart. Ideas and suggestions might include: We only want a few items. There are more shoe stores in the big shopping center. We are just going for groceries. We want to browse and talk to friends. There is a big sale at the department store. We have to buy birthday presents. We want to window-shop. The local stores don't have as much variety.

Students project generalizations related to both accessibility and agglomeration. Young people may propose that ease of getting to a center and the grouping of a number of businesses together affect their choice of shopping area. They will use the words *accessible* and *agglomeration* if these words are used naturally by the teacher during discussions.

The Trade Center Investigation: Putting Many Pieces Together

Upper graders are well aware of the variety of commercial activities in their local commercial centers—a variety that ranges from "mom and pop" stores to wholesale establishments.

Looking at Types of Trade Centers.

This knowledge can be used to categorize a nearby commercial area as to the kind of trade center it is. Is it a hamlet? a minimum convenience center? a full convenience center? a partial or complete shopping center? a wholesale and retail center? These are the types of trade centers that John Borchert, professor of geography at the University of Minnesota, found in studies he and his associates made in the Midwest. Dr. Borchert defines **trade center** as an entire city or village, not simply as a drive-in shopping center or a cluster of commercial establishments.

The chart of trade centers found in Figure 13.4 shows business functions arranged in three groups; from bottom to top they are convenience, specialty, and wholesale. The bar columns for each trade center type show which functions are always present and which may be present. For example, a minimum convenience center has a bank, a grocery store, a drugstore, a hardware store, a gasoline station, and an eating place. It also has two of the following: general merchandise, meat/fish/fruit market, variety store, and garage/auto/implement dealership.

R See John R. Borchert and Russell B. Adams, *Trade Centers and Trade Areas of the Upper Midwest*, Urban Report Number 3 (Minneapolis, Minnesota: Upper Midwest Economic Study, 1963). Figure 13.4 is based on this study.

Figure 13.4
Trade Center Types Defined by Business Functions

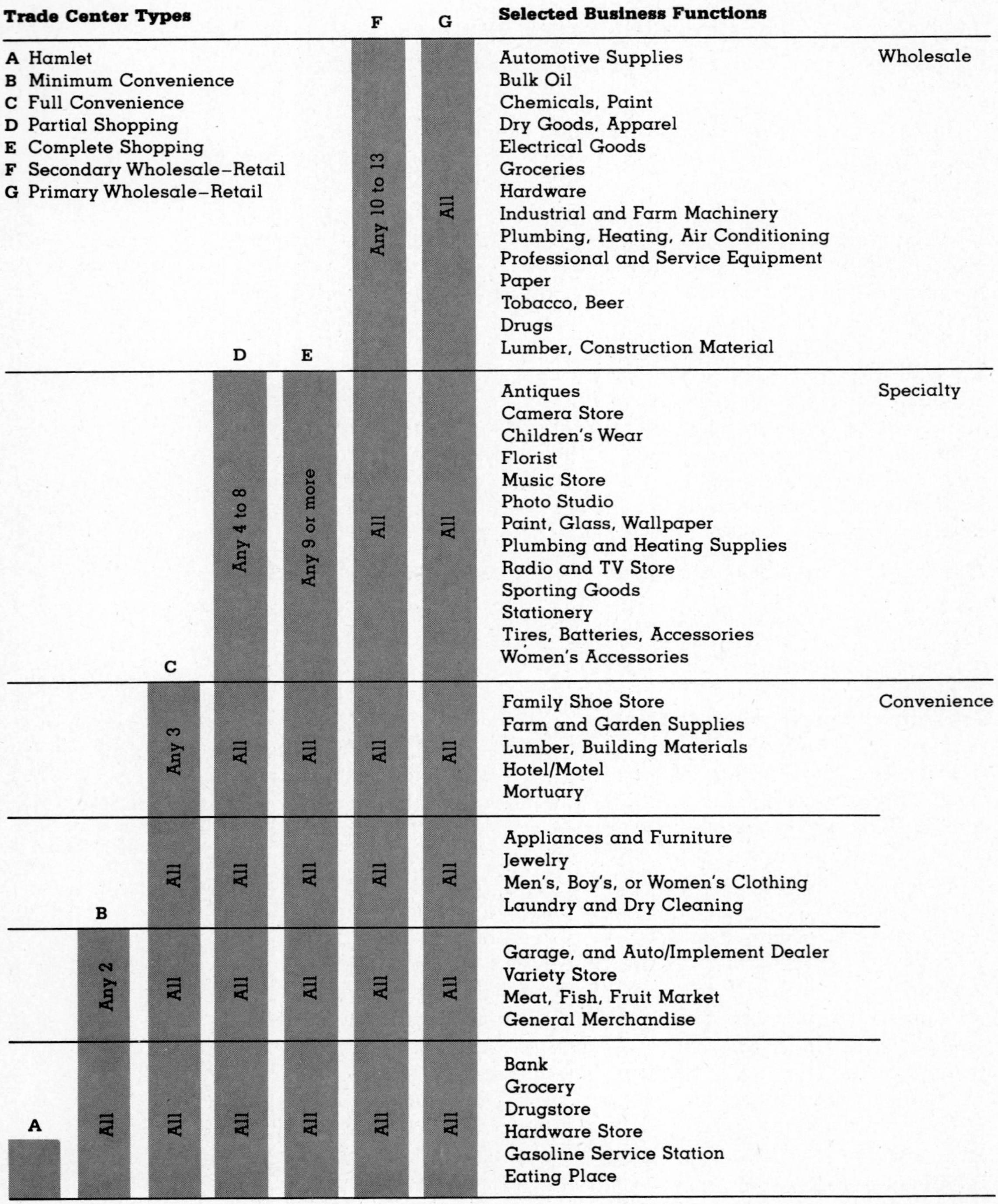

Trade Center Types

A Hamlet
B Minimum Convenience
C Full Convenience
D Partial Shopping
E Complete Shopping
F Secondary Wholesale–Retail
G Primary Wholesale–Retail

Selected Business Functions	A	B	C	D	E	F	G	
Automotive Supplies; Bulk Oil; Chemicals, Paint; Dry Goods, Apparel; Electrical Goods; Groceries; Hardware; Industrial and Farm Machinery; Plumbing, Heating, Air Conditioning; Professional and Service Equipment; Paper; Tobacco, Beer; Drugs; Lumber, Construction Material						Any 10 to 13	All	Wholesale
Antiques; Camera Store; Children's Wear; Florist; Music Store; Photo Studio; Paint, Glass, Wallpaper; Plumbing and Heating Supplies; Radio and TV Store; Sporting Goods; Stationery; Tires, Batteries, Accessories; Women's Accessories				Any 4 to 8	Any 9 or more	All	All	Specialty
Family Shoe Store; Farm and Garden Supplies; Lumber, Building Materials; Hotel/Motel; Mortuary			Any 3	All	All	All	All	Convenience
Appliances and Furniture; Jewelry; Men's, Boy's, or Women's Clothing; Laundry and Dry Cleaning			All	All	All	All	All	
Garage, and Auto/Implement Dealer; Variety Store; Meat, Fish, Fruit Market; General Merchandise		Any 2	All	All	All	All	All	
Bank; Grocery; Drugstore; Hardware Store; Gasoline Service Station; Eating Place	All	All	All	All	All	All	All	

The researchers found hundreds of minimum convenience centers in small communities throughout Montana, the Dakotas, Minnesota, Wisconsin, and Upper Michigan. These towns, aside from certain farm supply businesses, had few or no specialty outlets but did have sources providing items and services most often needed.

Categorizing.   A duplicated roster of business functions as set forth in Figure 13.4 can serve as a checklist for each student in a group involved in analysis of a local commercial area. Independently, students do a memory inventory, checking each item as they recall an example of it in their own community. A follow-up talk period allows comparisons of checklists. Students in pairs then proceed to label their community as to type; again a follow-up talk period allows for resolution of differences and support of ideas with specific examples.

The real value of an exercise such as this lies in the analysis that occurs in the follow-up discussion. Students begin to distinguish between kinds of commercial activity. They may make comparisons between their own communities and nearby communities. They ask:

What does the size of a community have to do with the kind of businesses located there?

Why might a minimum convenience center town have a hardware store but not a glass or wallpaper store?

Why would small communities always have an eating place, bank, hardware, drugstore, grocery store, and a gasoline station?

Space is available for rent in a complete shopping trade center. Which would more likely be a successful new enterprise—a camera store or a family clothing store? What factors must we consider?

How do sales compare in different trade center types? In which type would we find the highest dollar sales volume? lowest? Why?

G Students become more aware of basic relationships between spatial structure and human activity; they grow in their ability to process data.

Many children will know locations that have even fewer kinds of businesses than does the minimum convenience center. Dr. Borchert's investigators found 1800 such places, almost all with only a gasoline station, tavern or eating place, and a random selection of other businesses. He calls these places hamlets. Some students probably know of hamlets within larger political subdivisions such as townships. If so, they can list the services there, hypothesize why these services are available at that location, and categorize the site as a hamlet. Such activity can be carried out as part of unit study of the local community; youngsters plot all commercial sites, noting for each the kind of businesses found there. In this respect, community study can become an encounter with fundamental principles of geography, economics, and history as young people find out what has happened in the past to cause the site locations existing today.

A Problem to Ponder

A teacher took her first-grade class to visit stores in the local shopping area. Returning to the classroom, the children talked about what they had seen and developed a summary chart. The teacher guided the development of the chart to help achieve specific objectives she had in mind. The resulting chart is presented as Figure 13.5.

Figure 13.5
An Experience Chart

Our Walk to the Stores
Our class went on a walk First, we went to Priscilla's Candy Store. The lady gave us chocolates. Then we went to the pet shop. We saw dogs, fish, and an alligator. After that we went to the florist shop. We watched a man make bouquets. Our class had fun in the stores. We want to go again.

1. What objectives did the teacher have in mind?
2. What sequence of questions did the teacher project so that the chart developed as it did?

A second teacher took first graders to visit a similar series of stores. Their resulting chart is Figure 13.6.

Figure 13.6
An Experience Chart

Jobs People Do

Our class visited some stores. We saw different people at work in the stores. First, we went to Priscilla's Candy Store. The lady there sells chocolates. Then we went to the pet shop. The owner was taking care of the animals. At the florist shop we saw a man making bouquets. People do different kinds of jobs in stores.

1. How do the objectives reflected in Figure 13.6 differ from those of the first teacher?
2. Which teacher probably structured the sequence of questions to get at basic economic learning? How do you know?

Perceiving Relationships.   A look at businesses that fail can help young people perceive fundamental relationships among commercial services, human activity, distance, and time. Students start with a practical question that introduces them to factors of proprietorship: Why would you stop going to a particular eating place (hardware store, drugstore, etc.)? Reasons (the food is bad; there is a better place down the road; etc.) are recorded on the board to serve as data as students attempt a second question: What qualities must a shop have to be successful? Students generalize from their previous reasons, developing a list of items such as 1) courteous service, 2) reasonable prices, 3) desirable merchandise, 4) convenience, 5) attractiveness, 6) cleanliness, and 7) location near other shops. In identifying the characteristics of successful businesses, students will be identifying basic attributes of good business management.

T In contexts like this, encourage use of diagrams:

Children may need help in identifying two other factors critical in success: good money management and awareness of changing populations. If the proprietor spends more money than is taken in, he or she will soon be out of business. If the inventory stocked is too expensive for a population that is changing economically or if the proprietor does not change the inventory to meet the needs of a changing population, the business may fail. Analysis of these relationships aids students in developing understanding of factors significant in free enterprise: the profit motive, good management, hard work, and market conditions.

The Industrial Land-Use Investigation: Urban Patterns

When one flies over an urban area at low altitude to see how land is used, what geometric pattern appears? A classic model of urban land use, which was proposed about forty years ago based on the structure of Chicago, showed a bull's-eye arrangement (concentric circles). The innermost was a **high rent core**—a central business district with businesses, offices, museums, theaters, and other commercial and cultural features. Around the core was an area of deteriorating housing, some of it converted into light industry and business offices. A working-class residential zone formed the next belt followed by a ring of better single family houses and good apartment buildings. The bull's-eye pattern was fringed by **suburbs.**

T Use diagrams with children to clarify concepts.

A later model showed triangular sectors radiating outward along road and railroad routes from the central business district. According to this view of urban development, land-use districts such as light manufacturing, high-class residential, and older low-rent residential districts grow outward from the central bull's-eye forming triangles around a center. A subsequent modification of this theory proposes that a growing urban area results in an irregular star pattern. Points of the urban star reach out along highways and railroads.

Study of urban land-use patterns provides a productive vehicle for children to study factors that influence human activities. Such study can fit into existing social studies units that include consideration of city development or comparisons of city, suburban, and rural patterns.

Mapping.   A simple introduction to land-use study comes through map inspection. Students in pairs or small groups inspect state road maps:

They orient themselves by locating familiar places and highways.

They distinguish between small towns and large cities as shown on the map; they distinguish between major highways and minor roads.

They describe highway patterns in and around selected urban areas, contrasting older road patterns and superhighways with loops and bypasses.

They note the influence of rivers and terrain on road placement and even on the location of towns and cities.

As the need for more detail arises, students check more detailed maps of metropolitan areas. New vocabulary that will surface during follow-up discussion includes *radiate*, *perimeter*, *linear*, *hub*, *intersection*, *interchange*, and *city limits*; review words include *legend* and *scale*. To help students incorporate new words into their functional vocabularies, such words can be recorded on cards and suspended from lighting fixtures for use during writing activity.

Children can apply their findings in a graphic way by moving next to a map activity. On a large sheet, each mapmaker does the following:

He or she sketches a circle or rectangle in yellow to represent the downtown area of the local town (or of a nearby metropolitan area).

He or she draws major highways in red; lesser roads in black; and parkways and tollroads in green. Route symbols are then added. Commercial road maps aid in maintaining accuracy in scale and direction.

The mapmaker draws rail lines, rivers, shorelines, and mountain barriers.

He or she adds a legend to the map.

The mapmaker colors in other zones—orange for offices and retail businesses outside the central business district; brown for older residential houses and apartment buildings; purple for heavy industry and manufacturing; and green for suburban areas.

Looking for Patterns.   The land-use patterns that color-coded maps reveal may be striking. Are there concentric color bands around a business core? Are there colored sectors radiating outward showing different land uses? Is there a crude star pattern? Or is there only a random arrangement of color? Children can consider why the land-use pattern they have mapped exists: What happenings of past and present account for the current pattern?

R For an illustrated discussion of urban land-use patterns, see David Thomas, "Urban Land Evaluation," in John A. Dawson and John C. Doornkamp, *Evaluating the Human Environment* (New York: St. Martin's Press, 1973). The diagrams of land-use patterns furnish ideas for making transparencies that can spark discussion with upper graders.

T A Diagram Showing Land Use:

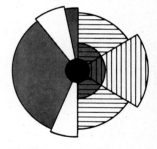

■ Central Business

□ Wholesale/Light Manufacture

▨ Lower Cost Residential

▤ Medium Cost Residential

▥ High Cost Residential

Diagram from David Thomas in *Evaluating the Human Environment* by John Dawson and John Doornkamp (New York: St. Martin's Press, 1973).

Working from a Large-Scale Map. In this and other similar contexts, the preparation of a large-scale map can help children gain an understanding of significant relationships and the ability to handle scale differences. To begin, an immense sheet of brown wrapping paper is tacked to the wall and the enlarged outline of the local area is projected using the opaque projector. Students plot key streets, highways, railroads, streams, and so forth. The scale should also be projected and drawn so that students have some concept of how distance is represented on the large map.

At this point the map can be placed on the floor so that students can work from all sides to add features: large buildings, manufacturing plants, schools, parks, shopping centers, oil storage tanks, power plants, and other important features. Mapmakers must decide whether symbols, initials, or names will be used for each item plotted. Deciding what to include and how to label things provides students with the opportunity to be selective. Often everything cannot be included; students must make decisions based on predetermined criteria about which items to include.

On their map, plotters draw a border around each distinctive land-use region with a colored line. A legend committee prepares a symbol and color listing on a smaller sheet that will serve as a legend. A title committee carefully designs a title. An evaluation committee later decides which features of the map worked well, which did not. Committees working on different aspects of a task are participating in a distribution of labor—an economic concept very easy to understand when one has been part of it.

The finished map, showing land-use zones, provides content for discussion. If the map shows heavy industry, discussion can begin most easily there, for reasons for site location are fairly obvious. For example, paper mills are located near a source of pulp logs and water. Heavy industries are located near rail lines to facilitate shipping. Light industry may be found on major interstate roads, again to facilitate the shipment of raw materials and finished goods.

At this point the teacher can ask a question that focuses on specific cases and leads to generalizations. What are the advantages of the location of Mill X? If asked similar questions about several industries, students begin to generalize that in choosing a location each industry considers factors such as availability of raw materials, workers, transportation, and markets for goods produced.

Collecting Data Firsthand. Although businesses supply people with necessary jobs, goods, and services, very often schools give only passing attention to economic processes so important to business success in a free enterprise system. A field trip to gather information about businesses can help children develop both an understanding and appreciation of the system. The school bus can take young investigators into one of the business areas mapped.

The bus moves slowly along the commercial streets as students record the name, location, and pursuit of each enterprise. On a second drive through the same area, students direct their attention to loading platforms and yards to spot the kinds of materials being loaded, unloaded, or stored. These are clues to raw materials used and goods produced. Students also may note how well the buildings and grounds blend with the environment. Do they have attractive façades? pleasant landscaping? litter? Is there evidence of air pollution? (These latter observations provide material for a related ecology lesson.)

Where sidewalks exist and buildings are close together, as in an industrial park, a walk can take the place of a drive. If a building name does not identify what business activity occurs there, a pair of students can enter to ask the receptionist what kind of business goes on. Of course, the students who do interviews of this type should know how to identify themselves and how to state the purpose of their investigation. If face-to-face interviews are impractical, students can obtain similar information by telephoning from the school. Practice in using the telephone directory as well as in telephoning for information is an extra dividend.

G A second benefit of this type of investigation is that students learn about places in their community that supply jobs for people.

Devising Classification Schema. Data gathered from a business tour provide content for classification. Through classification young people become familiar with the kind of business activity and jobs that exist. The teacher's role here is to devise questions that first ask students to identify clues to business activity, then to group related activities, and finally to label each group appropriately: What kinds of raw material did we see? What kinds of storage tanks were present? For what were they being used? What kinds of finished products did we see? Where did we hear a lot of noise? What does the word *manufacturing* mean?

The name of a company also provides clues as to the business activity carried on. Students may encounter terms such as *wholesaler*, *supplier*, *manufacturers*, *management*, *technical*, *scientific*, *contractor*, *repairs*, and *services*. Some terms will require dictionary investigation.

A classification scheme may include groups such as:

G Through classifying activity students develop key vocabulary necessary in talking about economic activity.

1. *Wholesale business:* breaks down large lots into small ones for resale
2. *Manufacturing:* assembles or converts raw materials
3. *Heavy industry:* refines or converts raw materials
4. *Office:* handles communication, computer, and paperwork of business.

Categories are suggested and then written on the board or on a chart. Other categories emerge through discussion. If, for example, contractor, repair, or other service activity appears on the list of businesses inventoried, students may add a Contracting or Service Industry category. Another scheme could be based on kinds of materials or processes used. The classification systems that emerge will depend on what the inventory produces and on the interests and maturity of the class.

Generalizing from Classification Systems. Having structured several classification systems, children next list the names of surveyed industries that fall into the category. With older students this kind of activity can lead to calculation of percentages within each category, to rank ordering of primary pursuits in the area visited, and to comparisons between different industrial sites.

Numerous generalizations can emerge from a systematic analysis of industrial activity, as shown in the following:

Level One Generalizations

The most common type of activity in this industrial park is light manufacturing.

Factory A is located by the river because its raw materials are transported by barge.

The automobile company needs a large flat area for its assembly operations.

Mill Y is in the industrial zone because it is not allowed in other town locations.

G Students learn to project more sophisticated generalizations based on specific cases.

Level Two Generalizations

Wholesale businesses need many retail businesses in their delivery areas.

Industries needing large numbers of workers must locate near large population centers.

Manufacturing ranks first, offices second, and wholesale businesses third in the percentage of all business enterprises in the area.

Level Three Generalizations

Some industries locate by a railroad, which can bring in bulk materials; however, they send out finished goods by truck because it is cheaper.

Some companies locate in the industrial park because there is good access for workers and easy movement of materials in and out.

When deciding on a location, a business or industry considers many factors including rent, taxes, transportation costs, availability of workers, and zoning regulations.

Considering Other Factors. As several of the previous generalizations imply, to be successful a manufacturing or processing industry has to have a market for its products and the labor it needs. It must pay wages, taxes, and the costs of raw materials, buildings, and machinery.

Richard Morrill, in *The Spatial Organization of Society*, states, "Resources and markets do not exist in all places, but rather at sporadic, specific sites. They are spatially separated and a successful manufacturer must overcome these distances." An industry seeks a location where the costs of obtaining and processing materials and transportation of goods to markets are minimized. Fuel and power costs may rank high in consideration. Formidable political barriers in the form of tariffs, zoning regulations, pollution standards, and banking and capital transfer regulations can push an industry away from an otherwise desirable location.

R See Richard Morrill, *The Spatial Organization of Society* (Belmont, California: Wadsworth Publishing, 1970), p. 81.

The Time Investigation: Another View of Distance

In his book *The Spatial Organization of Society*, Richard Morrill points out that travel time is an especially important determinant of "perishable central market place activities." Police, doctors, and fire fighters cannot be too far away in time. Even schools must be close to the serviced population. Similarly, people demand that their grocery and gasoline needs be met reasonably close by. Time is also a factor in decisions to use personal car, plane, or bus.

Constructing Time Maps. Today's geographers use maps to depict time-space relationships. Students who are knowledgeable about conventional land maps showing political divisions, cultural features, and topographic features can work with **time maps.**

In communities where commuting to work is common, young people can construct maps that show the relationship between commuting distances and commuting times; in so doing they will begin to perceive how distance shrinks as speed increases and travel time decreases. Mapmakers begin with a local road map attached to a flat surface. They fasten a piece of string to a central point in their neighborhood. Each student whose parents commute stretches the string to the point(s) where the parent(s) work(s). He or she pushes a pin into the map at that point and measures the distance the string stretches. If the map scale is

T Young children should get involved with time relationships. Ask them to estimate the time it takes them each day to get to school. Data are compiled in a simple experience chart: "It takes Mary, Timmy, and Martin only five minutes to walk to school. It takes Joseph, Jake, and Rose ten minutes to walk to school."

small and pins get crowded, students can lay out the measured distances on a large sheet of cardboard to form a graph based on distance, or they can enlarge the map. To emphasize "as the crow flies" distances, students then rule colored lines between the central pin and the work sites. The students have developed a space map and/or a graph based on distance.

Students now consider time. They measure out lengths of drinking straws with the length of each straw representing commuting time (obtained from parents). To do this, mapmakers must pick a practical scale; for example, ten centimeters may represent ten minutes. The time-proportioned straws are placed upright over the respective work-site pins to add the dimension of time to the flat map.

Relating Time and Distance.   Students who have made time maps can ask:

Do all time straws get taller as the distance from home increases? If true, a beginning statement might be: The farther one commutes, the greater the travel time.

Are some straws close to home taller than more distant ones? This observation could indicate a delay factor. Students can query parents, examine road maps more closely, and hypothesize why. Perhaps greater traffic volume, more traffic signals, more truck traffic, and/or poor roads are factors.

Are some travel routes by rail so that road traffic is avoided?

What seems to be the maximum time spent in travel to work? What seems to be the maximum distance traveled? Is there a relationship between time and distance?

Getting More Information Out of a Map.   When travel time becomes as important or more important to people than the distance between two points, decisions as to where to live, work, shop, and visit are no longer made only in terms of actual distance between points. In terms of human activity, places are brought closer together or moved farther apart by the time required to cover the distance between.

Students become aware of this relationship by converting their absolute space (commuting distance) maps into a relative space-time map. On such a map a large dot represents the neighborhood center. Youngsters each take their time straws from the map already constructed and lay them down with one end at the center and the other pointing toward the work location. Each marks a dot at the end of his or her straw and labels it with the name of the destination. When straws are removed, a relative space-time map has been constructed with time, not distance, as the significant dimension.

G Through this activity young people learn creative approaches to mapmaking.

Interpretation of satellite photographs requires
an adjustment of one's mental map of the world.

Since all straws have the same scale, circles can be drawn on the
relative space-time map using the center dot for the point of a pencil
compass. A bull's-eye effect is produced, with each circle representing
perhaps ten minutes from the town center. Geographers call these
lines **isochrones**—lines connecting all points of equal time out from a
center location.

Students can also construct relative space-time maps based on their
own travel times to school. The school is at the hub and the homes are
at the ends of the time spokes. Again isocrones in the form of concentric
circles are applied. Students can compare the space-time map to an
ordinary distance map of the area and discuss why the two are not
identical in shape. Do children walk to school or come by bicycle, car,
or bus?

Idea Page

Background information for the teacher. This Idea Page demonstrates how students can be made more aware of time-distance relationships. The activity set forth here is ideal to pursue in small work teams. Once the total class has decided on a scale, each team lays out one trip.

The aim. Visualizing shrinking distances around the world.

The introductory clues. Here are some voyages and flights that were at one time records in that they represent faster and faster crossings of the North Atlantic. They bring Europe and North America closer and closer together in terms of travel time.

Year	Means of travel	Time it took
1492	Columbus via wind power	71 days
1827	the steamship *Curacao*	22 days
1952	the steamship *United States*	3 days, 40 minutes, 10 hours
1927	Lindbergh's solo flight	33 hours, 29½ minutes
1974	Sullivan and Widdifield's supersonic flight	1 hour, 54 minutes, 56.4 sec.

The pursuit. Develop a scale through which you could lay out on the hall floor the time spans given above. Perhaps 1 m = 1 day will meet your needs. Using that scale, set out the time by placing a cutout of Europe progressively closer and closer to where you stand, which represents the East Coast of the United States.

The continuation. What are the advantages that you see coming from more rapid forms of transportation?

_____

_____

_____

What are the disadvantages of being closer in travel time to peoples across the world from you?

The Mental Map Investigation

Through investigations similar to the preceding ones, students can discover that human activities are not necessarily carried out in ideal locations. Many forces determine the actual sites where activity occurs—forces that are environmental, political, and economic, as well as social. However, these realities are not alone in influencing the location of human activity. There is a psychological factor as well, for people's perceptions of distance, space, and time differ. People's mental perceptions are not necessarily based on fact but are often influenced by desires, biases, values, beliefs, customs, and language. Propaganda, censorship, and lack of reliable information are also contributing factors.

Identifying Preferences.   Young people can come to understand their own perceptions by thinking about the question: Where do you prefer to live? Answers given depend in large measure on one's storehouse of information and misinformation about people and places. As that information changes, so does one's perception of the world.

Peter Gould and Rodney White in their book *Mental Maps* use space preference maps of people to see how perceptions are related to the real world. Youngsters in grades four and up can use this technique to explore their own mental maps. Later they can analyze their space preference maps and ask themselves why they have such preferences.

R Peter Gould and Rodney White, *Mental Maps* (New York: Penguin Books, 1974). A **mental map** is one's impressions of a geographical area.

Each student starts with an outline map of the fifty states, placing the numeral one on the state that he or she prefers to live in, followed by a two on the second preferred state, and so on to five. Students also make lists of reasons why they picked each state. A class space preference map is constructed with the resulting data. Starting with the home state, participants indicate by a show of hands how many picked each state as number one, two, and so forth. If the state name and the number preferring it are entered on the chalkboard in tabular fashion, the result will be a substantial amount of information for mapping and analyzing.

A class state preference map is made by coloring the state preferred by the most students a deep green, the next preferred state a paler green, the next a yellow green, and so forth. Individuals can shade their own versions of the space map in a similar fashion.

G This activity helps students become more aware of their own regional preferences and the reasons for those preferences.

Reasons for specific selections can be recorded in similar fashion. The class lists reasons for choices on five large sheets of charting paper, each headed by a state name. Students take turns recording reasons from their individual lists in the form of brief expressions: warm climate, seashore, good farmland, friends living there, winter sports, place where we now live.

Finished charts are posted where all can see, compare, and participate in categorizing reasons listed. Possible categories include environment, sports and recreational facilities, and social factors. Some items may fit several categories, which will illustrate the fact that boundaries separating categories of any system often are flexible.

Related questions that may lead students to explore the reasons behind their preferences include the following:

What characteristics did all the favored states have?

What factor was most influential in determining our number one choice?

What negative impressions caused you to avoid certain states?

Would adults have chosen states for the same reasons?

Was distance a factor in making some states more desirable?

Mature students may realize that economic factors such as job availability and the cost of living are important considerations. Professional investigators have found that people may rank as attractive their own state because they are most familiar with it or may list border states with warm climates or distinctive shapes as Texas, California, and Florida.

Identifying Ignorance.   A variation of the space preference map is the **ignorance surface map.** On blank outline maps students attempt to write in the names of all fifty states. Then, comparing their maps to a labeled one, they color the correctly named states red; states that are neighbors but have their names interchanged pink; and unknown states white. Youngsters look for patterns in their ignorance surface maps. Are there entire regions unknown? Are red sections mostly states neighboring their own? Are large white areas found distant from their own?

T An interesting follow-up is to select a distant state and hypothesize the ignorance surface map of young people living there.

Possible reasons for the resulting patterns can be projected. Where do students get information about other states? Do local newspapers, radio, and TV report much about distant states? What states have students visited? read about? talked about?

G Students learn how to tabulate data based on a number of instances.

Peter Gould and Rodney White in *Mental Maps* report that communication decays with distance; that is, messages and information decline with distance from the source. Students can refute or substantiate this statement through data collecting. Using newspapers brought to class, pairs of students tally the number of articles concerning other states by placing a check for each reference on the appropriate state on an outline map; they tally as well the number referring to their own state. (See Figure 13.7.) A more comprehensive approach is to save newspapers over a period of time so that when the tally is done, each pair of students has a paper for a different date. Summary tallies can be put on charting paper where each team enters its findings and totals are calculated.

Figure 13.7
A Tally Sheet

Newspaper Name _____

Number of items by state

	Home State	Neighbor State Name _____	Neighbor State Name _____	Neighbor State Name _____	Other _____	Other _____
Team 1						
Team 2						
Team 3						
Totals						

Students can be made aware of their own ignorance of vast parts of the world by constructing world ignorance maps. Students can compare their knowledge of countries of Europe to their knowledge of other countries located on different continents. Why can more children locate England, Israel, and Japan on a map than can locate Nigeria, Indonesia, and Colombia? Such examination can help youngsters recognize their own need for reliable information. Follow-up investigations of human activities, natural environments, and vocational opportunities in unknown states and countries can take advantage of heightened awareness of mental maps.

The Global View Investigation – Sitting on the Center of the World

North Americans often view other countries as somewhere over their horizons. Viewing a world map or globe, they see North America as the center of the world with Europe across the Atlantic to the east and Asia across the Pacific to the west. Is it harmful for students to perceive their own region as the center of a flat world? Perhaps not. However, young people must be aware of the distortions created by such an egocentric perception and of the fact that people in other places function with their own egocentric views of the world.

Viewing the World from Switzerland.   A simple way to widen students' perceptions is to gather a small group around a globe and to
turn it so that Europe is uppermost. The kind of globe that can be
removed from its cradle is best for this. Children select a country cen-
trally located, such as Switzerland, and mentally look at the world
from there, considering land and water trade routes, climate, population concentration, languages, topography, political boundaries, and
perhaps distances and travel times.

The easiest beginning is to think about the shape of land masses.
Looking eastward from Switzerland toward the USSR and then westward to Portugal, students see that much of Europe is a kind of irregular peninsula extending from the larger Eurasian landmass. Looking
northward across Germany and Denmark, they see Scandinavia jut-
ting down toward them. Looking southward they see the boot of Italy
and the fingers of Greece pointing across the Mediterranean Sea to
Africa and the Near East.

After this general orientation, the group can mentally construct a
"Swiss outlook" in terms of topography and trade routes, and then
sketch a world map with Switzerland at its hub.

1. The Lay of the Land.   If the classroom globe shows relief features,
it will be relatively easy for students to visualize the flatter lands
stretching from Brittany in northern France across Belgium and the
Netherlands, Germany, and Denmark into Poland. They follow and
trace the Loire, Seine, Rhine, Elbe, and Oder Rivers draining from the
mountains across the flatter topography into the Atlantic Ocean, North
Sea, or Baltic Sea.

2. Trade Routes.   Searching along the coastlines of the European
countries, investigators see the many large and small peninsulas jut-
ting into the Baltic, North, Mediterranean, and Adriatic Seas. They
take turns pointing out and identifying the straits, bays, rivers, and
estuaries that centuries ago provided navigation routes for the flow of
people, goods, and ideas. From Switzerland they peer down the African coast and the Atlantic, imagining what emotions and dreams the
early explorers experienced when they sailed westward from a Europe
that was to them the center of the world.

Viewing the World from Mt. Kilimanjaro.   The class can also view
the world from the top of Mt. Kilimanjaro, which is located near the
equator on the border between Kenya and Tanzania. It is the highest
point on the continent; from there students can look out over the landscape and vegetation of Africa and consider the climate. In their minds
they can imagine a journey downward from the summit, gradually
moving across the landscape toward the sea.

1. Landscape.   Looking off the African coast in a southeasterly direction, students see the island of Madagascar (Malagasy Republic). How does it look? In what way does its shape fit into the shape of the nearby eastern coast of Africa? Students may suggest that the land mass of Madagascar broke off the coast of Mozambique. Many geologists now think that this is what happened.

Westward from Kilimanjaro lies Africa's largest lake, Lake Victoria. Beyond are a curved row of long thin lakes: Malawi (Nyasa), Tanganyika, Albert, and Rudolf. All lie in deep valleys.

2. Vegetation and Climate.   A volunteer finds the Tropic of Cancer on the globe and traces with the fingers a band across Africa about seven degrees on both sides of the Tropic. This area gets fewer than twenty-five cm of rainfall a year and investigators can hypothesize the kind of vegetation found there. The teacher can point out that deserts are sometimes defined as areas receiving fewer than twenty-five cm of precipitation per year. Similarly, a student traces the Nile River northward through the Sudan and Egypt. Students hypothesize differences they would expect to find in human activity in the two areas. Using a population distribution map, they will discover that the population density in the river valley is several hundred times what it is elsewhere in the desert. They will begin to see the importance of water to humans.

Mini-Investigations: Branching Out into Related Areas

Investigations of space, time, and human activity can occur within a variety of contexts generally included in the elementary social studies. Perceptive teachers can help children uncover fundamental relationships as they investigate diverse geographical regions, routes of early explorations, community helpers and services, growth of nations, and social interactions. In these contexts children can begin to understand the influence of spatial location and travel time on human activity and the effect human activity has on the land itself. Human beings are affected by where they live; in turn they affect the land on which they dwell.

Below are a few ideas for inquiries that help children understand these effects.

1. Why and Where.   Children make maps of their state. Each map shows a different feature—rainfall, topography, rivers, rail lines, highways, population centers, industrial regions, or agricultural centers. Studying several maps projected on an overhead projector, students hypothesize why activities are located where they are.

2. More Why and Where. The same kind of inquiry with map comparisons can be made as children study regions, countries, or continents. Children consider why large centers of population developed where they did and why certain regions are primarily agricultural or industrial, and others are heavy in mining activity.

3. An Ideal Community. Students construct the design for a hypothetical town, placing services and trade centers in optimal locations and developing a rationale for the layout. Especially gifted students can go on to read about planned communities.

4. The Time's the Thing. Students studying the Westward Migration make a series of time maps of the United States, each map made to a time scale that gets progressively smaller as the covered wagon was replaced by the train, the car, and the plane.

T These activities are for use in primary grades. By making experience charts, young children talk about and record their direct observations about the space they occupy on earth. Children are, therefore, preparing for more complex study of geography and economics in upper grades.

5. Experience Charts. A list of where students go to buy basic commodities can be developed as an experience chart with very young children. If several charts are created over several days, a summary chart eventually can be developed with statements such as "Most of us buy our groceries at local shopping centers. We buy our clothing at bigger shopping centers."

6. Where We Work. In similar fashion young children make experience charts on which they record where their parents work. "Johnnie's mother works in San Mateo. Johnnie's father works in San Francisco. Martha's mother works in San Francisco." Later they generalize: "Most of our parents do not work in our community. Many work in San Francisco."

Spatial Location, Time, and Human Activity – A Summary Thought or Two

Concepts about the organization of human activity—its location in space and time—are at the heart of what might be called the new economic geography. Students handling these concepts will be going far beyond naming places and products to consider relationships and to hypothesize why the activities of the world are as they are. In investigating the new economic geography, today's young people will jump the artificial barriers separating the individual social studies disciplines to take into account economic, technological, and historic factors. In the process they will broaden the vocabulary they use to talk about structures and processes that relate to human activity.

A Problem to Ponder

In this chapter, you have seen numerous teaching tactics being applied to the study of relationships among human activity, spatial location, and time. These tactics are useful within other contexts as well. List on the left specific teaching tactics described in this chapter. Next to each, describe other contexts in which the tactic would be of value.

Tactic	Other Contexts
1. _____	_____
2. _____	_____
3. _____	_____
4. _____	_____
5. _____	_____

References

Abler, Ronald; Adams, John; and Gould, Peter. *Spatial Organization: The Geographer's View of the World.* Englewood Cliffs, New Jersey: Prentice-Hall, 1971.

Borchert, John; and Adams, Russell. *Trade Centers and Trade Areas of the Upper Midwest.* Urban Report Number 3. Minneapolis, Minnesota: Upper Midwest Economic Study, 1963.

Carter, Harold. *The Study of Urban Geography.* New York: John Wiley and Sons, 1976.

Dawson, John; and Doornkamp, John, eds. *Evaluating the Human Environment.* New York: St. Martin's Press, 1973.

Downs, Roger; and Stea, David. *Maps in Minds: Reflections on Cognitive Mapping.* New York: Harper & Row, 1977.

Gould, Peter; and White, Rodney. *Mental Maps.* New York: Penguin Books, 1974.

Morrill, Richard. *The Spatial Organization of Society.* Belmont, California: Wadsworth Publishing, 1970.

Thoman, Richard. *The Geography of Economic Activity.* New York: McGraw-Hill, 1968.

Wisniewski, Richard, ed. *Teaching About Life in the City: 42nd Yearbook of National Council for the Social Studies.* Arlington, Virginia: NCSS, 1972.

14 People on the Land: Population, Food, and Fiber

Diana's picture shows tribesmen of Kenya tending cattle.

There was an old woman
   who lived in a shoe;
She had so many
   children she didn't
   know what to do.
She gave them some
   broth without any
   bread;
She whipped them all
   soundly and put them
   to bed.

**Mother Goose,
   traditional rhyme**

Key Questions

How does a population distortion map differ from a conventional one?

Why are food, fiber, and population relationships significant issues today?

How can children be involved in enumerating, grouping, valuing, and research activities as they investigate foods they eat?

How can we involve children in making maps and graphs and in compiling information as part of investigations into world food production?

How can one use the study of fibers as a means of developing skills in making maps and graphs?

What kinds of activities are available for involving children in the study of population growth and movement?

What social science disciplines are being integrated through the study of food, fiber, and population relationships? What key concepts are being taught?

*economics   learn location
   geography   pop
      s.s.
   ecology*

**Figure 14.1
A Map for Today: The Fat Nations
and the Thin Nations**

The Fat Nations and The Thin Nations   Countries sized according to their populations

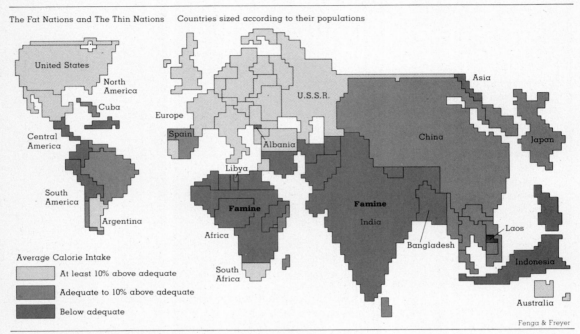

Adapted from Scholastic Magazines, Inc.

G
E
O
G
R
A
P
H
Y

E
C
O
N
O
M
I
C
S

D
E
M
O
G
R
A
P
H
Y

C
O
N
S
U
M
E
R

E
D
U
C
A
T
I
O
N

Introduction

Compare the map of fat and thin nations (Figure 14.1), which shows
countries sized according to their populations, to a conventional globe.
What has happened to the USSR landmass on the population distribution map? In contrast, what has happened to the space occupied by
countries such as China, Japan, Indonesia, and India? In a similar
way, study the changes in the sizes of European countries: England,
Italy, and Norway, for example. What is the population distribution
map telling the reader about the relative population densities of
countries?

Modern mapmakers supply the social scientist with numerous devices through which to express global relationships. One of the most visually exciting is the **distortion map,** in which the area of a region is sized in proportion to some factor other than land size and in which the shape of a country or continent approximates its actual shape. In the introductory map the factor is people; the map is built from small squares, each one representing a population of 200,000. These squares are assembled in the shapes of the countries of the world. Thus a country such as China occupies a much larger area on the population distribution map than on a conventional one, whereas a country such as the USSR is depicted as smaller.

A problem of mounting concern for the future is the unequal growth of populations in countries around the world. In some countries people are already crowded on the land, drawing on limited natural resources and food production. Dark shadows on the map emphasize the caloric differences. Often these countries must rely heavily on other countries to help meet basic food needs. In other instances, people are more spread out and have larger landmasses upon which to draw for basic needs. As population continues to increase disproportionately around the world, the problem will intensify, perhaps emerging as the most pressing issue to be faced in the years ahead. It is one that young people are facing today in social studies classes.

The introductory population map hints at the direction that school programs can take to make this issue relevant to young people. It depicts complex numerical relationships in a visual way understandable to young investigators, who can themselves build similar distortion maps with relative ease. Working in teams, youngsters cut hundreds of small squares (3 cm x 3 cm) of colored construction paper, with each square representing one million people. Now each team selects a different country, checks its population, counts out the number of squares necessary to represent the population of that country, and glues them into a shape approximating the shape of the country. If students have chosen a representative sample of countries, they can raise questions concerning social and geographic factors causing obvious differences. This task is simplified through reference to the population distribution maps students have devised. These maps make it easier for students to visualize large numbers and help them become aware of the relationships between people and the land.

In this chapter we will consider these relationships, focusing on activities through which students can deal with problems related to a mushrooming population, scarcity of food and natural resources, and an increasing interdependency among nations of the world.

R For a discussion of global education, see *Social Education*, Volume 38 (Nov./Dec. 1974), which focuses on this issue.

T Ask students to compare the sizes of Indonesia and Australia on a conventional map. Then compare them as they would appear on a population map.

Indonesia

Australia

New Zealand

Below adequate caloric intake

At least 10% above average in caloric intake

Is there any relationship between low caloric intake and high population density?

Demography and Agriculture - An International Concern

During the final centuries of the last ice age, glaciers melted to the approximate positions they occupy on the earth today, oceans filled to present levels, and humankind reached a population of about ten million—the present population of Mexico City. In the ten or twelve thousand years since, that population of ten million has grown to more than four billion. This dramatic rise did not come about in equal increments as the years passed by. It took perhaps two million years for the human population to reach the estimated ten million point attained at the end of the last ice age. Agriculture had not yet developed; food gathering and hunting could not sustain fast population growth. A high mortality rate existed as starvation, disease, and other calamities took their toll.

The development of agriculture about twelve thousand years ago triggered a spurt in population. By the beginning of the Christian era, as agriculture progressed from simple cultivation of wild crops to include domestication and improved yields, the world's population exceeded 250 million, reaching one billion by the beginning of the Industrial Revolution early in the nineteenth century. In not much more than one hundred years—by 1930—the world's population had doubled to two billion. During this time regional famines, plagues, and wars periodically slowed population growth, but never has there been a worldwide decrease in population.

Arriving in the 1980s, we find the world's population doubled again; we number a staggering four billion. This time, the world population doubled in fifty years. **Demographers,** those who study human population trends, predict that we will probably double again to reach a population of between seven and eight billion within the next twenty-five years. Therein today lies a problem of global proportions. Given the earth's limited resources, how will people stretch them to meet the needs of a population twice what it is now? This question leads to a value question: Is it wise to increase the population of the world so rapidly?

T A time line shows this growth.

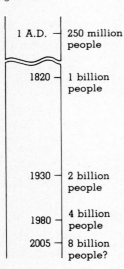

1 A.D.	250 million people
1820	1 billion people
1930	2 billion people
1980	4 billion people
2005	8 billion people?

Demographic Transition

A brief look at the past supplies some insights on this problem; we can see how closely agriculture, technology, and demographic changes are related. In the past, increased utilization of the world's grasslands combined with improved industrial and agricultural technology generally kept pace with the exploding population. Successive waves of emigrants moved from Europe to the sparsely populated Americas and to Australia and New Zealand. They and their descendants multiplied eightfold during the three centuries from 1650 to 1950. The great grasslands of the United States, Canada, Argentina, Australia, and New Zealand were farmed, producing cereal grains in such abundance that there was a surplus. Excess food could be sold or given away to those living in less productive and/or more crowded regions—given away not solely for altruistic reasons but to avoid huge storage costs and the price depressions resulting from surpluses on the market. During the same 300 years the population of the other countries of the world increased only threefold. In these countries high birthrates were counterbalanced by high death rates.

Decline in the death rate, particularly a decline in infant mortality, is a factor in the rapid population increases of Western nations. The number of deaths per 1000 people dropped significantly first as agricultural production increased, next as industrialization occurred, and then as health and medical technology improved. Simultaneously as the industrial-scientific revolution has progressed, Europe and North America have experienced a declining crude **birthrate,** or the number of births per 1000 persons. The decline, slow at first, gradually accelerated, particularly in more recent years. This decline in birthrate has diminished the rate at which the population is growing but has not stopped overall growth because of the parallel decline in the death rate.

The change in a population's birth and death rates that is associated with the process of industrialization and that over time slows the population growth is termed **demographic transition.** According to David M. Heer, this transition occurs in four stages as per capita income increases:

R David Heer, *Society and Population* (Englewood Cliffs, New Jersey: Prentice-Hall, 1968), p. 6.

First—High and irregular death rate; high birthrate; very slow rate of population growth

Second—Rapidly declining death rate; slowly declining birthrate; increasing rate of population growth

Third—Slowly declining death rate; rapidly declining birthrate; decreasing rate of population growth

Fourth—Very low stable death rate; low but fluctuating birthrate; slow to moderate rate of population growth.

Idea Page

Background information for the teacher. This activity shows how population concerns can be integrated into ongoing unit study.

The aim. Identifying reasons and relationships.

The introductory clues. Here is a time line of major events in the development and growth of the United States. Project it as a transparency.

1775   The beginning of the USA after war with England
1783   Settlement of the land just west of the Appalachians
1803   The Louisiana Purchase (from France)
1818   Agreement with Britain that the 49th parallel was the boundary between US and Canada
1819   Florida purchase (from Spain)
1845   Joining of Republic of Texas to the Union after defeat of Mexicans
1846   Oregon-Washington settlement
1848   California, Nevada, Utah, and Arizona taken from Mexico through war
1853   Gadsen Purchase of south Arizona (from Mexico)
1867   Alaskan Purchase (from Russia)
1898   Hawaii taken

The pursuit. (a class discussion). In what direction did the settling of the United States progress? Why did the settlers move in that direction? From where did all the people come to fill up the space? Why did they come? What do you think would have happened during the period from 1775 to 1875 if there had been no North American and Australian continents for people from Europe to occupy? What was happening to the world population during that time? **The continuation.** (a small group follow-up activity): Make a large outline map of the United States showing the boundaries of the individual states. Using an encyclopedia as reference, draw in each region indicated on the time line above and label it with the date when it became an official part of the United States.

More recently in the developing countries, transportation and communication have speeded the introduction of health and medical technologies so that improved care has occurred at a much earlier phase of industrialization than in the Western nations. As a result, death rates have dropped drastically while birthrates remain very high—critically modifying the second stage described by Heer. These high birthrates coupled with reduced infant mortality have raised the numbers of children so high that in more than half of the twenty most populous nations forty percent of the people are under age fifteen. This heavy population of children has a damaging effect on a nation's economy. First, a very large part of its resources must go to provide basic food, housing, health, and school services. Second, as the children reach childbearing years, the population has the potential to mushroom to still greater size.

Writing in *In the Human Interest*, Lester Brown points out that as infant mortality rates decline and life expectancy increases, birthrates will decline when people begin to realize that couples need not produce many children to have some survive to maturity. He finds that provision of health care is a prerequisite to this drop in birthrate. If improved health care is, however, to influence significantly a country's birthrate, health resources must reach beyond urban areas into the large populations found in rural areas. As the developing countries go into a stage of declining infant mortality, their populations are experiencing an interval of very high growth. The demographic transition has begun.

Many of the countries experiencing this problem are **have-not nations;** they have neither the land and agricultural productivity nor the economic base to provide food for a growing population. According to studies by the United States Department of Agriculture and the Food and Agriculture Organization of the United Nations, food production of the developing nations has risen over the last twenty years, but per capita food production has remained about the same. The population growth simply absorbs the increases. In contrast, the more developed industrial countries have seen a substantial rise in both total and per capita food production.

Food: Is There Enough for Everyone?

A corollary to population growth is the race against famine. We know that food production in both the developing countries and the industrialized nations rose at about the same rate between 1955 and 1975 and that this rate actually exceeded the annual growth rate of the world population. But because as much as eighty-six percent of this population growth is now occurring in the developing countries, it is little wonder that in these countries per capita food growth was less than 0.4% annually. Disruptions in food production resulting from natural disasters or from changes in governmental policies or other variables could quickly bring on food shortages and famine.

T Ask intermediate youngsters to hypothesize why today Americans live longer than those who lived several hundred years ago.

R Lester Brown, *In the Human Interest* (New York: Norton, 1974).

R The life of John Evelyn is a case in point. Evelyn had six children, none of whom survived him. Some children died in early infancy; some contracted smallpox. See *Diary of John Evelyn (1620-1706)* (London: Dent and Sons, 1907 or later editions).

Picture study can be used as children compare farming methods in different parts of the world; a natural question here is why do farming methods differ?

Increasing Agricultural Land and Agricultural Productivity.

One way to achieve greater food resources is to increase the land under cultivation; estimates by the USDA indicate that twice as much land is available in the world for crop production than is presently used. The problem here is that a very high percentage of arable Asian land is already in use; most available land is in the Amazon basin or West Africa where the cost of development would be tremendous.

A second approach is to increase the productivity of land presently tilled. To accomplish this requires not only water, seeds, fertilizer, pesticides, and herbicides, but also energy, incentives to farmers, and commitment by government. In this respect, the Chinese have made remarkable progress, producing enough food for 800 million people through massive efforts in land leveling, irrigation, and drainage; they have relied on heavy use of fertilizer combined with more than one crop per growing 'season. Yet the cost of agriculture is high; many nations simply do not have the necessary money.

Another tactic involves crop protection. Pests cause great losses in crops, livestock, and forests, attacking while plants and animals are growing, being transported, and being stored. Chemical pesticides remain a basic tool for controlling diseases, insects, and rodents—supplemented today with the development of disease-resistant plant varieties, of natural enemies that will attack the pests, and of improved storage practices.

R Read Norman Borlaug, "The World Food Problem–Present and Future," in *Shaping the Future,* John Roslansky, ed. (Amsterdam: North-Holland Publishing Co., 1972). Borlaug, a recipient of the Nobel Peace Prize, reminds us: "Each and every day when you eat whatever it is, you owe somebody in your society something. The food you consume daily is produced by the sweat of the brow of some person in some part of the world." Youngsters can identify the foods they have consumed so far on a school day and then identify those to whom they owe something in their society.

The Green Revolution: Natural Processes and Social Processes.

During the 1960s developmental research by Norman Borlaug and others resulted in the introduction of high-yielding strains of wheat into India and Mexico and of rice into the Philippines. By using the new strains Indian and Pakistani wheat crops were increased fifty percent; the Philippines turned from a rice importer to a rice exporter. This was called the **Green Revolution.** A relevant question for today is: Can this progress be sustained? High yields from new strains depend on high energy inputs in the form of fertilization, pesticides, and water pumping for irrigation. When farmers find fertilizer and pesticide costs impossible to pay or when government suppresses the market price of grain to keep urban living costs down, their incentive to innovate may disappear.

In *World Food Resources*, Georg Borgstrom states that grain provides humankind with two thirds of its calories and plant protein. Growing populations are forcing former grain exporting nations to become importers to provide people with calories and protein. To meet this need, Western farmers are supplying grain to many developing countries that are fast becoming dependent on that supply. Yet as populations continue to increase, existing surpluses become a less viable answer to the problem of feeding the world's hungry. Green revolutions provide some relief, but if populations continue to expand, neither sharing of surpluses nor green revolutions will suffice.

R See Georg Borgstrom, *World Food Resources* (New York: Intext, 1973), p. 12. This book includes many striking charts and graphs.

A Problem to Ponder

R From J. B. Hutchinson, *Population and Food Supply* (Cambridge: Cambridge University Press, 1969), p. 137.

J. B. Hutchinson states: "Agricultural production cannot be multiplied indefinitely. It is no more than common prudence to plan for the stabilization of human populations before the point is reached that food production can no longer keep pace with human multiplication and readjustment by catastrophe becomes inevitable."

What is Hutchinson trying to tell us? Do you agree or disagree with him? What facts do you have to support your point of view? What are the curriculum implications of his statement? What problems do you foresee today in introducing population concerns into school programs?

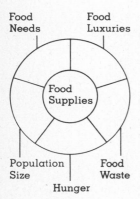

R See E. F. Schumacher, *Small Is Beautiful: Economics As If People Mattered* (New York: Harper & Row, 1973). This book sets forth the advantages of using small-scale technologies and muscle energy instead of large technologies and fossil fuels.

The Problem of People and Food Enters the Classroom

The relationships among food needs, food luxuries, food waste, hunger, and population size are ones that can be investigated starting early in elementary grades. This is a study in which concepts from economics, history, geography, and the natural sciences blend as young people consider the problem of limited resources and scarcity, the need for conservation, the need for modification of their own life-styles and desires, the changing nature of life on a crowded planet, and the interdependency of peoples.

Americans have been bred on a philosophy that bigger is better, a philosophy that has in the past been applied to everything from populations and cars to steak size and human consumption. Americans have been bred too on a throw-away philosophy; if you no longer need or want it, toss it away! More recently, people are realizing that small can be beautiful and that things thrown away in the past can be reused, sometimes with little effort. Through study of population-food-fiber relationships, young people can examine their own philosophy of consumption and may realize that their views and actions infringe upon others.

Investigating the Foods We Eat

Cassava and collards, mangoes and melons are common fruits and vegetables—but for whom? Investigation of the foods people eat leads students to an examination of their own preferences as contrasted to those of other people around the world and to an examination of the high production costs of some foods that are staples within their diets.

Enumerating. One way to introduce primary youngsters to the problems related to food consumption is through an identification exercise in which they enumerate the kinds of foods they eat every day. Children brainstorm and call out the names of foods; the teacher or students list each on the board.

Grouping. Young children enjoy talking informally about the foods they eat; they are eager to provide descriptions of taste, shape, color, and aroma. General discussion can flow into a classification activity in which students group the foods they have named into four or five categories. The teacher starts the process by focusing on one item such as orange juice; he or she circles it and queries, "What other food is like orange juice in that it comes from the same kind of plant?" Students will name items such as apples, grapefruits, and other fruits; as they do, they list the items in one column of a five-column chart. In like manner, children group cereals and grain products in a second column, vegetables in a third, meat in a fourth, and miscellaneous in a fifth.

This is the time to clarify labels through questions: What is a fruit? Are there some fruits that we eat that are sometimes mistakenly called vegetables? What are vegetables? What are some common grains? In this context, students check terms in the dictionary and encyclopedia. Older students can use information acquired to develop subcategories of fruits, vegetables, and meats as well as to distinguish among items listed as miscellaneous. The result will be a relatively complex category system, which can be set forth as a chart.

Once children have developed an understanding of the categories within their charts, they go on a Search and Decide Mission. Given names of less familiar foodstuffs not already enumerated—millet, sorghum, soybean, papaya, for example—teams or individuals race to find information and classify them. Before investigators start out, they should, of course, identify the kinds of facts they want to learn. Students and teacher develop categories of information: Description of Plant, Description of Edible Part, Climate Plant Needs, Food Importance, and Other Uses. Information researched is recorded directly on a guide like the one shown in Figure 14.2.

In the primary grades, a few liberties should be allowed in categorizing. The division of foods into vegetables, fruits, nuts, and so forth diverges from the botanical one. Youngsters may discover divergencies as they read in references to find additional items for charting. This discovery can help students understand that a series of items may be grouped in more than one way, depending on the categories chosen.

T Charts made by primary youngsters can be simple.

Fruits we eat	
apples	~~THH THH~~ I
grapefruits	~~THH~~ I
bananas	~~THH~~ III
peaches	~~THH~~ IIII

Meats we eat	
lamb chops	~~THH~~
bacon	III
hamburger	~~THH THH~~ ~~THH~~ II
hot dogs	~~THH THH~~

Vegetables we eat	
squash	~~THH~~ I
carrots	II
peas	~~THH THH~~ I
spinach	~~THH~~

T Use encyclopedia references such as:

World Book (Chicago: Field Enterprises) under "Fruits."

Golden Book (New York: Western Publishing Co.), sections under "Fruit," "Grasses," "Nuts," "Cereals," and "Vegetables."

Use specialty volumes too:

Francesco Bianchini, *Complete Book of Fruits and Vegetables* (American Heritage Publishing, 1976).

B. E. Nicholson, *Oxford Book of Food Plants* (Oxford University Press, 1969).

Figure 14.2
A Fact-Finding Guide

Plants Important to Us

Plant Name: *Papaya*
Probable Place of Origin: *Tropical America, probably Mexico and Costa Rica.*
Places Where it Now Grows: *Tropical places of world.*

Description of Plant—What It Looks Like and How It Grows: *A small green tree with big lobed leaves and long leaf stems. It lives 3 or 4 years.*
Description of Edible Part: *The fruits are green and turn orange when ripe. They are like orange melons with lots of seeds. They grow along the narrow tree trunk under the leaves.*
Climate Plant Needs: *The trees need lots of sun and warmth and protection from the wind. Frost kills them.*
Food Importance: *They are mostly eaten where they grow because papaya do not keep well. They are picked unripe for shipping*
Other Uses: *and contain a lot of Vitamin A.*
Papain, a meat tenderizer is made from it.

Investigating World Food Production

The activities described so far lay the groundwork for the study of food production across the earth's surface. This study is a productive context for refining young people's ability to make and interpret maps, graphs, and charts.

G Through this activity children refine their ability to work with map scale.

Mapping. Students who have completed fact-finding and writing guides for numerous food products can use the information to make large maps that display their data. This activity leads to heightened understanding of map scales, symbols, and legends. To begin, mapmakers trace the outlines of countries and continents cast by overhead or opaque projectors on large sheets of paper mounted on the bulletin board. Having made the transfer, students darken and refine borders and talk about the change in scale resulting from the blowup.

If the enlarged map of the world covers an entire board, the students can work together devising symbols for important fruits, vegetables, grains, and nuts, and then add them to the map, along with a legend.

Simultaneously, individuals or small groups can produce separate, smaller maps for each major food category, using the same symbol employed on the large version. Again students can compare the scale of the wall map with the smaller ones.

A diversity of symbols can be designed. Small pictures—a sheaf of wheat, a bag of rice, a bunch of bananas, or a coffeepot—can be drawn on the appropriate locations of the map. Where large areas are devoted to a crop, multiples of the picture designed to represent that crop can be drawn. Students can draw many of the small picture symbols on separate paper and paste them in the appropriate positions. Potato prints also can be used, with the appropriate symbol printed on the map. An attractive substitute for pictures is the repeated use of a word neatly printed across the map, filling in the appropriate geographic area:

rice rice rice rice rice rice
rice rice rice rice rice
rice rice rice
rice

As students prepare maps of this kind, they may want to add other features—mountains, deserts, cities, and so forth. Now is the time to help mapmakers realize that maps should not be cluttered with irrelevant features. As G. H. Gopsill reminds, "Each map is drawn for a specific purpose, which appears in the title; and. . .only that information which is relevant to this purpose should be shown upon it." At some point, therefore, student mapmakers should decide on a title for their map and limit the kinds of information plotted according to that title.

Deciding on the Most Important. As students research food production around the world, they will discover that some countries are key producers of certain food staples. Discovering such information, they can compile it in several different ways:

1. Sizing the label. On a world map, students print the names of the top five producers of a crop in large letters, the next five in medium-sized letters, and the next five in small letters, leaving all other countries unlabeled. On the same map, students print the names of the consuming nations using a different color. This is a simple group activity; each group produces a production-consumption map for a different food staple. The resulting maps provide content for contrasts and comparisons.

2. Putting countries together. Students who have identified the top producers of an important product make paper or cardboard cutouts of

T This strategy can be used as part of a study of regions of the world. Students learn how to handle map symbols in a meaningful context.

Bananas

Wheat

Citrus Fruit

R G. H. Gopsill, *Teaching of Geography* (London: Macmillan, 1958). This book supplies many interesting teaching suggestions.

the top three or five countries and print the name of each country across its cutout shape. Shapes are arranged as a collage and displayed on a bulletin board. For each group of countries, students select and print a clear label. Labeled country shapes can be colored and hung as mobiles. Suspended also are cards that depict symbolically the amount of key food staples produced and consumed.

3. Sizing countries in terms of crop production.   The population distribution map that opens this chapter suggests a way of handling crop production statistics. Students make a similar map showing relative production of specific food staples. It is probably too difficult and time-consuming to make a world map, but even middle graders can create cutouts of specific countries sized with regard to crop production.

According to the United States Department of Agriculture, the leading producers of wheat in 1975 (in millions of metric tons) were the USSR (65), the US (58.2), China (30.2), India (26), and Canada (17). Using these figures or more recent ones, young mapmakers make cutouts or drawings that show the five countries sized in proportion to their relative production. An easy way to do this is to project an outline map of the world on the wall and to trace the outline of the USSR. Then the projector is placed a bit closer to the wall, and the United States is drawn. To draw China, the distance between the projector and the wall is cut more; to draw India, the projector is moved in a bit closer, and so forth. This can be done for other food staples such as rice, where China is the main producer (80.2), then India (46), Indonesia (16.3), Bangladesh (12.3), and Japan (12). Students should compare the relative sizes of the countries in terms of rice production and then compare sizes on a political map.

4. Plotting symbols.   Younger children plot symbols for basic crops on outline maps that show the states and provinces of North America. Working from a list of food staples, children use references to discover where in North America these crops are produced. For each, they identify those three or four states and/or provinces leading in production and place the chosen symbol there.

Graphs.   Bar graph comparisons can lead to generalizations about production and consumption patterns. Working with major staples (for example, rice, wheat, corn, soybeans, sugar, and peanuts) and key countries (including the ones named above as well as Australia, Cuba, Vietnam, Thailand, Nigeria, and Brazil), students prepare three bars for each crop for each country. Arranged vertically or horizontally, one bar represents production, the second imports, and the third, exports. Of course, for some products there may be no imports or exports. Instead of solid-color bars, a row of symbols can be used, each symbol representing a million metric tons.

Investigating Consumption Patterns

Westerners today are among the highest consumers of food resources in the world. The average North American consumes about 3200 calories and ninety-three grams of protein per day, the European about 3100 calories and eighty-eight grams of protein. In contrast, the average Far Easterner consumes 2100 calories and fifty-six grams of protein per day.

Graphs. The significant differences in consumption patterns in countries of the world can be made striking by bar graphs. Georg Borgstrom presents numerous charts such as the one in Figure 14.3 that outlines information on animal-protein consumption (grams per person per day).

R From Georg Borgstrom, *World Food Resources* (New York: Intext Press, 1973), p. 195.

**Figure 14.3
A Chart That Can Be
Translated into a Bar Graph**

Country	Meat	Milk	Eggs	Fish	Total
China	5.3	0.3	0.9	1.4	7.9
India	0.6	4.3	0.1	0.6	6.6
Indonesia	1.5	—	0.3	3.4	5.2
Japan	6.1	3.7	4.4	15.5	29.7
United States	37.5	23.2	5.5	3.3	69.5

Upper graders can translate this type of chart into a bar graph in which measured lengths of colored paper represent different protein sources. These strips can be clipped to a line suspended across the room. Looking at their hanging graph, students can verbalize differences: that people in Indonesia and Japan consume animal protein mainly in the form of fish, whereas people in the United States and China use primarily meat sources; that people in the United States and Japan consume large amounts of animal protein in contrast to people in India and Indonesia.

Faced with visual evidence in graphs, young people generally want to know why. They can study the locations of countries relative to the seas in accounting for differences in meat and fish consumption. They can look at population size, population density, and wealth as factors that affect consumption.

Many books, encyclopedias, and almanacs include charts and graphs that show data systematically. This type of material is ideal for activities in which young people convert data found in charts into graphs and vice versa or in which they convert numerals into percentages. These charts and graphs can be made into transparencies that students can analyze together.

T Children in lower grades can make illustrated charts.

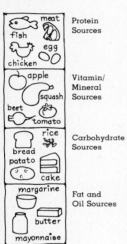

Collecting Data Through Observation.   Analysis of personal food consumption patterns provides young people with the opportunity to consider food groups important in the diets of people around the world. Using a chart, investigators record for a week or more the names and approximate amounts of foods consumed each day. Having compiled their data, they can group items into categories. Borgstrom supplies a helpful classification system: proteins for body building (dairy products, meat, fish, shellfish, beans, peas, and nuts); vitamin/mineral foods to maintain body processes (fruits, vegetables, and seaweed); carbohydrates for energy (bread, cereals, potatoes, and cassava); fats and oils for energy (lard, butter, margarine).

Such study can lead into sociological investigations. Young people compare the kinds of foods consumed at breakfast to those consumed at lunch and dinner; they compare their own patterns to their grandparents'; they look at the times when and the conditions under which they tend to eat. Students begin to consider why they do as they do. The result will be a listing of factors such as family tradition, national tradition, and ethnic tradition, as well as special factors such as availability and cost.

Valuing.   Data collection can lead also into valuing activity; youngsters look at their evidence and identify their favorite foods. Favorites are rank ordered—one through six—and analyzed in terms of the four food groups. Are favorites those high in calories? What problem could this trigger as students experience heavy growth spurts? What problem could this trigger as students get older and are less active? What other foods could we substitute for favorite ones high in calories?

Studies of favorite foods are open to analysis as to why certain items tend to be favorites. Students can listen carefully to commercials and critically read advertisements that urge them to buy and consume. A good beginning is to clip advertisements geared particularly for the youth market from newspapers and magazines and to record commercials on tape. Later students can identify the selling techniques being employed. There are a number of techniques in use. One is the use of glittering generalizations in which the advertiser implies that the product surpasses all others in all respects. A second is the testimonial in which a hero extols the virtues of the product. A third is the positive association in which the product is equated with success, acceptance,

T As part of social studies, youngsters should become wiser consumers. Read H. Wells Singleton "Consumer Economics Education—A Case Study Approach" in *The Social Studies*, 69:74-76 (March/April 1978).

and things young people want or like. A fourth is the bandwagon approach in which the suggestion is made that all those who are "in" use the product. A fifth, name-calling, tells of the horrors associated with competing products. Young investigators can identify all of these techniques through analysis of specific samples if the teacher guides thinking by asking appropriate questions. Once youngsters are familiar with some basic forms that propaganda can take, they can listen on television for further examples to share with classmates.

R See chapter 12, page 404, for an example of political propaganda.

Investigations into Fibers and Fiber Needs

Fibers for fabrics, mattresses, baskets; fibers for burlap, rope, and twine; fibers for paper and Panama hats! Plant, animal, and synthetic fibers are not as important to people as food, but their significance cannot be underestimated. In terms of international commerce they have tremendous importance; in terms of everyday use they are indispensible.

A study of fibers provides children with a concrete way of looking at limited resources as related to human consumption. It also helps them link common articles to sources, to wise use of the environment, and to human needs.

Enumeration and Classification. An impromptu classification of items made from fibers can serve as an introduction to the importance of fibers. The teacher can begin by collecting items and placing them on a display table. "Here is a ball of twine. It is made from a fiber. I also have a linen handkerchief made from another fiber. Who can add other items made from fibers to our display?" Students will quickly add things from around the room—things left visible for students to notice: a canvas sneaker, a piece of rope, a broom, a paintbrush, a woven basket, a sweater, a scrub brush, a piece of ribbon, and a stocking.

The game Animal/Vegetable/Mineral can be appropriate as a means of sorting fibers, modified slightly to include a fourth category—synthetics. Youngsters suggest to which category each item in the display belongs. Students check labels for clues as to the composition of items. The label for wool is a common one that youngsters should learn to recognize; labels such as Dacron, nylon, and polyester are ones that youngsters should recognize as synthetics.

T Young students can make category charts based on the kind of fiber contained in a garment.

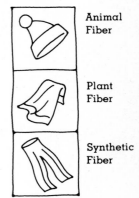

Animal Fiber

Plant Fiber

Synthetic Fiber

Gathering Relevant Data. Left with several unknowns, students can search for relevant information. During a brief visit to the library, youngsters gather essential information about fibers and practice separating relevant information from irrelevant. Each student is given one 3 x 5 card; on the card he or she records facts about one fiber chosen at random from a list that includes plant fibers such as flax, ramie, hemp, jute, kenaf, sunn, sisal, henequen, abaca, istle, Mauritius fiber, cotton, kapok, coir, piassava, palmetto, broomcorn, and papyrus; and animal fibers such as silk, wool, mohair, cashmere, camel hair, alpaca, and vicuna hair.

Search is limited to three considerations: 1) Tell what countries grow or raise the plant or animal. 2) Describe the plant or animal. 3) List several products made from the fibers. The advantage of using a small card is that youngsters are more likely to record relevant facts and to ignore unrelated ones. Clearly this is the time to refine skills in note taking and summarizing, as youngsters try to condense their thoughts to fit on small cards.

Clarifying Relationships on Charts. Back in the classroom, youngsters share the information gathered. They do not read their cards aloud; rather they speak from the cards as they describe their findings. Later a group of youngsters is chosen to gather all the cards and use them to compile a retrieval chart showing major plant fiber categories. A second group handles fibers from animals, compiling the results in a chart something like the one in Figure 14.4. Some teacher assistance may be needed in deciding on categories, but once these have been established, students continue on their own and will later share their charts with the total class.

G Students develop some skills of wise consumers; they learn to interpret fiber labels on items to be purchased.

Putting Pieces Together. Data-retrieval charts lead naturally into generalizations about interdependency. Students identify fibers originating close to home and those that must be imported. Relative costs of coats made from cotton, wool, cashmere, and vicuna can be determined by a trip to a shopping center; costs can be related to place of origin of the fibers. Comparative warmth of plant versus animal fibers can be analyzed and related to use.

Investigating Population Growth

R From a policy statement: "The Real Crisis Behind the 'Food Crisis,'" published October 30, 1975 in *The Wall Street Journal*.

An increase in food production must obviously parallel any increase in population if widespread hunger is to be avoided. As the Environmental Fund states, "It makes no difference whatever how much food the world produces, if it produces people faster."

Making Simple Calculations. Students who can handle simple subtraction can begin to get some feeling for how quickly population grows by computing **population increase.** An increase results when the number of births exceeds the number of deaths; for example, in the United States in 1978 there were fifteen births per 1000 population and nine deaths. This produced a population increase of six for every 1000 persons. For Mexico the birth and death rate figures were forty-one

Figure 14.4
A Chart of Fibers

Useful Animal Fibers

Fiber Name	Animal Origin	Country of Origin	Use
Silk	silk caterpillar	Japan, China USSR, India, Italy, Korea, Turkey	dresses, ties, scarfs, suits, and other clothing
Mohair	angora goats	USA, Turkey South Africa	worsted fabrics, knitting yarns, upholstery
Cashmere	cashmere goat	Tibet, China	coats, sweaters, skirts
Camel Hair	Bactrian 2-hump camel	Mongolia, China	coats, jackets
Alpaca	Alpaca	Ecuador, Peru, Boliva, in the Andes	coats and jackets
Vicuna	vicuna	Argentina in the Andes	coats and jackets

and seven, or an increase of thirty-four per 1000 persons. Egypt had an increase of twenty-six persons for every 1000 individuals. For India the difference between births and deaths per 1000 people was twenty-two.

This concept of population growth can be presented as a subtraction exercise; the class is given the birth and death numbers (per thousand) for a list of countries and must calculate how many more people for each thousand were added.

More mathematically talented youngsters can calculate the total number of persons added to a nation when they know the population increase; to do this, they apply the increase per 1000 to the entire population. For Egypt this would be [39.8 × (39-13) × (1000)] for a striking gain of 1,034,800 persons in one year. The chart in Figure 14.5 presents figures that students can handle in this way. It includes figures on growth rate as well, a concept that will be explained in the next section.

T
$$\text{Population increase per 1000 population} =$$

$$\text{Births per 1000 population} - \text{Deaths per 1000 population}$$

G Students apply their growing mathematical skills to a social problem.

Figure 14.5
1978 Population Figures

1978 Population Figures

	Population Figures in Millions	Birthrate Per 1000	Death Rate Per 1000	Growth Rate Percent
World	4365.3	32	12	2.0
Egypt	39.8	39	13	2.6
Nigeria	80.7	49	22	2.7
India	656.5	37	15	2.2
US	224.2	15	9	1.6
Mexico	65.8	41	7	3.4
Ireland	3.2	22	11	1.1
Italy	56.7	14	10	0.4
USSR	261.2	18	9	0.9

Figures supplied by The Environmental Fund, 1978

Hypothesizing Possible Relationships. Tables such as the one above are open to analysis of possible relationships. For example, youngsters can consider why the death rate per 1000 people is so much lower in the US, Mexico, Italy, and the USSR than in Nigeria, India, and Egypt. Students hypothesize reasons such as diet, medical facilities, and sanitation. Students go on to consider what the impact on population would be if the death rates in countries such as India were brought down to that in other countries shown in the table. In similar fashion students contrast birthrates and try to account for the differences they note.

T Daily consumption of calories per person in the world = 2500 calories.

Mathematically talented students can go on to calculate the additional calories needed each day just to handle the increased population in the countries given. It is at this point that youngsters should begin to hypothesize possible solutions—ways to provide food for an increasing population. Students will point to increased production through new strains, improved pest control, better irrigation, and so forth. Others will suggest bringing new areas into cultivation. Points suggested can become areas for individual investigation.

G This activity provides a meaningful context for sixth graders who are learning to calculate percent to apply their developing skills.

Working with Percent. The concepts of growth rate and doubling time are important in any study of populations. We often hear that the growth rate of a country is 2.5 or 1.3. To the uninformed, these numbers seem low. What do they actually imply about the added number of people in the world each year? Mathematically talented students can calculate growth rate if given figures relative to the actual gain in population.

In formula terms, **growth rate** is as follows:

$$\frac{\text{gain in population}}{\text{population}} \times 100 = \text{growth rate in percent}$$

Applying this formula to Nigeria, we can take the gain in population (49–22) and divide it by the population experiencing this gain (1000 people):

$$\frac{49-22}{1000} \times 100 = 2.7\%$$

Given a total population of 80.7 million, the growth rate means an actual increase of 2.18 million in a year.

Working with the birth and death rates provided in the chart, students can calculate the growth rate in percent and add it to the chart, as shown. They can then go on to figure out what the percent means in terms of the number of additional people joining the population.

Identifying Related Factors. Students who have manipulated birth and death rate figures will be ready to identify other factors that also cause changes in the populations of nations. Asked, "Besides changes in the birthrate and the death rate, what could cause an increase in a nation's population? What could cause a decrease?"

Students must consider the effects of immigration and emigration on the growth rate of a nation. In so doing, they may wish also to consider why nations faced with their own rising populations put a prohibition on immigration. A concluding question that tests young people's understanding of growth rate is "How do immigration and emigration affect the growth rate in the entire world?"

Interpreting Numbers. Doubling time–the length of time to double a population (assuming its annual growth rate were to remain constant)–gives one an estimate of future population growth or a measure of historical growth. Mathematicians give the social investigator an easy formula for computing doubling time, which if applied makes a striking point about population:

$$\text{Doubling Time} = \frac{0.693}{\text{growth rate in percent}}$$

T The number 0.693 has been determined by statisticians and is accepted as part of the given data.

A rough approximation of doubling time is found by dividing 70 (.693 rounded off and multiplied by 100) by the growth rate number:

$$\text{Doubling Time} = \frac{70}{\text{growth rate number}}$$

For example, in 1978 Ecuador had an estimated growth rate of 3%.

$$\text{Doubling Time} = \frac{70}{3} = 23 \text{ years}$$

This means that Ecuador's 1978 population of seven and one half million will be fifteen million by 2001, if the growth rate remains constant.

Materials to Study

Most up-to-date social studies series include population studies at some level. Here is a pictograph from the futures-oriented Silver Burdett Social Studies third-level book, *People and Resources* (Morristown, New Jersey, 1979), that handles population problems as they relate to available resources and services. How could you use this kind of graphic display in your classroom?

Figure 14.6
A Sample Pictograph

The Number of People Added to Mexico City Each Day

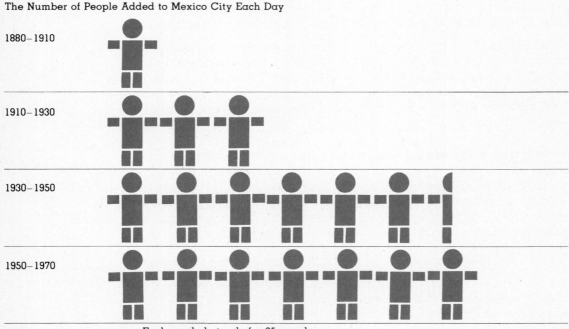

Each symbol stands for 25 people

To comprehend the significance of such massive increases, students can begin by computing their own ages in the year 2001. Looking into their own future, they can contemplate what impact a doubling of the population of their own community would have. What additional services would have to be provided? How many new schools would be needed? Working from this last question, students can create a change chart on the order of the one shown in chapter 2. On their chart they note changes they predict—changes that might include the construction of twice as many classrooms, the purchase of more school buses, the improvement of roads over which the buses travel, the hiring of more teachers, the training of more teachers by the universities, the purchase of more books, and the increase of companies that manufacture books. How will the people pay for all these changes? Students can also consider the impact on hospital facilities, shopping centers, fire and police services, and the community library. Identifying all the changes necessary in one local area helps students comprehend the immensity of the problem facing the world if population increases at its current rate.

Of course, the student of population growth must be aware that projected doubling times are crude approximations that are affected by a number of variables. Students can hypothesize events that could radically slow down or speed up growth. Brainstorming together, they can identify disease, famine, war, health and medical advances, changes in per capita income, and changes in family size as factors that may well alter the doubling time of the world's population.

Mini-Investigations: Branching Out into Related Areas

Work with food, fiber, and population relationships can occur in many contexts. Here are a few ideas for incorporating these fundamental relationships into the social studies program.

1. Empty Pots of the Past.   A series of stories such as "The Talking Pot" (in *Anthology of Children's Literature*, Edna Johnson, Evelyn Sickels, Frances Sayers, and Carolyn Horovitz, Boston: Houghton Mifflin, 1977), *The Magic Cooking Pot* (Faith Towle, Boston: Houghton Mifflin, 1975), and *The Magic Porridge Pot* (Paul Galdone, New York: Seabury Press, 1976) and rhymes such as "The Old Lady Who Lived in the Shoe" and "Old Mother Hubbard" can be part of a meaningful listening experience. Youngsters listen to figure out in what way all the stories are similar. They identify the common feature. (Each deals with the lack of sufficient food.) Listeners go on to consider why this theme has been such a popular one in folk literature of countries around the world.

2. A Population Mushroom. Most encyclopedias supply world population figures starting many thousands of years ago. This information can be plotted as a time line in which time and population cards are suspended from the ceiling with string, with time intervals accurately spaced out across the room. The fact that population has mushroomed in the last 100 years is made striking by the time line on which smaller population number cards (1 million, 2 million, 3 million) are spaced out at one end and larger ones are jammed together at the opposite end. Older students can suspend cards containing relevant historical events such as the Industrial Revolution that had an effect on population increase. The time line can be labeled "A Population Mushroom," and students can think about why the word *mushroom* is appropriate in this context.

3. Moving Around. Students can map significant migrations of people in the past by drawing arrows of different colors on a world map. Arrows extend from where the migrants started to where they went and are labeled with the appropriate time period and the approximate number of individuals involved. Students can brainstorm reasons for migrations, producing as lengthy a list as possible. Next to each item on the list, students place colored dots, matching specific reasons with specific migrations shown in color on their maps. Obviously there will be several dots next to each reason, for a number of migrations occurred for similar reasons.

4. Right at Home. Students can graph population changes during the last fifty years in their own state as well as in several other states. States such as California, Alaska, and Maine are productive ones to use for contrast. Students go on to study resulting graphs and consider why these changes have occurred.

5. Comparing Populations. Interesting conclusions can emerge from a study of graphs that show the number of men and women in different countries who are within different age groups. Studying a series such as that in Figure 14.7, students can begin by comparing the number of men and women who survive to specific age levels; the number of people being born today with those at higher age levels; and the relative percentage of people in each age level in each country. They can go on to hypothesize the impact if recent trends continue into the future. Gifted children can create similar graphs for other countries by working with numerical information supplied by population charts.

6. Stacking Us Up. Students can create original age group profiles for their own community. They start by obtaining the number of students in each age or grade group in their school district. After planning the scale to be used (e.g., 1 cm = 50 students), they cut bars for each age group from construction paper and tack one above another on a bulletin board. The result is a student population profile. Examining the profile, students decide if their graphic profile shows a shrinking school population or growth. They can offer possible explanations for changes they perceive.

Figure 14.7
Age Group Profiles –
A Way to Study Population Trends

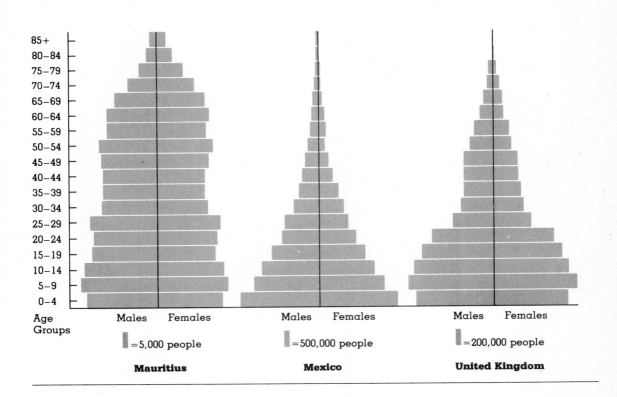

Food, Fiber, and People – A Summary Thought or Two

Scarcity versus personal preferences and desires! Limited resources versus unlimited desires! Mushrooming population versus limited usable croplands! These are conflicts facing the world today that give every indication of heightening in years to come. Some of the concepts—such as doubling rate and growth rate—inherent in these conflicts are rather sophisticated. Work with these must, therefore, wait until upper elementary grades. On the other hand, some aspects are open to investigation starting in earlier grades. Very young children can be asked to voice their preferences for foods, selecting from among all preferences the one or two they like most. Recorded in the form of experience charts, preferences become the content of discussion as children talk of what makes a wise choice when one must select from among desires.

Third and fourth graders can do much more, refining their developing graph and chart interpretation skills by working with data that relate to problems of food production and human consumption. At this stage children can become more aware of the needs of others who exist with far less than they do. Upper graders can go on to make judgments on issues, to predict future trends, and to hypothesize possible solutions. In this respect, study of the relationship between food and people is developmental; youngsters encounter aspects of the conflict between limited resources and unlimited desires within different units of study at each grade level. The result can be increased comprehension of the complex interrelationships among resources and populations and some understanding of what these relationships presage for the future.

A Problem to Ponder

In this chapter you have read about a number of different instructional strategies. Many of them can be applied in a variety of instructional contexts in addition to the one in which it was described. In the space below, list the strategies and indicate other contexts in which the strategy could be applied. One example is given to help you begin to ponder.

The Strategies

Possible Contexts

Strategy *Making a collage of countries that share a property*

study of language groups of democratic countries, of countries with plentiful coal reserves

Strategy _____

_____

Strategy _____

_____

Strategy _____

_____

References

Borgstrom, Georg. *World Food Resources*. New York: Intext Press, 1973.

Brown, Lester. *Increasing World Food Output: Problems and Prospects*. Washington, D.C.: U.S. Department of Agriculture, 1965.

Brown, Lester. *In the Human Interest*. New York: W. W. Norton & Co., 1974.

Czarra, Fred, ed. "Directory of Resources: Global/International Education." The *Social Studies 70*, September/October, 1979: 195-238.

Dalrymple, Dana. *Measuring the Green Revolution: The Impact of Research on Wheat and Rice Production*. Washington, D.C.: U.S. Department of Agriculture, 1975.

Eckholm, Erik. *Losing Ground: Environmental Stress and World Food Prospects*. New York: W. W. Norton & Co., 1976.

Emmel, Thomas. *An Introduction to Ecology and Population Biology*. New York: W. W. Norton & Co., 1973.

Handbook of Agricultural Charts. Agricultural Handbook No. 504. Washington, D.C.: U.S. Department of Agriculture, 1976.

Quick, Horace. *Population Ecology*. Indianapolis: Pegasus, 1974.

Toward the New: A Report on Better Foods and Nutrition for Agricultural Research. Agricultural Information Bulletin No. 341. Washington, D.C.: U.S. Department of Agriculture, 1972.

Walron, Ingrid; and Ricklefs, Robert. *Environment and Population: Problems and Solutions*. New York: Holt, Rinehart & Winston, 1973.

World Population Dilemma. Washington, D.C.: Population Reference Bureau, Inc., 1972.

World Population Estimates. Washington, D.C.: Environmental Fund, new edition yearly.

15 People Using Resources: Energy, Pollution, and the Environment

wooddu

Through a unit on environmental problems, children are becoming more aware of the effects human beings have on animals.

We declare that all aspects of environmental problems are the joint responsibility of all of us: developing the motivation to cope, gathering and interrelating pertinent information, making value judgments about action to be taken, and implementing the decisions.

A statement signed February 1975 by the editors of *The Science Teacher, Social Education, Chemistry/ Man /Society /Technology, The Physics Teacher, Art Education, and American Biology Teacher*

Key Questions

What is an ecosystem? What part does the sun play in ecosystems?

What stresses have human beings brought to bear on their environment? Why do humans use their environment in this way?

What kinds of solutions to environmental problems does humankind have available? Which solutions provide today's best hope for the future?

What are the goals of environmental study? Why is an integrated approach essential?

Describe how you could use these strategies: firsthand observation of local pollution and energy problems; social action activity; study of current events; reading and listening to stories; compiling data retrieval charts; cost studies; role-playing; simulations; behavior contracts; brainstorming.

What impact do I have on the environment? Do I respect the environment? Do I understand my own role as citizen aboard "spaceship earth"?

Figure 15.1
An Ecosystem Flowchart

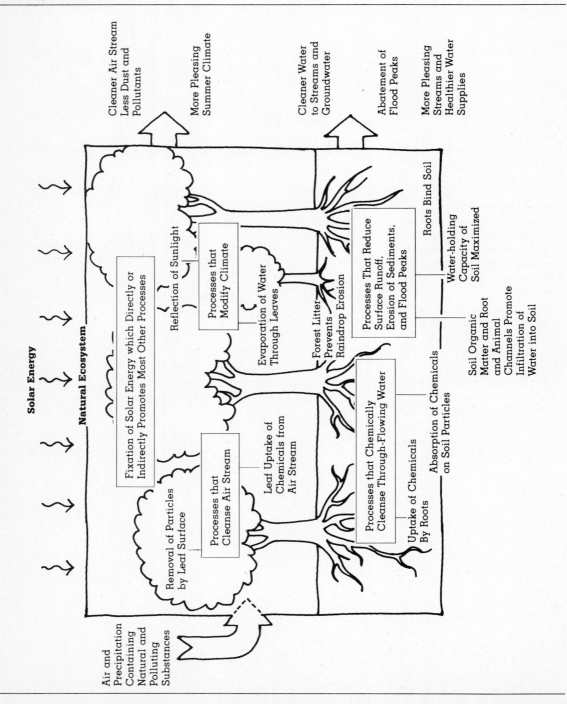

Introduction

Our early ancestors–many times fewer in number than we are today–scratched the earth, cut vegetation, and left refuse and organic wastes. Nature absorbed the disturbances and quickly healed the scars. Since these early human beginnings, growth in population, technology, and organizational power have drastically increased humankind's intervention in and disruption of nature's ecosystems.

Ecosystems are the functional units in nature. An **ecosystem** includes all the organisms of an area together with their physical environment, each interacting with the others and with the environment in an interdependent way and each operationally inseparable from the whole. Energy flows through the ecosystem from organism to organism in a complex of food chains. Energy is constantly being lost from all organisms and from all physiological and chemical processes to be dissipated; the energy flows through the system one way and cannot be recycled. Happily, for us, new energy constantly arrives from the sun and is captured by green plants to replenish the vital flow of energy through the system. However, to the extent that we destroy any ecosystem, it is less capable of carrying out its biological, geological, and chemical processes. It is less able to replenish depleted energy resources.

Linking ecosystem dynamics to human needs, the noted conservationist Paul B. Sears has written: "So far as the basic physiological resources–air, water, soil (i.e., food)–are concerned, the most serious effect of human activity has been to disrupt the great natural cycles that regulate their quality and abundance."

CONSERVATION AND ECONOMICS

POLITICAL SCIENCE AND LAW

R See Paul B. Sears, "The Earth's Natural Resources," in Huey Johnson, *No Deposit–No Return*. (Reading, Massachusetts: Addison-Wesley, 1970, p. 12).

Aboard Spaceship Earth – A Global Problem

The fact that human beings have a disruptive effect on natural systems was evidenced during the oil shortages of 1973-1974 and of 1979. Faced with higher prices and lines at service stations, people began to realize–perhaps for the first time–that they could not endlessly drain resources from the system and indefinitely dump wastes into it. Some began to realize that good citizenship requires more than pressing a lever on Election Day, good consumership more than getting the best price. We might have to change traditional ways of interacting with the environment.

The Energy Problem

The shock of OPEC's 1973-1974 oil embargo and the accompanying price rises sparked a search for new oil reserves and led to increased

R Read Lester Brown, *The Global Prospect: New Sources of Economic Stress* (Washington, D.C.: Worldwatch Institute, 1978) for a discussion of the global economic adjustments countries must make to the earth's natural capacities and resources.

coal prices as demand for coal rose. The price rises have given new impetus to the development of solar energy technologies.

Environmental Stresses.   In contrast, however, little attempt has been made to conserve; the world demand for energy rises each year despite price escalation and shortages. These demands are placing ever greater stresses on the environment. A few examples follow:

1. In Appalachia strip miners have removed trees and other vegetation from slopes and have dumped the rock covering the coal seams down these slopes. The result has been not only ugly scars on the landscape but also erosion, which has produced silted streams polluted with acid from coal residues.

2. Fossil fuels, burned in vehicles and power plants, produce fumes that can cause injury to human respiratory systems and to flora. Exhaust gases released into the atmosphere have as yet undetermined effects on the gas balance of the air and on the climate. With dwindling supplies of fuels low in sulfur, there has been pressure to use coal high in sulfur that results in even greater pollution of the air.

3. As we have increased the number of offshore drilling operations and have carried more oil around the world via tankers, oil spills have soaked beaches and covered mollusks and birds with oil. Ecosystems affected by these spills include the nurseries for many fish species and the feeding grounds of migratory birds; these systems may require long recovery periods following oil damage.

4. Although nuclear reactors can produce power without release of sulfur gases and particulate matter, many people oppose the use of nuclear power. As the Three Mile Island incident demonstrates, the hazard of leakage of radioactive gas exists. Also, as more nuclear reactors are built, the problems of disposal of radioactive wastes increase. Seepage from storage tanks and other disposal sites can occur.

T Clearly there is more to this popular bumper sticker than at first meets the eye.

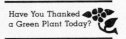
Have You Thanked a Green Plant Today?

Have children explain the significance of the saying.

Looking to the Sun.   Environmental stresses of the types just described have their origins in reliance on fossil fuels as sources of energy. In contrast, as the flowchart introducing the chapter shows, solar energy powers the natural system. Green plants harness solar energy through photosynthesis. They cleanse the air by removing particles and chemicals from it. Plants modify the climate through the evaporation of water from leaf surfaces and by reflecting sunlight and they chemically clean ground water that comes in contact with roots. Plants also reduce surface runoff, erosion of soil, and flooding. The result is an environment with little erosion, clear streams, a stable climate, clean air, and natural recycling of minerals and organic matter.

Since humans have interfered with these fundamental natural processes, we have had—in ecologist F. H. Borman's words—to "find replacements for wood products, build erosion control works, enlarge reservoirs, upgrade air pollution control technology, install flood control works, improve water purification plants, increase air conditioning, and provide new recreational facilities. These substitutes represent an enormous tax burden, a drain on the world's supply of natural resources, and increased stress on the natural system that remains."

Faced with these economic and natural problems, people today are looking to the sun. There is hope that eventually solar technology will provide a clean power to use for some heating and hot water needs. Indeed, some forecasters see direct solar electric power at reasonable cost in several decades. But such technology is still uncertain. During the intervening years, we must examine our energy demands, our sources of supply, and the stresses we bring to the environment. We must weigh benefits in terms of both economic and environmental costs, and in the end we must make value judgments.

R F. H. Borman, "An Inseparable Linkage: Conservation of Natural Ecosystems and the Conversation of Fossil Energy," in *BioScience*, 26:754-60 (December 1976).

More Problems Aboard the Spaceship

Even if we were to get our energy problems under control, other problems would still exist.

1. Urban sprawl has intensified the filling in of wetlands for home and industrial sites and the paving of farmlands for shopping centers and apartment complexes. Many trees have been cut, and sewage and other wastes have been dumped offshore and into landfills and rivers.
2. Highway construction has meant cutting through grasslands, marshes, pine groves, and deciduous forests.
3. Industrial processes introduce particles into the air, and concern grows as to the adverse health effects brought on by these particles.
4. Pesticides used to increase world food production have introduced foreign chemicals into the environment—chemicals dangerous to humans as well as to rodents and insects. Too, killing off one species in a food chain ultimately affects those at other levels.
5. Noise levels from machines, cars, buses, airplanes, motorcycles, trucks, and even transistor radios continue to annoy. How much noise can a body absorb before damage occurs? This is an unanswered question.
6. Plastic containers, bottles, and wrappers! Yes, we litter the land with the symbols of our civilization. A leaf falls to the ground; within months it becomes part of the soil, ready to support new life. In contrast, many synthetic materials are almost indestructable through natural processes.

The study of sources of energy should make children aware of ways we can become less dependent on fossil fuels (Solar home in Malibu, California).

Perhaps the reason we continue to put more stress on our environment is that it is difficult to assess the indirect benefits of a clean environment. We cannot assess the economic advantages of a cleaner environment. How is aesthetic enjoyment measured? What is the value of improved health in the twenty-first century?

In Search of Solutions

Problems related to misuse of the natural environment abound. In what directions should we look to find solutions?

The Scapegoat Solution.   There are those who, seeing the damage done to the environment, find applied science and technology convenient scapegoats. For social studies teachers to teach this negative view of science is to fail to realize how important science has been in making possible civilization as we know it. Stop to consider for just one moment the importance of some of the technologies that we take for granted: the printing press, vaccines, safe anesthetics, less hazardous travel, and improved strains of basic foodstuffs. We must teach children to respect science as we teach them to respect other human endeavors.

T Another scapegoat is big business. Most of us fail to realize that big business is giving us things we want: jobs, products for the good life, electricity. Be careful not to let children pass the blame.

Others have become so disenchanted with human systems that they have taken themselves out of the mainstream of society and attempted to return to what they conceive of as a simpler, better, more pristine way of life—as they imagine life was a few hundred years ago. It is doubtful, however, that any of us would care to walk the sewage-filled streets of the cities of the 1600s or 1700s or breathe their foul air. Through the words of Jonathan Swift, we see the filth of old London:

NOW from all Parts the swelling Kennels flow,
And bear their Trophies with them as they go:
Filth of all Hues and Odours seem to tell
What Street they sail'd from, by their Sight and Smell....
Sweepings from Butchers Stalls, Dung, Guts, and Blood,
Drown'd Puppies, stinking Sprats, all drench'd in Mud,
Dead Cats and Turnip-Tops come tumbling down the Flood.

R From Jonathan Swift, "A City Shower," 1710.

In London of Swift's day, a heavy rain was necessary to wash human wastes through the streets into the rivers. The technology of sewer pipes was developed in the 1840s and then merely to carry the wastes to the river or an open area on the city outskirts. The whole process of sewage purification was still to come.

Regarding air pollution, during the London winter of 1684 John Evelyn wrote:

London, by reason of the excessive coldness of the air hindering the ascent of the smoke, was so filled with the fuliginous steam of the sea-coal, that hardly could one see across the streets, and this filling the lungs with its gross particles, exceedingly obstructed the breast, so as one could scarcely breathe.

R From John Evelyn, *The Diary of John Evelyn*, ed. by E. S. DeBeer (Oxford, England: Oxford University Press, 1959).

Is the solution to throw away the fruits of science and return to an earlier day?

The "Technology Will Save Us" Solution.

It is a curious paradox that while in neo-Luddite fashion some people would be pleased to dismantle our technological achievements, others are not concerned about pollution and energy problems because they believe that a "technological fix" will always be found to make up for misuse of another technological contribution. According to this point of view, we will wake up one day to a miracle; the problem will be gone through the magic of new devices. Can we build the survival of future civilizations on dreams of a miracle?

T In 1811-1816, English workers rioted and broke up labor-saving machinery. People taking part were called Luddites after an earlier worker, Ned Ludd, who broke up stocking frames in Leicestershire.

Individual Responsibility – A Solution to Consider

Instead of looking on technology as either a scapegoat or a panacea or instead of pinning all the blame on big business, we need to look at the relationship between misuse of technological advances and our own personal value systems. Often it is in search of the good life for each of us that we do irreparable damage to the environment.

The Good Life and Conflicting Values.   If asked to list some of the things that translate into the good life, most of us would include items such as job satisfaction, a sense of security, and spendable income. To a large extent, these three elements are cut from the same cloth. They move us from an anxious day-to-day struggle to a calmer state of being. In one sense, these are reasonable desires, but in our industrialized society this desire for affluence has led us to demand comfort and convenience in many forms—air conditioning, fast cars, abundant hot water, throw-aways, electric gadgets, and convenience foods, to name just a few.

What is required to produce these things is generally not even considered. Take, for instance, what is required to produce that box of Chinese vegetables we pick from the supermarket freezer. 1) The vegetables were first machine-cleaned, chopped, and mixed with other ingredients. 2) The vegetables were precooked, sealed in a plastic bag, packaged in a colorful box, and frozen. 3) The box—along with others—was stored in a freezer. 4) The box was eventually transported in a refrigerated truck to the supermarket freezer. Contrast these steps with home preparation. Vegetables are washed and minced by hand, quickly heated, and served. No plastic (made from petroleum) is needed, no cardboard box (made from trees) is consumed, and no freezing (using energy sources) is required. But this method is not convenient.

This tale is neither a plea nor rationale for the abandonment of frozen foods, but rather an example to point out how voracious in energy use a convenience can be. As we make consumer choices, are we aware of all the implications? Have we weighed all the options? Today wise consumership is part of good citizenship, and good citizenship has always been a prime objective of social studies programs.

Within this educational context, the development of values clearly becomes a top priority. As Allen V. Kneese, economist and director of Resources for the Future, Inc., concludes, "Optimum rules, standards, or other techniques for controlling environmental quality must result from analysis of values, contrary to the usual approach which is still narrowly focused on physical effects and objectives." That people must reassess their traditional values associated with production, consumption, waste, and the environment is highlighted by a useful metaphor devised by economist Kenneth Boulding. Boulding views the earth as "a single spaceship, without unlimited reservoirs of anything, either for extraction or for pollution." On **spaceship earth** people must fit themselves within a cyclic ecological system, which is capable of continuous reproduction of material. This is a closed system without new

R See Allen Kneese, "Research Goals and Progress Toward Them," in Henry Jarrett's *Environmental Quality: Essays from the Sixth Resources for the Future Forum* (Baltimore, Maryland: John Hopkins Press for Resources for the Future, Inc., 1966).

frontiers and spaces into which people can expand and from which people can draw resources. The days of a "cowboy" economy, associated with "reckless, exploitative, romantic, and violent behavior," are part of the past.

In general, people have tended to discount the future, expecting that future problems will be taken care of by the people living then. We have tended to ask: "Why should we not maximize the welfare of this generation at the cost of posterity? Why should we not go out and pollute something cheerfully?" But futurist Boulding reminds us that an individual's welfare depends on the extent to which he or she identifies with others; "the most satisfactory individual identity is that which identifies not only with a community in space but also with a community extending over time from the past into the future." If we can help children develop this kind of identity, then we have given them a base for making sound value judgments today and tomorrow.

R Read Kenneth Boulding, "The Economics of the Coming Spaceship Earth," in Jarrett (1966), pp. 3-14. A striking article that all citizens should read.

A Problem to Ponder

The concept of spaceship earth is one that is useful in the elementary classroom as the basis for thinking about those needs that must be met for people to survive. Ask children: "Imagine earth as an immense spaceship flying through the universe. You are aboard. What things must you have aboard if you are to survive? These will be your inputs into your spaceship system. About what outputs must you be concerned?"
1. Design a chart for recording system inputs and outputs.
2. Devise an art activity through which children would be forced to think about aesthetic requirements aboard spaceship earth.

Investigating Human Impact on Ecosystems

During the 1973-1974 oil embargo and shortage, speed limits in the United States were reduced to fifty-five mph because vehicles traveling at that speed consume less gasoline per mile than at higher speeds. To keep consumption down, legal speed limits today remain at fifty-five mph. Yet even a brief ride along an interstate highway provides overwhelming proof of people's general lack of willingness to change their behavior patterns. Do people understand their dependency on limited resources of fossil fuels?

The Goals of Environmental Study

Increased knowledge and understanding of fundamental ecological relationships are surely of high priority if we are to live in balance with our environment. At some point elementary students must learn about ecosystems, food chains, food webs, photosynthesis, transpiration, weathering, erosion, sedimentation, and climate. These aspects of ecology, geology, and meteorology can be handled within interdisciplinary units that draw content from the natural sciences and simultaneously develop social responsibility and understandings. Study must be extended to get at basic values and beliefs. Programs must lead to:

1. Recognition of human beings as members of complex and interrelated ecosystems
2. Awareness of negative effects created by some patterns of human behavior
3. Recognition of human dependency on limited reserves of fossil fuel for maintenance of the good life
4. Respectful use of the environment so damage to natural systems is minimized
5. Ability to make wise value judgments in terms of environmental and energy use that go beyond personal wants and desires
6. Willingness to act upon sound judgments even if action means making do with less, expending greater personal effort, or ultimately changing habitual behavior patterns.

Beginning in Our Own Backyards

It is so easy to place the blame for environmental problems on others and accept little or no personal responsibility. For that reason, studies of self and neighborhood are particularly worthwhile; they provide firsthand evidence of our own negative impact on the environment.

R This investigation is from George and Dorothy Hennings, *Keep Earth Clean, Blue and Green* (New York: Citation Press, 1976), pp. 37-40. See chapter 3 of that book, "The Age of the Big Throwaway," for a detailed description of this and other activities for use at the intermediate level.

Finding Points of Negative Impact. Perhaps one of the acts people commit most without thinking is littering. As a result, litter within the environment abounds, making an investigation of the problem an easy one even for young students. A neighborhood walk can introduce investigators to the problem of randomly discarded trash or litter. Armed with clipboard, paper, and pen, students list specific items of litter they see. Lists will include wrappers of all kinds, ice cream sticks, cans, bottles, and cigarette stubs, as well as organic wastes from animals and plants. Older youngsters can convert their lists into tally sheets on which they check each recurrence of a particular item of litter and indicate the location at which that item was observed. Younger children simply identify pieces of litter on the spot and follow up with a talk time during which they consider where items come from and why people litter.

Classifying. Students who have collected litter data can process them by classifying into categories specific items found. Possible systems that students can devise include: 1) size of litter—small, medium, large; 2) kinds of litter—glass, metal, paper, plastics, organic wastes; 3) prediction of how quickly the waste will break down—will there be slow, medium, or rapid decomposition?; 4) location at which the litter was found—street area, wooded area, yard, vacant lot, and so on. This activity can increase children's awareness of how widespread the litter problem is. Students may generalize that people clutter their environment with all kinds of materials and that litter can be found in every kind of area where people exist.

Cleaning Up an Area and Doing a Time Study. Armed with gloves, shovels, rakes, and receptacles in which to place collected trash, students attack a site near their school or home and pick up the litter in that area. Especially curious classes can categorize items they pick up, focusing on the kinds of litter found. Helpful here is a simple recording guide, on which students tally items found in the appropriate boxes. See Figure 15.2 for an example.

T Other forms that data collection can take: sketching a littered scene, photographing it, and mapping an area using symbols to plot each item of litter found.

**Figure 15.2
A Data Retrieval Chart for Field
Investigation of Litter Buildup**

Litter Found in Our School Yard

Names of Investigators: _____ Date of Observation: _____

_____

I. Collect data: Tally each instance here.

	Total Tallies
Glass _____	_____
Metal _____	_____
Paper _____	_____
Plant Matter _____	_____
Plastics _____	_____
Animal Waste Matter _____	_____
A Combination of Materials _____	_____
Unknown Materials _____	_____
TOTAL OF ALL ITEMS:	_____

T Whenever young investigators record research data, they should start with some sort of grid for the collection of data and should include some means for analyzing findings.

II. Decide: Is the amount of litter buildup significant or insignificant? What kinds of material are most frequently discarded? Why do people litter?

Having cleaned up a site, young investigators return to it after two or three weeks. Repeating their collection and categorizing activities, they find out how much litter collects during a given time period. Teacher and students will be amazed at how unthinking people are! Faced with firsthand evidence, students themselves will ask why and may even become more aware of their own littering.

Taking Action to Change Behavior. In some instances, students will ask, "How can we make an impact on people's behavior?" Possibilities to explore in this case include the following:

Post *Please Do Not Litter* signs on the experimental site and return to clean up and tally after three weeks to see whether signs have had any effect on people's behavior.

Run a poster campaign in the school, if the experimental site is the school yard.

Develop an extensive public relations campaign in the school and neighborhood, including presentations to other classes, an auditorium program, patrolling and "ticketing" of those who litter, letters to the editors of local papers (perhaps with photographs), letters sent to community leaders (perhaps with data tables that present investigative findings), street corner presentations, and fliers distributed to residents.

This type of activity involves children in what has been termed **social action.** In this respect, participation shows young citizens the avenues of nonviolent action open to them. It also shows them the importance of having firsthand evidence if one hopes to convince others of the seriousness of a social problem. In addition, there is some indication that participation in a social-action endeavor may change the behavior of those who take part. In one urban area where children were setting fires in deserted buildings, teachers involved youngsters in a poster contest; posters were to depict the evils of arson and urge others not to burn. As a result of the contest, the number of arson cases in the community decreased significantly.

Applying Investigative and Social-Action Skills to Other Problems. The same kinds of activities detailed in the preceding sections can be used in a variety of environmental contexts. Here are just a few:

Air Pollution Problems. Students identify specific instances of air pollution in their community, categorize them according to the sources of pollution (pesticide, transportation, electrical generators, manufacturing, mining operations, waste disposal, heating systems in homes and schools, etc.), and generalize about the sources in their own community. Interviewing is a viable strategy here; young people talk with executives from companies that are known polluters.

Noise Pollution Problems. Students develop a category system for rating noise emissions: ear-shattering, annoying, acceptable, barely perceptible. Using their system, they list common noises found at home, at school, and on the streets and rate the noises. Similarly students can make subjective determinations, identifying the noisiest room in a house, the noisiest spot on a particular road, and the noisiest area downtown.

Water Pollution Problems. Upper graders can do pond, brook, or beach studies, starting with signs of physical pollution—objects clearly visible in the water or along the shore—and eventually analyzing the water chemically for pollutants. The teacher will need an environmental handbook at this point to supply specific information on water testing.

Land Misuse Problems. In rural areas, investigations take the form of identifying specific instances of misuse of agricultural lands; in urban areas, students look for instances in which more trees were cut down than were necessary for building purposes, where extensive paved areas were constructed unnecessarily, and where too few trees were planted around shopping areas and industrial buildings. Conversely, students may wish to identify instances of thoughtful use of the land, even awarding an emblem to worthy land users.

Eyesore Problems. Primary and intermediate students identify community eyesores: vacant lots filled with junk, buildings in disrepair, ugly signboards, buildings that are painted garish colors, and ugly road cuts. Photography is especially useful here; students compile a picture portfolio, with each photo described in a sentence or two. Sketching can take the place of photography where equipment is not available. Videotaping is a possibility where available; upper graders can produce a videotaped documentary that shows community eyesores.

Energy Problems. Young people identify specific instances of wasteful energy use they see over a period of two weeks. Keep a large chart posted; as investigators spot a wasteful use, they add it to the chart: air-conditioned buildings with doors or windows left open, car use when one can walk, keeping lights on when not in use, and so forth.

Keeping Abreast of the Current Scene. As youngsters undertake investigations of environmental misuse in their own area, they should keep alert for similar problems discussed on television news and in newspapers and magazines. Articles can be attached to a bulletin

R For additional activities, lesson plans, and excellent case study materials see V. Eugene Vivian, *Sourcebook for Environmental Education* (Saint Louis: C. V. Mosby Co., 1973).

R For specific information on testing water samples see Hennings and Hennings, *Keep Earth Clean, Blue and Green* (New York: Citation Press, 1976). See Chapter 4.

T As a contrast, share the poems and photographs in Lee Bennett Hopkins, *To Look at Any Thing* (New York: Harcourt, Brace Jovanovich, 1978). The photographs are spectacular!

T Remind students of the five Ws of news reporting: who, what, when, where, and why.

board, which becomes an independent reading center where students go to read items posted. Items picked up on television news programs and documentaries can be shared orally during general discussion times. Some experienced teachers have found that reporting on current events works better when children must contribute on a specific topic. This prevents children from clipping any article from the front page without analyzing its significance.

Also at times the teacher should orally share stories and articles that deal with human impact on the environment. In the lower grades, a story similar to Peter Parnall's *The Mountain* is ideal for this purpose. *The Mountain* tells about what happens when a virgin area is "saved" by being turned into a park; the destruction of it by people out to enjoy themselves is strikingly real. In the upper grades, a news story can serve the same purpose.

T See Peter Parnall, *The Mountain* (Garden City, New York: Doubleday, 1971). With early intermediate children, use Robert McCloskey, *Time of Wonder* (New York: Viking Press, 1957) and *One Morning in Maine* (New York: Viking Press, 1952). With sixth graders, share carefully selected portions of Henry Thoreau's *Walden* (any edition).

Identifying Environmental Relationships as Part of Ongoing Unit Study

Economist Boulding at the time of the 1973-1974 energy crisis pointed out the relationship that exists in modern times between economic growth and the use of fossil fuels. In Boulding's words: "Societies with primitive technologies, which rely mainly on immediate solar energy in the form of wood or cow dung for fuel and human or animal muscles for motor power, are of necessity poor." Understanding how dependent they are on fossil fuel, children may come to a heightened awareness of the importance of respectful use.

R See Boulding in Jarrett (1966).

Gathering Data About the Energy and Power Uses of Different Societies. As students consider societies of the past and present, they can identify the basic energy sources upon which people relied or rely for food gathering, production, preparation, and storage; for clothing production; for lighting; for transportation and communication; for entertainment; for heating; and for producing materials important within the culture (religious artifacts, war tools, etc.). Regardless of the society being considered, starting in the early primary grades, students can view pictures of human activity in their textbooks and the teacher can inquire: What kind of fuel are they using to cook the bread? What kind of equipment are they using to plow the field? Who or what is supplying the power to drive the plow? What kind of force is being used to grind the grain? Check the picture depicting Hopi food preparation techniques to see how such questions fit into an ongoing study and can be used in relation to pictures given in a text series (see page 374). In other cases, energy-related questions are appropriate: What kind of power runs the pottery wheel? What kind of power drives

T Use the same approach as youngsters view pictures from cultural picture essays, from *National Geographic* and *Smithsonian,* and on filmstrips.

the shuttle back and forth to make cloth? Comparative questions are appropriate too: What kind of power do we use today to plow a field in the United States or Canada? What kind of power do we use to grind the grain? run the looms that make our cloth? What fuel do we use to cook our food? Where do we get our bread? Do people today usually make bread at home?

Especially as children move up in the elementary grades, they can gather data more systematically using a retrieval chart of the type shown in Figure 15.3. In the column labeled "Time and Place" children list the name of a society they are considering as part of unit study as well as the name of the society they know best (their own). After picture reading, listening/viewing activity, or text or reference reading, children fill in the blanks of the grid. Students record a few words in each square on the chart. For example, under "Power used to move the plow, colonial Canada or America" children may note "oxen, horse, people." Children with verbal problems may use sketches drawn directly onto the chart instead of words.

Thinking about Data Gathered: Categorizing, Comparing, Generalizing, and Assessing.

Having filled in most of the chart, young data gatherers can move to a more demanding cognitive task: categorizing. They categorize entries in their charts as to kind: human muscle power, animal muscle power, water or wind power, plant or animal matter, fossil fuel, or nuclear power. Here students can use symbols to record classification information within the chart; for instance, HM can stand for human muscle power. Clearly young people themselves should determine the symbols to be used; they decide whether symbols will be abbreviations or pictures and what the specific symbol will be in each case.

Categorizing activity lays the foundation for making comparisons and contrasts. These can be expressed in the form of short summary statements recorded directly onto the grid system. Some statements can be rather specific: "In colonial times, muscle power drove the plow; today fossil fuels are generally used in our country." Some statements can be more general: "Back then, they tended to rely on human, animal, and natural power; today we rely more on fossil fuels and nuclear power to supply us with heat, light, and transportation."

Working at a higher level, students can project the advantages and disadvantages associated with the patterns of power and energy use they have identified. Here again students list their ideas directly on their charts, which can be created in wall-sized versions. Different groups take responsibility for collecting different segments of the data. Brainstorming is helpful as a way to get ideas flowing. Children may suggest, "It's easier; it's faster; it's more comfortable; it takes less effort

T An interesting country to analyze is China, where historically people have looked on nature with great respect. This is reflected in their art, which often depicts people as small units within large natural landscapes. It is reflected too in many of their land management techniques; one example is the graceful terracing of the hills. Students can hypothesize why the Chinese view of nature is so different from the American view.

R Read Christopher Joyner, "Energy and Social Studies: Designing a New Curriculum." *The Social Studies 70*, January/February, 1979: 16–19.

Figure 15.3
Comparative Chart

Data Retrieval Chart

Categorize according to area of human activity:
food-related, clothing-related, transportaion-related, etc.

Time and Place	Power used to move the plow	Power used to move ocean-going ships	Main forms of land travel	Energy source used for cooking	Energy source used for home heating	Means of lighting homes	Power used to grind grain	Power used to preserve foods	Power used to spin thread and weave material	Power used to make clothes from cloth	Form of air conditioning	Power used to supply a major form of entertainment	Power used for long-distance communication
I. Colonial America or Canada													
II. America or Canada Today													
Similarities and/or Differences	List specific ones you see.												
Advantages and/or Disadvantages of Way of Life	List specific ones you find.												
Time/Place You Would Prefer to live	Of the two included on this chart, select one and give the reason for your choice.												

Directions: In the blanks of the grid, name the specific power source. Then in the blank, classify according to the following system, using this key:

Human muscle power = HM
Animal muscle power = AM
Fossil fuel = FF
(oil, gas, coal)
Nuclear power = NP

Natural powers = NAT
(wind, water, sun)
Plant or animal matter = PA
(wood, dung, peat)

on people's part," as advantages of power based on fossil fuels. They may suggest, "It takes less time for a tree to grow than for coal and gas to form;" or "It requires no drain on stored energy," as advantages of power based on plant or animal matter and natural powers.

Based on all the data amassed and all their conclusions, students can select the time and place they would prefer to live. In stating their preferences, they must give reasons—reasons that draw upon all the information now available. This is a forced choice as described in chapter 6. Students must decide between two given options.

Using the Strategy in a Variety of Unit Contexts. The chart given as an example in Figure 15.3 is intended for use within a unit on colonial days. However, there are many other units where the same kind of chart is practical. Here are a few variations:

1. Study of a country of today in which there is much greater reliance on muscle power and much less reliance on fossil fuels than in North America. List that country as Roman numeral I and the student's home country as Roman numeral II.
2. Study of other key periods of the past. For example, as part of a study of the industrial revolution, students chart data about pre-industrial society in the first row; post-industrial society in the second row. Or, students gather information on the Bronze Age and on the Iron Age.
3. Study of several countries. Do this as a summary activity after children have been involved in a series of units about different countries around the world. They tabulate data about those countries and then categorize, generalize, and make value judgments.

A Task to Try

The data retrieval chart in Figure 15.3 can be varied for use at almost any grade level and within almost any study of time periods, cultures, or regions. Test this assumption by locating a text for first, third, and fifth grade. Select one unit from each. Devise a chart for each that could be used for data gathering that helps students comprehend energy use.

Making Decisions About the Environment

With regard to environmental problems, social studies must go beyond the collection of data and generalizing about relationships; social studies must be concerned with decision making. Every day—often with little or no thought—children and adults make individual decisions that directly affect their environment. These decisions are made as a matter of habit without conscious identification of alternatives and without examination and evaluation of various behavior options. People simply act. Let us look next at ways in which schools can make children aware of the decision-occasions they face almost daily and can foster growth in the skills of decision making.

R An important reference is Dana G. Kurfman, ed., *Developing Decision-Making Skills*, 47th Yearbook, National Council for the Social Studies (Arlington, Virginia: NCSS, 1977).

Identifying Everyday Decision-Occasions

A person is writing a first draft of a report. After completing one side of a piece of paper, he or she reaches for a second. This situation repeated every day represents a **decision-occasion** that many people approach without conscious thought. The possibility of using the other side is not even considered.

Primary youngsters can identify decision-occasions in which they function by habit rather than considering the alternatives. They start by focusing on classroom behavior patterns, asking: "What acts do we perform that are essentially wasteful but that we do without thinking? What acts do we perform that make our classroom environment a less pleasant place to live?" Over an extended period of time, youngsters watch for specific instances. They share discoveries during a general talk time or by recording on a bulletin board. Children will probably include some of the following classroom decision-occasions:

R This diagram is based on Edward Cassidy and Dana Kurfman, "Decision Making as Purpose and Process," in *Developing Decision-Making Skills* (Arlington, Virginia: NCSS, 1977), p. 11.

We do not turn off the sink faucet all the way.

We write just a few words on a sheet of paper and then throw it away.

We do not turn off the lights when we leave the room.

We drop litter on the classroom floor.

We pollute the environment with needless noise, especially when others are trying to study.

We open the window when the heat or air conditioning is on.

We leave audiovisual equipment running when it is not being used.

We put on the lights when the sun is doing the job.

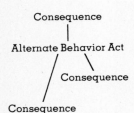

For each behavior pattern identified, children should note alternative behaviors and consider possible consequences of the habitual pattern and the alternative ones. During a trial period to follow the observational and decision-making period, students cooperatively work together to eliminate the polluting or wasteful behavior from the classroom. The teacher may have to work at modifying his or her own behavior as well, taking greater care to prevent waste of chalk, paper, paste, and other supplies.

Identifying Decision-Occasions Occurring Outside the Classroom

Once children have some understanding of decision-occasions, they can apply their knowledge to events outside the classroom. To begin, they can identify decision-occasions in which they take part at home and at play. Children can make lists of times when their habitual actions cause an unnecessary drain on energy resources or pollute the environment. These automatic decision-occasions may include times when they ask a parent to drive them in the family car rather than walking or biking; when they play their radio when others are trying to sleep, read, or talk; or when they fail to clean up a picnic site.

The same kind of thinking can take place as youngsters look at pictures found in textbooks. "What evidences of waste or thoughtlessness regarding the environment do we see in the picture?" is a beginning question the teacher can ask. "What other options did this person, organization, or company have?" is a second question. Particularly good pictures for this purpose are those showing homes ablaze with lights, cities aglow with neon lights, cars speeding along highways, bulldozers knocking down trees, areas paved over with concrete, rubbish strewn in a stream, and smokestacks emitting clouds of noxious materials.

Examining Probable Outcomes

Decision making should be based on a clear understanding of relevant facts and points of view. In classrooms, fact finding can include some of the activities described in the next section.

Identifying Facts Necessary for Sound Decision Making. Simple simulations are particularly effective as part of decision making. For example, upper elementary students in groups can function as a city or town council and can identify the particular kinds of information they would want to have at their fingertips before voting to install additional trash cans in a park where much litter has been found on the ground, require dog owners to clean up after their pets on public property, require all residents to separate clean paper and bottles from their trash so that these can be recycled, or allow a large industrial plant to dump its wastes into a local stream. It is important that students give the reasons why the information identified as necessary is considered basic to sound decision making. A student "council member" may, for instance, say that he or she wants to know whether trash cans currently in the park are being used. A perfectly valid consideration is whether people will use the containers if they are there.

Getting the Facts. Actual fact finding can take a number of forms—interviewing citizens, surveying conditions in the field, reading, and sending out questionnaires. In addition, especially when handling consumer decisions, students can conduct cost studies—cost being defined not just in terms of money spent but in terms of energy and environment as well. The steps in the processing and packaging of frozen Chinese vegetables given on page 496 suggests a direction that an energy cost study can take:

1. Students identify the probable steps in the production sequence of the item in question.
2. On a chart, next to each step in the processing sequence, they indicate the effect of the action on energy resources and possible environmental damage.
3. Students identify the steps in using a homemade product and the costs in terms of energy and the environment.
4. They identify the conditions under which the added energy costs are justifiable.

This design for classroom decision making can be applied to many different consumer questions:

Should I buy a new car, bicycle, coat, or baseball mit?

Should I buy model X, Y, or Z?

Should I buy the larger or smaller package of the same item?

Should I begin to use a product just developed?

In each case, students must consider both the direct money costs as well as the impact on the environment.

Realizing That Decisions Must Change as Circumstances Change. A decision appropriate today may be inappropriate tomorrow because the facts or relevant conditions may change. One way for children to see that a decision once wise may not always be sound is to compare automobile advertising before and after the oil shortage of 1973. The features stressed in today's ads reflect people's perceptions of a good car. Working from the firsthand data contained in ads from magazines of the early seventies and of today, young investigators evaluate the features stressed. See Figure 15.4 for a data retrieval chart to use. From their charts, students generalize: 1) What was considered a good car in 1970? What circumstances of that day led to that belief and influenced people's purchasing behavior? 2) What is a good car today? What circumstances led to this new belief and caused a change in people's buying behavior?

In handling these questions, students will have to go beyond quick answers to consider many factors: rising cost of the product in general, people's desire to do the "in" thing, rising costs of gasoline, fear of another embargo. Incidentally, a study of changing tastes reflected in changing consumer purchasing patterns is feasible with cigarettes, movies, heating and air-conditioning systems, and clothing.

Social decisions—whether they relate to the environment or not—reflect the prevalent ideas and beliefs of the time and place in which they are made. Once young people understand this, they have a

R Decisions also differ depending upon the geographic location of those making them. See James Aldrich and Anne Blackburn, "Should We Believe That Our Planet Is in Peril?" in *Controversial Issues in the Social Studies: A Contemporary Perspective*, Raymond Muessig, ed., 45th Yearbook of the National Council for the Social Studies (Arlington, Virginia: NCSS, 1975).

Figure 15.4
A Chart for Gathering Data About
Changing Perceptions

Automobile Advertisements: 1970 – Today

I. Directions: Locate ten car ads from 1970 by thumbing through magazines of
   that year. Locate ten random ads of today. Next to each feature listed, place a
   check each time that feature appears in an ad.

Features	Cars of 1970		Cars of today	
	Tally	Total	Tally	Total
Style (attractiveness)				
Large Size				
Safety				
Economy				
Luxury				
Comfort				
Power				
Maneuverability				

II. Directions. Generalize: Which features were very important in 1970?
   Which features were least important in 1970?
   Which features are very important today?
   Which features are least important today?

III. Rank order the features stressed today, from most often found to least often
   found. Then rank order the features as you feel they are important.

---

framework for interpreting past and present decisions and for changing their own minds on a question. In the words of historian José
Ortega y Gasset, "Progress is only possible to one who is not linked
today to what he was yesterday, who is not caught forever in that
being which is already, but can migrate from it into another." In this
respect, to criticize a person for changing his or her mind on an issue is
to fail to look at decision making in terms of the social and philosophical climate in which decisions are made.

R See José Ortega y
Gasset, "History as a
System," in *The Nature
of Historical Inquiry*, ed.
by Leonard M. Marsak
(New York: Holt,
Rinehart & Winston,
1970), pp. 7-10.

Making a Decision and Assessing Its Consequences

At some point, young citizens should be asked to make decisions about the environment based on a clear understanding of facts and defend their judgments with reasons. Simulations are useful here in allowing students to make a decision and assess its consequences.

A Simulation: An Example. Here is an example of a simulation game that requires upper graders to put themselves into a problem situation, consider related factors, and make a decision. Because of the sophistication of the economic principles involved, students will require considerable work with the fundamental concepts before attempting the simulation.

Stop Polluting

Step I: Share the following introductory materials with the full group:

The Story of Big Chemco

Big Chemco is a large industry found in Mistonville, Our State. Chemco has been located in Mistonville for at least fifty years. The company has grown bigger and bigger, and today is the largest employer of men and women within twenty kilometers of the plant. Many people have moved into Mistonville to work at Chemco. To handle the needs of all these people, a new shopping center with several department stores, smaller shops, and a large supermarket has just been built. Several restaurants have opened up. The construction industry in the area has been booming as a result.

Just recently the city council discovered that Big Chemco has been polluting the major river running through the city by dumping chemical waste into it. Simultaneously, they discovered that Chemco has been polluting the air through the fumes it was sending out. The city council, hearing of this, passed a law taxing all industries according to how much waste they each release into the environment.

Step II: Discuss the story to make sure students understand the key points. Why did the city council pass the tax ruling? How long had Chemco been in the city? Was Mistonville in good shape economically? Why or why not?

Step III: Introduce the simulation and divide the class into work groups. "Now we will divide into three-person teams. Each team will represent the major executives of Big Chemco. Your first job is to determine all the possible courses of action open to you. Then you must look at each course of action and identify what might happen if you decided on that action. To help in completing the work of your execu-

R See Fannie and George Shaftel, *Role-Playing for Social Values: Decision-Making in the Social Studies* (Englewood Cliffs, New Jersey: Prentice-Hall, 1967).

G The child is able to listen to acquire the basic facts of a case.

tive board, you will receive a set of cards. Some of the cards state possible courses of action you can take. Some suggest possible outcomes. See if you can pick out the possible action cards. Record these around the edge of the large piece of construction paper your board has on its executive table. Next to each action, write down the outcomes this action will trigger by taking items from the playing cards. You may write down actions and outcomes not on the cards.

Step IV: Distribute the simulation cards (Figure 15.5, p. 512).

Step V: When students have completed their actions/outcomes sheet, give them this problem: "Reconvene your executive board and select the course of action that seems most desirable, given all the factors that must be considered. Be ready to announce your decision to the city council and be ready to explain your choice."

Step VI: Convene the class as the city council. Teams must present their plans with the rest of the class asking questions to make sure they considered all aspects.

Step VII: Schedule a discussion. Ask, "What made this decision making so difficult? Whose rights did you have to consider? Is there any perfect answer? How did it feel to play the role of industrialist?"

Simulation: Some Related Points. One of the clear advantages of simulations is the possibility of thinking about problems from a point of view other than one's own. Faced with rising fuel bills and electrical costs, it is easy for a person to dismiss the problem by saying: "The company should absorb the costs of higher fuel charges, not pass them on to me." Quick solutions such as this one fail to take into account complex economic relationships at work in a capitalist economy. For example, lowering profits below a certain reasonable level forces investment money into other areas. Lower capital investment is one force that can lead to recession with all its associated problems. Students must comprehend the complexity of environmental problems and the economic impact of possible solutions. They must begin to see that all must participate in solutions and share a fair portion of the costs and the responsibility.

Deciding About Legal Questions – You Are the Judge

More and more today, court decisions seem to affect the everyday lives of people. For that reason, some social studies specialists advocate that law education be made part of the curriculum. Most proposals focus on social studies in junior and senior high school. However, some court cases, if explained with easy vocabulary and sentence patterns, can be understood by elementary students. The cases serve

G The child is able to see the relationship between a proposed course of action and possible results of that action; he or she can reason, "if this, then that."

G The child is able to select one alternative action from a number of actions, none of which is completely error-proof.

G The child is able to assess a decision of which he or she was a part.

G The child is able to ask questions concerning emotional issues in a polite, but pointed, way.

**Figure 15.5
Simulation Cards**

Continue to Pollute and Pay The Tax

Close The Plant and Move to a City Without a Tax

Raise The Cost of The Product

Fire Most of The Local Workers

Close Some of The Stores in The City

Hire a Team of Scientists to Figure Out How to Change the Process So That Fewer Wastes Are Produced

Install Expensive Equipment to Lower Pollution

Lower The Income of Investors in The Company

Ruin The Housing Industry in Mistonville

Ask Most Workers in The Plant to Relocate in a New City

Lower The Salaries of Workers to Cover The Increased Cost of Production

Make Less Profit on Each Item Produced

Cause The Stock of Chemco to Fall in Value

Cause Chemco to Go Bankrupt and Close Up

Go Out of Business

Ruin The Business of All The Stores and Shops in The New Shopping Center

Increase The Number of People on Welfare or Unemployment

Raise Taxes in General to Take Care of Unemployment Payments

Cause a General Recession in The Area

Increase Pollution in Another Area

Decrease Pollution in The Area

Lower Production

Shut Down Production Completely

as firsthand source materials through which children build understanding of current issues and events and refine their decision-making skills.

An example in point is the case of the Tennessee Valley Authority versus the Snail Darter. It can be the content of a simulation/role-playing activity in upper grades.

Step I: Share the following information with participants:

The Plight of the Snail Darter

A number of years ago the Tennessee Valley Authority began construction of the Tellico Dam at a cost of $120 million. This dam—like others in the Tennessee Valley System—was to be used to provide electrical, irrigational, and recreational facilities for the people in the area.

In 1973, Congress passed the Endangered Species Act. This act states that federal agencies must "not jeopardize the continued existence of endangered or threatened species or destroy a habitat deemed 'critical' to their survival." An endangered species is a kind of animal or plant of which very few still exist in the world. A habitat is the place where these animals or plants live.

In 1975, the Department of the Interior listed the snail darter as an endangered species. The snail darter is a three-inch fish. Its principal habitat is the Little Tennessee River. This river would be backed up and its flow halted by the proposed Tellico Dam. As a result, that would probably be the end of the snail darter on earth.

In 1977, a federal appeals court ruled that the dam—although almost finished—could not be completed. The Tennessee Valley Authority appealed that decision to the U.S. Supreme Court. Meanwhile, in July 1978, Congress voted to continue the Endangered Species Act—on which the entire issue hangs—for another three years.

Step II: Review the facts of the case by asking questions. What is an endangered species? When was the snail darter named an endangered species? When was the dam begun? How far along was dam construction when a halt was called? Why do you think Congress thought it important that the U.S. have an Endangered Species Act? Would you have voted for its continuation?

Step III: Divide the class into legal teams—some to represent the snail darter, some to represent the TVA. Teams should go to the library armed with research questions to find out more information about endangered species as well as about the TVA. Teams prepare briefs: "Why the dam should not be built" or "Why the dam should be built."

Step IV: Hold a number of mock hearings in front of the U.S. Supreme Court in which attorneys present their cases. After each pair of presen-

R See *Social Education*, Vol. 41, No. 3 (March 1977), which contains a special section on law education. See also the section on law education in John Jarolimek, *Social Studies in Elementary Education*, Fifth Edition (New York: Macmillan, 1977), pp. 187-190.

R More information can be obtained in *Science*, 200:628 (May 12, 1978) and *Science*, 201:426-28 (August 4, 1978).

G The child is able to come to a decision based on understanding of facts and opinions presented orally.

tations students should vote, ruling on the case based on the evidence presented.

Step V: Students, guided by the teacher, discuss the outcome of their voting and decide why they decided as they did.

The case of the TVA versus the snail darter suggests one way legal material can be handled in fifth and sixth grades as well as in junior and senior high. Students are given the facts in the case, but not the ultimate decision. They search for supporting information and prepare arguments representing one side or another. Arguments are presented before the court (the class), which finally must come to a decision. One advantage of this simulation design is that students learn about the way the judicial system in their country operates as they work with significant problems of today.

T Other cases to use include cases involving the construction of nuclear reactors (as in Seabrook, N.H.), the dumping of wastes (as in the Great Lakes), and the spilling of oil.

Taking Action

R See Edward Cassidy and Dana Kurfman, "Decision Making as Purpose and Process," in *Developing Decision-Making Skills*, ed. by Dana Kurfman (Arlington, Virginia: NCSS, 1977).

In the 1977 yearbook of the National Council for the Social Studies, Edward Cassidy and Dana Kurfman set forth a three-stage sequence for decision making: Stage 1—identifying decision-occasions and alternatives; Stage 2—examining and evaluating decision alternatives; and Stage 3—deciding and reflecting on the decision. In this chapter so far, ways of handling the beginning stages have been described, especially when decision making occurs as part of environmental study. All of the steps in Stage 3, however, are harder to work into realistic classroom study. Students may select an alternative, but implementation is often an impossibility. More specifically, young people may vote to halt dam construction as part of a simulation, but they never see the actual outcome of their decision. Assessment of the quality of the decision making must be limited to consideration of how the judgment relates to the facts.

Nonetheless, some opportunity to implement a plan of action and to assess real outcomes should be given youngsters in elementary grades. Let us look at two examples of how this can be done.

The Classroom as Environmental Microcosm. If the classroom or total school area is considered an environmental microcosm, it is possible for youngsters to make decisions about the use of that environment and then take action based on their decisions or plans. This can be carried out very simply in kindergarten and first grade as the teacher enlists students' aid in maintaining the attractiveness of the classroom. If general sloppiness and littering have become problems, youngsters and teacher call a class meeting. They consider the question: What action can we take to keep our classroom environment a nice place to live and work in? Children brainstorm suggestions, with the teacher urging students to identify specific actions that each person can take. A list may include items such as: We should always screw the lid on the paste jar; we should pick up scraps under our tables after cutting; we should put the scraps in the waste can.

From the list, each student selects those four suggestions he or she believes are the most important ones and agrees to follow those suggestions for the rest of the week. The child copies the appropriate items from the list and begins with an introductory phrase supplied by the teacher: "During this week I will remember to. . . ." Each child's composition, titled "My Contract with the Class," becomes a behavior checklist. At the end of each day, the child goes to his or her sheet hanging on a classroom wall and stars each suggestion that he or she followed during that day. In this respect, the child is held responsible for assessing changes in personal behavior. Later, children cooperatively assess the results of their environmental cleanup campaign.

Similar environmental action campaigns can be organized in terms of a playground area and children's respectful use of it. In addition, children can propose personal behavior contracts governing their use of the environment at large; contracts consist of statements identifying specific acts students will try hard not to commit during an agreed period of time. Again, time should be set aside for self-assessment. Did I carry out the things I agreed to do or not to do?

Study of the Good Life.   What are the things that we need and want to make life good for us? This question is a fundamental one that gets at basic values. It can be used as a stepping stone into environmental study as youngsters consider needs, technology, industrialization, diverse cultures, or the community.

Urged again to start by being specific, youngsters identify things "they could not do without." They identify also those things it is very nice to have. The result of this thinking time will be a board full of items. Now, individually, students are forced to make a choice; they must select fifteen top-priority items from the total list and write these on a piece of paper.

Following the individual thinking time, children identify those items that everyone chose, those that more than half the class chose, and those that fewer than half the class chose. Children then discuss reasons for their choices and consider what their choices indicate about their values. They then rank order their fifteen choices.

Working with a shortened list comprised of about twenty items rated high by many youngsters, students can create an Energy/Environment Drain Chart. Next to each item, they list the impact that satisfaction of the need has on energy resources or on the general quality of the environment. By doing this, youngsters begin to recognize their

T In kindergarten, the teacher records for children as they individually dictate their contracts.

dependency on natural resources. To drive that point home, students individually can draw up a plan of action–they draw up a list of things that are expensive in energy or environmental terms, which they agree to do without for a week. Here students' commitments will be in terms of riding a bicycle instead of asking a parent for a ride to school; not leaving the lights on; and not using paper towels. At the end of the experimental period, students talk together, admitting if they failed to keep their commitments and thinking through reasons why they failed. They talk about including some of the experimental actions in their everyday behavior patterns. Would it be hard? Why not try?

A Problem to Ponder

What does the good life mean to you? In thinking about this question, assume you have air, water, food, clothing, and shelter in survival quantities. What would you have to have to make life really worth living? Make your own list. Next to each item indicate the energy or environmental costs necessary to supply your desire. Then rank order the items on your list. You can list as many items as you want. Now assess your own concept of the good life. What does your concept tell about you?

People Using Resources: A Summary Thought or Two

R Eugene Odum, *Fundamentals of Ecology* (Philadelphia: W. B. Saunders Co., 1971).

R See "Editor's Declaration on Interdisciplinary Environmental Education" by the editors of *The Science Teacher, Social Education, Chemistry, Man / Society /Technology, The Physics Teacher, Art Education, American Biology Teacher* in *Social Education,* 39:72-73 (February 1975). The entire issue of *Social Education* focuses on "Integrating Social Studies and Science."

Human occupation increasingly is disrupting nature's finely balanced ecosystems. We cut down trees with abandon and dig deep into the earth to extract the resources that took millions of years to build up. In the process, we scar the earth and pile waste products upon it. We foul our earth by filling the air with particles and chemicals; we load our lakes and rivers with pollutants; we change weather patterns; we litter. In doing this, we generally fail to recognize that the very survival of the human race is dependent on an environment that can supply basic physiological needs.

Clearly these are problems that demand interdisciplinary approaches. In the past, environmental problems have been perceived as within the range of the natural sciences, but this is no longer true. In the words of Eugene Odum, one of the foremost ecologists of the century, "Success or failure in applying the principles of ecology for the benefit of man, at least for the next decade, may depend not so much on technology and environmental science as such, but on economics, law, politics, planning and other areas in the humanities that have up to now had very little ecological input."

Likewise, "the situation demands an interdisciplinary approach to environmental education." Programs must be designed so that youngsters acquire understanding of ecological relationships. But this is only one small part. Children must learn to perceive themselves as one component of the problem. Respecting the environment, they must make wise decisions based on understandings gleaned from the humanities and the social and natural sciences and learn to take action based on thoughtful analysis. These learnings are imperative if the future is to be better than today.

References

A Citizen's Guide to Clean Air. Washington, D. C.: The Conservation Foundation, 1972.

Energy Outlook: 1978-1990. Houston, Texas: Exxon Company, 1978.

Energy: Use, Conservation and Supply, Volume II– 1978. Washington, D.C.: American Association for the Advancement of Science, 1978.

Environmental Education in the Elementary School. Washington, D.C.: National Science Teachers Association, 1977.

Hennings, George; and Hennings, Dorothy. *Keep Earth Clean, Blue and Green: Environmental Activities for Young People.* New York: Citation Press, 1976.

Jarrett, Henry, ed. *Environmental Quality in a Growing Economy.* Washington, D.C.: Resources for the Future, 1966.

Miller, G. Tyler. *Energy and Environment: Four Energy Crises.* Belmont, California: Wadsworth Publishing Co., 1975.

Smith, Ralph. *United States and World Energy.* Publication 8904. Washington, D.C.: U.S. Department of State, 1977.

Studdard, Gloria. *Common Environmental Terms: A Glossary.* Washington, D.C.: U.S. Environmental Protection Agency, 1973.

Turk, Jonathan; Wittes, Janet; Wittes, Robert; and Turk, Amos. *Ecosystems, Energy, Population.* Philadelphia: W. B. Saunders Co., 1975.

U. S. Department of Agriculture, Soil Conservation Service. *Outdoor Classrooms on School Sites.* Publication PA-975. Washington, D.C.: Government Printing Office, 1972.

U.S. Department of Agriculture, Soil Conservation Service. *Teaching Soil and Water Conservation: A Classroom and Field Guide.* Publication PA-341. Washington, D.C.: Government Printing Office, 1977.

U.S. Environmental Protection Agency. *Don't Leave It All to the Experts: The Citizen's Role in Environmental Decision Making.* Washington, D.C.: Government Printing Office, 1972.

U.S. Environmental Protection Agency. *Noise Pollution.* Washington, D.C.: Government Printing Office, 1972.

Vivian, V. Eugene. *Sourcebook for Environmental Education.* St. Louis: C. V. Mosby Co., 1973.

Wagner, Richard. *Environment and Man.* 3rd ed. New York: W. W. Norton and Co., 1978.

Part Five   The Social Studies Curriculum

If you do not think about the future, you cannot have one.

John Galsworthy, *Swan Song*, Part II

The classroom teacher is also a curriculum designer. He or she must create ongoing sequences of instruction through which children develop understanding of basic social studies concepts and grow in cognitive and social-emotional skills. He or she must have an overall design in mind even as children become involved in specific lessons and activities.

Chapter 16 describes steps in the curriculum planning process leading to development of integrated units of social studies experiences. It supplies an example of a resource unit that the teacher can use as a guide in evaluating and designing others; it also presents a flowchart model for unit planning. Chapter 17 details some of the new directions that social studies programs are taking and provides the teacher with criteria for judging new programs and emerging trends.

16 Planning Units of Instruction: Objectives, Activities, and Sequences

Tara drew this as part of a
first-grade unit on Eskimo people.

These . . . times call for
the building of plans . . .
that build from the
bottom up. . . .

Franklin Roosevelt,
radio address, April 7,
1932

Key Questions

What curriculum decisions are generally made on the
school, district, or state level? What curriculum
decisions must the teacher make?

Why do curriculum specialists advocate the
development of behavioral objectives?

Write several behavioral objectives that could be part
of a third-grade unit on Colonial America or Canada.
What problems do you see in writing objectives that
identify interests, values, attitudes, and appreciations?

What is a resource unit? What kinds of information are
generally found in one? How does a resource unit
relate to a teaching unit? From what sources can one
get resource units?

What pieces fit together in a teaching unit? How does
the teacher decide what pieces to use in a particular
instance?

What is a flowchart? How can one be used in unit
planning? In planning flowcharts, what components
must the teacher include?

A Unit Mural

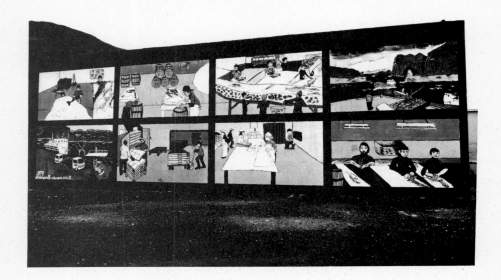

Introduction

Vestmannaejar is an island off the southern coast of Iceland. The eight-part mural that opens this chapter decorates an outer wall of one building of Vestmannaejar. Each segment of the mural depicts a step in the commercial preparation of fish. By following the sequence, one can learn how fish are brought to the small island port, cleaned, frozen, packaged, crated, and shipped out.

The economy of Vestmannaejar is dependent on the fishing industry; without it there would be little way for inhabitants of the cold, rocky island to earn their livings. Young people growing up on Vestmannaejar realize early the importance of fishing to them. Even in their teens, many begin to work in the processing plant, and they study the industry as part of the school curriculum. The large mural that adds a spark of color to the community was possibly a product of one group's study. It could have served as a culminating activity for a meaningful unit of work, in this case, study of a major economic activity.

Curriculum Planning in the Social Studies

Within most social studies programs, children's inquiry is organized around major topics taught as **units.** Some units focus on a period of time and some on a region or country of the world, a cultural group, a movement, or an aspect of human activity. Others focus on structures within society—the family, the neighborhood, or the school. Designing such a unit is a major task that at some point all teachers must undertake.

The School's Responsibility in Unit Planning

Planning for classroom units in the social studies often starts with two steps carried out in a school or district.

1. Identification of Goals—Committees of teachers determine the main goals of social studies instruction in the schools. These broad goals are incorporated into the school district's curriculum guide. Committees may indicate grade levels at which specific skills will be introduced and competency levels to be achieved at each grade.
2. Identification of Topics—Teachers in groups determine the topics through which the goals will be achieved at each level; these become the focus of classroom unit study. Often topics are chosen through selection of a textbook series or commercially produced social studies program. Grade levels at which topics will be introduced are generally those that parallel the chosen text series or program. At this stage too, major concepts and generalizations to be developed may be identified.

Because preliminary planning has occurred at the school or district level, classroom teachers are not free agents in the realm of curriculum. They operate within predetermined boundaries—the general goals, topics, concepts, and generalizations in the school curriculum guide and the content in the text or program selected by district teachers. In some instances, control of these fundamental curriculum decisions resides outside the school district; decisions about what topics should be taught and at which grade level each should be placed are made by state committees or curriculum specialists.

The Teacher's Responsibility in Unit Planning

The fact that the individual teacher must operate within the goal and unit framework established by school, district, or state does not mean, however, that the teacher has no responsibility for long-range planning. Just the opposite is true. In many schools the social studies teacher is responsible for carrying out these five interrelated **curriculum decision-making** tasks:

1. Setting Objectives—The teacher must identify the specific learnings to be achieved through study of each aspect of a topic assigned in the curriculum guide to the grade level.

2. Searching for Strategies and Materials—The teacher must decide what instructional strategies to employ to achieve general goals and specific objectives and must identify and produce necessary teaching materials.
3. Determining Evaluation Strategies—The teacher must decide the specific means to use in assessing student growth toward objectives and create assessment instruments.
4. Sequencing—The teacher must design an overall sequence of teaching and evaluation activities.
5. Planning Individual Lessons—The teacher must write plans for individual lessons within the sequence, identifying specific objectives, necessary materials, and procedures.

In summary, the teacher has considerable responsibility as a curriculum designer. Although decisions about what should be taught and at what grade levels specific topics should be placed are made earlier, the teacher still retains primary responsibility for deciding how to teach, how to evaluate teaching and learning, and what the sequence of instruction shall be. These are key decisions that must be made in designing units in the social studies.

Identifying Behavioral Objectives – Trying to be Precise

A major responsibility of the teacher is identifying what children will learn through a particular unit or lesson sequence. Where the subject content is complex, especially starting in grade three, an important step in planning is the development of a comprehensive content outline that goes beyond a given textbook. This insures that specific content material for each subtopic within a unit is clearly laid out. In addition, specialists in instructional design generally advocate thinking about **objectives in behavioral terms.** This means that the teacher must describe precisely the type of observable behavior a student will exhibit if mastery of the objective is achieved. It means that the teacher must also identify the conditions under which a desired behavior will be demonstrated and the level of success that is acceptable. Because teachers may encounter problems when they first begin to think precisely about student learning, this section attempts to clarify the process of identifying objectives.

R See R. F. Mager, *Preparing Instructional Objectives* (Belmont, California: Fearon, 1962).

Thinking in Terms of Observable Behavior

How does the teacher begin to describe objectives in behavioral terms? A starting point is to think of specific and overt actions that the student will know how to perform as a result of a projected lesson sequence.

The teacher, for example, may think: "By the end of this unit, I want each student to be able to outline, to use, to interpret, to write, to name, to solve, to describe orally. . . ." The infinitives in each of these cases identify observable acts. Specialists in instructional systems generally recommend that the teacher avoid less precise infinitives: to know, to appreciate, to value, or to understand. While these infinitives provide direction in overall goal setting, they supply little guidance in planning units and lessons because each act described has no directly observable component.

As the teacher thinks in terms of specific actions that students will be able to perform by the end of a lesson sequence, he or she must also think about the product that will result from that action. For example, having identified a specific action, the teacher asks, "What is the youngster to prepare?" The teacher thinks: "By the end of this unit I want each youngster to be able to prepare an outline of a three paragraph selection found in the fourth-grade social studies text. Furthermore, the outline should have three major headings; under each heading a student will have at least two subheadings." By thinking in such precise terms, the teacher now has a target for which to shoot. The objective as stated provides the teacher with a framework for planning classroom sequences through which students will learn to outline a written passage; it provides a framework too for determining whether each student has achieved the desired level of learning. Viewed from this perspective, statements of objectives serve a dual role; they provide guidance for both teaching and evaluating the results of instruction.

R Helpful in thinking in terms of behavior and product is Robert J. Kibler, Larry L. Barker, and David T. Miles, *Behavioral Objectives and Instruction* (Boston: Allyn & Bacon, 1970).

Translating Content Goals into Behavioral Objectives

Schools expect children to know factual information. After working with unit materials on South America, for example, children should have a general knowledge of the names and locations of key cities, major rivers, and mountain ranges. To translate this goal into behavioral objectives is an easy task for the teacher, who asks, "What specific acts will students be able to perform if they really know those facts?" Surely, students will be able to—

Pick out the South American continent and label it on a world map;

Locate and label the Andes Mountains and the Amazon on a map;

Label Caracas, Rio de Janeiro, Buenos Aires, Valparaiso, and Quito by writing the city names next to circle markers already plotted on a continental map.

Helpful infinitives for specifying objectives include *to pick out, to label, to plot, to name, to list, to fill in, to rephrase, to identify, to eliminate the one that does not belong, to put in chronological order, to define, to recall,* and *to recognize.*

Translating Basic Search and Communication Goals into Behavioral Objectives

Basic reading, writing, speaking, noting, outlining, observing, describing, graphing, charting, and mapping skills also lend themselves to statement in behavioral terms. In these cases, there is often a performance or product component that is observable.

A good example of a skills objective defined in behavioral terms is: The child is able to compose a paragraph summarizing at least three main ideas developed in an ongoing social studies discussion of which he or she is a part. Much can be gained from such precise thinking. A teacher who simply thinks, "I will help children develop their writing skills," or "I will help children grow in summarizing skills," is not taking direct aim. In contrast, the teacher who has identified the more precise statement of objective is on the way to planning activities that will lead to the observable behavior. Thinking about objectives has become a worthwhile planning endeavor, not an academic exercise as it is in cases where objectives are so general that they serve little purpose. Figure 16.1 sets forth several samples of functional objectives laid out to show the component elements.

Figure 16.1
The Behavior and Product
Components of a Skills Objective

The Behavior	The Product
The student is able to present orally	a two-minute report that explains the sequence of events leading up to the forced signing of the Magna Carta by King John I.
The student is able to locate	information on a physical map of Africa using the legend.
The student is able to compile	a list of key ideas about Guy Carleton after reading the appropriate selection in an encyclopedia.
The student is able to construct	a series of bar graphs depicting the comparative strengths of the Union and the Confederacy on the eve of the American War Between the States. The graphs will be carefully labeled and titled so as to summarize the content.
The student is able to skim write	an article from *Our Weekly Reader* and one sentence telling what the article is about.

Translating Cognitive Process Goals into Behavioral Objectives

Many teachers find that they can quickly learn to think out precise statements of behavioral objectives relative to factual content and basic search and communication skills. On the other hand, they find it more difficult to specify behavioral objectives that deal with intellectual activity in which much of the performance occurs inside the person who is learning.

In this context the teacher again must begin by asking, "What is it that I really want children to be able to do?" Using that question as a guide, the teacher who wants children to see relationships within data may be able to specify, "What I really want is that children are able to group items that share a common feature and invent a label to apply to the grouped items." The teacher who wants children to grow in the ability to solve problems may narrow the objective to, "What I really want is for children to be able to apply generalizations A, B, and C to explain the causes of the French and Indian Wars."

Infinitives helpful in thinking about cognitive process goals include *to group, to contrast, to compare, to create, to devise, to design, to relate, to set up, to distinguish between, to explain, to describe, to translate, to apply, to generalize, to propose,* and *to hypothesize.* These phrases define and limit the cognitive processes students are to learn to perform. Of course, the teacher must go on to ask, "What is it that children will be able to group, contrast, compare, and so forth?" Figure 16.2 provides specific examples of process objectives, showing both behavior and product components.

Figure 16.2
The Behavior and Product
Components of a
Cognitive Process Objective

The Behavior	**The Product**
Given two maps, one showing population centers and the other showing major rivers and the coastline, the student is able to hypothesize	reasons to explain the location of population centers. Reasons will be listed on a chart in written form.
Given basic facts about a community's needs, the student is able to design	a central market area that would meet those needs.

Translating Emotional-Social Goals into Behavioral Objectives

Interests, attitudes, appreciations, and values are other goals sought through the social studies. To translate these into specific objectives, the teacher must identify ways in which the student actually shows appreciation or interest or demonstrates a positive attitude or value. In some cases, it is possible to pinpoint specific acts through which the student shows, exhibits, or demonstrates emotional-social learnings. For example, the teacher who has as a general goal heightened respect for others may state as an objective: In a group situation, the student does not interrupt others who are speaking; in play situations, the student shares materials; when listening, the student makes non-verbal gestures that suggest receptivity to the ideas of others. These behaviors characterize people who respect others.

In some cases, however, teachers must stretch a bit to locate observable behaviors that are representative of internal feelings. Take, for example, an appreciation goal found in many social studies programs: The student appreciates the contribution of various and diverse ethnic groups to the character of the American and Canadian nations. One possible translation into behavioral terms is to state: The student writes a brief paragraph explaining the contribution of the Swedes to the settlement and development of New Jersey. Or the objective could be stated as: By the end of the unit on settlement patterns, the student will be able to list three specific contributions of Swedes to the American way of life. In both examples, the statement defines an observable behavior. Yet the reader can rightly counter: Just because children perform each of the stated behaviors is no clear evidence that they really appreciate the contribution of diverse ethnic groups to the growth of the nation. Then too, wise to the ways of teachers, some children express opinions, preferences, and values of which their teachers approve. They may believe far differently from what their classroom behavior suggests. Observable behavior, or lack of it, may be no indicator of growth toward feeling objectives.

Still another danger inherent in stating desired values, interests, appreciations, and attitudes as behavioral objecives is the possibility of coming away with too narrow a focus. Having defined a particular objective in terms of behaviors X, Y, and Z, the teacher may fail to recognize or accept as evidence of growth in learning a behavior different from the anticipated or defined ones. He or she may fail to recognize a child's product that is different from one designated in the statement of a behavioral objective, as comparable to the designated one. In searching for precision in emotional areas in which little precision exists, there is always the risk of becoming too rigid.

What does this imply for the teacher who is attempting to identify objectives as a framework for instructional decision making? The authors of this book believe that the teacher must proceed with care, realizing and accepting the weaknesses and dangers inherent in objective setting. In those instances where specific behaviors of an overt kind simply are rare or may not even be possible, the teacher comes as close as possible to identifying an acceptable observable behavior, knowing that the statement of objective is only a rough approximation. The teacher must also be alert during class sessions to children's overt behaviors that have not been identified as part of the objective yet are indicators of student achievement or nonachievement. A statement of an objective is not something that is unchangeable. Even as units progress, the teacher may think of other behaviors that suggest growth toward goals.

A Problem to Ponder

Common general goals of social studies programs are growth in appreciation of one's national heritage, ability to handle time relationships, and understanding of cause and effect relationships. For each of these goals, write one or more behavioral objectives that would give an instructional planner a clearer base for designing a unit sequence.

Gathering Ideas for Unit Teaching

Once the teacher has a clear concept of what children will learn through study of a topic and has determined how they already stand in relation to these objectives, he or she moves to the next step in unit development—designing activities and materials through which specified learnings will be acquired. Although the final design of learning activities is the responsibility of the classroom teacher, good takeoff points are the resource units available on a topic.

Resource Units – Gold Mines to Be Tapped

A **resource unit** is an organized collection of ideas and materials that relates to a social studies topic. Most units include some or all of the items listed in Figure 16.3. That list can be used as a format for construction of resource units by a teacher who finds it necessary to create one.

Figure 16.3
A Format for Resource
Unit Construction

Topic: _____   Intended Grade Levels: _____

I. **Introductory Statement:** A general overview of why this area is important, why it should be studied, and what general goals are being sought

II. **Content Background:** A statement or outline of background information

III. **Statement of Concepts and Generalizations:** A list of key terms and major generalizations from the social science disciplines that will be highlighted within the unit

IV. **Statement of Specific Objectives:** A list of learnings to be acquired, stated in specific behavioral terms where feasible

V. **Descriptions of Learning Activities:** Clear explanations of activities for large groups, small groups, individualized learning stations, and independent research for use with students—For each activity described in detail, behavioral objectives should be indicated

VI. **Actual Materials to Use:** Maps, charts, stories, poems, songs, simulations, value dilemmas, and games to use as part of unit study

VII. **Annotated Bibliography of Student References:** Story and information books that children can read as part of unit study

VIII. **Annotated Bibliography of Audiovisual Materials:** A list of films, filmstrips, tapes, records, filmloops, picture collections, commercial games, and so forth

IX. **Evaluative Means:** A list of ways to evaluate learning throughout the unit; in some cases actual evaluative instruments such as tests, checklists, rating scales, and interview guides

X. **Concluding Statement:** A review of important points developed within the resource unit; a summary of any general hints or limitations

XI. **Annotated Bibliography of Teacher References:** A list of books on the topic that the teacher can read to obtain necessary background

(Note: Not all units will include all items.)

Comprehensive units are obtainable, however, from many different sources. Commercial enterprises market units as part of audiovisual packets, picture collections, and text series. Nonprofit and governmental agencies also supply resource units on topics of concern to them. This is especially true when the topics relate to agriculture, health, population, energy, conservation, and consumerism. In addition, industries such as those involved in petroleum, gas, mining, and the manufacture of goods have compiled units often accompanied by free and/or inexpensive filmstrips.

Some school districts—especially those that encompass a large area and service many children—have developed **curriculum guides** that are really collections of resource units. Many are very complete, with picture sheets that can easily be converted into transparencies and/or handouts. Libraries in colleges and universities with a school of education often maintain files of resource units from representative districts throughout the United States and Canada. In some respects, these units and their associated materials are more useful than those from commercial sources in that materials may not be copyrighted and can be reproduced by the teacher in classroom quantities without requesting permission.

After finding comprehensive resource units, the teacher can easily be misled into believing that there is no need for further planning. Why not just use the resource unit as given? Resource units, however, are not teaching units. They have not been planned with a particular group of children in mind; in many cases they include far more materials and ideas than can be used in the amount of time generally allocated to study of the unit topic; and they may set forth ideas for which the teacher may not have the requisite materials. For these reasons, resource units must be viewed as a source of ideas. These ideas must be adapted to the particular classroom situation.

T Periodically some professional journals also include resource units and related activities. The teacher should develop a collection of those units that relate to topics generally included in the curriculum.

An Example of a Resource Unit Prepared in a School District

The value of resource units can be seen by analyzing a sampling of units compiled for different purposes. The section that follows includes a unit that is part of the social studies program for the second grade in Baltimore County, Maryland. It has as its theme "People Living in Communities." One unit in the program is titled "Looking at Communities." It was designed by district teachers to parallel a major curriculum topic; as a result it focuses specifically on the needs of children living in that county. Because the unit is comprehensive, only portions are reproduced so that the reader can get a general idea of the areas such resource guides include.

Unit: Looking at Communities—Second Year

I. Background Information for the Teacher

A community may be defined as a group of people who share a common place and common concerns. People satisfy their physical, social-emotional, and economic needs and wants in many different kinds of communities. In our country communities range from rural villages through suburbs to metropolitan areas and the inner city. They vary widely in size, density of population, physical features, climate, use of land, and cultural features. This study of communities is designed to help children understand that different communities in different places composed of different people are similar in some ways and different in others.

R This resource unit was prepared by teachers under the auspices of the Board of Education, Baltimore County, Towson, Maryland. The units in the Baltimore series are among the best available today. This one is reproduced through the kind permission of the Board of Education, specifically H. Clifton Osborn, Coordinator, Office of Social Studies.

In addition to helping children understand the meaning of *community*, this unit also provides many opportunities to plan learning experiences that teach inquiry skills such as observing and describing, classifying, comparing, inferring, and generalizing.
Question: How are communities alike and different?

II. Objectives

T Reading this page, ask, "What will be the major thrust of this unit?"

Pupils should be able to identify and describe different kinds of communities; compare and contrast the natural and human features of different communities; construct a model of the community; explain that a map is a special kind of picture; define map symbols as pictures which stand for real objects; interpret pictorial, semi-pictorial, and abstract map symbols; name and use cardinal directions; and identify and describe changes in communities.

III. Teaching Suggestions

Initiating Activities. To initiate this inquiry about communities, use one of the following suggestions or plan a similar activity.

T In this resource unit, many activities are provided for each major understanding being highlighted. Because they are so numerous, only a representative sample has been included here.

1. To arouse children's interest in learning about communities, write the word *community* on the chalkboard and ask: What is a community? As ideas are given, list them on a chart or tape-record them.
2. Show pictures, slides, or selected frames from filmstrips that depict different kinds of communities. Have the children discuss similarities and differences in the various communities shown and compare this information with their list of ideas. Teachers should not expect children's ideas about communities to be completely accurate at this time. Keep the chart or tape and have the class evaluate their original statements about communities again at the end of the unit. As the children discuss different kinds of communities, make a list of questions they want to answer during the study.
3. On a bulletin board or chalkboard arrange a variety of pictures depicting different kinds of communities. Use magazine pictures or study prints. Filmstrips, as well as pictures from the American Automobile Association and the Chambers of Commerce of different cities, will also be useful.
   Do not tell the children the types of communities depicted. After they have studied the pictures for a reasonable length of time, ask questions such as the following:

   Do you think each picture was taken in the same community? Why?
   How are these communities alike? How are they different? (For example, the land features are different; the land is used differently; the people are doing different things.)

Which of these communities do you think has the least number of people? The greatest number of people? Why do you think this is so?

What kinds of work might the people in each of these communities do? How do you know?

Which of these communities is most like your community? Give reasons for your answer.

The teacher should remember that the purpose of this initiating activity is to increase children's awareness of different kinds of communities with varying features. The discussion of the pictures might be taped so that the children can refer to it again and evaluate their responses after they have gathered more information about communities.

Developmental Activities

1. To develop the understanding that people live in many different kinds of communities with varied features, plan activities such as the following:

   Have the children study pictures of two different communities and discuss how they are alike and different. Ask them to compare these two communities with their own community.

   To help children define *community*, make a transparency with overlays entitled "What is a Community?" Draw an outline map on the transparency base and show items such as water, buildings, mountains, roads, and people on the overlays. (The teacher may prefer to prepare cutouts for a flannel board story.) As the overlay (or cutout) showing only natural features is added, ask questions such as the following:

   Does the land itself make a community? Why or why not?

   Would you like to live here as it is now? Why or why not?

   Place buildings on the land and ask similar questions. Add the overlay showing people and ask:

   Is this a community now? Why or why not?

   Would you like to live here now? Explain.

   Why are land, buildings, and people needed to make a community?

   Which of these do you think is most important in a community? Why?

   Children should conclude that people are the most important element in a community. People are needed to make a place a community; their needs and wants determine how the land is used and what buildings there will be.

T Many more questions are included in the actual unit. Note the emphasis on asking questions.

T Consider: What purposes are served by field excursions in this unit?

2. Children at this grade level should have many opportunities to explore their own community and observe its natural and human-made features. If possible, take several walking trips around the school neighborhood to observe the people and what they are doing, natural features, buildings, kinds of transportation, and other human-made features. In some areas of Baltimore County, the teacher may want to include nearby communities in the study to extend the possibilities for developing skills such as observing, classifying and analyzing data, and generalizing. To individualize instruction, use a variety of instructional materials and plan varied learning experiences to help children acquire knowledge and skills. Suggestions for activities are:

Divide the class into small groups and have each list or draw pictures of the kinds of land, buildings, and activities they might see in their own community. Discuss the lists made and construct a class chart or bulletin board to summarize the children's ideas.

Then have the children take a tour of the community and note the things they really do see. In some communities it may be possible to send small groups of children accompanied by an adult to different sections of the community. After the tour, help the children evaluate the accuracy of their initial responses and make any corrections that are needed.

T Notice the variety of teaching strategies suggested in the resource unit. Here is a suggestion for using a learning station.

To increase children's awareness of their own community, construct learning stations that encourage them to express their ideas about the community in different ways. For example:

Ask them to select a place in the community that they like, such as a park, a store, a friend's house, or a favorite place in their own yard. Have them write a story about the place selected to tell where the place is located, what it looks like, what they like to do there, and why they like it. In small groups, they may read and discuss their stories.

Have the children write a letter telling about the community to a real or imaginary friend.

To help children determine reasons why people decided to live in their community, have them interview parents and neighbors. Help them prepare a questionnaire similar to the following to use in the survey:

T Notice that in Baltimore County, even second graders are involved in the collection of firsthand data, in this case through interviewing strategies.

In my second-grade social studies class we want to find out why people live in our community. Will you please tell us why you chose to live here? Please check on the following list the reasons that are most important to you.

_____ The schools are good.
_____ There are good stores.
_____ It has good places to live.
_____ It is near work.
_____ There is good transportation.
_____ Friends live here.
_____ There are parks and playgrounds.
Name some other reasons.

_____

_____

Thank you.

Ditto the questionnaire or have each child copy it. The children should take it home and administer it to one or more adults. Help the class tabulate the results on a chart.

To develop children's ability to use the skills of comparing, inferring, and generalizing, discuss questions such as: Which reasons were given most often? Least often? Do you think people in other communities would have answered differently? Why or why not? Might children respond differently to the questionnaire than adults did? Give reasons for your answers.

To compare and contrast different parts of the community, groups of children may take short study trips to various sections of it. For example, one group might observe the community immediately adjacent to the school and another might go to a nearby neighborhood. Before the trip, have the children raise questions about the land, streets, buildings, and people that they want to answer.

T Evaluate the suggested activities provided in this resource unit in terms of the levels of thinking being stressed. Are students primarily involved in knowledge or are they beginning to analyze, generalize, summarize, synthesize, and evaluate?

To develop spatial concepts, have children construct a table or floor model of the community. Develop an understanding of what a model is by displaying models of trains, cars, or airplanes and discussing the characteristics of models. Transparencies 1, 2, and 3 from *Map Skills*, Set I (Hammond) will be helpful.

Place an oil cloth map base on a table or the floor and explain that the base represents the land of the community. Construct a model of the school and place it in the center. Using a street map of the area as a guide, help the children draw in the streets around the school.

The children may refer to the pictures they made after completing the tour of their community to recall the types of buildings they saw; how these buildings were arranged, e.g., adjoining, close together,

T Consider: What basic map understandings are being taught in this unit?

with vacant space or whole lots between them; what the buildings were used for; and how a person might travel from one building to another. They should use cardinal directions when describing routes. Discuss the size of the buildings to be made for the model to help children realize that the model is not as large as the community and therefore, model buildings will vary in size but will not be as large as the real buildings.

Using a variety of boxes, have the children construct models of the buildings in the school community and place them on the map base. Help them to understand that the model represents part of the community and the streets do not actually stop at the edges of it.

To strengthen and extend map skills, plan a variety of small group and/or individual activities such as the following:

Show and discuss the sound filmstrip, *What a Map Is*, from the *Maps Show the Earth* Kit.

In the classroom, have the children use a compass to determine cardinal directions. Write each direction on a card. As one child faces north, attach the "north" card to the north wall of the room. Then help the children identify the other directions and attach the appropriate card to each wall. Point out that east is to the right when one faces north and that west is to the left. (In some classrooms, it may be more helpful to make a weather vane by hanging the cards naming the directions from the ceiling.) Refer to these directions whenever it is necessary to express location.

To help pupils associate symbols on a map with places in a community, have them examine community maps such as the one on pp. 26-27 in *Man and His Communities*. As each community map is shown, discuss questions such as the following: What places do you see? How might people travel from place to place in this community? What kinds of work are done in it? How can you tell? Which places would you like to visit? Why? What places do you see on these maps that can be found in your community? Which ones are not in your community? If you were to make a map of your own community what new things would you need to show? What symbols might you use? How might a similar map of your own community help you? The pupils should conclude that since many communities have the same basic features, similar symbols will appear on the maps of different communities.

3. To develop the understanding that communities change over time and are constantly changing, plan small group activities such as the following:

T In this unit, reference is made to materials readily available in the schools of the district. What value do you see in this? Think about this statement: The most useful resource units are those developed by knowledgeable groups of teachers working at the school or district level.

T Think about this question: Do you think this district uses one or more than one text series? What evidence do you have to support your assumption?

Have the children interview parents, grandparents, or other long-time residents of their community to learn how the community looked when they were children, how the people lived then, what changes they have seen over the years, and how different people felt about some of the changes. Small groups may tape-record the interviews, write summaries of the information obtained, and/or invite the resource person to talk to the class. If old newspapers, maps, or photographs are available, children may use them to identify some of the changes that have occurred in the community.

Show the sound filmstrip, *The Everchanging Community*. Have the children compare the changes depicted in the filmstrip with those in their community. Point out that some communities may change more quickly than others.

Children might make a mural showing possible changes in a community such as new families moving in; people moving out; streets being widened; old buildings being repaired; new schools, homes, and other buildings under construction; buildings being torn down; and new parks and playgrounds being added.

Have children examine pictures such as those on pp. 124-125 in *Our Working World: Neighborhoods* to discover natural and human-made changes that may occur in a community. Ask questions such as the following: What kinds of changes are taking place in these communities? What effect might the changes have on the people who live in the communities? Help the children grasp cause-and-effect relationships by summarizing their responses in two columns on the chalkboard. In one column list the examples of change and in the other, the possible effects of each on the community.

Evaluation Suggestions

1. To evaluate children's understanding of the different features of a community, read the story *And to Think That I Saw It on Mulberry Street*. Then have the children play a game by completing the statement, "I think I saw a _____ in my community." They may name real things in the community, things not present in the community, or even fanciful things. The class should decide whether or not the statement is true for their community and explain why. The game may be extended to include different types of communities, e.g., "I think I saw a _____ in a rural community."

2. To assess children's ability to identify the features of different kinds of communities, have them play the game, "Just Imagine." Tell them

T The full resource unit supplies many additional activities that center on the concept of change.

T Additional evaluation suggestions are included in the full resource unit. They tend to be as informal and creative as the two samples.

to imagine the following situations, answer each question, and give reasons for their answers.

Can you imagine . . . a community that has only people in it? a skyscraper with a farmer plowing land next to it? a cowboy on horseback crossing a city street? a farm with a bus station next to it? a big baseball stadium or park with a launching pad next to it? people mending fishing nets in a desert? As the game is played, the teacher should note those children who are able to identify the features of diverse communities and to analyze and evaluate information.

Resources for Unit: Looking at Communities

Text References

T The full resource unit lists twelve text references.

Anderson, Edna A. *Living in Communities*. Morristown, New Jersey: Silver Burdett Company, 1976.

Brandwein, Paul F. et al. *The Social Sciences: Concepts and Values*. Second Edition. New York: Harcourt Brace Jovanovich, 1975.

Davis, O. L., Jr. et al. *Buildings We See* (Unit). New York: American Book Company, 1971.

Library References

T The full resource unit lists twenty-one titles of books for children.

Barth, Edna. *The Day Luis Was Lost*. Boston: Little, Brown and Company, 1971.

Luis knew well the community that made up his home, school and playground, but the day the water main broke, forcing him to find another way to school, he discovered a wider world.

Binzen, Bill. *Miguel's Mountain*. New York: Coward-McCann, Inc., 1968.

In an effort to stop the big pile of dirt in the park from being taken away, Miguel writes a letter to the mayor and so saves the "mountain" for the children to play on. Based on a real incident in Manhattan, this New York community is graphically shown by black-and-white photography.

Non-Print Materials

Filmstrips

T The full unit lists thirteen filmstrips.

City and Town. Learning Tree Filmstrips, 1974. (Set of 4 filmstrips: The Megalopolis, The City, The Town, and The Small Town)

Communities Are Different. Eye Gate House, Inc., 1971.

Finding Your Way (The Social Sciences Concepts and Values Sound Filmstrips–Green). Harcourt Brace Jovanovich, 1974.

Neighborhoods. Coronet Instructional Media, 1967. (Set of 6 filmstrips):

Multimedia Kits

Grossman, Ruth; and Michaelis, John. *Schools, Families, and Neighborhoods*. Addison Wesley Publishing Company, Inc., 1969.

Maps Show the Earth. A. J. Nystrom Company, 1971.

Study Prints

How People Travel in a City. Singer/SVE, 1966. (8 prints)
Keeping the City Clean and Beautiful. Singer/SVE, 1966. (8 prints)
The Northeast. The Fideler Company, 1967. (45 prints)

Transparencies

Map Skills, Set I. Hammond, Inc., 1969. (Color, 40 transparencies)

A Problem to Ponder

After studying the representative sections of the resource unit
reproduced on the preceding pages, the reader should consider
the following:

1. What decisions must the teacher make in planning an
   instructional unit that takes off from the resource unit? What
   clues are evident in this resource unit to indicate that it is a
   beginning point for instructional planning, not a finished
   instructional unit?
2. What additional avenues should the teacher using the unit
   explore?
3. In what ways might the teacher vary one or more activities to
   expand their value?

Designing Teaching Units: Putting the Pieces of a Puzzle Together

Having specified objectives and identified sources of materials and
ideas relative to a topic, the teacher must put together a **teaching
unit**–a creative sequence of activities for use with a particular group of
children. This task involves choosing from among possible activities
described in resource units and devising others. It also involves
sequencing pieces into an organized whole–a whole in which each
activity builds upon preceding activities and flows into the ones that
follow; a whole in which instructional and evaluative pieces blend
together. In sum, unit planning is like putting the pieces of a puzzle
together.

T Pieces of α Unit

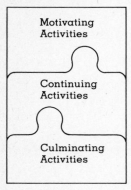

Motivating Activities

Continuing Activities

Culminating Activities

Deciding on the Pieces to Put into the Puzzle

Most units are comprised of three "pieces":

1. Motivating activities that establish the direction or directions the unit will take
2. Continuing activities through which major objectives are realized and fundamental generalizations are developed
3. Culminating activities that make the entire unit–or puzzle–fall into place.

These three components must fit closely together if the unit is to stand as α cohesive, integrated learning experience.

Deciding on a First Piece

What determines how teacher and students first make contact with unit content and processes? The word *motivating* applied to introductory unit activities suggests that beginnings should grab students both emotionally and intellectually. This criterion for determining what motivating activities to choose eliminates beginnings that ask youngsters to outline or to read α lengthy passage. More suitable unit starts include:

T See chapter 12, page 384, for a sample selection from Joseph Plumb Martin's *Adventures of a Revolutionary Soldier.*

1. Listening to α passage read dramatically by the teacher–For example, the teacher can introduce the American Revolution to upper graders by reading selected sections of Joseph Plumb Martin's *Narrative of a Revolutionary Soldier.* The teacher can follow with *Bang Bang You're Dead,* a story of playing at war, to help children see that war brings pain and suffering. Children react orally to the dramatic reading.
2. Viewing α series of pictures, a filmstrip, or a film and brainstorming background information for later generalizing activity–This was the motivational beginning suggested in the unit on communities given earlier in the chapter.
3. Interpreting large maps and globes with students describing what they perceive. Map and globe interpretation with follow-up map production can prove α good entry into regional studies.

T See the graph on page 64 of this book. It could be used in this fashion.

4. Interpreting α graph prominently displayed and considering the implications of the data shown–This can be α good beginning for upper graders working with world food or energy problems.
5. Handling related objects (realia or artifacts) and describing them–This can be α good entry into cultural studies.
6. Reacting to α questionnaire and talking about choices made— Wherever there is an element of controversy, this activity can strike an emotional chord with participants.

An Oral Beginning.   One feature shared by these possible unit beginnings is that all have an oral component, inviting children to talk together. There is a clear advantage to making unit introduction a class activity. The teacher establishes foundations upon which children will build later through independent research and learning-station activity. To throw elementary students out on their own at the very beginning of a unit without any preliminary group discussion is unwise. They begin without a clear perspective on the topic.

An Inductive Teaching Sequence.   A second feature of all the items is that they are relatively specific. Children begin by listening to a specific poem, story, or first-person account; by studying realia; or by examining pictures, maps, graphs, and so on. By beginning with specific instances rather than general ideas, students can use what they are first encountering as a base for later generalizing, hypothesizing, and relating. An inductive teaching model (Figure 16.4) demands movement from specific to general; it demands tightly focused beginnings.

Figure 16.4
An Inductive Teaching Model

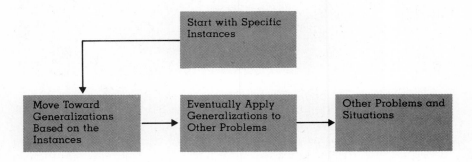

Rapid Involvement of Mind and Feelings.   A third feature of all the suggested unit beginnings is that children become involved directly from the very start. The teacher does not begin by telling or explaining. The class begins by doing! Neither does the teacher begin by laying out the work that groups will accomplish as part of library-centered research. Even though a unit may ultimately be structured as a library investigation, students need more than a brief teacher explanation of the topic and subtopics to excite them. They need direct involvement through talking, handling, viewing, reacting.

A Topical Connection.   A fourth feature of most of the suggested unit beginnings is that they interrelate with the unit topic in some way. As the teacher begins to plan, he or she may quickly conclude that—

Most units include talk times when children meet
to share their problems and their findings.

given the topic of the unit, the skills to be developed, and the previous
levels of student attainment—certain beginnings seem more appropriate than others. Thus regional studies may start with map or globe
interpretation and production; cultural studies with artifacts or picture
reading; or historical studies with listening time dedicated to first-
person accounts.

A Student Connection.   Yet another feature of most of the unit beginnings is that they take into account the maturity level of the children. Only an older elementary student could appreciate Martin's
firsthand account of time spent in the Continental Army. In contrast,
a picture storybook is more acceptable in lower grades as an
introduction.

In attempting to make "the student connection," the teacher may be
tempted to begin with a pretest that establishes students' previous understanding of the topic. He or she may introduce the unit by saying,
"We are going to study our town. Let's see how much you already
know. I will hand out a short pretest. Follow the directions. Write your
answers on the paper." To start this way is discouraging to students.

Pretesting is important, as was pointed out in chapter 10, but it should not be the introduction to the unit. Rather, pretesting can occur at an evaluation table. Independently, students go to the table to take a short test related to the content of unit study. They drop completed papers into a finished-papers drawer. With regard to skills, formal pretesting is not necessary at the beginning of a unit if the teacher is assessing student progress on a continuing basis. While working with children on previous units, the teacher is gathering data about their skill development. This ongoing input helps the teacher determine what skills to stress in the future.

Deciding on a Final Piece

Common sense suggests that, having tentatively decided how to begin a unit, the teacher should next decide on successive activities. However, common sense can be deceptive. Thinking in terms of possible culminating activities often proves to be a more productive next step. Culminating activities do not serve only as a means of tying loose ends together. In some instances, culminations are productions toward which participants work during much of the unit. A few examples will show how once a comprehensive culminating activity has been selected, it can determine many of the activities that form the core of unit study. Such culminations include:

1. a mock TV or radio show–Throughout the unit students gather information to include in the show, assign parts, and prepare the presentation.
2. a period newspaper or magazine–Students become newspaper staffs, each publishing a paper that tells something about the way people lived during a particular period. The culmination is the sharing of published papers.
3. a street fair or festival–Children, studying the way people live in an area of the world, identify a major holiday, celebration, or festival. Throughout the unit they gather data on this event; the culmination is a celebration in the classroom.
4. a meal—Students learn about food customs and prepare dishes representative of the people they are studying. The actual meal—served and eaten in the classroom—is the culmination of the unit.
5. a dramatization–Students work in groups to dramatize key events of a period they are studying. Data collection focuses on preparation for the dramatization.
6. a mural–Throughout the unit, data uncovered are developed as a mural. As a culmination of the unit, youngsters take turns reviewing key mural components for members of another class

who come to view the production. See the mural at the beginning of this chapter as an example of how comprehensive data compiled in this form can be.

Of course, not all culminating activities are this comprehensive. Sometimes a culminating activity is simply a talk time, when youngsters identify those customs, points, and people encountered in the unit that they believe were the most significant. They share their reasons for their choices. In other cases, an individual child or a small group may present a dramatic reading that sums up major themes developed. In still others, the culmination is a general sharing time when all children display products—written or visual—they have created during unit study.

Deciding on the Overall Unit Design

At some point, of course, the teacher must make final decisions as to which activities will form the nucleus of unit study. What determines the ultimate direction the unit will take? Basically there are three major determinants: the nature of the topic and the kinds of generalizations inherent in the content, the needs of the children, and the manner in which previous units have been designed.

The Topic as Determinant. As the reader may remember, the resource unit on communities presented in this chapter was organized with activities outlined under key generalizations. Activities in each section were structured so that children could discover those generalizations for themselves. In this case, the unit was primarily a geographic one, requiring considerable work with mapmaking and interpretation. Other units with a more economic focus may require work with basic mathematical relationships; others with an historic focus may require activity with time lines; still others with a cultural focus may require more craft and art activities.

The Children as Determinants. At times the teacher selects one activity rather than another because youngsters require more work with a particular skill. The chosen activity provides further practice with the needed skill; the omitted one does not. And so the decision is made.

At other times children's ability level is the deciding factor. An activity described in a resource unit may be too sophisticated or too simple for youngsters in the group. Another activity more in line with children's ability is chosen, or an appropriate activity may have to be created. At still other times the personality and interests of the class cause a teacher to reject one and select another activity. A teacher who knows a group may think, "My class would go through the roof if I tried that!" Or "My class would get bored with that."

The Unit in Perspective.   Variety is the spice of life—or so says the familiar expression. To approach every unit in a similar way or to rely always on the same limited selection of activities can cause children to lose their enthusiasm for social studies. Sometimes, therefore, a teacher selects one activity rather than another simply because the approach differs from those children have already experienced in previous units. Here the teacher thinks in yearlong terms: "In the first unit I emphasized library research. I focused the second on independent learning-station activity. Maybe we will complete most of our third unit as a whole class, having many class discussions. Children need practice communicating orally in group situations." At this point, the instructional planner is balancing one activity with others that are different so that youngsters' experiences will be varied and challenging.

Designing a Creative Whole

Having made tentative decisions about how to handle a unit, the teacher must develop a sequence of activities through which children will achieve the objectives identified earlier in the planning process. At this stage it is imperative that the teacher see how ideas fit together, how specific instances relate to generalizations, how one activity can be used to lead into others, how small group and independent activity can flow out of class brainstorming and discussion, and how small group activity can lead into total class discussion sessions.

A Flowchart Approach to Activity Sequencing.   Because a unit is a flowing sequence that generates further activity as it progresses, the **unit flowchart** is a useful technique for plotting out its design. A flowchart schematically depicts: 1) motivating, continuing and culminating activities; 2) the relationships among small group, independent study, learning-station, and class activities; and 3) the general direction of movement the unit will maintain. The planner begins by planning the motivating activity that will get the unit moving. By now, having spent considerable time weighing possible options, the teacher should have a clear concept of what that activity will be. Therefore, on the flowchart, he or she writes a very brief summary of the activity. If objectives have been clearly specified in terms of desired behaviors and if each has been numbered, the planner may place in the beginning block of the flowchart the number corresponding to the objective that may be achieved through the activity. Later, when writing daily lesson plans, the teacher can think through and elaborate on each step in the projected activity and include the full statement of objective or objectives in the plan.

In like manner, the planner plots continuing activities, identifying whether each activity will involve the entire class or only segments of it. Arrows indicate the direction of movement from one activity to the next. Objectives are noted next to the activity title.

The advantage of a flowchart approach to unit design is that the entire plan is visible at a single glance. Analyzing the projected design clearly laid out, the planner can note flaws—places where additional experiences will be needed if all objectives are to be realized, where the flow between activities is not logical, or where the sequence should be changed. A second advantage is that changes are easy to make as the unit progresses. The teacher can switch arrows around, add other activities to the chart, or delete ones previously included. A unit rarely functions just as its designer initially projects. Even the best plans must be modified as the teacher discovers that children need more time to complete a specific task or take less time to complete another.

An Example of Flowchart Planning.   A flowchart for a brief unit on the newspaper is given in Figure 16.5.

**Figure 16.5
A Flowchart for a Teaching Unit on the
Newspaper**

Objectives:

By the completion of the unit, the student should be able to:

1. Categorize items in a newspaper as news stories, editorials, features, classifieds, advertisements, letters, and so forth.
2. Identify (after analytic study) the overall design of a particular newspaper and tell where items tend to be located.
3. Contribute ideas to a full-class discussion session.
4. Present a brief summary of findings to a larger listening group and answer questions on the findings.
5. Identify editorial point of view and specific words an editor uses to communicate that view.
6. Write several paragraphs that express a clear point of view on an issue.
7. Contribute a product to a cooperative group project.
8. Produce a piece of work on an independent basis in response to a teacher's assignment.
9. Read a newspaper and come away with key details of information: who, what, when, where, and why.
10. Write a reportorial piece that clearly sets forth details of who, what, when, where, and why.
11. Categorize advertising appeals: glittering generalities, bandwagon, celebrity testimonial, and so forth.

12. Read a newspaper regularly to find out about his or her community.

13. Follow a set of written directions by performing the steps set forth in these directions.

The Plan

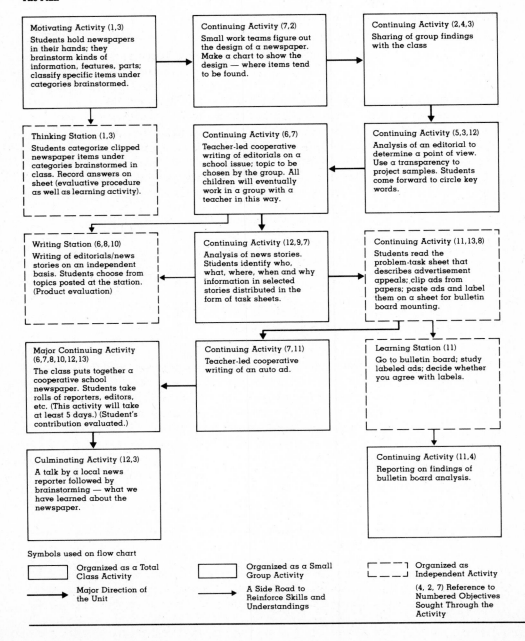

Motivating Activity (1,3)

Students hold newspapers in their hands; they brainstorm kinds of information, features, parts; classify specific items under categories brainstormed.

Continuing Activity (7,2)

Small work teams figure out the design of a newspaper. Make a chart to show the design — where items tend to be found.

Continuing Activity (2,4,3)

Sharing of group findings with the class

Thinking Station (1,3)

Students categorize clipped newspaper items under categories brainstormed in class. Record answers on sheet (evaluative procedure as well as learning activity).

Continuing Activity (6,7)

Teacher-led cooperative writing of editorials on a school issue; topic to be chosen by the group. All children will eventually work in a group with a teacher in this way.

Continuing Activity (5,3,12)

Analysis of an editorial to determine a point of view. Use a transparency to project samples. Students come forward to circle key words.

Writing Station (6,8,10)

Writing of editorials/news stories on an independent basis. Students choose from topics posted at the station. (Product evaluation)

Continuing Activity (12,9,7)

Analysis of news stories. Students identify who, what, where, when and why information in selected stories distributed in the form of task sheets.

Continuing Activity (11,13,8)

Students read the problem-task sheet that describes advertisement appeals; clip ads from papers; paste ads and label them on a sheet for bulletin board mounting.

Major Continuing Activity (6,7,8,10,12,13)

The class puts together a cooperative school newspaper. Students take rolls of reporters, editors, etc. (This activity will take at least 5 days.) (Student's contribution evaluated.)

Continuing Activity (7,11)

Teacher-led cooperative writing of an auto ad.

Learning Station (11)

Go to bulletin board; study labeled ads; decide whether you agree with labels.

Culminating Activity (12,3)

A talk by a local news reporter followed by brainstorming — what we have learned about the newspaper.

Continuing Activity (11,4)

Reporting on findings of bulletin board analysis.

Symbols used on flow chart

Organized as a Total Class Activity

Organized as a Small Group Activity

Organized as Independent Activity

Major Direction of the Unit

A Side Road to Reinforce Skills and Understandings

(4, 2, 7) Reference to Numbered Objectives Sought Through the Activity

In analyzing Figure 16.5, note particularly the following:

1. Objectives are number coded. By juxtaposing proposed activities and objectives, the teacher can quickly check to see that no objectives are being ignored.
2. The organizational patterns are symbolically coded. By highlighting the organizational patterns in this way, the teacher can see at a glance how one piece of the design relates to other pieces.
3. Arrows show the onward direction of the unit.

Working from the flowchart, the teacher develops plans for individual lessons within the series, prepares task sheets indicated therein, and collects the materials necessary for the study. In addition, the teacher sets up a reading table that contains related informational books, stories, and newspaper samples; sets up a listening-viewing station where students go independently throughout the unit to gather information from tapes and filmstrips; and sets up an individual conference center where he or she meets with individuals and small groups. Creative titles can designate specific learning stations in the classroom—for example, Book Nook, Listening Studio, Problems Lab, Writing Workshop, and so forth.

Planning Units of Instruction: A Summary Thought or Two

This chapter has described a flowchart model for planning teaching units based on resource units that describe numbers of activities to use for both instructional and evaluative purposes. The model assumes that the teacher who has projected a teaching unit will go on to design individual lesson plans that detail each activity in the projected sequence. This concept of unit planning stresses planning as a thinking process in which the teacher must consider numerous variables that affect decision making. The teacher as planner is essentially a decision maker, with the quality of his or her decisions influencing the quality of teaching and learning.

A Problem to Ponder

Based on the resource unit on communities found within this chapter, devise a flowchart for an actual teaching unit for use with a particular group of second graders. Before starting, make sure

you agree with the statement of behavioral objectives set forth in the unit; delete objectives that will have no component activity in your teaching unit; add other objectives that you believe you can also achieve through your projected sequence.

When you have plotted your plan on paper, analyze it to see whether there is a smooth flow of ideas and activity from one part to another; whether there is enough emphasis on independent study, total class interaction, and small group interaction; and whether there might be need for more learning-station activities to reinforce skills and understandings being developed in group sessions.

References

Bloom, Benjamin. *Taxonomy of Educational Objectives: The Classification of Educational Goals.* New York: Longman, 1956.

Callahan, Joseph; and Clark, Leonard. *Innovations and Issues: Planning for Competence.* New York: Macmillan, 1977.

Davies, Ivor. *Objectives in Curriculum Design.* New York: McGraw-Hill, 1977.

Gronlund, Norman. *Stating Objectives for Classroom Instruction.* 2nd ed. New York: Macmillan, 1978.

Hannah, Larry; and Michaelis, John. *A Comprehensive Framework for Instructional Objectives: A Guide to Systematic Planning and Evaluation.* Reading, Massachusetts: Addison-Wesley, 1977.

Hoover, Kenneth; and Hollingsworth, Paul. *A Handbook for Elementary School Teachers.* 2nd ed. Boston: Allyn & Bacon, 1978.

Kibler, Robert; Barker, Larry; and Miles, David. *Behavioral Objectives and Instruction.* Boston: Allyn & Bacon, 1970.

Krathwohl, David; Bloom, Benjamin; and Masia, Bertram. *Taxonomy of Educational Goals, Handbook II: Affective Domain.* New York: David McKay, 1964.

Lindvall, C. M., ed. *Defining Educational Objectives.* Pittsburgh: University of Pittsburgh Press, 1964.

Mager, Robert. *Preparing Instructional Objectives.* Belmont, California: Fearon-Pitman, 1962.

Popham, James; and Baker, Eva. *Establishing Instructional Goals.* Englewood Cliffs, New Jersey: Prentice-Hall, 1970.

17 Social Studies Programs: Yesterday, Today, and Tomorrow

Jessica is thinking about the way the world will
be when she is forty years old.

Key Questions

What is meant by a concentric circle, or expanding world design, as this term applies to the social studies? What can be a drawback of this design?

What major changes occurred in the selection and organization of content as a result of the new social studies? What triggered these changes?

What is a spiral curriculum? What is the function of facts in a spiral curriculum?

What is inquiry teaching? What is discovery teaching and learning?

What new emphasis appeared in the social studies about 1970? What renewed emphasis appeared about 1975?

What kinds of questions must the teacher involved in program selection ask?

What appear to be major directions for social studies programming in the 1980s?

Describe some ways in which society will probably change in the near future. How will the schools also have to change?

Figure 17.1
A Page from a Social Studies Program

Hamilton's influence on early American life was great. He created an alliance between government and the rich. Congress created the national bank. It put tariffs on foreign goods. Hamilton's suggestions helped build our modern industrial nation. But he paid more attention to the rich people and businessmen than to other groups in society.

Alexander Hamilton Tests the Social System

Hamilton tested the social system. He tested the idea that the government should not support any group at the expense of another group in society.

Test Yourself

1. What is a sound money system?
2. Why did Hamilton want the federal government to repay state debts?
3. How does specialized labor lead to greater production?
4. What is a tariff? How did Hamilton's tariff plans help American business?
5. What group of people benefited most from Hamilton's ideas? Did most of the American people belong to this group?

197

From *Our Working World: The American Way of Life* by Lawrence Senesh. © 1973, Science Research Associates, Inc. Reproduced by permission of the publisher.

The time was September 1959; the place was Woods Hole, Massachusetts; the event was a conference of leading scholars, educators, and scientists; the purpose was to talk about how education—specifically in science—might be improved. The discussions that occurred in that quiet Cape Cod community, as well as the events that led to the calling of the Woods Hole conference, were of major significance. They established a new direction not only for science education but also for programs in the social studies—a direction in which the fundamental ideas, or the **structure of a discipline,** became major organizing strands within the curriculum.

R The Woods Hole conference was reported in Jerome Bruner, *The Process of Education* (Cambridge, Massachusetts: Harvard University Press, 1960).

It was Sputnik, launched by the Russians in 1957, that forced educators to rethink ideas about the content and method of education. In response to Sputnik, the American nation clamored for tougher school programs, competitive with the Russians'. Congress allocated money for the development of curriculum projects that could be used in elementary and secondary schools. The first funded project was in the physical sciences; a National Science Foundation grant went to the Massachusetts Institute of Technology for the development of a high school program through which students woud acquire in-depth understanding of physics and the ways scientists pursue investigations in that discipline. In rapid succession, groups across the country began the development of new programs in mathematics, biology, and chemistry, often led by practicing mathematicians and scientists.

R See John Haas, "Social Studies; Where Have We Been? Where Are We Going?" *The Social Studies,* 70: 147-154 (July/August 1979).

As part of this new wave of scholarly interest in elementary and secondary programs, the noted economist Lawrence Senesh led a team in the development of an elementary program, *Our Working World*, through which young children were introduced to fundamental economic concepts and principles. Figure 17.1 is from the 1973 edition of that program. This series shows how economics is being integrated into the social studies. Appearing several years after the Senesh project was another more controversial program, *Man: A Course of Study,* which was developed under the leadership of Jerome Bruner and which drew heavily upon data uncovered by anthropologists and sociologists. The age of the "new social studies" had dawned!

Social Studies: Changes and New Directions

The age of the new social studies ushered in a changed view of the content appropriate for elementary programs, the manner in which this content should be organized for instruction, and the grade level at which specific content should be introduced. It also ushered in a changed view of the methodology and the fundamental goals to be achieved through instruction.

The Content and Organization of the Curriculum

In determining the content and organization of social studies programs, designers have tended to talk in terms of the **readiness** of a learner—whether a youngster is prepared intellectually, physically, emotionally, and socially for a particular learning to occur. Older programs—that is, pre-Woods Hole and Sputnik—typically were based on the assumption that learning is most meaningful when it begins with the immediate surroundings with which children are familiar and expands outward in concentric circles, so that youngsters gradually make contact with events and people farther removed from themselves. Accordingly, in the past, children encountered content about home and family in early primary grades and moved on to study the neighborhood and community, the state and nation, and finally the world, as shown in Figure 17.2.

Strict adherence to an expanding world design, however, is open to the criticism that it maintains both an egocentric and ethnocentric orientation. In some programs, students focused on *their* families, *their* communities, *their* region, *their* nation, and *the* European heritage, while the rest of the world was given only passing attention—if it were studied at all. Because the emphasis was on Western civilization, huge gaps as well as overlaps resulted.

A Different Approach to Content Selection and Placement.

R See Jerome Bruner, *The Process of Education*, p. 12, pp. 38-40.

Jerome Bruner set the tone for much of the curriculum reform of the 1960s when he offered a view of readiness that shattered the conventional basis for selection of content. He wrote, "The foundations of any subject may be taught to anybody at any age in some form." The key words in Bruner's statement are *in some form*, for content must be presented in terms of children's unique way of learning and of viewing the world. Accepting Piaget's learning stages, Bruner reminded that the teacher must deal with content in a manner consistent with the stage of cognitive development at which children are functioning. For elementary students, who function at the concrete operational level, this means that learning must derive from manipulation of objects and be internalized through manipulation of symbols.

Bruner also proposed that children can intuitively grasp the basic ideas of a subject area. Based on this belief, anthropology, sociology, economics, and political science—which were once considered intellectual fare only for high school and college students—were moved into the elementary curriculum. The result is that social studies programs today include not only history and geography, but sociology, an-

Figure 17.2
The Expanding World Design for
Social Studies Programs

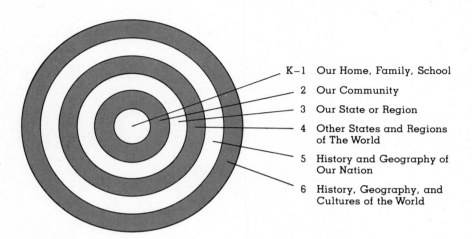

K–1   Our Home, Family, School

2   Our Community

3   Our State or Region

4   Other States and Regions of The World

5   History and Geography of Our Nation

6   History, Geography, and Cultures of the World

thropology, economics, political science, and sometimes psychology and ecology.

If all the social sciences are to be included in elementary social studies programs, an obvious next question is where in the curriculum one should place basic concepts and generalizations from these areas. In the past, history and geography were introduced in the third or fourth grade and continued through elementary and secondary schools. Should sociology, anthropology, economics, and political science be handled similarly?

Emphatically no, said the new planners. According to Bruner, students are more able to understand the fundamental conceptual schemes of a discipline if they meet them early in their schooling. The foundations of the social sciences should be introduced in primary grades. Youngsters encounter them over and over again, each time from a different perspective and in increasing depth. This is the design of a **spiral curriculum.** In a spiral curriculum, big ideas from all the social sciences are included at each grade level.

Let us take, for example, the concept of migration. First or second graders might deal with it by talking about why their families moved to Maintown, with the teacher summarizing points in a chart similar to the one shown in Figure 17.3. This simple chart shows the relationship between the specific reasons that brought individuals to Maintown and their actual move. Using it, primary students can consider related

R In the 1920s, Harold Rugg attempted a synthesis of the social studies. The junior- and senior-high school series he developed included ideas from history, civics, sociology, anthropology, and economics. See Peter Carbona, *The Social and Educational Thought of Harold Rugg* (Durham, North Carolina: Duke University Press, 1977).

R See Jerome Bruner, pp. 52-54.

questions: "Have other families moved here for the same reasons?" "Why did our families select Maintown and not Centerville?" "Do we like living in Maintown? Why?"

Figure 17.3
A Chart That Specifies Reasons
for Personal Migrations

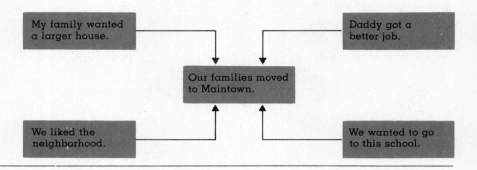

In the early primary years children focus on finding a place to live that meets personal needs. As these same youngsters encounter the same concept at higher levels, they consider other aspects: emigration and immigration, urbanization and flight from the cities, search for better living conditions, refuge from oppression and persecution, cultural diffusion, population patterns, and so forth. In this respect, and as Figure 17.4 suggests, the seedling of a big idea is planted in the first grade and extends its branches as it grows.

Integration of Content Through a Spiral Curriculum.   The traditional notion of readiness was based on the premise that one area of study should be mastered before the next was introduced. This led to the teaching of history and geography as discrete subject matter areas. A serious shortcoming of this arrangement, however, was that it compartmentalized learning and erected artificial boundaries—even barriers. It made the development of relationships between historical and geographic features almost impossible. When these two areas merged into the social studies several decades ago, the initial step in integrating social learnings had been taken.

The next step was taken with the introduction of concepts and generalizations from all the social science disciplines. This introduction

**Figure 17.4
The Branches That Can Grow
Out of a Concept Planted Early
in the Primary Years**

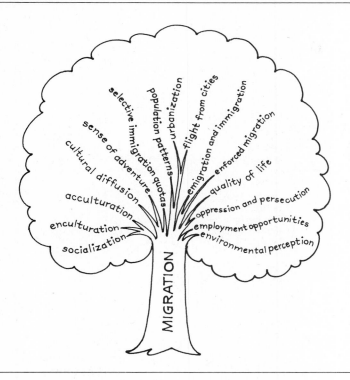

was not in the form of separate units based on each of the social sciences; rather the concepts and generalizations from sociology, anthropology, history, geography, economics, political science, and psychology were introduced as they related to human functioning. The result was an **interdisciplinary social studies** in which concepts from one area might be isolated for clarification or analysis but in which ideas blended as students used them to solve problems.

In practice, what does an **integration of the social sciences** mean? Let us look again at the concept of migration to see how integration of subject areas works. Starting in first grade, youngsters consider why their families moved to Maintown and talk about features in the community they like or dislike. In later years, they expand their understanding of the idea that the search for a better life is a persistent incentive for people to move. They learn that population shifts and patterns of migration have recurred throughout history. They look

R Check Robert Pearson, "Beyond the New Social Studies," *The Social Studies*, 64: 315-319 (December 1973) for a discussion of some of the problems inherent in the approaches of the new social studies. See also Martin Mayer, *Social Studies in American Schools* (New York: Harper & Row, 1964) for a critical discussion of some "sacred" approaches to the social studies.

at the role played by climate and topography and analyze the effects of movement on families and societies. In so doing, students work with big ideas of economics, geography, sociology, history, and even psychology, as can be seen in the spiral design depicted in Figure 17.5.

Figure 17.5
An Expanding Spiral Design That
Draws from All the Social Sciences

Why People Move

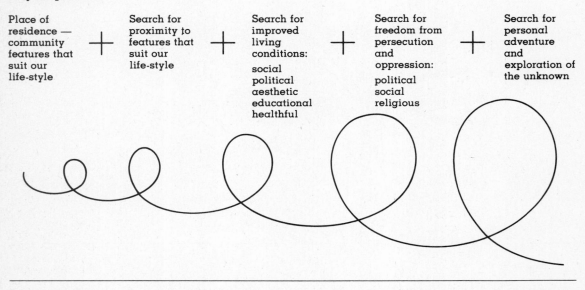

| Place of residence — community features that suit our life-style | + | Search for proximity to features that suit our life-style | + | Search for improved living conditions: social political aesthetic educational healthful | + | Search for freedom from persecution and oppression: political social religious | + | Search for personal adventure and exploration of the unknown |

Having studied historical migrations and having thought about moves they have made, by the end of elementary school, children working with a spiral curriculum should be able to express many important ideas in their own words. They should understand that people who voluntarily leave their residence or homeland may be motivated by a desire for economic, social, political, aesthetic, and/or salutary improvements; they are also looking for freedom from political, social, and/or religious oppression; they are looking for proximity to features that make possible a life-style they enjoy; and/or they are searching for adventure. This cluster of generalizations comes close to being a theory in that it can be used to explain past occurrences, to predict what may happen in the future, and to make decisions about actions that affect oneself.

T A theory is a broad explanatory statement that has stood the test of time. Although a theory is constantly refined as new information comes to light, a theory is usually accepted if no data exist that refute it.

The Function of Facts in a Spiral Curriculum. In older social studies textbooks, chronology in history and region in geography served as organizing features. History books typically started at some point in the past and continued until a later date. Books underscored the neat order of events, their causes and results, and the people largely responsible for them. Similarly, geography books focused on geo-political regions. Emphasis was on lists of crops, resources, cities, industries, and natural features. An unfortunate outcome of this form of content selection and organization was that many bits of information were stressed; meaningful relationships among them were ignored.

One way the new social studies deals with the problem of selecting and organizing relevant facts is to de-emphasize recall of specifics and concentrate on ways of processing information. Since no one can predict what facts will be relevant in the future, no particular pieces of information are singled out as all-important. Today's curriculum makers try to select materials from diverse places and time frames. A quick check of modern social studies programs illustrates the broad range of topics found—a Serbian village, the Aborigines of Australia, the Netsilik Indians of Alaska, and the Kpelle tribe of Africa. These topics are chosen to highlight relationships and to offer students the opportunity to search for and utilize facts in solving problems and formulating decisions.

A second way to deal with facts is to organize the social studies in terms of what Bruner calls the **structure of the disciplines,** the underlying principles, relationships, or big ideas upon which the disciplines are founded. These big ideas have wide application throughout students' school years and, indeed, throughout life. An organization based on the structure of the social sciences provides a meaningful framework for learning facts. Its advantages are fourfold, according to Bruner: 1) a content area becomes easier to comprehend; 2) memory of specifics improves; 3) greater transfer of learning occurs; and 4) the gap between elementary and advanced knowledge is narrowed.

R See Bruner, p. 18. See also two pieces by Philip Phenix: "New Concepts and the Crisis in Learning," *Teachers College Record,* 58: 137-143 (December 1956) and *Realms of Meaning* (New York: McGraw-Hill, 1964). Both suggest that the curriculum be organized around big ideas from the disciplines.

Generalizations are based on facts and, as with facts, can become obsolete. Since they represent the distillation of hundreds of facts about specific places, people, and events, however, these big ideas have greater application and a longer life.

Modes of Teaching and Learning

In the last decade the phrase **inquiry teaching** has come into general use to describe the instructional approaches of newer social studies programs. Inquiry teaching actually incorporates several related modes of thinking, teaching, and learning. It includes inductive and deductive thinking, intuitive thinking, and personalizing and valuing through in-depth study. Although much of this has been described in

R See, for example, Barry Beyer, *Inquiry in the Social Studies Classroom: A Strategy for Teaching* (Columbus, Ohio: Charles E. Merrill, 1971); see also Pearl Oliner, *Teaching Elementary Social Studies*, chapter 1, "Inquiry" (New York: Harcourt Brace Jovanovich, 1976), pp. 4-37; also Richard Gross, et al, *Social Studies for Our Times*, Section 4: "Inquiry Learning in Social Studies" (New York: John Wiley, 1978).

R See F. S. C. Northrop, *The Logic of the Sciences and the Humanities* (Cleveland and Silver Spring, Maryland: Meridian Books, World Publishing, 1959), pp. 35-58.

T See *People in the Eastern Hemisphere*, Book 6 (Morristown, New Jersey: Silver Burdett, 1979), chapter 16.

chapter 6, the following section highlights specific aspects that summarize the newer directions in teaching methods found in the programs of the 1960s and 1970s.

Analytic Teaching and Learning: The Inductive Stage.

Analytic thinking is the step-by-step, logical manipulation of data used by natural and social scientists to solve problems. It has become the backbone of inquiry teaching, for the cognitive processes inherent in inductive and deductive thinking are the processes through which children come to understand the social studies.

As the reader knows, **inductive thinking** relies on careful analysis of a problem to identify facts that must be known to solve the problem and on the methods of direct observation, description, and classification. Having analyzed the problem, a thinker observes the specifics of the case, expresses them in conceptual terms, and classifies the data. Translating these steps of thinking into teaching/learning terms, teacher and students begin by identifying specific instances and facts related to a problem being considered. Through skillful questioning and use of a variety of examples, the teacher guides students to uncover relationships for themselves and to organize their data to highlight these relationships. To encourage inductive thinking, the teacher questions rather than tells, draws out rather than explains. The result is self-discovery of the big ideas of the social sciences.

That discovery teaching and learning are integral parts of the new social studies programs can be seen by looking at a representative one. In the Silver Burdett elementary textbook series, upper elementary children read about the transmission of learning from generation to generation within three diverse cultures. They learn of the importance attributed to intellectual activity by the Jewish people from Biblical times to the present. They learn how apprenticeships operated in England during the Middle Ages. They learn too about the imitative forms of education prevalent in New Guinea at the time Margaret Mead carried out her landmark studies. Having encountered three instances, upper graders are asked to make a generalization that describes the relationships between the education of the young and the continuation of society.

Analytic Teaching and Learning: The Deductive Stage.

In deductive thinking, conclusions are reached by reasoning from general principles assumed to be true. From a practical standpoint, this is the purpose served by clusters of generalizations. In particular cases, the student, like the social scientist, can use the clusters to explain, predict, and decide.

The individual teacher is generally responsible
for planning the day-by-day activities of a class.

Deductive thinking is a component of many new text series. For
example, the 1975 edition of the Harcourt Brace Jovanovich series ends
each major chapter section with exercises titled "What Do You Think?"
and "What Should You Do?" At the fifth-grade level, youngsters who
have studied regional conflicts of interest and developed the generalization that people tend to pursue their own interests are given this
hypothetical problem:

T From *The Social
Sciences Concepts and
Values, Purple* (Fifth
Grade) (New York: Har-
court Brace Jovanovich,
1975), p. 223.

In 1789 Rhode Island and Delaware had only enough citizens to give
each state one vote in the House of Representatives. They knew that
even with two votes in the Senate they would not have as much
power as the bigger states.

What would those two states have gained if they had not joined
the union? What would they have lost?

In the text material preceding the problem, no reference is made to the
plight of Rhode Island and Delaware. This is a problem in which children are asked to predict the consequences of two opposite courses
of action based on generalizations they know. It requires deductive
thinking.

R See F. S. C. Northrop, *Logic of the Sciences and Humanities*, pp. 62-63.

Intuitive Thinking – Making the Big Leap.   When students apply their growing understanding of generalizations to the interpretation of a new problem, they are thinking in a logical manner. The leap they make between the known and the unknown is a small one. In contrast, when students think intuitively, they suddenly hit upon an idea without knowing exactly how or why they arrived at it. With a sudden burst of insight they have made a big leap from available data to the perception of relationships previously unknown to them.

Bruner explains that those conditions most conducive to intuitive thinking in classrooms include the following:

1. Teachers who themselves make educated guesses
2. Students who have considerable background in an area, especially a grasp of the structure of the discipline
3. Learners with confidence in themselves and their understanding of the subject
4. Minimal risks to the learners, who may resort to surer analytic modes of thinking when threatened.

R Based on Jerome Bruner, *The Process of Education* (Cambridge: Harvard University Press, 1960), pp. 61-63.

To teachers, it is sometimes disquieting to plan a step-by-step inductive-deductive sequence only to have it "ruined" by the student who almost immediately sees the point. Teachers may find themselves saying to the student, "Let's work through these facts systematically. You don't have the grounds to say that yet." But the fact remains that some of the greatest discoveries have come through intellectual leaps of insight; these leaps must be encouraged, not discouraged.

The instructional dilemma of teachers in this situation, however, disappears when they remember that immediate insights are only tentative and must be subjected to analytic verification. Teachers can respond, "That seems to be an educated guess, Keith. Let's go back now and check it out by identifying specific relationships." By using this tactic, teachers encourage the intellectual leapers and at the same time allow less able students to arrive at understanding step-by-step.

Intuitive thinking figures prominently in some of the newer social studies programs. Students are encouraged to make educated guesses, or **hypotheses,** based upon one or more activities and their own previous experiences. They then gather evidence either to prove or disprove their hypotheses. Hypothesizing is a valuable problem-solving tool that has lifelong significance; it enables one to make broad assumptions that can be used as a base for personal or group action.

T See *People in Families* (First grade), Teacher's Edition (Reading, Massachusetts: Addison-Wesley, 1972), p. 178.

In many newer programs, hypothesizing begins in primary grades. In Addison-Wesley's first-grade book, *People in Families*, a unit on one family, the Grossmans, opens with a picture of the boys of the family romping through the field. First graders are asked to hypothesize why no girls are in the picture. Later in the sequence, children are given the opportunity to decide whether their original hunch was right.

Personalizing and Valuing. In the period starting about 1970, many social studies programs began to emphasize the feelings and affective learnings of children. This was in contrast to almost total emphasis on intellectual functioning during the heyday of the new social studies in the 1960s. Much time today is devoted to the exploration of self; the examination of people's beliefs, attitudes, and values; and the exploration of similarities and differences of people. Two vehicles for developing affective learnings have surfaced: personalizing and valuing.

Personalizing has a distinctive meaning when used in the context of affective learning. **Personalizing** means that the learner is placed within the same setting as some other individual or group and from that perspective explores the feelings, choices, and/or decisions that these others have faced. Newer programs tend to advocate role-playing, sociodrama, debates, simulations, and so forth to involve children intimately in the content of the curriculum.

Values clarification and moral reasoning activities have also become major components of the social studies curriculum. In most programs, as youngsters decide how they would have reacted under the same conditions, they start by clarifying their own values. They identify their own feelings, attitudes, biases, preferences, and ideals relative to monumental historical events such as the relocation of the Japanese in the United States during World War II or relative to everyday problems encountered in the school or family. Emphasis is often on clarifying beliefs rather than accepting without question a set of societal values. Here is an example of a problem included in one text for third grade that encourages values clarification as children try to understand the concepts of rules and protest:

Reggie, Paul, Tito, Snooky, and Sal all belonged to the Sutter Street Club. The boys had built a tree-house to meet in, and they had made some rules. One rule said all the members had to pay ten cents dues each week.

One day Snooky said, "I don't have a dime this week. I'm not going to pay my dues."

"Well, it's a rule that you have to," Tito said.

"That's just too bad," Snooky said. "I'm not going to. It's not fair."

What do you think the boys should do? Why?

T From *The Social Sciences Concepts and Values*, Green, p. 225, 1975.

Multimedia Modes of Teaching and Learning. Inquiry teaching clearly necessitates the use of a wide range of materials and activities extending far beyond a single textbook. Many newer programs provide the teacher with instructional guides that describe supplementary activities and materials available for teaching and learning. The texts themselves include maps, charts, graphs, and pictures. Some include excerpts from original documents as well as from folktales, myths, legends, and autobiographies. Some also provide films, filmstrips, records, cassettes, and replicas of realia.

Using a variety of materials, students are encouraged to compare and contrast the facts given in different sources and to interpret them in terms of the biases of the people who prepared the materials. In this respect, students are encouraged to have a healthy skepticism. Working with first-person accounts and original documents, they analyze what the materials are telling them about a problem, time, or person. In this sense, many of the new social science programs are placing young learners in the role of the social scientist—albeit in a simple and unsophisticated way—to weigh conflicting evidence from varying sources and arrive at their own conclusions.

In-Depth Study. Inquiry teaching obviously takes time. To discover generalizations for oneself, to apply these to related instances, to hypothesize, and to consider one's values, beliefs, biases, and preferences takes much longer than to be told about the facts, generalizations, and outcomes.

Today's social studies programs generally provide for considerable concentration of time and thought on a more limited number of topics, with numbers of specific examples used as a basis for conceptualizing and generalizing. The one-year program *Man: A Course of Study* is a case in point. It attempts to find answers to only three questions: What is human about human beings? How did they get that way? How can human beings become even more human?

Less controversial programs such as the *McGraw-Hill Social Studies* series deal with people as they function under a variety of geographic, political, economic, and sociological conditions. Each book in the series deals with one major theme, as the titles verify: *Looking at Me*, *Discovering Others*, *Learning about People*, *Exploring Communities*, *Studying Cultures*, *Understanding the United States*, and *Investigating Societies* (1979). In this series students go beyond their own community, culture, and country to look at others. The fourth grade book, for example, introduces children to components of cultures found within four diverse groups: the Tasaday of the Philippines, the Mossi of Upper Volta, the Aymara of Bolivia, and the Uzbeks of the Soviet Union. By working with these cultures, children can generalize based on their in-depth understanding.

Basic Skills. The year 1975 witnessed a renewed emphasis on basic skills in the social studies. In the early 1960s, as curriculum makers began to consider anthropology, sociology, economics, and political science for inclusion in elementary programs, interest in basic skills waned a bit. Falling achievement scores nationwide, however, suggested a genuine need for more attention to these basics: reading and writing content material; locating information in references; interpreting maps, globes, charts, and graphs; getting information through listening; and taking notes. Thus, as the 1970s closed, many social studies programs began to highlight search and communication in addition to cognitive and social-emotional skills.

T That there is such a renewed emphasis is evidenced in advertising materials distributed by major publishers about their newest programs. For example, one publisher advertised in 1979 "a new edition with increased emphasis on the facts of geography and history, on map reading and other geography skills."

The Social Studies Today: Where It Is in the 1980s

In sum, it is possible to characterize the movements included in the term **the new social studies** as based on social sciences and inquiry. The new social studies brings children into contact with the major organizing ideas of history, geography, economics, political science, sociology, anthropology, psychology, and ecology in a spiral curriculum that enables learners to expand their understanding at each successive level. It provides opportunity for learners to function much in the manner of the social scientist. It provides opportunity too for learners to develop basic search and communication skills in meaningful contexts.

R Read NCSS Position Statement, "Revision of the Social Studies Curriculum Guidelines," *Social Education*, 43: 261-278 (April 1979).

Programs for Today and Tomorrow

The age of the new social studies not only ushered in changed views of the goals, content, organization, and methodology important in the social studies but also triggered a wave of curriculum projects and new or revised elementary text series that reflect these views. As a result of these changes, many good programs are available today, making the selection of text materials both easy and difficult—easy because text series can generally be found that harmonize with a school's stated social studies goals; difficult because with so many possibilities, the selection process becomes time-consuming.

In selecting social studies text series, teachers must consider the goals of the program, the accuracy and reliability of the content, and the manner in which the total program is organized. Figure 17.6 presents a guide for analyzing a social studies text series. As they analyze materials with such a guide, teachers must also begin to formulate value judgments about the comparative worth of the materials.

R See James Davis et al, "Evaluation of Curricular Projects, Programs, and Materials," *Social Education*, 36:712-72 (November 1972) for a comprehensive analysis of programs.

R Check Loretta Ryan, "Judging Textbooks: The Asia Society Project," *The Social Studies*, 68:236-240 (November/December 1977) for a discussion of treatment in textbooks of national and cultural groups as well as women.

Figure 17.6
A Guide for Analyzing a
Social Studies Text Series

I. **The Authenticity of the Content**
   A. Does the content reflect the real world as accurately as possible?
   B. Are the historical, sociological, anthropological, economic, geographic, and political generalizations valid?
   C. Are the data presented in charts, graphs, maps, and words up-to-date?
   D. Are the materials unbiased? Do they avoid stereotyped views of people and places? Do they give a comprehensive view of the topic rather than pushing a particular philosophical view?
   E. Were many educators and social scientists involved in the development of the program?

II. **The Goals of the Program**
   A. What kinds of skills are sought through the program?
      1. What kinds of problem-solving and decision-making skills are sought?
      2. What kinds of social-emotional skills are sought?
      3. What kinds of search and communication skills are being sought?
   B. What kinds of understandings are developed?
      1. What is the function of facts in the program?
      2. Are understandings from all the social sciences included?
      3. Are understandings about the unique nature of the human experience included?
   C. What kinds of attitudes, values, and appreciations are developed?
      1. What stress is given to self-awareness, career awareness, social awareness, and environmental awareness?
      2. Is the ability to clarify values a goal of the program?

III. **The Scope, Sequence, and Organization of the Program**
   A. What topics, concepts, and generalizations are part of the program at each level?
   B. How are the topics, concepts, and generalizations organized at each level?
   C. How is the program as a whole organized: spiral, expanding world, or modified expanding world?
   D. Are understandings from the different social sciences integrated into the program or treated as separate subjects?
   E. Do the topics, concepts, and generalizations harmonize with the stated goals of the program?

IV. **Modes of Teaching and Learning**
   A. Is the content presented so that students can discover generalizations for themselves and apply these in the interpretation of additional problems and situations?
   B. Are students given in-depth background on a problem or issue so that they can arrive at conclusions based on sufficient evidence?
   C. Are documents such as letters, articles, pictures, newspaper editorials and headlines, and diaries included in the text? Are folktales and/or songs included?
   D. Do the texts contain exploration logs, investigative data, and findings and writings of actual scientists so that students can function intellectually in the manner of a social scientist?

E. Is a wide range of people and actions depicted so that girls and boys of diverse ethnic backgrounds can see themselves reflected in the books?

F. Are many sides of an issue or problem presented?

V. **Writing Style and Vocabulary Level**

A. Are the writing style and vocabulary appropriate for the average reader?

B. Is the basic vocabulary comparable to that in the reading program?

C. When new, specialized words are introduced, are they explained in terms of the child's experience?

D. Is there a glossary in upper-level texts so that readers can develop skill in using this reference?

E. Does the prose style speak to children in nonpatronizing terms?

VI. **Format**

A. Are headings and subheadings utilized in a way that helps children see main ideas and relationships?

B. Are there periodic stopping points where students reflect upon and summarize their learnings, draw conclusions, arrive at solutions, hypothesize trends, and make plans?

C. What kinds of exercises are included? Do they require students to go beyond recall of specifics?

D. Is material laid out on pages in a clear, uncluttered way?

E. Are visuals used to supplement the written material?

F. Are pages bright and colorful without being distracting?

VII. **The Scope of the Teachers' Manual**

A. Does the manual clearly explain the goals, scope, and organization of the program?

B. Does it guide the teacher in developing logical learning sequences that require creative use of text materials?

C. Does the manual suggest specific activities for developing skills; for building attitudes, appreciations, and values; and for extending understanding beyond the text?

D. Is there a list of readings for the teacher who needs additional help?

E. Can the teacher function creatively and dynamically with the materials?

VIII. **Supplementary Materials**

A. What materials–tapes, filmstrips, pictures, realia–are available to use with the text?

B. What kinds of work sheets are available? tests?

C. How expensive are the supplementary materials?

Let us look at three social studies programs representative of the broad spectrum of materials that are currently in use:

1. *Man: A Course of Study* (Washington, D. C.: Curriculum Development Associates, 1974).

2. *Holt Databank System* (New York: Holt, Rinehart & Winston, 1976).

3. *Silver Burdett Social Studies* (Morristown, New Jersey: Silver Burdett, 1979).

In the section that follows, these three series are described briefly so that the reader can get some idea of current and future trends in social studies text material.

Man: A Course of Study

Man: A Course of Study, generally referred to as *MACOS*, is a full-year social studies program intended for fifth or sixth graders. It was developed by the Educational Development Center, Inc., under grants from the National Science Foundation. The first commercial edition became available in 1970.

R From Peter Dow,
*Man: A Course of Study,
Talks to Teachers.*
(Cambridge, Massachusetts: Educational
Development Center,
Inc., 1968), p. 6 and from
Janet Hanley et al,
*Curiosity, Competence,
Community, Man: A
Course of Study, An
Evaluation* (Cambridge:
EDC, 1969), p. 5.

Goals. The stated aims of the program are twofold: 1) "to stimulate children to think about the nature of humanness by providing them with interesting studies of animal behavior and human groups taken from recent work in the behavioral sciences and anthropology;" 2) to help children "come to understand that what we regard as acceptable behavior is a product of our culture." More specific pedagogical aims include the ability to 1) raise questions; 2) search for answers to questions raised and use the cognitive framework developed during the study in thinking about other areas; 3) use firsthand sources as a base for hypothesizing and drawing conclusions; 4) listen to and express ideas; 5) participate in open-ended discussions where no definitive answers are possible; 6) reflect on personal experiences; and 7) use the teacher as a resource.

R See J. S. Bruner,
Man: A Course of Study,
Occasional Paper No. 3,
The Social Studies Curriculum Program (Cambridge: Educational
Services, Inc., 1965),
p. 4. In the original,
Bruner speaks of *man*,
not *humankind*.

Scope, Sequence, and Organization. As Jerome Bruner outlined the program in 1965, "The content of the course is humankind." Three organizing questions serve as integrating strands: What is human about human beings? How did they get that way? How can they be made more so? In answering these questions, Bruner pointed to five "massive contributors" to people's humanization: toolmaking, language, social organization, the management of a prolonged childhood, and the urge to explain the world. To help children understand these characteristics of human activity, the program involves them first in a study of animals such as the salmon, the herring gull, the baboon, and the chimpanzee and then in a study of the life-styles of the Netsilik Eskimos who live in the Pelly Bay region of Canada. The entire second half of the year is dedicated to in-depth study of this small Eskimo group.

Materials. Three kinds of materials are part of the *MACOS* project: booklets, films, and simulation games. Instead of a textbook, the program offers thirty booklets that vary considerably in style, purpose, and amount of reading required. One booklet, for example, presents the field notes of anthropologist Irven DeVore, who studied animal life in Nairobi Park in the East African highlands. A second short booklet on structure and function includes simple sketches to illustrate major concepts. A third is a collection of songs and stories of the Netsilik. Maps, photographs, and posters related to the key ideas being studied are also provided. All these materials are intended for student use with minimal teacher direction.

Films and filmstrips are a major component of *MACOS*. The topics of these visual materials are the major topics of the program and parallel material presented in the booklets.

Simulation games are also an integral component. They enable fifth or sixth graders to participate in the life of the Netsilik. For instance, one game simulates seal hunting by the Netsilik. Students punch holes into a board in the hopes of catching a seal. Since chance allows some players to obtain more seals than others, participants readily discern the importance of sharing if those without seal meat are to survive.

Teacher Training. Because *MACOS* was one of the first programs to embody the content and inquiry mode of the new social studies, teachers participated in training sessions to learn to handle it. In addition, there is a guide for each section that explains the materials and offers ways of using them. The guides make very clear the instructional mode of the program: that students must be given freedom to think and interact with others with the teacher offering minimal direction.

Controversial Elements. Some of the content, teaching strategies, and materials that are a part of *MACOS* have come under fire as they have begun to be used in schools. Questions have been raised about their suitability for elementary children. Much has been written, pro and con, about this controversial program; the reader will want to read some of the articles and judge for him or herself.

Holt Databank System

Holt Databank, published in 1976 under the editorship of William Fielder, is a complete social science program for children in grades K-6. It is advertised as "a total systems approach" in which all the parts work together to achieve learning objectives.

Goals. The intended goals of *HDS* are fourfold: knowledge, inquiry, skill, and affective goals. The knowledge goals are expressed in terms of concepts rather than facts. On the first level, basic concepts include

R Read particularly: John Conlan, "MACOS: The Push for a Uniform National Curriculum," *Social Education*, 39:388-92 (October 1975).

Peter Dow, "MACOS Revisited: A Commentary on the Most Frequently Asked Questions About *Man: A Course of Study*," *Social Education*, 39:388, 393-396 (October 1975).

Bruce Larkin and the Executive Committee and members of the Board of Directors of NCSS. "The *MACOS* Question," *Social Education*, 39:445-450 (November/December 1975).

William Joyce, ed., "Social Studies and the Elementary Teacher" (a section containing five articles), *Social Education*, 38:441-457 (May 1974).

R Statements are from descriptive materials written and distributed by the publisher.

people, *earth*, *roles*, *social interaction*, *work*, *time*, *resources*, *language*, *seasons*, and *change*. In contrast, on the sixth level concepts are drawn from economics—*tools and technology*, *modern and non-modern people*, *market*, *production*, *price*, *supply and demand*, *resources*, and *ecology*—and from anthropology—*material culture*, *culture change*, *poverty*, and *interdependence*.

Inquiry goals are defined in terms of three mental operations: data gathering (observing, quantifying, interviewing, and experimenting); data organizing (classifying, comparing, defining, mapping, modeling, graphing, and charting); and data using (inferring, deducing, generalizing, explaining, predicting, and hypothesizing). Basic skill goals are defined as listening, speaking, reading, writing, chronology, and mapping. The affective goals being sought relate to values, attitudes, and self-concept. In sum, the goals of *HDS* are far broader and more inclusive than those sought through *MACOS*.

Scope, Sequence, and Organization. The scope and sequence of the Holt program are indicated through the level titles:

K—*Inquiring About Myself* (Emphasis: self, school, rules)

Level 1—*Inquiring About People* (Emphasis: how a person relates to others)

Level 2—*Inquiring About Communities* (Emphasis: the person, language, community, tools, and relationships between past and future)

Level 3—*Inquiring About Cities* (Emphasis: what a city is, has been, and can be; material primarily from geography and economics)

Level 4—*Inquiring About Cultures* (Emphasis: culture and cultural complexity; material primarily from anthropology and sociology)

Level 5—*Inquiring About American History* (Emphasis: the American nation; material drawn from history and political science)

Level 6—*Inquiring About Technology* (Emphasis: ways tools and technology have influenced human development; material from economics and anthropology)

Materials. The *Holt Databank System* has two basic student components: the text and the databank. The textbook at each level presents background information and introduces the problems for consideration. It differs from more traditional ones in offering numerous museum reproductions, cartoons, maps, drawings, and paintings as well as maps, charts, and graphs. With this emphasis on visual matter, the book does not prove a handicap for the limited reader, who still can perform fundamental cognitive operations using the visuals.

The databank is a collection of multimedia materials relating to the textbook units, or modules. Included are color/sound filmstrips, cassettes, simulations, foldouts, cards, pictures, and masters. These materials are packaged in compact units, which do not take up much classroom space. They are costly if the program is to be used with all youngsters in K-6, a factor that may deter some districts from considering the *HDS* as a program option.

The Teacher's Guide. A Teacher's Guide is available for use at each level. A relatively comprehensive aid, it explains how the system works, spells out behavioral objectives for each lesson, lays out daily lesson plans, and maps out materials to be used in each lesson.

Silver Burdett Social Studies

In 1979 Silver Burdett published an updated version of its textbook series titled *Silver Burdett Social Studies*. It is advertised as a complete K-8 program in which student textbooks and teachers' editions can be used alone or in conjunction with coordinated components that allow for considerable individualization.

Goals. The three primary goals of the program each receive equal emphasis. First, there is a knowledge dimension designed "to give children the strong foundation of facts, concepts, and skills needed for an accurate, in-depth, and useful understanding of today's world." More attention is given to factual knowledge than in the 1976 version of *SBSS*, but facts are still important primarily as a base for conceptualizing and generalizing.

R Statements are from descriptive materials written and distributed by the publisher.

Second, there is a social behavior dimension. Children in the program are involved in learning experiences that help "prepare them for intelligent, constructive, responsible citizenship." Finally, there is a values dimension. Considerable emphasis is given to helping children "explore, reappraise, and develop their own values and to understand the values held by people in cultures other than their own." These goals are treated at all grade levels.

Scope, Sequence, and Organization. Titles of the grade level components indicate the foci considered important as well as the fact that this is an interdisciplinary, integrated approach to curriculum design. The titles also show that students begin with what they know—the family—and expand outward from there. Level K: *The Earth, Home of People—Big Book* (a chart-like book with teacher's manual to be used with an entire class or small group); Level 1: *Living in Families*; Level 2: *Living in Communities*; Level 3: *People and Resources*; Level 3-4, Alternate: *People in Regions*; Level 4: *People and Ideas*; Level 5: *People* *in the Americas;* Level 6: *People and Change;* Level 7: *This Is Our World;* Level 8: *Man in America.* The reader should note that most of the sexist terminology included as part of titles in the earlier editions has been removed, except at Level 8.

Student Materials.   The textbooks in the Silver Burdett program can be used as a self-contained package. Texts in the latest edition have been written in a style and with a vocabulary so that even youngsters functioning two years behind their grade in reading can understand them. They include extensive case study materials that allow students to make discoveries about the nature of human activity and permit in-depth consideration of topics considered so important in the new social studies. They include primary source materials: letters, diaries, memoirs, newspaper stories, historic documents, and transcriptions of recent tape recordings. Using these materials, students can operate as junior social scientists, analyzing points of view, evaluating evidence, forming conclusions, and testing hypotheses. In addition, texts are filled with full-color photographs and drawings as well as maps, charts and graphs. Most of the newer social studies texts—as is true with those in the Silver Burdett program—are a joy to behold. They inspire one to sit down and begin to page through them.

Coordinated with the texts are picture packets, spirit-master activity sheets, problem-solving booklets, performance tests, individualized learning packets for slow readers, and sound filmstrip packages. These materials help students working independently perceive relationships and make discoveries on their own. As in the case of *Holt Databank System* materials, these are not inexpensive; but use of the *SBSS* program does not hinge on use of all the components. Texts can stand alone, or some components can be chosen to supplement the text.

Teachers' Editions.   The Teachers' Editions of *SBSS* are annotated student books with teaching aids provided in extended margins. These aids include behavioral objectives, major understandings from the social science disciplines identified according to the science from which each came, key vocabulary, motivational techniques, developmental and enrichment activities, answers to chapter questions, and ideas for helping slow learners.

Comparisons with Other Text Series.   In the late 1970s, many publishers of social science materials revised their programs, incorporating some of the same changes found in *SBSS:* heightened emphasis on social-emotional skills, renewed stress on basic reading skills and increased readability of materials, heightened concern with citizenship, renewed interest in American heritage, increased use of primary materials as a base for conceptualizing and generalizing, and the possibility of using the text without expensive companion materials. Examples in point include the *McGraw-Hill Social Studies, American Book Social Studies, Scott, Foresman Social Studies,* and Harcourt Brace Jovanovich's *Social Sciences: Concepts and Values.* Complete citations for these and other programs developed at the end of the 1970s are found in Appendix D.

Future Trends in Programming

Where are we going in the design of social studies programs in the 1980s? It appears at this point that we are moving in the direction of future designs that incorporate some of the following ideas:

1. Programs will provide children with clusters of generalizations to use in explaining human activity, predicting future trends, and deciding what personal action or position to take on an issue. In essence, the notion of a spiral curriculum, employed today in many programs, seems to be a direction for the future.
2. Children will be encouraged to build understanding of the way people function by observing human activity, by comparing and contrasting specific instances of human activity, by developing functional classification systems, by discovering relationships through inductive thinking, and by applying understanding deductively to the solution of problems and to decisions they themselves must face.
3. Programs will emphasize the acquisition of cognitive, social-emotional, and fundamental search and communication skills rather than the acquisition of facts. Facts are data upon which simple generalizations and more complex theories are built. For that reason, actual data that children can process for themselves—documents, pictures, models, artifacts—will probably become more important in future programs as students use them to find out and at the same time acquire basic skills.
4. Programs will take into account how children learn and think and what is most meaningful to them. Programs popular today tend to start with study of the child and his or her needs, move to the immediate family group, and go on to the community. Children start with what they know but, in contrast to older programs, they study not only their own needs, families, and neighborhoods, but needs, families, and communities in other places and times. This design makes comparisons and contrasts easier.
5. Children will be encouraged to recognize the uniqueness within themselves and respect differences in others. Comparative

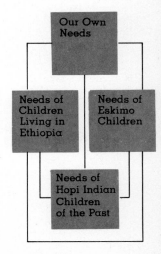

studies of the way people in different cultures function will be used for this purpose. Literature and autobiography will play a heightened role. Dance, music, art, and architectural traditions that give evidence of the rich and diverse heritages of different ethnic groups will also be highlighted. In this respect designs for future social studies may draw more from the humanities.

6. Programs will provide opportunities for values clarification and decision making related to events of both past and future. These include decisions having both ethical and legal dimensions, personal and worldwide impact–decisions concerning population increases, consumption of natural resources, environmental pollution, rights of the individual, migration and immigration, and discrimination because of sex, race, religion, or economic status.

In studying the designs of past and present, the authors of this book see an eclectic model for social studies programs emerging, one that combines the spiral design with a modified concentric circle design. In this model the big ideas of the social sciences serve as unifying strands, and the products of human activity as data through which children begin to comprehend what it means to be a human being. The result is an interweaving of strands into a curriculum fabric designed to prepare children to function cognitively, emotionally, socially, and ethically in a rapidly changing world.

The Future – A Prediction or Two for Educators

R See Lawrence Cremin, *The Transformation of the School* (New York: Alfred A. Knopf, 1961).

R Bernard Bailyn, *Education in the Forming of American Society: Needs and Opportunities for Study* (New York: Random House, 1960). Bailyn writes, "The past is simply the present writ small."

In analyzing education from an historical perspective, researchers today tend to look at educational developments of the past in terms of the social and cultural setting in which they occurred. Lawrence Cremin, for example, in *The Transformation of the School*, saw the progressive education movement as a reflection of progressivism in society at large. Studying education in colonial America, Bernard Bailyn saw the schools of the period as a reflection of the religious needs and beliefs of people who were trying to establish their own cultural traditions in an alien land. These and other historians have focused their interpretive lenses not only on specific educational institutions but on the societies that gave rise to them.

This approach is based on three fundamental assumptions about a society and the institutions it establishes; these are: 1) Institutions, including the schools, are an outgrowth of societal forces. 2) These forces in society are constantly changing. 3) Institutions that survive the changes occurring in society and continue to serve that society are ones that change with it.

Futurists can view educational developments of tomorrow in much the same terms as historians have viewed developments of yesterday—in terms of the social and cultural forces at work. To do this they need to predict to some extent the directions that social change will take. Predictions of this sort are tenuous, of course, but given the state of the present, some general future trends as well as educational implications can be projected.

R Read Paul Dickson, *The Future File* (New York: Rawson Associates, 1977) for a discussion of the blunders of futures forecasting and a list of the worst forecasts made over the past years.

Increased World Population

The population of the world continues to increase. Given that force, the future probably will bring more interaction among people occupying less space per person. Under these conditions people will have to accept ways different from their own and find privacy in ways other than through physical separation. The Japanese provide a model here. They have learned to adjust to life in smaller spaces and to retain their sense of personal identity and privacy. As a result they have achieved a heightened aesthetic sense and have learned to find pleasure in the beauty found in small things and spaces.

The educational implications of this worldwide change are twofold. First, schools must provide the opportunity for children to study themselves—their unique interests, beliefs, and abilities—and come to understand and accept themselves fully. As chapter 7 points out, the development of a positive self-concept and a future-focused role image is a necessary part of today's social studies programs geared toward the future.

Second, schools must provide personal resources so that each person can find contentment within smaller spaces. Here the humanities emerge as important within the social studies, for it is through literary, artistic, and expressive activities that people come to know what it means to be a human being. The result can be individuals with heightened personal understanding and inner reserves.

Increased Automation of Goods Production and Less Personalized Service

Today Westerners take for granted fast-food dispensaries, supermarkets, push-button "services," and computers that have taken over tasks previously performed by human beings. This trend toward depersonalized services means less face-to-face contact among people than in the past. In the future more individuals may work at home, getting data from computer terminals and using telephone lines to send work products to a central data bank. People may relate more and more to machines and less and less to other people. Depersonalization may become more a part of the future than it is a part of today.

R See Robert Fitch and Cordell Svengalis, *Futures Unlimited: Teaching About Worlds to Come*, Bulletin 59 (Arlington, Virginia: NCSS, 1979).

For education these trends mean that children need more opportunity to develop social skills and a sense of personal worth. Youngsters will have to seek out human contacts through social processes that are perhaps unknown today. They must learn to join and function in social groups that are distinct from their work activity and meet their personal needs in diverse ways. Again, people must come to understand themselves—what they enjoy doing and what they are good at doing—so they can use this knowledge to make sound decisions about how to use the increased leisure time that will accompany greater automation.

Greater Mobility of People

The availability of rapid forms of transportation has increased the mobility of people. In the future world, people will probably move even more frequently than today as they seek different life-styles. For the schools this means that teachers will be dealing with children with greater individual differences than are found in the present. The mix will include children with widely different experiential and ethnic backgrounds, physical and learning disabilities, and goals and ambitions.

How can schools accommodate their programs to the needs of such a diverse group? Educators as well as critics of education are beginning to talk increasingly of tailoring programs to meet individual needs. The problem here is that personalized instruction may conflict with established school routines and traditions. But as Robert Braun, an educational critic, questioned: "What after all is the purpose of schools? To teach children what they need to know or to maintain the bureaucratic traditions of the school?" In practical terms, personalized instruction may mean finding alternative experiences for the child who has already met basic learning goals.

Here the new technology that is so often decried may prove a boon. Computer-assisted instruction is becoming more and more a reality and is already in use at the college level. Children will be able to go to data banks—as well as to more traditional school libraries and media centers—to search for information to use in solving study problems. In the future there may be a new role for the media advisor or librarian. That person will help the teacher and children use the new technology efficiently. Children who have already acquired learnings that most of the class are pursuing should be able to investigate other areas with the assistance of the media adviser and use data stored not only in books but in computer memories. They should tap both print and nonprint media in personalized investigations. In this respect, diversity of school populations and hand-tailored programs can mean a broader experiential background within a class.

Increased mobility also means that children will come in contact with others who differ considerably from themselves. To learn to accept and appreciate the beauty of human differences will become even more imperative in the future than it is today. Chapter 8 of this book develops this point in detail.

Expanded Personal Choices – The Family in Transition

With increased technology, mobility, and leisure, people living today are faced with an unprecedented number of personal decisions. In the future occupational, marital, residential, recreational, and interpersonal choices will probably become even more extensive as a result of continuing changes in the structure of the family. Industrial and post-industrial society has seen a weakening of the extended family and kinship system and the diminution of male dominance. This has brought new freedom to individuals, a freedom that in turn has triggered new problems to be faced.

The **nuclear family,** comprised of parents and children, has become a primary social institution, taking the place of the **extended family,** comprised of grandparents, uncles, aunts, nephews, nieces, parents, and children. Investigating family systems of the West, Arab Islam, sub-Saharan Africa, India, China, and Japan, William Goode has identified a variant of the nuclear family as the dominant form of family organization in all these geographically diverse countries. Other investigators have related the rise in the nuclear family in China, Arab Islam, Russia, and Israel to ideological and political ferment. These findings have been confirmed by sociologists working with other cultural groups around the world.

R See William Goode, *World Revolution and Family Patterns* (New York: The Free Press, 1970), pp. 87-163 and 366-380 for descriptions of places where variants of the nuclear family are found. See also Rose Coser, ed. *The Family: Its Structure and Functions* (New York: St. Martin's Press, 1964), pp. 526-544 and 426-432; John Edwards, ed. *The Family and Change* (New York: Alfred A. Knopf, 1969), pp. 469-476; Norman Bell, and Ezra Vogel, ed. *A Modern Introduction to the Family* (New York: The Free Press, 1968), pp. 37-44.

The emergence of the nuclear family has had an impact on role statuses within the family and within society as a whole. Formerly a person's social status was dependent on his or her parents' status, in other words, on the social class of the family. One's social position, determined by birth, in turn influenced one's occupational and marital possibilities. Today personal achievement is replacing familial social position as the criterion for acceptance and job placement. Children need not depend on parents to learn a trade, nor must they await an inheritance; rather they can select a marriage partner or a job based on their own desires, standards, and/or abilities. They must make choices for themselves.

An even more striking change has occurred in the status of women. With increased economic independence and legal and customary rights, sharp sex-role demarcations are beginning to tumble, and the egalitarian family is emerging. Women no longer have a single career choice – marriage. They can choose marriage and/or a professional career in many diverse fields.

Two major implications for the school result. First, because the family unit is down to its minimum size, supportive relationships within the family have been reduced. As a result, functions once in the domain of the extended family have been assumed by governmental, industrial, and social agencies, including the school. This means that the school not only must pass on the intellectual heritage of the society but may move more into the area of personal development. As geographic mobility continues to increase, the demand for schools to take greater responsibility for children's personal development seems likely.

Second, because choices will increase, many more opportunities for decision-making and values clarification must be available for children in schools. Young children must make and evaluate their own decisions if they are later to handle the big choices they will encounter as adults. This cannot be postponed until senior high school, for important choices are coming at an earlier age as young children develop attitudes toward smoking, alcohol, drugs, and sexuality. If decision-making skills are not developed early on in schooling, we may have a generation of immature youth playing adult roles.

Obsolescence of Jobs

R An interesting article to ponder is Fred Best's "Recycling People: Work-Sharing Through Flexible Life Scheduling," *The Futurist*, 12:5-16 (February 1978).

In previous years one went to school to prepare for a lifelong career. In a rapidly changing world this is no longer possible, for a single technological change makes any number of jobs obsolete. Accordingly, mid-life career changes may be the norm, not the exception in just a few years. Today's workers, therefore, must become perpetual students if they are to have the skills to function in a time of rapid technological advance.

The implications of this trend are already being felt with renewed emphasis on skills. Children, armed with fundamental problem-solving, valuing, social-emotional, and search and communication skills, can apply them in a variety of contexts. The future may also see the expansion of the kinds of skills necessary. The ability to use technological devices—electric typewriters, computer terminals, calculators, mechanical devices—will gain importance as more jobs require skill in their use.

Information Management Systems

Today we are in the midst of an information explosion. As knowledge compounds itself, experts in all fields struggle to keep pace with information in their highly specialized areas. A single computer today handles enormous amounts of data; even this will pale in comparison to the phenomenal information stores that will be available in the future. Huge corporations have already found that they cannot function without complex information management systems. Smaller companies are discovering that they too need information management systems.

In the future, individuals will probably rely on information management systems in their personal lives. Computer terminals may be used in the home to store and manipulate information needed to manage household chores such as shopping, feeding the family, paying bills, and keeping accounts. For the school this means that students must learn how to use information management systems. Such learning may well be part of the social studies of tomorrow.

R See Edward Cornish, "Towards a Philosophy of Futurism," *The Futurist*, 11:380-383 (December 1977). Cornish writes: "The world that we will experience in five to twenty years is being shaped by decisions made now."

Greater Stress on the Essential Quality of the Environment

Larger populations, greater reliance on machines, more rapid transportation, increased automation—all these factors tend to put greater stress on the natural environment. Without doubt, people in industrialized nations must learn to rely less on costly fossil fuels and create less waste so as to pollute the environment in less destructive ways. With larger populations contributing to the pollution of the environment, each individual must take greater personal responsibility.

Here, too, there are significant implications for the schools. (See chapters 14 and 15.) Schools today, particularly through social studies programs, must develop more environmentally conscious citizens who have the skills and desire to carry out future planning.

R Read Kenneth Boulding, "Anxiety, Uncertainty, and Energy," *Society*, 15:28-33 (January/February 1978) for a discussion of the relationship between energy sources and the way of life on earth.

Social Studies for Today - A Summary Thought

Charlie Brown, Lucy, Linus, and Snoopy are friends to most of us. We know the kind of being each is, the way each tends to talk, and the way each typically reacts. In this respect, the "Peanuts" crowd is almost a twentieth-century institution.

What accounts for the continuing appeal of Charlie Brown and his friends? One possible answer is that Schultz puts a bit of each one of us in the strip from time to time. Periodically we see ourselves and our foibles reflected there. The strip in Figure 17.7 is a case in point. Who among us has not at one time or another acted just as Charlie Brown, panicking in a crisis situation caused by our own failure to plan ahead, promising ourselves that we will be better prepared tomorrow, and then, when the pressure is relieved—forgetting all our good intentions?

Figure 17.7
"Who Cares About Tomorrow?"

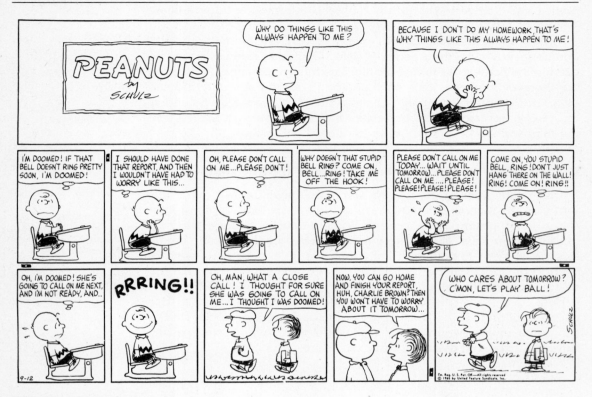

This reaction seems to characterize not only individual behavior but our collective behavior as well. Faced with a scarcity of fuel and long lines at the pumps, we conserve for a while only to resort to our old habits of wasteful consumption when the crunch has passed. As members of the crowd, we do this because we feel that somehow the problem really does not touch us or that for some reason we are personally exempt from the laws of scarcity and environmental dependency. At times we function as if we believe that closing our eyes will make the problem disappear.

But as with Charlie Brown's homework, the problems of increasing populations, increased demands on the environment, and new technologies will not disappear if we ignore them. Solutions must be found. Education today, especially in the social studies, has a major role to play in these solutions. Only if many citizens have a basic understanding of the complex interrelationships existing among political, social, economic, technological, and ecological systems and can make sound decisions based on their understanding will we be able to overcome the problems of today and tomorrow.

Who cares about tomorrow?

References

Bailey, Stephen. *The Purposes of Education*. Bloomington, Indiana. Phi Delta Kappa, 1976.

Commager, Henry Steele. *The People and Their Schools*. Bloomington, Indiana: Phi Delta Kappa, 1976.

Ferguson, Robert; and Proctor, Patricia. "Resources for Future Studies," *Social Education*, 43:226-228 (March 1979). A bibliography of materials.

Fitch, Robert; and Svengalis, Cordell. *Futures Unlimited: Teaching About Worlds to Come*, Bulletin 59. Arlington, Virginia: NCSS, 1979.

Gross, Richard, et al. *Social Studies for Our Times*. New York: John Wiley, 1978. See chapter 9 for a discussion of new programs.

Kauffman, Draper. *Teaching the Future: A Guide to Future-oriented Education*. Palm Springs, California: ETC Publishers, 1976.

London, Herbert Ira. *Social Science Theory, Structure, and Application*. New York: New York University Press, 1975.

Massialas, Byron; and Hurst, Joseph. *Social Studies in a New Era*. New York and London: Longmans, 1978. See chapter 12 on decision making.

Mayer, Frederick. *Education for a New Society*. Bloomington, Indiana: Phi Delta Kappa, 1973.

Mosher, Edith; and Wagoner, Jennings, ed. *The Changing Politics of Education: Prospects for the 1980s*. Bloomington, Indiana: Phi Delta Kappa, 1978.

Muessig, Ray. *Social Studies Curriculum Development*. Arlington, Virginia: National Council for the Social Studies, 1978.

Peshkin, Alan. *Growing up American: Schooling and the Survival of Community*. Bloomington, Indiana: Phi Delta Kappa, 1978.

Toffler, Alvin, ed. *Learning for Tomorrow: The Role of the Future in Education*. New York: Random House, 1974.

Appendices

Appendix A
Commercial Sources of Social Studies Teaching Materials

American Guidance Service, Inc. Publishers' Building, Circle Pines,
   Minnesota 55014. Offers kits of activities, props, posters, records,
   and cassettes for children K-4, designed to develop
   understanding of the self and others.

BFA Educational Media. 2211 Michigan Avenue, Santa Monica,
   California 90406. Offers 16 mm films on topics relating to business
   and industry, civics, community problems and services,
   economics, geography, minorities, and values.

Caedmon Records. 505 Eighth Avenue, New York, New York 10018.
   Features tapes and records on related themes in the humanities.

Coronet Co. 65 East South Water Street, Chicago, Illinois 60601.
   Offers sound filmstrips on careers, consumer education, families,
   energy, environment, folksongs, geography, history, Indians,
   map skills, and cultures. Also offers filmloops on cultures, history,
   climates, and map skills.

Denoyer-Geppert Co. 5235 Ravenswood Avenue, Chicago, Illinois
   60640. Products include globes; Canadian, U.S., and world
   history maps; regional maps; wall and desk outline maps;
   washable U.S. floor map; multimedia packages; map
   transparencies; and sound filmstrips on a variety of topics.

Documentary Photo Aids. Box 956, Mount Dora, Florida 32757.
   Features large black-and-white photos for historical and cultural
   studies.

Educators Progress Service, Inc. Randolph, Wisconsin 53956.
   Annual edition of *Educators Guide to Free Social Studies
   Materials* lists free films, filmstrips, slides, audiotapes, videotapes,
   scripts, audiodiscs, charts, bulletins, exhibits, maps, and posters;
   includes an index of items available to Canadian and Australian
   teachers.

Eye Gate House. 146-01 Archer Avenue, Jamaica, New York 11435.
   Products include filmloops and sound filmstrips on topics such as
   communities, civics, government, history, geography, ecology,
   energy, pollution, regional studies of the U.S. and Canada,
   families, and values; other products include transparencies on
   U.S. and world history.

Farquhar Transparent Globes, Inc. 5007 Warrington Avenue,
   Philadelphia, Pennsylvania 19143. Offers clear acrylic political
   globes.

Field Educational Publications, Inc. 2400 Hanover Street, Palo Alto,

California 94304. Offers sets of black-and-white pictures useful in teaching American history.

George F. Cram Co., Inc. 301 S. LaSalle Street, P.O. Box 426, Indianapolis, Indiana 46206. Offers globes and maps in various sizes and mountings, wall and desk outline maps, map transparencies, map skill sets, and sound filmstrips.

Guidance Associates. Subsidiary of Harcourt Brace Jovanovich, 757 Third Avenue, New York, New York 10017. Features multimedia packages particularly suited for developing moral reasoning.

Hammond, Inc. Maplewood, New Jersey 07040. Features atlases, globes, outline and wall maps, and transparencies on history, map skills, and climate-resource-population distribution.

Hubbard Co. P.O. Box 104, Northbrook, Illinois 60062. Offers land form and earth history models; American Indian and early civilization replicas of artifacts; maps, globes, and map teaching sets; slides and super-8mm filmloops on world cultures and people at work. Catalog: *Social Studies.*

InterCulture Associates, Inc. Box 277, Thompson, Connecticut 06277. Features cross-cultural study prints, records, and materials that can be used to compare traditions, customs, and physical differences of people of diverse backgrounds.

Learning Arts. P.O. Box 917, Wichita, Kansas 67201. Offers sound filmstrips on American history and government, Canadian geography, biography, children of other lands, cities, community helpers, economics, ethnic and world cultures, geography, law, map and globe skills, and values; offers records based on Random House Landmark Books; also offers transparencies on countries and states, economics, geography, immigration, map and globe skills, and outline maps.

Learning Resources Company. P.O. Drawer 3709, 202 Lake Miriam Drive, Lakeland, Florida 33803. Offers sound and silent filmstrips on human relations, careers, Indians, Colonial America, U.S. and world history, and cultures; offers audio lessons on awareness of world around you, U.S. history, women, and black Americans; also offers records of historical events.

Miller-Brody Productions, Inc. 342 Madison Avenue, Dept. 78, New York, New York 10017. Products include sound filmstrips on self-awareness; Newberry Award books and authors; filmstrips on oriental, black, Hispanic, and Indian cultures; filmstrips on consumer problems, American history, and folksongs of the American Revolution.

National Geographic Society. Washington, D.C. 20036. Offers books, films, filmstrips, globes, maps, and recordings on cultural, historical, and geographic topics. Catalog: *National Geographic Educational Services.*

Nystrom. 3333 Elston Avenue, Chicago, Illinois 60618. Products
include map and globe skills programs, raised relief maps and
globes, sculptured Canadian and U.S. maps with plastic sheet
overlays, desk and wall outline maps, and world history maps.

Prentice-Hall Media. Service Code KA2, 150 White Plains Road,
Tarrytown, New York 10591. Features sound filmstrips on careers,
ecology, energy, feelings, folksongs, history, Indians, minorities,
world area studies, and values; also offers silent filmstrips on
famous Americans, history, Indians, maps, and globes; offers
filmloops on history and Indians.

Rand McNally & Co. P.O. Box 7600, Chicago, Illinois 60680. Offers
maps and globes for the classroom; sound filmstrips and other
materials on American history; enlarged pictures for classroom
use.

Scholastic Book Services. 904 Sylvan Avenue, Englewood Cliffs,
New Jersey 07632. Features books, tapes, and records; multimedia
packages; and weekly news periodicals: *News Pilot* (grade 1),
News Ranger (grade 2), *News Trails* (grade 3), *News Explorer*
(grade 4), *Young Citizen* (grade 5), and *Newstime* (grade 6).

Social Studies School Service. 10000 Culver Boulevard, P.O. Box
802, Culver City, California 90230. Offers paperbacks, learning
center kits, simulations, skill development kits, filmstrips, posters,
charts, multimedia kits, and picture packets.

Society for Visual Education, Inc. 1345 Diversey Parkway, Chicago,
Illinois 60614. Offers sound filmstrips on Canadian provinces and
cities, communities, conservation, ecological crisis, energy,
folksongs, history, map skills, self-awareness, urban needs, and
values; also features picture collections on communities,
community helpers, history, black history, and world area
studies.

Troll Associates. 320 Route 17, Mahwah, New Jersey 07430. Products
include filmstrips on self-awareness, values, citizenship, the
world around us, government, history, Indians, and black
Americans; other products include color transparencies and
cassettes on the states.

Viking Press. 625 Madison Ave., New York, New York 10022.
Features *Jackdaws:* sets of reproductions of primary source
materials relating to historical events, eras, and figures;
facsimiles of letters, newspapers, posters, cartoons, and maps.
Offers sets relating to Canadian, U.S., and European history and
economics. *Jackdaws* are also available from other vendors.

Appendix B
Text Series for Use in Elementary Social Studies

Items are listed by series name rather than by author, for in most
instances text series are known by that name.

American Book Social Studies by Rosemary Hallum, Edith Newhart,
Dorothy Skeel, et al. New York: American Book Co., 1979.
Beginnings (K), *Self* (1), *Others* (2), *Communities* (3), *Environments*
(4), *Americans* (5), and *Cultures* (6).

Bowmar/Noble Social Studies. Los Angeles: Bowmar/Noble
Publishers, 1974. *You and Your Family* (1), *Groups and
Communities* (2), *Cities and Suburbs* (3), *People and the Land* (4),
Many Americans—One Nation (5), and *People and Culture* (6).

Follett Social Studies 1977 by Herbert Gros et al. Chicago: Follett
Publishing Company, 1977. *Exploring Our World: People* (1),
Exploring Our World: Groups (2), *Exploring Our World:
Communities* (3), *Exploring Our World: Regions* (4), *Exploring Our
World: The Americas* (5), *Exploring Our World: Eastern
Hemisphere* (6 or 7), and *Exploring Our World: Latin America and
Canada* (6 or 7).

Holt Databank System K-6, William Fielder, gen. ed. New York:
Holt, Rinehart and Winston, 1976. *Inquiring About People* (1),
Inquiring About Communities (2), *Inquiring About Cities: Studies
in Geography and Economics* (3), *Inquiring About American
History: Studies in History and Political Science* (5), and *Inquiring
About Technology: Studies in Economics and Anthropology* (6).

McGraw-Hill Social Studies by Cleo Cherryholmes et al. New York:
Webster Division, McGraw-Hill Book Co., 1979. *Looking at Me* (K),
Discovering Others (1), *Learning About People* (2), *Exploring
Communities* (3), *Studying Cultures* (4), *Understanding the United
States* (5), and *Investigating Societies* (6).

Our Land and Heritage. Fay Adams and Ernest Tiegs. Ginn and
Company, 1979. *Our School* (1), *Our Neighborhoods* (2), *Our
Communities* (3), *Our People* (4), *Our Country* (5), and *Our
World* (6).

Our Working World. Lawrence Senesh. Palo Alto, California:
Science Research Associates, 1973. *Families* (1), *Neighborhoods*
(2), *Cities* (3), *Regions of the United States* (4), *Regions of the World*
(5), and *The American Way of Life* (6).

People: Cultures, Times, Places. R. Grossman, J. Michaelis, P.
Bacon, et al. Reading, Massachusetts: Addison-Wesley, 1976.
Working, Playing, Learning (1), *People, Places, Products* (2),
Towns and Cities (3), *Regions Around the World* (4), *America: In
Space and Time* (5), *The United States and Canada* (alternate 5),
and *The Human Adventure* (6).

People in a World of Change. Robert Carter, Vernon Prinzing, and Edith McCall. Westchester, Illinois: Benefic Press, 1978. *Family and School* (1), *People and Places* (2), *Communities and Change* (3), *Earth and Its Regions* (4), *United States and Americas* (5), and *World and Cultures* (6).

Scott, Foresman Social Studies. Blair Berg et al. Glenview, Illinois: Scott, Foresman and Company, 1979.

Silver Burdett Social Studies. Edna Anderson, Norma Anderson, et al. Morristown, New Jersey: Silver Burdette, Inc., 1979. *Living in Families* (1), *Living in Communities* (2), *People and Resources* (3), *People in Regions* (3-4, alternate), *People and Places* (4), *People in the Americas* (5), and *People in the Eastern Hemisphere* (6).

Social Sciences: Concepts and Values, 2nd ed. Paul Brandwein. New York: Harcourt Brace Jovanovich, 1977. *Yellow* (K), *Blue* (1), *Red* (2), *Green* (3), *Orange* (4), *Purple* (5), and *Brown* (6).

Taba Program in Social Studies. I. Allen, S. Baugher, et al. Reading, Massachusetts: Addison-Wesley, 1973. *People in Families* (1), *People in Neighborhoods* (2), *People in Communities* (3), *People in States* (4), *People in America* (5-7), and *People in Change* (6-7).

Windows on Our World. Harlan Hansen, Frank Ryan, Everett Keach, et al. Boston: Houghton Mifflin, 1976. *Me* (K), *Things We Do* (1), *The World Around Us* (2), *Who Are We* (3), *Planet Earth* (4), *The United States* (5), and *The Way People Live* (6).

Name Index

Subject Index

Entries given in boldface are ones for which a definition is given in the text. Entries given in upper-case type are names of extended activities described in detail in the text.